IMPROVING MIDDLE SCHOOL GUIDANCE

Practical Procedures for Counselors, Teachers, and Administrators

Martin L. Stamm
Trenton State College

Blossom S. Nissman
*Central Burlington County Region for
Special Education
Mt. Holly, New Jersey*

Allyn and Bacon, Inc.
Boston • London • Sydney

Library of Congress Cataloging in Publication Data

Stamm, Martin L
    Improving middle school guidance.

    Includes bibliographical references and index.
    1. Personnel service in secondary education.
2. Middle schools. I. Nissman, Blossom S., joint author.
II. Title.
LB1620.7.S7   373.1'4   78-21006
ISBN 0-205-06449-3

Printed in the United States of America.

CONTENTS □

iii

FOREWORD

A school must always be more than a cognitive institution, for it contains growing people as well as growing disciplines. It must be, in actuality, an environment within which persons can develop, in accordance with their potentialities, satisfying self-images and confidence in their ability to become, in some measure, contributing, interacting members of society.

As children pass from childhood through the throes of adolescence and youth, the influences, opportunities, and requirements of the world and the future begin to produce with ever-increasing intensity forebodings, fears, anxieties—and concomitant aspirations.

It is a period rich in possibilities, and also fraught with perils. It is a time when all our professional resources should be utilized comprehensively in guiding, advising, and steering youth into rewarding, appropriate, and "fitting" growth patterns.

The authors of this useful and original book have considered the middle school as a continuum. The students in their development are not segmented, as they are in our educational system. The authors believe that students' growth directions move forward consistently, without abrupt modifications as grade and school levels change. In this book they describe a recommended program of guidance for approximately fifth- through eighth-graders. Within this range is included the somewhat new "middle school," which typically includes grades six to eight or five to eight.[1]

Throughout this time space students grow holistically, with every experience being absorbed accumulatively by the total organism. The guidance function, the authors claim rightfully, should be similarly holistic, insinuating itself into all aspects, day by day, of the educational program and working intimately and complementarily with all members of the educational team. In such a relationship personal interaction becomes the sine qua non, the essential open sesame, to success with students, associates, and parents.

If out of the gamut of changes in educational emphases today, one could be singled out, it undoubtedly would be the rising attention to individual differences. Guidance, certainly as much as any other field of educational endeavor, has felt and responded to this trend. In every contact with students, guidance counselors meet the now with a cautious eye on the past and an expectant eye on the future. Guidance, by its definition, can never be static; it must ever look toward the tomorrow, for that is where the person will live, contribute, and interact. And because the person must be the focus of attention always—although never separated from a present and potential setting—guidance in its techniques, its activities, even in its objectives, can never be rigid, formalized, or generalized. It too must be individualized, purposely fashioned to fit the needs of differentiated persons.

The authors stress, in their treatment of the guidance function, a new concept they call a Human Development Center, essentially a publicized available series of clustered services involving curriculum, community contacts, communication, counseling, crisis, professional growth, assessment, and career choice. There is little that is mechanical in the book. The humanistic approach is fundamental, with heavy accents on human and interpersonal relationships.

Under the concept of guidance described in this book, the counselor never considers his role as being distinct, aloof, or removed from school and curriculum objectives and content, discipline, extracurricular activities, in-service projects, public relations responsibilities, parent relationships, or group teaching. The school and community are considered as veritable treasure houses of resources, all of which are susceptible to utilization in the conceptualized emotional, social, intellectual, attitudinal, or career development of individual students.

---

1. The authors covered the field of guidance in the elementary grades in New Dimensions in Elementary Guidance (New York: Richards Rosen Press, 1971).

This book stresses the salient fact that in all of their activities guidance counselors are the partners of teachers, and proud of such categorization. Their professional services, however, are performed in many places—including classrooms, among many individual persons and groups, at many times, often outside school hours, in a variety of ways, and in pursuit of a variety of purposes. Perhaps, from one viewpoint, guidance counselors now are the last remaining "universal teachers," because of their pluralistic dimensions, in the sense that Leonardo da Vinci is conceded to be the last "universal man," masterfully at home in all fields of knowledge and activity.

The content of this book is offered as a challenge to present-day guidance counselors. The authors, with recorded practical experience, have researched and tested all of their recommended practices. They suggest what they believe will be both practical and helpful to earnest practitioners. They believe, too, that every practice tried will lead to still better practices and results. It is a recognized truth that every problem successfully resolved reveals and opens up new areas for study and attention, for adolescents in the middle school years are exceedingly complex beings, moving into a widening world which is continually becoming more complex, and more in need of the invaluable services guidance counselors are especially equipped to provide.

Thomas E. Robinson, Ed. D.
President Emeritus, Glassboro State College
Professor Emeritus, Rider College

PREFACE □

In our contemporary educational institutions, there is yet no set division of grade level grouping accepted as compatible by educational theorists. Most recently, the middle school concept has been advocated by leading educators as potentially a more effective approach to educating emerging adolescents than the "junior high concept." Tobin succinctly describes the purposes and functions of middle school when he states:

[The purpose and function of the middle school is] to provide a program for pre- and early-adolescents that is relevant to individual needs and societal demands in a world where there is constant change and a rapidly expanding body of knowledge. Such a program would consciously aim toward the continuing development of self-directing individuals, capable of solving problems through both rational and creative endeavors.[1]

Thus the merging of the preadolescent fifth- or sixth-grade student with the seventh- or eighth-grader, or both, laid the foundation for the boundaries for the middle school population.

---

1. Michael F. Tobin, "Purpose and Function Precede Middle School Planning," in *Middle School in the Making*, ed. Robert R. Leeper (Washington, D.C.: Association for Supervision and Curriculum Development, 1974) pp. 21-25.

The division is certainly not a new concept. The original one-room school house, as well as many elementary schools in service, including grades kindergarten to eighth, house these preadolescent and adolescent children. The primary change is the isolation of this group and emphasis on a program that is not limited to a self-contained classroom.

In this text we present our perceptions of the guidance role within this concept of the middle school. We feel that in light of social pressures, societal demands of the 1970s, and the general turbulence of our democratic society, there is a need for reevaluation and analysis of guidance services. We concentrate not on criticism of what is but rather what we feel can and should be. We support our theories with guidelines and practical examples for making these changes.

We strongly believe the middle school setting can provide the climate necessary to our present educational system, conducive to experimentation and flexibility in programming. Therefore, we propose an organizational plan for middle school guidance services to help build this climate in which both students and teachers can function productively. We attempt to open new vistas for the practitioner and the student of guidance, as well as the classroom teacher. This book was written to encourage counselors to use their teachers' and administrators' expertise, their creativity, and their energies to experiment and try new approaches, to throw away old guidelines, to dare to risk the undeveloped—with a new boldness—to provide services that meet the real and present needs of all who are involved with the middle school.

The transitional years between childhood and adulthood provide an opportunity to reinforce a sound foundation for future decision making within the school program. To accomplish this we believe there is a need for a clearly defined guidance role that concerns itself with the humanistic approach to education. We present such a program as a model for middle school guidance through the implementation of a Human Development Center (HDC). The HDC presents the services we feel middle school guidance ought to provide. We attempt to clarify these services so that all involved with the student can work cooperatively toward the mutual goal of better education.

Improving Middle School Guidance Services provides a rationale for this concept. The material has been exposed to school programs in New Jersey and Pennsylvania. It has been evaluated by teachers and counselors in graduate programs at Rider College and Trenton State College as part of the counselor training program. It has been published in professional journals[2] and supplemented by practitioners in the field who have broadened the scope of the concept as they worked in their schools. We are constantly researching the ideas expressed in the HDC concept of middle school guidance. We hope to continue to share our findings with our colleagues in our nation's schools through future publications.

As we identify the services of the counselor, we challenge those who care about the effectiveness of school and the students it serves to use these ideas and suggestions as a springboard in making school more relevant and more accountable to the demands of the modern changing society in which the student lives.

We encourage the reader to question our theory, to dispute our views, and to challenge our ideas. We also challenge the reader to examine his services and look objectively at himself and his role. The combined efforts of the reader and the authors should produce a clearer image of the school guidance counselor. For, once the counselor sees who he really is, and understands how others see him, he can begin to become what he wants to be—a productive member of his school personnel.

Note: Our use of the words *he, him*, and *his* throughout this book in reference to counselors, teachers, students, and others is not meant to imply sexism, but is simply to avoid awkward sentence structures.

Martin L. Stamm
Blossom S. Nissman

---

2. Martin L. Stamm and Blossom Nissman, "Middle School Guidance? What's So Special about It?" *The Administrator's Quarterly* (Spring): 6-11, 1973. Martin L. Stamm and Blossom Nissman, "How the Counselor Sees the Middle School Student," *The School Counselor* (September): 34-38, 1973.

ACKNOWLEDGMENTS

We wish to express our gratitude to those who have contributed their expertise to this book: Mrs. Mary Elisabeth Buhl, Director of Guidance, Matawan School District, Matawan, N.J.; Ms. Susan Caccese, social worker, Spottsville School District, Spottsville, N.J.; Mrs. Betty Demby, Director of Midway School, Lumberton, N.J.; Mr. James Dufford, New Jersey public relations official; Mrs. Harlene Galen, Principal, Edgewater Park, N.J.; Dr. Richard D. Hanusey, Assistant Superintendent of Schools, Philadelphia, Pa.; Mrs. Janet Kwiatkoski, school counselor, Lawrenceville, N.J.; Dr. Wayne I. Newland, Director of Pupil Personnel Services, Hamilton Township, N.J.; Dr. Thomas Robinson, President Emeritus, Glassboro State College, Glassboro, N.J.; Dr. Arthur Shapiro, County Director of Child Study Teams, State Department, New Jersey; Mr. Richard Strausser, guidance counselor, Mt. Holly, N.J.; Mrs. Esther Stroebel, learning resource teacher, Hamilton Schools, N.J.; Sr. Patricia Watkins, counselor, Gray Nuns Academy, Yardley, Pa.; Dr. David Winikur, county psychologist, New Jersey State Department; as well as the countless students and colleagues who patiently listened, evaluated, and encouraged us in our work.

Sampling the viewpoints of these professionals has provided us with the opportunity to present divergent opinions regarding the roles and functions of the middle school guidance concept. The reader must decide which suggestions and ideas are most appropriate for his particular school setting. We welcome the contributions, as well as questions and comments from those who read this book.

PART

I

THE MIDDLE SCHOOL, THE MIDDLE SCHOOL STUDENT, AND MIDDLE SCHOOL GUIDANCE SERVICES

CHAPTER ONE

What's Special about Middle School?

Rationale

Those involved in the evaluation of contemporary school organizations have recognized the fact that youth in the early stages of adolescence have special needs and problems in bridging the gap between elementary and high school programs.

Program changes have begun to evolve, with greater attention given to individual and group guidance in an attempt to provide clearer articulation with the high school programs. The input of the guidance staff was called upon to aid those planning the junior high curriculum with materials and assessment techniques. This led to instructional programs more appropriate to the needs, abilities, and interests of young people entering and passing through the early stages of adolescence.

The junior high concept was a good beginning, but only a beginning. Today's educational processes have been going through tremendous technological and sociological changes.[1] New devices for measurement, new family structures, and the mobility of present society reflect these changes. Also significant is the rapidly declining

---

1. The growth of the middle school and its characteristics are discussed in detail in Leslie W. Kindred et al., *The Middle School Curriculum* (Boston: Allyn and Bacon, 1976), chap. 1.

enrollment in K−12 schools throughout the United States, as well as inflation, recession, and outmigration in some areas.

In exploring these societal changes, educators have become aware of the need for better techniques for recognizing student uniqueness. The use of in-service education for the present population of counselors, teachers, and administrators, who accept the role of humanistic educators as well as academicians, seems to be the realistic approach. Thus we address this text not only to the counselor in the middle school but to the teacher, the administrator and the parent, all of whom work as a team in helping the child grow to his maximum potential.

The variations in growth and development of the middle school student demand that the program develop from the nature, needs, and abilities of the pupils involved. The middle school program is representative of preadolescents, early adolescents, and adolescents who have moved from the sheltered, protective self-contained classroom environment to the more independent departmentalized program of the secondary school.

In the middle school concept, there is stress on interdisciplinary programs of learning, team teaching, independent study, modular scheduling, learning laboratories, nongraded classes, minicourses, and individualized instruction. These unique programs challenge and channel the energy and enthusiasm of children in this age group. Grouping within this level of education is not designed to bring conformity of action among similar persons but rather to provide the kind of program that will serve pupils with unlike characteristics. The middle school parallels a unique period between the growing processes of childhood, adolescence, and adulthood. It provides time for a greater appreciation of the learning process.

Typical of the ten- to fourteen-year-olds is the contrast in social and physical maturation. A wide spectrum of rapid change among these students makes it difficult to identify the so-called norm. These children give the appearance of physical maturity but their social and intellectual growth do not keep pace. Since this is more often the rule than the exception, there is little or no group homogeneity. Middle school children therefore can be said to have the common characteristics of unlikeness rather than likeness. Their one commonality seems to be uncertainty about themselves. Realizing this, those involved with the growth and development of the middle school child must approach the task of this transitional period with sensitivity. It cannot be the sole responsibility of one staff member −

the counselor—but must become a way of communication and inter-action between the middle school child, his peers, and the adults within his life. The climate of the middle school, therefore, should be one of patience, understanding, guidance, and calm direction.

Because the middle school is involved in the transitional step on the educational ladder, it is free to provide a flexible program of greater choice for the student by encouraging exploration of interests and abilities. In order for the student to profit from this experience he must want to be part of it and feel he can succeed. The exposure to choices helps the student prepare for mature decision making, which is basic to future academic and vocational success.

The involved middle school staff seeks to humanize the educa-tive process by stressing the importance of the student, respecting his ideas, encouraging involvement of parents, and welcoming creativity of its teachers. A good middle school's primary goal is to provide learning as a pleasurable experience, within an atmosphere in which all feel important and essential. A vital, alive middle school environ-ment encourages curiosity and experimentation by providing the time and facilities to carry out new ideas and interesting innovations.

This level of education can provide a model for change to accommodate students typically plagued by problems of readjust-ment to changing bodies, changing interests, and changing personal relationships—often coupled with emotional turmoil. Characteris-tically, confused about themselves, their differences, and their simi-larities, they are looking for answers although they are unsure of the questions. They search for a self-identity acceptable to themselves. They demand of those who guide them an understanding of their level of comprehension within the scope of their world of expe-riences. The middle school student lives in a world of personal extremes and contrasts. He is beginning to shed his cloak of depen-dence as he takes up a shield of defense. He moves boldly with uncertainty; he declares his independence yet holds one hand on whatever gives him security. He is cautious about change yet shouts for it. He looks at himself and often sees a stranger.

The middle school becomes a special place because it has the unique opportunity of coordinating the individual needs of the child with the home, the school, and the community. Although this learn-ing environment continues to require emphasis on learning skills (processes), this emphasis must be flexible in recognition of the atti-tudes and values significant to this age level (procedures). A formula cannot be prescribed for the organization of an effective educational community, for the effectiveness of these processes and procedures depends upon its relevance to the variety of pupil needs it is designed to serve. It must continually change and challenge its own structure through evaluation and analysis by all those involved. Within this flexibility there are appropriate basic goals necessary to implement the philosophy of the middle school.

Primarily, in order to respond to any educational program, a person must have a quality of self-direction—a good feeling about himself. Each child and teacher involved in the program has to discover and accept his strengths and weaknesses to work up to his fullest potential. A person needs experience in making rational and responsible decisions, to understand and develop a tentative system of values, and to begin to appreciate himself as a thinking being worthy of active participation in his society. He must have enough confidence in himself to try and, if he fails, to try again. The middle school's primary goal should therefore be to reflect this attitude as a supportive measure through fair rules and regulations and realistic evaluative procedures. (William Glasser's *School Without Failure* develops this concept fully and should be in the reader's professional library collection.)

The second goal of the middle school is a commitment to learning skills. In the rush to provide experimental and innovative programs, educators should not neglect the basic skills needed to explore these programs properly. Such skills include communication, study, and manipulation skills. The presentation and use of these skills should be such that the student sees their serviceable value through an experiential approach supported by all school personnel, including the guidance staff. The counselor must know and understand the mechanics of the academic program within his school.

A third area of concern is the consideration of social development and interpersonal relationships. Without wholesome attitudes about others, as well as self, effective group interaction is not possible. Respect for property and another's opinion, for example, needs to be stressed as a primary life skill. Inability to interact with peers is a self-imposed roadblock that can seriously affect the learning process. Desirable social attitudes should be presented clearly, for children often find themselves being punished for a broken rule about which they had no previous knowledge. Behavior and good citizenship in the home and school community are important in developing a productive learning climate. It cannot be left to chance.

Physical well-being, as a fourth goal, needs to be considered in working with the middle school child. In this period of dramatic physical change, the child, his parents, and his teachers should be aware of good health procedures as well as danger signals significant to this age group. The principles of wholesome growth and development and the characteristics of physical maturation should be part of the curriculum. It helps to clarify misconceptions and fears typical of this age.

A fifth goal includes emphasis on creativity—consideration of a variety of options, experiences, and awareness of the multitude of horizons to be explored. Encouragement of creative and critical thinking and broadening the scope of future plans form the basis for this goal development. Each child should be encouraged to become all he is capable of being by challenging him to think, to try, and to explore.

The sixth and final goal is to help each child grow confidently and look to the future as an exciting experience yet to be met. He should be assisted in his exploration of the present in order to get a clearer picture of where he feels he will fit most productively in the future. He should look at education and learning as a developmental process because he is continually in the process of growing. He should see himself as part of a cooperative plan that has some definite sequential steps necessary to reach these goals.

The middle school is special. It seeks to provide a setting for something new—a change in the structure of the school organization of the past. Its thrust is toward development of more realistic communication between the child and his school as it functions within the community. It may well be the impetus sought by concerned educators to facilitate change for the entire spectrum of the educational process. Working as a member of the school community, the councelor must enlist the partnership of the guidance staff and other school personnel, as their cooperative involvement is of vital importance in providing the direction for fulfilling the unique goals of the middle school concept.

Supplementary Readings

Alexander, William M., et al. *The Emergent Middle School*, 2nd ed. New York: Holt, Rinehart and Winston, 1969.

Bondi, Joseph. *Developing Middle School: A Guidebook.* New York: MSS. Information, 1972.

DeCarlo, Julia. *Innovations in Education for the Seventies.* New York: Behavioral Publications, 1973.

DeVita, Joseph C., et al. *The Effective Middle School.* West Nyack, New York: Parker Publishing, 1970.

Edwards, Reese. *The Middle School Experiment.* London: Routledge and Kegan Paul, 1972.

Garvelink, R.H. "Anatomy of a Good Middle School." *Education Digest* 39 (February):14–16, 1974.

Garvelink, R. H. "Creating a Good Middle School: Through Revolution or Evolution?" *Clearing House* 49 (December):185–186, 1975.

Gere, A. R. "Focus: Middle and Junior High Schools: Symposium." *English Journal* 66 (April):25–51, 1977.

Huber, J. D. "Reincarnation of the One Room Schoolhouse: The American Middle School." *Clearing House* 49 (November):103–105, 1975.

Kindred, Leslie W., et al. *The Middle School Curriculum* Boston: Allyn and Bacon, 1976.

Leeper, Robert Rosborough, ed. *Middle School in the Making.* Washington: Association for Supervision and Curriculum Development, 1975.

McGlasson, Maurice. *The Middle School, Whence? What? Whither?* Bloomington, Ind.: Phi Delta Kappa Educational Foundation, 1973.

Romano, Louis, et al. *The Middle School: Selected Readings on an Emerging School Program.* Chicago: Nelson-Hall, 1973.

Stradley, William. *A Practical Guide to the Middle School.* New York: The Center for Applied Research in Education, 1971.

Tyler, Leona. *The Work of the Counselor,* 3rd ed. New York: Appleton-Century-Crofts, 1969.

CHAPTER TWO

The Middle School Student: A Quest for Personhood

Perhaps the most significant component of the middle school community is neglected in the literature on this new school grouping. Very little seems to be written concerning the examination and clarification of the student involved in this educational structure. Who is the middle school student? What are his needs? How can a program be planned and an organization of services developed unless this child is fully understood? Which staff members possess the expertise necessary to understand the growth and development of these students within this educational complex? Can it be one person on the staff or must it not be all staff members involved with the child? The guidance counselor as a member of this team, trained to accept this role, is a logical person obligated to accept responsibility for facilitating the humanistic aspects of the middle school child's education. The guidance counselor needs to share his expertise regarding the developmental patterns of the middle school child with parents, teachers, and administrators as part of a cohesive team with a mutual goal—providing the best school climate possible for learning.

Reflections

What if there is no counselor? The leadership needs to be accepted by other staff members. The administrator is the logical candidate.

Schools have been performing guidance services for a number of years without a counseling staff and have provided quality services. We believe that with a guidance staff many of these same services can continue in a more productive and organized manner, becoming more comprehensive and complete. Since all school personnel must be actively involved in a humanistic middle school environment, the designation of leadership and the success of the program depend largely on the quality and commitment of the leader. Since humanistic educational concepts are the heart of any guidance program, it seems logical that if a school can obtain a counselor, that should be a primary goal. In the interim, the needs of personalization of a school program, as presented in our Human Development Center, should be facilitated, with the staff member who is best equipped to do the job in the counselor's absence taking the lead.

Thus the leadership person has to become aware of who this student is in order to work with him. We have sought to provide a clear description of the middle school student and his unique qualities and basic needs. This is a difficult task, for the multitude of differences in physical, emotional, social, and psychological development between the ages of ten and fourteen are characteristic of the preadolescent and adolescent. To clarify and identify these differences, the authors have chosen to share with the reader the experiences of county psychologist Dr. David Winikur and school social worker Ms. Susan Caccese. Dr. Winikur presents his view from a psychological and parent vantage point, while Ms. Caccese's input deals primarily with the social implications. In order to present his point vividly, Dr. Winikur shares the following personal experience with the reader as he introduces his exploration of the middle school student's quest for personhood.

It was a cool night. As I rested from a tiring day of hiking and sightseeing, the warmth of the crackling fire and the glitter of the stars overhead in the cloudless sky comforted me. I gently sipped hot coffee and gradually began to unwind from the day's activities, our third day in Acadia National Park in Bar Harbor, Maine. I had thought through carefully all the things my wife and I had done in our efforts to be good parents, to provide a sound firm basis of love and respect in our children, tempered with discipline, responsibility and what we had hoped was good judgment. As objective as a parent could be in such a reflective situation, I kept coming to the conclusion that basically we had provided a sound family unit in which our oldest son's emotional state could flourish.

How then from where did this recently emerged monster come? What nourished this ogre that threatened to disrupt our whole family structure? He seemed to feed and thrive on teasing his younger siblings and grew stronger as they protested and cried. Previously when some discord developed, we could sit and talk about it. But no longer was this the case. He now withdrew quickly, turned his chin askew, rolled his eyes and responded to my questions with sharp retorts such as, "I don't know," or "I didn't do nothing." Other symptoms soon developed, such as weird noises and strange sounds (those familiar with the *Three Stooges* television show will understand), the purposes of which were to further unnerve his brothers and sisters and thoroughly exacerbate his parents.

"Where had we gone wrong?" "Where had we erred?" kept running through my mind as I threw another log on the fire and finished the coffee. He had always been a child who enthusiastically participated in activities. He was hungry for new experiences, and happy to accompany me on any jaunt that I suggested. But no more. Now he preferred to read in solitude, take long strolls alone and spend time alone in the tent. Where had this stranger come from? That precious thing whose picture we took on his first day of school, whose every report card, award, certificate, and other note of recognition we had meticulously saved and proudly displayed for grandparents, had been transformed. Like Regan MacNeil, he seemed possessed.

Such a description from parents is not uncommon. This actual case material reflects the kind of consternation and perplexing circumstances parents experience as their child gently eases out of childhood into early adolescence. The physical, social, emotional, and cognitive changes that occur in subtle and sometimes quick, unnoticed transitions are frequently devastating to parents and teachers, in the sense that they are so insidious. They creep in unaware; they sneak up on us when we are not looking and we find ourselves at a loss as to how to deal with this stranger to the family.

The material reflected in this chapter will endeavor to give a conceptual framework within which to understand these developments. Our purpose is to provide counselors, teachers, and parents insights into the "feeling networks" of these young persons. Our basic messages are simple. Adolescence is a difficult time for the youngster as well as for the adults in their life who must stand by as the changes take place. What appears to be strange, erratic, and aberrant behavior is, in most cases, normal for the age. The person we knew before these changes began still exists, and will prevail. These behaviors that seem so strange and alien are a result of a combination of factors. The many physical and emotional alternations occurring are difficult for the adolescent to integrate into his self-concept. New demands from society and the realization that adulthood is approaching all serve to confuse and frighten this child. Though our expectations of the middle school child change, we continue to confine them to a status of "powerlessness." They are clearly aware of and sensitive to this position. It is within this context that the developmental process of the adolescent years begin. This task of achieving an identity, charting a future, and defining oneself we call "a quest for personhood."

To better respond to the material presented here, we feel it is important that the reader try to recapture some of his own early adolescent experiences. A sympathetic if not empathetic frame of mind is essential to understanding these youngsters. At times we have found that an adult's current feelings create tensions and difficulties in relating to adolescents. These difficulties arise not so much in response to the behavior of the adolescent, but rather are a reaction within the adult to this behavior. This reaction stems from the adults' own need system. For example, realization to the adult that he or she is getting older and losing his/her sexual attractiveness is a common response to the adolescent's budding puberty.

Finally some direction will be provided in terms of dealing effectively with youngsters of this age and in promoting positive growth.

As part of our work in the schools, we have conducted numerous group counseling sessions with young people with whom we are thoroughly enamored. We find them sophisticated and naive, kind and selfish, considerate and rude, mature and childishly silly. Yet we feel a deep appreciation and sensitivity to the kinds of difficulties and frustrations that these behaviors can generate in adults. The "quest for personhood" of an adolescent is a groping, striving, searching period of life in which the boundaries are unclear, the final objective ill-defined and the resources for achievement undeveloped. At this point in life, most adolescents are aware that they are "becoming" but the frightening question remains "becoming what?"

The overriding themes of powerlessness and lack of focus—aimless wondering—characterized this nebulous period of time. Inconsistency is perhaps the only consistent thing about these youngsters. They are striving to attain individual personhood in a society that makes self-definition increasingly difficult. Parents, teachers, schools, and other social institutions place youngsters in tenacious positions by issuing conflicting demands upon them. (Acting grown up to an adult means that the adolescent should do as the adult directs. We understand the consternation a teenager feels when confronted by this logic.)

Largely because of confusing societal expectations, adolescents generally respond in an unpredictable manner, which disturbs the equilibrium of adults. No longer permitted the innocence of childhood, adolescents have not yet achieved the status and rights of adulthood. They are forced into a seemingly eternal compromise. Still dependent on parents emotionally and financially, they find themselves powerless to pursue their own ideas, suggestions, and inclinations. They struggle forward with a sense of commitment to some life-view, overcoming many obstacles along the way. As they search for an acceptable identity during a time when experimentation should be encouraged, they too often meet with objection and disgust from "experienced elders."

Many adolescents demonstrate great insight into adult behavior. One youngster related to us in a group session that his father read his own hopes, dreams, and fears into the behavior of his son, who then responded to him accordingly. Overwhelmingly, adolescents report that parental values, anxieties, and conflict are projected onto them. Adolescents recognize and internalize this disparity yet feel powerless to fight against it.

It has been said that "people who are determined to stay young resent people who actually are young." Surprisingly, adolescents are painfully aware of this resentment, which most often is strongly denied by adults. Many adults yearn to be at life's plateau once again, remembering only the excitement and ease of youth while choosing to forget the intense pain and powerlessness with which this period was fraught. In a further attempt to insulate their own teenagers from growing pains, they remember and share only the good times which their sons and daughters are expected to relive. Infrequently do they relate the unhappiness, the doubts and fears, the mistakes and the pains that they experienced.

That the peer group becomes exceedingly important during this phase of life is not surprising. Adolescents need the security, acceptance, and empathy of friends with whom they can be themselves. Peer pressure is strong and to be accepted is paramount. The external trappings of fashion, records, and other teenage symbols become vehicles for this acceptance and further serve to develop a subculture with its own code and language. Too, this subculture serves to effectively exclude those not of this age.

Adolescents are concerned about society's appraisal of them and their worth. As they move toward their own identity, they stop along the way to assume a less threatening peer identity as a first step toward "personhood."

A Developmental Perspective

Conceive of the adolescent period as a process rather than a product. It is an acquisition of skills, talents, and understandings rather than a period in time that is static and complete unto itself. With this in mind we can begin to provide a developmental framework about which to understand this age. It is an age of becoming, of transition into personhood. As a child stumbles down the path toward adulthood, for the first time there is an awareness of the great mystery of what is to come. The adolescent is permitted to view the vast panorama of this future, yet the long journey to the towering peaks of adulthood looms menacingly before him.

The adolescent has heard about or is aware of sexuality. Perhaps the youngster has begun to experience physical changes through the development of secondary sex characteristics. Facial and body hair may be developing. Menstruation and ejaculation are imminent, if they have not already occurred. Many hormonal changes are in process. Undoubtedly the youngster is aware that these bodily adjustments are occurring and realizes that they represent behavioral differences in his life which are both enticing and frightening. The idea of a career and having a responsible position reinforces the desire for independence and financial stability; yet it also represents awesome responsibilities and the requirements of a successful school experience to prepare adequately for the future. The opportunities for travel and independent activity are within this panorama. Yet these too represent vast increments of independence and responsibility which, to paraphrase Shakespeare, are more honored in the imagery than in the execution. Many new relationships are now available to the adolescent from a variety of previously unavailable sources. No longer confined to his immediate neighborhood, the adolescent experiences a more heterogenous peer group in schools, clubs, and in other activities. Increased mobility is characteristic at this age which further exposes the adolescent to a broader variety of people and life-styles.

As the youngster views these changes, he experiences the paradox of the adolescent age. This paradox takes shape as the adolescent desires all the trappings of adulthood and independent functioning, but balks at the realization that responsibilities, dangers, and commitments are required. The degree to which he is able to deal with these challenges as more independence accrues will determine the degree of successful social and emotional adjustment that will be realized.

It is little wonder then that budding adolescents demonstrate a *volatility* of emotion that is unsurpassed in the developmental process. Mood swings are excessive, ranging from high exaltation to deep depression. The inconsistency of pleasantness and head-splitting disharmony coexists so frequently that it is hard to reconcile. It is almost impossible for an adult to determine the adolescent's emotional status. At times the adolescent is excited, gleeful, and overjoyed, but in a few minutes can become sullen, skittish, and withdrawn. The insecurities of the adolescent are plentiful and obvious. At times the adolescent will function independently while on other occasions he will be whiny, whimpery, a constant complainer asking for direction. The adolescent may be mature and independent one day, straining to be allowed to perform in adult ways. The next day he can descend the stairs in a complete state of regressive dependency complaining that his parents do not love him because they do nothing for him. Such a youngster can be kind, thoughtful, and considerate of others, with insights into feelings that would astound any therapist. Within the same day he can be transformed into an impulsive, thoughtless, crass, insensitive bully whose parents, at that point, probably consider incarceration as the only option available. It is this type of inconsistency and paradoxical emotional coexistence that makes this age so difficult to understand. Parents and educators in their dealings with adolescents must keep in mind this consistency of their emotional inconsistency. Their lack of emotional stability must be viewed as normal within the context of this developmental period.

The process of adolescence has as its end product the establishment of a firm, coherent, and definable self-identity, the overriding goal and need toward which the adolescent strives. The child's task, as early adolescence begins, is formation of an understanding of the nature of this need to acquire the physical, cognitive, emotional, and social skills that will enable the adolescent to achieve the goal of self-definition. The youngster can then begin to stake out his self-image.

Counselors, parents, and educators must realize the importance and impact that success in these tasks at this early age has upon later years. As the child enters into this stage of development the paramount concerns are the child's beginning awareness that much of his behavior now becomes goal-directed. The adolescent gains a notion of this awareness and begins to accept it as part of the developmental responsibilities of the age. An adolescent who fails to give up earlier behavior styles, refuses to adopt more mature manners of functioning, fails to begin to assume more responsibility for his current and future behavior, who does not begin to make breaks with his parents, who continues to cling to immature coping styles, and who fails to develop the skills and talents that are needed for the later years is heading for a difficult future, one in which he will be ill prepared for emotional and social realities that will be confronted.

We know that as part of the young adolescents' search for a value system and formulation of an identity, a break with the past and a severing of family ties usually takes place. A challenge must be made of accepted beliefs and standards as part of the developmental process. This frequently has been the source of much discord within the family unit. In the popular press the phenomenon has been termed the *generation gap.* It is our view that this disruption of family relationships need not take place; frequently we have found that it has been avoided. For some reason Americans have overemphasized this generation-gap issue and responded too much to sensationalized media representations and descriptions of the adolescent's disharmony with his or her parents.

The more successfully integrated and mature the adolescent, the better able he or she will be to make this break from parents and be secure in his or her own identity. At the same time the adolescent can retain the ties within the family and community. The adolescent's task, as it begins in these middle school years, is not only to make departures from previously held standards and values, but to redefine them in terms of an emerging identity. There is the need during this time of life to reassess relationships within family and community. Out of this reassessment process should emerge richer, more mature, new relationships formulated upon the adolescent's emerging new sense of self.

The process of forming a self-identity that we emphasize requires a person to strike out emotionally on his or her own. Yet within the process of striking out there should always be a component of reassessment of previous relationships. The nature of family ties may change but the intensity need not. Reassessment may become more graphic if we consider the remark attributed to Mark Twain. He remembers feeling that when he was eighteen he found his father a terrible fool, but by the time he reached twenty-one, he was surprised to see how much his father had learned in three years. It is this same kind of phenomenon that continues throughout the teenage period and is a most normal and necessary occurence. Frequently parents and educators overreact to the questioning and attacks upon their value system by the young adolescent. It is more appropriate for adults to acknowledge this questioning as part of the developmental process and a necessary exercise for growth. These confrontations need not be construed as personal affronts or attacks. Parents and teachers should allow the teenager a system for reentry that allows for face-saving. The adolescent needs to be able to work back into the system with dignity. It is also helpful to view many of the adolescent's criticisms as having some validity. Graceful acceptance of criticism is a lesson that we adults need to learn and then teach our children.

Social learning theorists have pointed out the importance that "modeling" and vicarious learning experiences play in the development of a social interaction system. During the early adolescent period the impact of these learning experiences plays a vital role, in which the adolescent uses the mechanism of identification. This is the process of forming an attachment to another significant person and then emulating that person's characteristics by trying to incorporate them into his own personality and behavioral functioning style. At times the adolescent will identify and model his behavior after significant peers or older adolescents; this process can be maddening for parents and educators. New languages and styles of speech will emerge weekly. New slang expressions, dress styles, and values will be tried out. Support is provided by peers for disrespect toward authority. This at times, enables the adolescent to earn his spurs with his peers, with whom, at this point, there is heavy identification.

These processes of identification and modeling provide the adolescent with a crucial avenue for personality development. They let the adolescents try out, and possibly incorporate, differences of behavior and values—like rehearsing style of delivery before a stage production. Adults should view this as a muscle-building exercise rather than a personality change. Most likely the personality with which the adolescent enters this period is what will emerge; the end product will be broadened and of greater depth.

The well-adjusted adolescent, with a basic notion of his or her own identity and confidence in his abilities, will be able to go through this early adolescent period maintaining a strong sense of himself. He will be able to evaluate these other role possibilities and potentialities in a realistic and less tumultuous manner. Contact with adults outside the family—for example, teachers, community leaders, activity coordinators—provides an expanded presentation of potential role models. An adolescent who has aspirations toward becoming a mechanic may adapt behaviors and characteristics of someone at the gas station he frequents or where he has a part-time job. Another adolescent may learn a great deal about performing in the role of husband and father from his football or baseball coach because the coach's family attends many of the games and practices. Later the coach may invite the team to his home for a barbecue, providing further data as to role behavior.

The value of these experiences and relationships is difficult for adults to assess at the time they occur. The quality of these relationships and the impact they have on the adolescent's later life is frequently substantial, yet often goes unnoticed.

Other aspects of the adolescent's personality functioning are discussed elsewhere in this text. We feel the reader will be able to fit these other adolescent behaviors into this developmental perspective of an expanded range of normality. We refer specifically to such things as the adolescent's self-consciousness because of physical changes that appear. These physical changes inevitably lead to comparisons between themselves and peers, which is so typical of this age. This self-consciousness leads very quickly into probably the most characteristic aspect of the early adolescent—hypersensitivity and extreme responsiveness to criticism. The need for privacy is the need for a room for themselves and their belongings. Frequent squabbles erupt because other siblings enter this private domain, this sanctuary of the forbidden.

A tendency toward extreme reactions to criticism, particularly in a public setting, frequently leads us to recommend to teachers never to chastise, reprimand, or correct an adolescent in front of his peers. When requested to evaluate adolescents for school districts as part of our roles as school psychologist and school social worker, we have made it a point never to go into a classroom to get a young adolescent. Rather we very carefully guard their sensitivity and their responsiveness to peer group pressures by finding other means of meeting with them. The impact of the peer group and the important role it plays in the life of the early adolescent cannot be underestimated.

Another characteristic so frequently evidenced by these children is a theme we will develop shortly—their sense of powerlessness. Because they feel (and are) so vulnerable, they generate extreme defensiveness. The young adolescent frequently will respond to any criticism or perceived attack in a highly defensive manner. This is part of the hypersensitivity and self-consciousness that permeates this age.

The middle school child frequently displays what we term a *negative focus.* Early adolescents are almost possessed by what is wrong in their lives, what is wrong with their parents, what is wrong with their siblings, and what is wrong with their clothing. This kind of orientation and response is frustrating at best—and more likely exasperating—to adults with whom daily contact is a reality. This defensiveness and extreme sensitivity to criticism prevents youngsters of this age from developing an objective self-view. They are so self-conscious that their faults stand out like big red blotches on a clear background to them. Their overreaction prevents them from being able to deal realistically and maturely with their shortcomings. This self-view is characteristic of the age and should be tolerated. Parents, counselors, and educators can assist adolescents during this period by emphasizing that things are not as bad as the adolescent tends to view them. Further, adults may consider pointing out their own shortcomings, weaknesses, and failings as they remember from their own adolescence, delivering the message that it is appropriate, acceptable, and mature to deal with weaknesses and limitations. It is not an activity that opens oneself up to criticism.

A Sense of Powerlessness

In our group conversations with young teenagers about a variety of topics, they frequently recounted incidents and circumstances in which an underlying theme emerged. This theme we have termed the adolescent's sense of *powerlessness*, the inability to affect events and circumstances in one's life, as well as the lives of others. The impact of this sense of powerlessness, of total domination by the environment, can be devastating to a person struggling to form an identity. Consequently, for the young adolescent, frustrations of significant proportions result from this powerless stature. It is only with the acquisition of age and skills, and through significant turmoil, that the adolescent is able to propel himself out of the state of powerlessness into one of power, responsibility, and control of his own destiny.

Our conception of powerlessness as it relates to the middle school child, then, is the early adolescent's inability to have an impact upon the attitudes, opinions, and behaviors of others. This youngster has limited control over the circumstances of his own life and only minimal opportunities available for changing them. At times the feelings of powerlessness become so pervasive that the adolescent is unable to isolate and conceptualize them. More often than not, adolescents describe a generalized, vague situation that is disturbing and unsatisfying. "Negative focus" is a product of this pervasive powerlessness. However, there are adolescents who are sophisticated, mature, and articulate who can deal with this power-less position in which they find themselves. Even with this kind of advantage, the young teenager still lacks sufficient resources and stature in the eyes of adults to truly affect much change upon their powerless state.

The wellspring from which this powerless stature flows has its source in the institutions adults have established, which are basically unresponsive to youngsters of the early teenage years. Our society is so structured that people this age have minimal opportunities for accomplishment and production. The basic role of the middle school child in our culture is one of reception and intake rather than out-put. Yet it is only through production and accomplishment that recognition and identity are achieved. Athletically, the young ado-lescent is too underdeveloped to make significant contributions to sports teams that would result in the type of recognition and pub-licity that is possible in the later high school years. Academically, they are still too naive, unsophisticated, and cognitively undeveloped to make significant achievements. Nor can they deal with issues that are recognized as substantial in the adult world. Socially they are still awkward and ineffectual. Dating is, at best, only starting at this age—more so for girls than boys. In many ways, then, the adolescent at this early age is bound by limitations that dictate his own powerless state.

The young adolescent's emotional ambivalence, lack of direc-tion, indecisiveness, and limiting insight into his own emotional sta-tus, further relegates him to a powerless state. Frequently the middle school child is at the mercy of his feelings which are often unpredict-able. The lack of communication skills is probably most significant in rendering the young adolescent powerless. Most devastating is the fact that he or she is inarticulate. The youngster lacks the vocabu-lary, the conceptual framework, and the confidence to express his or her ideas and feelings concretely, succinctly, and forcefully which enables the young adolescent to be easily manipulated by others who are more articulate. Consequently he or she is at the mercy of those who can express themselves with confidence and retort any argument that the adolescent might muster.

Coupled with this lack of articulation capacity is a generalized lack of sophistication, a lack of exposure and of presence, that would enable an adolescent to handle himself and stand up for his or her rights and achieve recognition from others. Generally these social skills are absent, and the early adolescent is easily dismissed as inconsequential and immature.

Finally, because of the nature of the middle school age, many roles and styles are played. Changeability undermines credibility and causes the young adolescent to be considered unworthy of status and trust. Consequently the powerless role is assigned in the minds of adults, who think that if the youngster cannot make up his mind as to what his desires or opinions are, then one cannot attribute much to what he or she has to say.

This status of powerlessness becomes engrained into the adolescent and the resultant feelings influence behavior during this age. The overriding emotion is frustration. Frustration clearly results from the lack of impact that we have discussed, the inability to foster any change in circumstances that affect their lives and their lack of control over their own life circumstances. Frustration classically is defined as motivated behavior toward a specific goal, the access to which is blocked. The energized drive state behind the motivation remains and all this emotional energy then must be expended elsewhere. Frequently this pent-up energy is what we see in some of the adolescent's destructive behavior, in the negative focus, and in the randomness of much of his activity. Schools seem particularly to be a source of this frustration.

Too often young adolescents sense from the adult world the message that they are inadequate, insufficient, and incapable, which can only serve to reinforce a shaky self-image and lack of confidence. The feelings generated by powerlessness in the adolescent create a sense of distrust and alienation from adults—an unfortunate result as it communicates to the youngster that significant adults, needed by the early teenager to serve as models, are insensitive to their needs, are rejecting, and are further a source of frustration.

As we reflect so many negative reactions to these children, we could just as easily reflect positive responses that would foster emotional growth. It would not be difficult for adults to begin to structure school or home situations to enable the adolescent to receive recognition and achieve in a way that he or she could feel self-respect and gain the recognition of others. It is important that parents, teachers, and counselors empathize with these teenagers and let them know that they understand the frustrations that they are experiencing as a result of their powerless status. We need to convey the idea that we are trying to change this situation in whatever ways possible. It would be comforting to youngsters of this age if we reassured them that it is a transitory period, that others have gone through it, and that the adult world is attempting to mitigate some of the discomfort.

The Young Adolescent and Communication

Communication during the adolescent period is at once a fragile and complex phenomenon. As we have pointed out, in the quest for a personal identity the adolescent is exploring and experimenting with many roles. Often, the adolescent will assume a variety of postures in a relatively short period of time. These emerging roles are accompanied by changes in appearance, taste, language, and mannerism which necessarily preclude predictability and consistency in interpersonal relationships. Effective communication becomes difficult because of the changing nature of the partner in the communication process.

An obvious manifestation of powerlessness emerges when we consider the realm of communication skills. When relating to parents and teachers, adolescents are often placed in double binds. Their opinions are solicited, but accepted only if they are in agreement with the dominant adult view. If an opposing opinion is offered by an adolescent, it is rejected by virtue of the age of its creator. For example, "How could you possibly understand about World War II? I fought it—you were not even born, yet." Adolescents find such reasoning frustrating. They sense a flaw in the logic of such an assertion but lack the ability to articulate its fault. Adolescents find it difficult to take opposing stands on issues and rationally discuss controversial subjects, since parents tend to be egocentric about their own values. Many stimulating and revealing discussions are prematurely squelched under the guise of respect. Adolescents are painfully aware that the same issues or concerns that were cocktail party discussions the evening before are not condoned as topics for two-sided parent-child communication. "I felt exactly the way Mr. Jones did about the Vietnam War, yet my father listened to and accepted it from Mr. Jones but told me I didn't know what I was talking about," said one teenager.

Another limitation too frequently characteristic of adult–adolescent communication is that it is unfairly weighted to one side. In the adults' eagerness to be the "ideal" model for children to emulate, they fail to reveal their own incapabilities, limitations, mistakes, and shortcomings. In their attempts to be "above reproach," teenagers often find adults unapproachable. During a group discussion, some teenagers related that their parents "would like you to think they were perfect." They continued to explore the fallacy of perfection as related to human beings and then speculated on the reasons their parents chose to portray this facade. "Perhaps they are covering up their own lives," "They are afraid we will love them less if we know they were troublemakers when they were in school." If parents chose to remember and identify with some of their own negative adolescent experiences, it might help to "humanize" and promote parent–child communication during the teenage years.

Effective communication with a young adolescent is an attainable goal. The basic components are an atmosphere of openness, acceptance, and maturity of understanding. If such an atmosphere is established early in the relationship, a tone is set for later years that will outlast minor disagreements. Further, this approach to communication with a young adolescent reinforces for him a needed sense of value and self-respect.

The creation of an open and accepting relationship with a middle school youngster requires that the adult accept the responsibility for making mature communication work. It can be effected through some specific guidelines to the communication process. It is essential to realize, at the outset, that the young teenager, though at times reticent, moody, and withdrawn, has a great need for communication. He needs to talk, to express ideas, to be listened to, to be part of conversations, and to eavesdrop on adult discussions. Frequently at this age children do not leave the room after dinner. They sit and listen as their parents discuss the events of the day. Adults are put off by a teenager's terse, monosyllabic responses (sometimes sounding like animal grunts) to questions and assume, erroneously, that the young teenager is not interested in being part of the communication process. To the contrary, there is an embarrassment and awkwardness that inhibits them. The creation of an atmosphere for positive communication takes time and patience on the adult's part. Counselors, teachers, and parents should draw these teenagers out by asking their opinions. If this is unsuccessful, the adult should then relate opinions and express attitudes and feelings, and raise questions. Over a prolonged period, a basis for communication will emerge.

Too often adults are overly cautious in their conversations with teenagers. They fear that a contradictory opinion will be rejected by these young people who might then terminate the discussion. To the contrary, however, if an open communication relationship is in process, the adults need only be honest and sincere in their expressions and feel free to disagree with opinions of a teenager. To be effective, all that is required is that the adults be gentle in their disagreement, so that it is not construed by the overly sensitive, defensive, youngster as a personal criticism. When one disagrees, one should clearly state that it is a disagreement with an opinion or an interpretation. Adults should try to give specifics as to points of difference and acknowledge that there is room for varying interpretations. It is essential not to deal with young teenagers in a paternalistic, condescending manner. Statements such as "Well I used to think that way when I was your age," "You'll understand better when you grow up," or "You don't know what it's like if you haven't experienced it," all serve to terminate conversations and destroy relationships.

Particularly during the early teenage years, children are in possession of misinformation and do a lot of questioning. There is a strong need for open and frank discussions with informed adults. Unfortunately, the young teenager is frequently too embarrassed or awkward to raise these topics. The adult, be it counselor, parent, or teacher should take opportunities to bring up issues and deal with them forthrightly, openly, and maturely. Assumption of responsibility and initiative by the adult will serve a dual purpose. In addition to alleviating the teenager's discomfort and need for information, the adult's mature handling of the conversation will serve as a model for dealing with difficult issues. Such topics as sex, homosexuality, cheating, drugs, alcohol, all weigh heavily upon a middle school child's mind, generating much preoccupation and peer discussion. Though, at times, the teenager will be totally unresponsive to the adult's initiative, what is important is that the opportunity for a frank, mature discussion has been provided. The teenager has the right—and this should be acknowledged—to refuse such a discussion without recrimination. The youngster may be indicating such information is not required or perhaps he is too uncomfortable with the topic and is not ready for such information. Always provide a means for the child to raise the topic later. A statement such as "Well, that's O.K., maybe we'll talk about it another time," or "I can understand that you don't want to discuss it now, but if you ever have any questions feel free to ask me," is an easy means of maintaining a foothold on such discussions.

For the adolescent a by-product of an effective communication relationship with adults is a broadened perspective and improved thinking skills. One of the main functions of adult communication with a young teenager should be to help the young person think through situations. Seeing the different issues involved, isolating these issues, expressing them in an articulate manner, and being able to gain the perspective of different interpretations of similar events are skills that can be gained through interaction. Frequently, children of this age will come home and express opinions about another child that convey little information and much emotion. Such statements as "I can't stand him," "He's weird," "He's just so queer," do little beyond indicating a level of frustration and emotional discord. The adult may very gently acknowledge the teenager's frustration or anger and then proceed to help the youngster to think the situation through. It is helpful to pose such questions as "Can you be more specific about what things the person has done to make you so unhappy with him?" or "Why is it that you feel that way?" and isolate the specifics in a nonjudgmental manner. Teachers, too, are frequently the brunt of an adolescent's criticism. Such comments as "She is a terrible teacher," "He doesn't teach us nothin'," "She doesn't like me, she just likes per pets," are common. These opportunities may be used advantageously to help the teenager express himself in a more cogent and complete manner.

Much can be gained by allowing the teenager to participate and listen to discussions between adults concerning political, social, or personal issues within a family or school. Frequently, in forcing the young adult to offer an opinion about a political situation, for example, we are placing him in a situation that is difficult to handle. However, by mildly participating and passively listening, he can gain the perspective of differing points of view. Following a presidential address or a TV news special concerning the CIA, for instance, the adult can take time to review the issues carefully with the teenager, pointing out the various sides of the question. The youngster should then be encouraged to offer his or her opinion. It is important that the adult's presentation be specific and concrete in form, enabling the teenager to relate to the questions in a less abstract way. Such situations may also take place within the classroom. Issues relating to school functioning are wonderful opportunities for the development of this communication-thinking process. Discussions of this sort should be focused, by the teacher or counselor, on the issues at hand. Generalities should be substituted with specifics and emotions replaced with rational thinking.

Bridging the Gap

The alienation that develops between parents and their teenage children in the later adolescent years has its roots in the early middle school period. With an understanding of the adolescent's emotional state, with effective communication skills, with an appreciation of the difficulties a person in our society encounters as he enters the earlier teenage years, this so-called generation gap can be avoided. We acknowledged from the outset that effective relationships and communication skills with any person is a difficult task and more so with a youngster of this age.

What begins in the early adolescent years and becomes more noticeable during the later teenager period is that the nature of the parent/child relationship changes. It is the ability of parents and their children to acknowledge and adjust to this change that dictates the future nature and strength of their bond.

From the parents' perspective, they have to deal with the obvious fact that this youngster very shortly will no longer be a child. For some parents this can be a difficult adjustment. The maturation of a child means that the parent, too, is growing older. The implicit message here is that the parent is easing into middle age with its concomitant loss of vitality, attractiveness, and a general slowing down physically and mentally. Further, as the young teenager begins to mature, there is a lessening of dependency, in an overt sense, upon parents. Many adults find no longer being needed a difficult adjustment. Too frequently parents, perhaps more so with women, shape their lives around their children. We view the current trend toward women establishing careers and their independence a positive and healthy advent in our culture. Finally, what is most difficult for parents and school personnel to deal with is their loss of control of these youngsters, whom they generally were able to manage and direct with a fairly good response from the children.

From the middle school child's vantage point, there is a changing sense of their parents' vulnerability. The father who was omnipotent, able to repair anything, the strongest and most handsome man, now begins to be viewed as a fallible human being with limitations and foibles. The young teenager, at times, finds his parents embarrassing when some of these faults are revealed while friends are visiting. The values of parents are no longer accepted out of hand but are scrutinized closely and seen to be lacking in some places. It becomes hard for the child to maintain the same kind of responsiveness when these weaknesses are realized. At times the revelation and realization of parent weaknesses serves to reinforce the young teenager's hypersensitivity to criticism. He takes on the attitude that parents certainly are not perfect, "How can they expect me to do everything right?" This is a very difficult attitude to overcome.

With this kind of changing relationship going on, the maintenance of a strong bond between parent and child becomes a vulnerable process which requires much patience and maturity on the part of all involved. Too often we have noted that parents tend to give up. To some extent this is done because of the popularization of the concept of the generation gap. Rather than trying to find solutions to difficulties and attempting to understand the nature of the changing relationship, parents sit back, remove themselves, and, in a sense, cop out, by saying that "It's just the age, and he or she will outgrow it." In this sense the generation gap becomes a self-fulfilling prophecy, with much of what is predicted occurring simply because people do not try to work through some of the difficulties that arise.

This, too, is true of the school situation, where administrators and teachers continue to deal with these emerging personalities in an authoritarian and unilateral manner. Student councils are probably the least politically influential unit in a school system, yet they possess the potential for being the most effective. It has been our experience that children have very little input into a school's curriculum and management. Yet the children's behavior and learning are the reasons for the school's existence. The kind of modeling that a participatory relationship to a school would provide for these youngsters is immeasurable. Too often, adults lack the skills to effectively draw out the children's innate capacities to participate in the planning process. Counselors could be most effective in this role and have a significant contribution to make in this entire area.

Frequently, when questioning administrators and other school officials as to the level of participation and decision making within a school that children are provided, there is invariably a strong indication that, "of course the children have input." However, when you speak to the children involved they have understood the situation clearly. They recognize that they have been dealt with in a patronizing manner that was merely perfunctory and "lip service" was paid to their wishes, concerns, and ideas. In no way are we suggesting that children's wishes should be unilaterally adhered to. However, the middle school child certainly has the right to be respected for his opinions and to have such opinions evaluated on their merit. An example occurred in one of our groups where the students indicated a desire for a soda machine in the lunchroom. They had gone to the school administration to express their desire and had been told no, it could not be done. The following year they made the same request; again they were told no. The administrator indicated that he dealt with that issue the previous year, he was annoyed at being asked a second time, and he did not want to be bothered with such a question again. We discussed this situation with these eighth-graders and helped them to see some reasons why a soda machine was unacceptable to the administration. Once the children understood that there were dangers associated with the potential for broken glass from the bottles, they were much more amenable to accepting the administration's ruling. Frankly, we would have been hard pressed if they had raised the question as to why the machine could not have contained cans.

We do not feel that we did anything miraculous, that demonstrated tremendous insights or sensitivities, or that required special training. All we did was sit down and try to give rational reasons for decisions. Too often adults fail to do this. They see any request or suggested change in procedure a threat to their authority. A person secure in his or her position and identity is not threatened by such questions from young teenagers.

In summary

There is much that can be done by parents, counselors, and educators that will improve the quality of the relationship between an adult and a middle school child. The lives of all involved will be enriched by the more positive nature of such a relationship. The closeness and support that the young teenager will feel as he struggles through these years will be of immeasureable advantage in later life.

It may be helpful to try and highlight some of the points that have been made in this chapter. We have selected various behaviors that adults want or want not to do in their interaction with the middle school youngster. This type of presentation will serve as a reminder of points made within the body of the chapter and will be easily utilized as a quick source for further reference.

Paving a smoother road toward
personhood

Listen to adolescents. Give them time to talk.

Be honest and sincere in conversation.

Do not be patronizing and paternal. Accord them the respect you would an adult.

Talk to youngsters about feelings. Teach them about emotions and how they can be appropriately expressed. Be honest and discuss how you feel.

Identify feelings as they are expressed by other people, so that emotions become more comprehensible.

Be tolerant of inconsistencies and moodiness.

When criticizing, be critical of behaviors, not of personalities. Be sure to detail what is wrong with a behavior and how it is to be changed. When such confrontations occur, be sure that it is done privately—out of the presence of other children or adults. Do not embarrass the teenager. Always allow the opportunity to save face.

Be supportive and encouraging of ideas and goals even if they appear to be unrealistic. It is the fact that the youngster is thinking and planning that is important.

Help the young adolescent to tolerate, accept, and understand the inconsistencies of others. Encourage the youngster not to take everything so personally. Try to help the teenager gain a perspective.

Understand and convey the message that the middle school child is not always wrong or that adults are always right.

Be understanding about the weekly crises that arise in their lives.

Involve adolescents in your life. Do not shut them out. Tell them your hopes and fears. Discuss with them your involvements and plans. They will then involve you in their lives.

Do not preach, lecture, or shout.

Create an atmosphere and structure situations where the adolescent can be made to feel valuable. Let him or her make a contribution and feel that others are dependent upon him for good efforts.

Admit when you are wrong. Discuss honestly your own weaknesses and shortcomings.

Be understanding and accept imperfections. If you can do this you will be a step closer to your own perfection.

Supplementary Readings

Adams, James F. *Understanding Adolescence.* 3rd ed. Boston: Allyn and Bacon, 1976.

Bachelor, Evelyn, et al. *Teen Conflicts.* Berkeley, Calif.: Diablo Press, 1972.

Becker, H. S., ed. *Social Problems.* New York: Wiley, 1966.

Briggs, Dorothy Corkille. *Your Child's Self-Esteem.* Garden City, N.Y.: Doubleday, 1975.

Brunk, Jason. *Child and Adolescent Development.* New York: Wiley, 1975.

Buxton, Claude F. *Adolescents in School.* New Haven, Conn.: Yale University Press, 1973.

Coles, Robert, et al. *Twelve to Sixteen, Early Adolescence.* New York: Norton, 1973.

Disque, Jerry. *In Between: The Adolescents' Struggle for Independence.* Bloomingdale, Ind.: Phi Delta Kappa, 1973.

Dreyfus, Edward A. *Adolescence: Theory and Experience.* New York: Norton, 1973.

Ginott, Hiam. *Between Parent and Teenager.* New York: Macmillan, 1969.

Goodman, P. A. *Growing Up Absurd.* New York: Random House, 1960.

Gross, Ronald, and Osterman, Paul. *Individualism.* New York: Dell, 1971.

Hawley, Robert C., and Hawley, Isabel L. *Developing Human Potential.* Amherst, Mass.: Education Research Association, 1975.

Hebeisen, Ardyth. *Peer Program for Youth.* Minneapolis, Minn.: Augsbury Publishing House, 1973.

Joseph, Stephen. *Children in Fear.* New York: Holt, Rinehart and Winston, 1974.

Jourard, Sidney M. *The Transparent Self.* New York: Van Nostrand, 1971.

Maslow, Abraham. *The Farther Reaches of Human Nature.* New York: Viking Press, 1971.

Peters, Herman. *Counseling Youth Series.* Columbus, Ohio: Merrill, 1972.

Piaget, Jean. *Science of Education and the Psychology of the Child.* New York: Viking Press, 1972.

Purkey, W. W. *Self Concept and School Achievement.* Englewood Cliffs, N. J.: Prentice Hall, 1970.

Salk, Lee. *What Every Child Would Like His Parents to Know.* New York: Warner Books, 1972.

Stamm, Martin L., and Nissman, Blossom S. "As the Counselor Sees the Middle School Student." *The School Counselor,* September 1973.

Stradley, William E., et al. *Discipline in the Junior High School.* New York: Center for Applied Research in Education, 1975.

CHAPTER THREE

Assisting the Middle School Student in Coping with Pressures

There is significant pressure placed upon the middle school child by his peers to conform. One of the major concerns in society today is helping the preadolescent and adolescent cope with these pressures in a positive and productive manner. We believe the greatest service that can be provided in a preventive approach toward drug and alcohol abuse and development of healthy social patterns is through insight and awareness of environmental, attitudinal, and emotional needs of the child passing through these impressionable years of growth and development. The middle school student, through parental concern and specific educational techniques, can be given guidance in self understanding that will aid him or her in making more realistic and rational decisions when these decisions have to be made.

Six Fundamental Characteristics of Growth

All human beings share the basic needs of security, acceptance, love, self-fulfillment, physical well-being, and a need for a positive self-image. These are normal desires that must be given proper priorities. The child who feels he is denied these basic needs seems to be a likely candidate for drug abuse and social conflicts. Underlying these basic needs are six fundamental characteristics that have been found

31

significantly *lacking* in those persons who are involved in socially unacceptable behavior in the middle school. They include: (1) attention and love through family and school relationships; (2) ability to face issues; (3) rational proportion of desire for fun, pleasurable sensations, and experiences in contrast to self-discipline and a sense of responsibility; (4) resistance of peer pressure—an ability to be independent in making decisions or judgments; (5) compliance with rules, regulations, adult direction, and structured activity; (6) direction in a search for success (the desire for instant gratification seems to prevail).

Recognizing and channeling these desires into constructive and positive action is of primary importance. The early and formative years play a vital role in establishing sound approaches to discovering techniques for achieving success in these areas of normal emotional development. The teacher or parent who provides guidelines for the child will help negate the need for the child to search for artificial means of tranquility or ways to blot out problems and misunderstandings through the use of drugs, alcohol, or sexual promiscuity. The fact that these involvements merely mask problems and distort viewpoints must be exposed and explained in a logical and realistic manner on a level that the middle school child can understand. Materials explaining the content of drugs and alcohol are plentiful, but these are not the answer. We believe that this information has to be supplemented by an awareness of the basic fundamental characteristics as the initial step to understanding. Providing acceptable experiences that fulfill these needs is the second and most crucial step of preventive procedures. Specific techniques, activities, and examples that have been used effectively in child development are provided to help strengthen these characteristics. The ideas are presented as guidelines in initiating ongoing programs of awareness between parent, child, and teacher. The counselor has to take the responsibility for providing insights which will aid in stabilizing the child's personal concepts so that he or she may live a happy, productive life within his environment. Further clarification of the fundamental characteristics basic in developing sound attitudes and stability follows.

Attention and love

The need for attention and love is basic to mankind. If these needs are not met, the person may seek other sources of compensation. How can a parent or teacher identify these needs and provide experiences that will fulfill them during the impressionable years of life in the middle school? We have identified six areas that commonly are a part of every child's life that provide an opportunity for the home and school to reinforce this feeling and need for acceptance, approval, and self-worth. They include: (1) listening to a child with sincere interest, (2) being aware of sudden changes in attitude and behavior, (3) developing a good relationship with a child's friends, (4) developing a good relationship between home and school, (5) establishing wholesome standards of living within the home and school community, and (6) demonstrating affection. The counselor must assist the teacher and parent in carrying out and identifying techniques for fulfilling these needs. Some examples follow.

Listening to a child with sincere interest may be achieved through commenting on the discussion taking place and showing understanding and sincerity even though the topic may seem trivial to an adult. The parent or teacher who continually moralizes and pronounces judgment that is negative will close the open door of communication and force the child to seek other sources of attention and love.

Illustration: *Mary, the ten-year-old daughter in a family of four, was interested in cheerleading tryouts at her middle school. She practiced for weeks with her friends and anxiously awaited the days of trials. Although she felt that she had performed well, she was not selected by the teacher-sponsor to be one of the cheerleaders. Several of her friends were. She felt rejected, embarrassed, and a failure. As she discussed her feeling with her teacher, she sought assurance and understanding. Her teacher's patience and interest were helpful but even more important was her teacher's wisdom. She helped Mary understand that there will be many occasions in her future when she will have to accept rejection. She stressed the importance for her to understand that this rejection was for her skill in cheerleading, not as an insult to her personality, appearance, or attitude. It showed Mary that she needs to evaluate situations in the proper perspective. If her teacher had said, "What's so important about being a cheerleader? I can see you getting upset about something important—but cheerleading—that's just a lot of nonsense!" or "Perhaps the teacher that made the selection knew the other girls better because you certainly were as good as the rest!" This would have been an excellent example of not listening to the child. At that moment cheerleading was one of the most important happenings in her life and the beginning of a valuable learning experience of accepting one's limitations. Blaming the teacher or refusing to accept the decision is of no help to Mary. Taking the time and effort to listen provided Mary with the*

opportunity to evaluate the situation on her own level of compre-
hension and better understand how to accept disappointment ration-
ally.

Being aware of *sudden changes in attitude and behavior* is also important in helping children mature socially and emotionally. Parents and teachers should be alerted by the counselor to be sensitive to a child who suddenly seems to lose interest in things that previously interested him, seems to be content to sit alone instead of joining the *usual* activity with his friends, and in general seems to exhibit character traits that are not his usual behavior patterns. The key to this situation is *sudden change.* What is normal for one child may be abnormal for another. The middle school years have been described as years of turmoil. Changes are not unusual but the teacher and parent should be aware that dramatic reversals in behavior and attitude require attention. Each person is unique and must be evaluated according to his or her own limitations and personal characteristics.

Illustration: *Charles was fascinated by cars and airplane models. He spent hours working with his friends constructing these models. The usual quiet concentration of the past seemed to be disrupted more and more frequently with outbursts by Charles and the sessions became less populated with his friends, who seemed to get the brunt of his impatience. Charles seemed irritable and impatient with everyone. The first reaction of his parents was to pass it off as growing pains and the usual adolescent conflicts. But as this continued the parents sought out the counselor who followed up with a talk with Charles's teacher. This revealed that the teacher too was concerned about Charles's work for the past few weeks. She questioned whether anything was wrong at home. With their concern for Charles and upon the teacher's and counselor's recommendations, Charles was taken to the family doctor by his parents for a check-up. The doctor discovered a deterioration in Charles's vision. After medical treatment for vision correction, with new glasses selected by Charles, the boy seemed to be able to return to his past behavior pattern and was again busily working at models and improving in his school work. The problem had been that he could no longer see the details necessary in his work and therefore he could not live up to his own expectations. The quick concern and interest of his parents and teacher, with the help of the counselor, alerted by his sudden loss of incentive and change in behavior, helped avoid much unpleasantness for Charles.*

Parents should be encouraged to develop *good relationships with their child's friends* as another logical means of communication. Encouraging children to bring friends home and treating these friends in a way that helps them and your child know that you really enjoy their being there makes it unnecessary for the child to seek other places to go.

Illustration: *Lizabeth's mother encouraged her to invite a few of her friends to lunch one Saturday. It was the kind of lunch that showed her daughter and friends that because they were special she wanted to treat them special with a favorite food or a well-liked dessert. Mother was home but did not interfere with their activities. She complimented their behavior when one child left by saying how she enjoyed having them. She treated them with the same courtesy that she would have showed to her friends. The children were obviously comfortable having her around. Rather than a buddy relationship, it was an adult–child relationship that the friends and daughter could appreciate. The initial meeting and the follow-up occasions when friends came and felt welcomed in the home set the stage for good communication between the child and parent.*

It is not necessary for the parent to organize or manage the activity in any way. It is important that the parent be there. Children are quick to sense when they are not wanted or when they are being tolerated. Active children can disturb the neatness of a home. The decision has to be made as to what is more important, everything neatly and untouched in place or the joyous laughter of youngsters dancing and sharing the excitement of the day. Carpeting can take much more punishment than the stifling of individual growth and development. The guidance of children should be realistic and values should be considered when determining rules and regulations in the home or classroom.

The counselor should emphasize the *importance of good home-school relationships* to the parent. The home and school need to work hand in hand to provide the best environmental climate for the child. It is important for parent, teacher, principal, and counselor to have respect and trust for one another. They should have an open line of communication. A conference between a teacher and parent or a teacher and counselor with the parent should not be a threatening situation.

Illustration: *Mrs. G., a sixth-grade teacher, made it a point to talk to each parent early in the year to establish a positive relationship with the home. Her conferences generally were occasions where she encouraged the parents to ask her questions and tell her about their child. After this initial meeting, it was a simple matter to call parents concerning any problem that arose as well as providing information on special achievements. The first reaction to this contact was one of surprise and even suspicion by many parents for their only contact with teachers previously had been for their child's poor performance in school. The teacher's positive approach started school out on a pleasant note for both student and teacher. The contact by the teacher had made them want to be more involved, for they felt the teacher displayed a respect for them that many had never felt before. This interaction has a two-fold consequence. In addition to the direct contact with parent, the attitude toward the teacher was one of cooperation and there was less "blaming of the teacher" in problems that arose.*

Establishment of wholesome standards of living within the home and school community is of vital importance in providing a foundation of behavior patterns on which the child can rely. Most families and classroom teachers feel that their present standards within the home or classroom are adequate and see no need for change. Since situations occur that demand change, there must be room for flexibility. The following considerations must be kept in mind. Is the discipline fair? Are the rights of every person, adult or child, respected? Do you play favorites among the children? Children are quick to detect deception and insincerity. A child expects to be corrected when he has violated a clear-cut rule of home or school. If ignored, he is most likely to get into more severe difficulty because he rationalizes that no one cares. If he is treated too severely he cannot justify the treatment and may not be able to correct the mistake if not clearly told the error he has made. Correction is not necessarily physical punishment but rather a fostering of better understanding of a more acceptable and positive alternative.

Illustration: *Steven needed a pen for school and couldn't find one in his desk, so he took his sister's without asking. Upon arriving home that afternoon he looked in his pocket and found the pen missing. Meanwhile his sister had searched for the pen in vain. Mother then recalled Steven had a pen that morning and asked him about it. After much discussion it was revealed that he had taken it and lost it. The points of concern discussed were: Steven's lack of consideration for others because he did not ask to borrow it and the need for him to replace what he had lost. Through careful investigation, Steven found his own pen and agreed to either give that to his sister or purchase a new one with his earnings. Steven could not argue with these alternatives. The entire situation was handled calmly and logically. Steven was made aware of his responsibility to others yet he was given a chance to accept a punishment that was positive and served a purpose. It showed that those involved cared enough about him to give him a chance to right a wrong. The same procedures could be used effectively in the classroom.*

It is vital that children understand that love is not used as a pawn. A *youngster must feel he is loved* even when he is being disciplined or corrected. The feeling that a person cares enough to correct and help must be the underlying concept. A parent or teacher who reacts in a rage and an uncontrolled manner at an infraction of a rule shows the child he lacks respect for the child as well as for himself. He also presents a negative communication model. What a parent or teacher does and how he acts is more meaningful than what he says.

Demonstration of affection must be the result of a sincere feeling that is spontaneous reaction to something you honestly find pleasing.

Illustration: *June was sitting at the kitchen table studiously writing an assignment for school. She was obviously concentrating and doing her best. Her mother was watching her as she finished washing the dishes from the evening meal. The affection between mother and daughter was seen in the instant when June, upon completion of her work, sighed heavily and looked to her mother for response. Mother's returned smile of obvious pride and affection was the unspoken word. In a way it was June's security blanket. Not one verbal exchange was spoken but the glow on June's face reflected the warmth of the moment. June had no doubts that she was loved as she picked up her books and headed toward the phone to call a friend.*

Caution must be taken that overprotection is not mistaken for love. This may destroy instead of build. It may destroy self-confidence and pride and question sincerity. An overprotective parent may have so many rules that a child is prevented from exploring and experimenting on his own. His creativity will soon be stifled and he will begin to question his own judgment. This child may become afraid to venture out on his own or perhaps react with resentment to the lack of confidence exhibited by his parents or teachers and no longer look to them for guidance and advise. Thus the door to future communication between parent and child and teacher and child begins to close. The middle school child seems filled with doubts and most especially needs to know that both parent and teacher can be trusted to be concerned for his welfare, happiness, and success.

Ability to face issues

As soon as a child enters the world he is faced with decision-making experiences. He is required to face up to experiences in which he plays a part or to be shielded from these experiences. Parents are often tempted to do the latter. By preventing a child from accepting responsibility for his actions, he will find each action more and more irresponsible. He will find it impossible to make his own decisions in long-range planning, for he will have no past experience on which to base his new decisions.

Illustration: *Helen, a fifth-grader, was given the responsibility to care for the class pet hamsters for the weekend. There were two. During the weekend, one of the hamsters got caught in the exercise wheel of his cage and died. Helen was naturally quite upset and sought her parents' advice. The mother's suggestion was to purchase another hamster to replace the one that died and not mention it to the class. This was done and Helen returned to school on Monday with the two hamsters. Although the change was not noticed by the teacher, several children seemed to notice one hamster looked different, and the two were not getting along as before. After many tears, Helen admitted that one had died and been replaced. The teacher, fortunately, was able to console Helen and explain to her that all realized it had been an accident. She explained to Helen how fortunate it was that the hamsters were home with her for otherwise they would have been alone for the weekend. She also explained that there was no need to replace the hamster secretly, for all would have understood that this accident was not her fault.*

The parents, in their attempt to cover up for Helen had not only encouraged her to lie but by their actions, had declared her guilty of something for which she was not to blame. In their effort to shield Helen they had condoned a negative behavior pattern. After consideration Helen saw this was wrong and began to question the wisdom of her parent's solution. The experience of facing issues helped Helen understand the importance of truth, courage, and the possibility of being confronted with a difficult situation through no fault of her own.

Fun, pleasurable sensations
and experiences

All children enjoy fun, pleasurable experiences, and sensations that produce pleasure. The area of concern is the degree of participation in such activity. The drug user, the alcohol user, and often the sexually promiscuous youngster have been found to seek this activity in exclusion of all else. The youngster has to find satisfaction in this area in proportion to other emotional, social, and physical needs. These can be met through encouragement of a hobby or by creating situations in which the youngster can experience real joy without artificial stimulation or socially unacceptable behavior. Satisfaction may also be achieved by bringing enjoyment into the classroom and home through exhibitions of good sportsmanship, admitting the imperfections of adults, being able to laugh at silly little things that go wrong around the house and classroom, and providing and fulfilling reasonable standards of accomplishment by clarifying goals and aims.

Illustration: *Marcia was an extremely quiet child—a loner—unable to make friends among her peers. (Seeking acceptance is a primary motivator of deviant social behavior.) Because she was a quiet and cooperative child, no one paid particular attention to her. She had developed through the years a friendship with an elderly couple in the community whom she often visited after school. She had found the couple's bird collection fascinating. She would listen enthusiastically to the endless tales of the sources of these beautiful woodcuttings. When Marcia mentioned this at school, the teacher perceptively decided to take advantage of this interest to stimulate Marcia's social life and helped her begin her own collection of carved dogs. Each time the family went on a trip all would search for a dog for Marcia's collection. As this hobby grew, Marcia became more discriminating in her choices and was soon talking to the salespersons with a more assured and relaxed attitude. She began to seek out further information through investigation at the library, where she met youngsters with similar interests. New-found friends were brought home to view her treasures. Having this extensive collection gave Marcia the support she needed to build her self-confidence and self-esteem. She became the class "expert" on identification of dog breeds and eventually was recognized for this skill within the entire school. Looking back it seemed impossible that this was the same shy middle schooler who had so little to contribute to class previously and now was seriously planning to become a veterinarian.*

Cooperative planning of the school and home gives some good guidelines for helping children in their adjustment to their environment. The family should become involved in a supportive manner. There are many opportunities within the home to further the development of the individual child as a member of the family group as well as a member of the school community. The family discussion time during dinner is an excellent time for developing concepts. Having all the family together on at least one occasion during the day helps to provide a stronghold of solidarity. It encourages the use of those within the family as sounding boards for ideas, problems, and general clarification of concepts and interpretations of values. It opens doors to communication. It helps all involved understand the importance of caring for someone else as each member of the family shows respect for the other. This can also be the mode of operation in the classroom. The interaction among students should reflect a sense of respect and responsibility toward peers.

Illustration: *Jean was unusually quiet at the dinner table that evening and all in the family were aware of this change from her usual animated manner. As the conversation moved into discussion about the events of the day, Jean mentioned her concern over cheating in class. It seemed someone had asked to see her paper during a test and she was torn between her desire to help her friend and her feeling that it would be wrong. It was interesting that neither parent demanded that she tell what her decision had been. The family talked of alternatives. With this unthreatening relationship, the entire family concluded that Jean had to make her own decision. The responsibility one has to a friend was discussed. Young brother Tom made the point that he felt giving the answer for friendship's sake was really just like buying a friend. The experience Jean had and shared with her family provided a realistic evaluation of peer pressure, loyalty, and honesty in everyday situations and cooperation and trust within the family unit. All who were part of the discussion had learned something from the experience.*

Had Jean's parents said, "That's terrible! Don't ever let me hear about you letting someone copy off your paper!" they would have been unfairly judgmental. Jean would think twice before asking another opinion that would evaluate a judgment or decision she had made or was considering making. For she was not seeking to be judged and evaluated but rather to be given alternatives from which she could make future decisions.

Parents and teachers must be aware of peer pressure. It is a real and powerful force of motivation. The middle schooler has to learn to discriminate between right and wrong and to have developed enough self-confidence to react rationally to peer pressure. This can only be achieved by building positive feelings about self, understanding self-limitations and potential, and finding a measure of success in something that is respected by someone else.

It is also vital that parents and teachers set reasonable standards of accomplishment for youngsters. Unrealistic standards adopted by children guarantee failure and lead to reluctance to try new experiences.

Illustration: *Henry, an eighth-grader, suddenly had a seizure which was diagnosed as severe epilepsy. He had been active in sports and a star quarterback on the middle school football team. He had already been approached by the high school coach to become a member of the freshman team when he entered ninth grade next year. This was a crushing blow to Henry, for medication was not stabilizing his condition and the medical prognosis demanded that all athletic involvement be curtailed. He was told he must learn to live a more sedentary life. Henry was crushed. He rejected this decision and, because of his inability to accept it, compounded his problems and brought on more intense seizures. It soon became a nightmare for Henry and his family. His school work suffered; his illness became more difficult to control; his attitude became more and more negative every day. Henry became involved in drugs. He was counseled by the school staff but to no avail. He became truant in school and belligerent at home. On several occasions he was brought home unconscious after passing out on the street from either drugs or drinking. Finally, in desperation, he was committed by the family, with help from the community guidance clinic, to the state hospital. While in the hospital he became more involved in the drug culture and seemed to be on a self-destructive course. The hospital doctors warned his parents that his continued actions would most certainly shorten his life. At seventeen, two years after his commitment, the chief psychiatrist said there was nothing they could do to help Henry. He stated to the parents that this previously all-American boy would not last another year.*

It was felt by those who examined the situation that Henry had felt that his athletic success was all that gave him self-worth. When this was denied him, he saw no reason for the future. Until he could find life of value and see a place for himself, no therapy, specialists, family, or teachers could seem to reach him. The importance of moderation was clearly illustrated here. The need for alternatives to save this youngster's life was urgent. The family decided to remove him from the area, with its familiar pressures and surroundings, and try

41

to give him a new lease on life. On a trip to Florida they discovered a ranch that sought young men to work with wayward boys. Henry seemed interested and voiced the opinion that maybe he could help prevent some other young kid from fouling up his life as he had. Two years have passed and Henry continues to serve as an instructor in this ranch commune. He is receiving much feedback from his "charges." He now has responsibility toward others. He may make it; time will tell. His parents and teachers communicate with him and his responses have increased, reflecting his enthusiasm for his new-found purpose in life. His parents and teachers wonder how they could have prevented this trauma in what they all believed to be a stable, well-adjusted child. The need for children to learn to cope with pressures, changes, disappointments, and rejections is illustrated dramatically here. How many youngsters have not made it? We must be constantly aware of each child's needs so that he can move comfortably into alternative choices when that is necessary. Henry, like others, needed support and guidelines. He could not do it alone.

Sometimes the family or the teacher is too close to the situation to help. Outside help should be sought. Time is of great importance. Reinforcement, magnification, and distortion occur when a problem is ignored. Clarification is needed and the best source of aid should be sought at the earliest moment. All individuals like fun and pleasurable experiences and sensations. The youngster must be given direction in order to understand how these experiences may be acquired in an acceptable manner within the society in which he lives. A child has to be taught by example and direction that these experiences cannot be at the expense of others, that they have a place in, but cannot monopolize, one's life, that they may be shared at appropriate times, and what appropriate times are. Direction is the key to understanding. Channeling these feelings and desires into acceptable behavior patterns results in rewarding and fulfilling experiences basic to sound personality development.

Peer pressure

In the battle for individuality we see the child strive to conform. He does not want to be different. As he grows older he becomes more conscious of his desire to be like everyone else, be accepted and also find his own identity. So within the structure of our society we bring children up in conflict. The need for self-understanding is basic to maturity yet peer pressure demands likeness in all. Adults often reinforce this theory by encouraging early dating (because the girl next door is dating), long hair on boys (because the fashion magazines display this as "in"), participation in tumbling class, dancing class, baseball teams, football, and so on (because everyone else does it). Peer pressure is exerted among adult peers as well as children. It is the image passed down to the child—that of conforming to others. We adults continually express our desire to encourage children to be individuals, to develop their potential, to be themselves. We are giving lip service to a belief and encourage the exact opposite. Then we question why a child is so greatly influenced by his peers. The child is merely following the example of the adult. If this is our way of life then we must face it realistically. We must not downgrade these peer influences as negative relationships but rather help the child learn to be discriminating in his peer interactions.

Illustration: *Joy was a member of the girl's softball team. Thursday afternoon there was a planned practice and all team members were expected to be there. Joy was hoping to get the position of pitcher and that practice was to be for tryouts for this position. On that same afternoon, class pictures were being taken for her church choir, of which she was a member. Her mother had told her to go for the picture and her teammates were trying to persuade her to stay for practice. She decided to stay for practice and miss the picture taking. She had decided to take the consequences of her mother's anger, her absence from the picture, because she wanted to be on the team. She was surprised that she was not punished when arriving home but merely told by her mother that she felt she had made a poor decision. Several months later, upon publication of the church yearbook, she was conspicuous by her absence. The softball season was over. She had pitched a few times but that was past and she began to evaluate what she had done. She realized then that she could have had another chance as a team member but there was no second chance for the picture for that year. She had learned an important lesson. She, not her persuasive peers, had to live with her decisions. Her mother's attitude was a wise one. If she had severely punished Joy the lesson of responsibility for one's actions would have been clouded by the reprimand. Joy had to account to herself for her actions. This is much more difficult than accounting to someone else. Her future decisions will probably be more logically weighed when peer pressure becomes one of the criteria.*

Peer relationships can be positive. They can provide models of excellence. A child who seeks out others who are considered unacceptable within society and chooses to emulate their behavior has usually found relationships with those considered acceptable unsatisfactory and unfulfilling. It is the parent's or teacher's role to be aware of this child's problem before he is forced to find acceptance that is socially unacceptable in his search for self-worth.

Illustration: *Joan was born with a severe birthmark on her face. It was bright red and could not be ignored. Nothing could be done to remediate it medically until she was sixteen years old. Her parents were concerned about her adjustment to the stares and comments of her peers (and strangers) until cosmetic surgery could be performed. The neighborhood children seemed to accept her appearance casually (after the initial shock of her younger years) and Joan managed to live with the situation. In sixth grade, several of her friends started to show interest in boys and were beginning to go to movies and parties with boys. Joan was never included in dating plans. Fortunately, her teacher and mother saw this situation beginning to arise and provided supportive measures for Joan by introducing her to makeup that helped cover the redness, inviting boys and girls to the house for parties, and generally encouraging Joan to face the issue squarely. It was concluded that it wasn't exclusively an appearance problem for Joan, but that she really didn't want to date boys yet and in a way she was glad that she didn't have to. It developed that many of the children felt that way and welcomed the open house that Joan's mother provided because it didn't demand that they "pair up" and made most of the youngsters feel more comfortable and relaxed with each other. It was the teacher's belief that this realistic viewpoint of Joan's problem had prevented her from using it as a rationalization for anything she couldn't do or have. It is not uncommon for a person who feels different or neglected to use the false security of the drug culture to cover up these feelings. Joan had no need to seek this outlet.*

The handling of Joan's problem was an example of preventive procedure through the working together of all those involved in her growth and development. Without this interrelationship and mutual concern, preventive procedures cannot be initiated and carried through. It must be an ongoing process to be successful for attitudes, values, and goals are not overnight accomplishments. They are the result of living experiences in the lifetime of the person and are influenced by all experiences and people with whom the person comes in contact. As long as we as adults put so much weight on conformity and being like our neighbors and friends, our children are going to reflect this attitude in their relationships with their peers.

Conformity, structured activity, and
rules and regulations

Our society today stresses conformity, structured activity, and compliance with rules and regulations. It is a way of life and is usually reacted to with varying degrees of acceptance or reluctance by the middle school child. Each person is asked to conform to family procedure, fulfill a specific role as a functioning member of this group, and follow through on rules and regulations. The degree of these functions is of significant importance. It is possible for the rules and regulations of the home to be in direct conflict with those of the school. A parent in the home and a teacher in the school, must take this fact into consideration. Are these restrictions realistic or are they unreasonable?

Illustration: *Ellen, a fifth-grader, was a member of the tumbling team in her middle school. The group was invited to perform for a neighboring PTA. The event was to conclude at 9:00 P.M. on a school night. Ellen's parents had a bedtime rule of 10:00 P.M. for school nights and it would be impossible for Ellen to meet this deadline if she joined the team in a refreshment stop after the performance. Her parents decided to go along with Ellen and bring her home on schedule instead of extending the curfew they had set. They felt that relaxing this rule would be lax on their part and perhaps thus encourage bad habits of irresponsibility. This inflexibility on the parents' part prevented Ellen from participating in a far greater experience of team spirit and the excitement of being with her friends on this special occasion. The overprotectiveness of her parents showed little respect for Ellen's needs. The parents' priorities could be challenged. Would the extra half-hour of sleep justify Ellen's restriction from the activity?*

Rules and regulations should be flexible and continually evaluated. Parents and teachers have to be able to accept changes and thus help the child to accept changes. The highly structured life of a child leaves little room for self-discipline, decision making, practice in good judgment, and weighing alternatives. A child who is "programmed" to perform in a certain manner at all times is stifled creatively and stunted in his or her emotional growth.

Illustration: *Sidney was always a quiet child who could be depended upon to respond to any direction by the teacher. Entering seventh grade in the middle school program, Sidney was to experience his first departmentalized classes. He had worked carefully with his parents and teachers setting up his schedule. In fact, his mother had come to school with him before opening day to be assured that he would be able to find all his classes and would be off to a good start. Sidney and his mother led a very structured life. His military father insisted on a very organized routine, from which there was no deviation. Meals were prompt, bedtime exact, trips planned well in advance, and any reluctance to conform resulted in severe punishment. In a conference with the teacher, the mother proudly related how perfectly Sidney behaved and how cooperative he always was. She was proud to say that he had never felt the wrath of his father's discipline as had the other two boys. The first day of class in the new program, one of Sidney's classes was changed and a note was placed on the door for the student's direction. For some reason, when Sidney arrived at the classroom the note had either fallen off or been removed, but the classroom was empty. Sidney looked at his schedule and panicked. He had no idea what to do. His solution was to retreat to the boys room where he hid until the end of the period. Why did this happen? It is logical that Sidney, who had never been asked to make decisions nor to adjust his routine on the spur of the moment was unable to cope with a change. Fortunately, the situation was brought to the attention of the school counselor who immediately contacted the parents, with Sidney's permission, and held a four-way conference to alert them to the possible problems that could occur unless Sidney were given the opportunity to have some freedom of choice. What may be seen as the "perfect child" who responds to adult needs may be an empty child with no direction or self-motivation to depend upon when he needs to make his own choices or accept changes in his routine.*

The opportunity to explore, experiment, and sit quietly and think is needed to help a youngster accept his own imperfections as well as the imperfections of others. He needs to be able to function without a preplanned timetable if he is expected to function independently. Without experience he will be unable to do this. The parent and teacher, therefore, should provide:

1. Experiences that will give the child a chance to be flexible and make changes.
2. Opportunity to make decisions and judgments on his or her own.
3. Acceptance by the adult involved of variations of rules and regulations when the need arises.
4. Minimum amount of rules and regulations so that these restrictions are realistic.

5. Continual reevaluation of appropriateness of guidelines that determine the rules and regulations within the home and school.

Consideration of needs and sensitivity and a practical awareness of our constantly changing society in which a child functions is basic in providing a good foundation for future decision making and healthy acceptance of change.

All human beings strive for success. The child has to be exposed to success and the process of achieving it. A child who never has known disappointment, has had all his limitations rationalized as the weaknesses and inefficiencies of others, will have a difficult time accepting his own limitations. This leads to false expectations and therefore an inability to accept everyday disappointments. Drugs provide instant gratification but mask the problems that lead to their use. The child must be made aware of the fact that this is only a temporary solution, for when the impact of the drug wears off the problem is still there. In addition to this, the child becomes less capable of coping with the problem than before the use of the drug. Instant gratification is only a way of delaying the decision-making process.

Illustration: *Jerry's parents had always considered him a good boy who never gave them too much difficulty. On several occasions, when Jerry was involved in neighborhood vandalism (scratching his name on a neighbor's car, ripping a neighbor's backboard down in anger, for example) his parents excused it as "boys will be boys." Jerry wanted a minibike and was promised one for his birthday. After he got the bike, he wanted a motorcycle, which he received for Christmas. He then wanted a basketball court in their backyard, since the boys in the neighborhood didn't like the facilities at the local schoolyard. Each request was granted and seemed to lead to more and more disturbances in the neighborhood. Finally the parents were called to school because Jerry was involved in a gang fight. He was quite belligerent to the principal and remarked "You can't do nothing to me. You touch me and my Dad will sue you and you'll lose your job." The parents were shocked at this behavior. Plans were made for Jerry to be evaluated by the Child Study Team and Jerry was found to be under extreme tension as well as a very angry boy. Much to his parents' surprise he expressed the feeling that they didn't love him, that they had no time for him and were trying to buy him off with all the material things he requested. He had actually asked for all those expensive things hoping they would refuse his requests and show more interest in him as a person. His parents were*

47

sincerely concerned and anxious to mend these broken fences between themselves and their son. This is not an unusual situation. Parents need to be aware of a child's messages for help and attention. Providing everything for a child that he requests is the easy way. Helping him to build restraints and restrictions within himself is more difficult but nevertheless essential.

Success — instant gratification

The infant in the home clearly defines his needs by crying and making the appropriate noises and movements until his needs are satisfied. He cannot wait. As a child grows older, he learns to wait a little longer to satisfy his needs. The child who has never been permitted to learn this has difficulty in adjusting to school, relationships with others, and being a part of this competitive world. *Success*, according to Webster's dictionary, is "a favorable termination of a venture." The child who has not had the experience of striving for success, but rather has always had assistance in achieving needs, is usually unable to make his own decisions and have enough stick-to-itiveness to follow through on a project. Formulating the habit of looking to others to fulfill needs leads to the false assumption that success is the product of another's work. It is often heard, "Why did Johnny do that? We have given him everything. There was no need for him to steal!" The need was not for the product he stole but rather to be accepted by his peers. In a way, the child who begins performing unacceptable acts such as this is finding success in his relationship with others. His need for success is instantly gratified by the theft and sometimes, when he is caught, he finds this a rewarding experience. It is more difficult to help a child develop successful experiences on his own than to cater to his needs. But it is essential that each child be exposed to successful experiences that have been the result of his own endeavors.

Information, statistics, threats, warnings, and precautions concerning drugs, alcohol, and sexual promiscuity are only superficial approaches to the problems. Each person must be reinforced with adequate emotional stability and security that will provide the strength, logic, knowledge, and desire to make intelligent and practical decisions when they have to be made. Often the aftereffects of these involvements with drugs, alcohol, and sex are irreversible. There is no turning back. Abuse leads to involvement with a culture different from that acceptable to the society in which the person lives. One who decides upon involvement and loyalty to the drug culture, for example, must therefore reject his former cultural codes. This is a tremendous commitment and is not a casual decision to be made in one rash moment. We strongly believe that through reinforcement of the individual's self-worth, those who are involved with the child's growth and development can do much to provide him with the armor necessary to cope with the pressures that may lead to avoidance of the problems and issues that confront him. He will have had enough self-esteeming experiences to give him the self-confidence and know-how he needs to make realistic long-range decisions. He will not need artificial support to help him endure life but rather accept his daily experiences as an exciting challenge. He will have enough faith in himself to look to the future with hope and courage as well as enthusiasm. He will be aware that there is no future in a drug oriented life.

Awareness is the key. The middle school counselor, administrator, and teacher who respond sensitively to all students seeking direction and guidance, who work cooperatively with parents and colleagues, and who look beyond the immediate behavior for reasons and solutions will be fulfilling a major service to the school community.

Supplementary Readings

Ginott, Haim. *Between Parent and Teenager.* New York: Macmillan, 1969.

Glasser, William. *Identity Society.* New York: Harper and Row (paper), 1975.

Glasser, William. *Schools Without Failure.* New York: Harper and Row (paper), 1975.

Stamm, Martin L., and Nissman, Blossom S. *Your Child and Drugs.* Rancocas, N.J.: Guidance Awareness Publications, Box 106, revised 1978.

Wisconsin Clearing House Publications. Booklet no. 101, *Take the Time*; Booklet no. 102, *What's There to Do Besides Drink?* Booklet no. 104, *Alcohol: The Number One Drug*; Booklet no. 106, *The Manual for Group Facilitators.* Madison: Wisconsin Clearinghouse (420 North Lake St.), 1977.

CHAPTER FOUR

A Model for Middle School Guidance Services: The Human Development Center

Alert and sensitive educators are seeking solutions to the repressive practices and archaic barriers to the educational process. Emphasis is on programs of total development. Elementary and secondary school professionals have been caught up in a lock-step, marking time to the tune of regimentation, low budgets, administrative short-cuts, and packaged learning for such a long time, that it is difficult to accept change. Perhaps it is time to listen to the sound of a different drummer. Within the continuum of the educational process—early elementary to high school level—comes this relatively new concept based on a philosophy and a belief about the nature of growing children—the middle school. Recognizing the significant differences in the needs of children from ten to fourteen,[1] middle school personnel look to leadership charged with the responsibility of developing this philosophy. The counselor, trained to understand the social and emotional development of the child, therefore, accepts a coleadership role with teachers and administrators in developing a comprehensive, humanistic middle school.

Those working with the middle school student, therefore, need to be aware of the guidance responsibilities of the middle school as a

---

1. See James F. Adams, *Understanding Adolescence*, 3rd ed. (Boston: Allyn and Bacon, 1976) for an excellent discussion on the needs of the adolescent.

51

unit. How will this school work most effectively in coping with the needs of these children at this crucial stage of their development? The authors view middle school guidance services as a *Human Development Center* (HDC) that deals with sensitive human beings (students, teachers, parents, and the community as a whole) developing a rapport between these persons and coordinating the services to provide the most productive program possible. The HDC seems a most appropriate label for guidance in the middle school. This concept accepts the involvement of the counselor with scholarship, educational counseling, vocational and career counseling, and program development as well as social and emotional growth and development. It is a means of helping the students and staff discover more about themselves as well as improving the learning environment. The counselor becomes an advocate of the student, often fulfilling the role of ombudsman. The counselor is child-centered and flexible. The counselor is cognizant of the fact that the school is in a position to provide a workshop for the humanistic aspects of education and that his role must be in coordination and cooperation with all other staff members, with the classroom teacher as his extended arm of communication.

Through an HDC approach, where the student can be selective and the counselor available when needed, to be discussed in the following chapter, this developmental all-inclusive view of education is possible. The HDC therefore become the nucleus of the school services. It includes services in curriculum, community, communication, counseling, crisis, professional growth, assessment, and career resources. Each cluster functions independently as well as being part of a unit mutually interested in providing services to meet needs of the professional staff, students, parents, and the community. These services can be performed effectively only when all these facets are considered. Through the HDC the school provides a place where students, teachers, counselors, administrators, and parents can communicate with ease. It provides many open doors and eliminates duplication of responsibility. It calls upon these persons to share their skills and work as a cooperative unit with the students, each as a vital member of the guidance team.

Educators today talk about students having more say about education, yet there is rarely a platform provided for them to say it. This model provides guidance services as a focal point in the school program and demands that the counselor include team involvement, with the active participation of students. Through this cooperative process, the counselor will aid the administrator, teacher, parent, and student in helping each discover how he can be of greater service to the school and to himself. In turn, each becomes more aware of himself and his functional role in his school and home community. In a way, it demands that all involved in the education process become aware of the activity outside his role as well as recognizing his own responsibilities. Responsibilities are more clearly defined and, therefore, more willingly accepted and more frequently requested and followed through. It is the unknown that causes fear and stagnation. Once people are aware of what is available to them and how they can use these services, the services become part of their everyday experiences and are accepted as basic to their needs. The guidance service is no longer exclusively crisis-centered but rather a preventive service available to all. How then are these clusters identified and defined? (see fig. 4–1).

Curriculum Service Cluster

The *Curriculum Service Cluster* is clearly identified to the student and used to facilitate course placement and readjustment of academic programming. This is implemented through the use of para-professionals and will free the counselor from the bulk of clerical duties that presently tie many counselors to their desks. In addition to this service, the curriculum cluster can provide isolation areas accessible to the student when he needs to work alone. These are specifically designated for this purpose and are set up in a similar fashion to a carrel in a typical library study area. A counselor or counselor-trained teacher assigned to this area on a rotating basis is available to the students. Within this cluster is the resource center supplied with materials and book exchanges on topics dealing with work study and interpersonal relationships in school. Peer tutors are obtained upon request from the students for assistance in curricular work. Daily group sessions are provided to discuss predetermined topics requested by students and/or faculty. The group sessions, led by either teacher, counselor, student, or administrator, or even parents, deal with further explanation of upcoming standardized tests (such as the SAT) or other current problems of interest to the school community relating to curriculum needs, changes, or additions.

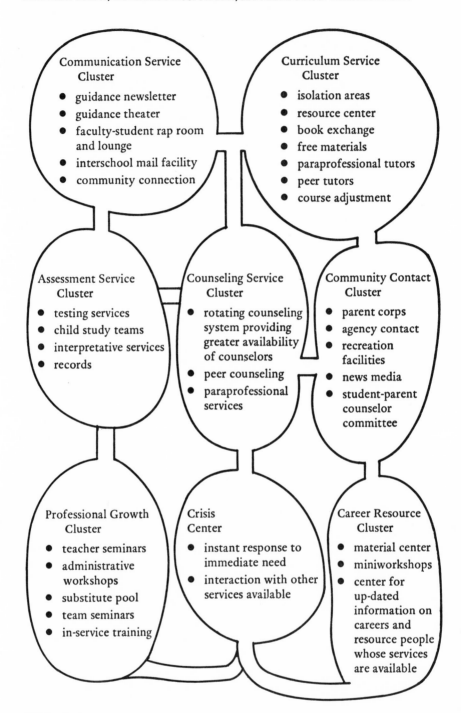

Figure 4–1
The Human Development Center

Illustration: *Jean arrived at Center School after the semester had already begun. Her guidance counselor met with her in determining class placement for general information as an introduction to her new school. The counselor checked the curriculum cluster schedule and noted that a group of freshmen were meeting in an open forum to discuss implementation of new extracurricular programs. The chairperson, student Sally S., was sent a note requesting that Jean be invited to the meeting and given some insight into the program and activities at Center School. This was followed up and Jean made some interesting suggestions to the committee as the result of her experiences in another school. The first day at Center School for Jean was one of acceptance. The teacher working with the committee saw to it that Jean had an escort to all her classes through this group. The transition from another community during the school year was made gracefully and naturally for Jean and did not necessitate a large block of clerical time from the counselor's day. There was no question that this helped Jean move more quickly into the swing of the school's activities and feel more at ease in her schoolwork because she was no longer a stranger.*

Community Contact Service Cluster

The *Community Contact Service Cluster* is composed of a parent corps that is available as an extention of school services. These parents are selected for services as resource people, school chaperones, teacher-aides, and group leaders. One professional (counselor, teacher, or administrator) accepts the responsibility of contact person to provide an open line of communication with the local agencies and the news media. This committee acts as a liaison between the school and these outside agencies. A school representative from the faculty and student body accepts joint responsibility for keeping up to date the community and school recreation roster as the source of information for community and school needs. A teacher or counselor accepts the leadership role for the overall program and works closely with a student-parent-community involvement and interaction. If the school has a PTA organization, it can be coordinated with the work of this group.

Illustration: *Pete is one of seven children. His teacher in the fifth grade, as well as teachers in previous grades, consistently describe him as quiet, withdrawn, yet cooperative in school. His sixth-grade teacher felt that Pete was lost in the crowd at home and was con-*

cerned over his lack of interaction with his peers. Gradually a relationship of trust grew between the teacher and the child. In conversation one day it was brought out that Pete had been given a bowling ball by his uncle but had never used it because he had no one to go with and no way to get to the community bowling center. There was no economic problem since the father, an engineer, made a more than adequate living for his family. Being a passive child, Pete had never asked to join his brothers for he felt they would bowl so much better than he. He knew no one his age that bowled. His brothers and sister, according to Pete, had their own circles of friends and he had learned to function satisfactorily as a loner. But, through the conversation, the teacher felt that Pete would enjoy learning to bowl. The teacher then contacted the student leader of the Community Contact Service Cluster and requested information on local bowling groups. In addition he requested that the group assist Pete in finding a beginning group and a means of transportation. The student-parent-counselor committee obtained a placement for Pete in a car pool of a Saturday morning bowling group. Pete was brought into the group and for the first time in his life was actively a part of a peer group situation. It was a beginning for Pete and an easy step for the teacher, since the Community Contact Service Cluster was available. In this case only the service functioning under the cluster dealing with placement was brought into play with the counselor freed from the responsibility fulfilled by the committee established for such a purpose.

Communication Service Cluster

The *Communication Service Cluster* acts in a public relations capacity. The leader need not necessarily be a counselor but may be a teacher and/or student leader interested in this type of activity. This cluster accepts the responsibility for a monthly guidance newsletter and presents a guidance theater with current materials dealing with personal development significant to the teenage student. This cluster also accepts responsibility for the faculty-student rap room lounge. This teacher–student relaxation area is open to those who choose to sit together over a Coke or coffee to become better acquainted and relax in a nonthreatening environment. Many schools have found such an arrangement most successful when the room is located off the main corridor of the school. A classroom may easily be converted to a lounge by the students through the addition of posters and a few comfortable chairs donated by the PTA or a local merchant.

This cluster also implements interschool mail facilities with emphasis on sharing among other schools in the district. It is available to students, faculty, parents, and community organizations, with all groups represented on a committee. This committee has the responsibility of deciding what is acceptable for interschool mail and choices for the guidance theater. Also within this cluster is a community resource such as a local restaurant or recreation center that is used as a source of communication by providing an outlet for announcing upcoming activities.

Illustration: *During the past year, a neighboring state experienced a severe flooding crisis. Entire communities were washed away. Many families were left homeless. Several of the students in the school had relatives who lived in this community and were directly affected by the tragedy. Through the Communication Service Cluster concept the students decided to explore the possibility of aiding these victims. The student group of Explorers (a camping club sponsored by the school) requested communication with all the schools in the area to obtain volunteers for aid for the victims. A bus was borrowed from a neighboring community church; parent volunteers made several trips into the area with students and parents as clean-up crews to help these families get their homes back in living condition. The communication services enabled the group to involve all who were interested without interrupting any normal school services.*

Counseling Service Cluster

The *Counseling Service Cluster* involves services traditionally considered part of the guidance staff's major role. Within the HDC in the middle school, this cluster provides for a rotating counseling system that allows for an available counselor before, during, and after school hours within the school personnel center. Many parents have employment responsibilities that prevent them from participating in counseling programs and services that occur during the school day. The availability of counselors at off-school hours is essential. The parent and the student know that the center is open to be used when needed. Group counseling, peer counseling, and individual counseling services are provided. Each counselor accepts this responsibility the same night each week so that those wishing to use the services have not only the option to seek out the service but to select the counselor of their choice. The counselor's evening time is compensated by an afternoon or morning off on the day that this professional accepts responsibility for evening hours. Peer counseling is provided through the counseling center by interested students who have been involved in an internship program as counselor aides for one year prior to becoming a peer counselor. Peer counselors are used effectively in assisting new entrants, working with groups younger than themselves, and working with the counselor as part of a group.

Illustration: *Jan's school work seemed to have taken a noticeable drop in the past two report periods. Her parents were concerned but because of their working schedules could not get to the school during school hours. With the new schedule of counselors available printed in the monthly guidance bulletin, her parents were made aware of services available before, after, and in the evening of school hours. They wanted very much to seek the counselor's help together. Because of this new organization it was the first time the parents could arrange to be at the school and see the counselor without losing time on the job. Appointments were made with the counselor for 6:00 P.M. the following week. Jan contacted her counselor and arranged to see her before her parents' appointment. The fact that both her parents were to be there was important to Jan. This meeting provided an opportunity for the counselor to give the parents some insight into the school curriculum and to clarify services available in helping this family get the most out of their daughter's school experiences. Follow-up meetings were planned and the parents felt a new closeness to the school. The previous assumption that the parents were not interested was dispelled. A new attitude was assumed by all who had worked with Jan. The availability of the counselor had made a tremendous difference to these parents in their understanding of the school. It also assisted Jan in helping her realize the sincere involvement of her parents and the school as a team.*

Crisis Service Cluster

The *Crisis Service Cluster* provides an instant response to an immediate need. The other clusters are used as follow-up services. A guidance team member (teacher, counselor, administrator) is designated as the crisis person throughout each school day. The team members are on a rotating schedule that is posted so that the person seeking guidance has an option to consult the person of his own selection. With this as an initial service, coupled with the availability of resources of the other clusters, there is an opportunity to work with the causes of the problems that arise in the normal school environment rather than the consequences alone. Without acknowledgment of a crisis outlet, guidance personnel and administrators spend a disproportionate amount of their working time responding to emergencies. There is much overlapping of services and very little time for long-range planning and actual counseling. The Crisis Center acts as a sorting system that directs people to the most appropriate service to respond to their needs.

Illustration: *Several seventh-graders were having difficulty in their math classroom. There finally was a "show down" and the math teacher sent all four to the Crisis Center. They brought this note: "These four boys are disrupting my class and have been doing this for the last few days. Help!" The scheduled person in the center gave the boys an opportunity to "cool off" and then discussed with them their need to develop better school attitudes. The crisis center person did not work out the problem with the boys. It was decided they would profit from a counseling session as a group, and perhaps individually, so contact was made with the Counseling Cluster to meet with these boys at an appropriate time on their schedule. As soon as they calmed down, they were permitted to return to their class and arranged to go to the counselor in the Counseling Service Cluster at the scheduled time. The teacher was aware that the crisis cluster was not a "dumping ground" for problems but rather a place where plans were made to work out the situations that had arisen and allow for minimum disruption of her class. The Crisis Center provided a place to reorganize one's thinking and make plans for alleviating the situation that had become unacceptable.*

Assessment Service Cluster

The *Assessment Service Cluster* provides the testing services for the school. Here the teacher, student, or parent inquires about test results and students are given test batteries as recommended by the school or agency personnel. Such tests could include occupation and vocational information, those that analyze strengths and weaknesses of the student and provide a basis of career development information, and those tests specifically designed to provide objective data in responding to concerns about the student. The Assessment Service Cluster works closely with the *Career Cluster* as a career laboratory and provides a vital service through its tools of measurement. The cluster is ideally manned by a psychometrist trained in this area. A counselor or teacher with testing training and expertise should be able to follow through adequately on this responsibility if a psychometrist is not available. Today many classroom teachers have completed counseling training programs and are fully qualified to accept this responsibility. The assessment service cluster personnel interprets, administers, and works cooperatively with the staff in test selection. The Child Study Team that traditionally assesses learning disabled children works closely with this cluster. The assessment service cluster also plays a role in determining time and procedure for assessment programs in the school by working closely with the administrator, counselor, and teacher representatives.

Illustration: *A standardized test was to be administered to all eighth-grade students at the X school. Previously, the teachers were involved in administering the tests, and this resulted in disruption of the school program for all the other grades. The plan had been to cancel all classes for all other grades for three consecutive Wednesday mornings from 8:00 A.M. to 10:30 A.M. while the eighth-graders took the test. The teachers generally disapproved of this system for they felt they needed this time with their classes. The Assessment Service Cluster personnel made arrangements for the test to be given through a staggered program as an alternative to the previous plan. There was no need to delay classes for unaffected students for the eighth-grade students would take the test during their English and math periods on Monday and Tuesday. Since there was no need for a change in schedule, there was no disruption of the school. The counselor also was able to go personally to the classrooms and supervise the test, combining the groups that had classes the same period. The teachers were used as proctors during the exam. Because all the tests were given by the same person—the trained counselor—there was much more assurance of validity. Upon receipt of test results, the counselor returned to the classes and gave an overall explanation of the terminology and procedures used to score the tests, as well as the format of the results that would be sent to their parents. In addition, the counselor worked closely with the teachers through in-service sessions to assist them in greater understanding of test and most productive use of student records in general. Students were reminded of the availability of the information at the Assessment Service Cluster and teachers were provided a summary of results for their review. The mystery and confusion that so commonly follows a standardized test experience was eliminated and resulted in better understanding by both teachers and students of the value of the standardized test experience.*

Professional Growth Service Cluster

The *Professional Growth Service Cluster* provides for in-service programs for teachers and paraprofessionals in staff development. Such programs are most productively developed as an outgrowth of administrative staff and faculty needs. This cluster also functions as a liaison agent with local training schools as a practicum source. Its main thrust is to encourage and train guidance oriented teachers and provide guidelines for improving interpersonal relationships within the school and community. In response to school-community needs workshops dealing with current concerns are provided for teachers and administrators. These workshops are sponsored by the counseling staff but may often be directed by selected experts whose presentations are tailored to concerns and interests of the school community. Participation in seminars is encouraged as a means of developing better staff coordination and guidance skills. In order to facilitate these activities one school district provided one half day a week for release of all staff and early school dismissal. Another school developed a substitute pool with funds to provide a substitute for teachers involved in a particular student's problem that needed group discussion. Minigrants were made available in New Jersey to pay for substitutes so that teachers could be released from class to participate in training sessions dealing with mainstreaming. Team teachers rotated their large group activities so that alternate team members could attend seminars of interest. The interest of the staff and their involvement is characteristically directly related to the quality and relevance of the seminar topics.

Illustration: *A new policy was presented within Memorial Middle School. All children with learning disabilities, who had previously been isolated in special classes, were now to be mainstreamed into the regular classroom for varying periods of time. The staff's immediate reaction to the idea was negative. The problem was brought to the Professional Growth Service Cluster committee. They decided there was a need to clarify the directive and determine the validity of this program through the coordinated efforts of those teachers who would be involved in the change in placement. A committee was selected to visit schools that had experienced mainstreaming and their reports and comments seemed to support the plan. It was decided that these people would be sought out as resource persons to help the school in adjusting to this plan. Teachers who had experienced the transitional process of mainstreaming were invited to be on a panel to present a brief resume of their experiences. Representatives of the special education classes were also on the panel. The workshop consisted of a half day meeting where the teachers could question the panel members. The program was developed on a volunteer basis and, with the clarification of goals, most of the teachers were willing to become involved. Through prompt action of this committee in response to teacher concerns, much confusion and conflict was avoided. Sound relationships among these professionals (regular and special education teachers) developed and their service as resource persons was quickly recognized.*

Career Resource Service Cluster

The final cluster identified is the *Career Resource Service Cluster.* This cluster is a source of up-dated information to help the student answer questions and clarify concepts and philosophies concerned with future goals. It also aims to provide opportunity to interact with professionals already successful in the working world. Miniworkshops directed by community resource people are available as a technique used to expose students to careers. Local industry, merchants, and advanced training institutions are actively involved as contributors to the career cluster. Today we talk of providing students with serviceable skills as one of the goals of school. Through emphasis on career orientation, decision making, and projections toward future planning, a giant step is being made in this direction. Each guidance office should provide a source of current literature dealing with careers. (This is discussed in greater detail in the chapter on career orientation.)

Illustration: *A middle school located in a small industrial town on the east coast houses a population of students who, upon graduation from high school, either go directly to work in the steel industry or go to college. The latest statistic from the community high school shows 8 percent of the senior class planning to attend college in the fall. All others plan to work in the community or are still seeking employment. Most of the students were unaware of the many opportunities open to them outside of their community. A survey completed by an eighth-grade class studying community structure disclosed that most of the students assumed that they were limited to the work about which they knew and saw in the community. The Career Service Cluster student-staff committee decided to provide a wider exposure to work experiences for the students. They set up a calendar of monthly work experience areas. Using the* Dictionary of Occupational Titles *and the assistance of several social studies and English classes, they determined job groups based on interest. Each month featured another area. The first month's jobs were concerned with those of people interested in art. Bulletin boards around the school reflected this information. Material was fed into classrooms for teachers to use as part of their lessons. Community people who worked in the areas of art were presented at the Guidance Theater (see Communication Cluster for details) for students interested in this area. All attendance was voluntary. The general feeling was that of amazement at the number of jobs available that used art talent as one of the criteria for success. Interest developed for individual follow-up, material on training, and financial potential. English and social study classes used this interest to enrich their class activities. The entire school became a part of the program. Materials were plentiful for industry and local merchants were willing to send it free for the asking. The Career Service Cluster actually became a student activity club; much of the material was provided by the social studies staff, and ideas and interests were stimulated through interaction with the students.*

The illustrations of these clusters are actual experiences in middle schools throughout the nation. Many of these examples were *not* identified as part of a Human Development Center organization but are just that. Each offers services suggested by the HDC we propose. The following chapters of this book should provide school personnel presently involved in the middle school community with ideas and techniques for using the services and facilities presently at their disposal in the most efficient and productive manner with the HDC concept as a model base—one kind of organizational plan for the middle school.

This multifaceted approach to guidance in the school seems to respond to the flexible needs of the modern school's environment. To provide a functioning model in a school of two thousand students, four counselors working closely with the teaching and administrative staff could implement the services outlined here that would be appropriate for that particular school. Each school community is different and needs its services based on clearly identified needs.

The HDC model, in many cases, differs little from the present ratio in most schools. The main advantage of this plan is its management base. Each counselor, teacher, administrator, or parent involved is aware of his responsibilities as a member of the guidance team.

All are active members of the team. Each plays an important role through a clearly identified organizational plan.

To effect a successful HDC, the professional leader must be equipped with the skills necessary to guide the cooperative interaction of many persons. The counseling skills defined in a subsequent chapter of this book are highly significant. A complete and efficient counseling service center will provide the counselor, and the guidance team as a whole, with greater credibility, a clearer identity and an opportunity to determine the area in which he is most effective and can provide the best service within the school. Ideally a director of pupil personnel should coordinate the Human Development Center model. Teachers, administrators, parents, and students are actively involved in both leadership and service roles. The evaluative process needs to be continual, with a flexibility that welcomes change brought about in response to the needs of the people it serves.

Supplementary Readings

Benjamin, Alfred. *The Helping Interview.* Boston: Houghton Mifflin, 1969.

DeVita, Joseph C., Pumerantz, Philip, and Wilklow, Leighton B. *The Effective Middle School.* West Nyack, N.Y.: Parker Publishing, 1970.

Featherstone, Joseph. *Schools Where Children Learn.* New York: Liverright, 1971.

Field, Fred. *A Theory of Leadership Effectiveness.* New York: McGraw-Hill, 1967.

Glasser, William. *Positive Addiction.* New York: Harper and Row, 1976.

Glasser, William. *Reality Therapy.* New York: Harper and Row, 1965.

Gordon, Thomas. *Teacher Effectiveness Training.* New York: Peter H. Wyden, 1974.

Hansen, John H., and Hearn, Arthur C. *The Middle School Program.* New York: Rand McNally, 1971.

Margaritis, Stephen. *In Search of a Future for Education.* Columbus, Ohio: Charles E. Merrill, 1973.

McCarthy, Robert J. *How to Organize and Operate an Ungraded Middle School.* Englewood Cliffs, N.J.: Prentice-Hall, 1967.

Murphy, Judith. *Middle Schools.* New York: Educational Facilities Laboratories, 1965.

Popper, Samuel. *The American Middle School: An Organizational Analysis.* Waltham, Mass.: Blaisdell Publishing, 1967.

Shertzer, Bruce, and Stone, Shelly C. *Fundamentals of Guidance*, 3rd ed. Boston: Houghton Mifflin, 1976.

Silberman, Charles E. *Crisis in the Classroom.* New York: Random House, 1970.

Storen, Helen F. *The Disadvantaged Early Adolescent: More Effective Teaching.* New York: McGraw-Hill, 1968.

U.S. Department of Labor. *Dictionary of Occupational Titles*, 4th ed. Washington, D.C.: Government Printing Office, 1977.

Yamamoto, Karoru. *The Child and His Image.* Boston: Houghton Mifflin, 1972.

CHAPTER FIVE

How to Initiate a Human Development Center in the Middle School

Philosophy

Guidance services are initiated in the belief that a primary goal is to help each person seeking its services make the most of himself in order that he may function effectively and productively within his environment. Guidance services within a school are all encompassing. They include *all* who are a part of the school community — teachers, administrators, specialists, students, and parents. It is often a problem to use the guidance and counseling services effectively because of the generally narrow approach to the guidance concept. In fulfilling the goal of self-discovery and self-growth, the guidance services must become a functional part of the learning environment of the school. They cannot be isolated in a small annex and considered apart from the mainstream of the school.

Much of the work of the guidance team is organized around the pivotal points of self-discovery and awareness of opportunity.[1] It

---

1. In presenting guidelines for the HDC, we refer to the counselor as the facilitator of guidance services. It is essential that the reader understand that guidance services can effectively be part of the school with other staff accepting the leadership role. The guidance team, therefore, consists of teachers, administrators, parents, students, specialists, and other school personnel.

67

involves helping students explore strengths and limitations, how to use them for the greatest benefit personally and in relationships with others, and how to change what can be changed to increase each person's capabilities. The line of responsibility for support of guidance systems includes both the superintendent of schools and the community which supports the total educational program. The Director of Guidance usually accepts the role of coordinator of these guidance services.

The middle school provides a fertile ground for a meaningful and effective guidance program when the program of learning concentrates on the needs of the learner. Within this structure, the guidance program supports this concept by providing services that will help the curriculum function smoothly. It is important that a sound and practical philosophy be determined.

The role of guidance in the public schools is essentially that of furthering the individualization of education against the quickening pace of change and the rising complexity of life which this change has brought about.[2] Each generation brings with it new problems on learning and living in a changing world. The new technology provides instant feedback on these changes and procedures. Often these rapid changes lead to confusion and conflict in the educational process. Children are learning today from books that may be presenting facts that will be denied tomorrow. Whole new cultures of the past are being discovered to change the face of history. Today's jobs will be obsolete tomorrow, as discussed in the chapter on career guidance. Guidance personnel and educational leaders must join hands in helping to stabilize educational concepts in order for school to provide a foundation for future needs. Through emphasis on self-growth and techniques of seeking answers, education can become functional. The basic philosophy for guidance in the schools therefore should consider the following:

1. The counselor is *one* member of a team. Each member of the team is involved in the educational process and in the combined effort of being of service to each child within the school community.
2. The child is a unique being, with his own values and beliefs. He is entitled to his uniqueness and in no way should he be manipulated into a mold of conformity that strips him of this uniqueness.

---

2. Excerpts from *Educational Improvement Center* Concept Paper: "Middle School" (Pitman, N.J.: 1974).

3. The student, teacher, or administrator has the choice of using or not using the guidance services. Guidance services should not be mandated but rather grow out of mutual need and desire of those participating in them.

4. All involved in working with these students are welcomed into the guidance function, as a member of the team.

5. The philosophy of the guidance services complements the philosophy of the school.

6. Guidance and counseling form a continuous and sequential process as an integral part of the educational climate.

7. The guidance role includes responsibility toward the home, community, and society as well as the school.

8. Counseling emphasizes assistance in providing information and sources of exploration so that the student may build skill for making wise decisions, interpreting situations, and being able to face reality.

9. Those involved in guidance accept with sincerity and interest the responsibility of working with people and possess adequate skills to function effectively.

10. Guidance and counseling services are continually in the process of evaluation by those who perform and by those who receive the services.

There are many different philosophies expounded by experts in the field of guidance and counseling. What is important is that the counselor develop a consistent philosophy utilizing those aspects of theory which have meaning for him in his work with persons in a school setting. The theories may suggest different operational procedures and techniques for different kinds of student needs. It's the counselor's desire to meet all student needs, which makes it unrealistic to rely on one theoretical model: He becomes eclectic in his approach for he is aware of and able to consider a variety of approaches, choosing the one that will best serve his purpose at that particular time. Thus flexibility, a key in the guidance program, has to be compatible with the school curriculum. The curriculum must also reflect such flexibility in meeting the changing needs of the student. If this flexibility is not evident, the counselor, as an advocate of the student, accepts the role of an agent of change.

Why do we concern ourselves with a philosophy at all? Are not these "lists" just words rather than actual deeds? Doesn't each individual have his own philosophy by which he lives—written or unwritten? True. But as we work in an organizational concept there is a need for mutual understanding—an operational foundation, so to speak. Formation of a basic philosophy is a fundamental need for the advancement of professional growth. Through a written philosophy a group organization such as a school clearly defines its direction. It provides a basis for periodic review of this direction in order to take changing times into consideration. A school counselor is an educator. Teachers and counselors are involved in the same process and with the same people. They are mutually concerned with assisting each young person develop meaningful values and realistic goals appropriate to self and society. The school counselor and teacher are both sensitive to and aware of factors that affect a child's behavior and learning. Recognition of these factors in a team approach provides a springboard on which to help each child grow holistically.

What are these factors? What aspects of a child's mental and emotional growth are important in the learning process? Such factors include: (1) realistic attitudes toward self and others; (2) insight into his potential for growth and achievement, (3) self-discipline through the acceptance of responsibility for his own behavior; and (4) skills and attitudes that will enable him to achieve his goals. A philosophy provides structure for the counselor by supporting the concept of the individual's right to locate his special areas of strength and his most promising growth potentialities. A philosophy is unique to its own community. Basic concepts may be presented but the team formulating the services must determine the areas that apply to their particular services.

Projected Goals and Objectives

Upon formulation of philosophy, the subsequent development of the Human Development Center model is to determine behavioral objectives. These state specifically what the staff plans to achieve through their functional services. Examples of such objectives would include:
The guidance team shall:

provide choice of guidance services through selective scheduling. This is illustrated in the description of the HDC clusters.

have available current materials on career information.

have personnel equipped to provide information supportive of materials.

provide a system of communication between agencies and the school.

provide an ongoing evaluation of services through questionnaires and follow-up studies with a cumulative report at the conclusion of each school year.

provide individual counseling services for students, parents, and faculty.

provide communication weekly and monthly with parents, students, and faculty through bulletins, news releases, and in-service workshops.

provide group counseling services for students, parents, and faculty.

schedule regular meetings with faculty and students convenient to the school community and in coordination with the curriculum planning.

maintain updated records and cumulative folders.

provide services to help each person develop a realistic understanding and acceptance of himself.

provide services to help each person formulate his goals and understand the range of opportunities available to him for the realization of these goals.

provide services for orientation of new students and new teachers.

provide leadership for an organized program of research for the development of new services and implementation of programs that would aid in the upgrading of the school as a whole.

make known the services available to the community, students, and school personnel.

keep well informed on the new and effective procedures of individual growth and development.

assist students in long- and short-range planning.

develop and maintain a cooperative relationship between the guidance staff and other members of the school community.

develop a plan of communication with local, state, and federal agencies and organizations, both public and private, which offer educational and vocational programs, employment, or assistance to students.

provide complete student assessment services including administration, diagnosis, and interpretation of evaluative instruments.

assist all students, whether they are part of the regular curriculum or of the special classes and services.

These, and other behavioral objectives unique to the school in which they are to be implemented, concentrate on getting the most effective use of guidance services and letting those involved with the student know that these services are available.

Getting Started: Procedures and Facilities

After the development of the philosophy and objectives by the guidance team priorities have to be set that would most adequately meet the needs of the school being serviced by the guidance staff as part of the Human Development Center.

The guidance team should include representatives of all who are involved in the growth and development of the child within the school and community. Thus, a good team would include a counselor, principal, teacher, a member of the specialist staff, and the school nurse. Decisions would then represent a good cross section of interest within the school. This team assesses, through group meetings or questionnaires, the most urgent needs that the guidance program could serve. This team also serves as a link between the home and school community and the Human Development Center model. The team would develop a clear but brief explanation of the HDC services. This information would be made available to the parents, the superintendent, the principal, and the students as well. A proposed form follows:

Guidance Office
Date

Dear Concerned Parents:

The guidance team has been planning a program that concerns you and your children. In order to facilitate maximum services from our school staff, we have organized what we call the Human Development Center model. This model will involve the counseling staff, teachers, administrators, specialists, paraprofessionals, students, and you.

Briefly, we have tried to delegate responsibility to avoid overlapping of services. In order to provide more rapid response to you and your child's needs, we have developed specific clusters of responsibility in the areas of curriculum, assessment, counseling, career resources, community contacts, and professional growth. We have also made plans to extend the counseling services with a rotating system of our staff, to be available to you Monday through Friday from 7:00 A.M. to 10:00 P.M.

For further details of this program, please consult our next newsletter. We welcome any questions. We plan to have a meeting to respond to your questions and concerns on____. We hope you will find it convenient to attend either the morning or evening session.

Sincerely,

Guidance Director
Telephone number

It is important to caution those initiating a program that directives, communications, and plans should be made available to the superintendent and principal so that they too may be currently aware and supportive of the progress of the program because they will be involved and familiar with the procedures being implemented.

If there has been no guidance staff in your middle school, the plan for implementation must be directed initially to the Board of Education for approval. The person in charge of the program should be able to present clearly outlined plans of the program with support from those on the planning team. Since it is a new program, there will be a need for a money allotment for personnel and materials involved. This often is the primary roadblock in initiating a program. It is not an insurmountable task. The first source of inquiry for funding should be through state, local, and/or federal programs. These are often available on a partial reimbursement basis. If this is not possible, the team has an even more difficult job, which would involve the presentation of the program as a vital part of the school curriculum. A pilot program with part-time programming should be the initial move. Teachers qualified as counselors could be given reduced schedules of instruction for released time to participate in guidance services. The choice needs to be made as to what should be done first to serve the school's urgent needs. Quality services rather than quantity should be emphasized.

During the first year, a school that previously had no counselors could implement the *assessment* and *crisis clusters.* Through these services, the validity of assessment procedures and service itself could be justified. The crisis cluster would illustrate vividly the need for other clusters of the HDC. Careful records and accounts of procedures and services rendered should be kept and constant communication with the superintendent, the Board of Education, and the school community will help provide an awareness of these services.

Each year, services may be added as the scheduling of staff allows. The provision of these services and the extent of their use will determine how rapidly those who hold the purse strings will expand the program. Organization of guidance services as a service to the school do provide financial savings in the overall picture through preventative procedures such as assisting a child in making a better adjustment to school and providing a better learning environment for each child. This is of great interest to school boards and superintendents who are continually in the throes of budget problems. By acting as a buffer in many problem situations, the guidance team lessens the need for outside services.

Through the guidance services, the teacher is given the privilege of concentrating on teaching, which is his role and is encouraged to seek out the counselor to assist in helping each child become better equipped to respond to the learning situation provided within the normal confines of the school community. The entire school climate is affected as the faculty works together in making school a place where teachers and children want to be.

Upon approval of the services and objective, the faculty is involved further through requests for referrals and suggestions as to how the guidance services may be used most productively. The following form (5—1) placed in the counseling center mailbox upon completion, has been used effectively to encourage faculty involvement. Upon receipt of this form the counselor would respond with Form 5—2.

It is important that this contact be prompt and that all appointments be followed through. The guidance team member determines from the referral which cluster would best suit the student's or teacher's needs. If the student or referral agent requests the services of a specific team member, the student could be assigned to the appropriate cluster when it is being serviced by that member.

The success of a guidance service center such as the HDC model described depends on several factors. These include the support of the administration, the dedication of the guidance staff, the support of the teachers, parents, and students, the promptness of the services, and the availability of skilled guidance staff and adequate facilities within the school plant.

Adequate facilities does not imply a large expenditure of money from the community. In examining the Human Development Center model, one may easily see that the facilities already within most schools could be used more efficiently. What are presently used for counseling offices could be developed into cluster centers. Where there are no offices, the reduced enrollment in schools has opened classrooms that could be used effectively as clusters in the HDC model. Furniture could be obtained through community service organizations. Beautiful facilities do not guarantee a good counseling program; the staff does. With the enthusiasm and cooperation of all staff members and the support of the administration, much can be done with facilities already on hand. The initiation of a school guidance program is a group endeavor. It is well worth the frustration, the conflicts, and the roadblocks that greet all who attempt to bring about change.

Form 5-1

Name of student _____ Home room _____

Most convenient time to contact student _____

Referral agent* _____

Most convenient time to contact referral agent _____

Reason for referral (briefly stated)

*Referral agent may be teacher, self, administrator, parent, agency, other (identify).

Form 5-2

To: (Referral Agent) _____ Date _____
     (Student)

From: (Counselor's name) _____

Counseling Cluster (or other cluster) Location _____

Re: (Name of referred student)

Message: I will be able to meet with _____
during your _____ period. Will you please confirm this appointment
and return to my mailbox. If the time is inconvenient, please give a more
appropriate time with one alternative. Thank you.

Please check: _____ This time is convenient.

_____ This time is not convenient but _____ or _____ is.

Supplementary Readings

Billings, R. L. "Musts for Middle School." *Clearing House* 49 (April): 377—379, 1976.

Gatewood, Thomas E., and Dilg, Charles A. *The Middle School We Need.* Washington, D.C.: Association for Supervision and Curricular Development, 1975.

Geisenger, Robert W. *Reasons for Developing Middle Schools in Pennsylvania and the Implemented Characteristics.* Harrisburg: Pennsylvania Department of Education, Bureau of Research, 1971.

Gibson, Robert L., et al. *The Development and Management of School Guidance Programs.* Dubuque, Iowa: Brown, 1973.

Gowan, John, and Demos, George (eds). *The Guidance of Exceptional Children*, 2nd ed. New York: David McKay, 1972.

Rogers, Carl R. *Freedom to Learn.* Columbus, Ohio: Merrill, 1969.

Samuels, Mimi, and Samuels, Don. *Peer Counseling: A Complete Handbook.* Miami, Fla.: Fiesta, 1975.

Shertzer, Bruce, and Peters, Herman. *Guidance Program Development and Management*, 3rd ed. Columbus, Ohio: Merrill, 1974.

CHAPTER SIX ⬜

Accountability: ⬜
Evaluation of Guidance Staff

Developing an Evaluation Tool

Searches of current literature indicate that little has been done to help counselors determine their success or failure in meeting their identified goals. In this current desire to provide "accountable" education it is necessary to determine how to measure this accountability and to whom each professional within the middle school structure is accountable.

Customarily those involved in the helping profession of counseling are evaluated by their administrators on criteria pertaining to the functions and responsibilities of the classroom teacher. Often the very same evaluative tool is used for all staff members. Rarely is this evaluation reflective of effectiveness with students, parents, teachers, and administrators. The role of the counselor is unique and therefore difficult to measure in terms of completed goals. The success of the counselor cannot be measured by the number of students counseled, the quantitative listings of telephone calls, student contact, completed schedules, or the like. Much of what a counselor does can only be identified after a long-range observation or in conjunction with the work of the full school team of teachers and administrators. Cooperation of parents also is vital in achieving goals.

Counselors therefore need to be accountable to teachers, parents, school administrators, board members, students, their colleagues, and themselves. Each school needs to determine the role of the counselor in relation to students' needs. Each school must determine how each staff member can best utilize his time and energy to serve its community most effectively. Specifically, how then can a district measure the quality of a counselor's performance? Roslyn Gross, Director of Pupil Personnel Services and Evaluation of the Woodbridge School District in New Jersey, developed such an evaluative tool. The procedure for setting up an evaluation program for the entire school district, including the middle school, as described by Mrs. Gross is as follows.

At a meeting of all the counselors in the district, the question of counselor effectiveness was raised and volunteers were requested for a district committee that would explore the area of counselor effectiveness. After a number of stormy meetings and changes in composition of the committee and chairmanship, a very serious nucleus of counselors continued to meet. These counselors decided that prior to attempting to evaluate effectiveness of counselors, it would be necessary to clarify and state goals based on what the counselors thought they could and should do. This task was not easily accomplished. Perseverance and extreme dedication on the part of many participants made it possible to produce a list of guidance department goals acceptable to the entire committee, which was a good beginning. (Form 6–1 lists these goals.)

Form 6–1

Guidance Department Goals*

1. Be as available as possible for counselees at all times, but always in emergency situations.

2. Help the counselee understand his personal problems and aid him in seeking and evaluating alternatives so that he can become familiar with and competent in decision-making processes.

3. Be available and accessible for counseling with parents regarding the needs and concerns of their children.

4. Assist each counselee in making the best possible choice of available courses based on his needs and abilities.

5. Counsel and consult with school administrators, teachers, school nurses, special services personnel, and other counselors on matters

which are of concern to our counselees and be an active participant in curriculum planning and instructional improvement reflecting input of counselees.

6. Be visible and accessible both in and out of the guidance office.

7. Improve teacher-pupil relationships.

8. Be available to discuss any concern of the individual counselee.

9. Seek assistance for pupils who have learning problems.

10. Interpret test results for all counselees, administrators, staff members, and parents.

11. Maintain confidentiality in order to protect pupil welfare.

12. Use all available resources to help students think about future plans.

13. Familiarize all incoming students with the physical plant and programs offered.

14. Supervise and administer the township standardized testing program in our school.

15. Provide students with information and activities necessary to familiarize them with post–high school educational and occupational opportunities.

16. Meet with all new counselees.

17. Make available to all staff members data pertinent to a successful student transition from school to school.

18. Prepare pupils and teachers for all testing situations by discussing purposes of testing and uses which will be made of test results.

19. Maintain an atmosphere in which graduates and dropouts will see the guidance department as a source of information and constructive advice.

20. Familiarize parents of all incoming students with the physical plant and programs offered.

21. Make available test data for curriculum improvement.

22. Provide job placement services for all counselees.

---

*In priority order as established at the Guidance Workshop in which counselors, administrators, and Board of Education members participated. This is Stage 2 in the work of the committee exploring *Evaluating Counselor Effectiveness.*

The following step was a meeting of Board of Education members, central administrators, and school administrators. The approval of the stated goals was obtained. This was a very important stage of the total program. Acceptance of the goals by these important groups made possible the progress that followed.

Following the statement of goals, it was obvious that it would be necessary to determine if these goals were met and how well. This was no easy task. What would be the best source for answers to questions about how well stated goals were being met? Who would be in a better position to tell counselors how effective they are than the various populations they serve—teachers, parents, administrators, and, most important, students?

The committee felt that it was important for each of the groups served to have an opportunity to make a judgment on how effective counselors are. Working within this framework, it was decided that four evaluative instruments based on the goals set forth would be developed and then submitted to each of the target groups.

Development of the instruments was a painstaking process, which was frequently discouraging, but they were developed and used on a pilot basis the second year that the committee was at work.

Between the time the committee prepared the goals and evaluation instruments, much groundwork had to be laid to make this evaluation plan palatable to counselors and administrators. No effort was spared, because unless there was support and agreement to this plan, there was little hope of accomplishment.

(In retrospect, the most difficult task was to convince counselors that they should want to take a good hard look at how effective they were and that students should be included in the evaluation process. All of the counselors on the committee and in the district had to be willing to accept the fact that there would be criticism from the groups being served and there was the risk that some of the criticism would be severe. What most of the counselors failed to realize was that many good things might be said about them as a group and as individuals.)

In order to increase the acceptability of the evaluation process, it was decided that for the first year the results would serve only for each counselor to look at himself introspectively. The returns from each student's questionnaire would be seen only by his own counselor.

Questionnaires given to teachers and parents were designed to elicit responses concerning the performance of the guidance department, not individuals. The department then would decide what implications the results held for them collectively and individually.

Once the premise that evaluation would lead to professional growth had been accepted, it was simply a matter of time and energy to devise appropriate evaluative instruments.

Guidance department goals

In the first step the twenty-two goals that appeared reasonably attainable by counselors were stated. For each goal several methods or techniques for achieving the stated goals were cited. From there it became a matter of posing a question for each of the evaluation groups to see if they felt that the goal had been met.

The example following goal 10 (Form 6–1) illustrates the technique utilized. Following the goal statement is the technique identified for reaching the goal, and then questions to be used for each target group.

Goal: To interpret test results for all counselees, administrators, staff members, and parents.

Techniques: Use of group guidance and individual conferences.

Objective Measures:

Students: 1. Were the results of the standardized test explained to you? Yes _____ No_____
If yes, was it done in a group situation _____ , individual conference _____ , combination of both _____ ?

2. Did the explanation of test results help you to understand more about your strengths, weaknesses, and/or interests?
Yes _____ No _____

Teachers: 1. Were the results of standardized testing programs made clear to you? Yes _____ No _____

2. Has the testing program aided you in understanding the strengths and weaknesses of individual youngsters?
Yes _____ No _____

3. Do you have any suggestions for improving the testing program? Yes _____ No _____

Administrators:

1. Interpretation of standardized testing program results to counselees, administrators, staff, and parents.
Highly effective _____ Satisfactory _____
Needs improvement _____

Parents: 1. Do you feel that your child's guidance counselor is
available to you for explanation of test results concerning your child? Yes _____ No _____

A meeting of central administrators, school administrators,
Board of Education members, and counselors was held to discuss the
purposes of the process of evaluation of counselors, the actual instruments, and the anticipated gains in improvement of the guidance services in the district. Strong support was shown and counselors were
complimented for showing willingness to have their effectiveness
evaluated. The forms were finalized. (See Forms 6–2, 6–3, 6–4,
6–5.)

Form 6–2

Student Questionnaire

The information contained in this questionnaire is designed to give us
answers which will help us to do a more effective job with students we
counsel. In our job it is very difficult to know when we are doing a satisfactory job and the only way to find out is to ask the people we serve. We
hope that you will take the time to answer the questions in a most honest
fashion. Feel free to omit any questions that do not apply to you. Placing
your name on the paper is an option that is left up to you, but please fill
out the other pertinent information.

Name _____ Grade 5 6 7 8   Male ____ Female ____
(circle one)

Counselor _____   Yes   No

1. Were you made familiar with this school and its   ☐   ☐
   programs before you entered the school?

2. Do you feel that the annual orientation program
   provided was helpful to you? If answer is no, offer   ☐   ☐
   suggestions for improvement.

	Yes	No
3. Have you met your counselor?	☐	☐

4. Have you ever requested a meeting with your
   counselor?
   Frequently _____
   Occasionally _____
   Seldom _____
   Never _____

5. If you requested a conference, was it honored within   ☐   ☐
   a reasonable time?

6. Do you feel that your counselor is the person to whom
   you would come with _____

   a. a personal problem
   b. a school problem

7. If the answer to either a or b above is no, to whom
   would you go?

8. Did your counselor listen to your problem?   ☐   ☐

9. Did your counselor offer any help?   ☐   ☐

10. In time of emergency, have you found your counselor
    available?
    Always _____
    Most of the time _____
    Sometimes _____
    Never had an
    emergency _____

11. Do you feel that you are better able to cope with
    a personal problem as a result of conferring with   ☐   ☐
    your counselor?

12. As a result of having discussed a school problem with
    your counselor, to what extent were you helped?
    Considerably _____
    Somewhat _____
    Not at all _____
    Situation made worse _____
    Question not applicable _____

	Yes	No
13. Did your counselor follow up on your problem?	☐	☐
14. Have your parents ever contacted your guidance counselor?	☐	☐

15. If yes, did your parents' contact with your counselor benefit you in any way? If yes in what way?

16. To your knowledge, has your counselor consulted with any other school personnel on your behalf? (Check appropriate person)

Principal   _____
Nurse   _____
Teacher   _____
Psychologist   _____

	Yes	No
17. Would you have wanted your counselor to consult with other personnel on your behalf?	☐	☐
18. Did you ever discuss a teacher problem with your counselor?	☐	☐
19. If yes, did the situation improve for you in your class after the discussion?	☐	☐
20. Do you feel that information discussed with your counselor is kept confidential?	☐	☐
21. Do you ever meet your counselor outside his or her office?	☐	☐
22. Do you ever see your counselor at after-school functions?	☐	☐
23. Was the purpose of the standardized test you took this year made clear to you before the testing session?	☐	☐
24. Did the explanation of test results help you to understand more about your strengths, weaknesses, and/or interests?	☐	☐
25. Were course offerings fully explained to you?	☐	☐
26. Were your test results explained to you in reference to selection of courses?	☐	☐

	Yes	No
27. Were your career objectives discussed prior to course selection?	☐	☐
28. Did you accept the suggestions for course selection made by your counselor?	☐	☐

29. If no, check:

Parent disagreed   _____
Student disagreed _____
Other influence   _____

30. Was vocational information made available to you?	☐	☐

31. If yes, individually ____ in groups ____

32. Check which of the following were made available.

Field trips ____ Tapes ____ Pamphlets ____
Career Kits ____ Books ____ Speaker ____
Movies ____ Film Strips ____

33. Were you kept informed concerning high school opportunities?	☐	☐
34. Did your counselor have a conference with you concerning high school planning?	☐	☐
35. Were job placement services made available to you?	☐	☐
*36. Is it necessary to have a guidance counselor in middle or senior high school? Why?	☐	☐

*37. What are your personal feelings about your counselor?

*38. What advice could you offer your counselor so that he or she might do a better job with the next group of counselees?

---

*If necessary use reverse side of page to complete statement. Please number accordingly.

Form 6-3

Community Questionnaire

The guidance personnel of the _____ school district are continually seeking to provide the services that are needed and desired by our youngsters and their parents. Because of this, a committee of counselors devised this questionnaire.

We would very much appreciate your responses to the questions listed below so that we might have an idea of the areas the community feels are most important. This will help us establish priorities.

The choice of submitting your name on this form is optional, but we would appreciate knowing the name of the school.

My child attends _____ Middle School in the 5, 6, 7, 8 grade.

(circle one)

Signed _____

(Optional)

1. Does your child have plans for (check one)

   Vocational school   _____ ?
   College   _____ ?
   Immediate employment
   after completing high school _____ ?
   Undecided   _____ ?

		Yes	No
2.	Has the counselor ever contacted you regarding your child via phone call, letter, or through your child?	☐	☐
3.	Have you ever met your child's counselor?	☐	☐
4.	Are you hesitant about calling your child's counselor regarding any problem your child might be having? If yes, state why.	☐	☐
5.	Have you found your child's counselor willing to discuss your child's welfare with you at any time?	☐	☐
6.	Have you requested help from your child's guidance counselor?	☐	☐
7.	Was the counselor helpful?	☐	☐
8.	Did the counselor follow up on your child's progress?	☐	☐

		Yes	No
9.	Have you been informed about the availability of your child's standardized test results?	☐	☐
10.	Do you feel that your child's guidance counselor is available to you for explanation of the test results concerning your child?	☐	☐
11.	Did you attend a meeting on course offerings and selection?	☐	☐
12.	Were course offerings and grouping adequately explained to you?	☐	☐
13.	What do you consider to be the most important functions of the guidance department?	☐	☐

Form 6–4

Teacher Evaluation of Guidance Services

The purpose of this questionnaire is to determine the effectiveness of the guidance department in this building as it relates to the teaching staff.

We sincerely value your opinions concerning the services we offer, and, although at times we seem to be at odds, we are all striving to obtain the same result: happy and successful youngsters.

Placing your name on this form is optional, but we would ask for candid answers.

Name: _____ Grade level 5 6 7 8
(circle one)

		Yes	No
1.	Have you received helpful advice when speaking with your counselors regarding student matters?	☐	☐
2.	Would you readily speak with the counselors regarding students' problems outside the academic realm?	☐	☐
3.	Do the counselors initiate interviews with you regarding individual students?	☐	☐
4.	Were the consultations pertinent and productive?	☐	☐

	Yes	No

5. Did you refer any students with learning problems to the guidance counselor? ☐ ☐

6. Did the counselor offer any help to the students? ☐ ☐
   If yes, to some _____ to all _____ .

7. Did the counselor report actions taken to you? ☐ ☐

8. Did the counselor's intervention produce a positive change in the situation? ☐ ☐
   If yes, frequently ___ sometimes ___ rarely ___

9. Do you believe the guidance department has a responsibility to describe course content to students? ☐ ☐

10. Do you feel that your students are properly grouped? ☐ ☐
    If yes, always ___ most of the time ___ seldom ___ never ___

11. Were you given adequate preparation and directions for testing sessions? (Does not apply _____) ☐ ☐

12. Were you provided with the opportunity to examine test results from the pupils you teach? ☐ ☐

13. Did you understand the significance of these results? ☐ ☐

14. Has the testing program aided you in understanding the strengths and weaknesses of individual youngsters? ☐ ☐

15. Do you have any suggestions for improving the administration of the testing program? ☐ ☐
    If yes, explain:

16. Upon your request has the guidance department made available to you materials to use in your classroom? ☐ ☐

17. Do the counselors exhibit professional attitudes in maintaining confidentiality regarding pupil welfare? ☐ ☐

18. Do the counselors respect confidentiality concerning what you tell them about the youngsters? ☐ ☐

19. Have counselors assisted you in contacting parents? ☐ ☐

	Yes	No
20. Did the guidance department make available to you information derived from the follow-up study of graduates?	☐	☐
21. Have you seen guidance counselors attempting to be helpful to you or your students in areas other than the guidance office?	☐	☐
Do you approve of this?	☐	☐

Form 6-5

Administrator's Appraisal of Counselor Effectiveness

Counselor's name _____ Date _____

Appraiser _____ School _____

Purpose: The purpose and use of this form is to evaluate the counselor's effectiveness with the hope that constructive suggestions will be made to improve the counselor's effect on the total school program.

Procedures: 1. The appraiser will evaluate each category as Very Effective, Satisfactory, or Needs Improvement by checking the appropriate box.

2. Areas designated as needing improvement must be accompanied by specific suggestions for improvement.

Evaluation Criteria	Very Effective	Satisfactory	Needs Improvement
I. Professional Performance			
A. Counselor is available and accessible at all times, but always in emergency situations to:			
(1) Counselees	_____	_____	_____
(2) Parents	_____	_____	_____
(3) Staff Personnel	_____	_____	_____

Evaluation Criteria	Very Effec- tive	Satis- factory	Needs Improve- ment
B. Counselor helps counselees understand personal problems and aids him in achieving a degree of competency in the decision-making process.	_____	_____	_____
C. Counselor exhibits professional standards in utilizing confidential information known about youngsters.	_____	_____	_____
D. Counselor has provided me with helpful advice regarding student matters.	_____	_____	_____
E. Counselor's attitude allows for a free exchange of ideas regarding students' problems outside academic realm.	_____	_____	_____
F. Counselor expresses opinions about the need for curriculum changes.	_____	_____	_____
G. Counselor has been instrumental in improving teacher-pupil relationships.	_____	_____	_____
H. Counselor creates an atmosphere in which graduates and dropouts will see the guidance department as a source of information and constructive advice.	_____	_____	_____
I. Counselor assists in identifying students with learning problems.	_____	_____	_____
J. Counselor makes appropriate services available to students			
(1) with learning problems	_____	_____	_____
(2) with personal problems	_____	_____	_____

Evaluation Criteria	Very Effective	Satisfactory	Needs Improvement
K. Counselor conducts follow-up on counselees.	_____	_____	_____
L. Counselor assumes the responsibility for establishing a working relationship with staff members.	_____	_____	_____
M. Counselor familiarizes			
(1) incoming students	_____	_____	_____
(2) parents of incoming students with physical plant and programs offered.	_____	_____	_____
N. Counselor makes available to all staff members data pertinent to a successful student transition from school to school.	_____	_____	_____
O. Counselor meets with all new counselees.	_____	_____	_____
P. Counselor adequately explains course content, grouping and consideration for course selection to:			
(1) students	_____	_____	_____
(2) parents	_____	_____	_____
Q. Counselor prepares students and staff for testing.	_____	_____	_____
R. Counselor supervises the administration of the township standardized testing program.	_____	_____	_____
S. Counselor interprets standardized testing program results to			
(1) counselees	_____	_____	_____
(2) administration	_____	_____	_____
(3) staff	_____	_____	_____
(4) parents	_____	_____	_____

Evaluation Criteria	Very Effective	Satis-factory	Needs Improvement
T. Counselor provides and analyzes test results for the staff for their utilization.	____	____	____
U. Counselor provides counselees with			
(1) vocational (career) information	____	____	____
(2) transcript services	____	____	____
(3) college information	____	____	____
(4) job placement information	____	____	____

Personal Qualities:

	Very Effective	Satis-factory	Needs Improvement
A. Sensitivity to students	____	____	____
B. Objectivity	____	____	____
C. Appearance appropriate for position	____	____	____
D. Emotional balance	____	____	____
E. Acceptance of suggestions	____	____	____
F. Adherence to school policies	____	____	____
G. Professional committment	____	____	____
H. Evidence of professional growth	____	____	____

To be used by evaluator: Comments and suggestions:

Signature _____ date _____

To be used by counselor: Comments (Optional)

Signature _____ date _____

Only for year-end evaluation _____ Reappoint for next school year _____
Do not reappoint for next school year _____ .

Principal's signature _____

The populations to be polled were then identified and arrangements were made for feedback indicating areas of strengths and weaknesses to be returned to counselors so that steps would be taken to improve services.

From the realization of the need for a critical look at the job the counselors say they do, in this school district, many valuable side effects accrued. Among these were:

1. Counselors, as result of working with their peers on this project, learned from each other in a highly professional manner.
2. Specific guidance department goals had been identified, prioritized, and broadcast to the entire school community. There was no doubt that the guidance department was alive and well and active.
3. Teachers, parents, and students were pleased to be asked to react, and some positive feelings toward the guidance department were generated.
4. Teachers, parents, and students became more aware of the couneslors's role and function.
5. Counselors now knew how they rate.
6. Feedback led to reexamination of goals as well as individual counselor self-assessment.

There are no shortcuts to obtaining these outcomes. The goals and questionnaires included in this chapter are examples of what can be done. It is not suggested that another school district use these identical forms, for each school district is unique. Its personal needs must be assessed for an evaluation to be effective. In addition, it is obvious that participation in the process of development of an evaluation is a necessary component for those who are to use it and reflect on its results. Therefore, if a district needs guidelines to rate a counselor, or help for counselor's self evaluation, this is one procedure that has proved to be an effective evaluative tool.

Perhaps motivated by the success of this school district, guided by the ideas, and cautioned by obstacles surmounted by this guidance staff, a school district can begin the momentous job of rating the effectiveness of the counseling staff and program.

Supplementary Readings

Glasser, William. *Positive Addiction.* New York: Harper and Row, 1976.

Sullivan, Howard J., and O'Hare, Robert W. (eds.). *Accountability in Pupil Personnel Services* (CPGA Monograph: No. 3) Washington, D.C.: APGA, 1976.

CHAPTER
SEVEN

Public Relations Techniques:
Selling the Programs!

A student assigned to a counselor knows what the counselor's job is and how he or she can help him in his adjustment to school—or does he? Some do; but unfortunately most do not. Many teachers and parents are not really sure what services the counselor provides. Administrators assign counselors responsibilities that the counselors feel are out of their domain. Uninformed teachers, administrators, and parents can handicap the counselor's work by demanding inappropriate services from the counselor. A student unaware of the services guidance staff offer may be deprived of much needed assistance.

The logical solution? The counselor must find effective ways to "spread the word!" Clear communication is the key. Communicate and these problems may be avoided by the guidance staff. The guidance counselor today can be and often is a vital force in public education. The effectiveness of his job often depends heavily upon the aid of dynamic public relations with all those for whom guidance services are available.

Most counselors realize that counseling students is only one part of their multifaceted role. Among their many tasks counselors include aiding teachers, advising parents, and, like all educators, seeking ways to show accountability to the taxpaying community. The counselor who accepts this challenge needs to have working knowledge of the basics of sound school public relations. Those educators sensitive to public need realize there is a demand for more specific information dealing with what is going on in the schools. The counselor is placed in the center of a fast changing educational picture.

> If we [think] of the school system as a wheel with the pupil at the hub, we can think of the counselor as a structural frame which supports the various spokes of different teachers [administrators and parents], involved in helping the wheel maintain balance and move forward on a steady course.[1]

Suggestions for Community Contact

The counselor must, therefore, be prepared to communicate effectively with all of his different "publics"—students, teachers, administrators, parents, and those who are not directly involved in school at all but do pay taxes. Communication is an approach to meeting this need and should be seriously considered a major responsibility of the guidance staff.

How can this be achieved?[2] In order to perform this service, the counselor has several alternative procedures at his fingertips. Following these suggested procedures with a flexibility most effective in meeting the unique needs of each school and community, the counselor should become more productive, more meaningful in his role and more truly an accepted part of the mainstream of the educational process.

The initial step in public relations is to plan a course of action. The counselor needs to know exactly what he wants to say and to whom he wants to say it. This communication should begin internally. He needs the support of the school staff. To achieve this he should consider the following suggestions:

1. Offer the services of the guidance department through in-service programs.
2. Introduce the staff to the faculty and clearly define the services each offers, the procedures for communication, and the open-door policy for the faculty.
3. Schedule regular after-school hours once or twice a month and encourage teachers to stop by to discuss current problems, suggestions, or just to talk.

---

1. Paul Mok, *A View from Within* (New York: Carlton Press, 1962), p. 169.
2. Much of the material in this chapter was submitted by James Dufford, Public Information Officer, New Jersey Department of Defense, formerly Public Relations Director for Cumberland County College.

4. Plan "kaffeeklatches" on a periodic schedule. This is an excellent occasion to discuss mutual and community school concerns.
5. Schedule individual appointments with all teachers at the beginning of the year. Often teachers prefer to talk over a concern privately and will hesitate to take the initiative for they may feel it signifies their own incompetence.

It is important to clarify the role of the guidance staff to the faculty. Assuming that the role is understood is a mistake that is frequently made by the practitioner. Teachers who know and understand the counselor's job will realize that the guidance department is, in reality, a department concerned with people and not a "memo mill" or schedule center.

Another effective method of communication is through an inexpensive and easily developed brochure distributed at an early in-service session. This could include information concerned with:

1. The counselor's role, simple and realistically stated. (There is nothing that turns off a teacher faster than a job description written in textbook style or in idealistic and impractical terms. This impersonal approach gives an impersonal view of the guidance staff.)
2. The guidance department's area of responsibility and how these services can and should be used. This should not be determined by the guidance staff alone but should be the coordinated effort of the guidance team and general staff input.
3. The department's philosophy, which should agree and complement the philosophy of the institution it serves.
4. Suggested ways teachers can aid in the guidance process.
5. Samples of guidance forms and circulars.
6. Test information that is current, accurate, and briefly describes the program of the school concerned.
7. Office hours should be stated and strictly adhered to. There is nothing more damaging to the image than to be left waiting for an appointment or to find the entire guidance office vacant as all counselors go to lunch or a meeting at the same time.
8. A listing of all counselors' names (preferably accompanied by a picture of each counselor) and the listing of students assigned to each counselor.
9. Brief biographical sketches of the counselors that give the faculty, parents, administrators, and students some idea of the skills and training of the guidance staff as well as a picture of the "humanness" of the person. (Often these sketches include such general impersonal facts that they are of little interest to the reader. Including some personal facts makes the counselor a unique human being.) It is of course important that these written communiqués be supplemented by person-

97

to-person contact. If the public doesn't come to the counselor, the counselor must go to the public. The image of the counselor needs to be that of a person qualified to help, a person who cares to help, a person able to provide the humanization of the educational process.

Accurate and timely information is vital in public relations. Special reports may be used effectively to keep parents, faculty, students, and the community informed regarding future plans and procedures. For example, one of the quickest ways to alienate a teacher is to disrupt his instructional schedule without warning. Good public relations can help prevent this. Before guidance-sponsored tests or special programs are conducted, the counselor should notify the teaching staff. These reports, notes, notices, and memos to faculty and parents should emphasize a positive approach rather than imply a "command from above." They will be accepted by a wider audience and help build a sound image of the counselor as a specialist working cooperatively with the staff. These special reports may be individual flyers or included in a guidance bulletin printed and distributed when needed to keep all persons aware of plans that involve them.

The student as a vital component of success in the counselor's role is often overlooked. Before the school year begins, a letter may be sent to all the students to whom the counselor has been assigned. This is the initial step in establishing an open line of communication. It should provide information that will help the student discover the how, the why, the who, and the where of the guidance department. A map of the school should be included for the school freshmen. Often the most frightening and frustrating problem a new student faces is finding his classrooms and locating the guidance office in the commonly large and complex middle schools of today.

This first contact may be followed by a scheduled group meeting and individual contacts as soon as possible. Plans for the year may be shared at this time. Students will appreciate being informed realize how important they are to the counselor in determining the services most appropriate for their educational and social growth and development. Good student public relations means cooperative involvement by both student and counselor. The middle school student will not tolerate spoonfed, teacher-directed programs and activities. He wants to be a part of the planning and should be. It is paramount that the guidance staff understand how the student body feels about what they, the counselors, are doing to be effective.

A strategy for improving the students' concepts of guidance would be through student rap sessions and group counseling. Group guidance provides a cohesive climate where people who feel the effect of social distance may communicate with peers in an ongoing and supportive way. The counselor can be effective in organizing the groups, helping to define the problems and laying the ground rules. Strategies for the middle school could include groups who share a specific problem. These students should be approached by invitation (passes issued) and attendance encouraged rather than enforced. A "trouble team," comprised of counselors and voluntary faculty members whose schedules provide for their immediate availability when trouble strikes, could be organized. An on-the-scene rap session could provide remedies before polarization. Existing groups such as clubs or problem groups could be used for rap sessions. A suggestion box for student initiated concerns would be helpful. Rap sessions could be held to ease discipline problems; disinterested learners could be motivated by use of field trips and visitors, followed by group discussion; after-school teamwork training could be implemented through sports. Some target groups could include:

1. Students concerned with drug information.
2. Students with problems involving sex.
3. Students with problems coping with teachers perceived as unfair.
4. Students with home problems.
5. Students with physical problems.
6. Students considering dropping out of school.
7. Students concerned with changes in the school.

Good human relationships within the educational system are obviously not unlike good human relationships in other settings. We intuitively know that warmth, understanding, and caring are crucial ingredients in social relationships. The function of a guidance person is to help facilitate the development of these warm, empathetic, and caring relationships throughout the school. Honesty and consistency in communication with the student are necessary. The counselor who transmits these qualities to the students will succeed in improving the point of view of the guidance system.

The following approaches were found to be helpful in attempting to improve the guidance point of view with students in the middle school.

1. Establishment of a health careers club, open to fifty middle school students. The counselors have physicians, nurses, and other medical personnel speak to the students, set up field trips to hospitals, laboratories, show films, and conduct discussion sessions.

2. A career club for students having interests in vocations such as automotive lines. Field trips and films are used. A stock car is brought to the school and the students (boys and girls) have an opportunity to examine it and ride it. The culminating activity may be a trip to the stock car races.

3. Other career areas may be highlighted as time allows the counselor to develop them in coordination with the staff and the curricula. The discussion sessions with small groups (six to twelve persons) were found to be most productive. Students require time to develop confidence in counselors and counselors are responsible for respecting all information as confidential.

4. A telephone hot line is another idea. This would be available to students as another effective technique of communication. It needs to be adequately publicized and accepted by those whom it will serve. (Recently such a hot line was developed to respond to students' questions regarding venereal disease. Those responding to their questions were teenagers provided with a training program to supply them with the facts.) Counselors may use this telephone aid to help students directly and to involve more student and parent volunteers. Student and parent volunteers can be trained to function as part of the hot line. Once it has been identified as a source of help to students it can be expanded to aid other age groups in the community. Open-line communication affords many opportunities to use the skills and talents of many people to supply instant responses to individual needs.

The actual physical appearance of the guidance center—with the materials available there—is another aspect of public relations. As the Human Development Center model stresses, it should include a colorful combination rap room, resource center, and publications clearing house for students and teachers. A well-decorated and up-to-date bulletin board, the hub of any guidance center, should have job, social agency, school, and training information currently displayed.

The guidance office should be stocked with removable and replaceable brochures and publications that the student may take and keep to think about when he has the time. Publications should be concerned with scholarships, future tests and their dates, financial aid information, details about family counseling agencies, job openings, procedures for applying for medical aid, and sources of specific information about the community.

As an information center, the guidance office can provide good public relations with students by supplying an answering service that would not necessarily demand the identification of the person submitting the question. This can be achieved by limiting one bulletin board area to answers to questions submitted in a question box. Often students are embarrassed to ask their parents or the counselor about personal concerns and would willingly ask these questions anonymously. Surprisingly, it is soon discovered these questions are of common concern and the posted answers aid many students. Such questions as, "Who can I go to to find out if I have VD?" or "I am still afraid of the dark. Does that mean I am crazy?" or "Whom can I see without telling my parents?" or "I took something from _____ Department Store. I would like to return it without getting into more trouble. How can I do that?" and so on. Often the response suggests local agency help, seeing a specific counselor, or directions on whom to contact or where to go that the student can follow through on his own. In no way is the student identified unless he chooses to identify himself. The availability and confidentiality of the counselor is stressed in each response.

Public relations is an ongoing process. It is important for the students to be reminded that the guidance center is there for them. They should be part of the continual evaluative process that assures them the guidance staff exists for their needs. Parents and administrators, students and teachers need to know what the guidance staff offers to them. The extent of this understanding can logically be determined through a survey conducted periodically with all involved to explore the effectiveness of the guidance staff. Form 7-1 is an example of a survey that may be used for this purpose. It can provide the counseling staff with a more realistic and meaningful approach to their role of service with their school. Such a survey assists the guidance counselor in gaining accurate information, taking account of himself, and providing a rationale for adjusting and changing present procedures. New programs may be conceived, old procedures supported and strengthened and better relations among colleagues pro-

---

Form 7-1

Student Survey Form

This student survey is designed to help any worker determine weak areas in a program and let the whole student body know the guidance department cares by the fact that they respond to the questions

. . . .

Directions: Do not put your name on this survey. Carefully read the statement or question and then make a check in the space of your choice or fill in the blank. An honest answer will help your guidance department serve you better.

Check one: Boy ( ) Girl ( )   Your Grade 5 ( ) 6 ( ) 7 ( ) 8 ( )

1. What is the last name of your counselor? _____

		Yes	No
2.	My counselor has been helpful to me.	□	□
3.	Do you see the guidance counselors as being the same as the principal?	□	□
4.	Have you ever been turned away by a teacher when you have asked to go to the guidance office?	□	□
5.	Have you ever wished the guidance office would be open evenings so your parents could get to see your counselor about a problem you were having if they were unable to come during the day?	□	□
6.	Would you prefer to keep the same counselor in all grades?	□	□
7.	Is homeroom guidance of any value to you?	□	□
8.	Do you like your guidance counselor?	□	□
9.	Do you feel you can trust your counselor?	□	□
10.	Do you feel you understand the function of the guidance department in this school?	□	□
11.	Do you prefer a male for your counselor?	□	□
12.	Do you mind having your counselor teach a class in which you are a student?	□	□
13.	Do you think that a function of the guidance department is to discipline students?	□	□

Use the remaining space to express any other feelings you may have regarding the function of the guidance department in this school. We welcome any ideas you may have to help us serve you better.

moted. Through the process of a student survey, the student will become more a part of the guidance services within the school.

Since students are the counselor's primary concern, a great deal of guidance public relations needs to be centered around the student. The task of keeping students informed may seem endless at times. A colorful but brief brochure (not a bulky handbook that will never be opened, much less read) is a workable idea. It should list all the services offered the student. Brief and clearly stated information and examples of how important these services are should be included. This brochure should be designed exclusively for the student and contain many of the suggestions made earlier in this chapter in regard to the teacher's handbook.

There is also a need for an attempt to overcome two commonly observed problems in guidance: criticisms concerning the actual services of the counselor and clarification of what the counselor does, beyond clerical services, explained to parents, board members, and the community at large. Orientation programs are helpful here. A program that is both visually and auditorially stimulating can make a more meaningful and lasting impression. Major presentations could take the form of a series of skits or dramatic presentations that should depict areas to be stressed. A typical example of such a problem and possible solution could be the introduction of a comprehensive program of guidance services to the students of a middle school who are first entering the school. With the aid of some talented students or a few members of the drama club, a format could be worked out and a script written. This script might deal with common situations affecting students in which guidance could assist. The first scenes could show the situation without the services of the counselor followed by scenes showing the same situation with the assistance of the counselor. (This would work well with the school board also.) Many problem areas, from scheduling to social adjustments, could be dealt with and effectively presented. The guidance department plays a major role in selecting and directing the scenes to be used with or without the actual participation of the counselors in the actual performance.

These live productions of such a dramatic presentation could be effective for large groups such as an assembly program or a PTA meeting. In addition, the program could be videotaped for future use with smaller groups as a source of information, a basis for discussion, self-evaluation of the counseling staff, and/or for particular individuals seeking such information.

The counselor should also keep in mind that parents can often be the prime motivators of change in the schools, as they are the bulk of the external public. Will they be a help or a hindrance? Will they feel included in the school planning or threatened by the new programs? The unknown poses a threat in any situation. Many parents do not understand what the counselor's job involves. Most are not aware of the techniques and trends in guidance today. Their contact with guidance services most typically is in time of trouble. As taxpayers, they may be skeptical of the counselor's role in public education. Generally, the best rule is never to assume anything. Provide as much information as possible as a preventative measure to avoid parental conflict.

We recently were given the following memo as a student project. It illustrates clearly the "parent's-eye view" of the counselor's role.

Parents' View of the Counselor's Role

A Parent's-Eye View

It's not often that a veteran parent gets a chance to tell off a principal and get applauded for it, but Mrs. Marian Fox found herself living that dream of glory recently, and then some. Her captive audience numbered more than 200 school administrators, and she drew on an admitted 47.5 kid-years of experience with the public schools to rub the principals' noses in some of the messages they send, even when they don't know they're communicating.

As guest speaker at a PR workshop sponsored by the Montgomery County (Md.) Public Schools, Mrs. Fox presented herself "not as an expert in PR, but a victim of it." Most of the listeners were seen to wince at least once as she ticked off some bad memories and some good advice:

"Where's your welcome mat?" she asked, wondering if the bulletin boards in the building will convey warmth, and whether she will wait in a hard chair in a cold hall longer than in a doctor's office. One school, she recalled, had a teller's cage—"or maybe it was a used door from a speakeasy or the partition from the visiting area in an abandoned prison" through which visitors spoke. "How warm!"

"When you write to me, communicate," she begged, noting that throughout her parenthood she has been the victim of both feast and famine. Some years the most informative message she got was the impact aid questionnaire. Other years she was the champion contributor to the Boy Scout paper drive. And the tone of the messages: "Your child needs a quarter," to another that referred to the "milieu in which our students will fulfill their potential" and ended, "It is the desire of the team at your school to provide the utmost in horizontal enrichment experiences and involve important members of the community in the learning situation." Yes, she recalled about the latter one, she agreed to chaperon the third-grade field trip.

"Look who's tampering with your image," she warned: "everybody." At a back-to-school night—the only time some parents ever set foot in the building—does the visitor leave with an upbeat feeling or the idea that the teachers had taken whining lessons? And does the custodian grumble when he's asked to roll a blackboard down the hall for a community meeting? "Every one of you has a press agent," she cautioned the principals, "whether you're aware of it or not."

"Honesty is the best policy . . . honest it is." She reminded the principals that suburban parents ride in carpools, belong to clubs and churches, and talk to each other—often about the school. "You may talk to parents one at a time and tailor some of your answers to what you think that person would like to hear," she said, "but remember, we compare notes."

"Pass thou not the buck," Mrs. Fox warned, recalling how she used to think the superintendent and the board were responsible for every little thing that ever happened in the local school. It was a great day when she ran across a copy of the system's policy manual and discovered that the buck stops on the principal's desk for lots of things. "Everybody's got problems—why should you be an exception?" she asked, recalling principals she has known who insisted that everything was sweetness and light hours before the roof fell in or the teachers took to the picket line. "I might become your best salesman in the community for your plan if you let me know you have a problem and let me think I helped solve it."

"Get your priorities straight," she cautioned. One of her sons, she related, once had to call home because he had split his trousers. When she raced to school with a replacement pair, she was greeted by a bill for a dime for the phone call. Not too long after that, a note came home from the principal soliciting trading stamps to get a silver tea service for the teachers' lounge. "Needless to say he got his dime and you can bet your used tea bags he didn't get a Top Value stamp from me. I'll even admit that I held a small, intimate victory celebration when that principal departed."

"Don't bruise my ego and smash my self-concept," she begged. In running parent conferences, principals always seem to forget that the parents had an education too and tend to believe they turned out pretty well. "If I gripe about something in the school, will you tell me I'm old-fashioned? If I see my child as a bit more brilliant than you do, how are you going to keep me from feeling like the overambitious parent of a dumb kid?"

"Parent conferences can be the best or the worst public relations you engage in," Mrs. Fox said, describing grim hours perched on tiny chairs while teachers, the principal, and other assorted visitors whisper just out of earshot before confronting her with some psychological gobbledygook that sent her and the boy off to see a psychiatrist. A few hundred dollars later the doctor decided the kid's problem was that the school was messing him up."

This spokesman for everyman—or everyparent—drew a lesson from all those painful reminiscences: "Your public relations with me is the sum total of the experiences I have with your school. It's all those notes and memos and newsletters. It's how I feel when I come into your school. When I come, I wear lots of different hats and I look at you through different colored lenses—a harried mother bringing a forgotten lunch, a chaperone or a volunteer, a concerned parent, a worried parent, a defensive parent, and even a parent who just received her tax bill in the mail.''

Now that she is about to graduate to nonparent status as far as schools are concerned, Mrs. Fox reminded the administrators that she'll still vote and pay taxes. "I'll still be getting messages from you," she warned, "and for both our sakes, I hope I receive the message that you think you're sending." (provided by James Dufford)

In summary, parents would appreciate:

contact through letters explaining to them the services the guidance staff is equipped to perform and how they can use these services. Many parents are not aware that the counselor will assist them as well as their children. This will encourage parents to get to know and trust the counseling staff.

encouragement to come to the school at every opportunity. Do not reserve contact with parents for punitive or negative information about their child.

encouragement to become involved in school programs.

provision of evening time for parents who work outside the home to lessen the burden put upon them to come to the school.

receiving copies of guidance department publications at students' homes. Parents appreciate the effort and they'll be kept aware of what's going on in the guidance department.

invitations to participate in committee work, hot-line assignments, and other guidance projects.

publication and correct interpretation of test results. Plan public forums to explain and discuss test results. Results from district tests always hold an attraction for people, so never pass up an opportunity to interpret test findings with the community. Technical terminology should be avoided.

prompt communication of any guidance-based poll or questionnaire. Hesitation in releasing results or assuming that the public is not interested leave the guidance staff open to criticism.

being made aware of external communication efforts. Guidance news always interests them once they know the staff is there to help.

Many schools have approached the problem of internal communications by establishing an advisory council as in the HDC Community Cluster. This type of council includes counselors, teachers, students, and community members. By establishing advisory councils, counselors and administrators can obtain feedback, opinions, develop rapport, and generate an atmosphere of trust among all groups involved. An advisory council can be particularly useful in choosing test series, discussing school and guidance problems, reviewing and interpreting test results, and in planning and executing follow-up statistics on graduated and dropout students.

Follow-up studies concerning students are more likely to be accepted by the staff and community in general when they are presented by the advisory council. There is a feeling of involvement by the representation of many groups in this council. Thus the counselor will be able to keep his finger on the pulse of the school community as well as the outside community he serves.

In this discussion of public relations, staff, students, and parents have been highlighted. Communicating directly with these groups is a commendable beginning. Even so, communication responsibilities are not yet fulfilled. There are others in the community who must receive the message. They do not have contact through the schools but they have an investment in the schools. They too pay taxes. The link to this segment of the population, as well as all others, is through the media. Most newspapers and local radio stations welcome guidance news because it concerns and interests a large number of people.

If a school district's community relations person is available, his services should be used. Keep him informed of all the news of your department. Feed him ideas about human interest stories. Offer him all the cooperation that time allows. If the media are the link with the community, then this office of community relations is a link with the media. If a school district doesn't have an assigned public relations person an alternative plan can be put into action. One member of the guidance team should act as a receiving agent for all information to be publicized. Find service organizations and other community-based support for guidance projects such as rap centers, drug abuse centers, and so forth. The involvement of community organizations with the schools will draw the attention of the news media. Establish a contact with a local newspaper reporter and radio station manager. Talk to them about communication needs and seek their advice in publicizing your programs. Suggest ideas for photo features and human interest stories to reporters. Send simple, well-written news releases to all the local media and don't forget the weekly papers (or the area weekly "shopper" publications). Local radio stations may be willing to provide air time for a weekly program of guidance happenings. These stations are also receptive to airing public service spot announcements. These may be fifteen- or thirty-second taped messages informing the community of back-to-school night, public forums about test scores, or any other guidance programs. Consult the local stations about format and any other technical assistance. Develop a regular column of guidance news to be carried in local or weekly newspapers.

Effective use of the media demands acceptable timely and interesting materials. It is wise to delegate this responsibility to a staff member who writes well and enjoys working with this responsibility. All news should then be fed to this counselor who will present it in an organized, professional manner. If something is to be said, it should be said well. Keep in mind that:

> guidance news should be centered around people (especially students—respecting confidentiality, of course) and not things or general statements. The human element should be the basis of all communications.
>
> all counselors should be made aware of what is being sent to the media. Duplication is inefficient and may cause confusion.
>
> the district newsletter should always include a guidance department story. An entire issue may be dedicated to guidance-related information periodically.

Whether the counselor is talking to a student or writing a news release, he is involved in communications. He is in the "people business"—the most challenging and rewarding business there is. The degree to which he gets information across will greatly influence the effectiveness of the services he offers. Public relations cannot be left to chance. It provides the support to get done what has to be done in any situation that involves people.

Supplementary Readings

Ginott, Hiam. *Between Parent and Teenager.* New York: Macmillan, 1969.

Gordon, Thomas. *Teacher Effectiveness Training.* New York: Peter H. Wyden, 1974.

PART
II

THE MIDDLE SCHOOL COUNSELOR

CHAPTER EIGHT

The Middle School Counselor: What Must He Be?

As we look at the middle school counselor, we must observe him within the changing role of today's society. The counselor accepts the responsibility of consultant and resource person. To do this, he must know the community in which his students live. He must be aware of the unique needs of his clients and alert to changes as they occur.

The adolescent or preadolescent student is in the throes of change. New, undefined pressures can cause added stress to the conflicts already part of his life. As he moves through school, he is asked to make decisions that influence him dramatically for the rest of his life. In some middle schools, the student is required to make a major course selection that will box him into his future vocational choices — the choices with which he must live for the remainder of his productive life! And, with the extended life-span due to medical breakthrough, he may be committing himself to over a half a century of work he will come to despise. Not a very bright picture to paint for a person of any age. The counselor must understand the developmental stages of the middle school student to help him in making wise decisions and coping with the changes that are so significantly a part of the middle school years. It is the counselor who provides the meeting place for the student and has his hand on the pulse of the school. With the counselor's assistance, the student can explore all the avenues before him and then prepare to make the decisions that need to be made.

The middle school student has reached the stage in his life when he is interested in fitting into place all that he has learned both in and outside of school. He seems to be trying desperately to make sense to himself—his feelings, his ideas, and his ideals. The guidance counselor must be willing to participate in this self-exploration with an open mind and sufficient skill to channel the typically critical, negative viewpoint of this age child into more positive, rational viewpoints.

The Role of the Counselor

How can the school counselor fulfill these responsibilities? What kind of person must he be? If we can view the middle school community as "characterized organizationally by flexibility, environmentally by sensitivity to changing needs, and instructionally by individualization," as proposed by Atkins in "Rethinking Education in the Middle School,"[1] we can envision the counselor's role.

The effective counselor supports the student's fundamental need to assert independence. The counselor must be able to provide the expertise in human growth and development as a supportive service to teachers and parents in understanding the special needs of this age group. Accepting this challenge, the school counselor needs to broaden the scope of his image to include that of staff member involved in all aspects of the learning process. What kind of person must he be?

Let us begin by reviewing the image of the counselor through a well-known adage with a slight twist, "The I's have it!" The counselor's role demands *Intelligence, Information, Interest, Involvement, Initiative, Inquisitiveness, Imperfections, Inspiration, and Indestructibility.*

The school counselor must be *intelligent.* He needs to be skilled in counseling both individuals and groups. He must understand developmental needs of children. Thus he will be able to serve this function with faculty and parents as well as students. He must be *well*

---

1. Neil P. Atkins, "Rethinking Education in the Middle School," *Elementary School Principal*, November 3, 1973, p. 119.

informed through continual study of techniques and theories. He must be able to use these techniques and theories appropriately. The counselor must be sincerely *interested* and *involved* in each client seeking his assistance. He must be able to accept change yet not seek it just for its own sake. He must know his school community and be active within it. He must know his clients' parents, know his clients' teachers, and be aware of school policy within which all must function.

The counselor must show *initiative* in seeking out new ways and different procedures to aid in coping with situations that arise. The counselor needs to be *inquisitive*, to question, for through these questions he will discover answers and errors, both necessarily a part of the learning experience.

The counselor needs to realize his *imperfections* in order to accept the frailty of individuals—the imperfections in others. In realizing his own imperfections, the counselor is capable of growing as a person and becoming more competent in his role.

The counselor needs to be *inspiring*—to have the ability to communicate trust, hope, courage, and strength in his respect toward others to assure them of their self-worth and make them feel comfortable interacting with him and others.

The counselor must be *indestructible*, with a willingness to try again and again when all else seems to fail. He must truly respect his fellow men of all walks of life and strive to see the good in each one. The counselor must have enough personal strength to recognize that growth and change are often a relatively slow process. He must be able to view all aspects of the situation and supply alternative approaches. He must be patient. The school counselor needs to accept an open-door policy that not only means prying loose the door to his office but also the door to his mind and actions. The counselor acts as neither judge nor jury but rather as facilitator urging each person who seeks his services to think and act for himself—to accept responsibility for his own actions and to come to his own decisions.

The middle school counselor of today needs to be committed to people. He must possess a special kind of courage that enables him to show he cares. He should be able to see his clients as part of many environs—home, school, and society. He must recognize the uniqueness of each person and avoid judging others by his personal standards and codes of ethics. He needs to be accessible for a brief talk, to listen, to observe, or to provide information as well as extended counseling sessions past the usual closing hours of the school day. Each client's needs must be as important to the counselor as they are to the client himself.

What must the counselor be? He must be aware of himself and his own limitations so that these human traits do not cloud his associations and professional competency with those he serves. A counselor must be a sensitive and dedicated person who cares enough about others to give unselfishly of his time, talents, energies, and expertise in trying to help all who seek his services. In this process of dedication, he must continue to grow as a normal and stable person who will be a model for his client because he supports his actions with his attitudes. He must resist the temptation to play God.

A middle school counselor who is part of the community in which he works not only exhibits a respect for this community but has a more intimate understanding of the environment of his client.

The counselor may acquire many of the skills and qualities suggested here. The most difficult is gaining rapport. It is a sensitive process of complementary personalities. All persons cannot relate to all others. A secure counselor will not feel professionally threatened if he must refer a client to another counselor because he becomes aware of his inability to communicate. He recognizes his limitations and refers a client to more sophisticated services than he personally can offer.

There is no one image of a counselor that can be prescribed or described, for each counselor is an unique as his client and he should preserve that uniqueness in himself as proudly as he does in his client. For the counselor who understands himself and his role, and who is aware of what those he serves desire of him, can provide services compatible with these viewpoints. Then this counselor will be able to move within the climate of the school and community as a productive member of the guidance team—a most noteworthy goal for the practitioner. As we describe the idealistic view of the counselor, it seems most appropriate that the counselor actually functioning in a middle school should have an opportunity to describe the realities of his job. How does this middle school counselor see himself? What are his services and how do these services relate to the HDC model described? Is this model realistic or idealistic? How better can the potential of this model be presented than from the viewpoint of an active middle school counselor?

Janet Kwiatkoski, middle school counselor in Lawrence Intermediate School, New Jersey, speaks out.

The 1960s emergence of the middle school concept was born of necessity. The Soviet scientific breakthroughs of the late 1950s had caused many Americans to look upon local school systems as their real life "Rip Van Winkle." Something had to be done if the United States was to be inherited by its youngsters and remain the leading world power.

Common agreement was that educational reorganization was long overdue. True, the theories espoused by Piaget and Skinner were well known. If then, children do indeed pass through various levels of maturational development perhaps it was time to further investigate these levels and provide fertile fields for additional experimentation. But many parents and educators alike projected that the pendulum seemed destined to swing uncontrollably to the radically progressive side. Among the most innovative of plans was the proposal to reorganize the long standing 6−3−3 educational structure. Progressive child specialists theorized that the existing two- or three-year junior high school period could perhaps be put to better use if it were redesigned to include the upper intermediate grades as well. More conservative people chose to visualize the redesign as a means of at least partially alleviating the problem of pupil overcrowding. The middle school then, as it was most commonly called, became a product of the times. It promised to be the cure-all for what many Americans were calling an ailing educational system.

During this same period, physician, psychologists, and psychiatrists began to substantiate new theories regarding child development from birth to adolescence. The new theories were so complex that it was soon apparent scientific specialization would be necessary to fully explore all the ramifications which heretofore had not held a particularly major priority.

The middle school concept was a bold movement which caught on quickly in the more progressive sectors of the community. Gradually as it proved its capabilities, as noted throughout this text, it became a widely accepted new concept in education. With more and more data being revealed pertaining to the nature of children, how they "learn" and what they "feel," it seemed fitting that learning specialists and guidance counselors would enter the middle school scene through a team approach. Of the two new specialists, guidance counselors have been in the past and still remain a controversial issue. Often middle school counselors have met with such disfavor that the job description has been modified to accommodate a more palatable title, i.e.: child advocate, educational humanitarian, and child development specialist, to name a few.

A part of the unpopularity of the role of the counselor has no doubt filtered down from the ranks of the high school counselors who have long been the scapegoats of the secondary educational system. Taxpayers in the past, but more specifically in view of the recent money crunch, questioned the need for a salaried educator to "talk to kids." (Especially when the talking in a middle school setting seldom deals with tangibles such as college entrance or vocational and career guidance.) Thirty years ago that's what parents felt was their role, or perhaps when a parent was not available the teacher could fill this need. Many present-day educators still can be found to support this concept. [The HDC model in this book presents a compromise that encourages teachers to work in partnership with the counselor though the counselor sharing her expertise and providing the teacher with basic guidance skills.] The reason for disenchantment with the counselor as a member of the middle school staff does not rest with any one person or group. Specialists and classroom teachers have been professional rivals on and off over the years and in many cases poor administrative planning has created such situations. Equal pay for equal work is a human heritage and all too often the specialist has had privileges which have been the bone of contention in more than one school system. In presenting typical examples of a counselor in action, this writer will illustrate the extent of the counselor's role, often unknown by her colleagues. It is not uncommon for many classroom teachers to believe the fantasy that counselors, through their magic methods will "right all wrongs and make all the bad things go away!" In too many instances counselors are considered administrators and have many administrative privileges such as an office, telephone, often the services of a secretary, and what at times appear to be unlimited coffee breaks and unending lunch hours. Hardly does this add up to be an endearing situation, particularly in view of the fact that the strength for a successful program must come from within and of course the guidance program is no exception. But the important issue is that a counselor or a guidance position must be judged by what it is rather than what it seems to be. As illustrated in the following daily description, in reality counseling is many hours of frustration, redtape, and heartbreak, all of which can vanish when a child, parent, or teacher is genuinely helped by the professional humanitarianism of a counselor.

Basic Needs for Successful Middle School Guidance Program

What then is it really like to be a middle school counselor? Before that can be answered this writer must define what she believes counseling to be. Counseling must be a personal thing; it cannot be all things to all people. A philosophy must be flexible enough to change to meet new needs as they emerge. Counseling is for all children. Children involved in the guidance program described were not thought of as necessarily "in trouble" or "strange" by their peers, parents, or teachers. The challenge then was to establish a comfortable, pleasant environment which would be made accessible to all the children in the school. The services provided, if measured by the HDC model, would include the Counseling Cluster, the Crisis Center, the Assessment Cluster, and the Communication Cluster headed by the counseling staff. The counseling office houses another middle school counselor, the child study team (Psychologist, Learning Specialist, and Social Worker) and the guidance secretary. Support of the administration was found to be essential. The following guidelines served as a basis for the middle school program in this school.[2]

---

2. Lawrence Intermediate School, 66 Eggerts Crossing Road, Lawrenceville, N. J. 08648. *Statement of Philosophy*, 1977.

The role of the guidance counselor must be that of a child advocate. During the critical years of ten to fourteen the counselor shall work with the school staff to oversee the emotional, social, and educational development of his counselees to the best measures possible. When priorities must be set, the best interests of the child must be served first. With that goal foremost in mind the following job description was designed reflecting the team approach to counseling services:

1. The counselor should meet with each classroom teacher early in the school year to go over any information which will enable the teacher to more fully meet the needs of her children.

2. Early in the school term, specialists should receive an *awareness list* consisting of the names of children who are academically remedial and need special consideration in academic assignments.

3. The counselor should be included in administrative meetings on any or all levels which include decision making about his or her counselees concerning their emotional, social, and academic well-being. He or she should not be held responsible for decisions which do not include his or her involvement.

4. The counselor should coordinate Assessment Testing and Achievement Testing. This includes scheduling, issuing directions for, and supervision of the actual testing as well as dispersal and collection of testing materials and follow-up on test interpretation.

5. The counselor should take an active part in the orientation of new students and their parents to the school. This includes evening orientation meetings and classroom orientation for 5th graders in early September and 7th grade (into 8th) students in the spring.

6. The counselor must establish and maintain lines of communication whenever possible between parents and himself or herself. This can be done by office meetings or by 'phone conferences. Office conferences can be scheduled as early as 8:15 A.M. or as late as 4:00 P.M. by previous appointment.

7. The counselor should be involved in noontime problems between students or aides and students when the offense is of nonphysical nature. When an offense involves disciplinary action then the counselor will turn the problem over to an administrator.

8. Classroom guidance is of prime importance and should be offered to all students. Fifth-grade children are scheduled regularly and sixth- and seventh- or eighth-grade classes when and if the need is seen by the classroom teachers or the counselor.

9. The counselor should be as accessible as possible to staff and meet their needs in impromptu conferences as counselor time permits. Those teachers she or he does not meet in impromptu situations should be scheduled from time to time so that a sharing of information can take place.

10. The maintenance of student records in a well-organized manner is of prime importance. With the help of the guidance aide and/or secre-

tary this should be an ongoing process. In the spring of the year, when student data processing is especially heavy, an aide would be appropriated to guidance to help meet these heavy demands.

11. The counselor should continue to act as a public relations agent between other school systems and educational institutions. Such responsibilities should not supersede the needs of counselees, however.

12. The counselor should function as an important part of the Child Study Team and be particularly responsible for the processing of referrals.

13. The counselor, in order to maintain a favorable working relationship with staff, should not become involved in situations between parents and educators that seriously question professional standards. In such cases the counselor should put the parent in touch with an administrator.

14. The counselor should meet with administrators, staff, and parents in the spring in order to determine the best placement of each child. The scheduling of classes is not a part of the regular school year counselor responsibilities. It is suggested that adequate time be allotted for such scheduling during the summer. Such lists would be put in the hands of the administrator before the counselor leaves for final summer vacation. The counselor does not assume responsibility for changes made in class lists after that point.

15. The counselor is responsible for the formulation of a yearly guidance budget, a monthly log which reflects day-to-day activities, and a monthly administrator's report.

Setting Priorities

A setting of priorities is important in order to function in an orderly, effective manner. But priorities can and must change from time to time. Usually a counselor will notice a need to make some changes with each new school year. Over the summer months children often change physically and emotionally. Last year's shy boy may be this year's terror and the parents or teacher may need many hours of counseling help. In the case of such emergencies one must be prepared to reorganize one's time.

A consuming involvement can also be with the child who is experiencing the grief syndrome. Whether it be divorce, temporary separation from a loved one, or death in an immediate family, the results can be tenuous. The counselor must be prepared to research various situations which arise and be able to make sensible recommendations to the family, teacher, and child based on what authorities in the field suggest. It is important for the counselor to gain insights from many sources and be prepared to suggest further reading in the problem area. A counselor must consistently guard against being "all knowing." It can be dangerous for all concerned.

Typical Days in the Life of a Middle School Counselor

All counselors should continually be involved in self-evaluation. This writer found it helpful to keep a guidance diary from time to time. It fosters an appraisal of use of time and helps to evaluate personal attitudes that may be developing through the fulfillment of the responsibilities of the job. Following is an example of two days in the life of a counselor. The reader is urged to note the continual interaction with other school personnel.

Day 1

8:08 A.M.	Arrived at school. Opened up the office.	*Thought how clean it looked—colors are good—the plants add a lot.*
8:15 A.M.	Discussed the schedule for the day with the guidance secretary.	*Probably the key to keeping our sanity is being organized—I can imagine what it would be like if one of us was and one wasn't organized!*
8:30 A.M.	Began working on final copy of the new district-wide cum folder.	*My two work copies are too messy to take to the administrator's meeting tomorrow. Too many hours have gone into this project to do it halfway now.*
9:00 A.M.	Met with new 5th grade teacher who replaced substitute. Went over her class list child by child.	*She sparkles! I like her. She'll do O.K.—she has confidence but is not overbearing. She took copious notes.*
10:45 A.M.	Saw previously scheduled children. One counselee has real hangups about missing special school activities due to remedial instructions.	*Tried to explain that getting a firm base now is important —can get into more activities in a few years and it will matter more then.*
11:10 A.M.	Made appointments to see various other children tomorrow. Spoke with special services' secretary re: continued absences of two students.	*Will see these children later this afternoon. Asked special services' secretary to ask attendance officer to check on these two counselees.*

11:40 A.M.	Saw 5th grade boy in outer office waiting to see the assistant principal.	*I spoke with the boy—he was frightened but trying to be brave—he called his teacher a name. Teacher came and we all talked. The teacher looks about 14 years old himself. It was like a 14 year old and 10 year old who had squabbled and neither wanted to give in. When I left they were ready to talk—I'll check later.*
12:25 P.M.	Lunch at my desk.	*Good way to get paper work done but not too great on the digestive system—what I need is a place to hide to get anything done—the phone rings, people popping in and out—I really have to stop taking the paper work home every night—I'm cheating my family.*
1:00 P.M.	Saw the young male teacher from 11:40 entry.	*Student and he talked and all is well. Nice young man to work with—I suspect he will have to tighten classroom management, though.*
1:25 P.M.	Spoke with the school psychologist by phone about procedure for getting parental permission for learning evaluations and psychological testing.	*This is presenting headaches. Psychologist needs permission to test—teacher who referred the child won't ask parent for this permission. I hesitate to call for it makes parents defensive toward guidance when this is our initial contact.*
2:05 P.M.	Planned schedule for next week. Wrote out memos to teachers and placed the memos in their mailboxes.	*Thank goodness all my life I have written lists—maybe all that time someone up there knew I'd be a guidance counselor and got me ready!*
2:30 P.M.	Returned three parent calls.	*Being a mother is a help in this position—and I think my age is in my favor—parents who give very young teachers*

		trouble often soften a lot when I get involved. Parents are generally cooperative.
3-20 P.M.	Mrs. D. stopped in (teacher of grade 6.)	*She's feeling low. It's hard to take another teacher's place in midstream. She's having trouble individualizing everything. She seemed pleased when I volunteered to come in and do a special unit with her class. I want to get a feeling of why her class is having trouble getting along. The teacher left a little less down —we all need someone to care.*
4:10 P.M.	Left school.	

Day 2

8.05 A.M.	Arrived at school.	*It was good to feel ready for the day. This is a good idea— writing down the next day's appointments before leaving the day before.*
8:20 A.M.	Review of day's schedule with the secretary.	*Many interruptions by 'phone today. I'm thinking about discussing with the principal the possibility of holding calls to the guidance office until 8:30 A.M. We need time to get organized.*
8:35 A.M.	M. dropped in.	*She loves children. Is it possible to be a born teacher? She loves her class and they love her. It is a pleasant note on which to begin a day.*
9:00 A.M.	Made an all school "Brotherhood Week Announcement."	*I'm using a soft sell and it seems to be working. I checked yesterday and very few kids have been sent to the asst. principal's office on disciplinary charges. Are they really listening and trying to be nice to each other? I think so.*

9:10 A.M.	My guidance intern and I met to discuss her plans for the day as well as the progress of her independent project.	*She'll be a good counselor. She has a very open face which seems to convey "I like you," and children need to get that feeling from an adult. A guidance intern is a great deal of work but it is such a necessary experience for the future counselor.*
9:40 A.M.	Sixth-grade classroom guidance group.	*A lot of cruel name calling in the class reported by the teacher. After talking with many of the children privately and in small groups, I suspect a tug-of-war between students and teacher. The teacher and I discuss my suspicions and she is willing to try a few new approaches. Hopefully this session today will build some guidlines for the class and teacher to use in building a better relationship.*
10:30 A.M.	Five educators from another district arrive to visit our school.	*We spoke with them briefly about the school and the various programs including guidance, toured the building, and placed them in classrooms to observe. Original greeting was with the principal and guidance counselor. The teachers in our building seemed pleased to have visitors but I am glad we had their visit planned in advance. I'm not going to be able to spend as much time as I would like with them. The children seem restless today—it must be the weather—they haven't been out to play in days!*
11:45 A.M.	My four girls are back.	*These four fifth-grade girls can't get along together but won't stay apart. So very typical for their age. But I see many hours with these girls—very mature for their*

age but at the same time so silly.

12:30 P.M.	Made sure our visitors had lunch.	*Hope I can speak with them later today. It's a great way to get ideas for new programs to try.*

12:40 P.M.   The great watch mystery . . .   *R. says his watch was taken from his desk yesterday. M. is wearing it today—What can I do about it? We agreed to talk it over with M. M. says he found the watch in the Boys' Room yesterday. I admired his telling me he found it—no story about "it's mine." I said the choice must be yours, M., but a boy who has been as honest as you will have to choose the right thing to do. He gave it to R. M. is sad; R. is happy; I think it all worked out well.*

1:35 P.M.   Lunch break.   *Saw the "watch mystery" teacher briefly. Discussed results of conference with R. and M. Had an interesting conversation with a group of young teachers about the high cost of living—it's hard for them to make it.*

1:55 P.M.   Secretary told me three girls had been sent from the cafetorium for unbecoming conduct. The lunchroom aides would like me to talk to the girls.   *It seems there was a discussion in the cafetorium among these three girls about fruit cocktail. Eventually a bet was made to determine whether peaches, gooseberries, or pears would fly off the tip of a spoon at a different rate of speed and distance. Things got a little messy. We talked about how lunchroom would look if 250 children all tried this experiment and then gave them moral support while they cleaned up the "experiment."*

2:35 P.M.	Returned to office.	*The visitors were winding up their visit and had some questions. The administrator had a lot of questions about our guidance program and our secretary prepared packets of materials to take back with them. They seemed to have enjoyed their visit.*
3:20 P.M.	Two boys stopped by after school.	*They needed to talk—the boys are having trouble since they were assigned to safety patrol—other children say they are trying to "act big"— we talked about responsibility and what goes with it . . . some of these children have beautiful minds . . . we really need to listen to them more . . . they left so happy→I felt good!*
3:50 P.M.	It's Friday—the school is quiet—nearly everyone is gone.	*I need to get away—the week has been long and hard—but that's the job and in spite of it all I love it.*

The report of two days' activities from the view of the middle school counselor provides some insight into the multifaceted role of the counselor. The real goal of the counselor—that is, to serve children—is never far from mind. The counselor depicted here is one who listens, who has boundless energy and patience, and who respects the needs of the staff with whom she works. This one counselor's view of her role and herself gives a vivid picture not only of what her clients gain from her in their relationship but what she gains from the experience—a sense of worth and well-being. It is a sensitive partnership—that of the counselor, teacher, child, and administrator. It demands an open mind and extreme patience. Is it not helpful for the counselor to explore his own strengths and emphasize these strengths as part of the counseling services he provides? Is it not also wise to be aware of one's weakness and seek out from the talent within reach in the school and community to supplement the counselor's own strengths to better serve the child? In the middle school, where there is a counselor, his role should be to organize the management of these skills and services available to the school community so that the most productive interaction can take place between children, parents, teachers, administrators, and the counselor himself. No one can determine the most appropriate goals or a blanket approach to counseling in the middle school. The counselor must seek his own direction and be sure this direction reflects the needs of those who use his services as well as the use of his and his colleagues' skills to the greatest benefit.

Supplementary Readings

Avila, Donald L., Combs, Arthur, and Purkey, William W. *The Helping Relationship Sourcebook*. Boston: Allyn and Bacon, 1971.

Kealy, Ronald P. *Middle Schools in the United States: 1969–70*. Nashville: Faculty Research Committee, George Peabody College, 1970 (multilithed).

Kohl, John W., Caldwell, William E., and Eichorn, Donald H. *Self-Appraisal and Development of the Middle School: An Inservice Approach*. University Park, Pa.: The Pennsylvania School Study Council, 1970.

Lawrence, Gordon. *Measurement of Teacher Competencies: Final Report of Research—Project MPACT for Middle Schools*. Gainesville, Fla.: University of Florida, July 1971 (mimeographed).

Mellinger, Morris, and Rackauskas, John A. *Quest for Identity: National Survey of the Middle School, 1969–70*. Chicago: Chicago State College, Chicago, Ill., 1970.

Rice, Philip. *The Adolescent: Development, Relationships and Culture*. Boston: Allyn and Bacon, 1975.

Smith, Daniel. *Educational Psychology and Its Classroom Applications*. Boston: Allyn and Bacon, 1975.

CHAPTER NINE

The Middle School Counselor and the Special Education Student

The services of the counselor often ignore the child who has been identified as "special" and placed in a particular educational program. The misconception seems to be that this special placement will provide all the academic, social, and emotional support the child will need. Sensitive educators are aware of the fallacy of this premise. Dr. Wayne I. Newland, Director of Pupil Personnel Services, Hamilton Township, New Jersey, provides the following as support for the need of counselor involvement with the special education student in the public school setting.

A man planted a young tree in the ground and left it to grow. While he was away one day, a windstorm came. The tree was bowed, first in one direction then another. A neighbor, seeing that his friend's tree was about to be uprooted, went into the gale, propped the tree upright, and secured it to a fence.

When the first man returned from his journey, he saw that his neighbor had been responsible for saving his tree, and he was grateful. He said, "This is my tree, but now it is also your tree. You have contributed to its life. You shall enjoy its beauty and rest in its shade."

—An ancient parable of unknown origin

The importance of the middle school counselor in helping to mold young lives has become obvious. The resulting joys and rewards have been stressed for decades and are retold again in this book. However, a significant part of the school population has been virtually overlooked in the evolution of the counselor's role. Only in recent years has work with special students, those with identifiable learning handicaps, begun to receive the attention of preparation institutions, authors, and counselors themselves.

The ancient parable epitomizes the work of the counselor. How much more, though, does it apply to helping those youngsters who, like undernourished trees with very weak roots, need particular kinds of attention and concern as they try to face the windstorms of learning and growing up. Those who work closely with educationally handicapped children often relate with enthusiasm some tiny but significant growth in a retarded youngster's progress toward decoding; or a slight lengthening of a hyperactive child's attention span which opens a little wider the door to learning; or the adolescent with neurological problems who has finally attained the independence and self-reliance to participate in a job-placement program. Unique relationships develop between faculty and these students, their parents, and families. The weaker tree is braced in the wind, and becomes their tree also.

Counselors Can Have a "Piece of the Action"

Counselors should and must contribute to the program of special education students. "But how can I work with the specials?" we might hear. "I taught regular classes before becoming a counselor. I've had no special training. Besides, children like that upset me." These attitudes are quite understandable. But anyone with the basic equipment to be a *good* counselor of the majority of students has what it takes to work with the educationally handicapped as a middle school counselor, given professional commitment and concern.

Some technical knowledge is useful and can be picked up along the way through reading,[1] in-service sessions, meetings with special services personnel and special education faculty, and college course work. But the main ingredient to success is a genuine effort to be of service to these special young people.

For purposes of this chapter the term *special education students* refers to pupils who have been diagnosed as having some identified and classifiable handicapping condition which interferes with learning. The presence of this condition necessitates prescriptive teaching designed to teach to the child's specific level and pace of achievement, exploit strengths, and, where possible, remediate the handicap. *Exceptional* is also used here interchangeably with this restricted meaning.

---

1. An excellent book of readings on this subject is *The Guidance of Exceptional Children*, ed. John Curtis Gowan and George D. Demos (New York: McKay, 1965).

While further definition will follow, it may be helpful to describe children *not* in the focus of this chapter. Although they are certainly as deserving of counselor time, we are not concerned here with the bright or gifted student, nor are we speaking of culturally, economically, or socially disadvantaged, per se. They may all have special educational needs, but are not technically considered "handicapped." Special education and these other categories are not mutually exclusive, however. A student may have a handicap in his auditory or visual perception and yet possess a potential for functioning well above average intellectually. Some children from disadvantaged backgrounds also have specific learning handicaps which add to their difficulties in school.

The numbers and categories of educational handicaps vary from state to state. Some uniformity will probably result, however, from the passage of the Education for All Handicapped Children Act of 1975 (Public Law 94–142). This federal legislation sets forth the following classifications (see Appendix B for detailed description of the Child Study Team of the New Jersey School System that is authorized to determine these classifications):

Mentally retarded
Hard of hearing
Deaf
Speech impaired
Visually handicapped
Emotionally disturbed
Orthopedically handicapped
Other health impaired
Specific learning disabled

This taxonomy is not too dissimilar from that used in most states. One example of variation is in New Jersey, a pioneer in mandating education for the handicapped. That state's law includes an additional category, socially maladjusted, and dichotomizes specific learning disabled into neurologically impaired and perceptually impaired.

Since this chapter is concerned with the role of the counselor in the middle school, further discussion of the technical aspects of education for the handicapped is not warranted here. The reader is referred to a vast literature in the field of special education which ranges from basic introductory materials to the most scholarly work.

There has not always been a variety of special education programs available. From the late 1800s there have been isolated educational and/or training programs for the severely retarded. Not until the third quarter of the present century have special education programs for a wide range of handicaps been instituted in the U.S. public schools.

This response to the particular needs of handicapped children generally did not include counselors or their preparation institutions. Hunt,[2] in 1960, pointed out that "the training of counselors is frequently inadequate to allow for acceptance or understanding" of the student who is handicapped. Ten years later Rutman[3] surveyed the middle states region and found that nearly 27 percent of school counselors never attempt to deal with the handicapped and that more than half of those who do spend less than 5 percent of their time with exceptional children. Rutman logically posited this glaring inadequacy to be a result of the lack of training that guidance counselors had received in the field of special education. In a survey of major counseling and special education journals of the 1960s Cormay[4] found only sixteen articles dealing with the counselor's work with the exceptional student.

In the early 1970s, however, we saw the pendulum swing in the direction of special education counselors—specialists trained to work just with the educationally handicapped. At the start of this decade Texas became the first state to provide local districts with funding for such positions.[5] In 1972 the Economic Opportunity Act stipulated that at least 10 percent of the Head Start program's national enrollment opportunities should be available to "special children" previously ignored. Counselors were to be trained to work in this area.[6] In 1974 the Bureau of Education for the Handicapped increased its services for identification of the handicapped (the unserved and the underserved) child. Counseling was considered an essential consideration for these new clients.[7] The thrust of the times

---

2. J. T. Hunt, "Guidance and Exceptional Children," *Education* 80:364, 1964.
3. Joyce Rutman, "An Examination of the Work of School Counselors with Handicapped Children" (Ph.D. dissertation, Temple University, 1970).
4. R. B. Cormay, "Returning Special Education to Classes," *Personnel and Guidance Journal* 48:641–646, 1970.
5. *Texas State Plan for Special Education*, Senate Bill 230, 1974.
6. Norma Radin, "The Impact of a Kindergarten Home Counseling Program," *Exceptional Children* 36:251–259, 1969.
7. T. P. Lake, "Keeping Posted," *Teaching Exceptional Children* 7:57, 1974.

served to generate interest in counselor specialists who would work exclusively in this area. This was advocated as a new role by Carl Hansen in 1971. He wrote:

Special education in America has now progressed to the point numerically, financially, and professionally whereby special educators should seriously consider fulfilling the total counseling needs of the special education student through the services of a special education counselor—a counselor knowledgeable about handicapped conditions and a professionally trained counselor for and about the exceptional child.[8]

Now, however, a centrist approach to counseling special education students seems to be emerging. It is hoped that this text will contribute to the acceptance of this position. The typical counselor's case load should include special education students as well as all other types of pupils. While the counselor in all levels of our school systems should be a generalist, it is especially important in the middle school. This is where students are moving from the cocoon of the usually self-contained elementary school classroom into the routines of changing classes and greater independence.

Mainstreaming

The most significant factor, however, that has made the regular counselor a vital part of the educationally handicapped student's program is the concept of *mainstreaming*.

Education, perhaps more than most fields, is subject to "bandwagon jargon," with some new term emerging periodically as the "in" word. The special area of educating the handicapped is no exception. That word for the 1970s is *mainstreaming*. It is being promulgated from the highest levels of federal and state departments of education, is the frequent focus of professional writings in the field, and is a conference topic on virtually every agenda when special educators gather. Mainstreaming is echoing (sometimes reluctantly) throughout the halls of the nation's schools. What is mainstreaming?

Too many special education students have been regarded as more "special" than they should have been (that is, different, un-

---

8. Carl E. Hanse, "The Special Education Counselor: A New Role," *Exceptional Children* 38:69, 1971.

usual, odd, weird, less deserving, should be isolated, and so on). Mainstreaming is premised on the recognition of the right of these children to be in the mainstream of the school along with pupils with no learning problems. If other students receive art, music, and physical education instruction, the handicapped should also. Special education classes should not be placed in substandard, isolated rooms while "normal" children have regular classrooms located in bright areas of the building. Athletics, clubs, counseling services, cafeterias, and school playgrounds should not have unnecessary special restrictions against these children. Each child should be as much a part of the mainstream of the school as he is able to be. This approach is often referred to as placing the handicapped student in the "least restrictive environment." The recent federal legislation mandates "procedures to assure that, to the maximum extent appropriate, handicapped children ... are educated with children who are not handicapped, and that special classes, separate schooling, or other removal of handicapped children from the regular educational environment occurs only when the nature or severity of the handicap is such that education in regular classes with the use of supplementary aids and services cannot be achieved satisfactorily."[9]

To further clarify the process of mainstreaming, two distinct approaches are described. Application of these alternatives depends on the individual student's capabilities and needs. The terminology is an attempt to aid in communication, not just to expand the jargon.

The first approach is the "integration" of the student into the mainstream of the school. Some mildly handicapped students can function well if *not* placed in self-contained special education classrooms. A minimally or moderately handicapped student may make overall progress effectively in a mainstream or regular class or homeroom, doing much the same things as the other students. However, he would need to receive selected, prescribed assistance from a special education teacher in a resource room or skills center for a portion of his school day. Such students tend to feel a part of the "normal" school population, have more positive self-images, and progress well if the extra help they actually need is administered. The key to this approach is to integrate the student well and carefully into the mainstream, but also to provide him direct assistance in the special ways appropriate to meet his academic or social needs.

---

9. *Education for All Handicapped Children Act of 1975*, Public Law 94–142.

The second strategy of mainstreaming is "exegration." Many educationally handicapped students do need a more intense program than is possible in an "integrated" setting. These children are assigned to self-contained special education classes with other children having similar problems. Although segregated, these young people are often capable of being exegrated (worked out into the mainstream) to some extent. A student may join a regular class of his own age group for art or music. He may take science, shop, physical education (or even reading or math—if he can handle it) with regular classes. The aim is to provide special class students with *carefully selected* activities and mainstream involvement, so long as it is consistent with his growth needs.

The implications of mainstreaming for the counselor must be recognized. It is assumed, by definition, that every child who has been classified as handicapped in the middle school has received a careful and thorough evaluation by special services personnel and that this has resulted in a prescribed educational plan which includes appropriate strategies for mainstreaming. Such a study usually involves psychological testing, a learning assessment, and a social case history. A comprehensive medical examination may be done to recognize or rule out physical problems contributing to the learning deficits. Other specialists, such as a neurologist or psychiatrist, may have been included (see Appendix B for details of a child study team). It is important that teachers and administrators be given the opportunity for input into the study. However, it is of utmost importance in middle schools for the counselor to be involved.

Today's approaches are a far cry from when the teacher of "specials" was expected to keep his students completely in his control, to himself, virtually unseen by the rest of the school. Too frequently the administrator and other teachers were most happy not to bother *that* class and for *that* class not to bother them. As a result, the teacher provided everything he could for the children: academic prescription and instruction, Band-Aids, TLC, physical education, art, music, and whatever counseling he could give the students and their parents. Even so, much good was done for a lot of exceptional children. In many cases, however, such teachers considered themselves martyrs for the cause of their students, at the same time being possessive of this exclusive role. Mainstreaming has not necessarily been easy for regular classroom or special education teachers.

Focus of the Counselor's Role

The counselor's role in the middle school is vital. Someone should be close at hand to oil the complex machinery that is a specially designed program including mainstreaming. The counselor is there and has an overview that is the basis for exercising oversight. The special services staff members who perform the evaluation are probably not located on site. The teachers who have been and are involved in the case are busy teaching most of the day. The principal is busy with his myriad of duties. Aside from the fact that the counselor is on site and may have a flexible schedule for availability, he is the logical staff member to be the program expediter for a number of reasons.

Ideally, the counselor has known the student since entry into the middle school setting, whether or not he was classified as a special education student at that time. He should have been in touch with the specialists who had been involved, and can provide the necessary bird's-eye view as the specially designed program is implemented for the child. Further, and very important, the counselor knows and should be able to work with the personalities of the staff members serving the student and be an effective expeditor.

This does not require as much technical background in the field of special education as it takes insight and a keen interest in performing the role of counselor to the full extent with every student. Some approaches may be different, some objectives extraordinary, some relationships frustrating. Overall, though, it will be successful and rewarding.

The counselor's role with the special education program in the middle school is a varied one. For the middle school student to realize his fullest potential there must be a liaison between the pupil, the parent, and the teacher, as well as between the school and community. In our schools today the counselor generally serves this function well for the "normal" child. A counselor should serve handicapped children as well. The areas of concern are similar for all children, but the emphasis, techniques, and goals may vary.

There are several broad areas of focus for the counselor in working with special education students in the middle school: identification of potential learning handicaps, personal adjustment counseling, career guidance, and parent counseling.

Identification of potential
learning handicaps

Many, if not most, students who have learning handicaps are found during the primary or early intermediate grades. Such early identification should be a prime goal of every school system. Because of the subtle ways certain handicaps manifest themselves, the seriousness of some problems may not appear until the middle school years when the child falls significantly behind his peers in one or more areas of development. Too frequently a student passed on as "merely a slow learner" meets frustration levels he can no longer tolerate in socially acceptable ways. A student with average intellectual capacity but with a perceptual development lag can become maladjusted or disturbed if he has been treated by his peers or by his teachers as "dumb" or "slow."

If such a child comes to the attention of the middle school counselor, he should be alert enough to consider whether there might be some educational handicap present that warrants a specialized program. The counselor should work with the teacher(s) and administrator to effect referral for a special services work-up. However, the counselor with insight will act, not only react. He will inquire of teachers, particularly of incoming classes and new children, concerning learning or behavioral difficulties that may be present but not too apparent.

As the counselor develops greater sophistication in recognizing what may be potential learning handicaps, he must retain two perspectives. First, since some teachers may not recognize what may represent learning handicaps, the counselor should seek descriptions of behavior and progress and make his own close observations rather than depend on brief characterizations by the teacher. Second, the counselor must be careful not to "play doctor" or become a pseudo-diagnostician, but to refer questionable cases for consideration by trained specialists.

In addition to helping identify students who have never undergone a child study evaluation, the counselor may detect weaknesses in a classified child's prescribed program. He can then recommend a reevaluation or updated assessment and prescription.

It is important for the counselor to develop a relationship with the parents of special education children. A counselor in the middle school is the most logical person for a parent to contact for information, and he is the person most likely to be able to maintain liaison with parents during referral, evaluation, and program implementation. More will be said later in this chapter regarding work with parents, however.

Personal adjustment counseling

Because of the handicapping condition, nearly all special education students have adjustment problems. They may be stigmatized in the eyes of their peers and adults. The handicap may have certain obvious physical characteristics. Since the middle school is a transition between elementary and secondary approaches, it is a busy place, usually with some type of departmentalization. This often necessitates tight scheduling of classes and teachers, allowing little time for faculty to meet informally with students. The school counselor is, again, the logical person to help in this area.

Counseling in relationships is vitally needed by the special education pupils of middle school age. They usually need help in adjusting to themselves—accepting their own limitations and recognizing their own strengths. They need help in relating to other handicaped students, to their own and other teachers, to students in the mainstream, to their parents, and to the public at large. By virtue of assisting the students to achieve personal and social growth, the counselor can help the student become more teachable, more comfortable, and more cooperative and self-reliant in the school setting and at home. Group and individual counseling are appropriate means of modifying self-concept, reducing anxiety, and improving behavior. This may be done during a class or at a separate time and place. Counseling can and should be a major tool in helping these students adjust within the school and community.

A counselor may be available for crisis intervention when a handicapped student meets frustrations he cannot handle alone. Too frequently the special education student responds or acts out in a manner which is brought to the attention of the school disciplinarian, when what is actually needed is a counseling approach. An alert and available counselor can capitalize on such an event so that the experience becomes a part of the student's growth and learning rather than an interruption or setback in it.

Career guidance

Special education students should receive formal career education or orientation as early as the middle school years. The competent counselor need add but little to the knowledge and awareness which is the base of his mainstream career counseling. The counselor's goal is to help a student with special handicaps and needs to consider exploring a particular range of careers. Expediting the student's discovery of his aptitudes and interests is a necessary and major contribution to an effective educational program.

Some study and research of this focus has been conducted in recent years. During the summer of 1972, two University of Iowa professors, one in counselor education and one in special education, conducted a cross-disciplinary seminar in career guidance.[10] The success of that program exemplifies the effectiveness of work in this area.

Parental counseling

Frequently the parents of handicapped students feel inadequate; sometimes they assume responsibility for their child's problem and are confused by this guilt. At times there may be outright rejection or inability to accept the child as he is—or to recognize that there is any problem whatever. The parents may need more help than the teacher, special services staff, and counselor can provide. However, the middle school counselor should coordinate the relationship with the parents and do what seems possible with the resources at hand. The counselor should also be familiar with community agencies from whom help can be sought by the parents.

A very effective way the counselor and teachers can assist parents is to bring together mothers and fathers of several special education students. This should not be considered group therapy performed by the counselor, but rather giving these parents the opportunity to be accepted and to accept others with similar concerns. They can share encouragement and woes with one another in a type of Alcoholics Anonymous approach. Often it is helpful to bring in a specialist of some type (pediatrician, psychologist, learning specialist, and so forth) as a guest. This can provide the basis for getting together and definite contributions can be made to the people involved.

There are usually many kinds of students in the middle school—bright and slow, athletic and clumsy, culturally advantaged and dis-

---

10. D. Jepson and P. Retich, "Cross Disciplinary Approach to Teaching Career Guidance," *Exceptional Children* 40:514—518, 1974.

advantaged, and many average "just-plain-kids." It is quite likely, also, that some educationally handicapped students are or ought to be in special education programs. They may be in appropriate classes, they may be identified but underserved, or they may not be identified at all and become more deficient every day.

The middle school counselor must accept a responsibility to all children. He or she must help good programs to continue to run smoothly; must help get weak or out-of-date prescriptions revised; and must be alert to children with potential handicaps and help them obtain the diagnosis and needed program.

In short, he or she must be a full-time counselor to the whole school—to every student who attends. A counselor who can do a good job with regular students can do a good job with and for exceptional children. It takes time, awareness, concern, and often even emotional commitment. But like that old parable, when you help the weak tree live through the windstorm, that tree also becomes yours, with its beauty and joys.

Finally, two pats on the back for middle school counselors: the first one is placed high and given heartily—for the steps they have already taken to help handicapped kids. The second is a little lower and a little firmer—to propel them on to more and better service in this field.

Supplementary Readings

Manni, John L., and Pica, Louis, "A Consultation Model for Counseling Parents of Handicapped Children." Paper presented at the National Association of School Psychologists Annual Convention, Kansas City, Missouri, 1976.

Newland, Wayne I. "Are They Forgotten in Your School?" *New Jersey Guidance News* (a publication of the New Jersey Personnel and Guidance Association) 38 (Spring):18—19, 1974.

Newland, Wayne I. "The Password for This Year Is 'Mainstreaming'," *Bureau Briefs* (a publication of the Curriculum and Instruction Branch of Special Education and Pupil Personnel Services, New Jersey State Department of Education) 4:1, 1973.

CHAPTER TEN

The Middle School Counselor and Career Guidance

The middle school counselor must provide effective career guidance for all children. During these crucial formative years the child develops patterns and attitudes toward work that will carry over into adult life. Career guidance in the middle school years should continue to provide opportunity for occupational exploratory activities that, it is to be hoped, had been initiated in elementary school. Youngsters need information about the world of work and a chance to examine their attitudes toward work.

The student who is given the chance to explore occupations and relate his school work to potential careers is more likely to be meaningfully involved in the daily activities of the curriculum. He or she sees purpose in learning and has a more realistic view of the educational process.

The emphasis on career development throughout the school experience is based on the concept that education in public schools should provide every child completing school, or even upon early departure of school, with a serviceable skill. Schools are to aid the student in making the transition from student to productive member of society. Research shows that educators and psychologists have found that a person's vocational choice is not a short-term process but a continuous collection of experiences that influence this choice. Career awareness, therefore, becomes the joint responsibility of the home and school well before these choices need to be made.

Career guidance in the middle school is action-oriented. It provides students with the opportunity to be involved in processes that will expose them to various careers. It helps students learn attitudes of respect and appreciation for all types of work. It explores the relationship between work and leisure time. It helps to broaden career interests and find relevancy between school curriculum and the world outside school. Through these processes all students become more aware of themselves, their own capabilities, and how these relate to various career choices.

If we can agree that children are naturally curious and exploratory, they will be quite capable of learning on their own, given the opportunity. Given frequent chances to be creative, they will progressively develop creativity. Provided the opportunity to learn by doing will reinforce abstract concepts with concrete experience. Keeping these points in mind, we recommend that the middle school guidance program reflect a "hands-on" concept that allows the student to visit, touch, question, and develop various career components in order that he may better understand the varying aspects of a particular career. Career guidance in the middle school does not wish to narrowly prepare a student for one specific lifelong career. Its goal is to give the student a broad general knowledge of opportunities, challenges, and responsibilities by familiarizing him with the many work activities of adult life. The student is then encouraged to develop his own self-perceptions in relation to how he feels about what he sees. How can this be implemented? The following techniques and activities are intended to help the teacher and/or counselor introduce the idea of career development within the school community. Working with the classroom teacher, the counselor can provide a source of motivational techniques that will encourage each student to explore his own interests and talents in relation to future planning and career decision making.

Role-Playing Techniques

Children enjoy creative activities and opportunities to express themselves. As a follow-up activity of a visit to a community business establishment or to a professional office such as that of a dentist or doctor, the students can act out how certain workers perform on the job. By acting out the behavior of workers in specific situations they are exposed to two important aspects of understanding a career: the many responsibilities of a job still unknown by the observer, showing the need for in-depth exploration of the role, and the dependence of one job upon other jobs in order for it to be productive. This role playing may be part of a classroom activity where the children observing the role playing must determine the role being acted. The students involved in the actual activity can project themselves into a wide variety of jobs, thus becoming more intimately involved with that career area. The "actors" soon find that they need much information in order to play a role and are stimulated to explore further into the areas of their interests.

Television Survey

Viewing television for several hours in one day will expose students to a variety of jobs. An interesting assignment is to have students record all the jobs mentioned or taking place within a certain period of time on television. Most will develop an impressive list but usually neglect to include all the workers necessary to get the show itself on the air! A visit to a television studio is often a surprise to most students. The small studios, the numerous technicians (never seen on their TV screens) and the detailed planning (cue cards, props, and so on) give a vivid example of the need for training in many areas by many people in order to produce a show.

Field Experiences

"Seeing is believing," a well-known adage, reflects an important concept of career awareness. The youngster who sees the action of the job is more sensitive to whether or not this job appeals to him. In planning field experiences one should take two important factors into consideration. (1) What jobs will actually be observed? Many industries and businesses provide tours that demonstrate their operation rather than the jobs which the employees perform. Other plant tours take students where they can observe workers but fail to explain the nature of the work itself. (2) Students should be alerted to what should be observed. It is also helpful to orient students to plant rules and regulations prior to taking the trip. These rules may in themselves lead to interesting conversations about jobs in that particular plant. Follow-up is a vital factor. The youngsters should have the opportunity to review what they saw and how it relates to their previous perceptions of the jobs. It is surprising how often this view of an activity may be misinterpreted by the observer. It is necessary for the counselor and teacher involved in this visitation to have previously visited the site and have accurate information to respond to student questions. It is also worthwhile to have a representative from the site come to the classroom at a later date to respond to student concerns in areas where there seems to be significant interest. The school counselor should keep an updated resource file to assist teachers in selection of visitations. Previous staff member visitations should be noted with brief evaluations and suggestions that may be helpful to others in selecting a field experience site for a class trip. This information should include: (1) appropriate age level for visitation, (2) contact person, (3) jobs demonstrated, and (4) recommendations that would be helpful, for example, visiting in the afternoon is better than the morning or students should wear comfortable shoes as the tour is long.

Learning Center Stations

As mentioned throughout this book, we believe there is merit in cooperative planning in a school. Therefore information should be shared at any opportunity. Materials may be collated and stored in a central location for use by others, becoming coordinated through the school learning center as an interest center activity. Each month the counselor and resource room teacher could feature a particular job or job cluster. A job cluster indicates jobs that can be grouped in certain categories, for example, jobs in the health fields, jobs in the service fields, and so on. Students studying the *Dictionary of Occupational Titles* will find a multitude of jobs available in each cluster. Through investigation of their interests they can determine the cluster area most appropriate and then discover the many jobs available in that area. Information provided at learning stations can stimulate class and personal involvement.

Interest Surveys

Interest surveys may be formal or informal. Formal surveys are discussed in Chapter 11. Informal interest surveys help in the search for better understanding of careers. It helps the students learn more about a large number of career opportunities in terms of their interests. A career interest survey may be developed in the following manner. Classes or class groups may be divided into eight interest areas. These include: (1) artistic, (2) business, (3) scientific, (4) health services, (5) technical and mechanical, (6) clerical, (7) outdoor jobs, and (8) personal services. Each group is assigned to investigate jobs that fall in their specific areas. After designating these jobs, the group is to determine at least four questions that would demand a positive response if the person expressed interest in the job. For example: Do you like to work with soil and gardens? If the person responds yes, it indicates he is interested in an outdoor profession. The questions need to cover a wide spectrum of professions. In formulating the questions, students discover much about the jobs of their interest. They also begin to discover the many variations of jobs reflecting the same basic interests. It helps a youngster see that there are many sides to his personality that determine future career choices. As investigations of jobs becomes more detailed, the student discovers the education needed to fulfill the responsibilities of the particular job, the ability levels of performance necessary, and such health factors as endurance, good coordination, and perhaps size. The student soon discovers that interest is only one ingredient in the determination of job success.

Occupation File

As students investigate the jobs of their parents, their local merchants, the professionals who provide services for them, and their individual interests, an occupation file should be developed. Each job description should be listed on a 3 × 5 card with the following information: (1) job title; (2) office, plant, or industry where job may be viewed in action; (3) contact person; (4) brief description of job qualifications with respect to education, physical aspects, age, and experience. Students may then use this file for follow-up of their interests and also to obtain part-time jobs for "trying out" the job of their interest.

"You Are There" Dramas

It is fascinating to discover how jobs came into being. What social pressures stimulated the demand for the job? How have jobs changed

143

over the years? To respond to these questions and provide students with some insight into how needs for jobs are determined "You Are There" dramas can be developed. The idea is to investigate the types of work characteristic of a certain time period in history. The social studies teacher will find this very helpful in developing an interest in history. For example: In our early American history tradesmen were artists in their area of skill. The apprentices who trained with them had to train for many years before they were permitted membership in the trade. Each person was a specialist and his goods usually bore the initials of the creator. Using this information, students act out the experience of shopping in a colonial American shop comparing the differences in products and materials used today. Today's technology has taken much of the personalization out of production, and purchase of an "original" product is extremely expensive. Students could compare the advantages and disadvantages of both types of sales markets. They could investigate the causes of changes in demands for products. They could relate the events of history to the development of certain jobs. For example, the need for more sophisticated defense mechanisms led to a demand for more scientists; the increase in population demanded a quicker means of production; and the decrease in the availability of such raw products as wool, fuels, and lumber necessitated the development of synthetics. Such exploratory study by the students puts life into history and provides a connection between the past and present.

Bulletin Boards

Of course the bulletin board should not be neglected in exploring careers. Each month the counselor may select a topic dealing with careers and have students respond to the areas of interest with papers, samples of materials, and other sources of information. For example, the fifth-grade students could supply material for a bulletin board dealing with information concerning their parents' jobs. The sixth grade could develop a bulletin board display concerned with people in the community whose services they use. This is very effective if pictures of the actual people are provided to make the presentation personal. Many students will be surprised when they interview the local druggist whom they all know so well and find out the many responsibilities he has as proprietor of his store. The seventh-grade students could develop a bulletin board recognizing the jobs that their teachers have had in addition to teaching. This is a popular display which is set up with the teacher's picture in the center and lines drawn from the picture showing all the jobs that have been part of that teacher's life. The number of work situations in which most people have participated is amazing.

Some children find it interesting to note that their teachers have been waiters, gardeners, dishwashers, and so on, before becoming teachers. The eighth-graders could develop a display of the jobs they have held and details on how to apply for a job. Many children find this difficult and need guidelines. Getting pointers from their peers seems to be an effective approach. Once the school designates an area for the Career Bulletin Board, students will look to it for information. There is much free material available that can be placed in the bulletin board area for students to take home and review. Once interest has been stimulated, students and teachers will have ideas to develop through monthly displays.

Much material on the market and free material from manufacturers may be obtained by the counselor for distribution to the teachers. The ideas presented here are only a few of the vast area of exploration on careers. The career development process begins at home, even before the child enters school, as he is exposed to the attitudes and jobs of parents and neighbors. It continues through school to the adult years. Because of the extention of the life span, many people experience success in several careers. It is no longer necessary to be locked into the first job experience of your choice.

Career education and guidance, therefore, is a process and a program which includes awareness, exploration, and preparation experiences. It is recommended that a total career education program begin with the awareness stage in elementary school and continue in the middle school with the exploration component. In high school the student is engaged in a preparation phase.[1]

Each school must determine the needs of its school community. Contemporary education suggests that such exploration be open-ended as the mobility of our society demands this. Students need to be exposed to the satisfying experience of doing a job well and the wide range of work experiences open to them. The importance of learning should be clearly combined with exploration of the world of

---

1. Edward G. Johnson and Charles W. Ryan, *Career Education in Maine* (Augusta, Maine: State Department of Educational and Cultural Services, Bureau of Vocational Education , 1974).

work. An effective career education program will include students, faculty, administrators, parents, and counselors working together to respond to community needs.

Career guidance includes all children. Counselors do not limit themselves to college-bound students or vocational-education students as special categories. When designating careers one means whatever life-style the individual seeks for his future. College is not a career but a means to a career. Vocational training is also a means to a career. The dropout student also needs help in preparing for a work experience. He too needs to develop a serviceable skill. School then accepts the responsibility to provide this serviceable skill appropriate to the needs of the student—every student. Each school needs to determine the best plan for its school that will most adequately use its community resources and most appropriately serve its students' needs.

Supplementary Readings

Anderson, Judith, Lang, Carol, and Scott, Virginia, *Readers Guide: Focus on Self Development, Stage One: Awareness.* Chicago: Science Research Associates, 1970.

Dinkmeyer, Don, and Caldwell, E. *Developmental Counseling and Guidance: A Comprehensive School Approach.* New York: McGraw-Hill, 1970.

Etheridge, Bessie D. *Implementing a K–12 Career Development Program in the District of Columbia*, final report. Sponsored by Bureau of Adult, Vocational, and Teacher Education, Department of Health, Education, and Welfare. Washington, D.C., 1973.

Goldhammer, Keith, and Robert E. Taylor. *Career Education: Perspective and Promise.* Columbus, Ohio: Merrill, 1973.

Hansen, J. S. *Career Guidance Practices in School and Community.* Washington, D.C. National Vocational Guidance Association, 1970.

Hoyt, Ken, et al. *Career Education—What Is It and How to Do It.* Salt Lake City, Utah: Olympus, 1972.

Isaacson, Lee. *Career Information in Counseling and Teaching.* Boston: Allyn and Bacon, 1971.

Booklet

Nissman, Blossom S., and Stamm, Martin L. *Proceedings: Technology for Children Spring Conference of New Jersey—1976.* Trenton, N. J.: State Department of Education, 225 West State Street, c/o Dr. Fred Dreves, Director, 1976 ($2.00). This booklet provides over 50 specific ideas on how to implement "hands-on" activities as part of the regular school curriculum.

CHAPTER ELEVEN

Test and Nontest Procedures for Student Appraisal

The major task facing those who use tests in counseling and guidance is the translation of test results from statistical terms (the language of the professional) into easily understood behavioral terms (the language of the layman). This chapter will emphasize test interpretation as it relates to the middle school child. We feel there are ample sources available in the literature (see Suggested Readings) that provide descriptive analysis of standardized testing instruments as well as the rationale and cautions concerning their use. The counselor needs to be cognizant of statements contained within the codes of ethics of the American Personnel and Guidance Association and the American Psychological Association with respect to utilization of testing instruments and the levels of training necessary for such use.

Effective use of an assessment instrument within the counseling processes requires that it be employed by a person competent not only in the administration but in the interpretation of the results. We feel strongly that proper training and experience with an instrument prior to its utilization is essential for sound guidance practices. The counselor should carefully read the instructional manual and other information available, making sure that the technical aspects of validity and reliability are sound. The instrument needs to be appropriately selected for the population upon which it is to be used. If at any point the examiner is uncomfortable with the results or unsure of the appropriateness of the material, this information should not be used. It is our belief that it's better *not* to test than to test and provide wrong, misleading, or negative information.

Another factor to be considered as the counselor proceeds in the assessment process is that a test is merely one of many behavioral samples of the client. In addition to standardized tools, such supplement information as observational data, cumulative record information, and insights gained through counseling sessions, as well as impressions by others working with the client, must be considered. These tools are utilized in an attempt to generate certain hypotheses which are continually checked against further data. There needs to be a constant process of cross validation in order to insure the accuracy of observations and conclusions. Self-insight as to limitations as counselors and testers, as well as limitations of the instruments, is an important component in such a process. Finally, a counselor should not allow a test to dictate outcomes. A test is a piece of information based upon a minute sample of behavior that at best only provides a direction for further exploration. In making assessments and utilizing testing instruments the counselor is beginning to form hypotheses about probabilities for the future. The instrument itself tells us nothing. The interpretation the counselor provides the client may then be used in the client's decision-making process.

Clearly then, tests do not describe right or wrong choices nor do they imply what students should do as a consequence of their test scores. Tests can only yield probability estimates of future performance. They are silent regarding what the person should do in light of their predictions and it is the counselor's responsibility to help the student make such value choices. Counselors who use tests should be alert to the student's need to identify and confront the choices available. The student must then be encouraged to assume personal responsibility for courses of action and decisions to be made.

It needs to be emphasized, in addition to those points mentioned above, that test results can be psychologically threatening to the client if they are not presented in a manner which tends to minimize this threat. The counselor must realize that at times test results can challenge the person's view of himself, thereby mobilizing psychological defenses that are necessary for the individual to maintain his positive self-image. For example, a student hoping to enter an academically oriented high school program is going to resent and reject test results that indicate his low achievement is indicative of low ability that would predict failure in his college-bound course selection. A contrasting situation might be created by a student confronted with the evidence that his poor school performance is not reflecting low ability but rather a lack of effort.

The middle school student has been identified as typically frustrated about his or her growth and development—physically, emotionally, and intellectually. Concern for adjustment to a more independent learning environment and future career planning may be constructively investigated through assessment tools. To illustrate the use of tests with middle school students, the following descriptive studies are provided:

Examples of use of standardized assessment tools:

Case A

I. Preliminary Statement

David is a thirteen-year-old boy who will be entering the eighth grade in September. He appears to be a normal, healthy youngster, who achieves well in school. David has many friends and enjoys watching sports and particularly playing basketball. His love of basketball has inspired him to think about pursuing a career in this field, if he has the talent. If he cannot be a basketball player, he has indicated a desire to be a microbiologist. David has expressed concern about the overprotectiveness of his parents. He feels the need for independence but cannot successfully express this need to his parents. David's parents do appear to be very cautious with him yet give him just about everything he desires.

II. Summary of Available Data

A. Present Status

1. Age: 13
2. Sex: male
3. Grade: entering eighth grade

B. Physical Status

David appears to be in excellent physical condition. According to his medical records, he has not had any severe illnesses and has had the usual childhood diseases.

C. Educational Status

David maintains an A and B average at school. He excels in the areas of social studies and science and has expressed enjoyment of these two subjects.

D. Personal-Social Traits

David appears to be a well-mannered, likable youngster. He is very friendly and has many friends. He enjoys being with people and entertaining them with jokes. He has participated in summer drama presentations.

E. Home and Family

David is the youngest of two children. He has an older brother, seventeen, who will begin college in the fall. David's father is an operating engineer. His mother does not work outside the home. David's parents provide him with almost anything he wants and are interested and supportive of what he does. They do appear to be somewhat overprotective of him and he senses this and argues about it with them from time to time.

F. Assessment Procedures

David was administered the Lorge-Thorndike, Iowa Test of Basic Skills, Gates Macginitie Reading Test, and the Academic Promise Test (APT) as measurements of achievement and aptitude. He also was administered the Strong-Campbell Interest Inventory to examine his vocational interests.

G. Assessment Interpretation

Scoring 135 (verbal), 151 (nonverbal), and a total of 143 in the Lorge-Thorndike, with a composite score of the 96th percentile in the Iowa Test of Basic Skills, 96th percentile (speed/accuracy), 99th percentile (vocabulary), 96th percentile (comprehension) in the Gates-Macginitie Reading Test, and 99th percentile (abstract reading), 90th percentile (numerical), 97th percentile (verbal), 85th percentile (language usage) in the Academic Promise Test.

The Lorge-Thorndike tests reveal this client to have an above-average I.Q. in verbal and nonverbal areas. The series of Iowa Tests show that Dave ranks consistently in the 96th to 99th percentile. The APT and the Gates show the same kind of consistency which leads one to believe that the validity of these tests is what they say they are. Client's scores are excellent in the area of mathematics as indicated by the Iowa, which corresponds with his school grades noted on his cum folder. Areas of minor weakness are indicated by his performance in spelling, punctuation, and capitalization skills. Strong-Campbell Interest Inventory: David scored highest in the area of math-science, showing a high interest in medical service and social services. Interest also was indicated in the areas of recreation and engineering. Low interest was indicated in the areas of office practices, teaching, and advertising. This seemed to reflect David's interests and future planning and has provided him with some direction for further exploration.

Inquiry:

What data presented here are of special significance to you as a counselor?

What level of counseling training does assistance to this client demand?

What are immediate counseling goals in this case?

What are long-range counseling goals in this case?

What is your evaluation of the tests selected to complete an assessment of this client?

What assessment or appraisal tools or instruments would you have used in assisting this client?

Whom would you involve in working with this client, outside the counseling office?

What information do you find lacking in this case description that you need to do a thorough study of David?

What are the advantages/disadvantages in working with this client, who is recognized as a "normal" student? Do you feel such a student is the concern of the counselor? How do you determine who should receive your services as a counselor?

How would you summarize, to David's parents, the information you have learned about David?

How would you summarize to David what you have learned about him?

What kind of input would you desire from David? from his parents? from his teachers? from his peers?

Case B

I. Preliminary Statement

Darron is an above-average student, who recently consulted the counselor because of concern about his grades. His mother and Darron seemed anxious to have the counselor explore his potential and determine to some degree if the drop in Darron's grades is academically or socially based.

II. Summary of Available Data

    A. Present Status

        1. Age: 10
        2. Sex: Male
        3. Grade: Promoted to 5th grade

    B. Physical Status

        Appears healthy, well-exercised, well-groomed
        1. No physical problem
        2. Good eyesight—examined past month
        3. Complete physical examination within past two months

    C. Educational Status

        1. Received mostly A's and B's
        2. Promotions and no retentions
        3. Relationships with individuals and teachers excellent; positive attitude about school and teachers.

    D. Personal-Social Traits

        Prefers to be alone; however, enjoys the company of other boys his age. Enjoys reading mostly science fiction. Very sensitive to feelings of others. Does not wish to become too involved with personal problems of others.

E. Home and Family

Pleasant, neat-appearing home in middle-class neighborhood.
1. Father: accountant
2. Mother: part-time secretary
3. Siblings: sister aged 3½

Darron's mother is very pleasant, soft-spoken and seems most concerned with her children; that's why she works only part time. The young sister attends private nursery school for three hours a day. Mother feels Darron "is a smart and kind boy whose feelings are easily hurt."

F. Special Interests

Darron is involved in baseball, has been a Boy Scout for two years, is on the safety patrol and a member of the school orchestra and choir. He takes guitar lessons and accepts the responsibility for practice on his own. He cares for his dog and fish and is responsible for the cleanliness of his room. In an interview with the counselor, Darron seemed pleasant and well-mannered. He demonstrated awareness of most current news and the interest he has in outdoor activities. He is an avid reader who enjoys school experiences.

G. Assessment Information

Darron was administered the following tests and his performance is noted.
a. Wepman Auditory Discrimination Test—perfect score
b. Stanford Achievement Test (grade equivalent scores): Word meaning, 5.5; paragraph meaning, 4.5; spelling, 5.9; arithmetic computation, 4.3; arithmetic concepts, 3.7; arithmetic application 4.1.
c. Nelson Reading Test: Vocabulary 41–48; paragraph, 43–44; Summary: Vocabulary 96th percentile band.
d. What I Like to Do Test
   High interest academic life, arts, sciences, performing.
   Occupation profile: active work and desk work highest.

Assessment Summary: Darron scored well on all his tests. His interests are geared to academic life. Reading skills compared to national norm on the Stanford Achievement are good. Reading near national norm. Weaknesses in the areas of paragraph meaning and arithmetic concepts. Darron seems to fall in the average range and tends to set higher expectations for himself with reinforcement from his mother. As illustrated in the Stanford scores, he scored on grade level only in the area of spelling and word meaning—in fact, above grade level in these two areas. His enjoyment in reading is reflected in his excellent performance on the Nelson, which emphasizes vocabulary and comprehension. The interest test gives some insight into his awareness of vocations but in no way provides a firm picture of future vocational choice or limitations. The general agreement among the test results seem to indicate that Darron's grades do reflect his potential. It is cautioned that expectations for Darron should be more realistic and he should be encouraged to look at his achievement in a positive way, taking each step of progress as a move forward toward sound growth and development both socially and intellectually. Clarification of meaning of test scores is a sensitive task for the counselor that needs to be provided in language clearly understood, with emphasis on the positive aspects of Darron's performance on these limited assessment tools.

Inquiry:

Do you feel the assessment instruments selected by the counselor were appropriate in responding to the client's and the client's parents' concern?

What was the complete role of the counselor in regard to the assessment interpretation?

What are the cautions the counselor must consider in interpreting these test results to the parent? the client? the teacher?

What do you see as the real problem that may influence Darron's academic and emotional growth? Is it clearly identified in this description?

What services could the counselor perform that would generally assist parents with similar concerns?

What further information would you, as counselor need to provide a complete response to the parent's concerns?

Whose services would you possibly seek to assist you with this client?

What is there about Darron that is typical of a 10 year old?

Case C

I. Preliminary Statement

Connie is an eighth-grade student who sought out the attention of the counselor. On several occasions she was directed to come to see the counselor by several teachers for acting out in class. She seemed to enjoy talking about her concerns to the counselor at times and yet at other occasions she was very reluctant to discuss anything—just wanting to sit quietly in the counselor's office as she "got her head together," as she put it.

II. Summary of Available Data

   A. Present Status

      1. Age: 14
      2. Sex: female
      3. Grade: eighth grade

   B. Physical Status

      Connie is physically a large girl for her age and developed more than many of her peers. She seems to be torn about many things in her life—especially her growing sexuality as a female. She is quite preoccupied with an interest in sex and doing things that she feels are opposed by an adult. She says she likes to do things for the fun of it. She is especially anxious and concerned about not being "different." She becomes upset and angry when she feels she has done something that does not meet with approval of people she likes. She also has trouble in expressing her affection to people who are important to her, therefore seeks their attention through negative behavior or verbal responses.

C. Home and Family

The problems described by the counselor seem to have some relation to the home situation. The counselor notes that early in her relationship with Connie, she felt, and Connie confirmed to some degree, that she does not get a lot of personal attention from the mother and father unless she has gotten into trouble in school or done something in the home that the parents disagree with. Connie felt that this may be because the mother in the home is not her real mother. Her mother died during her early childhood.

D. Educational Status

Connie's past educational achievements rank from average to below average. Her records indicate that her achievement was stable until she reached the middle school. Before that she had little indication by her teachers that she was having any special problems in doing her work. Some did comment that she was probably not working to her fullest potential. Since she has been in the middle school, however, her record indicates a number of conflicts and behavior problems. As a result, her subject-matter grades dropped in areas where she had little interest or little compatibility with the teacher. A number of comments were made in reference to her behavior in class and her relations with others. According to Connie and one of her past teachers, there have been a long series of encounters with the principal on discipline matters. Her present class grades vary a great deal: typing, A; science, D; math, F; English, C; physical education, A, ranking her below average on major academic subjects while ranking high on nonacademic subjects. Scores reported on standardized tests rank Connie as average; intelligence quotient also was listed as average.

E. Personal-Social Traits

Connie is very moody. Her moods change within minutes and may be set off by almost anything that she feels is not in accordance with what she wants. Her moods may cause her to pout and refuse to talk or interact with others. At other times she is resistant and uncooperative. Connie talked to the counselor a great deal about "getting even" or revenge on people she feels have wronged her, denied her her wishes, or have done something that hurts her feelings. She carries this attitude with her peers as well as with adults. The counselor observed that Connie has developed a number of defenses or ways to defy requests made of her. She often defends her position or ideas by proclaiming that "everybody else is doing it" or denying matters altogether. In defying adults she often makes angry facial expressions, mumbles things that are inaudible, refuses to obey requests, or accuses the adult of not having explained clearly what is expected of her. Her parents complain of this defiance also.

Connie has engaged in a number of unacceptable activities in school. These include drinking in school to the point of intoxication, smoking pot, and cutting classes to be with friends during their lunch periods. She also speaks of indulging in sexual activities because her friends do so. In her social interactions, Connie often displaces the blame for her failures, punishments, and responsibility of getting into trouble. She fails to see the part she plays or refuses to accept the responsibility for her actions. It is interesting to note that she enjoys writing and art and often writes about herself in fictional stories.

Social interaction with her teachers is distant and strained. She prefers to keep her relationships with her teachers at a distance even if she likes the teacher. She avoids being touched or any closeness whether it be where she sits or the extent of her conversation. She choses to keep a physical distance between anyone, including her parents, talking to her.

General Information from Counselor's Report: Connie is one of six children in the family. Two siblings younger than she and three older. The family is a part of the military and could be classified as lower middle class. The father will soon retire from the military with maximum rank for enlisted men. The mother works on the Army post also. The home is well kept; the family members dress appropriately, except for Connie. The parents admit to having a number of problems with Connie, but say that she is quite capable and has not been reared to be as belligerent as she now behaves. The mother seems to be the dominant figure in the home. Connie seems to fear her mother and favor her father.

F. Assessment Information

Connie was given the following tests: Super's Work Value Inventory, Strong Vocational Interest Blank, Differential Aptitude Test, and School College Ability Test.

Results were as follows:

Super's Work Value Inventory: Connie's highest scores were on the creativity, security, and prestige scales, with scores of 15 each. These scales indicate the following:

Creativity: associated with work which permits one to invent new things, design new products, or develop new ideas; consistent with liking art, drawing, and writing.

Prestige: associated with work that gives one standing in the eyes of others and evokes respect. Seeks others' respect rather than power status; consistent with her desire to have acceptance from peers.

Security: associated with work which provides one with the certainty of having a job. It also reflects a degree of interest in getting the rewards of work. Most often expected of high school students. The three lowest scores on the inventory were: management (11), associates (10), independence (11). These scales indicate that she does not have a strong interest in these areas.

Management: associated with work which permits one to plan and lay out work for others, characterizing business students; not consistent with high typing grades.

Associates: a value characterized by work which brings one in contact with fellow workers whom one likes; not consistent with her desire to be with friends.

Independence: associated with work that permits one to work in his own way, as fast or as slowly as he wishes. Connie seems to express a need to know what is expected of her.

On the Strong Vocational Interest Blank Connie's highest scores were in relation to occupational therapist and X-ray technician. Basic interest was reflected in military activities, medical service, office practices, and merchandising.

On the Differential Aptitude Test, Connie scored in the 5th percentile in numerical ability, 20th percentile in verbal reasoning, with a total composite percentile score of 24. This supports her grades in math and English as demonstrated in her middle school records.

In the School and College Ability Test, Connie again fell into the 6th percentile in verbal and 15th percentile in math, with a total composite percentile score of 10.

As a result of the test information, the counselor planned to continue to keep in contact with Connie in an attempt to help her feel better about herself and have a more realistic understanding of her strengths and weaknesses. The counselor hoped to help her work through her inability to accept responsibility and improve her school behavior by helping her clarify the values she had adopted in an effort to be accepted by her peers. The counselor will arrange to meet with Connie's teachers in an attempt to clarify her level of comprehension in order to provide more successful learning experiences.

Inquiry:

What information has been provided here that helps you most to understand Connie?

What other information would you seek?

What other areas of assessment would you explore? or is this adequate?

What do you see as the problem most urgent in regard to meeting Connie's immediate needs? How would you work with Connie if you were her counselor?

Taking into consideration the normal growth and development patterns of a middle school child, what do you see as typical behavior in relation to Connie's actions?

What do you see as a long range-plan for the counselor? teacher? How valid do you feel the evaluation of the test results are? If you were to write a brief descriptive paragraph about Connie, what would you emphasize, using the test results as guidelines?

These three cases illustrate how middle school counselors used standardized testing instruments to assess students. No person can be completely evaluated through standardized tools alone. There are many other aspects of the whole person that will help the counselor understand the child. The classroom teacher often finds children in his group who are difficult to measure or even to teach because they need detailed direction with respect to self-management before they can begin to perform academically.

The counselor knowledgeable in human behavior can develop, with the classroom teacher, management skills that would provide a classroom climate conducive to learning. Often students score poorly in tests or other assessment measures primarily because of their inability to follow directions and maintain a productive degree of attention to the lesson. By elimination of these distractive behaviors through specific management techniques tailored to the child's needs, the child may be more responsive to a learning experience. A child cannot be evaluated if he does not perform the task. If a child does not try it should not be assumed he cannot learn. Every effort must be made to encourage and motivate the child to participate actively in the learning process.

Teachers concerned with management techniques will welcome such counselors' suggestions on classroom management as the following:

In the middle school program of a Hightstown, N.J., school, teacher Mrs. Esther Stroebel has had a great deal of success with the following procedures for better classroom management.

Procedure 1—verbal contracting: individual reward system. Typical of the middle school child is the need for acceptance in peer relationships, in the search for which competition becomes significant. The following management technique helps to provide students with individualized instruction while they are still a part of a group. This plan may be used for one child, a small group, or an entire class. Each child has a schedule. He must complete all the work assigned, individually or in a group, and exhibit acceptable behavior in order to receive a check for the day. The work is assigned by the teacher; the behavior guidelines are those formulated by the class. At the day's end, individual evaluations take place and a check is placed on the child's personal chart. A note telling parents that he earned the check is sent home. At the end of the week, five checks earn him a decorated statement of the fact. This is a continuous report of accomplishment which may be shared with parents and friends.

Each morning starts a new day. Reward folders are empty. After each lesson, class, small group, or individual lesson, paper cutout rewards are given to the students who have attempted or completed their work and who have exhibited acceptable behavior according to the class rules. The reward is given or not given with a brief comment and sincere concern. This routine continues throughout the day for all subjects and activities. At the end of the day, rewards are collected and evaluation takes place individually. Each child knows why he did or did not get a check. The children find it very serious to discuss their progress and ways of improving their work. All evaluations are constructive and noncompetitive. The written statements read: "Dear Parents, I earned a check today." Parents are informed of the plan and many have places where they display the notes. Each Friday, the specially decorated reward is given each child who gets a check for each day of the week. The personal charts recording the checks are a continuous record and are available to the child for observation at all times. If a child does not get at least three checks a week, he and the teacher have a conference. This teacher's experience has shown that the children look forward to and request the conferences. They need to talk over ways to obtain their checks. Toward the middle of the year, the rewards and conferences become unnecessary. Everyone does his own thing habitually. Each one has learned how to do what is expected of him in order to earn a check. This method is especially effective with fifth- and some sixth-graders.

The secret ingredient of this method is that the teacher guides and modifies all academic and social behavior in a friendly, palatable, and constructive way. As the behavior becomes secure, the teacher gradually raises the requirements for a check for the individual child. Parent involvement usually comes about naturally. Children show parents their daily checks or parents ask to see them. Some parents treat the child to a popular event or buy a desired gift when several perfect weeks are attained by the child. There are parents who have no contact with the school and never see the checks. In such an instance, the teacher and the child are involved alone.

This type of loose verbal contracting alleviates the threat of a competitive schedule required by the teacher. Each child progresses at his own rate of speed and according to his ability without any severe pressures. All that is required is to attempt to do the assigned tasks and to fit into a productive classroom atmosphere. For most children the schedule is comfortable, and they thrive on it. Happily, the system also seems to help children with personal problems. They find that they are able to join the class in many ways and are rewarded for any small and realistic production. School guidance counselors find that such children's self-image improve dramatically as they boast of their reading or math rewards and general progress. This method is a good basis for many kinds of classroom instruction. It lends itself to individualized instruction, interdisciplinary instruction, and programmed reading and math.

Procedure 2—time-work units. This plan is for the student who is unable to be a part of the class because of hyperactivity or disruptive behavior in a group. The goal of this plan is to teach the child how to accept the responsibility of completing a task independently. The learning situation could be an individualized class reading time. The plan is implemented as follows: (1) Isolate the child and give him his own corner. (2) Give the student an academic task at his instructional level and do it with him. Begin with a short unit of time (about five minutes). When the lesson is completed, allow the child to have a free choice of activity at the same location. Stay with him for a few minutes and then leave. His job is to try to stay in the assigned area and not go anywhere else. When he does this, mark his work on a chart made especially for him. The chart should be prominently displayed. National Wildlife stamps are often used. The child watches his progress and shares his success with others. This is his first positive step to belonging.

(3) This process continues until the child accomplishes the time-work unit alone. The task assigned is gradually increased. At this time, the student times himself at the task and also accepts the responsibility to choose his free time in his area. He is still isolated. (4) When the student accomplishes a fifteen- to twenty-minute task and has controlled his behavior during free time, he may share his free time with another child. When this is successful, he may join a small group lesson. Each time he fails in any situation, he returns to the preceding activity module. At this point, the student is in control of the regimen and usually needs little support from the teacher. The student measures his success in the number of times he accomplishes the teacher-prescribed tasks and is able to function socially in a group. (5) This process continues until he is integrated into the class. In every step in the process, the child knows that he belongs to the class and that he will always have the teacher's support. The teacher

is involved in all the steps as a resource person. In addition to having the teacher's support, the student learns, as he gets closer to his peers, what is expected of him as a member of the class. At this time, he is secure enough to be able to follow and understand his work and play schedules as well as the other children's schedules. He is capable of functioning within the entire class program. (6) There is never any punishment and there is always the chance to start over from a proved emotionally comfortable and successful situation. The initial time the teacher spends is well worth it because the time is less than that spent with a miserable, disruptive, and lonely student.

Procedure 3—parents' workshops. A very small percentage of parents are disinterested in their children's problems; the large majority want to help. Usually they do not know how to help. Parents of children with learning problems want to help "cure" their child. They are eager to help but their experiences with their children have been frustrating for all concerned. In an attempt to eradicate this rift in the all-important relationship of the parent to child, the teacher began a series of parent workshop meetings that took place afternoons or evenings every other month. Parents who wish to be included in the program contact the teacher and a program ditto is circulated to parents through their children or the mail. They are requested to respond.

One such workshop on homework included role playing by the teacher and her aide, who emulated the behavior of both parents and children to demonstrate ways of initiating more productive relationships. The role playing depicted such typical communication problems as listening to parents and accepting responsibility for the task to be completed. Specific suggestions for helping students with their homework were also given. A suggestion to a parent who was having a severe communication problem with her child was not to do homework with him at this time. However, most parents were able to improve their teaching skills and enjoy a measure of success. Usually the homework workshop held early in the school year is most helpful. It is a popular request. Most parents believe that they help their children best by supervising homework.

Another popular and necessary workshop is one on involvement. It emphasizes the need for parents with learning disabled children to involve themselves in and enjoy the child's world. Change of attitude in a parent (who is usually trying to teach the child proper social behavior) is the best insurance for improving the child's self-concept. A new and different relationship with a parent is an ego-builder. In this workshop, involvement exercises are used, guidelines are formulated, and parents apply the principles to their particular parent–child relationships.

Such workshops are good for sharing knowledge. A parent or a teacher prepares a discussion on such topics as nutrition, hyperactivity, development of speech, theories of learning, and so forth. The staff also has workshops on how certain subjects are taught, the speech therapist's role, the school psychologist's response to questions, and job descriptions of other school personnel invited to join in the parent group discussions. Parents are invited to wander in and out of the classroom during the school day in order to see the class activity and their children in action. Workshop topics help to clarify any questions parents may have as the result of these observations.

The afternoon workshops are held in a classroom from three to five o'clock. Refreshments are served and there is opportunity for exchange of ideas. Child study team members, principals, supplementary teachers, and other grade teachers all receive announcements and many attend workshops on topics that interest them.

The evening workshops are held in a parent's home and are usually lengthy. These meetings are dominated by parents who discuss common problems and gather strength in seeking solutions in a group. At these meetings there is a concerted effort to understand the nature of problems, try to find solutions, and to realize that some problems will take longer to resolve than others.

Procedure 4—student (peer) interaction. The main objective of this procedure is to make the learning of basic arithmetic facts (flash cards) more interesting. This procedure also involves students in the academic and social structure of the school. Traditionally, special education students have been removed from the mainstream of school society. The main objective was accomplished and the additional benefits were very exciting and beyond the teacher's greatest expectations. She attempted this teaching method with much trepidation, never having really seen or heard about its working for an academic subject with students who had learning disabilities.

The procedure was implemented as follows: Each student in an individualized math program is given basic facts in addition, subtraction, division, and multiplication for study. These facts are put on personal flash cards. There may be one or twenty cards, depending on the students' progress. The student studies these cards in the manner used in the classroom. Some students are in special classes; others are in regular class situations.

Two kinds of colorful and imaginative tags are made—the teacher's tag of a bespectacled college cap and gown face and a student tag of a student's face with lightning flashes eminating from the brain. At a designated time, students from different grade levels and ages meet and pair off as teacher and student. Each student carries his flash cards with him. One student is the teacher; the other the student. They wear their tags. The "teacher" takes the students' cards and flashes them. The cards that receive the correct response are placed in a pile before the student. The missed cards are reshuffled and flashed again. Each time a card is missed the "teacher" turns it around to show the answer. Finally, when all the cards are piled in front of the student, the students exchange roles.

The students also take a card showing progress and fill it in. The students return their cards to a personal (shoe rack) pocket. Students study the cards at home and in school. At another time, students may take a test. The known facts are refiled and new facts are added to their pockets for study. The number of cards given to a student to study is determined by the teacher. The visiting teachers handle the basic cards of their students in their way. The only uniform teaching procedure is that children pair off with their personal cards or any cards given by their classroom teacher.

Preparation for student interaction is a few minutes of study with the cards and then a fast test with a teacher's aide. The correct answers are rewarded by allowing a child to shoot a toy racing car toward a target. The game is varied during the year. As a teacher's aide is occupied with this, the teacher gives the requested tests at the beginning of the period before any practice. In short, the students must know the basic facts "cold."

The only requirement for all children who participate in this program is to know at least the numbers 1 to 10. They may not be familiar with division but are able to determine the correct answer on the back of the flash cards and are able to function as "teacher." Needless to say, children of limited ability get quite an ego lift when working with other children who are obviously ahead of them in math skills.

The results were as follows: (1) Students learned their basic facts without embarrassment. (2) The students were inspired to study at home and in school in preparation for the interaction encounters. (3) Students enjoyed traveling to other classrooms and inviting other students to their room. (4) Students gained friends. (5) Students learned to study from one another. (6) Students with difficult behavior problems assumed the responsibility of adjusting their behavior because any student causing friction could not participate. The alternative was to role play with a *real* teacher. So the result was that students made an effort to conform and participate with the student group.

Procedure 5. The most important aspect of living in society is communication, a point which is clearly taken in discussions throughout this book. The greatest handicap of all the categories is that of speech and hearing. Children who are legally deaf are contained in special schools. However, children with speech problems are present in the public school systems. Therefore, Mrs. Stroebel devised the following teaching procedure for these children because speech once a week with the speech therapist, available in most schools, is not adequate remediation.

The classroom teacher needs to work cooperatively with the speech therapist. When the therapist lists objectives for future lessons and includes suggestions and choices of materials, it is vital that the teacher follow through on these developmental skills. The teacher can do this by making short (ten- to twenty-minute) lesson plans. A student from an upper grade may be assigned to work with the speech-handicapped child. The student is usually excused from seat work during reading or math time. The student is taught how to give the lesson. Often students prefer assisting in this tutoring situation to attending study hall. The interchange between student and tutor usually is in the form of a language development game: "John, see if you can get ten out of ten" (ten words with beginning consonants or digraphs the child needs to develop); "John, look around the room and tell me what begins with the sound of the first word listed." Some lessons involve repetition of certain sounds and practice in self-evaluation. The child says the word; the teacher-student evaluates its production. Then the child is taped and hears how well he has managed the sound in question. He then develops the technique of evaluating his own delivery and the student-teacher tells him how well he has done the job. This procedure goes on throughout the year. In this way, the students get speech every day and are under the supervision of the speech therapist. (The "tutor" may also be a student with a speech problem who needs remediation and, through working with a younger student, will be actually helping himself by improving his listening skills!).

Results indicated that: (1) the students had fun and enjoyed the program; (2) the teacher-students enjoyed the experience and were very conscientious and concerned about their assignments; (3) the classroom teacher noted the accelerated language development and reading progress. The teacher, since she was part of the speech program, was able to interrelate the contents of the speech lessons with other class subjects: Find all the shells that are identified by the beginning letter *S* or list all the foods the Pilgrims ate that begin with *br*; the speech therapist especially applauded the results gained from the self-evaluating techniques learned by the students.

These brief descriptions, provided by a master teacher, illustrate techniques for responding to particular child needs through "nontest procedures." The counselor needs not only to alert the teacher to learning deficiencies, but provide specific techniques and professional tools for responding to these needs. This can be achieved by being sensitive to staff expertise and encouraging the sharing of ideas among staff members. The counselor who is willing to become involved in classroom activities will be providing the meaningful service that most teachers and parents seek.

Supplementary Readings

Anastasi, Ann. *Psychological Testing*, 4th ed. New York: MacMillan, 1976.

Chauncey, Henry, and Dobbin, John E. *Testing: Its Place in Education Today.* New York: Harper and Row, 1964.

Goldman, Leo. *Using Tests in Counseling.* New York: Appleton-Century-Crofts, 1971.

Green, John. *Introduction to Measurement and Evaluation.* New York: Dodd, Mead, 1970.

Kiley, M. A. *Personal and Interpersonal Appraisal Techniques for Counselors, Teachers, and Students.* Springfield, Ill.: Thomas, 1975.

Meyering, Ralph. *Uses of Test Data in Counseling* (guidance monograph). Boston: Houghton Mifflin, 1968.

Nunnally, J. *Introduction to Psychological Measurement.* New York: McGraw-Hill, 1970.

Pepin, Arthur C. "The I.Q. Test: Education's Bugaboo," *Clearing House* 45 (5): 278–80, 1971.

Stamm, Martin L., and Nissman, Blossom S. *What You Always Wanted to Know About Tests . . . But Were Afraid to Ask.* Box 106, Rancocas, N.J. 08073; Guidance Awareness Publications, 1973; reprint, 1977.

Stamm, Martin L., and Nissman, Blossom S. *The Implications and Application of Assessment Instruments for Counselors in Training.* Box 106, Rancocas, N.J., 08073; Guidance Awareness Publications, 1976.

Tyler, Leona E. *Individual Differences: Abilities and Motivational Directions.* New York: Appleton-Century-Crofts, 1974.

Warters, Jane. *Techniques of Counseling.* New York: McGraw-Hill, 1964.

CHAPTER TWELVE

Approaches to Understanding and Communicating With Middle School Students

Recently, in a conversation we had with an innovative and creative counselor, Richard Strausser of Folwell School in Mt. Holly, New Jersey, he defined his role in working with students as follows: "As a counselor working with fifth-graders, I find I must first understand the developmental aspects of this stage of growth. Secondly, I must realize that each child's world has been shaped by his home and community environment even before he has been exposed to school. As he progresses through the school community, he adjusts his pattern of behavior to meet his needs as he sees them. It is important to note that the child often perceives himself differently than the adult or even as his peers perceive him."

Working with Fifth-grade Children

On any particular day and at any time the fifth-grade child may confront the counselor with a variety of emotional characteristics. These emotional displays may range from the confident, self-assured posture to the shy, introverted behavior pattern. The counselor may be given responsibility for calming the belligerent and agressive child or stimulating the passive, nonagressive underachiever. The counselor learns quickly that outward verbalizations and actions often mask the child's true inward concerns, frustrations, and conflicts. The very characteristic of self-uncertainty identifiable with the middle school child presents a roadblock to the counselor in communication. The ability to identify the student's actual concern is vital in meeting each child's unique needs. What then are the common characteristics this counselor finds in working with the fifth-grade student?

Every child needs to be loved and liked. Sometimes you may perceive that a child does not want love or wants to appear independent of someone caring. There is the strong possibility that this attitude was developed as a defense mechanism against people who misuse him. He frequently learns to mistrust the motives of people who show affection if his open affection has previously been rejected or criticized negatively.

Every child wants to be kind and good. Basically children learn that goodness and kindness multiply this reaction in others. However, again they sometimes learn that others take advantage of them if they initiate the action. Therefore, to prevent being hurt and disappointed, they may perform unkind acts to others.

Every child wants to be considered normal and assure himself and others that there is nothing wrong with him. This is especially significant to the middle school child who is confused about body changes and growth in general at this age. If experiences with authority figures have, over a period of time, and in many subtle and overt ways, indicated that the child is not normal, he will assume this posture. He has often been told he is slower than his sister or lacks the talent in sports his father expected him to have or is clumsy or lazy. In addition, his feelings are reinforced when adults do not let him think for himself or make his own decisions. Adult actions frequently imply that a child is not to be trusted with his own decisions. By emphasizing negative aspects of behavior, the behavior is reinforced. After a time the child comes to believe that he is not up to par and thereafter succumbs to below-average performance. Often he may entertain deep resentment of others who so classify him.

Most children attempt to do things to the best of their ability. In accepting this premise, the counselor provides positive reinforcement in helping the child become all that he is capable of becoming.

All children want to be accepted by their peers. They want desperately to be selected as group members and considered an asset to that group. Children who are rejected by their peers often seek other methods for attention—for example, acting out and bizarre behavior.

It is not suggested by this counselor that these five points are new or unique but rather that they are basic in understanding and communicating with children of all ages, but most specifically the middle school child.

The counselor must accept the role of helping the child cope with his present environment, assisting the child whose equilibrium is upset, working with the child whose personality characteristics are not acceptable to his classmates or the adults of his life by allowing each child the opportunity to communicate his concerns. The most difficult role of the middle school counselor is providing a comfortable, nonthreatening environment for children to seek out as a means of airing these concerns. The counselor who seeks to bring some stability to such children's lives needs tools to bridge this gap and enhance the understanding of each client.

Working with the fifth-grader, Mr. Strausser has found the individual conference, group conferences, discussions with mothers, special-purpose groups, and puppetry effective communication tools. These programs are explained in detail so that counselors may use the ideas, adjust them to meet their needs, and share with Mr. Strausser the good feeling of success in opening doors of understanding and windows of the world to the fifth-grade middle school child.

The individual conference

In this situation the child is one-to-one with the guidance counselor. In as nonthreatening a manner as possible, the counselor seeks to find out many things about the child. How does he feel about his school, his teacher, his classmates, his home, and school activities? What makes him saddest at home and school? Whom does he like the best and what is there about the person that makes him feel good? Whom does he like the least and what is there about the person that makes him unhappy? These questions merely show the direction of the inquiry. Not all questions need to be answered. The fifth-grader is just one step from elementary school and transition to the middle school has to be gentle and secure. A sensitive counselor will extend the direction of any question wherever the answer indicates in order to bring the problem into proper perspective. During the probing the counselor is attempting to understand the child and the forces that precipitate undesirable conduct or the problem with which the child seems to express concern.

There are several advantages to the individual conference with a child of this age. The individual conference enables the counselor to reach a deeper understanding of the child in a minimal amount of time. It enables the counselor and client to develop a singular attack in solving a particular problem. It provides individual attention which might be one of the child's needs.

There are several disadvantages to the individual counseling method. The counselor does not see the child functioning in a normal setting and may be misled into misguided interpretations of his actions and responses. However, this may be compensated for by observing the child in various school situations as well as when he is alone. A counselor is limited in the number of contacts he can make in a day. Since the counselor normally has schoolwide responsibilities, he must be highly selective with respect to the number of one-to-one counseling sessions he may have.

Group Counseling

An effective method for meeting the needs of many children is to have group counseling conferences—a group of children meeting with the counselor for the general purpose of learning to live productive and happier lives. Such an objective may cover a wide gamut of directions or activities. Meeting with the counselor in a nonjudgmental and nonappraising situation grants a freedom of development that is readily accepted and quite productive. Group conferences or meetings may have specific purposes, as will be noted later; however, for a point of departure and discussion, this counselor describes the Discoverers, the name assigned to several groups meeting in his school.

The Discoverers

The Discoverers are groups of fifth-grade boys and girls who meet once a week. Members are nominated by their classroom teacher, who considers whether or not the children wish to attend. Groups are separated by sex. Membership is open to all; it is not restricted to the problem child. Group size is limited by the size of the room. The preferred seating arrangement is in a circle and around a table.

The general purpose of this group is to learn how to live happier lives and how to cope with adverse situations. It helps the counselor to appreciate the fact that children want to be happy and that many forces operate to create conditions to make them unhappy and distrustful. General guidelines for the members are found in <u>Steps for Winners</u>, which they attempt to incorporate into their lives to guide their conduct.

STEPS FOR WINNERS

1. We decided to be happy today and planned to be happy tomorrow. We love in the present and for the future. We found that most unhappiness stems from too much thinking about the mistakes and failures of the past.

2. We avoided being angry at others. We found that keeping a grudge against someone or something makes you unhappy. A grudge is poison to your happiness and control.

3. We resisted the desire to feel or say that one has the right to be upset at someone or something.

4. We didn't waste time and energy fighting things we could not change. There is little you can do about the house you live in, your brothers and sisters, your family, your school, your teachers, your classmates. Don't let them make you unhappy.

5. We were friendly to other people instead of retreating within ourselves and building a prison of loneliness when we found ourselves wanting to be unhappy, sad, or mad.

Although the steps imply that an action is completed or is part of the life of the person making the statement, it is seen as a goal to be achieved. A person could live a lifetime and never be successful in following the steps totally and completely. Assuming that a member does these things seems to be more positive and uplifting than having a goal by which one can be measured. It is true that one could make a judgment and state that a Discoverer is not living up to the steps. However, such a judgment cannot be made by another Discoverer, for a Discoverer attempts to build another up rather than belittle one!

An important feature of a Discoverer meeting is that the children act as chairpersons. The following outline guides them:

AGENDA FOR MEETING

1. Call to order (tap gavel 3 times): This is the _____ Group of Discoverers. We will now read our Welcome.

2. Members read the Welcome

3. Chairperson starts reading of Statement of Pride and Humility. Each member makes own statement.
4. Reading of Steps for Winners.
5. Chairperson asks for anyone with a story or experience to share with the group. (The stories should relate to a situation where a member used one of the steps to make his life better.)
6. Comments from guidance counselor.
7. Reading of instruction item or discussion as selected by chairperson.
8. Reading of Closing.
9. Chairperson closes meeting: "The ____ Group of Discoverers meeting is now closed. Live a happy life until we meet again."
10. Chairperson selects someone to be chairperson for the next meeting and advises the counselor of the selection.

To further clarify this agenda the following information is provided. After the Call to Order the chairperson requests one of the members to read the Welcome statement, which is typed on a card passed around, and each member reads a sentence or two. The third item on the agenda calls for each member to make his Statement of Pride and Humility. This, too, is on a card which is passed around the room. The chairperson begins.

WELCOME

We welcome you to the ____ Group of Discoverers.

We are glad you came today and hope that here you will find happiness and friendship.

A Discoverer understands what it is like to be lonely, frustrated, hassled, sad, mad, angry, and jealous. We have had these feelings and still have them. We try to learn how not to let them get us down. We are learning how to be happy in everything we do.

The Discoverer program is based upon the Steps for Winners as applied to our lives. By sharing what we read and telling each other our experiences of successes and failures we move closer to our goals a little bit at a time.

Remember: Everything that is said here in this meeting must be held in confidence and treated as secret. This enables all to share, trust, and care for one another.

STATEMENT OF PRIDE AND HUMILITY

1. I am _____ (state name).
2. I am a Discoverer,

3. (Choose from one of the following)

_____ and I have problems.

_____ because I have problems.

_____ because I have hang-ups.

_____ because I want to understand.

_____ because I want to understand my problems.

_____ because I want to know about me and others.

_____ because I want to learn what makes me and others do what we do.

_____ because I want to learn how to control my thoughts and actions.

CLOSING

Thanks for being here, for listening, for being tolerant and forgiving of our failures, and for helping us all to grow in peace, love, and happiness.

Remember: What was said here should be treated as a secret. Use what you need to guide you in the things you do and say. We hope that through sharing and using the Steps for Winners you will have more fun and feel better about yourself and others.

Come to the aid of another Discoverer who is temporarily failing in his efforts. Help the Discoverer who is down. Help bring happiness with a smile and an act that shows you care.

Use of a card has the effect of controlling and designates the person who has the floor for the moment and aids in the orderly progress of the activity. In this statement the person makes three points. The first two declarations encourage pride in himself and his group. He states his name and announces that he is a Discoverer. He then chooses from one of the suggested reasons for being at the meeting and announces it to the group. This declaration of a fault shows some humility.

In the development of the statement there was a lesson in giving freedom to children. During the early days of the program, when the statement was found necessary, the fact of the three separate parts was rather clear. However, the particular wording of the humility part offered decision problems. The form of the statement as it now exists was originally designed as a form on which children could vote and designate their preferences. However, observation over a period of time showed that the children liked all the choices. It became clear that restriction of choice would be an unnecessary limitation and an encroachment on a child's need for an opportunity to make his own decision.

The fourth agenda item calls for the reading of the Steps for Winners. Like the opening routine items, these are on a card which is passed around; each member reads one step. Usually only the first sentence, which is the key idea, is read. The weekly repetition and reflection on the steps is important for the child's understanding of the program.

The fifth item on the agenda gives the members the opportunity to share their successes and failures since the previous meeting. The reading of the Steps immediately before this assists the members in recalling incidents. A member has the option of talking about or explaining a step. Extra copies of the Steps are on the table.

To reduce the amount of anxiety and excitement among children when several want to talk at the same time and are wildly waving their arms, the chairperson has the option of two techniques. He may start with a certain child in the circle and follow around the circle in order. He is subject to showing favoritism only on his first selection of a person to talk. As a result it is rare for a child to criticize the chairperson for not being called upon when this technique is used. A child who does not want to talk when his turn comes says "pass." This simple procedure is important; each child knows he had the opportunity to express himself; he knows he was not shunned. A second technique of controlling the excitement level discourages the waving of hands to indicate a desire to talk. Instead, the floor seeker simply extends a thumb upward from a clasped-hands position. It does not take long for the children to use and appreciate this method of gaining attention. Secondary values are that the chairperson must be alert to the small quiet actions of the members and much greater eye contact between the chairperson and members seems to take place.

Comments from the counselor follow the members' talks. At this time the counselor may interject specific items or activities he deems constructive for the particular group meeting. The agenda, guided by the chairperson, is selected before the meeting in consultation with the counselor. Various books, listed in the Supplementary Readings, provide ample material from which appropriate material can be selected. Pictures and printed cards relating to values or feelings are available from publishing companies.

The eighth agenda item calls for a reading of the Closing by the members, using the same method as in the opening activities. After this the chairperson raps his gavel and closes the meeting. The last agenda item calls for the selection of the chairperson for the next meeting. In this selection he may not pick one from the same classroom if more than one classroom is represented nor may he select one to serve a second time before all others have served. These conditions assure fairness, which children appreciate. The procedure also protects the counselor from unconsciously showing favoritism or being accused of it. The counselor does maintain a log to assure that the two selection conditions are followed.

Throughout the meeting the counselor makes a strong attempt to be nondirective or nonauthoritarian. In the early part of the year the students find this difficult to accept. Amazingly, groups comprised of disruptive children are more desirous of having the counselor assume a domineering and prescribing authority role. However, in good time the students will exhibit responsible leadership conduct. The physical position of the counselor should be in the circle with the other members. A counselor sitting outside the group seems to set the stage for negative feelings, creating obstacles to having a productive and happy meeting. A successful meeting occurs when the children leave with inner pride and the thought that they have done something worthwhile.

Special Purpose Groups

Approximately one out of eight children in a school may come from a home affected by a drug or alcohol problem. These children generally have unique problems of adjusting to troublesome situations. Frequently, the troubled parent is very demanding, harsh, self-centered, and sometimes abusive when he or she is in the throes of his or her problem—alcoholism. The person is controlled by the drug—the drug demands; the person responds. The child has no choice but to live within this environment. The very harshness of this truth is the basis for one's learning to accept the situation and to have empathy for the alcoholic parent. Nevertheless, it is difficult for a child to accept and to understand this truth, and may be quite damaging to the child's emotional development and attitude toward life.

The guidance counselor can help. A special group may be arranged for these children, in which they may discuss and seek solutions to this threat to their happiness and comfort. The book *Alateen—Hope for Children of Alcoholics*[1] is a fine source for understanding and developing discussion activities. Special care to protect the anonymity of the members of such a group, and their families, must be taken, and the counselor must structure the meetings with the paramount thought of not embarrassing a family or child. The counselor will be surprised at the extent to which alcoholism affects the school community. It is especially noticeable within the middle school where the child is going through tensions of his or her own in the growth process and has the additional burden of family disruption and uncertainty. It is also the time when family groups are under excessive strain resulting in separation and divorce primarily because of this social stigma. It is therefore vital that the counselor involve himself or herself in indicating to the affected child that someone cares. These crucial years of decision making often determine whether the child himself or herself will turn to alcohol and drugs to face the challenges of society.

Several procedures are followed to help the children and yet guard their and their families' privacy. First, a child is usually identified after being referred by the classroom teacher or school nurse. The child is brought to the counselor for discussion. During the course of the talk the subject of the commonness of drugs or alcohol problems is introduced, and the detrimental effects of such problems are explained to the child. The counselor may review some of the symptoms that are common and affect the family constellation. It is extremely important that the counselor be sure of his or her facts and not attempt to generalize. Somewhere during the counselor's talk the child may volunteer the situation that exists in his family. This is usually the case, for the child does want to be able to talk to someone he can trust. If the counselor has developed this kind of image in the school, free interchange will take place. The counselor may then suggest that this child meet to discuss ways to cope with this situation with other children who share the same problem. Interestingly, at this point children often suggest the names of other children who have similar problems and request that they be invited to join the group. And thus the identification process grows.

---

1. *Alateen—Hope for Children of Alcoholics* (New York: Al-Anon Family Group Headquarters, 1973).

Before attending a meeting, it is advisable that the child tell at least one of his parents what is planned and have verbal or written permission granted to be part of the group, according to school policy. Meetings of these children may follow the plan of Alateen.[2] Such meetings stress the need for continued protection of the identity of the members, the need never to cause any child or family embarrassment, the need to learn how to love and accept the afflicted family member, and the need to learn how to be happy in the existing situation.

Discussion Group for Mothers

In the United States there is a growing sociological problem that is touching the lives of more and more middle school children—the problem of the father-absent family. This is, of course, not isolated and unique to the middle school, but is highly conspicuous in this age grouping of children. Perhaps parents hesitate to separate when the children are so small that the mother cannot leave the home to earn a living. Whatever the rationale, divorce, desertion, and separation seem to spiral during the tenth to fifteenth years of marriage. In addition, death or job relocation for the father leads to the father-absent family. It is estimated that one out of five or six school children is so affected. Among the middle school aged children, the number reaches one out of two in some areas of the population. This means that in a class of twenty-five children, about five of them will be from a home that does not have a father present.[3]

This phenomenon has been the subject of study by psychologists and sociologists with increasing tempo over the last twenty years. A comprehensive report reviewing findings of many studies is that of Henry Biller.[4] Biller's extensive bibliography may serve as a basis for further investigation by the counselor. The essence of the situation is that children in these families have a strong tendency to develop some undesirable personality characteristics as well as being adversely affected in scholastic achievement.

---

2. Ibid.

3. Martin Stamm spent six months touring middle schools throughout the United States and found counselors felt the most significant home problem expressed and exhibited by children in this age group was the broken home caused by desertion, separation, or divorce.

4. H. B. Biller, "Father absence and the personality development of the male child," *Developmental Psychology* 2:181–201, 1970.

The middle school guidance counselor has or may assume a particular responsibility in this situation. He may familiarize himself with the literature to better understand the potential problems in his school and develop aid programs.

This counselor has found that the mothers can assist themselves, and consequently become more sensitive to their children's needs, by forming a talk group through which they can discuss the problems that commonly confront them, search for solutions, and learn through exposure to others experiencing the same concerns that they are not alone. Knowing what has happened to other families may serve as a point of departure for prevention in their family. Aiding the mother is well worth the time and effort for it will subsequently have an effect on the child by encouraging an awareness of the child's needs from the remaining parent and the parent's needs from the child.

Using Puppets

A group of puppets may serve the middle school guidance counselor in several ways. By observing children in special play situations a counselor may gain considerable insight into the children—he can learn of their values, their communications in the home, school, and playground, their feelings in any number of subjects, and their desires. He can gain all of this just by listening to the children stage puppet plays. In addition, if he takes a stage, puppets, and scenarios into a classroom for a play-acting program he will develop a trusting relationship with children rapidly. The teachers of the classrooms he visits will appreciate his assistance in the development of the children's verbal and expression skills. All these values come to the counselor with a portable puppet stage, lights, about fifteen cloth hand puppets (made by the children), and a set of scenario cards.

A portable puppet stage (fig. 12–1) has been found suitable for the middle school classroom, as the counselor can easily transport it from room to room and it will withstand the manipulations of the children. The stage is made of 5/16 inch plywood and trimmed with molding. It sits easily on two desks. Three children can be seated comfortably behind to perform. A cloth cover which attaches to the bottom front of the stage with Velcro hides the performers from the audience. A pole lamp from which the center lamp has been removed provides an acceptable stage light. Clamp-on lamps would also do. To complete the stage, one needs only a dark see-through backdrop cloth which is suspended from the top of the side wings with a curtain rod.

The hand puppets are simple and easy to make (fig. 12–2). Size and construction instructions are available in many puppet books. The scenarios are also uncomplicated. Contrary to what is normally practiced, children do not need to write a script before they can put on a play. Providing a scenario as a guide for their play is all that is necessary. The extemporaneous talk and actions that they provide is frequently quite satisfying. After a group of children present a play that is accepted by their classmates it becomes an easy and joyful task for them to write it out as a reinforcement of their effort and a language activity, if that is desirable.

Following are some scenarios that may be used. Note that they are problem situations which the children solve. Each is typed on a separate card and is passed to pairs of two puppeteers. They then are given time to organize their thoughts. The pairs are called one at a time to make their presentation. If there are several pairs and there is concern about who shall be first, each pair may pick a number card (as in the supermarket); their presentation order will be determined by the number they select.

Scenario 1

Your mother wakes you up to go to school. You don't want to go because your teacher is going to give a test. You tell your mother that you don't feel good and want to stay home.

Scenario 2

Your friend comes to your house to play with you. While playing she knocks a dish off the table; it breaks and she begins to cry. You calm her down. She then spills a bowl of crackers and cries. You calm her down. Next, she stumbles over a chair and cries. You calm her down. The play continues and she makes a series of errors, cries, and you calm her down.

Scenario 3

You and your sister share the responsibility of setting the evening table, preparing the vegetables, and serving the meal. Tonight your sister comes home from school and she is sick and cannot help. Just as you are about to start working, some friends come and beg you to go skating with them.

Scenario 4

You and your family are driving to the shore for a picnic and swimming. It starts to rain.

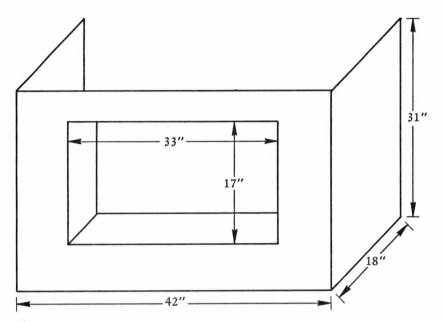

Figure 12–1
A Portable Puppet Stage

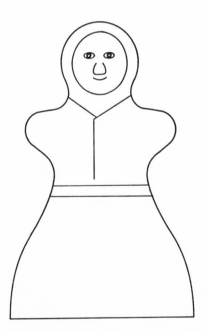

Figure 12–2
A Typical Hand Puppet

Scenario 5

You are at an amusement park with your brother and parents. You and your brother become separated from your family and can't find them.

Scenario 6

It is Saturday morning and you just want to lie around. Your mother asks you to help clean the room.

Scenario 7

Your mother wants you to stay in and do your homework. You have friends at the door waiting for you to come outside and play.

Scenario 8

Your mother and father are riding in a car. Your mother keeps telling your father to watch this and that. Your father gets angry. Your mother continues to tell him what to watch. They have several near accidents. You're frightened.

Scenario 9

You are watching your favorite TV show. Your big brother comes in to see a different show. He wants to change the channel. You argue.

Performance evaluations cover several aspects. A person is concerned about the development of the physical skills relating to the manipulation of the puppets. The children want to do well. The counselor might develop a few skills before the presentation starts — for example, how to manipulate the arms, where the fingers go, and so forth. After each performance the actors themselves become the best critics of their own show. Give them a chance to analyze and explain. The counselor and teacher may lead the class in a discussion of the values or feelings displayed by the puppets and relate these to day-to-day activities in the school and home. By listening, the counselor may perceive many of the forces acting on a child in his home, at school, and on the playground. He may learn how the child reacts to problem situations. He may learn some of the outstanding characteristics of several family members and how they affect the child. These insights can be of great value to the alert counselor.

Communication is the basis for human interaction. If children can learn to live with themselves, they will have less difficulty living with others. The counselor must accept the responsibility of encouraging positive communication skills in order to provide each child with the strength and self-confidence he needs to live a mentally and socially healthy life.

Working with Sixth- to Eighth-grade Children

Sixth to eighth grades are usually identified as the stage at which the middle school student has survived the adjustment to a more independent school situation as opposed to the protective environment of the elementary school. A serious effort by the middle school counselor to assist the fifth-grader in adjustment provides the opportunity for wider growth in the years to follow in the middle school.

Sixth grade is crucial to decision making for the plans and programs decided upon in sixth grade often determine the entire school experience until graduation. Students and their parents are customarily assembled yearly in large auditoriums to be cautioned by the counselor that course selection and decision making should be done with much careful planning. It is not unusual for the parent and child to walk away from such meetings confused, frustrated and feeling very inadequate. It is vital, therefore, that the middle school counselor work closely with the classroom teacher, parents, and the child in assisting in decision making. This necessitates clearly defined course descriptions, time allotted for each child to see the counselor and discuss alternatives, and counselors spending a large portion of their time in the classrooms responding to questions before final decisions are made. The counselor cannot rely on the student's self-motivation in most typical cases. The child needs direction and this direction, in the form of a counselor appointment, is the beginning process that exposes the student to the services of the counseling office. Too many students, usually those who have no outstanding problems, do not know how to see the counselor or what services the counselor can provide. As part of the *Counseling Service Cluster*, procedures must be clearly identified to respond to these needs. A booklet or part of a permanent bulletin board display should clearly state: (1) each child's counselor, (2) counseling hours, (3) what to do in an emergency, (4) whom to see and when, (5) where materials may be found, and (6) a listing of all counseling services.

As described for the fifth-grader, one-to-one counseling services should be encouraged on a self-referral basis after the first-year work with the fifth-grader has clearly identified each child's counselor.

Group counseling is effectively used with middle schoolers as interaction with peers seems to be compatible with their life-style. Comparing mutual concerns and questions helps the middle school child feel normal—a vital concern at this age. The counselor often has little to say in group discussions as the students interact. Topics of major concern include: changing growth patterns and physical appearance (usually the cocounseling of the school nurse helps here), feelings of depression—a very serious concern—hopelessness with respect to future planning, lack of communication and friction at home, competition with peers and siblings, athletic ability or lack of ability, belonging to an "in group" or not belonging, moodiness, and fears. The goal of such group interaction for these sensitive subjects is not the search for a solution but rather to recognize the fact that such feelings and concerns are normal and shared by others.

Techniques for organizing group sessions through counseling services may be implemented through counselor involvement in after-school clubs dealing with interpersonal relationships, in-service workshops with students to develop peer counselors as a service within the school, and allowing the alternative of selecting a group activity during study-hall time that can be facilitated by other school faculty who have worked with the counselors as part of the *Counseling Service Cluster.* Procedures for organizing these services are as follows:

After-school interpersonal relationship clubs

Teachers and students alike enjoy talking about themselves and learning about others in a relaxed, nonacademic atmosphere. If the school has a place available where the students can sit in comfortable chairs and share a Coke or the like, much good interaction can take place. In such after-school activity, designated as *interpersonal relationships*, the student and teacher leader or facilitator establish goals that meet their particular needs. Usually the first concern is personal—getting along better with others or helping others get along. As the group develops and the members become more aware of each person their goals usually become broader and include restructuring of routines and procedures in the school that aid in facilitating better school communication. This may involve such physical changes as doors for school entrance in the morning to more sophisticated concerns as communication with administrators about evaluative systems used in the school or new procedures for school management. The relaxed atmosphere and the opportunity to share ideas, no matter how radical, is rarely available in the public school situation. The middle school child has gone halfway through his schooling and in many—too many—instances it has led him to plans for dropping out. Here, through open-ended interaction, a person may air his concerns and evaluate his plans with the interest and involvement of others who really care. It is important that such a club not become a catch-all for the "rejects" nor a rap session for all the school "stars" but rather a heterogeneous group of all children planning together and caring about the school and each other.

In-service workshops for students

Middle school students enjoy sharing concerns and helping others younger than themselves after they have "survived" a level of growth and development. Peer counseling is an effective means of using this interest productively. Counselors and teachers can work with those students interested in helping them develop good counseling skills. Limitations of their role need to be clearly defined. Their help in areas of adjustment and course selection can be invaluable. Rules that respond to the particular needs of the school should be set up by the group. Peer counseling usually works most effectively when the counseling relationship is always with the "counselor" at least one grade level above the counselee. The use of peer counselors is of tremendous help to the counseling staff, as it provides immediate response to concerns that often can be better answered by students who have just recently been through that particular experience. Peer counselors may be trained through assisting in the counseling office, working with a particular member of the school staff, facilitating a particular group dealing with school plans or management, or specific workshops dealing with a definite area—for example, that of a new school entrant, a teacher-student problem, or assisting a student to find the proper person to help in handling a special problem. Peer counseling is very helpful to the peer counselor as it provides the rare opportunity for one student to help another—a role accepted by his peers within the school. The middle school child is often so intent on receiving peer acceptance that he will hesitate to do what he believes to be "authority approved actions." Making peer tutoring part of the everyday activity at school establishes positive behavior and caring about someone else, is considered acceptable, and provides the opportunity for sound emotional growth for the "doer" as well as the "receiver."

Group activity as an alternative
to study hall

The traditional study hall experience is rarely a productive one in the middle school. Long periods of concentration and quiet are not typical of the middle schoolers' makeup. Providing an opportunity to select group meetings to participate in during study hall has been quite successful in middle schools. Discussions on sexuality, self-image, boy–girl relationships, and future planning are popular among the students. Providing facilitators to encourage interaction or outside consultants from the community to share their expertise and then encourage small group discussion is very helpful.

Instead of the usual large assembly presentations on a topic of concern, where students hesitate to ask questions and react before such a large group of sometimes hostile peers, small group sessions are set up and limited to the participation of ten per group on a first-come, first-served basis. This is an excellent way to provide career information on a personal basis. Students select the group they wish to attend and converse easily with each other and the expert in attendance. Other groups are set up on a five or ten-meeting basis, where topics of concern are discussed with the same persons on a long-range basis. This is often done with the involvement of parent groups, who need to be considered important in the middle school community. The new child they no longer seem to recognize, who neither communicates with them (or does so in a negative way) nor wants to share concerns, is confusing and frustrating to the parent. Parent groups that later join with students (preferably not their own children) have great potential for providing understanding between children and their parents. The commonality of their problem seems to be the key factor.

Middle school children are characteristically in the "coming-out" stage of their lives. They need, more than at any prior time, to have an opportunity to ask questions, listen to others, find out where they are in life, and start thinking seriously about where they wish to go. Counselors have a serious challenge when working with the middle schooler. It is for this reason that middle school counselors should make every effort to organize their services so that they can use the major part of their time counseling children, interacting with parents, teachers, and administrators, and helping each grow personally. This can be done only if counselors accept the responsibility of helping each person who comes to them identify his goals and assist him to work toward achieving his goals. William Glasser[5] emphasizes that children of today are role-oriented before they are goal-oriented. They demand that educators, parents, counselors— all who interact with them—accept them as people before they will listen to what they need to become a specific kind of performing person in our society. Counselors must accept the responsibility of helping the child identify his role, helping those who influence his life accept the role he has identified, and then freeing the child to make the appropriate choices for finding his place in society.

Supplementary Readings

Adams, James F. *Understanding Adolescence: Current Developments in Adolescent Psychology*, 2nd ed. Boston: Allyn and Bacon, 1973.

Berne, Eric. *A Layman's Guide to Psychiatry and Psychoanalysis.* New York: Simon and Schuster, 1968.

Collins, Vincent P. *Me, Myself and You.* St. Meinrad, Ind.: Abbey Press, 1972.

Elkind, David. *A Sympathetic Understanding of the Child: Birth to Sixteen.* Boston: Allyn and Bacon, 1974.

Ernst, Ken. *Games Students Play.* Millbrae, Calif.: Celestial Arts, 1972.

Harmin, Merril L. *Got to Be Me.* Niles, Ill.: Argus Communications, 1975.

Harris, Thomas A. *I'm O.K.—You're O.K.* New York: Avon Books, 1969.

Hornik, Edith Lynn. *You and Your Alcoholic Parent.* New York: Association Press, 1974.

James, Muriel. *What Do You Do with Them Now That You've Got Them?* Reading, Mass.: Addison-Wesley, 1974.

Jungeward, Dorothy, and James, Muriel. *Born to Win: Transactional Analysis with Gestalt Experiments.* Reading, Mass.: Addison-Wesley, 1974.

Powell, John *Why Am I Afraid to Tell You Who I Am?* Niles, Ill.: Argus Communications, 1974.

Robert, Marc. *Loneliness in the Schools.* Niles, Ill. Argus Communications, 1975.

Simon, Sidney B., Howe, Leland W., and Kirschenbaum, Howard. *Values Clarification.* New York: Hart, 1972.

Stamm, Martin, and Nissman, Blossom. *Your Child and Drugs: A Preventive Approach.* Rancocas, N.J.: Guidance Awareness Publications, 1973.

---

5. William Glasser, *Positive Addiction* (New York: Harper and Row, 1976).

CHAPTER
THIRTEEN

Ideas for In-service Workshops

In-service workshops, seminars, conferences, sunbursting, and various other titles indicate an endeavor to plan an activity that will help stimulate professional growth. This chapter will provide brief descriptions of such activities. The counselor or administrator may find these suggestions helpful in developing concepts and fulfilling goals set by the school community. There is, of course, no firm prescription that will serve all educational needs equally well. Each counselor or administrator should examine the ideas presented in light of his program and the specific needs of the students and staff in that program.

There is no set plan that will ensure success but the basic approach recommended in all work sessions should include the following: (1) careful planning to avoid such loose ends as confusion over meeting location, lunch arrangements, alternative activities if technical equipment fails or if the main speaker is detained, and clear delegation of responsibility; (2) involving representative members of the staff in the selection and planning of each activity and rotating the leadership role frequently; (3) showing sincere enthusiasm about the topic and/or activity, making sure the presenter is capable of providing an interesting approach; (4) limiting the number of activities taking place at once so that participants will not feel overwhelmed by all that is offered to them; (5) always requesting an evaluation of all aspects of the activity and using the suggestions in meetings and programs that follow; it is extremely helpful if the program chairperson responds with a personal note to a comment that is especially thoughtful or helpful in an evaluation response—this not only is good public relations, but it assures those who participate that their comments are read and acted upon.

Specific ideas for professional growth activities include:

Feedback from College Courses

Because of the constantly changing educational programs and the common desire among educators to upgrade skills, many school staff members participate in graduate study. A productive seminar could be centered around the input of these professionals. Characteristically, graduate courses require extensive research in the form of a written paper or oral report. Most students perform this task and submit it to the professor for evaluation. No one else profits from all this work. People welcome the opportunity to share their knowledge and discoveries with their colleagues. This can be done through small group meetings for specific subject areas or as a combined school experience. We believe that the lack of awareness among educators regarding subject areas other than their own reinforces the communication gap between teachers and administrators. If each were made aware of the goals and objectives the other seeks to achieve there would naturally be greater sensitivity in their professional relationships. In addition, such seminars would stimulate faculty interest in upgrading skills and provide a source for enrichment of the school curriculum.

Current Pocket Books Review

A plethora of excellent books dealing with educational theories and philosophies and written in laymen's language is available. These books are not only extremely interesting and enlightening to the classroom teacher and counselor but are also read and enjoyed by parents. Therefore, we see the merits of reviewing these books as twofold: as a means of personal enrichment and in order to be aware of what the parents of the children in the schools, and sometimes the children themselves, are reading about educational processes. Such books as Virginia Axline's *Dibs, In Search of Self*, Theodore Rubin's *Jordi/Lisa and David*, Howard Jones's *Children in Trouble: A National Scandal* (see Suggested Readings for others) may be used as excellent motivational tools for discussion among staff members experiencing common problems. Availability of these books in the school's professional library will encourage their perusal and stimulate spontaneous and informal discussion. How much better than the usual "gripe sessions" heard in the typical teachers' lounge at lunchtime!

Clarification of New Laws

Both federal and state laws are constantly changing with respect to the responsibilities of educators and the involvement of parents and community in the educational process. Too often the counselor and teacher receive little clarification of these laws and directives for they seem to be only part of administrative discussions and board meetings. A person is usually more responsive to change if the change seems logical and is clearly understood. Administrators should be sensitive and take the time to identify these laws as they pertain to staff responsibilities. This can be accomplished easily by providing copies of the laws and distributing them to the entire staff. Those interested in further clarification should be provided the option to attend a session where they are encouraged to ask questions and air their concerns. This is a wise preventative procedure that will consequently create a more cooperative atmosphere.

Book Company Demonstrations on a Single Theme

Most schools are aware of the availability of members of publication companies as consultants to schools. To use this resource effectively, we suggest that their services be used in a discriminating manner. Provision of a general material display usually does not allow the educator to enjoy full exposure to all that is presented. Therefore, an attempt should be made to present such material workshops in a cluster arrangement. For example, one seminar or workshop sponsored by the counselor could deal exclusively with materials concerned with developing a self-image. Each publisher should be given specific directions on this limitation and be prepared to display material in that area. Thus, teachers and counselors would have the opportunity to compare products and concentrate on one area of concern.

Classroom Management

The environment in the classroom is of major concern to both teachers and counselors. Assisting teachers in developing a positive climate is of primary importance in developing a good learning environment. Techniques for classroom management may be presented through the following procedures: (1) role playing and evaluation; (2) tape recording open-ended situations and allowing the participants to determine techniques for follow-up in groups or individually; (3) video taping of a classroom for private evaluation by the teacher so that he may view his reaction to student behavior; (4) sequential seminars introducing such behavioral techniques as behavioral modification, transactional analysis, and reality therapy; and (5) team visitations where two teachers and/or counselors work together in assisting each other in improving classroom climate. (The availability of another "place" for a disruptive child often is all a teacher needs to help that child gain control of himself or herself.) If classroom management and discipline were recognized as common concerns, more teachers would be willing to involve others in coping with their problems.

Curriculum Development

Guidance counselors often express reluctance to become involved in curriculum matters in the school. We think this is unrealistic for, unless a child can cope with the curricular demands, he will find school adjustment difficult. He will be unable to achieve success through learning and therefore will be tempted to search for success in other ways. The counselor must be sensitive to the needs of his clients. Basically, he should constantly be evaluating whether the student's problem is because of poor class placement and if so how he can amend that situation. It is as detrimental for the student to be in a course that is too easy as it is to be a student in a program beyond his level of comprehension. Counselors should arrange to attend department meetings and provide input regarding clients to those teachers involved with their educational development.

Mainstreaming Techniques and Procedures

The mainstreaming process, as discussed in Chapter 10, indicates that the special education child is involved in regular class activity. The success of this process depends upon the coordination of professionals: the special education teacher and the classroom teacher. Often the regular classroom teacher fears that the special education student needs a more sophisticated instructional program than can be provided in the typical classroom. Therefore it is essential that the regular classroom teacher be given enough information on the special education student's disability to determine his limitations in the class. This is an important point of consideration. When a student is mainstreamed, the major concern is adjustment. The classroom teacher who feels comfortable with this child in his room, who knows what is expected of him, and who is realistic in his approach to meeting this child's needs in the new class environment will probably meet with success. Seminars presenting this information and assuring the classroom teacher that there is a possibility that the mainstreaming will not be successful provides the teacher with a realistic view of the situation. Classroom teachers and special education teachers should work together in an open seminar, responding to each other's concerns and questions.

Evaluation Procedures

Ongoing evaluation is necessary in any good school setting. Evaluation should be a two-way approach with all in the school being able to voice opinions about school management. Several chapters give examples of evaluative tools that allow the students and parents to evaluate counselors as well as the teaching staff. Those who are recipients of services should be able to voice their opinions and suggestions about these services. Teachers should be able to evaluate principals, parents teachers, teachers students, and so on. The procedures of evaluation need to be carefully developed and this is the reason for workshop and seminar approaches. To prevent such evaluations from becoming complaint sessions, constructive comments should be emphasized. Suggestions for procedures should be the combined effort of all involved in the evaluation. Evaluation need not only dwell on individuals but can productively involve procedures and processes within the school. This can be initiated through a suggestion box technique where unsigned (or signed) suggestions may be submitted for consideration by a "task force" interested in and qualified to discuss that particular area of concern. Once a format for evaluation is developed it can evolve into two forms: it may be confidential to the person evaluated or it may be generalized in content and open to group reaction. The topic usually determines the type of evaluation.

Assessment Tools

Testing procedures and materials are constantly changing in an attempt to develop culture-fair instruments. Workshops need to be held to keep the staff aware of these changes and provide insight regarding the best and most effective use of test results. Assistance given to teachers in test interpretation procedures by counselors would be extremely helpful to the teacher in responding to questions by parents at conferences. Although the teacher may refer the parent to the counselor for further detail, it is essential that the classroom teacher have some knowledge about the meaning of testing scores in relation to the child's performance in his class. Miniseminars or workshops that give them this foundational knowledge could be provided for teachers. It is important that professionals share their expertise in order to upgrade the quality of communication with parents.

Interpersonal Relationships

The number of school in which administrators and teachers never share the same educational experiences is surprising. Programs for administrators are not open to teachers and administrators rarely attend teacher seminars except perhaps to introduce the speaker or welcome someone to the school. This is a tremendous loss to both professionals. Providing a workshop activity that involves not only teachers and principals, superintendents, and specialists, but secretaries and custodial staff, is the basic ingredient of an interpersonal relationship activity. Procedures of communication, relating to one another, listening skills, and the like can be introduced as those who work side by side communicate perhaps for the first time. In such seminars teachers in the same building talk with their peers for the first time—not because they didn't seek each other out previously but because they were on different lunch schedules and never chanced to meet in the teachers' lounge. Superintendents interact with teachers and principals with custodial staff in an attempt to learn who they are and how they feel about common concerns in the school. It is truly an exciting experience, for each person begins to feel a responsibility for the school in a different way than before. Listening to each other on an equal level of interest helps to foster a school unity that is worth working toward. The bond of a staff determines the degree of individual involvement. Eliminating the unknown through personal interaction leads to a cohesive school staff. There are many programs available that will help the counselor work with personnel in this area.

Current Educational Concerns

Educators should be aware of the national and local problems facing the educational programs. Schools can help their staff keep current on such information by providing update sessions on a monthly (or weekly basis). The guidance staff may act as the collating agent and assemble a bulletin that feeds this information to the staff through their department meetings or bulletin board displays. Follow-up discussions should always be available for those interested in details or further clarification. This could be a joint endeavor by the counselor and another staff member best equipped to respond to the questions in the area of concern. Community problems and school problems could be handled successfully through this process, for they could be dealt with promptly. A concern becomes a problem only when it is allowed to ferment and continue to grow out of proportion. If dealt with immediately, through clarity and truth, it can lead to change rather than disruption of progress.

Teacher/Counselor Idea and Resource File

Cooperative efforts of all staff can lead to the development of an idea and resource file for use of the entire staff. We all agree that it is foolish to reinvent the wheel, but this is the process that continues to prevail in many schools. Idea workshops on a specific topic could lead to building this file for other teachers' use. For example, one teacher may have only two students in his class who have difficulty learning the symbols for chemical formulas. Another teacher may have devised a procedure for teaching these symbols and could share the worksheets with his colleague. Teachers, over the years, develop their own procedures and techniques that have been modified from techniques they have learned from others. Sharing these ideas in a "rap" session and providing the use of teacher-made materials among the staff helps develop good rapport among the staff and enriches the curriculum for the students. This resource file may be housed in the office near the ditto machine. Each time a teacher develops a new worksheet and makes copies, one copy is placed in the resource file, with his name noted, under the topic to which it applies. Other staff members may then feel free to share these ideas and go to the teacher who created them for further clarification or follow-up if necessary.

Effective Counseling Technique

Counseling techniques should not be a secret. An excellent workshop experience for all staff is demonstrations by the counseling staff of their techniques. Many teachers and administrators have no idea what "goes on" in the counseling office. Role playing demonstrating teacher–parent counseling, child–teacher–counselor sessions, administrator–counselor interaction and counselor–teacher sessions help teachers and administrators understand the counselor's role more clearly. In addition, the counselor may be of assistance to teachers with respect to their communication skills with parents and children.

Orientation Programs

There are many times in school activities when children and teachers are in the position of entering a new situation. New students move from elementary to middle school. New teachers join a new staff. Students move from the middle school to high school. A student may enter a school in the middle of the year. All these situations demand involvement of many staff members in helping these people in their adjustment. The fact that the counselor accepts responsibility for carrying out most of these services is not enough. All the staff should be given insight into what the counselor is doing, why he is doing it, and what each staff member needs to know to help facilitate the transition that will take place.

Career Conferences

The counselor is usually involved in providing opportunities for students to learn more about careers. In coordination with social studies and English teachers, counselors may take the leadership role in coordinating their career conferences with the interests of the students. The staff works with the counselor in providing follow-up of the areas presented in the conference. This subject is discussed in depth in Chapter 12. Generally, it may be stated here, all staff should have correct and complete information regarding any conferences on careers offered the students so that they are in a position to use the information to supplement their class activity or plan their program to make the career conference meaningful to their students. Too often the career conference is announced for a certain evening, with no details given as to who will attend or special areas of interest. Often the same schools and industries are represented each year at what is becoming a traditional event, with very little input from students or staff. It is suggested that the career conference be the result of the combined input of those it seeks to serve and those involved in working with the students who must make the decisions: students, teachers, parents, and counselors. Career conferences do not have to be a one-day activity but may better serve student needs if presented in clusters of interest areas, to allow students time to review the spectrum of jobs that surround them.

In-service workshops and seminars are developed as the result of needs of the staff and students. The school that functions as a vital unit will seek out such activities in order to grow professionally and personally. Providing such an outlet to discuss concerns openly, encouraging the use of experts in the particular areas of consideration, opening the door to suggestions and change, and stimulating the school community to share ideas and resources can only lead to a productive and happy school climate where teachers and students want to be. The counselor, therefore, needs to accept the responsibility of providing such workshops and encouraging staff participation. Good school management is based on understanding of all involved. The counselor, as a human relations expert, must first explore the areas needing professional growth and understanding and then provide this information. The *Professional Growth Cluster*'s personnel have responsibility for all areas of the school and may choose any aspect of the program for an in-service workshop. It should not be limited to those areas we customarily think of as guidance-oriented, such as human development and interpersonal relationships. Understanding curriculum needs, the responsibilities of mainstreaming, the place for evaluation and assessment all are essential in developing a school that provides the most productive learning environment. Counselors need to think of themselves as generalists rather than specialists in the middle school so that *every* aspect of the child's world becomes an important concern for the counselor and teacher.

Supplementary Readings

Pocket Books

Axline, Virginia. *Dibs: In Search of Self.* New York: Ballantine Books, 1971.

Fox, Jessie Gray. *Gone Is Shadows' Child.* New York: Pyramid Books, 1971.

Hopkins, Lee Bennett. *Let Them Be Themselves.* New York: Scholastic Book Services, 1969.

Jones, Howard. *Children in Trouble: A National Scandal.* New York: Pocket Books, a division of Simon and Schuster, 1971.

Moustakas, Clark. *Psychotherapy with Children: The Living Relationship.* New York: Ballantine Books, 1970.

Rubin, Theodore Isaac. *Jordi/Lisa and David.* New York: Ballantine Books, 1968.

Wexler, Susan Stanhope. *The Story of Sandy.* New York: New American Library, 1970.

Others

Benjamin, Alfred. *The Helping Interview.* Boston: Houghton Mifflin, 1969.

Berkowitz, Newman. *How to Be Your Own Best Friend.* New York: Random House, 1971.

Berne, Eric. *Games People Play.* New York: Ballantine Books, 1964.

Branden, Nathaniel. *Breaking Free.* New York: Bantam Books, 1972.

Glasser, William. *Positive Addiction.* New York: Harper and Row, 1976.

Gordon, Thomas. *Teacher Effectiveness Training.* New York: Wyden, 1974.

Gross, Ronald, and Osterman, Paul. *Individualism.* New York: Dell, 1971.

Hawley, Robert C., and Hawley, Isabel L. *Developing Human Potential*. Amherst, Mass.: Education Research Association, 1975.

Jourard, Sidney M. *The Transparent Self*. New York: Van Nostrand, 1971.

Perrone, Vito, et al. "In Service Program for Teachers: Center for Teaching and Learning," *Today's Education* 65 (November):50—56, 1976.

PART

III

THE GUIDANCE FUNCTION OF MIDDLE SCHOOL TEACHERS, ADMINISTRATORS, AND PARENTS

CHAPTER FOURTEEN

Guidance Skills Needed by Classroom Teachers and Administrators

Throughout this book the authors have emphasized the necessity for teachers and administrators to assume a partnership with the school counselor in order to develop a comprehensive guidance program. Across the nation, escalating costs demand a cut-back in staff and a reorganization of school services compatible with the shrinking economy. Additional personnel is not the answer to implementing the services of the Human Development Center (HDC). Idealistically, the presence of a counselor in the leadership role identifying and providing guidance services needs to be acknowledged. Realistically, a middle school unit cannot import a special staff to fulfill humanistic goals. In fact, it is questionable if this would be the ideal solution even if costs were not the issue. The involvement by teachers in concern for good mental health among students they teach is to be encouraged and applauded. If the adoption of the HDC model necessitates the active involvement of teacher and administrator it has served a twofold purpose: it has added a greater depth of communication between teacher and student and it has provided guidance services for a greater number of people.

The Teacher's Role in
Guidance Services

What then is the teacher's role in guidance services? The teacher who is sensitive to his students' emotional as well as academic needs will be a more effective teacher. He will be able to relate to each student as an individual person as well as part of a group. He will be more aware of instructional and personal problems and know where to go and how to deal with these problems. He will feel comfortable as part of a team and be able to clearly identify his role on this team. He will also feel more comfortable with student progress as he considers and understands the capabilities and potential of each student. As a guidance-oriented teacher, he will understand the need for a classroom climate conducive to learning—one with minimal distractions and maximal supportive materials on varying levels of achievement.

The guidance-oriented classroom teacher in the middle school needs to demonstrate qualities similar to those designated as important for the guidance counselor. The teacher and the counselor work in parallel to achieve their goal. Thus we believe the classroom teacher needs to possess the following personal qualities: (1) sensitivity, warmth, and understanding; (2) organization skills; well-informed in his area of expertise; (3) creativity, patience, and flexibility; (4) in good physical health; have strength and stamina; (5) ability and desire to work with others; able to appreciate their talents as well as his own; (6) truly respect the uniqueness of children, including their personal values and moral codes, even if they differ from his own; (7) respect for the privacy of others, allowing for individuals to select alternatives in the academic and social processes; (8) the ability to listen intently and react to another's point of view in a calm and rational manner.

In addition to these personal attributes, the classroom teacher needs to demonstrate specific essential skills and concepts in order to provide a comprehensive approach to education in the middle school. These skills and concepts include: (1) knowledge of normal growth and development patterns of the middle school student; (2) awareness of current concerns both on the national and local scene; (3) awareness of services available within the community that support school needs; (4) awareness of the basic aims and functions of the family unit characteristic of the school community; (5) knowledge of life cultures other than his own and appreciation and recognition of differences—intercultural awareness. The teacher who is aware of the need for these competencies and is continually involved in an on-going self-appraisal plays a vital role in the development of good mental health in the classroom.

In the HDC model the classroom teacher can successfully function in a leadership role in the following clusters:

The community cluster. As the liaison between home and school, the classroom teacher is the natural link to bind and solidify this connection. The classroom teacher knows the student better than any staff member. He can enrich his own understanding of his students by becoming more intimately knowledgeable about the community in which the students live. The classroom teacher accepting responsibility within the community cluster serves himself professionally as well as the students and community persons with whom he comes into contact.

The curriculum cluster. The curriculum cluster is a natural extension for the classroom teacher. Having a thorough understanding of his own subject matter, the classroom teacher can be very helpful to the student in his course decision-making process. The teacher will personally and professionally benefit from the interaction with other teachers, gaining knowledge about their area of expertise and how each supports or reinforces the other in the learning process.

The counseling service cluster. This cluster must be supported by the classroom teacher. Through attendance at in-service workshops the guidance-oriented teacher will become knowledgeable in identifying students who could benefit from individual or group counseling and then be able to follow up on this service through his interaction with the student as well as with the student's parents and peers.

Through the use of the *Assessment Service Cluster* the classroom teacher can provide support for the direction and emphasis of his subject matter. The overall progress of students can be easily evaluated through data provided by standardized and teacher-made assessment tools. Teachers who understand the terminology and purpose of the testing instruments can use this knowledge to personalize student goals.

Through involvement with the *Crisis Cluster* the sensitive classroom teacher can assist the student in finding appropriate guidance services to alleviate a particular problem before it becomes a major conflict in the student's school program.

By participating in the *Professional Growth Cluster* the classroom teacher can develop skills that assist him in understanding the varied dimensions of the student with whom he works. Most important, this cluster provides the teacher with a direction regarding the services available for assisting the student within the school and community. Naturally the relief of a student's frustrations and conflicts will enable the student to be more receptive to the knowledge and learning environment the teacher presents to him as part of the curriculum.

The *Career Resource Cluster* is often based in varied classrooms as an integral part of the curriculum. Through a guidance-oriented teacher, the student can receive assistance in lifelong career goals—a realistic educational approach to learning. It therefore supports the concept that basic skills are part of the working world by using these skills in exploring the working world. The student will then develop a greater appreciation of the importance of the educational process and its relationship to the life he will lead.

A guidance-oriented staff is essential in providing a successful HDC. Through complete involvement, the teacher adapts subjects and teaching to the needs of students, contributes to the overall staff's understanding of each student, and seeks to further the development of students through recognition of the students' successes and failures. This obvious respect and concern for students provide an educational climate that encourages creativity and learning. It cannot help but develop a feeling of self-worth in students as well as in the staff members who are part of a cooperative school community.

In order for the classroom teacher to feel free to broaden the scope of his involvement, the school administrator must be supportive of this humanistic approach to education. The administration of a school district greatly influences the extent of staff involvement. The administrator needs to view the roles of teacher and counselor as complementary in order to facilitate the HDC as described in this book.

The Administrator's Role in
Guidance Services

The teacher (as well as the school counselor) is customarily responsible to the school principal. The specific guidance responsibility carried by the principals themselves is dependent upon the size of the administrative unit. In some middle schools the principal delegates guidance responsibilities to counselors and teachers. Some leadership in guidance is to be expected from principals, who have the responsibility to:

1. see that guidance roles are compatible with staff, facilities, and the school community needs;
2. delegate responsibility of actual operation of the school program to appropriately trained persons;
3. provide facilities and materials for carrying out identified goals and responsibilities;
4. support the services identified as part of the HDC;
5. provide opportunities for community involvement in guidance functions;
6. coordinate guidance planning with educational planning so that appropriate personnel will be available for participation in guidance activities;
7. support in-service education;
8. employ a counseling staff with appropriate credentials and skills who can accept leadership in the HDC model;
9. encourage and assist in evaluation of guidance and overall school services;
10. be supportive of constructive change and improvement in school management;
11. allot instructional periods for group counseling;
12. work cooperatively with teachers and counselors with respect to specific and general student needs and school community problems;
13. encourage active community involvement in the school programs;
14. clearly identify the guidance services available to students and the community.

The principal who provides this support allows and encourages the counselor and the guidance team to become visible to the school and home community. Dr. Richard D. Hanusey, regional superintendent of an inner city school district in Philadelphia, Pennsylvania, is a staunch supporter of guidance from kindergarten through twelfth grade. When we requested him to express his views about the counseling role from the administrative point of view he stated:

In this day and age, wherein the budget is the "tail that wags the dog," where constant attempts to save money are often translated into dropping of services, where all supportive services are always under scrutiny and often listed as educational frills, counselors have a definite role to play. Counselors must by action-direct services prove to all who challenge the need for counselors that you do offer valuable services. Visibility, especially within the community, is a key factor.

In essence, I am saying—based on my own biases and perceptions—that I perceive the counselor as a most important and valuable member of the educational family (school team, if you will).

I say you are important.

I know what you can do and the impact you can make on the learning climate of a school—upon a child—upon a parent.

What you must decide are: How important is your role based on your own perceptions? How important are you willing to make your role? How much effort will you expend in making the guidance counselor's position one that cannot be eliminated regardless of the financial climate? I, as an administrator, will support you if you are the kind of counselor I need. And that kind of counselor is one whose physical constitution is impervious to fatigue and frustration, whose heart runs on automatic energy, whose mind is clear and makes incisive decisions, whose drives insist he assume a leadership role and views aggressive action as the modus operandi and defensive and apologetic actions as mortal sins and who finds the four walls of his office as constraints and above all possesses a willingness to serve and neither knows nor recognizes any limits regarding service. If you do, perhaps you will receive a note such as this one:

Dear Miss K,

I couldn't figure out how to show my appreciation so I sat down and wrote what may pass as a poem but whatever else it's true.

> Everytime I left a yelp
> Who was there to be of help.
>
> It was a pleasure
> Without measure;
>
> To watch a pro
> Defeat the foe;
>
> You helped a friend
> Without no end [*sic*] ;
>
> Your [*sic*] the very best
> You pass every test;
>
> This fails in form
> But who conforms.

Robbi really loves going to school now and it certainly is a big difference.

Thank you,

N.D.

The administrator seeks commitment. The teacher searches for assistance; the counselor strives for cooperation and teamwork; all reach for the same goal—to assist the child. Through an awareness of each person as part of the team—the educational team with a humanistic attitude—guidance services become an essential part of the school program.

CHAPTER
FIFTEEN

Guidance Techniques
for Middle School Teachers

Developmental Guidance Techniques

The teacher's role in guidance services in the middle school is an important one. A classroom that does not provide activities that take into consideration individual differences and the special needs of the middle school child (described throughout this book), will have little success in developing well-rounded, stable students—those who learn most readily. They do so because they are receptive to learning, know why they are in school, and basically feel good about themselves. The teacher must work continually to build this kind of classroom climate.

Once a teacher becomes actively involved in teaching he or she will begin to create his own methods of making classroom activities more meaningful to his students. If the teacher is continually aware of the middle school child's feelings of insecurity, uncertainty, and need for self-worth, he will build his activities around experiences that reinforce the child's self-image as a positive one and provide many experiences that allow for success.

While teaching in a middle school, Mrs. Harlene Galen provided such a curriculum for her fifth-grade students. She feels that many of the techniques used can be adjusted and modified to meet the needs of older middle-schoolers as well. Mrs. Galen sees the role of the middle school teacher as highly guidance-oriented, for it presents a double challenge—the teacher is required to help each child gain or maintain his emotional equilibrium in addition to introducing subject matter. In other words, the program in most middle schools is child-centered, or should be. The teacher needs to be a practitioner of developmental guidance. Thus, functioning as an effective middle school teacher is not one procedure which the teacher masters and executes. Flexibility in choosing techniques and methods is necessary if the teacher is to achieve effectiveness.

What then specifically does the teacher try to include in presentation of curricula that is based on a guidance orientation? The following four categories of procedures are illustrative of how the teacher may augment this type of presentation. Each assures every student that the teacher cares about him and wants to get to know him better. These categories are: (1) environment-setting techniques, (2) listening techniques, (3) vehicles for expressing feelings about the teacher, and (4) vehicles for expressing other feelings. The counselor who helps the teacher become aware of these four categories of communication and understanding will be assisting the teacher in developing a classroom climate conducive to learning. The teacher will learn more about the child and become more aware of his strengths and limitations over and above the knowledge provided on the child through testing and other teacher comments. Techniques such as those following provide a guidance-oriented classroom, for they give the child the opportunity to tell about himself and illustrate in many ways how he sees himself as a person, as a member of the group, and in relation to his family and the teacher. This most certainly gives the classroom teacher a closer bond with the child and a much higher degree of understanding of him as a unique person.

Let us examine these categories as they were implemented in Mrs. Galen's class.

Environment Setting Techniques

Environment setting techniques are directed toward the child entering a new school situation. A child who is about to enter a middle school for the first time experiences varying degrees of conscious and unconscious apprehension about this new adventure. Often he expresses his anticipation that the work will be boring, dull, and irrelevant. Almost never will the fifth-grader admit to himself or to his peers his main concern—the teacher. The middle school teacher can take action to allay the child's fears about the educator and about the school work through these suggested techniques.

An introductory letter. A letter mailed to each student the week before the opening of school will not only dispel some of the middle school neophyte's concerns about the teacher, but will also begin to establish pupil–teacher rapport. If the middle school is departmentalized, the homeroom teacher will send the letter. If it is partially self-contained, the teacher with whom the child spends the major part of his day will be the correspondent. The guidance counselor can work with teachers in developing the contents of the letter, if the teacher seeks this assistance. The following letter, sent by Mrs. Galen to her new fifth-grade middle school children, illustrate this suggestion.

> Name of School
> Address
> Date

Hi (name of student),

That day is coming! On (date), at (time), school begins once more. However, I promise that if you and your classmates are willing to be good sports and give me a fair chance, you'll prove to yourselves that fifth grade is fun!

You're probably curious about me, your teacher. My name is (teacher's name). I've been teaching full and part time for over fifteen years. My students have ranged from tiny three-year-olds to tall fourteen-year-olds. I learned something new from each of these students. In addition, I learned something new from sharing happy and sad times with children outside of school in my experiences as a Scout Leader, a camp counselor, and a youth group director. And do you know what? I'm sure I'll learn something else brand new from you. That's right. A teacher learns just as much from her pupils as her pupils learn from her.

The enclosed photograph shows two nonhuman members of my family (picture of guinea pigs). Meet C.B. and Pipsqueak, our guinea pigs. My husband and our children, thirteen-year-old Robyn, eleven-year-old Pamela, and soon-to-be-seven-year-old Steven, have agreed to share these pets with you. In return they ask that you treat them well. I'm sure you will take good care of their guinea pigs. Perhaps you can find out what these animals like to eat and can bring them a small snack on the first day of school (date and day).

Have you heard of the F.F.F.F.? These initials stand for the name of a secret organization whose membership is open only to members of your class. You and your classmates may join but nobody else in our school is eligible; not even our principal! On (first day of school) you'll learn more about this club. Maybe you can figure out what

F.F.F.F. means before the first day of school. These hints may be helpful. One F means the opposite of frightened. Another F stands for your grade this school year. Two of the Fs have something to do with detectives. Happy guessing!

> Sincerely,
>
> Teacher's signature

The teacher tape-recorded the children's comments about the letter on the first day of school. The children related that they enjoyed the letter for varying reasons. Some comments made were: "It told me about the teacher"; "I love animals and the picture of C. B. and Pipsqueak was so cute"; "I don't get much mail for me. This letter and picture were mine and even Mom said my brother couldn't share this!"; "I wanted to belong to the club"; "I had fun figuring out what the club's initials meant. It was sorta hard to wait to find out if I'd guess right though."

Parents' reactions to the letter were favorable as well. Almost all remarked about it at the first parent–teacher conference in November. They reported that it helped to decrease their fears about their children's adjustment to the middle school years.

Not all teachers will be able to use this same type of material in their introductory letters. Following the few guidelines below should help teachers construct a letter which appeals to varying age groups.

1. Make sure that the tone of the letter conveys the teacher's understanding of the children's feelings.
2. Appeal to the interests of the age group. In the example, interests included animals, secrets, clues to a mystery, and the exclusion of the authority figure (principal) from the organization, the F.F.F.F., which incidently stands for *Fearless Fifth Fact Finders.*
3. Offer tangible ways in which children can become contributors to the class. Note in the sample the snack for the animals and the clue for the club's name.

A work questionnaire. No matter how hard a teacher tries, no matter how much expertise he possesses, he will never make all aspects of school appealing to every one of the students. The educator is able, however, to make his students aware of the fact that even adults, whom the child may resent for their supposed license to do whatever they want, dislike certain things about their jobs. A work questionnaire, an actual sample of which follows, is one means of creating this awareness.

212

Work Questionnaire

Purpose: To find out what adults think about their jobs.

Due: Upon your arrival on <u>(day and date)</u>

Student's name_____

1. Think about your dad's *or* your uncle's *or* your grandfather's *or* a neighbor's job.
   (a) Describe the job.

   (b) Ask this one man to tell you what he likes most about his job. Write the answer in the following space.

   (c) Ask this same man to tell you what he dislikes most about his job. Write his answer in the following space.

2. Think about your aunt's *or* your grandmother's *or* your mother's *or* a neighbor woman's job.
   (a) Describe her job. (Remember that being a mother and a homemaker is a job too!)

   (b) Ask this one woman to tell you what she likes most about her job. Write her answer in the following space.

   (c) Ask this same woman to tell you what she dislikes most about her job. Write her answer in the following space. (Use the back of this paper if you need more space.)

The sample work questionnaire was given for homework during the first week of school. The lively discussion that followed the reading of the answers to this sheet did much to increase the students' perceptions of the real adult world. Several children drew parallels between what each liked about "my job," school, and what they disliked about it. The teacher participated by telling what she liked about her teaching and what she didn't like. The final outcome was a decision by the students to try and "get through with the part we like least first, whenever we can, and then get on to the not-so-bad parts."

The students accepted responsibility that they might have been reluctant to accept if the teacher had not taken time to involve them in this discussion and planning. The counselor can expose the teacher to such techniques to provide new approaches to helping him develop a sense of responsibility and self-discipline among middle school children.

Listening Techniques

Another procedure to develop a skill basic to the learning process is the emphasis on listening—counselor to child, child to counselor, teacher to child, and child to teacher. Listening is a skill important in everyday life. Counseling training programs list this as an essential quality of the counselor—to be able to listen.

Total listening involves not only the teacher's acceptance of verbal expressions but his recognition of nonverbal talk in the form of body movements, posture, and facial expressions as well. If the teacher is truly listening to all the student has to say, he will not correct the child's grammar, manner of speech, use of terms. Neither will the educator reproach the student or express dissatisfaction with either body or verbal messages, even the use of swear words, often added by the student to test their reported adult shock value. Furthermore, the teacher will strive to keep uppermost in his mind the fact that a student will seek a teacher's guidance freely only if he is certain that the information he gives will be kept in confidence.

Timing is of crucial importance in successful listening. The young middle-schooler who has a problem needs to be heard immediately. The teacher's listening at the time when the student feels the greatest urgency is a preventative measure. In most cases, waiting will not cause the student's problem to decrease in intensity and may even cause additional problems to arise. It is at this time that the teacher should be aware of the availability of the counselor to assist in serving the student. Facing the problem as soon as it occurs often means less time expenditure for the teacher than if the problem is handled "later when there is time."

The following narrative, based on a real occurrence in Mrs. Galen's class, is typical of situations in which the middle school teacher can beneficially apply the techniques of total listening.

"I hate you," Hazel shouted through clenched teeth. She glared defiantly at me, hands gripped tightly together in her lap, chin thrust forward.

"Yes, I know," I replied, consciously forcing my voice to remain calm.

"I said, 'I hate you!,'" Hazel repeated with added vehemence. "Aren't you going to send me to the office?"

Twenty-three pairs of eyes jerked quickly up from their work and riveted on the action at Hazel's desk.

"No, I'm not going to send you to the office," I replied with conviction, "because the problem is here. Isn't it?"

"Yeah . . . I guess so."

"Then we'd better work this out here, hadn't we?"

"Yeah. But ain't ya gonna have me suspended 'cause I talked to you like that?" asked Hazel petulantly.

"Would suspending you solve the problem?" I persevered.

"No, but I talked bad."

"You were angry at me, Hazel," I replied in a controlled tone.

"Yeah, and I still am," she insisted, vainly trying to recapture her intensely belligerent attitude. "I hate you when you make me do that stupid damn math. I can't do it!"

"Maybe you can't do it alone," I answered, "but perhaps we can do it together."

"Well, maybe," she pouted, "but you can't help me anyhow 'cause ya were just gonna let the other math group come up. Ain't that so?"

"I was going to," I replied, "but I'm sure they won't mind waiting a few minutes. Now, let's look at that word problem."

As we can see, this total listening encompassed many areas. The teacher did not moralize but concerned herself with the immediate problem—the frustration of Hazel. The teacher did not become defensive but listened to what was being said rather than concerning herself with her image. The class was captured by the discussion and brought in to assist by waiting for the teacher and Hazel to come to a conclusion. The harmony of the classroom helped weather Hazel's storm. The student needs to be able to express his feelings and concern for his teacher. He needs to discover how this can be done in an acceptable manner. These are guidelines that will help him in accepting authority. This teacher may find the services of the middle school counselor helpful for Hazel as she could work with a counseling group in developing more acceptable self-management skills at another time when she is not burdened by the additional problem of academic success.

Vehicles for Expressing Feelings

The middle-schooler's right to express feelings about the teacher and the adult world he represents is one area to which the teacher should give open-minded consideration. Perhaps because they view it as threatening, many educators ignore the abundant evidence that not only is the middle school-aged child constantly declaring his independence from adults, but he is also becoming more dependent upon, and in many cases even permitting himself to become subservient to, a gang or group for support and reassurance in standing up against adults. Peers have greater influence than parents in most matters and *adult* is often defined in a negative sense. The preadolescent's or early adolescent's relationship to adults is further colored by his discovery of adult hypocrisy. The child notes proof of this hypocrisy in adults' reaction to sex, to telling the truth, to being honest in paying traffic fines and income taxes.

Experts in child growth and development report that, in spite of his vigorous protestations to the contrary, the middle school child still needs and wants adult support and guidance. However, because of the child's nature at this age, adult authority cannot be absolute.

The prime obligation of the teacher of middle-schoolers is his acceptance of things as they are. Once he has done this he can concentrate his energies on providing vehicles which will permit each young person to express attitudes and feelings toward adults in socially acceptable ways, those which do not impede his progress toward emotional maturity.

Some teacher-tested methods that work with young middle-schoolers in helping them communicate and resolve their conflict regarding adult authority are presented here. The counselor can help the teacher by bringing these ideas to the teacher's attention. Additional ideas of helping the child cope with his peers also are presented.

Idea 1: grievance box

Early in the school year let the children cover an empty box and lid with decorative material and label it "Grievances." Discuss with the children the purpose of this box—to serve as a repository for complaints about either the teacher's behavior or the behavior of a peer which the criticizer thinks the teacher can handle. Elicit from the children the rules for the box's usage and refrain from insisting upon the inclusion of a specific rule or you will only reinforce the children's observations about adult hypocrisy.

A word of caution should serve the teacher well. Seeing oneself through another's eyes is often unsettling, so the teacher must prime himself to be tolerant. Also, the educator can be certain that some children will utilize the grievance box as a vehicle for testing the teacher.

Every grievance deserves the teacher's acknowledgment in some appropriate way. Speaking to the child, incorporating his suggestion, changing what is bothering the student, are examples of means of assuring him that you considered his thoughts.

Below are some samples from an actual grievance box. Only the names have been changed but everything else, including the spelling, is authentic.

I don't think you had any right to drag my personal business outside the school into our talk this morning. I know you were right about me thinking about what was going on with the boys and just daydreaming and whispering and bothering the other kids with notes. But you had your nerve! Edith.

Plese [sic] Plese. Stop Herb from berping [sic]. He keeps doing it and it's so vulgar that I can't get my work done. Thank you, Beth.

I don't like it when you move my desk like you did this morning. Every time George and I start acting up, you move my desk. Next time move George's. O.K.? Sam

I'm really so ashamed of that note I put in the grievance box yesterday. You were right when you talked to me about my note-passing and giggling and pinching Leah and Jane. I knew you were right but I got angry so I wrote that nasty note. I'm sorry. Please forgive me. Brenda.

Jake was throwing spitballs too. You didn't catch him. I think he should come in at recess time with me starting tomorrow and make just as many spitballs as I have to. That's only fair. Matt.

When you want to make a point, yew [sic] always shake your head up and down. That's a bad habit. Don.

Idea 2: teacher's report card

A report card for the teacher is another legitimate outlet for the young middle-schooler's feelings about his teacher. The provision of an envelope for each child's teacher's report helps to convince the child that his responses will be kept confidential. A self-explanatory example follows. The children were given it during the last month of the fifth grade. The comments were quite interesting. Teachers as well as children learn as they work together. Establishing the kind of rapport that permits this interchange certainly will affect classroom climate.

Dear Students,

A teacher may get a report card too. Now is your chance to think about your experiences in _____ grade this year, the daily living in your classroom, in the library, on trips, your teacher's successes and failures from your point of view.

I believe that you know by now that anything you say will not be used against you by this teacher. However, if you feel better about speaking freely about me if you do not have to sign your name, do not sign it.

Please be truthful. The answers to these questions are to be your own, not your parents' or your friends' or your neighbors'. After you have answered these questions, please fold this sheet and seal it inside the attached envelope. Return it to *Hector's Homework Box* tomorrow morning as soon as you come in.

Sincerely,

(Teacher's signature)

P.S. I will use the answers to your questions to improve myself during the next school year. Your thoughts are very important. *Please be truthful.*

Directions: Circle the best answer.

1. (teacher's name) is fair to me.

   Most of the time   Sometimes   Almost Never

2. _____ listens to me.

   Most of the time   Sometimes   Almost Never

3. _____ can take a joke.

   Most of the time   Sometimes   Almost Never

4. _____ uses my ideas, suggestions, and creations.

   Often   Sometimes   Never

5. _____ raises his voice.

   Mostly when   Often when he   Never
   its necessary   should not

6. _____ likes me as a person.

   Yes   No   I don't know.

7. _____ helps me do my best.

   Most of the time   Sometimes   Almost Never

8. _____ keeps his word.

    Most of the time   Sometimes   Almost Never

9. I like to add these things about _____ (some good and some not so good).

10. Other comments:

When one middle school teacher announced that the children would be making out report cards for her, she received several doubting comments. One good student who had repeatedly proved her integrity seemed particularly upset. The girl stayed after school under the pretense of straightening up the supply closet. Once all the other students had left, she confided, "I know what you mean when you say we're going to give you a report card. You're going to give us the report during the last week of school, right?"

"Yes," replied the teacher, somewhat puzzled.

"One teacher in my old school told us the same thing and do you know what?" queried the child.

"What?" responded the teacher.

"She didn't give us a report card for her. She gave us a wicked test on all the arithmetic we'd had all year!"

Only after the teacher showed this child the ditto master of the report card would the child believe that what her current teacher had promised was not some kind of trick as had been the previous experience. Trust is built on trust and neither teacher nor parent can hope to establish a trusting relationship if behavior is not reciprocal.

Idea 3: letting-off-steam writings

A time when students are especially antiteacher is just after discipline has been imposed by this representative of the establishment. It is time for "letting off steam." If the teacher promises what the child writes will not be held against him and that he will destroy the child's communication in the author's presence, he can ask the child to write a few paragraphs about his dislike of the discipline and any unfairness on the teacher's part. Some teachers permit the child to use any swear words he desires in this comment.

Equipped with the child's writing, the teacher can encourage the student to justify his feelings rather than to search for negative attitudes. The end result of such a child/teacher conference should be formulation of a positive alternative to replace the original action which necessitated the discipline. Sometimes this means a modification of the teacher's, as well as the student's, behavior.

Idea 4: two-minute complaining

A compulsion for accelerated action is felt by most children experiencing strain and anxiety. Direction of such action into harmless physical expression similar to "two-minute complaining" can be accomplished easily in the classroom. The "enemies" stand back to back. On a signal from the timekeeper each begins shouting his reasons for wanting to fight the other(s). Rules of the "game" demand that body contact be maintained and that the shouting must be sustained until the timekeeper signals that a full one hundred and twenty seconds have elapsed. The usual result is that the participants quickly run out of words and find this first a frustration and then a comical position to be in. Laughter reigns, and aggressive feeling is lessened.

Idea 5: role playing

Role playing serves to legitimatize children's feelings about each other. By participating in a hypothetical misunderstanding, children who clash in daily classroom living can freely express their thoughts about each other without fear of censure. This technique further sharpens the participants' perceptions about others' feelings if each one assumes his adversary's role for the duration of the make-believe situation. Areas for discussion and role playing may be determined through suggestions of the student. It is helpful if a special area is set aside where students can place their suggestions to be reacted upon by the group. This can be simply a brief note or description placed on a 3 X 5 card by the teacher or student to be used later during a role-playing experience.

Idea 6: forewarning

The early middle-schooler, with teacher's guidance, generally begins to develop greater self-awareness. He becomes tuned in to the feelings he experiences and can communicate these to others. If the child can be encouraged to alert his teachers to his potentially trouble-causing feelings, unpleasant occurrences can often be prevented. Through small group sessions, the teacher can work with the counselor to help the student understand these feelings in relation to his personal growth and development. Consider the following illustration:

At his own suggestion, Alex had been coming to his homeroom before school each morning for additional help in arithmetic. One Wednesday morning he stomped into the room, plopped into his chair, yanked a piece of paper from his notebook, slammed it on the desk, and announced, "This is going to be a bad day. I know it."

"Would you tell me why?" asked his teacher.

"It's my dad," exploded Alex. "He did it again. He is always threatening to take me out of our youth group's baseball league. He wouldn't let me go to the game last night and I was the pitcher. And if I'm out anymore, they may disqualify me altogether."

"Mmm," said the teacher in a sympathetic tone. "And did your dad have a reason for keeping you home?"

"Yeah," blurted out Alex, "but it wasn't a good one. You see, Mom came home from work and the house was a mess. My sister and I were s'posed to have straightened it up but we didn't. So my dad, he turns on me and hollers that I'm the oldest and that I'd better get busy. Well, I got hot under the collar and shouted that I thought he was unfair 'cause Stacey hadn't done her part and he didn't say anything to her."

"I get the picture," replied the teacher.

Five minutes later, with a minimum of teacher guidance, Alex had figured out that his dad really was concerned about him, that he was proud of Alex's performance in the baseball league, and that Alex's behavior had forced his father to make the threat out of anger. Furthermore, Alex admitted that he himself could help eliminate such scenes in the future if he really worked hard at it. By the time his classmates entered the room, Alex had his own emotional house in order and his day progressed fairly well.

Idea 7: write it and destroy it

When a child gets angry or upset at another, the teacher may suggest that he stop whatever he is doing, write that person's name on a piece of paper, and then add either a description of what the person did to make him angry or what he'd like to do to that person. Any type of message is permissible since the writer must agree that he will not let anyone else see that paper and that he will destroy it as soon as he has completed writing the message on it. After he has finished putting his comments on the paper, the child can destroy the paper by whatever means most appeals to him—ripping, cutting with scissors, crumbling, shredding, poking holes.

One child expressed his satisfaction with this technique.

"I thought of the paper as Brian himself. It made me feel good to get back at him by poking holes all over him and hurting him just as much as he'd hurt me. After poking most of the paper, I began to feel less angry. Then I was glad that the paper was just paper and that I really had not hurt Brian."

Idea 8: physical outlets

Even though the teacher may consider many of these outlets to be too unsophisticated for the middle school student, actual experience has proved that students of that age find them effective. Such releases include socking a punching bag while pretending it is the person or the problem the puncher detests, tossing beanbags at a backboard on which have been painted the words "What I'm Mad At," manipulating clay, creating and breaking down checker towers, boardwashing, desk scrubbing, and floor cleaning. These provide harmless scapegoats for the troubled child if he is permitted to use them when he most needs them. Just pacing up and down the hallway outside the classroom for five minutes works well for some children. The important point is to know the student and permit him to suggest ways to compensate for his immediate needs that will make his actions socially acceptable.

Idea 9: art

Drawing serves as an excellent medium for helping many a child "get himself together" when he is feeling mixed up or indecisive, two emotional states especially typical of the middle schooler. Doodling serves as a common release for tensions and should not be criticized if it does not interfere with the learning process. Creating with wood scraps, collage materials, tempera paints, watercolors, and so on, also serves as good "therapy." In classrooms where middle school children are given the responsibility for using these items whenever they feel a legitimate need, little misuse of the materials occurs and the emotional climate tends to be a healthy one. It must be clearly understood that the teacher should not attempt to interpret drawings or analyze artistic work to determine the possible disturbance of the child. Art in the sense we discuss here is a form of release for the child and is left to his personal interpretation. He has the option of whether or not he wishes to share his work.

Idea 10: clubs

The gang is an integral part of the lives of students at this level of learning. Clubs provide accepted outlets for debates, expressions of interests, and concerns. In fact, in-school clubs often carry over to out-of-school activities. Developing their own club organizations offers middle-schoolers worthwhile experiences in accepting responsibility to others as well as to themselves.

Vehicles for Expressing Other Feelings

All people desire the opportunity to express themselves. This is often a difficult task. Students need to convey their feelings about themselves or their peers. Physical means are often the most expedient— and frequently the only method these children employ. While throwing things, kicking, fistfighting, and similar outlets may sometimes be the easiest way to express feelings, even preadolescents are mature enough to learn alternate techniques.

The teacher should aim to set the stage for a cooperative— rather than resistant—experience in working through difficulties caused by some form of unfavorable behavior. Therefore the teacher should focus the student's attention on the real problem. A simple statement by the educator to the effect that "I still like you but I don't like what you just did" is frequently all that's needed to accomplish this. Once the trouble has been properly identified, one or a combination of the procedures described may be effectively employed.

The ideas presented here are neither unique nor completely original. They reflect the attitude of teacher concern for students and a climate of people caring about each other. The normal conflicts and pressures that confront the teenager need outlets. Providing such outlets as suggested by Mrs. Galen makes her job within the classroom that much more productive.

If we subscribe to the idea that teacher expectations have a tendency to become self-fulfilling, then we can conclude that a teacher will help these children progress in self-understanding and self-direction if he truly believes they are capable of such growth.

The teacher who has faith in his students' potential to look at themselves objectively and try to change what displeases them is involved. He is receptive to student needs and secure enough in himself to know that he too must be able to accept change and be flexible in his reaction and interaction with his students and colleagues. These illustrations of Mrs. Galen's class reflects this concept through the examples of open-mindedness and commitment to the children for whom she is responsible. By putting action into activities, the teacher permits each child to begin learning how to become a productive and rational member of society.

It is significant to note that the teacher's role in guidance is crucial because the teacher has the immediate and direct contact with the student. It is essential that the teacher be sensitive to special needs of students in order to respond correctly to these needs—whether they be academic, social, emotional, or physical. It seems so logical that when a child complains of a slight physical pain—for example, a headache or small abrasion—there is no question about sending this child to the nurse. It is important that the emotional and social aspects of a child be as seriously considered as the more obviously observable physical problems. The teacher's alertness and response to personal and social needs can most certainly affect the quality of a child's performance in school.

A View from Within

Often, in an attempt to determine the guidance role of the teacher, emphasis is placed on adjustment. The view the student has of himself must also be considered. How can the teacher explore this view and discover whether the child's expectations are compatible with those often preset for him by the school? The counselor, working with the teacher, can encourage this understanding by providing procedures for the teacher to use in finding out about the child's concerns and self-image. In addition to the technique presented earlier in this chapter, we will share with the reader a technique, used by Sister Patricia Watkins, that clearly illustrates a guidance approach to better teacher–student understanding.

In a coordinated effort between counselor and teacher, middle school students were asked to explore their feelings and concepts in response to the following open-ended sentences developed by Sister Watkins.

224

1. I am . . .
2. People think I am . . .
3. What I really want is . . .
4. I feel that I am not . . .
5. I am important because . . .

The students were given no other direction than to complete these statements with the first and most appropriate thoughts that came to mind. The students found it a very interesting experience and took time to elicit thoughtful responses. Upon completion of the exercise each child met with the teacher privately to further explore the comments. On some occasions the counselor was also part of the conference with the student. It provided an excellent means for the teacher to open interaction with the child on a subject other than academic performance. The teacher often called upon the counselor to follow up with a child who now wanted to talk further to the counselor. The experience had served several positive purposes. (1) It provided opportunity for a closer relationship between child and teacher. (2) It helped the counselor by developing an opportunity for the counselor to work directly with a teacher in a preventive role as well as providing a better understanding of the counselor's role to the student. (3) It helped the teacher develop a greater sensitivity to his students' emotional and social needs.

The responses of the ten- to fourteen-year-old middle school children provided a most interesting view of the students and their personal feelings about themselves and others. Not only are the reactions interesting for each child, but a vivid picture of the conflicts and concerns of teenagers as a group come into view. Following are samplings of student responses that seem to illustrate the effectiveness of this technique in providing the counselor and teacher with greater insight into the concerns of students in the middle school. As this information is pursued further, through individual and group counseling, the students begin to see clearly that these professionals sincerely care enough about them to listen. We have added comments following each student's statements to illustrate how the student's remarks may be used to enrich the learning environment.[1]

---

1. Samplings provided by Sister de Chantal of the Grey Nun Academy, Yardley, Pennsylvania. Sister deChantal was the school guidance counselor.

Beth:

1. I am a person who can be happy and sad at the same time. A sensitive person.
2. People think that I have grown tall in the past year. Also that I am a sensitive person. And also a nice person at times.
3. What I really want is a real true friendship, a person who would really like me, my whole self, and a person who I would really like. I want to look nice in the eyes of some people.
4. I feel that I am not a person who could be shy. A person who cannot take a shock or a sudden thing.
5. I am important because I love my family and other people, and my family loves me. Because I'm here I exist in life.

Comments: Beth sees herself as a sensitive person and feels others see her with the same feeling. She values the worth of a good friend and feels that love of family is important in life. She respects her own uniqueness and seems to be aware of the changes in her feelings that are characteristic of the preadolescent/adolescent age group. The counselor and teacher can help Beth by assuring her that her fluctuating feelings are normal for her age. Group sessions would probably be a comfort to her, for she will be able to share these feelings with her peers and see their normalcy.

Tim:

1. I am, I think, a nice person, at least I like to be. I am also an animal lover and don't like shooting other animals.
2. People think that I am disagreeable and mean. People also think that I am dumb and try to take advantage of me but most of the time it doesn't work.
3. What I really want is our pet cat Mickey back and to make the man who hit him suffer the same way that he did.
4. I feel that I am not wanted in games and other things because none of the boys want me to do anything with them and when I play with the girls they always ask me why don't I play with the boys.
5. I am important because I am a person. Some people think that people are important if they're famous or something like that but that's not true.

Comments: Tim is obviously upset about the recent death of his cat and wants to strike out at the "unknown man." He then tends to group all others as being against him, not seeing him as a good or intelligent person. He shows a lack of self-confidence and a strong concern for his masculine identity. He feels rejected by his peers and suspicious of "others." The counselor and teacher need to be sensitive to Tim's concerns and help him build his self-image and make some inroads in improving relationships with his peers.

Karen:

1. I am a person who really does like everyone in some way.
2. People think that I am different and not like them, not everybody, only certain people in my class.
3. What I really want is for everyone to be happy.
4. I feel that I am not liked by certain people in my class, but it's not really them, it's that if they like me, someone will not like them.
5. I am important because . . . I don't feel that I am important. Nobody is important no matter who they are, or what they do. Being important is what you feel. If someone thinks they are important, it's not that person that is important, it's what they do, or what they think they are.

Comments: Karen sees herself as loving all and wanting nothing but good for everyone yet she does not get this response from others. In her desire to be "good" she tries to rationalize her failing to have the friends she seeks. She too seeks friendships and acceptance among her peers. With the counselor, she could explore her feeling with a small group of her classmates to determine how she can gain the acceptance she seeks.

Linda:

1. I am a girl who is lonely and has only a few friends and try to be nice to everyone. I try to be in everything that they include me in. I am also a girl who always gets teased.
2. People think I am nice; I mean my parents, and maybe my teachers. Some people might think that just because I don't do something they do I am chicken or a baby.
3. What I really want is people to stop teasing and calling me names, and also telling me to wear what I don't want to.
4. I feel that I am a nice and sweet girl that doesn't have very many friends. I feel that other kids don't like me.
5. I am important because . . . I don't know.

Comments: Linda is confused by the reaction of her peers to her behavior, for she sees it as readily accepted by her parents and teachers. She seems to express the opinion that she must lower her standards to gain acceptance by her peers. She seems to have conflicts in her thoughts about right and wrong behavior. She too seeks acceptance by her peers and seems to lack direction in achieving her goal.

227

The counselor can assist Linda in clarifying her feelings toward others and her interpretations of others toward her through individual or group counseling sessions.

Bill:
1. I am a human being.
2. People think that I am a nothing.
3. What I really want is for people to like me in my class.
4. I feel that I am not fit for this school because none of the boys in my class like me.
5. I am important because I am my mom's and dad's child.

Comments: Bill's comments, combined with those of his classmates, make it obvious that there is a serious need for the teacher to work with this class in group dynamics. The feeling of rejection again permeates the child's comments and seems to echo the hopelessness of several of the other students with respect to group acceptance. The counselor needs to work with the teacher in exploring this class's climate. Is there a small group blocking out the less social students? What is causing this rejection of some and not others? How can this be changed?

Joanie:
1. I am myself, someone who not everyone understands and even dislikes. I am a person who dislikes others and sometimes myself. I am someone sometimes forgotten and not noticed. I feel unsafe and used.
2. People think that I make excuses for the actions I do. People think I am ugly and don't have a personality. People think I lie.
3. What I really want is to be liked more than I am and not used. I want to be noticed and do things I want without being scared or being disliked completely.
4. I feel that I am not liked because of my faults and opinions. I am not nice all the time. I'm not like everyone else.
5. I am important because people may think I'm important because I hang around popular and important people.

Comments: Joanie tries to look at herself objectively and admits her imperfections. She wonders if she has to give up her individuality to be liked. She fears that people use her yet states she seems important because she uses the importance of others to give the image of importance. Joanie is trying desperately to decide what kind of person she wants to be and questions how much of what she feels she is will have to be given up to make her acceptable to others. The teacher and counselor can work with Joanie and her peers in evaluating their talents, and likes and dislikes, in relation to their aspirations and self-perceptions. With direction, Joanie can begin to see more clearly her position in the school and home community as a productive and pleasant place to be. She will explore whether the expectations she has set for herself and others are realistic. Upon determining this, she will then be able to determine a plan of action that will help her reach these goals without compromising her beliefs and feelings about herself and her relationships with others.

Neil:
1. I am Neil, one person in billions.
2. People think I am . . . I don't know what people think of me!
3. What I really want is to have the power and the money to change certain things in the world.
4. I feel that I am not important.
5. I am not important because I am only one person that can only make minor changes.

Comments: Neil sees himself as unimportant as measured against the vastness of the universe. He expresses the need for change and his desire to bring it about. The counselor and teacher can work together in helping Neil see how vital each person is by encouraging him to define what these changes he would make and how he would go about making them. Neil's comments reflect an interest in science and obvious intelligence. Encouragement to create and expound on his thoughts would probably help Neil in his school progress as well as give him the motivation he seems to seek to encourage him to investigate those things that interest him. Neil would be a good candidate for independent study and responsibility for the science interest areas in the classroom. This identity with some specific skill would help him see himself as a unique and worthy human being.

Ellen:
1. I am lonely because I don't have any brothers or sisters and no friends at home except for one girl across the street, but I am too afraid to go over and ask her if she likes me, anyway. I don't have any real pets that could go around with me, so I am lonely.

2. People think I am lucky and happy. That I laugh and joke a lot and have fun because there is nobody to bug me. They think I'm not shy and am happy.

3. What I really want is to have lots of brothers and sisters and dogs and friends and one best friend, and Christmas all the time because at Christmas it's warm in the house and people are happy and there are lots of people around and I'm not lonely anymore. But this year it won't be because Mary Ellen is married and I don't have friends at home and no brothers and sisters and it will not be as good as before.

4. I feel that I am lucky and all that but not really all that happy. Also I am not always shy.

5. I am important because I am the only kid in my parents' life and because I am a person who thinks and feels in a way that is all my own.

Comments: Ten-year-old Ellen is concerned that others see her "only child status" as positive while she sees it as lonely. In revealing this feeling she tries to assure all that it has nothing to do with her love and respect for her parents. Ellen feels that others see her as she is not and she seeks to find a way to be the way she feels she is. The teacher and counselor could respond to Ellen's desire to discuss her concern about Mary Ellen and the loss of Mary Ellen to marriage. A group session or an individual session with Ellen could emphasize her identification of what makes things good for her and how she can bring more of this goodness into her life. Often, if a child is given the opportunity to sort out thoughts that are general into specific feelings and actions, she can cope more easily with situations that arise. Ellen's interpretation of happiness in discussion with her peers may help her become more aware of her goals and desires and how to achieve the kinds of relationships she seeks with others.

Brian:
1. I am feeling happy.
2. People think that I'm not what I should be. I'm not myself; I am always copying.
3. What I really want is the Mona Lisa painting by Leonardo DaVinci.
4. I feel that I am not living up to what I should be and am not too aware of what's going on.
5. I think I am important because I am me.

Comments: Brian feels that people don't see him as he really is and he is not too concerned about it. He seems to express the feeling that people will realize his value in good time. He is obviously comfortable with himself. The counselor could reinforce his feeling of self-worth by having him try to express what he feels he is capable of being, how he expects to achieve his goals, and how school can serve him most productively. Brian is an example of a child who may not excel in school because he is satisfied with minimum performance. The question is whether or not the teacher can accept this and whether or not children like Brian should be allowed to be satisfied with less than their best. We feel that being comfortable with oneself and knowing one's abilities, although not using them to the maximum, is much healthier than constantly striving to reach the highest level of achievement and missing the joy of life surrounding each person—that of being happy doing what you are doing at the time you are doing it. Often children are so pressured to succeed in something, they are unaware of the purpose or overall goal of the striving for success and learn little in the process. A good example is memorizing a very long and complicated poem and never understanding the thoughts and feelings it transmits through its passages. Brian's contentment with his world should be nurtured, for it will provide him with the strength of character he will need to grow into a productive mature person capable of making a worthy contribution to society because he feels worthy as a person.

Robert:
1. I feel nobody likes me, so I try to get their attention. I feel like a person who is never wanted. I feel left out!
2. People think that I am a person who would do anything to get things. And that I am a real jerk and don't know how to do things.
3. What I really want is people to pay more attention from people I would like to be with in the group.
4. I feel that I am not wanted because some of the boys were playing football and I wanted to play and they would not let me play; they would say the game is locked.
5. I am not important.

Comments: Robert expresses his frustration at being unable to join the group and belong to the team. He joins his peers in his concern for acceptance. Robert's comments should help the teacher see the importance of helping Robert and his peers understand the obligations of people to each other and the need for exploring positive approaches to developing friendships within peer groups. There are many good filmstrips and open-ended stories available to assist the teacher and counselor in developing these concepts.[2] (See Suggested Readings at the conclusion of this chapter.)

John:

1. I am disgusted with the hostile world around me. We should be free to say what we want or do what we want to without being jeered at. I feel that I'm not important, and that I am a complicated person who is not understood or treated right, and I am intelligent.
2. People think I am stupid; not in subjects in school, but as a person. They also think me boring and uninteresting. I just am not interested in certain subjects.
3. What I really want is to have a lot of close friends who really like me and not just say they do, and who are my kind of person.
4. I feel that I am not well liked, understood, or treated right, because of reasons mentioned above.
5. I am important because I'm a person with feelings.

Comments: John expresses his doubt of others' sincerity and his disappointment with the world about him. He too expresses the desire for friends who accept him as he truly sees himself and not as they want him to be. John would profit from group interaction that strives to establish channels of communication among his peers. John sees others as viewing him in a negative light. It would be helpful for him to discuss with the counselor why he comes to this conclusion and what he can do to change this image so people see him as he sees himself.

In reviewing the concerns and comments of these children, we are in no way recommending that all counselors become "armchair psychiatrists" and try to analyze the words and thoughts of all students. Rather, we recommend that counselors and teachers take time to listen to the concerns of these children and react in a logical manner—by following up on these concerns through further discussion and interaction directed to the questions presented by the students. Looking closely at the statements of this sampling of middle school students, the counselor can see their general concern for belonging and acceptance.

---

2. Open-ended stories may be developed through the creativity of the students, use of actual school problems, or supply of the beginning of any good story to the students for their original completion.

Most of the students express the feeling of loneliness and the feeling that the perceptions of others do not seem to relate to their self-perceptions. The counselor and teacher who take these concerns literally and seriously will be able to take steps in aiding the student to meet his personal needs.

It is difficult to learn when a person feels defeated, confused, or personally neglected. The middle school child presented in these brief examples seems to express a plea for help in understanding "self." The counselor must accept the responsibility for assisting the student in this search.

The student in the middle school is a challenge to the counselor. The counselor who can work with the staff in encouraging this self-exploration and striving toward acceptance and normalcy is providing a most important service to the school. He is functioning as a humanist who is aware of these extremely fragile and sensitive stages of development in the adolescent. He acknowledges the concerns and conflicts of pupils as being most important in their lives—important enough to care about them as individual persons. The counselor is involved with the people who surround each client within his school and community—how he works with them determines the effectiveness of his role.

In addition to the counselor's good communication with the student, other important influences in the child's life determine his needs. The parent and home life exert definite demands on the child. Often the fact that the student must function successfully within his family to feel successful himself, is overlooked. If the child's family represents a community of trust, the child will know how to function in the larger school community with this kind of security. If the home is unstable, conflicting, and a constant battle for recognition, this will carry over in school performance.

Therefore, the family's ethical standards and moral codes must be understood and respected by the school. The sociological aspects of the community reflecting the home make each school unique. The needs of a factory work-oriented town differ drastically from a suburban executive-based bedroom community and an inner-city community of relief recipients. Yet these communities also have the basic commonality of containing human beings with wants, needs, and aspirations leading to the intangible goal of happiness and success.

There is of course no one answer, no one supreme goal but rather a vast variety of goals custom-designed for each person. The effective counselor is instrumental in helping teachers, parents, and administrators view each child "from within"—within his thoughts, within his background, within his goals, and within his abilities and talents. The counselor has the tools to acquire this information; he has but to take the time, then add interest and work at gaining the support needed to follow through. All children are not verbal—some can talk to the teacher and counselor through the written page and other children communicate through behavior.

It is the professional educator's responsibility to gather this information and reach out to the student to give the support needed to help him grow to his fullest capacity intellectually, emotionally, and socially. The rewards of his efforts will be reaped by the child, the counselor, and the community in which the child will live as a mature, productive, and responsible citizen. That is the true purpose of school—a complete educational experience that involves the whole child.

Supplementary Readings and Materials

Berkowitz, Newman. *How to Be Your Own Best Friend.* New York: Random House, 1971.

Berne, Eric. *Games People Play.* New York: Ballantine Books, 1964.

Branden, Nathaniel. *Breaking Free.* New York: Bantam Books, 1972.

Buscaglia, Leo. *Love.* Thorofare, N. J.: Slack, 1973.

Frank, John. *Complete Guide to Co-Curricular Programs and Activities for the Middle Grades.* West Nyack, N.Y.: Parker, 1976.

Harris, Thomas. *I'm O.K.—You're O.K.* New York: Avon Books, 1969.

Jules, Henry. *Culture Against Man.* New York: Vintage Books, 1963.

May, Rolo. *Love and Will.* New York: Dell, 1969.

Moustakes, Clark. *Loneliness and Love.* Englewood Cliffs, N. J.: Prentice-Hall, 1972.

Perls, F. S., et al. *Gestalt Is.* Moab, Utah: Real People Press, 1975.

Powell, John. *Why Am I Afraid to Tell You Who I Am?* Chicago: Argus Communications, 1975.

Robert, Marc. *Loneliness in the Schools.* Niles, Ill.: Argus Communications, 1973.

Rogers, Carl. *On Becoming a Person.* Boston: Houghton Mifflin, 1961.

CHAPTER SIXTEEN

The Community Involved: When? How? Where?

When?

To involve the community in the school is to bring reality and purpose to the curriculum and to the lives of those who are a part of the learning process—student, teacher, administrator, and parent. Community consciousness, pride, and understanding are essential components of a productive learning environment. The school accepts the responsibility of working with families when it accepts the responsibility of working with the whole child. The family and school need to clearly understand each other's goals and communicate with each other to determine if these goals are compatible or in conflict with one another. There is a very subtle but real interaction between individual well-being and environmental factors,[1] which presents a distinct challenge to counselors and community persons in their cooperative venture of developing responsible citizens. School personnel need to be sensitive and flexible. Each member of the school community needs to be aware, informed, and interested in the changing needs of the community in which the students live. Is it typically transient? Is it stable, reflecting family constellations from several generations? It is primarily urban? rural? inner-city? blue-collar? pro-

---

1. Mike Lewis and Judy Lewis, "The Counselor's Impact on Community Environments," *The Personnel and Guidance Journal* 55 (6):356–358, February 1977.

fessional? Each group presents different pressures and needs. Each reflects different directions for the children it spawns.

Lewis and Lewis consider the importance of the counselor with respect to understanding the community and its impact on the child:

Negative aspects of the community environment may be detrimental to the growth and development of individuals.

Positive aspects of the community environment support individual growth and development.

Counselors working alone, and individual citizens, working alone, are both powerless to make the community responsive to the needs of community members.[2]

There is a need to define a commonality of purpose between community and school. There is a need for an open line of communication and a mutual trust that provides the productive field of learning that is the goal of the school.

When then does the counselor develop this relationship with the community? It is an ongoing relationship that is part of the counselor's interaction with teacher, child, parent, and community services. It is a consciously developed process of communication that shows the counselor is aware of services within the community and uses them properly. It is the eye-to-eye contact between counselor and parent formally within the school and informally within the community. It is the sincere involvement in the community by the counseling staff and school staff in supporting changes that need to be made and providing appropriate services that arise through community need.

How?

How does the counselor develop this relationship with families and the community as a whole? What specific techniques and procedures foster this school-community partnership? There are many procedures used successfully with middle school students and their parents. This is such a crucial time to reinforce the bond between parent, child and school, for there is typically a strain in communications between parent and child, as discussed in previous chapters.

---

2. Mike Lewis and Judy Lewis, *Community Counseling: A Human Services Approach* (New York: Wiley, 1977), pp. 156–157.

Counselors and/or teachers throughout the country are recognizing the need to make themselves available to parent groups. Through in-service seminars counselors work directly with parent groups discussing school programs, discipline, student responsibilities, guidance services, future planning, and specific community problems involving the school. Such sessions usually require three or more consecutive meetings and encourage participation by all adult family members (parents or guardians). The counselor or teacher acts as facilitator of the group by providing supplementary sources of information. The leader keeps the discussion within professional boundaries and oversees group participation so that a few verbal group members do not completely monopolize the discussion. Resource people may be presented in a guest capacity at some of these meetings. These may be parents themselves with certain community responsibilities, other specialists within the community, and those who provide services that could be used to help the community grow and develop. Most communities have specialists of their own who will willingly, competently, and freely share their expertise with local groups. In addition, involvement of students themselves through panel discussions provides on-the-spot information for parents. It is comforting for persons, whether students or parents, to find others who share their concerns. Interchange of ideas and procedures used to cope with mutual problems is quite helpful. The teacher or counselor's role as motivator and reinforcer is supportive to the participating parent. The awareness of the commonality of problems that arise in those trying years of the teenager seem less threatening to parents when these concerns and ideas are shared.

The parent who observes the counselor or teacher as listener and resource person rather than advice giver and decision maker feels more comfortable in communicating with the school representative. Community-school open interaction provides the staff with credibility to the parent and helps increase the effectiveness of the services the teacher and counselor seek to provide.

The parents and guardians of the school population should be involved in the school processes. For many parents, the child's entrance into middle school places more demands upon them as they find helping their children with work becomes more difficult—contact with several teachers instead of one, as in the elementary school, is an impossible task. The complexity of the curriculum and the changes taking place within the child with respect to social adjustment demand assistance and understanding. The parent is reluctant to seek out help for fear of rejection, so the counselor or teacher must seek out the parent. The most important initial role of the teacher and counselor relative to parent relationships in the middle school may well be the initial contact that says clearly, "We understand. We know it is difficult. Working together we can get through it with a good chance of success in reaching the goals we all seek to achieve—that of providing a productive and happy learning environment for our children."

As discussed in the chapter on public relations, parents need to be offered the opportunity to be a part of decision making and planning within their child's school. Through parent representation in community councils, curriculum committees, discipline policy committees, and program committees there is greater acceptance of change by the community because they, in essence, have had a part in making the change. Parents are generally concerned about their children and want to know how they can help. Reluctance to participate may often be caused by feelings of inadequacy, lack of personal educational background, or actual fear of the authority of the school—reflecting their own perceptions of school from their own childhood experiences. The guidance team—teacher and counselor working together—should show parents a sincere respect for their life experiences through school programs, personal attitudes, and general warmth and receptivity to the cultural differences of each and every person within the school community. This is illustrated in the chapter on career guidance where community specialists, small and large industry, and local businesses are equally encouraged to share their skills with the students. Community organizations—for example, those emphasizing the Italian culture, Greek culture, and so forth—should present programs that help children (and teachers) see and appreciate the importance of differences in a community—giving them the wealth of knowledge accrued from sharing part of another person's heritage.

Where?

School-community interaction is certainly not limited to the family alone. All those involved in services to the community become a living extension of the school. The school can reach out to the community through many sources to assist in the social, vocational, personal, and educational needs of students. Such community services may include:

Social

Local game centers, hamburger hangouts, churches, community centers, where bulletin boards and announcement centers can be kept to keep students updated on important school and community functions.

"Y's" and youth groups, 4H clubs, and other organizations that cater to individual interests. A resource file for students and parents should be easily accessible in the student lounge and counselor's office so that students can consult it freely.

Community events should be posted in a special place. This information could be forwarded and kept current through the Community Service Cluster by a responsible student.

A local community radio station may be receptive to student reporters giving taped updated announcements at specific times during the day. This is a common practice, especially in rural communities where school is so far from home and most children are bused to school. Therefore early announcements on the local station can alert students and parents to daily events and plans for after-school activities may be made more easily.

Vocational

Many suggestions regarding vocational and career community connections may be found in the chapter on careers. In addition it is suggested that the middle school personnel implement the following:

Develop a student placement directory listing students employed by local and surrounding industry for a personal contact for present students. It may also provide first-hand information on job openings for younger students when older students move on to college or different jobs.

Develop an occupational handbook based on one-page statements by parents about their jobs. Have them respond to three basic questions: What is your job? What do you do on your job? What training did you need before you could do your job? This would be extremely helpful to students in considering job preparation. The personal aspects make it so much more real and interesting.

Service organizations may be contacted for support of scholarship and health programs. These organizations—Kiwanis, Rotary, Lions Club, and so forth—are usually active in every community and very much interested in establishing service groups within middle schools.

Involvement with local government is of great interest to middle-schoolers looking for input regarding future interests. Most communities encourage student participation in government and will often encourage middle school students to spend extended periods of time observing the political setup of a community. Many communities provide time for middle school student representatives to exchange positions with political leaders. It is an invaluable experience.

Personal

National, state, and local agencies can often provide financial support for school needs and should not be overlooked. Many such agency staffs are highly qualified consultants who will come—at no cost to the schools—and work with the staff to resolve problems. These agencies are a vital source of community aid and include such organizations as

1. The Division of Vocational Education
2. Public Employment Relations Commission
3. Department of Labor and Industry
4. Rehabilitation Commission
5. Occupational resource centers
6. Occupational training centers
7. Employment services
8. Youth opportunity centers
9. Department of Health, Education, and Welfare
10. County colleges
11. League of Women Voters
12. Chamber of Commerce
13. Youth employment services
14. Industrial Development Commission
15. Businessmen's commissions
16. Children's bureaus
17. Welfare boards
18. Agencies for unwed mothers
19. Drug rehabilitation centers
20. Medical clinics

This general list of organizational groups typical of communities is just the tip of the iceberg. The reader who questions the relevance of this list to the middle school child is not aware of the problems within the middle school of today. Children seem to be more involved with parent problems. Pregnancy is found in the elementary as well as middle school. Child abuse is being recognized as one of society's major problems. Drug abuse through misuse of alcohol and drugs is common within the middle school. VD is running rampant. The counselor, teacher, or parent can no longer hide his head in the sand and hope these social ills will disappear. The agencies provided by the community are available and ready to assist the child, parent, and educator in working with these problems. Many such services offer privacy to the child by not involving parents. It is the school's responsibility to make known to the child and parent the availability of these services. It is the counselor and/or teacher's responsibility to be sure the services recommended through the school *do* perform the services they promise, for often this is the last port in the storm for the parent and child. The school should welcome agency personnel into the school to speak to teachers and parents (as noted in the description of the Community Service cluster) and provide clear and honest facts as to what they do provide for their clients. The services of the community should be supported as helping services and not thought of as stigmatizing the person seen entering their doors.

Educational

Educational services within the community vary. Many provide services to the school and others act as an extended arm to the school's services. Examples of extended services provided to the school include:

1. The Commission of the Blind—assisting the classroom teacher in working with a blind child integrated into the mainstream through braille books and teaching the child typing.
2. Specialist services contracted by the school as needed, as discussed in the chapter on special education.
3. Visitations provided to local industry or historical settings within the community or state for enrichment of academic programs and work-study programs that actually bring students into the community as part of their curriculum.

One middle school provides such a work-study program as an orientation program to prepare students for more extensive work-study in the secondary school. This school in northern New Jersey buses *all* eighth graders, one day a week for an entire semester, to a specific industrial or business facility where the student spends the day learning about the mechanics and procedures of that particular job. A fantastic learning experience.

The counselor and teacher working together need to accept the role of liaison between community and school and in doing so know how to encourage the school to use the community's resources most effectively. It is a source of program enrichment, social growth opportunity, personal growth, and career orientation. It may be as expansive as the school staff's creativity, imagination, and energy permits it to be.

The community is involved. When?—at every opportunity that the counselor and teacher can use its rich resources to illustrate a learning tool or make a more meaningful adjustment to life. Where?—as close as the corner store and as distant as the school cares to travel. How?—by being there and providing the source of materials for the student, family, and school. And by using all available time, materials, and facilities to put life into the school by opening the windows of the classroom to the world that surrounds it.

Supplementary Readings

Cook, David R. *Guidance for Education in Revolution.* Boston: Allyn and Bacon, 1971.

Directory of Human Services. Camden, N. J.: Community Planning and Advocacy Council of Camden County, 1976.

Lewis, J., and Lewis, M. *Community Counseling: A Human Service Approach.* New York: Wiley, 1977.

Lewis, M., and Lewis, J. "The Counselor's Impact on Community Environments" *The Personnel and Guidance Journal* 55 (6):356—358, February 1977.

Ross, Murray G., with B. W. Lappin. *Community Organization.* New York: Harper and Row, 1967.

CHAPTER SEVENTEEN

The Team Approach to Guidance

If the reader, thus far, has fully understood the HDC concept, he now recognizes that the team efforts of school personnel are basic to successful guidance services. Each member of the team plays a vital role. Briefly stated, the teacher functions in both guidance and referral roles, the administrator provides support and facilitates services through provision of working areas and materials as well as direct contact with students and staff, the counselor acts as consultant, organizer of services, leader in counseling services, and community contact proportionally to the number of students within the school and the number of colleagues working with him. Other professionals are called upon for their unique skills in response to teacher, student, administrator, and parent needs. Parents are partners in the guidance services, working with the team in setting and carrying out goals. The student is the person upon whom all these services focus.

This chapter will discuss some ideas and proved techniques for developing effective and harmonious professional relationships among school and special services personnel who are characteristically part of the guidance team. The suggestions and ideas presented here are those of Mrs. Mary Elisabeth Buhl, head guidance counselor at the Lloyd Road Middle School in Matawan, New Jersey. These techniques were used by this middle school to establish rapport with community agencies, to assist parents with implementation of guidance team recommendations, and to provide the most efficient guidance services possible to this school community. Mrs. Buhl states:

The approach employed here is clearly pragmatic. However, this is not meant, in any way, to attenuate the importance of a sound theoretical base. There is a plethora of material dealing with the multidimensionality of counseling theory. To mention just a few, one might consult Osipow's *Theories of Career Development*, Hall and Lindzey's *Theories of Personality*, Stefflre and Grant's *Vocational Psychology*, and Hilgard and Bower's *Theories of Learning*. These selections are arbitrary, but classic. There are many others. Mention is made of these examples simply to guide the reader to a theoretical framework for counseling; for without a solid grounding in counseling theory, the purely practical focus here will have little more than mechanistic value. There is undoubtedly a need to translate theory into operational dimensions; such is the *raison d'être* of this chapter. Yet it must be kept in mind that there *is* theory behind all good practices.

This middle school counselor, therefore, presents her interpretation and understanding of the team approach in the middle school setting.

Team Composition in a Middle School Setting: Primary and Extended

The primary guidance team is composed of persons bringing to bear a wide range of expertise on the many phases of child development. They include the school administrator, a number of teachers, and the guidance counselor.

There is a secondary, or extended, team composed of additional professionals who are invited to attend a given series of team meetings because of their special relationship to and involvement with a particular student. The extended team is composed of one or more of the following: learning specialist, nurse, psychologist, speech therapist, medical doctor, probation officer, psychological therapist, police detective, or public agency representative from, for example, the welfare board, mental health center, or family service agency. The primary team forms the trunk; the extended team provides the branches. A child's parents are frequently invited to attend some of the staff meetings pertaining to their child. In New Jersey it is mandated that parents be closely involved in educational changes suggested for the child by the school. In a broad sense then, parents become part of the extended team as well.

244

When this description of the guidance team is related to the HDC, it may clearly be seen that the HDC concept provides an organizational plan for the productive functioning of the team and the identification of the roles of its members, whether primary or extended. We shall examine in detail the functions and processes of the team as part of the school community.

Functions of the Team as a Whole

The guidance team is a superb example of the gestalt concept at work. A new whole is brought to the conceptualization of many adults who have viewed a child from their differing vantage points. They gain a perspective from each other which would not be possible if they were each dependent solely on their own observations. The total effect demonstrates once again, in social science, that the whole is much greater than the sum of its parts. Legislation in some states has wisely created such teams and the benefits of this process to the child can be witnessed repeatedly. The guidance team provides the vehicle through which the goal of interdisciplinary communication may be realized.

The Team Meeting

Team meetings are most frequently held in the school building in which a child is located. The reason for this is simple logistics—most of the people on the primary team are already there. In addition, such meetings are usually scheduled for the time of teacher preparation periods, so that the teachers may participate.

Atmosphere and Agenda

The specifics of the agenda vary according to the needs of each case, but the general format remains the same. The team meeting is usually chaired by the counselor, though in some cases the principal may wish to exercise this role. In formal settings, agendas are printed in advance of the meeting. At the conference itself, there is often a "hidden agenda," which bears mentioning. For example, a teacher who is not yet tenured may have very little to say at a team conference for fear of offending his principal. Such a person needs to be encouraged by the counselor, after the conference, to present any material he feels is relevant. This possibly will reveal some highly significant observations about a student's performance, attitudes, health, behavior, and so forth. In another instance, one team member may be tempted to dominate such a meeting or steer it in a particular direction in order to impress the administrator who later must evaluate him for renewal of his professional contract.

The point is that the hidden agenda may be as significant as the formal agenda. It is well to be sensitive to its existence, understand the dynamics, and place in perspective the role each team member has chosen to play.

As the meeting progresses, each person reports his views of the child in question, from the vantage point of his area of specialization.

Record keeping

At the outset of these presentations, someone should be designated as the person to keep records of what transpires at the meeting. If there is no team secretary, it is recommended that the school counselor take notes, for the following reasons: (1) his office is located in the school building where the other records of the student are maintained; (2) there is a guidance office in which such notes may be secured and confidentiality observed; (3) the counselor plays the linking role among all the other professionals who work together in the child's behalf.

Great care needs to be exercised in recording comments. Not all team meetings will be amicable. Not all professionals will view the critical issues in the same way. Nonetheless, records must be kept, and as accurately, as concisely, and as dispassionately as possible.

Confidentiality

Because such meetings deal with highly sensitive issues, strictest verbal confidentiality must be maintained to protect the rights of the student and his parents. This also applies to note taking. If one has to stop and think about whether or not he ought write something down, a good rule of thumb is "when in doubt, leave it out!" Many states have wisely enacted "sunshine laws," giving parents the right to view the entire contents of a child's file. Such laws have helped not only the parents but the professionals as well. They have alerted the latter to exercise great care in what they say and write about a child's behavior.

If the material discussed at a team meeting has been of a highly sensitive or controversial nature, it is well for the counselor to pass his notes to each member present, so that they may be read, amended if necessary, and initialed. Such a procedure protects the rights of all concerned—especially the note taker!

Implementation of Team
Recommendations

How counselors and teachers
work together

The goals of counselors and teachers are similar—they are interested in maximizing student growth. The guidance-oriented teacher carries a double responsibility, for he is concerned with the emotional and social growth of the child as well as responsible for imparting information and helping students to develop wisdom and knowledge. The focus of the counselor is to facilitate personal growth in students, so that they are better able to take advantage of what their teachers have to offer. The term *facilitate personal growth* is an umbrella. It includes everything from working with a child's parents to group counseling with students to implementing changes in a school's environment, and many things in between.

The best way for teachers and counselors to work together is to concentrate on their mutually shared goals, and then develop objectives which will in fact accomplish each of their aims. The ultimate goal in a teacher-counselor relationship is to develop a healthy respect for each other's strengths accompanied by a conscious effort to minimize each other's shortcomings.

Counselors may facilitate this process in many ways. Counselors understand that their title, "counselor," is a misnomer. Counselors spend precious little of their time counseling, and considerably more of their time performing either guidance or personnel tasks. Recognition of this fact of life in public education makes the task of cooperative adult behavior much easier. Therefore, we turn to some of the techniques that facilitate cooperation between teachers and counselors, which are in fact personnel techniques: (1) Providing guidance reading materials for the faculty lounge. This indirect approach may give some insight and information to teachers who might otherwise not ask about it. (2) Written communication in the form of memos is important, but care needs to be taken in the wording of such messages. (3) Arranging meetings with the small group of teachers who work with a given student is an extremely important vehicle of communication. (4) Meeting with parents and teachers in conference can be a very effective means of helping to implement team recommendations. It helps to ensure the accuracy of transmitting such information, and in fact can be a supportive technique for both parents and teachers. It often happens that such three-way conversations are followed by separate conferences with counselor and parents, and with counselor and teachers. (5) The distribution of a questionnaire by counselors to teachers often facilitates the implementation of team recommendations. It gives teachers the feeling that their comments and observations have value, and that other adults care about the methods they are using to help a child in the classroom. (6) There is also no substitute for socialization. This includes having lunch together, meeting after school, working together on committees, or being part of the same extracurricular activities in which given students participate.

How the counselor and specialists work together

For our purposes, the specialists constitute the school psychologist, learning disabilities teacher consultant, social worker, and speech therapist. These professionals, in most suburban and rural school districts, serve several schools and are therefore housed in some central office apart from the school building. This geographic arrangement necessitates a different kind of working relationship with schools, and counselors have a critically important role to play. The counselor often has the unspoken task of creating the atmosphere in which cooperation may take place. The counselor is the person who has the office and telephone. He is, hopefully, the one who is most tuned in to individual student needs in the school. He therefore forms a very logical and necessary connecting link between special services and a school. The interpersonal relationships the counselor forms with these specialists often determine the amount and quality of service a given school receives. Therefore, techniques may be employed to help ensure this service. Specialists often feel like intruders; they need to be made to feel especially welcome. This creates an atmosphere where communication may take place. Specialists need a place to work when they come into a school building, but space is often at a premium. Therefore, they may use the counselor's office while the counselor uses this time to do group guidance in a classroom. Perhaps there is an empty classroom in which they can work—counselors may arrange for its use. The counselor should accept the responsibility of keeping the specialists informed and use their expertise.

How the counselor and the nurse work together

The school nurse is a repository of all kinds of information which can help the counselor help the students. A good working relationship here is especially important, because what may appear to be a student's behavioral problem may in fact be a medical one. It is most helpful for the nurse to prepare a written list of the names of each student with a medical complication and the nature of the problem. It would be well for the counselor to commit this to memory. The nurse is often one of the first people in a school to detect that a student is a drug user, has poor dietary habits, is frequently absent because of preventable illness, and so on. Because it is imperative for the counselor to have this kind of information, the counselor will find it helpful to initiate frequent contact with the nurse. A cooperative informal relationship is probably best.

How the counselor and the administrator work together

If the counselor and the administrator cannot work together successfully, both will be deprived of services, and the school, and ultimately the students, will suffer. Therefore, no matter how far apart a counselor and administrator may appear to be, it is to the counselor's advantage to make every effort to facilitate communication—the administrator is the power base. Historically, counselors have occupied a powerless position. This is changing, and counselors are beginning to develop a power base of their own. But until this happens, counselors can function as change agents, primarily in relationship to administrative power. Counselors, then, need to integrate the power of the administrator in order to receive his cooperation in attending to the atmosphere in which students learn to manage themselves. The counselor must be visible to the administrator, so that he is aware that the counselor is an active person within the building. Keeping the administrator well informed of counseling activities will help to ensure his support. Seek his ideas and ask for his help. Write down a counseling job description, based on the needs of a particular school. This will give the administrator some concept of what counselors do. And it will give both counselor and administrator a base on which to build more specific annual counseling goals and objectives. In effect, this becomes a counselor's contract. In these days of accountability, it can function most advantageously in defining the often nebulous role of the counselor. Encourage the administrator's input in defining one's counseling role. As a team member, the administrator should receive copies of pertinent reports, position papers, newspaper articles, journal articles, and the counselor's own reports of research. The administrator may not read them all but, again, he will be aware of the impact of the counselor.

The point of all this is that while the administrator discovers what the counselor is doing, the counselor is becoming more aware of the administrator's perceptions. And this provides the counselor the atmosphere in which to function as a change agent. This frame of reference gives the counselor the opportunity to initiate committees set up to facilitate various kinds of change and to function as a member of other committees as established by the administrator. The most effective way to facilitate communication is to meet regularly, in formal session, once a week; it is advisable to meet informally more often. If the administrator does not assume responsibility for scheduling such meetings, the counselor should be the initiator. The issue here is keeping communication ongoing—not whose job it is to provide for it.

This approach is not in fact an invitation for counselor and administrator to become overly dependent upon one another. There is no need for the administrator to be concerned with all of the details of what a counselor is doing. The emphasis on administrator-counselor interaction is on brief, succinct, regular contact through which trust and cooperation may be established.

How the counselor and outside consultants work together

An outside consultant may be one of many different kinds of professional personnel who is treating either a student or his family in some particular way. Thus, the outside consultant might be a medical doctor caring for the child because he is epileptic. Or he might be a clinical psychologist, a physical therapist, a clergyman, or a community social worker chosen by or assigned to the family. He might also be a

250

consulting psychologist or psychiatrist selected by the school district either to evaluate or treat the child.

In this latter case, when a school district selects its consultants, care should be made not to formulate long-term agreements. Such agreements often preclude a district's receiving continuing services at a uniformly high level. Consultant services should be the best obtainable and also those that are compatible with the philosophy of the school and its personnel. Recommendations of outside consultants should be weighed carefully and taken seriously. If their suggestions are incompatible with the thinking of a majority of the other professionals involved, it may be time to get new consultants. Counselors can work effectively with outside consultants by clearly respecting their opinions and demonstrating this accord, by being conscientious about implementing consulting recommendations, and by following up on these recommendations with other staff members. The counselor should accept the responsibility of reporting results of implemented recommendations, observations, the need for changes in procedures, and so forth, by telephoning or sending periodic written reports to the consultant regarding a child's performance in school and by inviting the consultant to stop by the school informally on occasion to observe the child's in-school behavior. There will be times when the school staff and the consultant will differ on their procedural recommendations. Some very careful analysis is suggested in response to such a situation. Following this, if accord is not reached, the school staff ought to bring in one or more additional consultants from the same field—or, simply, get a second opinion. This usually solves the problem. Yet, there will be some instances when resolution is still not achieved. In such cases, the staff should invite the team from the county level of the Department of Education to participate. At this point, the county specialists will at least indicate the most advantageous methods of dealing with a child's problems when he is in school.

How the counselor and the county
office staff work together

The staff of the county office of special services rarely become part of the team at the school building level. However, they are in frequent contact with a school district's own team of special services. They are sometimes called in to participate in just such situations as that described above. In addition, they function as a valuable resource on interpretation and implementation of state legislation and county regulations for school districts. They have a particular interest in the problems of special education students and the learning problems of children with various disabilities. The school counselor will probably have minimal direct personal contact with the county team, as county services are usually facilitated through local special services teams.

In larger school districts, the school social worker usually functions as the contact person for community agencies; in small districts, this function often falls to the counselor. It is common practice for a counselor and therapist in a community mental health center or guidance clinic to be in frequent phone contact regarding the specifics in school behaviors of a child. One of the best ways for the counselor and community agencies to work together is to build a feeling of mutual respect so that two-way sharing of information may occur. Another is for the counselor to build key relationships within each agency—better to have one person with whom there is real rapport than a bevy of persons functioning in a superficial relationship. A note of caution might be injected here. In community agencies, the wheels of progress often grind slowly. It would be naive to assume that a case has been handled unless evidence substantiating that it has been is presented. Persistence is essential when working with any bureaucratic structure, and agencies are no exception. Therefore, don't hesitate to make repeated phone calls to inquire about progress of a case. In dealing with social agencies, especially, it is easy to forget that one is a counselor instead of a social worker. School counselors have to be careful to remember that their function is to provide a strong link, not a strong shoulder.

How the counselor and parents
work together

There are some important sociological factors that influence the degree and manner in which the counselor and parents work together. They are based on the socioeconomic level of the local community the school serves, as well as on the nature of the community. Whether the geographic region is inner-city urban, suburban, or rural has a highly significant effect on the parental contact factor.

In a rural setting, geographic distance plays a role. Because it takes more time and effort for a parent to go to the school, there is a lower frequency of personal parental contact. Because of the feeling of being personally removed, there may also be less telephone contact. Parents in this setting are more inclined to leave the educating to the school, and play a relationship role with the school only if their child's difficulty with learning or lack of adjustment demands it. Parents frequently work either on farms or in processing factories scattered throughout rural regions. The socioeconomic level is generally below the median. All these factors contribute to decreased parental participation. In this setting, the counselor has to exercise his initiatory skills to produce significant parental involvement.

In suburban settings, one witnesses the gamut of involvement. It is generally higher, however, because of the higher educational level and awareness of parents, higher incomes, drive for upward mobility, smaller percentage of mothers working full time outside the home, and so forth. Suburban schools are unique in having concerned citizens' committees, active parent organizations, and larger numbers of parental volunteers participating in school programs and assisting with clerical duties. Parents in this setting almost demand a higher degree of counselor involvement.

In inner-city urban schools, the pattern of parental involvement is much like that in rural areas. Upper-class residents often send their children to private day or boarding schools. They have little contact with public education. The bulk of the city school population is derived from the lower socioeconomic stratum, with its concomitant descriptors. There is a higher percentage of both parents working longer hours, of welfare families—many of whom do not take an active interest in school affairs, and so forth. Meaningful involvement between the home and the school is therefore more difficult.

The concept of how a counselor works with parents has been interjected here because parents often become part of a guidance team conference. (But they do not always. Sometimes it is necessary for the special services, counselor, administrator, and outside consultant to discuss a child's problem in relation to the familial dynamic. In such cases, neither parents nor teachers participate.) But in a more open conference, where teachers have a role to play, parents usually are invited to attend. This is especially important for the parents, even though they may be overwhelmed by this collection of "experts." They are probably able to absorb only part of what transpires at such a meeting, because their own feelings operate at a high level that interferes with their integration of the material discussed. They hear the counselor's comments regarding a child's management of himself, his relationships with others, his approach to the dynamics of counseling (without revelation of the content of the material discussed between their child and the counselor). They also hear a report from each of their child's teachers regarding his classroom behavior and his progress in learning. The nurse gives her input regarding the frequency and nature of a child's complaints, and the administrator comments on his observations, which may include the need for in-school disciplinary measures.

The parents are also asked to give their observation of the child at home and in the community. These are integrated with the observations of the professionals, and a remarkably accurate picture of the child and his needs—both in and out of school—will then be drawn. It is at this point that specific recommendations are made both by and to each person participating in the conference. Parents may ask that teachers handle their child in a given way in school, based on their observations of what works at home. The psychologist may suggest a given topic or method to be used by the counselor when he works individually with the child. The teachers may suggest special techniques for the parents to use in reinforcing learning at home. And so it goes.

Now let us take a look at some specific techniques. Following the conference, the counselor begins to work with the parents in a different way than he did before the conference took place. When counselor and parents first began to work together, it was probably several months ago, when the first observations were made that the child was having difficulties in school. A series of conferences had taken place between parents and counselor. Various measures were discussed and implemented, both at home and in school. But the child's problems persisted, and the counselor suggested that the child then be referred to the special services team for evaluation. The counselor does the spade work in these situations, helping to relieve some of the parents' anxiety, and getting them to the point where they are ready to accept help both for their child and for themselves.

The team conference, in which the parents have just participated, is the end of one process and the beginning of another. All the available data about a child's functioning have been collected, and the role of the counselor, in working with the parents, is now to help them to implement some of the recommendations made by the team. For example, perhaps one such recommendation was that the parents take the child to a community mental health center for treatment. The counselor either calls the parents after the conference or makes an appointment with them to help them to follow through on this recommendation. He gives the parent the names of several community agencies or individual therapists from which to choose. He describes what intake procedures are used, how to make the contact, how long it will be before the child is seen, whether the parents will also become involved in the therapeutic process, what the approximate costs will be, the range of time that therapy may take, how to discuss this whole process with the child, how the school will handle the release of a child from class so that he may maintain appointments with the therapist, what to do about classwork that a child has missed, and on and on. Again, one can see that just one small item in the guidance team's list of recommendations has a great many details to be attended to. The counselor is once again acting as an anxiety-reduction agent, by providing support, and is preparing the parent for the new dynamic which is about to take place. The counselor is also reinforcing a specific behavioral objective emanating from the team conference. In addition, the counselor makes frequent use of telephone contact to report on the child's progress in school and to see if there have been any changes at home. It is especially important here to reinforce positive behavior change. At this stage in the process, telephone a parent specifically to let him know about a positive development that has occurred in school. It is not a good idea to call the parent to report yet another negative incident. He already receives enough of these from other sources. During this relearning process, the child is still going to revert to his undesirable behaviors until new patterns have been firmly established. Therefore, the school administration may have to exert disciplinary measures in response to specific undesirable behaviors. The parent often becomes hostile and defensive at this point, viewing the school as undermining all the good that's being done, being insensitive to the fact that the child is really trying, and so forth. The counselor now functions as an intermediary in *three* ways: he helps the parent to release his anger, he helps the administrator to moderate his disciplinary approach; and he helps the child in incidences of regression by recognizing positive effort at self-management.

Sometimes there are children who present very similar dynamics both at home and in school. In such cases, a counselor may want to try working with the parents of these children in small groups. There are some excellent source materials available. A body of literature is slowly developing which describes some specific goals, techniques, and expected outcomes in working with parents of children who present a wide spectrum of problems both at home and in school.

A few brief words of caution are in order before leaving this topic. Working with parents presents its hazards as well as its rewards. Great care needs to be taken in both what and how communication takes place. A counselor may think he is helping when in fact a parent may be reacting with greater anger, hostility, and defensiveness than he did to begin with. An understanding of this is endemic to the relationship process. However, being understanding and being alert are two separate issues. Better to say too little than too much. Better to write comments and conference reports with an eye to parsimony than verbosity. It is well to remember to have parents sign release forms for the transfer of confidential information, and to have them read and initial any written reports of conferences in which they have participated. In this day of legal sensitivity, the wise counselor will assume as a priority the protection of the rights of all persons concerned.

Conclusion

In retrospect, we find some common threads running through each of the preceding topics. One is the need to establish select meaningful working relationships with the other adults who are involved in creating an impact on a child's home and school life. The element of developing sound interpersonal adult relationships is one of the basic tenets of becoming an effective counselor. It can be demonstrated, even in this limited discussion, that upon good interpersonal adult relationships hinges the effectiveness of a counselor's interventions. A counselor with serious relationship problems will have difficulty meeting the demands of the various situations described, which only produces frustration for the counselor and a lack of confidence in the counselor as a professional.

Another commonality is that of initiative and action. The days of a counselor sitting in his office, doing primarily individual counseling with students, is over. Counselor case loads are far too heavy, the needs of many students too great, and guidance programs too extensive for counselors to retreat behind closed doors. A counselor must be a visible, dynamic, initiatory kind of person in order to be able to function within today's guidance framework. If he isn't that kind of a person by nature, then he may need to seek the kind of training which will help him to operate in this way on the job. What is being suggested here is not personality change in the counselor but rather behavior change within the context of his employment setting.

Yet another common thread is that of being able to create an atmosphere of warmth, acceptance, and trust. This holds true for all the different adults with whom he must relate, in addition to the students who are in his care. At the same time, working conditions demand that he be an analytical and cautious person, have an awareness and sensitive understanding of where people are coming from, and be able to deal with the realities of life.

This is a large order for a counselor to fill. But no one within the field ever said that counseling was easy. A counselor may have his critics, may feel discontinuity, ambiguity, and isolation. Yet he will also have great satisfaction along the way, watching relationships develop, seeing behavior modified, and watching systems change — knowing that he played a major role in making it possible for the lives of children to be different in a school which dared to grow.

Supplementary Readings

Dinkmeyer, D., and Carlson, J. *Consulting: Facilitating Human Potential and Change Processes.* Columbus, Ohio: Merrill, 1973.

Dinkmeyer, Don C. *Guidance and Counseling in the Elementary School.* New York: Holt, Rinehart and Winston, 1968.

English, H. B., and English, A. C. *A Comprehensive Dictionary of Psychological and Psycholanalytical Terms.* New York: McKay, 1974.

Gorn, Janice L. *Style Guide.* New York: Simon and Schuster, 1973.

Hollis, J. W., and Hollis, L. U. *Organizing for Effective Guidance.* Chicago: Science Research Associates, 1965.

Peters, Herman J., and Aubrey, Roger F. *Guidance Strategies and Techniques.* Denver: Love, 1975.

EPILOGUE

The counselor's role in the middle school is one of child advocacy. Middle school guidance should help foster the best educational environment possible and then seek to help the student participate to the maximum level of his talents. The counselor must be sensitive to the needs of the teacher, the child, the parents, and the administrator, while keeping a clear focus on helping establish a school climate in which learning is a natural pleasure. Such a school climate keeps the mind open and receptive to experiences. The counselor needs to assist the student and those who accept responsibility for his growth by providing pertinent information to help determine the direction in which this creative growth can go. Learning should extend one's life into new dimensions that increase in scope with the passage of time.

Knowledge cannot be internalized in isolation of emotional growth. Positive feelings about oneself provide the confidence needed to be daring and adventure into the unknown. The middle school years have been identified throughout this book, by a variety of experts, as years of trial and conflict. It is a crucial time for the child in determining his values and ideas that will provide the foundation upon which he will base not-too-distant decisions. It is essential for the schools to deliver a trained person who can help the child discover his strengths and cope with weaknesses. Consequently, wise contributions may be made to difficult situations. Many of these choices will be the decisions with which the youngster must live in his adult years. Middle school guidance counselors should strive to develop a harmonious individual. Middle school is the place to start searching for the characteristics needed to live and lead a productive life in this contemporary world.

Self exploration is extremely difficult for the middle schooler, who is characterized as explosive, exploratory, and insurrectionary by those who live and work with him. Instead of integrating talents and interests, these youngsters seem to seek outward and move in conflicting directions simultaneously meeting insurmountable road-blocks and frustrating obstacles. To provide a realistic self-view of a student's direction, it is necessary for the counselor to emphasize the importance of looking at the total person as a harmonious unit. In essence, guidance services should accept the responsibility for cementing the components of the person and bringing into focus a harmony with the person's self concept.

Guidance and counseling services must attempt to identify and accept positive and productive attitudes which help one to grow intellectually and socially. The counselor, teacher, or parent who encourages the young child's searching curiosity will help the middle-schooler prepare for a balanced life. The guidance of the youth of today, which allows for and encourages differences and emphasizes the struggle for achievement as a worthy experience, provides the setting for a better world.

APPENDIX A

Forms and Organizational Guidelines

Guidance services are oftimes misused or unused for a very simple reason—lack of clearly defined organizational guidelines. Various aspects of the guidance services necessitate clarity of contact and services. Answers are needed to such questions as: Who is responsible for what services? What are the time schedules for special activities and where are these schedules available? What forms are used to obtain contacts and materials? What is the internal organizational pattern? What techniques and forms are used to communicate with the school community and receiving agencies? Each school will need to formulate its own forms and guidelines to facilitate maximum use of its services. We have provided here samples of forms used effectively by middle school guidance staff to aid teachers, students, and parents in their school activities and classroom management, to identify appropriate personnel to fulfill specific needs, and to provide techniques for a smooth running coordinated active school environment.

Form A–1 is made available to teachers at the school office. It is completed by any teacher who feels that a specific child needs specialized attention from the guidance staff, the school psychologist, or any specialist in the school.

Form A–2 identifies staff members who have special responsibilities in servicing teacher and student needs. This is an especially helpful form that should be in each teacher's possession. It has to be kept current. The new teacher finds it a welcome time-saving device

261

Form A–1

Name of School
Referral to Pupil Study Team

Pupil's Name _____ Grade _____

Birthdate _____ Address _____

Referring Teacher _____ Subject _____

Description of Problem:

Achievement:

Behavior:

_____   _____
Date of Referral   Signature of Teacher

Form A-2

WHO DOES WHAT?

Teacher A—Room 2

Textbooks
Supplies
Parking system
Student insurance
Magazines
Student lockers
Grade books
Buzzer schedule
Announcements
Lunch
Student guide
Substitutes (phone: 872-7328)
Assembly seating
Morning meditation
Calendar

Teacher B—Room 104

Athletic program
Activity sponsors
Audiovisual aids
Television
Film orders

Teacher C—Room 5

Master schedule
Rotation system
Class assignment
Available records
Warning notices
Guidance procedures
Study halls
Teacher assignments
Counseling

Teacher D—Room 27

Data processing
Duplicating materials
Telephone
Office forms
Report periods
Attendance

Teacher E—Library

Special reservations for use of library
Magazine orders
Special interdistrict book needs

in the confusion of adjustment to the multitude of responsibilities that are part of his new job.

Most middle schools send some form of progress report to parents before the actual report card. Parents who receive failing notices usually respond by calling the school office. These calls are directed to the counselor to whom the particular student is assigned. The follow-up responsibility of the counselor is to respond to the parent by either arranging a parent-counselor-teacher conference, arranging an appointment convenient to teacher and parent alone, or involving the student in the conference. The most appropriate procedure is determined through the response to parent request and teacher and counselor coordination. One form used is the letter mailed to the student's home (Form A-3) and sent midway through the marking period. Supportive of this letter to parents is a report completed for the student's and counselor's records by the classroom teacher that identifies the underlying cause of the unsatisfactory performance. This will assist the counselor in his response to the initial parent inquiry (Form A-4).

One of the goals of middle school is to help the student become more self-directing in his learning than he could be in the traditional school program. Forms and guidelines made available to the students assist in making the goal a reality.

Often the guidance staff follow through on placement of students needing specialized instructional services. Working with a teacher-sponsor, the counselor may provide the contact for the student who desires tutoring or is recommended for this supplementary aid by his teacher. The following forms have been found helpful in providing this service. Form A-5 is completed by the student available to tutor.

Form A-6 illustrates student tutor request form information giving details of area of needs. The student may request a particular tutor, if desired.

The third form (A-7) is sent to the tutor to provide him with basic information and determine his acceptance of the responsibility.

The student receiving the tutoring is sent Form A-8.

This program has proved very successful as a supplementary aid to teachers. Once the initial planning is completed, it may be carried out entirely by students. The availability of students' schedules, grades, and records to the guidance staff provides a practical location for this service.

Form A-3

Name of School

Phone: _____

Date

Dear Parents:

We have not reached the midpoint of the first marking period. As is our custom in this school we have consulted all of our teachers to determine the progress being made by each student.

According to our records _____ is experiencing difficulty in the following subject areas:

(subject) (Teacher)

_____   _____
_____   _____
_____   _____
_____   _____
_____   _____

The purpose of this letter is to seek your cooperation in correcting this problem. We ask that you encourage your child to meet immediately with his or her teachers. We also invite you to call your child's guidance counselor for a more detailed report on the problem.

The first marking period will end on _____ so there is still time for your child to achieve on a satisfactory level.

Thank you for your attention to this matter.

Very truly yours,

Guidance Counselor

Form A–4

(5 × 8 card)

Student _____ Grade ____ Year ____

Address _____

Instructions: write course title, identifying numbers, and your initials.

Course	1st Marking Period	2nd Marking Period	3rd Marking Period	4th Marking Period
Math I	1, 4, 5, 8 JA			
Home Ec.	2, 7 GP			

Explanation:

1—Failing the marking period as of this date
2—Passing but working below capacity
3—Work shows a marked decline
4—Homework assignments incomplete or not turned in
5—Response in class poor
6—Test preparation inadequate
7—Excessive absence
8—Unprepared
9—Disruptive behavior
10—Other (explain)

Form A-5

Name _____

Address _____ Telephone _____

Home room number _____ Grade _____

Free periods _____

After-school time and days free (if any) _____

Subject can teach _____ Level _____

_____   _____

Form A-6

STUDENT REQUEST FORM

Name _____

Home Room _____ Grade _____

Subject _____ Period _____

Free Period _____

Teacher _____ Counselor _____

Comments or requests _____

Form A-7

TUTOR INFORMATION FORM

You have been requested to tutor

Name _____ Home Room _____ Subject _____

Teacher _____ Counselor _____

during your free period on _____
                                          day   time

Please contact _____ within the next
                         name of student

three school days. If you have any questions or problems, please contact
me.

_____

Tutor program secretary

Form A-8

STUDENT TUTORING APPOINTMENT

_____ has been assigned to you as your tutor
            name of tutor

in _____ . If he or she does not contact you
            subject

within the next few days see me.

He or she will tutor you during _____ . He or she will be in contact
with you within the next three school days. You may contact him or her
if you wish. It would be helpful to contact your teacher for materials.

268

Communication with the counselor must be a simple procedure. Various schools use different techniques for this vital contact. Often a mail box that is equipped with request forms (A–9) is used. This is followed by return forms which provide the time for the appointment, but should not prevent a student or parent from coming to the guidance office without previous notice.

Probably one of the most significant forms is the evaluation of the services provided by the guidance staff. It is important to determine if the guidance staff's services provide what they feel they provide and whether these services are the services wanted and needed by the staff, students, and community (Form A–10).

These samples illustrate the importance of simplicity in forms and organizational guidelines of any guidance function. All material distributed by the guidance staff should be clearly identified as a guidance service so that questions, comments, and criticism may be directed to the sender for change and follow-through. A notification of a service not identified will usually be discarded. But identification has a two-fold purpose. The administrator who knows and sees the steady flow of identifiable services from guidance personnel will not be so inclined to place busywork on the already busy guidance staff. The lament concerning inappropriate activities of counselors will be eliminated for the counselor who is too busy performing identifiable counseling-related tasks.

The initial step in organization of a guidance staff is to look critically at the services you perform, decide how these services can be managed more efficiently and proceed to delegate the responsibility to the staff for putting these ideas into action. Never overlook the suggestions of teaching staff, administration, and students. Through ongoing evaluation and a team approach the guidance services of a school can become a maximal functioning team working cooperatively to provide fast, efficient, and appropriate responses to staff, student, and community needs.

Teachers and administrators are often unfamiliar with the counselor's responsibilities. To assist in clarification of the middle school counselor's role, these responsibilities have been clearly defined (Form A–11). The guidance program description identifies *what* the teacher can expect from the counselor and *when* specific activities such as testing, group activities, and other special events will take place. These forms are also helpful for the school that has few or no guidance counselors, for they clearly identify the services that a

Form A–9

COUNSELOR CONTACT FORM

Name _____ Home Room _____

Free Period _____

Question or problem _____

Your Counselor _____

Form A–10

GUIDANCE EVALUATION FORM

Please rate in order of importance in Column I these guidance services provided by our staff. Please rate in Column II the services you personally used this year. Thank you.

	Column I			Column II			
	Definitely	Maybe	Not Important	Often	Sometimes	Never	Unaware that this service is available
1. Placement of new students within class							
2. Resource person							
3. Helping in transition and adjustment of new students in school							
4. Periodic evaluation of progress							
5. Counseling of students referred by faculty							
6. Testing service							

	Column I				Column II			
	Definitely	Maybe	Not Important		Often	Sometimes	Never	Unaware that this service is available
7. Follow-through on referred cases								
8. Follow-through on special recommendations as to pupil placement								
9. Orientation in preparation for school transition								
10. Cumulative folder updating								
11. In-service programs for teachers								
12. Public relations with community								
13. Consultation with teachers and visit to classroom upon invitation								
14. Orientation program for new teachers								
15. Group guidance services								
16. Career information								
17. Group counseling services								
18. Tutoring program leadership								
19. In-service program for parents								
20. Crisis counseling								
21. Consultation services for parents								

Adaptation from form courtesy of Patricia Kerr, Counselor, Bensalem Township, Pennsylvania.

Form A–11

RESPONSIBILITIES OF THE GUIDANCE OFFICE

1. Coordinate California Achievement Testing program
   a. Set up test schedule
   b. Be responsible for all supplies
   c. Interpret test results to teachers
   d. Interpret test results to parents

2. Plan and coordinate 3 back to school nights—grades 5–7 (October)

3. Plan a daytime open-house program for grades 5–7 during American Education Week

4. Coordinate orientation for incoming 4th grade—students and parents (spring)
   a. Visit and speak with all 4th-grade students
   b. Meet with each 4th-grade teacher concerning each student—take notes to help make placement
   c. Hostess evening open house for parents
   d. Meet with concerned parents concerning placement for the following year

5. Make sure all cum folders are up to date
   a. Each fall folders of incoming students are sorted out
   b. Each spring supervise updating of current information on cards

6. Make sure confidential folders are up to date
   a. Make a list of all evaluations and dates of latest tests
   b. Furnish data to teachers

7. Help specialists become more aware of students who need special consideration because of particular learning, emotional, or discipline problems

8. Serve on committees—both districtwide and school
   a. Chairperson
   b. Member
   c. Advisor

9. Coordinate college tutorial program
   a. Rider
   b. Trenton State

10. Coordinate parent-aide program
    a. Screen applicants
    b. In-service program for aides
    c. Assign aides to classes that desire aide help

11. Supervise guidance practicum teacher(s)

12. Coordinate visitors' program (approximately 300 per year)
    a. Administrators from other districts
    b. Professors and students
       1. Trenton State
       2. Rider

13. Submit a monthly guidance report

14. Meet with various community agencies who service our children
    a. Private physicians
    b. Child guidance
    c. Therapy clinic
    d. Local community center

15. Conduct teacher in-service for teacher-parent conferencing techniques

16. Prepare awareness list for 8th-grade counselors

17. Act as a consultant to E.T.S. on their testing program

18. Responsible for guidance secretary and constant updating of her job description

19. Take part in career awareness day in May (part of Operation Quest)

20. Accompany some 6th-grade teachers on industry field trips

21. 5th Grade
    a. Orientation
    b. Help teachers to become aware of individual students' problems
    c. Classroom guidance sessions once a week (Sept.–Dec.)
    d. Individual meetings with each child
    e. Crisis counseling
    f. Parent-teacher-counselor conferences

    6th Grade
    a. Helping teachers to become aware of individual students' problems
    b. Classroom guidance (Jan.–May)
    c. Individual meetings with each child

    d. Crisis counseling

    e. Small group counseling (Sept.–Dec.)

    f. Parent-teacher-counselor conferences

7th Grade

    a. Helping teachers to become aware of individual students' problems

    b. Crisis counseling

    c. Teacher-counselor meetings

    d. Parent-teacher-counselor conferences

22. Setting up classes

23. Writing up teacher-parent-counselor reports based on conferences

24. Attend Mercer County guidance meetings

25. Meet with 4th-grade principal on an ongoing basis

26. Meet with the following administrators on an ongoing basis

    a. Principal

    b. Vice-principal

    c. Assistant superintendent (in charge of elementary schools)

27. Take an active part in public relations

    a. Neighborhood coffees

    b. Evening parent testing seminars

28. Attendance at district principal meetings by invitation to discuss pertinent information

ADDITIONAL YEARLY COUNSELOR RESPONSIBILITIES

1. The writing of department goals, objectives, and indicators (fall).

2. P.T.O. Executive Board meetings (monthly—8:00 p.m.).

3. Attendance at Faculty Council meetings.

4. Attend "Back to School Nights" (5, 6, 7)

5. The writing of the monthly Counselor-Guide Letter.

6. Keep a daily log of all guidance-counselor related activities.

7. Preparation of a monthly administrative report.

8. Write lesson plans for classroom guidance sessions and submit them to administration.

9. Record minutes of Special Services Meetings.

10. Coordinate seventh-grade assessment testing.

11. Coordinate sixth-grade California Achievement Testing.

12. Ongoing membership in Student Records Committee (Chairperson 1974–75).

13. Coordinate visitations of Trenton State students and their professors.

14. Lead grade level parent seminars (fifth–fall; sixth–winter; seventh–spring).

15. Prepare yearly guidance budget.

16. Process student referrals.

17. Ongoing professional agency contact.

18. Supervision of guidance intern.

19. Meet with ongoing contact with admission people from area private schools.

20. Coordinate parent-aide program.

21. Coordinate visitation schedule of educators from local school systems.

22. NYPUM Advisory Committee member.

23. Coordinate Trenton State College volunteer tutors.

24. Coordinate "American Education Week."

25. Coordinate seventh-grade students' and parents' orientation to eighth grade, as well as supplying applicable data to South Campus counselors.

26. Coordinate fourth-grade students' and parents' orientation to fifth grade.

27. Set up classes for all grades (spring).

---

counselor performs; these responsibilities may be assigned to teachers or other school personnel with guidance training.

The awareness of the counselor's schedule (Form A–12) helps the teacher plan for interaction with the counseling staff at the appropriate and convenient time for both teacher and counselor. The counselor's schedule can only suggest a general routine, for crisis and emergency situations are typical throughout the school day. Presenting even the briefest schedule also helps the teacher become more aware of the counselor's role. For those schools that desire more specific organizational guidelines, Form A–13 may be helpful. Here the counseling staff lists specifically in greater detail the areas of emphasis during the school year.

Form A–12

DAILY GUIDANCE SCHEDULE
(Tentative)

8:10 A.M.	Arrive at school
8:30–9:00	Consultation time: teachers, parents, or children (in order of most frequent occurrence)
9:00–9:30	Check with LDS, nurse, vice-principal, and principal concerning student matters such as: truancy, absences, parent information, new insights into student behavior (Thursday—9:00–10:00 special services meetings)
9:30–10:00	Return calls from parents from late preceding P.M. and early present A.M. Call parents regarding newly acquired information from present 9:00–9:30 A.M. conferences
10:00–12:00	a. Classroom observations of students b. Checking of guidance data, i.e., updating enrollment numbers, scanning newly arrived student data from preceding schools or special services office c. Occasional home visit d. Call agencies that are used by our school, i.e., learning clinic, child centers, etc. e. Meet with teachers concerning classroom problems f. Parent conferences (both with and without teachers) g. Crisis counseling—brought to my attention by the nurse, teacher, parent, or child h. Paper work—involving planning to testing seminars, American Education Week, in-school testing programs, orientation programs for parents and students, planning classroom guidance schedules, writing of notes to teachers concerning arrangements for parent conferences i. Conferring with student practicum counselor(s) about assignments and progress
12:00 P.M.	Return phone calls to parents which have come in from 10:00 to 12:00 or when I've been out of my office
12:15	Lunch—usually in my office to continue work from 10:00 to 12:00 time slot

1:00	6th-grade guidance group each day (behavior modification with the emphasis on improving social attitudes and behavior)
1:45–2:15	5th-grade classroom guidance—6th-grade individual
2:15–2:30	Check in at guidance office for any emergencies
2:30–3:00	5th-grade classroom guidance—6th-grade individual
3:00	Return phone calls for afternoon
3:15–4:00	Leave school between 4:00 and 5:30—Mon., Tues., Wed. and Thurs. and 3:15 Friday

1. College students and their professors tour our school facility on a regularly scheduled basis each semester. These visits are generally twelve times a year. Also administrators and teachers from other school districts are generally accompanied by a counselor during their half-day visit.

2. Visits to agencies who service our children are made when more information is needed on the part of the agency or the school. These usually occur four or five times a year.

3. If a *crisis* situation occurs—*all previously scheduled activities must be cancelled.*

Form A–13

THE MIDDLE SCHOOL GUIDANCE PROGRAM

The guidance office actually begins the new school year the last week in August. At this time, parents and counselor confer by appointment, new registrants are placed in classes, new staff members are met and helped to understand the guidance services, and incoming student data is checked and noted. Incoming fourth-grade cumulative folders are cleared of incidental materials.

I. Fall (September–December)

A. Each of the classroom teachers meets with the counselor to discuss the characteristics of the children with whom he is working.

B. After the initial meeting, teachers are encouraged to seek help from the counselor on an ongoing basis. This usually involves seeing four or five teachers a day.

C. Each teacher is seen on a check conference basis once a month even if he hasn't initiated a conference.

D. All student referral cards are directed by teachers to special services through the guidance office:
   1. Teacher-counselor conference
   2. Pupil observation by the counselor
   3. Counselor gives referral to special service team
   4. Joint action on referral as to how to handle referral
   5. Follow-up
E. Administrative personnel—counselor consults with administrators on an ongoing basis:
   1. Counselor-assistant superintendent of elementary education
   2. Counselor-helping teacher
   3. Counselor-4th grade principal
   4. Counselor-principal to discuss many facets of the school program
   5. Counselor-vice-principal to discuss discipline crisis cases
F. Developmental guidance program in grade 5 begins weekly in September. Topics included in the afternoon classroom visitations at which classroom teachers are asked to remain are:
   1. Coming to a New School
   2. Friendships
   3. Feelings
   4. Interesting Life Experiences
   5. Group Behavior
   6. Individual Behavior
   7. School Problems
   8. Home Problems
   (This program generally continues until Christmas.)
G. Sixth-grade guidance is based on fall afternoon meetings with each student or in a small group of 2 or 3 to discuss "self." Goals are:
   1. To help each student see the counselor as a friendly, humane person
   2. To help middle school children feel comfortable in a guidance office atmosphere
   3. To help the child feel that in spite of the size of the school, he and his opinions are important
   (Behavior modification groups for 6th-graders are held as needed. This need is brought to our attention by the classroom teacher.)

II. Winter (January–March)

    A. Fifth-graders are seen individually or in small groups to discuss "self." Each group or individual meets with the counselor for about 20 minutes.

    B. Classroom guidance for 6th-graders begins:

        1. Rap sessions—the ideas for discussion come from the students.

        2. Discussions motivated by the SRA Focus Series

        3. Teachers often suggest topics or classroom problems and attitudes which concern them.

    C. In the past, the 8th-grade guidance program has been (in addition to the spring 8th-grade orientation program):

        1. A group interest inventory to establish a basis for individual or small group counselor-student conferences (twice a year).

        2. Weekly counseling sessions with kids with school or peer adjustment problems.

    Note: Classroom guidance and individual meetings are arranged for the afternoon, as teachers prefer this. Reading and math are generally in the morning. We also work around the specialists' schedules when possible.

III. Spring (April–June)

    A. Orientation of incoming 5th-graders (currently 4th) and their parents.

        1. Meet with 4th-grade principal.

        2. Meet with each of the 4th-grade teachers to discuss each child and his individual needs and possible 5th-grade placement.

        3. Meet with special service team from 4th-grade school to discuss children with outstanding problems.

        4. Place children in classes for the incoming year and share these lists with 4th-grade principal to make sure chemistry is favorable.

        5. Hold an evening orientation program for parents.

            a. Introduction of staff

            b. Brief presentation of school goals

            c. Tour of the building

            d. Coffee and question time

B. Orientation of out-going 8th-grade children and their parents to the South Campus (High) School.
1. Meet with each child to set up 8th-grade schedule.
2. Set up mutual visitations between middle school staff and South Campus staff.
3. Evening meeting with parents to acquaint them with 8th-grade program (counselors from both schools).
4. Prepare an awareness list for South Campus counselors, learning specialist, and psychologist.
5. Check cum folders to make sure all student data are updated and standardized test results are on.

In order for classroom teachers, administrators, and counselors to work toward common goals, these goals need to be defined. One middle school developed goals and objectives describing the general responsibility of the counselor followed by specific activities that reflected these responsibilities (Form A–14). The general goals remain firm each year while the objectives are modified to meet the recognized needs of the students, staff, and parents.

Forms and organizational guidelines are essential in bringing an efficient and competent guidance service to a school. It is important that flexibility be practiced, for without this the very guidelines developed to give structure can become restrictive and handicap the growth of the program. As the guidance program becomes an integral part of the school, forms can be lessened and the natural interaction among persons will provide much of the structure previously outlined. Therefore, the staff is continually involved in an ongoing evaluation that includes the processes and procedures it uses to function.

A brief evaluation by parents (Form A–15) and students (Form A–16), or a detailed evaluation as described in the chapter on accountability, will provide the counseling staff with feedback helpful in determining their structural and organizational needs within the school community.

Form A–14

Name of School

Guidance Department

The guidance and counseling program is geared to reflect these goals and objectives.

Goal 1

The middle school counselor must be committed to the concepts involved in helping the children bridge the gap between the growing processes of childhood and adolescence.

Objectives (grades 5, 6 and 7, 8).

1. The counselor must be a leader in helping the child develop internal moral control and a set of values (Piaget); i.e., personalized learning (Hummel).
2. The counselor must strive to help appropriate counselees alleviate the feelings of anxiousness, poor adjustment, unpopularity, and defensiveness which result from a poor self-concept (McCandless).
3. The developmental counselor must be concerned for all children in the school population, and not just the problem oriented child (Dinkmeyer).

Goal 2

The guidance staff provides the needed leadership and resources for creating an awareness among administrators and teachers for the purpose of providing an environment which is necessary to meet the needs of middle school youngsters.

Objectives (grades 5, 6 and 7, 8).

1. The counselors must help all staff understand that the social and emotional needs of the middle school child are of significant importance.
2. By serving in the role of consultants to staff, the counselors can encourage the understanding of the child as he moves from dependence to independence as a learner (Bloom-Piaget-Kagan).

Goal 3

The middle school counselor, as a specialist in child growth and development, can help parents provide an atmosphere which will encourage the child to develop self-assurance, self-awareness, and good learning habits.

Objectives (grade 5)

1. The counselor must make a concentrated effort to help parents of incoming students feel comfortable in the environment of the middle school and encourage their participation in parent orientation programs.
2. Through individual communication with parents of fifth-grade children, the parents will become increasingly aware of the services offered by the counselors.
3. By assuming the leadership role in parent seminars, the counselor can encourage the parent to be the liaison between the school and home by encouraging his child to search and explore for a better understanding of the world about him.

Form A–15

Name of School

Parental Guidance/Counseling Survey

_____ Counselor _____ Counselor
      (name)   (name)

_____ Principal
          (name)

Please underline the appropriate response when possible.

1. The counselor with whom I communicated was
   a. Mrs. (name)
   b. Mr. (name)
   c. both counselors
2. We met in
   a. the counselor's office
   b. spoke by phone
3. Those involved were
   a. mother and counselor
   b. father and counselor
   c. both parents and counselor
   d. child, parent(s), and counselor
   e. other (please explain)

4. I felt that I was treated cordially by the guidance secretary and the counselor(s).
   a. yes
   b. no

5. In my opinion, the time allotted for my conference was
   a. more than adequate
   b. adequate
   c. less than adequate

6. I left the counselor with the feeling that I and the matter at hand had been treated with
   a. sincere concern
   b. adequate concern
   c. impersonally

The following responses require short narrative answers.

1. In what ways, if any, do you find the guidance services at the middle school are helpful to you and your family?

2. Do you believe your child views his or her counselor in a positive or negative way? Please explain.

3. As a parent, do you believe you understand the role of the middle school counselor? Would parent seminars, guidance newsletters, or more information at parent orientations and Back to School Nights be helpful to you? Please clarify your answer by explaining which would be most beneficial.

4. We would be most receptive to any suggestions you might care to make.

Thank you for taking your time to answer this questionnaire. It is not imperative that you sign your name.

Form A-16

STUDENT QUESTIONNAIRE

My counselor's name _____

Instructions:

a. Please read each question carefully and check only one space for each answer.

b. Do not answer any question that does not apply to you.

c. Do not sign your name.

Questions:

1. I think my counselor tries to understand the problems boys and girls have.

   _____ yes _____ no _____ sometimes

2. Does it matter if your guidance counselor is a lady or a man?

   _____ yes _____ no _____ sometimes

3. I have visited alone with my guidance counselor.

   _____ yes _____ no

4. I feel my guidance counselor genuinely cares about me.

   _____ yes _____ no _____ sometimes

5. I feel better after I talk with my counselor.

   _____ yes _____ no _____ sometimes

6. I can trust my counselor.

   _____ yes _____ no _____ sometimes

7. I like my counselor to visit in my classroom.

   _____ yes _____ no _____ sometimes

8. When my counselor visits our classroom, he shows a real interest in what we are doing.

   _____ yes _____ no _____ sometimes

9. My guidance counselor is a fair person who listens to all sides of the story.

   _____ yes _____ no _____ sometimes

10. I have been sent to the guidance office for discipline.

   _____ yes _____ no

11. I went to the guidance office to complain about a student misbehaving.

    _____ yes   _____ no

    (only if you answered yes to either question 10 or question 11 should
    you answer this next question 12.)

12. I feel my counselor tried to handle this discipline fairly.

    _____ yes   _____ no   _____ sometimes

13. My counselor really tries to help work out a problem.

    _____ yes   _____ no   _____ sometimes

14. My counselor is interested in the things that interest me.

    _____ yes   _____ no

How do you think your counselor can help boys and girls more?

APPENDIX B

The Role of the Child Study Team

In order to clarify how children are diagnosed as "special education students" we requested that the role of the Child Study Team be clearly defined. Dr. Arthur Shapiro, Coordinator of Child Study Teams for Central and Southern New Jersey, offered the following information:

Some children have problems that are chronic and whose causes are often not easily discernible. Regular classroom procedures do not reach them and temporary remedial measures prove ineffective. These are the children who are most likely to be referred for an in-depth analysis as well as an individualized program based on that analysis. In order to plan effectively for their education, it is necessary to know as much as possible about their deficits, abilities, and the educational environment in which they function. All exceptional children should be provided with a clinically designed educational program based on a thorough understanding of the characteristics and needs of the person.

When learning does not progress at a normal rate for such a child, it is essential that the teacher and counselor be able to call upon the services of specialized personnel to help pinpoint the exact nature of the educational problem. The group of educational specialists whose particular skills are necessary to identify, evaluate, and devise an appropriate strategy for ameliorating or circumventing these problems is the diagnostic, or child study team. Because of the various specialties represented and the need to coordinate their efforts to be effective, these professionals must function as a team in a joint manner.

The actual composition of the child study team may vary from case to case, depending upon its nature. Many states have legislation mandating such teams. For example, a basic child study team in New Jersey consists of a school psychologist, a school social worker, a learning consultant, and appropriate medical personnel. The child study team may also include such professionals as medical specialists from the fields of neurology, psychiatry, pediatrics, the school nurse, educational personnel from areas such as reading, speech, vision, hearing, adaptive physical education, special education, classroom teaching, administration, and, of course, guidance.

How does a child needing help come to the attention of the child study team? Children who fail to make an adequate school adjustment emotionally, socially, or academically may come to the attention of the team in one of several different ways. Parents themselves may ask the superintendent of schools, the principal, or the director of special services to consider their child's special needs either before or after he enters school. Or the child may be brought to the attention of the team by the school principal, the guidance counselor, the school nurse, or the regular classroom teacher.

The process of identification is very important at the middle school level. It is important for the child study team to work with teachers in the middle school to develop a frame of reference for selecting students in need of help in order to prevent serious long-term consequences that happen in the lives of children because of unrecognized physical and psychological problems. It has been demonstrated time and again that one of the most important people in the child's life, when it comes to the early recognition of such problems, is the classroom teacher. Very often, it is the teacher's knowledge of normal developmental patterns which alert her to early difficulties and thereby initiate the process of diagnosis and remediation by the team. Because many problems, both physical and emotional in nature, may be discovered at this level of interaction, every school should make an effort to encourage this type of awareness on the part of the total faculty.

Once a referral is made, the child study team obtains as much information as possible regarding the child through testing, observation, and conferences with the school staff and parents. Information from other sources may also be requested by the team or submitted by the parents. In approximately one out of every four cases of children referred, the case study by the team may reveal other needs. The school district may then seek the services of ophthalmologist, otologist, audiologist, neurologist, and other specialist. Such in-depth studies thus necessitate many hours of professional services.

Once a child has been referred to the child study team, the school psychologist will usually see him on a one-to-one basis and administer tests to explore his social and emotional functioning as well as his intellectual strengths and weaknesses. Tests and techniques have been developed that permit the school psychologist to discover the signs of potential emotional problems, often before parents, themselves, are aware of them. In addition, the tests can determine the existence of such phenomena as mental retardation, developmental or perceptual lags, and neurological impairments.

Other diagnostic tools aid the psychologist in measuring the child's intelligence, potential aptitudes, achievement levels, skills, and interests. The results of each diagnostic study are confidential and are discussed only with those school staff members who are intimately concerned and involved with the child's case.

Although the basic function of the school psychologist is diagnostic rather than therapeutic in nature, the formation of counseling groups is rapidly becoming a part of child study team procedures. At the middle school level the role of the psychologist should also stress counseling, psychological procedures, and effective in-service work with teachers, young adolescents, and parents.

The learning consultant is a teacher with extensive classroom experience who has had additional special training in making educational diagnoses of a child's learning disabilities. He must have the experience, training, and ability to bring to the teaching situation the appropriate learning methods and materials and knowledge of how children learn. The specific diagnostic areas in which the learning consultant is primarily responsible include visual perception, auditory perception, levels of abstract thinking, visual and auditory memory, discovery and measurement of interest, and specific disabilities and learning aptitudes in reading, arithmetic, and work-study skills. Once a child is referred to the team, the learning consultant will usually arrange to see the child within the classroom setting. Through this pupil observation the consultant hopes to get an indication of the child's interaction with his peers as well as his reaction to authority figures, his individual behavior characteristics, his independent work habits, his participation in a group setting, and an overall evaluation of the child's classroom work. The learning consultant is the basic liaison between the child study team and the classroom teacher, with respect to development of academic skills.

Based upon the findings and recommendations of the other members of the team as well as his own, the learning consultant can work out an educational prescription and procedural plan of action with the classroom teacher which may include new or different techniques or special materials depending upon the individual needs of the child.

The school social worker represents the liaison between the school and the home in the joint effort to maintain and sustain a child receiving special educational services. He generally works with the parents and the home in order to obtain information from and about the family that will be of use in the case study. In turn, he also presents the goals and objectives of the school to the family for the purpose of effecting mutual responsibility. The school social worker will usually make a home visit to determine the developmental history of the child, the dynamics of the family group, the current social adjustment of the child, the family's involvement with other community agencies, areas where he can be of present or future service in referring the family to other community sources, and the parents' perception of the child's school situation.

The social worker interprets the role of the home environment as it affects the child's behavior in school to the educator. In addition, he also interprets the team's findings to the parents in order for them to better understand their child's needs. As a practitioner in the field of mental health, the school social worker contributes expertise in interviewing techniques, ability to use community resources, and human relationships. He also provides the needed communication channels between the child study team, parents, community agencies, and the school. In his training, the school social worker receives a background in casework and groupwork techniques.

At the middle school level, the social worker must be able to relate in depth to those agencies that deal with preadolescents and adolescents. In addition, the social worker must be in contact with the courts, the probation department, welfare agencies, the rehabilitation commission, narcotic treatment centers, clinics, and so forth.

After reviewing their findings on the child, the members of the team then consider the educational alternatives which can be offered. Parents of handicapped children must be notified in writing when a child has been referred to a child study team. And the child study team must then notify the parent of the classification, educational plan, and the recommended program, which parents have the right to dispute.

At present, the most common educational setting for handicapped children is the special class in the local school district. A recent and accelerating trend is to move children from special class programs into the mainstream of nonhandicapped children's programs, whenever possible. There are many variations in mainstreaming programs, from occasional experiences by handicapped children in integrated programs to complete participation, with supportive services, in the curriculum programs designed for nonhandicapped children. Many handicapped children are given instruction at school supplementary to their regular programs. This additional instruction must be based on the specific recommendations of the child study team. Supplemental instruction may be provided for a child assigned to a special education class as well as for a child maintained in a regular class program. The resource room is one plan which provides special supplementary instruction to handicapped children participating in regular classes. The resource room provides the special equipment and instruction that the pupil needs to succeed in the regular grade. The pupil may receive individual or small group instruction. A comprehensive review of a child's classification and his special education program must be made by the basic child study team within a three-year period after classification.

The mainstreaming concept puts a premium on the interaction between counselors, special education teachers, regular classroom teachers, and child study teams. The mainstream philosophy for the handicapped is based upon the following basic assumptions regarding educational practice:

That interaction with nonhandicapped peers and adults is educationally beneficial for the handicapped.

That it is educationally beneficial to the nonhandicapped to interact, understand, and value the handicapped persons in our society.

Along with the foregoing assumptions, there is a need for the following educational commitments:

1. To provide as many program alternatives as there are needs of handicapped children.
2. A commitment to the educational goal of moving the handicapped from restricted (segregated) educational programs to less restricted (integrated) educational programs and that educational efforts be directed at helping handicapped children enhance the benefits of the integrated setting.

3. The removal of all educational barriers to providing appropriate programs for the handicapped.
4. That all educational programs provide the handicapped with the opportunity for interaction with nonhandicapped peers and adults in some aspects of the educational program.

In order to assure that a mainstream education be provided to children with learning problems, the following programs and services are needed:

1. Preservice or in-service training programs for the regular education teacher which insures:

   Maximum management skills for handling atypical pupils.

   Increased educational, diagnostic, and remediation capabilities.

   Positive attitudes toward keeping handicapped children within the regular class program. (This need also includes school administrators and special education personnel.)
2. Services to prevent and alleviate educational problems for all children before such problems result in handicapping conditions. Such services should minimally include remedial reading, guidance and counseling, and teacher and administrative flexibility to modify the educational program as needed.
3. Potentially handicapped children shall be provided a thorough and complete evaluation by a basic child study team. Such evaluations should include a psychological evaluation, a sociocultural study, a medical evaluation and an educational and learning assessment. This professional evaluation should be available to all children within a school district.
4. The primary purpose of the diagnosis, evaluation, and classification of a handicapped child is to develop an educational prescription and program to best meet the child's educational needs.
5. If mainstreaming can best serve the needs of the handicapped child, the concept should be employed. However, the regular class program must be enhanced by supplementary instruction and/or participation in a Resource Room/Learning Center program.
6. The handicapped child should be provided the services of certified personnel in the areas of art, music, physical education, home economics, and industrial arts on the same basis as nonhandicapped children. Teachers of the handicapped should not be required to teach these subjects to the handicapped children they serve.

Another aspect of the child study team is its role in educational planning and curriculum development. Often, when the child study team participates in education planning, it can propose ways in which the curriculum can be developed to promote academic gain, proper mental health, and the prevention of emotional disturbances. The team should also seek ways to provide opportunities for enrichment of superior students as well as to provide help for slower students. Often the team works closely with the guidance department to help those students who are having difficulty adjusting to the middle school.

The guidance counselor in the middle school should be fully aware of the services within the school district and the community and should help coordinate these services to help the child. It is most critical that guidance counselors in the middle school be both efficient and well prepared. As members of the pupil personnel staff they should know the assets and disabilities of each child. It is up to the pupil personnel services staff to work with the classroom teachers in developing the student's total program. It is from the pupil personnel services team that the classroom teacher receives an additional dimension in the consideration of the many facets of individual development and educational growth. On the middle school level, the classroom teacher should be able to look to the team, including the counselor for helpful information relevant to the child's development and his individual needs, which may not be readily apparent in the classroom, particularly in a departmentalized situation.

Although handicapped students do not display distinctive and unique personalities, they generally do display a larger number of personality problems than their nonhandicapped peers. The reasons for this are (1) the larger number of frustrations they encounter in attempting to solve their problems, (2) the many more situations of nonacceptance and misunderstanding they encounter, and (3) the difficulties they encounter while attempting to develop realistic and healthy self-concepts. Coupled with the developmental stress of preadolescence during the middle school years, the student may find himself overwhelmed without supportive services and special provisions which will help him overcome his learning handicaps. In order to overcome these problems a complete diagnosis coupled with a total coordinated program involving the services of all school personnel must be provided.

INDEX

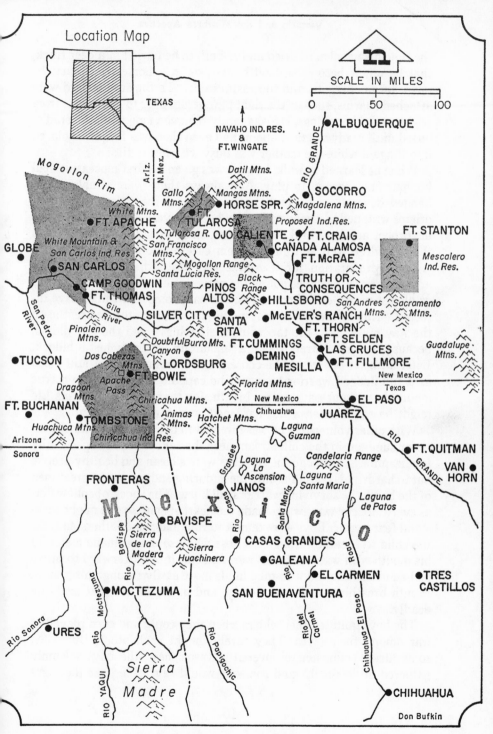

Region of Mimbres Apache Activity, Including Indian Reservations

the time his navel cord dried and fell off, to be buried in a deer track, that he might become a good hunter, or in a horse track, that he might be an energetic and successful raider. To the cradleboard were attached charms, such as the right paw of a badger to guard him from fright, and other things. He was rarely removed long from the cradleboard until ready to crawl about, and even then was frequently laced into it again while the mother was busy with her duties.

When he learned to walk, he soon was given his first moccasins, had his hair cut, learned to play. And always there were rituals, many handed down from beyond the memories of the oldest ones, their origins wrapped in legend and myth, but each very necessary to assure his proper and healthful development, stage by stage. Apaches loved their children well and guided them carefully during their growth. A boy's preparation for war ever was stressed. If, when playing around the *rancheria*, he got on the nerves of his elders, he was never, or almost never, cuffed or beaten. Instead, some adult may have directed, "Run to the top of that mountain! Do not stop to breathe on the way up. Run to the top without stopping!" and the boy did so, because he must. Rarely was it a "mountain" at first; just a hillock. Later a higher one would be chosen, and then one greater still, until as a full-fledged warrior he would be capable of running up a true mountain without pausing for breath, for that was one way his life might be saved when a less-hardened enemy was in pursuit.

With other youngsters he was directed to bathe each morning, winter or summer, in the chill stream near the *rancheria*, not specifically for cleanliness, although the Apaches were a clean and healthy people, but to harden his body, for only the enduring endure, as the great men of the band, the surviving warriors, all knew. The shock of cold water, as every Apache was aware, made the heart strong, so one might withstand fear in war. Boys were taught to run, and some fathers, to train the child to breathe through his nose when so doing, made a son fill his mouth with water before a race and spit it out afterward to prove he had not swallowed it to take in air more easily through his mouth. Mouth breathing made one thirsty, and in the desert that could be deadly.

The boys imitated their elders when they could and even played at war among themselves. They rarely fought each other. But when some lucky youngster discovered a wasps' nest, the boys solemnly gathered in "council," and someone would say, "We hear there are

10

some mean things living over there. Let's go to war with them!" Before a gallery of their elders, gathered at a safe distance, they attacked the nest. Though frequently stung severely, they carried it off in triumph, if they could endure the assaults of the infuriated insects, tore the nest apart, and rubbed themselves with it, saying ritually, "Make me brave!"[27]

While growing, the boy was taught the names and characteristics of the life around him, the trees, the smaller plants, the animals, birds, insects, snakes, about tracks and how to trail, for the keen-eyed Apache was among the world's great practitioners of this subtle art. When old enough, he accompanied his elders on hunts, first serving an apprenticeship with toy bows on small animals and birds about the community. Approaching manhood, he might accompany the men on hunts after deer and perhaps elk. And, while his body was hardened and trained, so was his mind.

He must have seen, from earliest cognizance, the killing of prisoners taken in battle or on raids. A Chiricahua informant told Opler that the captured men were slain quickly, or brought back to the camp to be killed by women who had lost some relative on a raid or war party, and hence merited this ritualistic revenge. Grown men, he said, never were kept alive, either to be married into the tribe or enslaved, because "a mature man is dangerous." The ethnologist quoted several informants to the effect that the Chiricahuas treated Mexicans "in a rough way," largely because the Mexicans did the same to Apaches when they could catch them. Prisoners of the Indians had their hands tied and "then they turned the women loose with axes and knives to kill the Mexican prisoner. The man could hardly run, and the women would chase him around until they killed him." Sometimes the women mounted horses and, clutching lances, dashed at the prisoners, spearing them to death.

On the other hand, children from four to six, when captured, frequently were adopted into the tribe. Women captured were brought back, the men never having sexual relations with them before they reached the *ranchería*, because if they did, "their luck would be spoiled." Even at the camp, such women usually were not sexually disturbed, although eventually they were expected to marry an Apache warrior.[28] Many became well loved, in the Apache way, and quite accepted. The favorite wife of the famous Mangas Coloradas was a Mexican,[29] and so was a wife of his son, Mangus.[30]

11

The Apache boy often was a delighted witness of the victory dance which followed a successful raid, when a captured beef or mule would be butchered and roasted, and the people were happy.

Opinion generally credits the Apaches with being the cruelest, or at least the most merciless, natives of the American continent, but the extent to which this is justified is not established. Certainly they did not make torture a ritual, as did the Iroquois, although there is abundant evidence that cruelty frequently was practiced upon prisoners. There were cruel Apaches, just as there were cruel whites. It is not clear that the one represented a larger percentage of his population than the other, although perhaps there was less social restriction upon Apache cruelty than upon white cruelty. This is not proven either, however. Conner said accurately that "savage civilized men are the most monstrous of all monsters."[31] And, just as there were whites who could not stomach torture of a human being, so there were Apaches who avoided it. "Alien enemies were generally killed instantly, and prolonged torture was not practiced, although a captive sometimes met with a cruel death," wrote Goodwin. "More than one instance was recorded where [Apache] men, knowing this was going to take place, withdrew until it was over, because they could not bear to watch human suffering of this kind."

Nor was cruelty or brutality toward animals universally, or even commonly, practiced, despite the general belief. "Occasionally a man will beat his horse . . . but it is uncommon and considered cruel and likely to bring horse sickness upon the individual. . . . In former times, riding horses with sore backs, or sometimes until they gave out, was not considered cruel because the horse was meant to ride. Not being highly valued, dogs receive rougher treatment than any other domestic animal and frequently go about half-starved. A dog being attacked by others is often left to fight until badly bitten, and dogs who get in the way about camp are likely to get a whack over the back or a boot in the side, but the Apache does not consider this as being cruel. Dogs naturally fight; food is often too scarce to waste on them; they are expected to forage for themselves to a certain extent, and . . . they must be made to get out of the way when underfoot. On the other hand, it is considered cruelty when a child or adult kicks a dog without reason."[32]

The Apache boy grew almost to manhood before being taken on the first of his four apprentice raids, for raiding was dangerous business and he might have to endure what the most hardened men could withstand in order to return safely. Usually he began this exhilarating occupation at about sixteen, although the age varied with the individual. Some boys refused to go out at all, to the scorn of the society, or proved untrustworthy or otherwise unfit and were rejected by the warriors after a raid or two. Obviously, Victorio made good in this rigorous, exacting profession, for it also was a training for war, at which he was to prove a past master. War and raiding, it should be noted, were thought of by the Apaches as distinct endeavors.

During his novitiate, adult warriors sought to prevent his being killed, because that would reflect upon their leadership, but they spared him no hardship. He must fulfill a man's role from the outset, although not ordinarily permitted on his first raids to undertake tasks of great danger. He must go through an earnest preparatory ritual. Relatives and older men told him what to take, how to conduct himself, particularly if separated from the other raiders, to travel only by night unless in the mountains, how to find water (and to avoid searching for it by day no matter how thirsty), where to sleep by day, to avoid deep shade, because that is where an enemy would search for him, how to endure inclement weather, how to conceal himself in grass or brush, and the proper use of smoke signals. These intriguing devices were not, as some would have it, a primitive semaphore, but rather an announcement of some fact such as one's location or the location of friends, or an order to bring in comrades or, with other related signs, to muster strength.

The Apaches used a special vocabulary, almost a distinct language, on war or raiding parties. This, too, must be learned and followed ritually.

The boy was given a drinking tube by a shaman who had to do with things of war, for his lips must not touch water on these first missions; that might bring disaster. With the drinking tube he was given a scratching stick and a special hat, and these three things must be returned to the shaman after the raid, when other boys might inherit their use. His actions on the raid itself were controlled by deepseated beliefs: to turn quickly and look back would bring bad luck; if he failed to use the scratcher his skin would become soft as a woman's; if he did not use the drinking tube his whiskers would grow in an un-Apache way; he must not have sex while out; he must use the warrior's words, or he would be unlucky; he could not eat warm food, for if he did horses would be worthless to him; he could not eat entrails or meat from an animal's head; he must speak respect-

13

fully and not laugh at anyone; no matter how weary, he must not sleep until given permission; he must do the heavy work around the camps, to toughen him.[33] All of these things the young aspirant must understand and do, if he would be a success and one day perhaps become a leader of his people. And Victorio learned them well.

At long last, after his four apprentice missions, he became a fullfledged warrior, for it was only so that successful Apache fighters were developed. He had become an adult. He could raid, fight, and make war. He could smoke, and he could marry. By this time, hopefully, he had acquired horses or mules from some hapless enemy, for these were needed to obtain a wife.

The Chiricahua Apaches were a chaste and modest people with regard to sex. Not only did they avoid carnal relations with whites, but blatant sexuality was frowned upon even among themselves. There was perhaps as little promiscuity among them as in any people of that day, or this. Girls particularly would rarely tolerate advances of this kind, although, of course, there were exceptions, as there are among all people. Boys, who like others elsewhere felt the powerful urges of maturation, tended to confine experimentation to an occasional woman known for looseness, or to a rare girl who might reciprocate, or even to women of other tribes who had not the reserve of their own people.[34]

One above-average agent, who knew them well, described Victorio's people even as late as 1873 as "virtuous." His medical report listing various ailments among them pointed out that "there is no taint of syphilis" in the band, in marked contrast to Indians of many other tribes. This in itself was good evidence of their avoidance of promiscuity and their general sexual restraint.[35]

Somewhere, perhaps at a dance, Victorio found a girl to whom he was attracted, and who liked him, and the odd, casual-appearing courtship ensued. During this the couple might not even hold hands, yet would come to agreement upon sharing a life. He would be prepared to pay for her with a horse or two; if he had been very successful in his early raids, and desired her very much, and if her father demanded a great deal, perhaps the price would be four or five horses, and maybe a saddle or something like that in addition. Such gifts were less tribute than an indication that the young man was economically worthy, and could provide well for a wife. The gifts were accepted by the father and his wife who, as mother-in-law, could never afterward come in face-to-face contact with the husband of her daughter, but who was nonetheless respected and cared for by him and her daughter, his wife. Affection between Apache couples ran as deep as among whites, but to non-Apache eyes and traditions it seemed less profound, a concept very mistaken.

Polygamy was permitted by Apache custom, but Victorio, who apparently could have supported additional wives better than most by reason of the wealth he acquired through extraordinarily successful raids, appears to have loved and remained constant to his one wife throughout his life. At various times censuses were taken of the Mimbres. Typical is that of 1876, when he is listed first on the compilation. He is shown as possessing only one wife, five children, and four sisters or widows for whom he must provide.[36] In no census now extant is he given more than one wife. Victorio must have been a loyal husband and devoted, as was his woman to him, and this says something for the quality, the character, of both.

Having come this far, Victorio could concentrate henceforth on the proper business of a man—raids, war, and, perhaps, if he were more than ordinarily successful, council and leadership. The Apache world, being a self-sufficient community, was surrounded by enemies, near enemies, occasional enemies, or, at any rate, outsiders one must view with suspicion, if not always with hostility. Not all raids were directed against the Mexicans. The Pimas, Navahos, and, on rare occasions, other Apache bands, were also targets. There was room here, plenty of it, for such an active man to develop his unusual potential.

II

The Races Meet

The Mimbres may have joined other Indians in welcoming the bearded white intruders from the south, but hostilities were inevitable, given the warlike natures of Apache and Spaniard, the relative poverty of the one and the riches of the other. At some time, probably in the seventeenth century, the hostilities commenced, to continue for two centuries.[1] By the time Victorio was born, and while he grew to manhood, they seemed endemic, although this problem was not uniquely one of Spanish-Mimbres relations. Spain's whole northern frontier was rimmed by tribes actively or potentially hostile, from the fierce Seris on the west to the belligerent Comanches on the east. The Mimbres, central geographically, also came to be central in Spanish projects for defense.

It is difficult to distinguish clearly the Mimbres from other Apache groups in the numerous Spanish reports of frontier activities. The ethnologist Opler binds the various New Mexico bands together, calling all of them "Eastern Chiricahua," or, as they were known to other Chiricahuas, the Tcokanene, or "Red Paint People."[2] Frequently they were lumped by the Spanish with the "Gila Apaches," a vague term apparently at an early date covering the Yavapais, a non-Apache people living between the Colorado and Gila rivers; the Chiricahuas, central, southern, and eastern; and the San Carlos group, among them the Pinal and Aravaipa Apaches.[3] Occasionally, however, reports refer specifically to Mimbreño Apaches, or in some other way definitely point to that people. Teodoro de Croix, commander general of the interior provinces of New Spain from 1776 to 1783, all but brought peace to that troubled frontier, although weighted with problems, a shortage of manpower, and chronic lack of funds.[4] He reported that the war with the Apaches generally began in 1748 in Nueva Vizcaya, the territory that included modern Chihuahua and some bordering lands, and continued intermittently from that time forward. Even earlier it had become endemic in Sonora, although a troubled peace was established now and then at Janos,

16

in western Chihuahua, and other centers; such intervals never were of long duration. In 1777 Croix reported that the Apaches were overrunning Sonora "with impunity,"[5] horse herds were swept off regularly, and presidio garrisons hard put to defend their posts and herds, let alone engage in punitive operations. All of the road from Fronteras to Janos, crossing a principal Apache raiding route, was "exposed to the most serious blows of the Gila Apaches."[6]

Even more successful than Croix in pacifying the frontier was Commandant General Jacobo Ugarte, from 1786 to 1791 in command of the *Provincias Internas*. He believed in peace with those Indians who would accept it, but unremitting campaigns against the persistently errant. His men reported killing hundreds of Apaches, but still they raided, and even when the Mimbreños and others made a peace they often broke it.[7] Ugarte was perhaps the first commander to use Chiricahuas who had come to terms as auxiliaries against hostile Apaches still out, including, usually, the Mimbres.[8]

Had Croix and Ugarte been followed by men of equal vision and integrity, the northern frontier might permanently have been pacified and thousands upon thousands of lives saved, countless millions of dollars spent for purposes other than war, but this was not to be.

In 1787 eight or nine hundred Mimbres, or almost all of that people, had been settled near San Buenaventura, on the Santa Maria River in western Nueva Viscaya, but for some unremembered reason they were flushed out in the first of their long history of *émeutes*, precipitating a lengthy series of pursuits, engagements, and depredations in which the Spanish suffered perhaps as much as the Mimbres, but in any event congealing Apache antipathy toward the whites.[9] Small bands of Mimbres and other Apaches later settled at Janos and San Fernando de Carrizal in about 1790[10] and became the nucleus for what were known as the "Apaches *mansos*," who have remained quiet until the present day. By 1796 the Apache problem appeared well on the way toward solution under a generous reservation system.

In 1810, however, the Mexican Revolution caused withdrawal from the north of troops, and, in the resulting turmoil, reductions in rationing and loosening of control over the Indians set bands to depredating. By 1821, when independence was achieved, the frontier was in chaos. It was necessary to begin its pacification all over again. But now the strong central policies were no more. Military and administrative weaklings, upstarts, opportunists, had taken over. The

17

Indian problem became virtually insoluble. Victorio was born into a time of ceaseless war.

In the heart of the Mimbres country lay the legendary Santa Rita copper mines, so well known that Victorio's people were frequently called the Coppermine Apaches. The origin of these mines, as worked by white men, is not clear, and there are reports that prehistoric Indians secured pure copper from the site. Copper bells and other artifacts are found in some ruins, and human remains dating to pre-Spanish times were said to have been discovered in primitive pits there. About 1800 an Indian told Lieutenant Colonel José Manuel Carrasco, or Carrisco, about the deposits. He lacked capital to commence operations and four years later sold his interest in what he called Santa Rita del Cobre to Francisco Manuel Elguea, a Chihuahua banker. Elguea obtained a crown grant to cover the site, built a settlement and a triangular fort,[11] and set Indian slave labor from Mexico to work extracting ore, while free Apaches watched wonderingly from nearby hills.

Mining methods were primitive. From vertical shafts horizontal passageways were driven along fractures until native copper was found. "The miners, working on their hands and knees in the tiny pitch-dark holes, picked the rock to pieces and put them into rawhide bags. Then, carrying the bags on their backs, they climbed out of the shafts on nearly vertical 'chicken ladders' (poles in which notches had been cut for footholds . . .). On the surface the ore was carefully sorted, to remove any barren rock." The purest copper went direct to the mint. Rich ore later was crudely smelted. In 1807 Lieutenant Zebulon Pike reported that the mine produced twenty thousand muleloads of copper a year, sent to the Royal Spanish Mint in Mexico for coinage.[12] He estimated that a muleload was 300 pounds, although in fact it was about half that. Because of Indian troubles and for other reasons, the mines were shut down about as often as they were worked, but they were a Spanish, later a Mexican, outpost in southwestern New Mexico, and they drew explorers, trappers, and travelers as a magnet. They also brought Victorio's people into frequent contact with the Spanish from the south, and with lean, cold-eyed Americans from east and north.

About the time Victorio was born came the Patties, Sylvester and his son, James Ohio, ostensibly on a beaver-trapping mission, though actually they were typical border rovers, restless, out for any adventure and equal to most. Thus while James Ohio Pattie concentrated on trapping, hunting, and Indian scuffling, Sylvester leased the copper mines for $1,000 a year and began diligently to turn a profit. When a clerk ran off with his gains of $30,000, he was ruined, and philosophically returned to trapping and roving, eventually expiring in a California prison.[13] There were others lured by the mines, however, to take his place.[14]

Colonel José Joaquin Calvo, commandant general and inspector of Chihuahua, here entered into a "treaty" with twenty-nine Mimbreño chieftains, promising them rations in return for tranquility, but the rations failed to arrive and depredations and warfare gradually increased, so that Victorio matured in a period of waxing hostility.

Because nothing else seemed to work, Sonora readopted extermination as a public policy and on September 7, 1835, resumed an earlier program of payment for Apache scalps, 100 pesos (a peso was roughly equivalent to a dollar) for an adult male. Chihuahua soon followed suit, adding fifty pesos for the scalp of a woman and half that for a child's.

One authority relates in grim detail the utter chaos this grisly business generated in Chihuahua and Sonora. On May 25, 1849, Chihuahua had upped the price, enacting the "Fifth Law," which provided a reward of 200 pesos for each warrior killed, 250 for each taken prisoner, 150 for a female captive or Indian child. Acceptable proof of a slaying was a scalp, and the bounty soon came to be paid for any scalp, adult or child, male or female, Indian or, very often, Mexican. It was a bloody business. In 1849 alone 17,896 pesos were paid out. But the Indian menace was not erased; instead, Chihuahua was in an uproar. Many of the scalp hunters were from north of the border, white or Indian or runaway Negroes; others were Mexicans or Apaches themselves. Some organized into raiding parties. Others worked alone, or with a few companions. They were everywhere, but so were the hostiles, the Gileños among them, along with other Chiricahuas, the Mescaleros, and the Comanches. After this sordid year, scalp hunting began to taper off, but the damage was done.[15] Implacable hatred, if it had not existed before, was now firmly implanted in every Mimbreño breast against the Mexicans, and there was no longer any hope of settlement. So much for the evil wrought by evil.

One of the first and most portentous results had been the notorious massacre of Juan José Compa, head chief of the Mimbres, and an uncertain number of his people on April 22, 1837, probably in the

19

Animas Mountains, south of Santa Rita.[16] This deed was engineered by a scalp hunter, John James Johnson of Kentucky,[17] and, while a momentary success in that it was a brief victory over the Mimbreños, it in fact touched off many years of bitter fighting between the races, demonstrating anew that murder most commonly begets murder, rather than peace.

Victorio, a lad of ten or twelve at the time of the Juan José assassination, may have witnessed it, or survived the assault. If so, it no doubt made an indelible impression upon him, or tales of it recited about *ranchería* campfires in subsequent years surely would have, but he was too young, by four or five years, to have taken part in any retributory actions.[18] The immediate results of the massacre were disastrous for the whites. Parties of trappers were annihilated. Santa Rita was shut down and abandoned because of Mimbreño hostility, one account affirming that its people were virtually wiped out fleeing toward Chihuahua,[19] and only the vultures and rattlesnakes occupied the site for eighteen years.

Yet during this period contact with the Americans increased,[20] reaching a crescendo at the time of the Mexican War, which began in 1846. Brigadier General Stephen Watts Kearny, with Major Edwin Vose Sumner in command of his dragoons, reached the Mimbres River en route to California in October, 1846.[21] On the sixteenth of that month, according to the journal of First Lieutenant William Helmsley Emory of the topographical engineers, the command entered the Mimbres Mountains, or Black Range, and the next day crossed the trail to Janos, which followed the old Mimbreño war trail along the river. The Mimbres valley was "truly beautiful, about one mile wide, of rich fertile soil, denseley covered with cotton-wood, walnut, ash &c. It is a rapid, dashing stream, about fifteen feet wide and three deep . . . filled with trout. At this place we found numberless Indian lodges, which had the appearance of not having been occupied for some time." On the eighteenth, at the foot of Ben Moore Mountain,[22] the command passed the deserted copper mines, where they found "the remains of some twenty or thirty adobe houses and ten or fifteen shafts sinking into the earth. . . . We were disappointed in not meeting the Apaches yesterday and to-day. This afternoon some [Indians] came in dressed very much like the Mexicans, mounted on horses. They held a talk."[23]

October 19 the command made thirty miles westward to a tributary of the Gila, Mangas Creek, which heads between the Big and Little

Burro Mountains, and here, the following day, they met Mangas Coloradas and some of his people, the chief swearing "eternal friendship to the whites, and everlasting hatred to the Mexicans," assuring Kearny they would never harm the former, to which the veteran scout, Kit Carson, "with a twinkle in his keen hazel eye," commented to Emory that "he would not trust one of them."

One of the chiefs, not necessarily Mangas himself, offered the Apaches' help if the Americans would invade Chihuahua, Sonora, and Durango, adding that "the Mexicans are rascals; we hate and will kill them all!" Emory graphically describes this motley band of Apaches, of which Victorio and the later-famed Loco may well have been part:

A large number of Indians had collected about us, all differently dressed, and some in the most fantastical style. The Mexican dress and saddles predominated, showing where they had chiefly made up their wardrobe. . . . Several wore beautiful helmets, decked with black feathers, which, with the short skirt, waist belt, bare legs and buskins, gave them the look of pictures of antique Greek warriors. Most were furnished with the Mexican cartridge box, which consists of a strap round the waist, with cylinders inserted for cartridges. . . . Their hills are covered with luxuriant grama, which enables them to keep their horses in fine order, so that they can always pursue with rapidity, and retreat with safety. The light and graceful manner in which they mounted and dismounted, always on the right side, was the admiration of all. The children are on horseback from infancy.[24]

There were various other contacts with Americans during this period and, once the Southwest was secured, Washington took steps to establish a formal relationship in order to obtain, if possible, the tranquillity necessary for orderly development of the region. The redoubtable John Coffee (Jack) Hays of Texas Ranger fame, was named subagent for the Río Gila, New Mexico, on April 11, 1849.[25] The Office of Indian Affairs, which had operated informally within the War Department, was transferred to the new Department of the Interior that year. It had established two principal types of field jurisdictions: superintendencies and agencies. The superintendents had general responsibility over several tribes in a given area, the agents over a single tribe, group, or band. Agents normally reported to superintendents, but sometimes directly to the OIA, and on occasion were virtually diplomatic representatives, attempting to restore or preserve peace, perhaps induce the Indians to cede land or remove to other areas, and carrying out provisions of treaties, distributing gifts, rations, and so on. In the early days the governor of a territory frequently served also as Indian superintendent. Because Congress limited the number of agencies, the OIA established "subagencies," some of the subagents becoming full agents in effect, although often with less salary; or "special agencies" might be established, the special agents usually being regular agents in all but name. Superintendents and agents were allowed much latitude in the choice of sites for their headquarters, particularly at first.[26]

Jack Hays, an uncommonly resourceful man, found his task impossible. He could not even establish relationships with the Indians he was supposed to supervise. From San Diego he reported to the secretary of the interior on January 3, 1850:

... I sought to have an interview [with the Apaches on the Gila], but I failed in every effort to see them. They were shy and hostile, with feelings aroused against the whites by an attack recently made on them by some Americans employed by the Gov. of Chihuahua expressly to fight Indians [the Johnson debacle]. . . . I went into the country of the Gila Apaches, and sought by every means to establish a friendly intercourse with them without success. At one time a few were preparing to come into our camp, and had actually collected within two or three miles of us, but were unfortunately dispersed by a Mexican force of four hundred men, the day before they were to visit us. . . . I deemed it folly to attempt to affect any good with these Indians. If I remained long in their country it was at the very great risk of life and I accordingly felt myself forced to abandon as an impossible thing the undertaking of treating with or conciliating these dangerous and refractory Indians. From all I have seen and known of the Apaches, they are treacherous, warlike and cruel, and need severe chastisement before they can be made to know the policy of observing good faith with the white people. Some of my own companions were killed by them at the very time they were intimating an intention to treat with us. It is exceedingly hazardous for any but large parties to attempt to pass through their country. . . . I have had no other opportunity of reporting to you before arriving at this place, to which I came for the purpose of tendering my letter of resignation.[27]

Hays's report is interesting in part because there is a recollection among descendants of Loco of the abortive attempt at agreement, interrupted by a "Mexican force of four hundred men," although the family memory places this at Cañada Alamosa, almost twenty years later. So large a band of armed Mexicans could not have reached Cañada Alamosa, northwest of Fort Craig, at that late date without arousing comment in official reports. However, the recollection, preserved by the Loco family, suggests that this noted chief knew of the event and, if this be true, Victorio no doubt also was involved, in view of the close bond between the two.[28]

So ended the initial essay at regularizing relations with Mangas and the Mimbres. Not for four years would another attempt be made, although contacts continued, not all of them amicable, by any means. A small dragoon force "defeated" a large party of Apaches near the copper mines, August 16, 1849, severely wounding the officer in command.[29]

The next major meeting concerned the Apaches only incidentally. It resulted from the prolonged stay at Santa Rita of the United States Boundary Commission, headed by John Russell Bartlett. On February 19, 1852, he wrote a lengthy communication—all of his communications were lengthy—to Secretary of the Interior Alexander Hugh Holmes Stuart, about "the establishing of more pacific relations with the Indian tribes" of the area traversed, commenting also on the eleventh article of the Treaty of Guadalupe Hidalgo about the duty of this country to suppress raids by Indians into Mexico and to discourage traffic in captives. This provision was abrogated by the Gadsden Treaty, ratified in 1854, but when Bartlett was in the Southwest it still was in force.

He reported that he had covered the country from the copper mines to the San Pedro River in Arizona, and southward into Sonora, and although relations between the Chihuahua Mexicans and the Indians were in an uneasy lull, in Sonora the situation was sadly different. Nothing of Apache depredations there had been exaggerated, Bartlett reported.

None but those who have visited this state can form any adequate idea of the widespread devastation which has marked the inroads of the savage. Depopulated towns and villages; deserted haciendas and ranches, elegant and spacious churches falling to decay; neglected orchards, teeming with fruit, and broad fields, once cultivated, now are overgrown with shrubbery and weeds, shew to what an extent the country has been overrun. But it is not only scenes like this that mark the course of the savage. There is scarcely a family in the frontier towns but has suffered the loss of one or more of its members or friends. In some instances whole families have been cut off; the Father murdered, the mother and children carried into captivity."

He said that "on my journey south toward Ures, the capital of the state, the inroads of the savage were equally apparent quite to the capital itself." In the direction of Fronteras, Arispe, and other parts of Sonora the story was the same, with the northern and central part of the region "abandoned to the Indian." Confined by illness at Ures, Bartlett reported that scarcely a day passed without reports of Indian depredations. "So bold have these Indians become, and so little do they stand in fear of chastisement from the citizens, that they visited the capital during my tarry there, and rescued several of their associates who were confined in the state prison."

A party of one hundred raiders was chased by forty armed men from Hermosillo, but the pursuers were ambushed and twenty-three slain within five leagues of Ures. Bartlett said that the raiders were mostly Apaches, from the Mimbres to the Tontos, keeping up "a constant warfare for about fifteen years" past—that is, since the Juan José massacre.

"The Copper Mine Apaches have been among the boldest of these depredators, and the names of their chiefs, Mangas Colorado, Del Gadito, Coleto Amarillo and Ponce have struck terror among the people of Sonora, Chihuahua and those portions of New Mexico and Texas which border on the Rio Grande." During his stay at Santa Rita, Bartlett added, he had had a friendly intercourse with those very Indians.

I had several talks with Mangas Colorado, the head Chief of all the Apaches (as he calls himself) with reference to a more peaceful life on his part. I recommended to him to cultivate the soil, and raise his own corn, mules, horses &c., instead of stealing them from the Mexicans. He listened with attention to what I said, and in reply observed that he was too old to begin to raise corn or to cultivate the soil, and that he must leave these things for his young people to do. He expressed a most earnest desire to be at peace with the Americans and spoke in the highest terms of their bravery and knowledge. But why we should defend the Mexicans, after being at war with them, was to him incomprehensible.

Mangas, continued Bartlett,

unquestionably possesses a great influence among the several Apache tribes. . . . He is a man of strong common sense, and discriminate judgment; he has none of the savageness delineated in his appearance or manifested in his action or bearing, that we anticipated from the many vague rumors afloat; he is evidently a councellor rather than a warrior. . . . Ponce and Del Gadito are also men of more than ordinary character, intellect and influence and seem reasonable and practicable in their views and expectations. Hitherto, however, they have all been viewed by the inhabitants of this country as cruel, bloodthirsty, implacable enemies, and too often assuming them to be so, they have been treated when occasion offered worse than brutes. No attempts have been made to conciliate them, but on the contrary, many flagrant acts of injustice have been committed against them and much done to exasperate them and increase their hostility.

Bartlett suggested

the establishment of an Indian Agent at the Copper Mines . . . ; also the assembling of the chiefs, at once, and the distribution among the tribes of presents to the value of 4,000 or 5,000 dollars with a promise that if they continued faithful, to make them yearly presents of clothing and corn, until they were able to sustain themselves. . . . To carry out the object proposed, there would be required an appropriation of about $25,000. This would include the purchase of goods for presents and the transportation of the same to the Copper Mines, the salary of an Indian Agent, and other necessary attendant expenses, the pay of an Agent or Commissioner to make treaties with these and other neighboring Indian tribes, the compensation of guides, the purchase of mules, horses, camp equipage, &c., &c.[30]

Bartlett was less than successful in his boundary survey.[31] But his recommendations for treating with the Mimbres were intelligent, practicable, and were to be closely followed.

III
Victorio Signs a Treaty

Victorio first comes into sharp focus with the "provisional compact" of April 7, 1853, to which he affixed his "X" along with eleven other chiefs and subchiefs, although the name of Mangas Coloradas, at that period the greatest of Apache leaders, is not found there. The agreement never was ratified by the United States Senate. Perhaps it was intended to complement and define a treaty of July 11, 1852,[1] concluded by John Greiner, acting superintendent of Indian affairs for New Mexico,[2] filling in during the fatal illness of Governor James S. Calhoun,[3] and Brevet Colonel Sumner for the whites and, for the Apaches, Mangas, Capitan Vuelta, Cuentas Azules, Blancito, Negrito, and Capitan Simon. Among the "witnesses" to it was Brevet Captain John Pope, who, years later as a major general, would command the department and have his fill of directing the chase of Victorio and the wild Mimbres.

The treaties were a logical development.

The casual raid and peace, depredation and occasional retaliation might have continued as the pattern for life in the Southwest, had not a more brittle, aggressive people swept in with the Mexican War. Then came the California Gold Rush, with countless groups of treasure seekers hastening via little-known trails through the Indian country. Their course was retraced by wandering prospectors who had failed to strike it rich in the Sierra Nevada and now were pecking their way back through the mountains, range by range, all demanding "protection" from the savages whose lands they blithely seized, of whose way of life they were wholly ignorant, denying that these red men had any rights whatever, if they interfered with the holy search for gold, silver, and copper. Thus the Treaty of 1852 and subsequent agreements became urgent.

The treaty followed numerous confrontations, some serious and others less so, involving the Apaches along the Río Grande and west of it, that is, the Mimbres and Gila bands particularly.[4] Late in January they attacked a unit of fourteen soldiers under a noncommissioned officer, killing four, wounding three, and running off stock. "Murders after murders, depredations upon depredations, and innumerable other evils to the people," complained Calhoun from his sickbed. The trouble was lack of munitions and lack of money to finance punitive operations, he thought. In February conditions were no better. A wagon train loaded with stores for Fort Webster, at the copper mines,[5] was attacked, the mules killed or driven off, and the wagons plundered, although the teamsters escaped. A few days later the Apaches ambushed and killed three noncommissioned officers in advance of a Third Infantry unit commanded by Major Israel Richardson somewhere north of El Paso. The Reverend Juan F. Ortiz, vicar of the Territory, had all his animals stolen. The mails were robbed. Other men were murdered, parties attacked. "These wholesale robberies and murders are of such uninterrupted continuance that the inhabitants of this Territory are in a state bordering on despair," said Calhoun, gloomily.[6]

In April he wrote again. "Our Territory is in a more critical condition than it has ever been before, a combination of the wild Indians who surround us is threatened. . . . If the Government of the United States intends doing anything for our protection for Heaven's sake let us know it."[7]

The 1852 treaty, ratified by the Senate and signed by President Franklin Pierce March 25, 1853, provided that the Mimbres recognize the jurisdiction over them of the United States, establish amity, avoid depredations against citizens or livestock, refrain from predatory incursions into Mexico, permit establishment of military posts among them, rely "upon the justice and liberality" of the government to establish fair territorial boundaries, and accept "such liberal and humane measures" affecting them that Washington "may deem meet and proper."[8] The pact was to establish the control of the United States over the Mimbres, secure their submission, and accomplish little else. Mangas, "a magnificent looking Indian," and "undoubtedly the master spirit of his tribe," brought his delegation to the pueblo of Acoma for the signing. There he met Greiner, Sumner, and others.

When the Article in the Treaty was read and explained to him that his people were not to cross over into Old Mexico and they were to remain at peace with the Sonoranians also, he said, 'Are we to stand by with our arms folded while our women & children are being murdered in cold blood as they were the other day in Sonora? That people invited my people to a feast—they manifested every shew of kindness towards us. We were lulled

27

into security by their hypocrisy, people drank and got drunk and then the *Sonoranians* beat out the *brains* of fifteen of them with clubs. Are we to be the victims of such treachery, and not be revenged? Are we not to have the privilege of protecting ourselves?"[9]

Greiner commented, truthfully, "It will be extremely difficult to keep these Indians at peace with the people of Old Mexico."

Stories of such slaughters of drunken Apaches occur so frequently during the frontier years that one must accept them as basically true, but one can only speculate how they were engineered so often as the Apaches report, and why the Indians fell into the same old trap with such regularity. Perhaps peaceful relations between Mexicans and Apaches were as common as war, and for purposes of trade and perhaps other reasons a tenuous relationship always existed; the occasional massacres were abuses of this relationship, rather than chance incidents in a long period of generally hostile dealings between the peoples.

No sooner was the treaty signed than Greiner went south to the copper mines to locate those Apache chiefs who had not yet assented to the pact. He wrote Luke Lea, commissioner of Indian affairs,[10] that "these Indians are very wild." When contacted, Ponce and the other chiefs said they were for peace—with the Americans—"but are by no means willing to promise that they would not continue the war with Old Mexico." Greiner added that "the people of Sonora & Chihuahua have treated these Indians very badly, and they have been bent on having satisfaction, and I fear it will be almost impossible to prevent hostilities between them." Already white settlers were eager to obtain choice Apache lands along the Mimbres and a hundred miles north of El Paso along the Río Grande for agricultural purposes, but the Mimbres refused to abandon them without compensation, a foretaste of what was to come.[11]

The chronic state of hostility improved dramatically with the 1852 treaty, which the Apaches obviously took seriously and whose terms they meant to keep. On September 30 Greiner reported that "all the Indians on our Southern Boundary are anxious to live in peace with the United States Government, but," he hastily added, "evince the most decided hostility to the citizens of Old Mexico. They complain bitterly of the bad faith & treachery of the people of Sonora & Chihuahua, and if half their statements are true, the Indians would be justified in seeking revenge."[12] Had the Americans been as diligent

28

and trustworthy as the Indians in keeping the bargain, had the treaty been as central to the whites and observed by them as scrupulously, the Apache-white hostility might never have resumed and the history of the Southwest become a happier one. But greed and ignorance and callous disregard for the rights of others entered in, and interminable misunderstanding and bloodshed resulted.

Edward H. Wingfield of Georgia reached Santa Fe in October and Governor William Carr Lane, who had succeeded Calhoun, ordered him to Fort Webster "amongst the Apaches for duty," to succeed Charles Overman, sent to the copper mines as special Indian agent only in July of that year. Overman had proven inept and Wingfield was not much improvement. It was difficult to obtain honest men who also were intelligent, kind, and capable of empathy with the tumultuous Apaches, yet these qualities were essential for an agent. Greiner pointed out that "the more I see of Indian character, the more I am convinced that a proper spirit of kindness toward them is the best mode of governing them, and by pressing this policy, and seeing justice done them, we [would] need have but little more trouble with the Indians of New Mexico."[13] His observation was true enough, but difficulties were mountainous.

The problem had remained. Lane wrote the commissioner of Indian affairs on the last day of 1852 that for six months there had been no report of depredations by Navahos or Utes, "but against the miserable, starving, thieving Apaches, complaints are made in every direction."[14] Therefore, on February 28, 1853, he had journeyed southward to see what might be done. He reached Webster April 2, and found that Wingfield had brought in about three hundred Mimbres under Ponce and other chiefs. Instead of being prepared to raise corn, as he had hoped, they "were perfectly idle." Not only that, but all of the bottomlands near the fort not taken to raise food for the soldiers had been turned over by Wingfield to his interpreter, Francois Fletcher. Fletcher had put Mexican peons to planting for his profit, "an embarrassing state of things," as Lane acknowledged. Nevertheless, he negotiated the provisional compact of 1853 with those chiefs who could be contacted and left the original of the document with Wingfield, instructing him to obtain "signatures" from such absent chiefs as he could. Apache signers, in addition to Victorio, whose name appears as "Vitoria," included Ponce, José Nuevo, Cuchillo Negro, Josecito, Sargento, Veinte Reales, Riñon, Delgadito Largo, Tusho, Placera, and Corrosero. Lane signed for the government, and there were nine white witnesses, including Major Enoch Steen[15] and Wingfield.

With an escort of sixteen dragoons commanded by Steen, Lane journeyed on to the Gila River to reconnoiter the Mimbres country. He found but a single chief on that stream, "and from him I learned that the young men were down in Chihuahua and Sonora on predatory excursions," while the other Indians were in distant mountains collecting mescal.[16] He estimated the Mimbres and upper Gila Apaches at "about 1,000 souls," but noted that no contact had been established with "the Coyoteros, Tontos & other bands of Apaches, who live lower down the Hela."

His compact had included a number of visionary provisions, impossible of fulfillment in the New Mexico of the 1850's. Among them:

Art. 1st: Said confederate Indians solemnly agree and promise henceforth to abandon their wandering & predatory modes of life; and to locate themselves, in permanent camps, & commence the cultivation of the Earth, for a subsistence, and as soon as possible, to build for themselves dwelling houses, and to raise Flocks & Herds.

One might as well covenant with the wind to still or the tide to cease. Or Article Two:

They also agree to make laws, to prevent their people from doing any manner of Evil; & faithfully to execute their Laws. They promise hereafter, never to resort to the ancient custom of retaliation, for any injuries which they might suffer; nor will they ever attempt, to right their own wrongs, in any case whatever; but in all instances will apply to the proper authority, for a redress of their grievances, and will abide all decisions thus made.

If this was translated accurately to the chiefs, which is to be doubted, how they must have howled with glee when they discussed it later in their secluded *rancherías!* These provisions went against the whole fabric of Apache custom and social organization; they would have caused them to become what they were not, and never pretended to be. The compact could only have been conceived by a white man wholly ignorant of Apache ways, his mind perhaps influenced by the example of the Pueblo Indians, a totally different people.

Elsewhere the compact provided that the Apaches would choose, "in their own manner," two chiefs for each band, a captain and a second captain, to be avenues of communication and responsible for the conduct of their people. This presupposed that Chiricahua chiefs were chosen like political leaders and performed similar functions. Such was not the case.

A chief or subchief won his position either by hereditary right or his own superiority in war and council, and even a man from a line of chiefs must exhibit superior qualities before becoming one. The leader class was something else. A man who became an outstanding leader might be termed a "chief," but that did not make him such. A chief came to his position either by heredity and ability, or by ability alone, but if he had not the latter—plus persuasiveness, or charisma—his blood line alone could not keep him a chief. A leader, on the other hand, "has no absolute control," as an informant told Opler, who commented, "The head man's rank is assured only as long as his direction is effective." An informant said, "If the group is dissatisfied with their leader, if they are tired of him and don't like him, they may just move away and camp elsewhere and recognize another leader." Obviously if a "chief" satisfactory to the whites had been chosen, his status would have endured only so long as he had no unpalatable directions to carry out, and his control over his people would be, by Apache custom, more that of persuasion than anything else. This is not what the whites had in mind, but it was all that was possible in the Apache society of the mid-nineteenth century.[17]

The 1853 compact provided that the government would feed the Apaches for a limited time and supply them with breeding stock and farm instructors. It also urged the maintenance of order, promised protection against illegal traders, defense against their enemies. If, on the other hand, warriors depredated upon Mexicans, the United States forces would "intercept the return of the marauding party, & permit the Mexicans to exterminate the robbers," a provision also doubtless providing the Apaches amusement.

Despite its aura of unrealism, the compact had a salutary effect on Apache-white relations, for the Indians abided by it better than did the whites. Perhaps, again, they took it more seriously. Had the government regularly provided honest amounts of good food, breeding stock, instruction, and care, the long and dreary series of Indian wars in this area might never have developed, but these obligations were not fulfilled.

About six weeks after Lane returned to Santa Fe, he received a glowing letter from Caleb Sherman, Indian trader at Fort Webster, whose license, of course, depended upon the good will of the Indian superintendent. It congratulated Lane upon "the complete success of your efforts to induce [the Mimbres] to settle down and cultivate the soil. . . . The manner in which they have prepared the ground, and planted it far surpasses any thing of the kind I have seen in the Territory for neatness, and would compare favorably with the best cultivated farms in the states."[18] Lane was far away, might never return, and a little flattery never hurt any trader wishing to continue to function.

With this rosy report, Wingfield sent along a letter dated May 18 which reported:

Mangus Colorado came in today. I assure you he is a noble speciman of the genus homo. He comes up nearer the poetic ideal of a chieftain, such a one as Homer, in his Illiad, wrote describe [sic], than any person I have ever seen. No feudal lord, in the palmy days of chivalry, can lead his vassals under better subjection. His manners are stern, dignified & reserved; he seldom speaks, but when he does it is to the point, & with great good sense. You may be satisfied that he is the Master Spirit amongst the Apaches.

Wingfield paid high tribute to the Mimbres, praise so lofty, indeed, that it becomes suspect, particularly in view of his conclusion:

The more I see of these people, the better I am satisfied that the process of assimilation, to these manners & customs of civilized life, will be much easier, than our Government has had any experience of. . . . If I had time I could detail to you hundreds of instances . . . of the development of amiable habits of character & a nice discrimination between right & wrong, exhibited by the Apaches [that would do credit to those] who have been raised under the teachings of the Decalogue, & Christ's Sermon on the Mount. Now would it not be cruel, most cruel, in our Government, not to foster and develop these beautiful elements of character, in these people. When I think of the probable withdrawal of the aid of the Govt. from these people . . . it makes me sick at heart.

The notion of all that cash ceasing to flow through his agency for beef and corn for the Indians made it unlikely that he exaggerated his anguish; frequently somewhat of a gulf developed between what the government paid for and what the Apaches consumed.

Wingfield said he had explained, article by article, the compact to Mangas when he came in and that the Indian "gave his cordial assent" to it. In an accompanying letter Major Steen assured the governor that "Mangus is well pleased with your treaty," and wanted a military post on the Gila, probably for protection from Mexican raiding parties. He had recently fought with the Mexicans, Steen said, "about 50 miles south of where we were [near Lake Guzman, and] lost only 3 of his warriors, but had, as he says, hard work to save his party; that when he told the Mexicans that the Apaches were at peace, & asked them why they killed his people, the Mexicans replied that they were not at peace, with the Apaches, Americans, or Texians, & that they had come to fight." He hinted thus at the colossal difficulties of bringing tranquility to the southwest at that time.

Mangas, Steen added, "has more sense than all the rest" of the Indians "put together."[19] But he had never seen Victorio in his maturity.

Lane terminated his brief governorship, which had commenced September 13, 1852, being succeeded on August 8, 1853, by David Meriwether, who held office almost four years, departing Santa Fe in May, 1857. When Meriwether journeyed from Independence to New Mexico to assume the post, he brought with him one of the most able and dedicated men ever to hold the position of agent for the Mimbres Apaches, Dr. Michael Steck.[20] This was Steck's third trip to the Territory.

He was sent by Lane to Fort Webster to relieve Wingfield July 8, 1853, under a stinging letter of instructions in which the governor seemed outraged that the agent had been feeding all comers, even bringing in bands from the Gila for rationing. "Has the agent been insane?" Lane wondered angrily. "The compact with the Apaches was made upon the express condition, that it should be approved at Washington; & with the express understanding that there was no bargain made, unless it was there approved. And it was never intended, from the first, to feed any Indian, but those who were employed in raising a crop." Lane charged Wingfield's "mismanagement will cause great embarrassment, not only to me, but to you also, & to my successor, by creating expectation, amongst the Indians, which must be disappointed."[21] With this gloomy forecast Steck left for Fort Webster, but apparently his mission was shortly interrupted, for James M. Smith became agent, or subagent, there on September 1 for the brief period before his untimely death in December.[22] Perhaps during this period Steck served as agent for the Mescaleros, east of the Río Grande. For many years the Mescaleros and Mimbres had the same agent, under the reasoning that both were Apache tribes and they were culturally akin. It may be that the supply of agents was limited by a penurious Congress. Steck reported August 13 that he had visited the Mimbres camps, hoped to take a census shortly, had issued some rations, and looked upon "the feeding of Gila Apaches as the only means of preserving peace. Their immense numbers, the scarcity of Game and the great disproportion between the number of men and that of the women & children renders it entirely out of their power to support themselves from hunting. The men have from two to five wives and often from ten to fifteen are dependent upon a single hunter."[23]

Smith, when he took over in late summer, estimated there were six thousand to seven thousand Indians "within range of this Agency." He listed them carefully, although some of his bands are not clearly identifiable today. Perhaps he was forced to gather information from frontiersmen, who supplied locally accepted labels for encampments. Smith estimated the Mescaleros proper at 80 lodges (a lodge was probably calculated as indicating five Indians, including women and children), and other Apaches, perhaps of the Mescalero division, the Agua Nuevas, 100 lodges, and the Paseños, 80. The Mimbres he calculated at 100 lodges, and the Mogollons, Eastern Chiricahuas like the Mimbres, 125 lodges. The Gila Apaches had 150 lodges, the Coyoteros, or "wolf Apaches," 300 lodges, the Tontos and Garroteros, 400 lodges (although the "Garroteros" usually were considered Coyoteros, a corruption of that name; in describing them Smith indicates he included the Yavapais, a non-Apache people, among them). The "Penol," or Pinal, Apaches he put at 150 lodges.

Smith added that Indians "in Mexico," but who, he said, joined the Apaches in depredations, including the Maricopas of 400 lodges (who were enemies of the Apaches and did not raid with them), the "Ceieros" (Seris), 50, the Janeros (an Apache people), 100, the Carisals, 80, and the Carinals, 80. Plainly he was guessing on the last two. Smith said the Indians living on the Mimbres and in its vicinity numbered from five to eight hundred souls.

With few exceptions, Smith reported, the Indians under his supervision were "poor, miserable and filthy. They live on game when they can get it, on the mescal, the piñon [nuts], the cedar and other berries and in some cases, grass with salt. When pressed by hunger they eat mules and horses of their own or if they have none, infest the roads and settlements for the purpose of stealing them and at the same time take many of the lives of our most valuable citizens. It is estimated that not less than 400" lives had been lost since the Mexican War. Smith stressed, what was "obvious to everyone," that the Indians must be fed, taught to support themselves, or "be exterminated," adding that "the expense of feeding would not be a tithe of what it would cost to destroy them." He suggested a deputation of Apaches be sent to Washington, the first of numerous such proposals by various officials, but the difficulty was twofold: to get Washington to agree, and to get the Apache leaders to go. Victorio, Mangas, and others adamantly refused for years to make the trip, fearing perhaps that once beyond reach of their people they would be imprisoned or destroyed. Yet, Smith argued, "a similar course having been pursued with other tribes, no reason can be assigned why the Apaches, wild and cruel as they be, should not be civilized in a like manner."

Smith complained of the arrangement by which Fletcher, who was supposed to train the Apaches in the mysteries of agriculture, had contracted with the government for a Mimbres River bottom for a farm to be used for instruction and now, with few Apaches "trained," desired to sell the farm back to the government for $1,600. No more than twenty-five acres had been put under cultivation, with an expected yield of only ten to fifteen bushels of corn an acre. Yet this neglected and near-worthless field "has been parceled out to 13 bands, numbering 199 [Indians], and turned over to them for preservation. As Indians eat corn (stalks and all) in a green state and much of this has already been destroyed by them, it is doubted whether, by the time corn should ripen, there will be any field to gather. . . . I know not what to do."[24] The Indians desired issues of corn, meat, tobacco, knives, powder, and lead and "complain that we have not complied with our treaty and will not understand it's being disapproved at Washington. . . . They say they have worked as we desired they should and have not stolen our animals . . . and that we should comply with our word. . . . If [rations] are stopped altogether I believe [they] will commence hostilities. . . . A small amount of money will prevent this but millions will be necessary to whip and exterminate them."[25]

Fletcher, Smith continued in a subsequent letter, apparently had become quite a rascal. In addition to being a supposed farming instructor, he traded with the Indians, was visited periodically by illegal Mexican traders from the river towns "who doubtless contrive to bring whiskey into the country & sell it to them." Fletcher denied knowledge of any such contraband but, Smith added, "it is hard for me to believe he does not know it, as I am told, he succeeds in getting from them a large number of mules which nothing but whiskey scarcely will induce them to part with." He believed Fletcher was "a partner, no doubt," of the Mexican traders.

"Unless this kind of trading can be broke up & put a stop to it will be impossible to manage the Indians," Smith warned.

A deputation headed by Delgadito, "a powerful man and a warlike chief of great influence, second only to the great Mangus Colorado," visited Smith to talk about it, "and to complain of the murder of their women" as the result of drunken brawls resulting from the illegal whiskey. The talk was "long and friendly." Although the key to the problem was breaking up the unscrupulous trade, an agent's authority to do so was indistinct. Smith urged that Congress clearly define his power and duties, and, if this had been done, much trouble would have been averted, then and later. But the traders were "free enterprise" figures, and free enterprise meant votes; restrictions upon them would cost votes, and Congress was reluctant to act responsibly upon such distant matters. "I have no doubt there are many such claims as Fletcher's in the heart of the Indian country here which, if recognized, in any manner, will forever defeat the humane policy of the U.S." in regard to the Indians, Smith opined. He was right. He digressed briefly and illuminatingly on conditions at Fort Webster, a typical southwestern agency of the period:

> The Agency is the common resort of all the Indians. They always expect to be invited in the house and to take a seat, if hungry to eat &c. They expect storage for anything they have and the use of the corral. This is the only way to bring them over to civilization. They must be indulged and treated with kindness or they will not come to see the agent. At present the houses of the Agency are not suitable nor are there rooms enough. They consist of one room built of sticks & mud in the roughest manner for the reception of Indians & all persons having business with the office. Of a second to store corn, horse furniture and such articles. . . . Of a third about 8 or 10 feet square for a kitchen almost in a state of dilapidation. The Agency requires an interpreter, a man to keep the stores & make issues and another to herd animals and to be a keeper of packs. The interpreter occupies the Indian reception room. The keeper of stores the storeroom and the herder and packer the kitchen. The agent has no room at the Agency and is indebted at present to Major Richardson at Fort Webster for his quarters and for the storage of his baggage.

Such were the makeshift facilities of the first Mimbres Agency. Even so, it was not well constructed. The rickety condition of the corral already had allowed stock to be stolen, Smith complained.[26] Yet the agency had preserved a shaky peace, and thus fulfilled its primary mission.

Smith knew of the impending transfer of the fort from the Mimbres to the Río Grande Valley, and, thinking it "unsafe to remain at that place after the military force is removed," wanted to take the agency east, also. Meriwether, after conferring with gruff old Brevet Brigadier General John Garland, a veteran of the War of 1812, the Seminole War, and the Mexican War, new commander of the New Mexico military district, authorized Smith to remove to the new post at Fort Thorn, when it should be established.[27]

During these months, while becoming informed of territorial matters and his new duties, Meriwether took a decisive step with regard to a prime object of Apache trade, captives from Mexico. Many of these were absorbed into the tribe, but others were seized simply for purposes of trade, since the price, or ransom, for a captive was apt to be generous due to treaty obligations assumed by the Americans and to the natural desire on the part of officials to see all such hapless creatures returned safely home. But Meriwether saw instantly the peril in ransoming victims, since to do so would encourage the Indians to capture more. On October 30 he informed Smith that traffic in captives "can never be tolerated."

"Whenever you have it in your power to do so you will reclaim and if necessary take by force any captives belonging to Mexico or the United States which may be found in the possession of the Indians," sending Mexican prisoners to the consul at El Paso, he instructed.[28] On occasion this humane purpose was frustrated when Mexican officials refused to accept the rescued captives. Nevertheless, the practice became part of the established policy of the United States, and the ransoming of captives for relatively high prices was discontinued. The Indians were disgruntled, but there is nothing to suggest that it led to any increased butchery. Perhaps the slaughter could not be increased; it was savage enough already.

Smith died December 15, 1853. After some confusion, Dr. Steck became agent May 9, 1854, establishing his headquarters at the new Fort Thorn.[29]

IV

By Any Name

With the Steck Papers at the University of New Mexico are a number of notebooks. In one are jotted thoughts for an address Steck delivered in August of 1854 to the Mimbres, and perhaps later to other bands of Apaches (the notes are neither clearly identified nor dated). On one page of this worn little notebook, however, a question is penciled, the reply to which Dr. Steck apparently intended to seek from Mimbres Indians he met. The question:

"Why is Lucero Victoria?"

This clear suggestion that at this point Victorio bore the name of Lucero, meaning in Spanish "Morning Star," is strengthened by various other references to a Mimbres chief named Lucero in Dr. Steck's records, but no further mention of Victorio, by that name. This despite the fact that occasionally he includes lists which he believed complete of the names of Mimbres chiefs. For example, in his abstract of issues for the quarter ending December 31, 1854, Steck lists the band of Lucero among those of Delgadito, Cuchillo Negro, Josecito, Losho (Loco?), and "Beinte" (Veinte) Reales as drawing rations and supplies. For the quarter ending March 31, 1855, noted Apaches also drew issues, including Lucero, Poncito ("Little Ponce"), and Itan, or Etan, who, incidentally, is another Apache appearing frequently in records of the period, but otherwise unknown unless by the name of Loco or some other.[1]

On January 31, 1855, Steck sent Indian Commissioner George W. Manypenny the first of newly required monthly reports from Indian agents. In it he said:

> During the month I have seen every captain in the tribe, viz.: Mangus Coloradus, Delgadito, Itan, Laceres [Lucero], Josecito, Cuchillo Negro, Serjeanto, Rinion, all of whom have visited the agency and received rations of corn & Beef. They are scattered over the country from the Gila to the Rio Grande and from the line between Mex. and the U.S. to the country occupied by the Navajoes. . . .

38

They were strewn so widely partly because the amount of presents he was authorized to give them was too trivial to hold them in closer, Steck added.

Without one exception the principal chiefs seem willing to attempt the cultivation of the soil if means can be furnished to assist them. They already feel their dependence upon the Govt and by the judicious expenditure of 1,000$ during the present year many hundred bushels of corn can be produced principally by the labour of the Indians themselves. They can be made to see the advantages of this course and in a few years be permanently located.

As politely as possible Steck urged more help for his Indians.

"I hear complaints among them of the bad faith of the Govt. towards them," he reported. "They say they have been promised assistance but that [they have] waited now two years and not recd it and any one acquainted with the peculiar Indian character will at once see the evils that would result from another year's delay, to say nothing of the actual good that would follow from civilization." He added that his Indians had been at peace with the United States ever since the 1852 treaty, and any minor stock thefts and depredations were promptly corrected following investigation.[2]

Yet this was not true with regard to Mexico. Numerous reports from that country indicate that murder, rapine, and other evils by the Mimbres continued unabated. On November 9, 1856, Ballasar Padilla, *commandante* of the Presidio of Janos, wrote to Governor Meriwether listing, among many other depredations, the theft of a woman, Prudencia Abilos, by the Mimbres Indians, Lucero and Monteras. The latter cannot be identified, but Lucero may well have been no other than Victorio.[3]

Many place names in New Mexico, Chihuahua, and Sonora bear the name "Lucero," even as numerous others bear "Victorio," as, for example, the border crossing, "El Lucero," mentioned in a State Department communication of 1880, the year Victorio was slain, and Ojo del Lucero, Sierra del Lucero, and others. These are not clear-cut evidence of the prominence of an Indian Lucero, of course, since there were noted Spanish families of that name.[4]

Be that as it may, Victorio does not reappear by his familiar cognomen in any contemporary official records from the time of the 1853 compact until 1865, although he is then described as a well-known and powerful chief. Mentioned or not during this time, he was a leader of growing importance, as witnessed by his evolution into the leader of the Mimbres. During this period their history was his history.

On August 12, 1854, Dr. Steck with two companions made a six-day sweep from Fort Thorn to the Mimbres and up it for a dozen miles,[5] contacting Apaches of the several bands, conferring with many, but uneasy because he met none of the principal chiefs. "They have since sent me word that they did avoid me, and gave as their reason that some Mexicans had told them a campaign was to be made against them, and that we were coming out as spies, &c.," he wrote Meriwether. Because his supplies were so scanty, he had been forced to deal out presents and food quite sparingly, and the Apache agriculture he had observed seemed very inconsequential.[6]

Notes for a speech Dr. Steck intended to deliver on this journey have been preserved, excerpts illustrating how an agent of that period addressed his wild and turbulent charges:

When I left here I told the chiefs that I would see their Great Father & tell him that I had seen them and that they were at peace & willing to cultivate the soil. Great Father was pleased & has sent me back and said if they continue to do well that he would help them. He said it was bad to be at war. That road to war was always red with blood—full of women & children weeping & starving—but the road to peace is easier to travel and in it you will find safety for yourselves and plenty to eat for your wives & children. You know this is so. When you are at war you must hide in the mountains, when you are at peace you come in and trade and talk with the people without the fear of being molested.

Where is [a long blank space follows in which no doubt he intended to list warriors killed, if he could learn their names].

They were killed in battle and their wives & children mourn their loss. Why is it you have so many more women & children? Because you have been at war and your braves have been killed.

You must not steal or rob any more or I will have nothing to do with you. If I hear that any one does steal and I find it out they must be punished. The Captains must look to this—if any of Delgadito's band steals I will look to him. . . .

The Apache when one of his men is killed don't ask for the man who killed him, but the first American they meet they kill &c. The Great Father wants to be at peace. . . . But it is not because he is afraid for he has more soldiers than you can count, they are like the grass on the prairie or the leaves on the trees. . . .

Take my advice and stick to your word—you have promised to be good men and don't forget your promise.[7]

That autumn Steck again visited the Indian country, inspecting the camps of most of the important chiefs west of the agency, was "kindly received and everything seems to indicate the most friendly feeling. Since the compact [of] 1853 their conduct toward our people has been entirely pacific. . . . No depredations have been committed by the Gila Apaches and some property stolen by them has been returned." Steck noted that the Indians were destitute, however. Formerly they had subsisted upon stock stolen from Mexico, but now with their wants "partially supplyed by the Government," they remained generally at peace, hoping for better. If the rations were not increased, at least to subsistence levels, and if overly frugal authorities were not more generous, the Apaches would have no recourse but to resort once more to plunder to keep their people fed. "Much has been promised them," he pointed out. They expected the promises to be fulfilled and in this expectation they endured semistarvation and destitution, but they could not be expected to do so indefinitely. No people would.

Their agriculture was limited in part because they must plant corn and keep it cultivated with sharp sticks as their only tools, the government never having felt a compulsion to provide even hoes. "Yet notwithstanding all these disadvantages they have many small paches [sic] that they have kept clean . . . and will yield them some recompense for their labour." Much more could be done, with a modicum of assistance, the agent urged. "Cultivation of the soil is the surest road to civilization," he reminded his superior. Now, while their mood was favorable, was the time to encourage them. "No time [should] be lost in the accomplishment of an object that promises so much good."

Dr. Steck outlined the Indians' food cycle: the game was scant and during summer and early fall they resorted to mescal, acorns, juniper berries, and, when these were exhausted, devoured their horses and mules. When the animals were consumed, they must steal or starve until the following summer—and they would not starve willingly.

"If we wish to maintain peace with those Indians we must feed them a portion of the year. I look upon that as the only means of preventing depredations. Reverse our positions, place the white man in a starving condition and I doubt whether he would consult the right to property more than the Indian. He to [*sic*] would steal and justify himself by declaring that 'self preservation is the first law of Nature'."[8] His appeal was strong and well reasoned. Only a very small amount of money might save the Southwest from disaster. Yet for many years such a calamity hovered on the horizon simply because the dollars supplied were so paltry, given so grudgingly by a penny-pinching Washington, and came forth so belatedly.

Depredations reported from time to time rarely turned out to be the work of Indians, whom the settlers almost invariably accused initially. In January, 1855, Steck reported that mules and horses stolen from a ranch near Doña Ana had been taken, not by Indians as first supposed, but by Mexicans. "The name of the principal thief is known & he is from near Chihuahua," he reported. Other thieves "generally supposed to have been Mexicans," stole more stock from near Socorro that month. A third rustling, of fifty-three mules, was charged to Indians, but Steck was not convinced. "I am very confident they were not stolen by Gila Apaches," he reported.[9] There was so much lawlessness in New Mexico at the time one could never be certain who was stealing from whom.

With mid-spring, Steck journeyed forty-five miles northwest of Fort Thorn to the headwaters of the Animas River, a tributary of the Río Grande heading in the Black Range, where Cuchillo Negro had his camp. The Indians had cleared about three acres in hopes they would receive from someone seed, tools, and encouragement for planting. Since the government would not pay for instructors, Steck, himself a onetime Pennsylvania farm boy, would lend a hand, first to Cuchillo Negro, then to Mangas, Delgadito, Ponce, Lucero, and others, all of whom "seem willing to plant," as he wrote.[10]

Meriwether interrupted this laudable endeavor, however, writing Steck April 28 that the President finally had constituted the governor special commissioner to fashion treaties with the Indians. The official directed Steck to assemble the Mescalero and Gila Apaches at Fort Thorn on June 7. "This will be the day of the full moon, which will enable you to designate the time so that the Indians will understand and recollect it," he reminded him.[11]

The agent agreed, believing that although the Río Grande, which the Mescaleros must cross, was very high, the conference could be held. All the chiefs would be present, he wrote, "except Mangus Colorado, who ... is still very sick, but promised to be here if well enough to attend."[12]

Unlike the earlier treaties, that of 1855 was aimed, for the first time, at getting the Mimbres (and Mescaleros) to cede large areas of their land, allowing themselves to be restricted within definable limits, their first reservations. Only the failure of the Senate to ratify the pact postponed such a delimitation for fifteen more years.

"There was a very full attendance" at the negotiations, Meriwether reported, "and I was very particular in ascertaining whether the chiefs, captains and head men were authorized by their respective followers to treat with me, and ... to ascertain if there was any objection on the part of the Indians assembled. . . . . I am happy to inform you that no objection was made to any provision of the treaties. . . . .

"I desired very much to treat with the Gila Apaches at the same time and place ... but many had gone on an expedition against the Mexican provinces of Chihuahua and Sonora. . . . The Mimbres Indians are generally classed with and considered as a part of the Gila Apaches, but they live separate, claim different tracts of country, and have separate and distinct interests and organizations."

Steck was a formal witness to the treaty.

"The two bands treated with are of about equal strength and numbering from six to seven hundred souls and their reservations will be about equal in extent also, each containing between two thousand and two thousand five hundred square miles of land ... and each band has ceded to the United States from twelve to fifteen thousand square miles," continued Meriwether. Although the proposed reservations seemed large, the governor noted that neither had more than fifteen square miles that could be cultivated, and each contained mountain ranges with the game and mescal the Indians desired. He conceded that the annuities he had arranged might bulk large, but deemed it best to be "generous" with Indians so nearly hostile until they could support themselves without stealing and depredating.[13]

Mangas Coloradas, doubtless told by his lieutenants of the content of the treaty, proved strangely reluctant to sign it. Statesman that he was, he saw more clearly the restrictions it placed upon the Indians than the illusory benefits it promised them and decided he would never be a party to it. Without his assent it would be meaningless for anyone, white or Indian.

He informed Steck that indisposition had kept him from the negotiations, and promised to accompany the agent to Santa Fe in August to sign. Later he said it was too hot to go there in August. Besides, he added, he feared the diseases he had heard were rampant there. Anyway, whatever Delgadito and Itan agreed to was all right. But he would not formally acknowledge this fact by touching pen to the document. Mangas Coloradas would not sign away the lands of his people.[14]

Mangas was becoming increasingly aloof, and Victorio took his cue from that great chieftain. From this time forward one may detect a growing aloofness in Victorio, too, although he was ever ready to listen to the whites, to bargain with them, to agree when what they said made sense. But he grew increasingly distrustful of them; while Loco and others were ever more amenable, Victorio more commonly now lurked among the shadows.

In early September Steck granted a trader permission to visit Mangas' camp and bring him in, but once more the big Indian refused. He said that the Sonorans were making a strong campaign into his country, and he must remain to take care of his people.

"I have no doubt his fears are well founded," Steck admitted in a letter to Meriwether.

The Indians reported to me some twenty days since that a party of Mex. soldiers on the trail of the returning Apaches struck the Gila about 150 miles west of the Coppermines and followed it this way one day then turning off again towards their own country, that they had one piece of artillery &c. The Indian spies followed this command into the Cierra Larga where they joined the main force, say they were encamped on a small river . . . and had music and fandangoes every night. The account given by the Sonora people were that five hundred citizens and soldiers had went in pursuit with a determination to follow them [the Indians] into their country. If they do come they will have a warm time of it as the Indians are prepared for them, but I fear it will result like most of their campaigns, a big smoke but little fire.

You will recollect my stating to you when here in June that most of Mangas young men were off in Sonora. They joined the Mongolloneros [sic] and Coyoteros, entered the country at different points and have since returned with a large number of captives, horses, mules & cattle. . . . One party brought 20 captives, another 12, and another 10.[15]

For the quarter ending September 30, Steck listed supplies given to Mangas, Cuchillo Negro, Riñon, Ponce, Itan, Delgadito, and other leaders, but neither the name of Lucero nor Victorio appears.[16] Thus it is probable that he was of the great raiding party that swept northern Mexico that season and returned with so many prisoners. He may well have led it.

Among the reasons the Senate failed to ratify the 1855 treaty perhaps was the suspected existence of "Spanish or Mexican Grants of Land or mines of Gold, Silver, Copper, Lead, &c.," within the proposed reservations. For a riches-mad nation, this might seem a substantial obstacle. Steck conceded that near the center of the Mimbres reserve was a Mexican grant of nine square leagues,

the well known copper mine Grant . . . successfully worked as late as the year 1838 or 1839. The Houses and Fort of its former ramparts are still standing, also many of their fruit trees, and has the appearance of once having been a flourishing town of some 300 to 400 inhabitants. It was abandoned on account of the hostility of the Indians who attacked and killed many of the inhabitants, and the remainder were compelled to fly for safety.

"South and west, of the copper mines and also within the limits of the contemplated Mimbres reserve, there are gold mines which were extensively worked and also abandoned on account of Indian hostility. There is also found within this reserve the ores of Iron, Silver & Lead.

In the letter reporting this, replying to a request for information from the General Land Office surveyor-general of New Mexico, William Pelham, Steck also broached what was to become the key issue that ultimately drove Victorio on his final warpath and caused havoc, conflict, and turmoil in the Southwest for a third of a century to come: removal. He proposed that, better than the suggested reserves for Mimbres and Mescaleros, would be removal of these bands to the remote Gila, where they could live with relatives far from the communities and thoroughfares of whites and from the predatory traders who steadily smuggled contraband to them. "There are always bad men among them [the Indians], they would give much trouble to settlers and endanger the safety of the U.S. Mails," he pointed out, if allowed to remain on the suggested treaty lands. Not only that but, remove them farther from the frontier, and "you throw open for settlement the finest and most desirable portion of New Mexico."[17]

Meriwether, thinking his proposed treaty sabotaged, was furious when the contents of Steck's letter were revealed. He had been in constant touch with the agent, the governor fumed, and Steck never had revealed knowledge of any mining grant, or objected in any way to the negotiations, while the agent himself was aware of a fight between Mescaleros and Mimbres at the parley in which a man had been killed and several wounded, demonstrating the ill-advisability of throwing them together on some common reservation.[18]

Steck replied soothingly that he had meant no offense. He supposed the copper mine grant was well known to the governor, and the wisdom of establishment of a common reservation was a matter of opinion. So the issue passed. The Senate failed to approve the treaty in any event.

In his annual Indian affairs report for 1855, Meriwether sent the commissioner fresh estimates of the Apache population: Mescaleros, 150 warriors, 700 to 750 souls; Mimbres, 175 warriors and 800 to 850 souls; Mogollons, 125 warriors, 500 to 600 souls; Coyoteros, 750 warriors, 3,000 to 4,000 souls; "Garroteros," 150 warriors, 700 to 800 souls; Tontos, 200 warriors, 800 to 900 souls. For the Apache nation in all that region: 1,600 warriors, 7,500 souls. His summary was probably about 25 per cent too high.[19]

V

A Fateful Sequence

Scattered incidents from time to time in southern New Mexico rarely could be blamed upon the Mimbres once they had signed their treaties. Quite the reverse. These Apaches appeared to dread retaliation upon them for the sins of others. On November 15, 1855, William Watts Hart Davis,[1] secretary to Governor Meriwether and acting for him in his absence, wrote to Manypenny that four Indians had stolen 150 mules from José Chavez in Bernalillo County, but were hotly pursued by Second Lieutenant Isaiah N. Moore of the First Dragoons and twenty soldiers. The command recovered about 120 of the animals. This depredation, wrote Davis, apparently had been the work of Mogollon Apaches, since they and the Gilas "have been in the habit of making annual robbing excursions into the same section of the country in the fall of the year to procure food to last them through the winter." He had written Steck, nevertheless, directing him to learn whether any Mimbres were involved.[2]

The agent already had a similar matter on his mind. Just before Christmas a party of Socorro citizens called to report that raiders had stolen twenty-one horses and mules and thirteen head of cattle, were trailed to the Mimbres camps, but the Indians prepared to fight them off. Discretion being indicated, the citizenry backed off. Steck already had heard of this incident from an Apache and threatened his people that, if the charge were true and the stock not returned, he would terminate their rations.[3] This was a serious threat at the beginning of winter, the hard season for survival, and the chiefs were concerned.

Steck did not doubt that the Mogollons and perhaps others of the Gilas had been involved in some of the depredations reported.

He wrote Davis on January 9, therefore, that he had taken "great pains" to discover whether the Mimbres were guilty. "So far as the chiefs and the tribe generally are concerned, I know that they are as desirous to remain at peace as we are that they should do so," he reported. A tour of their country revealed very few bones of plundered

47

and devoured cattle; therefore he assumed the chiefs were not trying to cover up any wrongdoing.

Steck warned at the same time that he had heard that "volunteer companies" were clamoring to aid in "punishing" Indian thieves. If this were done from "patriotic" motives, that was one thing. But if the posses were not under firm control of responsible officers they might wreak much mischief, especially if they desired to steal stock of peaceful Indians, a consideration not beyond possibility. Steck also wrote General Garland of his trip through the Mimbres country, informing the officer that the chiefs "seemed to regret that the robberies had been committed, and were much alarmed for their own safety."[4]

They had promised to prevent depredations by their own people and to point out the guilty ones if any by chance occurred. Steck believed them. Delgadito and Itan both hoped troops would be stationed in the Mogollon country to the west, "as that would stop their [the Mogollons'] stealing, a great deal of which was laid" to the Mimbres. Steck thought establishment of such a post a good idea. He described the two points of practicable entry into the rugged Mogollon Mountains and thought a good place for a permanent post would be where the Gila emerges from the range. "You would have the Mogollon Indians around you but principally to the N. East you would have the Mimbres Indians, south Mangus Colorado & those of Cierra Larga, & West the more powerful tribe of Coyoteros and within striking distance of them all." Wood, water, grass, and farming areas were all abundant, Steck reported.[5]

Davis, unconvinced by Steck's reassurances, replied on the twenty-first that "if the Mimbres chiefs are as well disposed for peace as they tell you, they must control their bad men, or in case they cannot do so, they must report them to you, and assist you in having them punished. It is ridiculous for them to say that they cannot control a few bad men of the tribe—the truth is that they do not try."[6] The letter revealed the official's woeful ignorance of Apache social organization and the limitations it set upon chiefs and head men.

Steck replied on February 15, giving evidence once again of the good faith of his Indians.

He reported that on one occasion they had closely watched the minor band of one, Cigarito, a subleader whose people were suspected of depredating:

About ten days ago five of the thieves left their camp for the settlements.

48

Delgadito immediately sent an express directing me to put the people on their guard which I at once done writing to Mesilla. The five thieves went directly to Mesilla, stole four oxen the next day. They were followed and overtaken and three of them killed, one of them the son of Cigarito. They also stole some horses from the Miembre [*sic*] Apaches who followed them and killed two others. About a month ago a Mexican (usually called California Jo) who has been living with the Apaches for two years and whom I have suspected was engaged in much petty stealing charged to Indians, was employed by me to invite the Indians to the Agency. . . . He borrowed a horse and left, but instead of doing as he agreed, went to the Indian camp and told them not to come in, killed the horse he had borrowed. The Indians . . . declared that Jo must return a horse. He refused, a quarrel ensued and Jo was killed on the spot. This is the Indian tale—and the only part of it I can vouch for is that Jo was killed. . . . Thus we have got rid of six thieves in the last month. The remainder of Cigarito's party have gone south into Mexico where I hope they will remain.[7]

Such were the difficulties facing chiefs and head men seeking to "control a few bad men," and, no matter what the official in distant Santa Fe believed, the fact is that they did try to manage them, though it was a very hard thing to do.

To further complicate matters, there occurred a tragedy in April, 1856, which might have had catastrophic effects upon the Indian situation had Steck not been an extraordinary agent and had the Mimbres not been determined, come what might, to remain at peace with the Americans.

Steck had accompanied a military force commanded by Brevet Lieutenant Colonel Daniel T. Chandler into the Mogollons,[8] where a camp of presumed raiders was attacked, an Indian killed, three or four wounded, and 250 sheep and 31 horses and mules recovered. On their return from the Gila, by way of the Burro Mountains, the expedition passed the copper mines and moved on toward the Mimbres. Here the soldiers had a clash with peaceful Mimbres Indians "without a provocation." To Steck it was "so unexpected and may be productive of so much evil," that he reported it in detail:

The night previous to this unfortunate affair the whole force encamped about 7 miles from the Mimbres, and here considering himself out of the enemy country he [Chandler] resolved upon the following morning to leave the main body of men and tired animals in command of Maj. [Oliver Lathrop] Shepherd and with one company of infantry and a detachment of dragoons to go on in advance to his post, Ft. Craig. After marching about 6 miles toward the Mimbres and one mile from that stream he discovered

49

the camp of Delgadito, Itan, Ramon and other friendly Indians who were assembled to see the command as it passed, and to see their agent by appointment. He approached with his command, about 60 men, within musket range and fired into their camp without knowing or stopping to enquire who it was he was firing upon. The firing was continued at least 20 minutes. The Indians, with a few exceptions, scattering in every direction into the Mts. with the loss of one woman killed, another wounded, three children wounded and at this date one child still missing.

Delgadito and Costales, the Mexican-born subchief, finally made contact with the officer, who told them he thought they were Mogollons and agreed to pay them for their losses. Yet, Steck pointed out, repayment was of slight importance "when compared with other evils that must result from such a rash and unguarded step. To manage our Indians he must have confidence in your kind intentions and how can he confide in you if when he had been promised a friendly salutation you greet him with musketry and the shrieks of dying and wounded women and children?"[9]

Steck's letter ultimately reached Washington. A demand for an explanation brought from Chandler his version.

He said his troops had been following up a trail of depredators when "we discovered on the hillside a horse, which we captured, having the same brand" as one stolen.

The spies who were sent out returned and reported that the Indians of whom we were in pursuit were encamped in a small cañon close by, and hidden from view by an intervening hill. Lieut. Moore, with a detachment of Dragoons, was sent to the left and front, to cut off the retreat on that flank, and Lieut. [Matthew L.] Davis, with an Infantry command moved up the cañon. As soon as these troops arrived in sight of the Indians a fire was opened upon them, and the men advanced rapidly, the Indians returning it and retreating. Moving up to the mouth of the cañon, it was seen that the warriors were outstripping the squaws in their flight, and accordingly the fire was stopped the troops advancing and endeavoring to get within gunshot of the men. As we advanced it was discovered that the camp was an extremely large one, too large, in fact, to consist of those only whose trail we had followed. Seeing at this moment an Indian advancing on horseback waving his hat, as if desirous of holding a talk, I made signal for him to approach, which he did. He proved to be Costales, interpreter and subchief of the Mimbres Apaches, and informed us that this was Delgadito's camp. I immediately sent for Delgadito and dispatched an order to Maj. Shepherd who was moving on the hill in their rear with the remainder of the troops, to halt and not to open open [sic] fire on the Indians.

50

Chandler said he agreed to compensate the Indians, and that they were satisfied.[10]

Garland passed Chandler's version on to the adjutant general with the comment that "the homily of Agent Steck might just as well have been omitted, for he was not present at the unfortunate occurrence, and the officers of the army have too much intelligence and humanity of feeling to make a ruthless attack upon even savage foes."[11]

Jefferson Davis, secretary of war, wrote to Secretary of the Interior Robert McClelland that Chandler's explanation "is satisfactory to this Department,"[12] but Steck was not mollified. He wrote Manypenny on October 28 that he had heard the War Department had ordered an investigation, but that no one had inquired of him, nor, to his knowledge, of any officer who had taken part in the incident. "I have no desire to follow up this unpleasant affair but in self defense I beg leave to place before your Honor the enclosed letters written by officers accompanying the expedition. . . ."[13] The only surviving letter was from Lieutenant Davis, who said he was aware that the command was in Delgadito's friendly territory, rather than in hostile country, when the attack was launched.[14] There the matter ended. Although the fault was of ignorance rather than viciousness, it was a narrow squeak and, had Delgadito been less level-headed, might have become a major tragedy. Only the determination of the Mimbres leaders, including Victorio, of course, to remain at peace under any provocation prevented a holocaust.

Yet in another way the Chandler expedition did bring further tragedy. An Indian had been slain in the Mogollon Mountain attack, and in the Apache view, this must be avenged. As a consequence death came upon an innocent man, and his demise, too, must be avenged by the whites. Revenge and counterrevenge comprised a grim ritual on that bloody frontier, although in this case it is probable that most contemporaries failed to link the incidents.

Henry Linn Dodge, an attorney and Mexican War veteran, had been named agent to the Navahos in July, 1853. A member of a distinguished family, he had married a Navaho girl and in some ways was an odd man, given to garish dress and other idiosyncrasies, but for all of that he was an effective agent.[15] On November 16, 1856, he disappeared while hunting alone near a Zuñi pueblo. Twelve days later Meriwether wrote Steck that he had been informed that "a party of Indians, either Mogoyons or Gila Apaches, had captured Agent H. L. Dodge and taken him towards the Gila, and the object of this

51

letter is to instruct you to endeavour to procure his release as soon as possible." Steck was told to send out small parties to ascertain the facts and, if possible, to ransom Dodge.[16] The agent sent into that country José Mangas, a brother of Mangas Coloradas, and Tenaja, a Mimbres, "with instructions not to return without bringing positive information."

They came in January 2, reporting that "an american was killed about one day's ride or more from Zunia by a party of Mogollon & Coyotero Apaches. That they found him hunting in the mountains alone and that he was shot dead by one of the Indians. They further report that on the same day the same party killed several [other reports said nine[17]] Mexicans." Steck believed there was little doubt the American was Dodge. He then added the reason for the apparently casual slayings:

"They say further that some time previous to that time the same party stole some stock from the settlements, were followed, most of the stock retaken and one Indian was killed and that this party went to revenge his death," a practice normal and right from the Apache viewpoint, but outrageous from the American. The Chandler expedition had slain an Apache—ergo, the Apaches would even scores by slaying an American. To further improve the situation, the Indians then split into two groups "and went into the settlements and stole two large bands of sheep and nearly one hundred head of cattle and horses." These were divided up on the headwaters of the San Francisco River, most trailed west into Arizona, but the remainder southward down the identical trail Chandler had followed. This group, of eight or ten lodges, was the party Chandler earlier had attacked, led by Cautivo, or "captive," and Tsana. Captain Thomas Claiborne, commanding at Thorn, listened as José Mangas reported, and added that the raiders had threatened the Mimbres Indians if any retaliatory attack were made upon them.[18] Retaliation would come, nonetheless, though much later.

The whites were not the only people sinned against, Steck reported. On the evening of December 29 sixteen horses were stolen from Delgadito's camp by two Mexicans who were trailed the next day, eleven of the animals recovered, although the thieves escaped with "five of the fleetest horses." Steck hurried an express to Mesilla and recovered one more, then dispatched two noted leaders, Costales, the Mexican-Apache, and Ratton, to work out the trail and see if they could recover the other animals.

"They followed the trail to near Mesilla and returned to San Diego [a crossing of the Río Grande about ten miles southeast of Fort Thorn, north of Mesilla], where they intended staying all night." A vague rumor of trouble reached Thorn next morning, December 31, and Claiborne sent Second Lieutenant Alexander Early Steen to San Diego to investigate. Steen left the post at 4:00 P.M. with a corporal and five private soldiers, accompanied by Ammin Barnes, who leased the government ferry boat at San Diego. Steen reported on New Year's Day:

I arrived at San Diego at about 9 o'clock P.M., and encamped near the ferry house for the night, and after clear daylight this morning I commenced an examination which resulted in finding in the sleeping room of the ferry house a quantity of blood on the floor, and a butcher and table knife, lying on the floor, perfectly filled with gore, and a hat and wrapping sheet of manta and a sack, at once recognized by myself, Mr. Barnes, and some of the men to be that of Costales, . . . and from the trail of blood leading from the house to the banks of the river, I concluded the person killed had been thrown into the river, and after searching probably an hour and a half, the body of Costales was fished up, he had evidently been killed while asleep; his head was split open with a blow from an axe, his throat cut and the entire scalp taken off.

The body of Ratton was never found, although signs indicated that he too had been murdered.[19]

It was then that Dr. Steck revealed his remarkable influence over the Mimbres, extracting from Delgadito a pledge that he would not allow his people to retaliate or seek revenge,[20] although the fact that Costales was of Mexican birth might have helped. Meriwether gloomily doubted Delgadito's "ability to restrain his people from retaliating upon some of our innocent people. . . . I have instructed Agent Steck to use his best efforts to have the murderers arrested and punished, but the murder was committed only about seventy-five miles from the southern boundary of this territory, and as the supposed murderers formerly resided in the province of Chihuahua to which they have probably returned, it is highly probable that they cannot be arrested."[21] Some time later he added that "I am inclined to the opinion that but little effort was made to arrest the murderers."[22] The victims were only Apaches, anyway.

The Mimbres, if occasionally targets for injustice, were not entirely without fault. Steck conceded in mid-March that several depredations had been committed by his Indians. On the eighth, eight had stolen seven mules near Robledo, were followed by Brevet Captain Alfred Gibbs thirty miles to the west, and six killed. "They were undoubtedly Mimbres Apaches," Steck admitted, one being identified as such. In a letter to Lieutenant Colonel Dixon Stansbury Miles on the nineteenth, he noted that the Mimbres had gone to Janos, where they and the Mogollons were engaged in "extensive" trade in stock with the Mexicans, most of it doubtless pilfered from northern ranges.[23] Other thefts were by Mescaleros,[24] just as avid for white man's stock as their cousins. But such thefts suggested neither general hostilities nor that all Mimbres were so engaged, the agent pointed out.

Today one man & a large number of women came in & state that all the Mimbres Indians are gone south to make Moscal. This corresponds with the report of a man whom I sent out to ascertain the cause of their strange conduct [that is, their seeming aloofness toward the agency] who states that there are no Indians on the Mimbres or in the Mts. near there except one camp. . . . I have required of them that all who wish to remain at peace must be on their reserve by the next full moon, and have warned them that all who are caught off of it will be treated as enemies and that no doubt war would be made against them.

While admittedly there were some "bad men" among them, Steck added, "there are many in whose professions of friendships I have the utmost confidence."[25] Steck had good reason for hurriedly ordering his Indians back into their usual camps.

For it was now spring and what has been called the "campaign of the clowns" was making up. This was an effort, in a general way, to exact payment for the Dodge murder, which, as we have seen, was in retaliation for an Apache slaying, which was—etc., etc. Anyway, the expedition was to be led by Colonel Benjamin Louis Eulalie de Bonneville, sixty-one, whose frontier career had been long and useful, but who now was regarded by his officers as "a hulking bag of wind in his dotage."[26] One of its two principal components was commanded by Colonel Miles, Third Infantry, whom Governor Lane considered a martinet and a "walking sponge."[27] The other wing was under command of one-armed Colonel William Wing Loring, a North Carolinian who was to become a major general in the Confederate Army. They were considered by the most able junior officer of the expedition "men who don't know what to do or how to do it if they knew what they wanted."[28]

On May 1 Loring left Albuquerque with the northern column, the regiment of mounted rifles and other units, including Pueblo scouts. That day and on the second, Miles and Bonneville left Thorn with the southern column, including dragoons, infantry, and guides. Bonneville had been alerted by Steck that in view of the "proximity of your operations it will be of the utmost importance to keep the [Mimbres] within their reserve and prevent the Mogollon Band from seeking refuge around the friendly band which they will be apt to do if tightly pushed."[29]

The two columns converged on the Gila near Greenwood Canyon, where a depot was formed,[30] and a long and indecisive stay ensued, while small units coursed the nearby mountains looking for the enemy. Loring's Pueblos found and attacked a Mimbres band about ten miles east of the upper Mimbres River in the Blank Range, where there were no hostiles, killing six or seven, including Cuchillo Negro, the important chief, and capturing some stock and nine women and children at the chief's little farm. Bonneville took Miles's column down the Gila until, near Mount Graham in present-day Arizona, on June 27 they found a camp of Coyoteros peacefully gathering mescal and, with Captain Richard Stoddert (Baldy) Ewell and his dragoons in the vanguard, launched a murderous attack, killing twenty-four, wounding others, and taking twenty-seven prisoners. The success of the attack must have surprised Ewell, who had written to his mother earlier that "I am very tired of chasing a parcel of Indians about at the orders of men who don't know what to do or how to do it if they knew what they wanted. . . . We are now starting in a 'solumn' (solid column) of 600 men, we will NOT be apt to see Indians, and mules and horses will be the only sufferers."[31] The Coyoteros had not been charged with committing depredations upon New Mexico,[32] except for the Dodge incident involving Cautivo's small band, but one Apache seemed as worthless as another to many soldiers.

Returning in mid-September Bonneville wrote to James Collins, new superintendent of Indian affairs for the Territory, that "we were operating in what has been known as the Gila country for more than four months, had detachments of troops scattered in every direction bringing on their return sketches of the country and information from every quarter. . . . [First] Lieutenant William Dennison Whipple [Third Infantry] was sent into the Mogollon mountains. He remained in them near twenty days—visited the headwaters of the Gila, and described it as a most elevated and tumbled up region, perfectly worthless, except for a limited space on the northwestern slope of the mountain."³³ His report was fairly accurate, though it was a favorite range of the Apaches named for it and for the Mimbres as well. To this day it is a lovely, challenging wilderness.³⁴

While Bonneville was rummaging about the mountains, most of the Mimbres, in order to be well out of the way, drifted down into Mexico, made a treaty of sorts with the citizens of Janos, and negotiated fruitlessly for the liberation of some of their people held by the Mexicans as hostages, not for wrongs done by the Mimbres, but for those alleged against the Gilas to the west.³⁵ Delgadito had informed Steck that his Indians remained uneasy after the Chandler affair and because of a still more recent incident when, approaching troops with a white flag, they again had been fired upon. Steck believed it "unsafe" for the Indians to remain on the Mimbres, too, and urged those who had not gone to Mexico to move in closer to Fort Thorn where he could look after them.³⁶

The Apaches, increasingly rasped by contact with the Americans, had perennial trouble with Mexicans below the border and discovered anew that all the world was still their enemy, closing in upon them.

Toward the end of the summer of 1856 a party had visited Janos, and thirteen were thrown into prison. One was released and sent with a letter from Padilla, the Janos military commandant, to Mangas Coloradas, informing him that his people were to be "held in confinement" until "certain property stolen by his people was restored to the citizens of Janos." This letter was brought to Steck and its contents sent to the governor. Meriwether, under guidance from the agent, wrote Padilla, pointing out that the prisoners held, and the Indians charged with depredations, "were of different and distinct bands, and one should not be held responsible for the conduct, or punished, for depredations committed by the other." He requested that the Mimbres be released from confinement, promising to do everything possible to cause the property to be restored.

He sent his letter by a Mimbres woman, who returned from Janos with a reply dated November 9 in which Padilla said he had conferred with his superior, José María Zuloaga,³⁷ an embittered old Indian fighter who told him to hold on to the captives despite Meriwether's plea. Padilla added that the prisoners had been taken during "the attack made upon this place by them, in company with Mangas Coloradas, Cascos, Cautivo, Barbonsito, Galimbo, Perea, Durazelle, Tapaye and many others, and when they carried off a large quantity of property." By holding them, he concluded, it was hoped that "a permanent peace can be secured." He remarked pointedly, "We are satisfied that you will use every means in your power to restrain the Indians who reside in the United States from coming into this Republic to steal and murder as they have done up to this time, and also will not consent to the traffic of the inhabitants with the Indians, purchasing the animals which the Indians have stolen from this country." The veiled charges were serious ones that would be frequently echoed in the future, as would corresponding allegations by American settlers, soldiers, and officials against what they considered occasional Mexican collusion with the Apaches—when it suited their purposes.

Padilla made clear his conviction that the Mimbres were equally responsible with other Indians for "the ruined and miserable condition to which they have reduced the settlements of this State," which, he said, "is worthy of the compassion of all civilized men and it is impossible to look upon those Indians or the captives innocent."[38] It would tax the wisdom of a Solomon to determine the right and wrong of all the charges and countercharges leveled during those confused years, and to administer justice, and there was no Solomon in the Southwest.

By late November of 1857 most of the Mimbres who had been camped near Janos, or between that place and the border seeking the release of their people, had given up and struggled back to the Mimbres River, sick and disillusioned. Apparently the Mexicans, unable to get from them what they did not possess—livestock other Indians had stolen—had resorted to more cruel methods of retaliation and to satisfy their bitter hatred against these, their foes of generations past. Steck reported of his returned charges:

They are . . . almost naked and actually in a starving condition. They . . . have occasionally received rations from the Govt. of Mexico. They have suffered much from disease and many of them have died. . . . Scarcely a family returned but has their hair cropped short, the badge of mourning for some relative. They believe they have been poisoned, and I have but little doubt that many of them have, as reports have reached here from the citizens of Janos that many of them had been poisoned, and the symptoms as described by the Indians resemble those of poisoning by arsenic, probably administered in whiskey as that formed a part of their rations. . . . The Mogollon Band . . . also visited Mexico and have there contracted diseases from which many of them have died, and I am informed by Mangas Colorado, their former chief, that they are now willing to . . . make peace.

Steck's long training and practice as a physician lends weight to his

57

suspicion of the use of arsenic against these Indians. Arsenic, next to whiskey, was often the prime civilizing agency of the whites, and not only of Mexicans, either. It also was employed by unscrupulous Americans, some in high places, and not alone by Americans against Red Indians, but by Englishmen and many other peoples. It, or strychnine, was used to decimate the Bushmen in South Africa, where waterholes were doctored with the poison, and to remove troublesome Australian aborigines. "Civilized" man employed murder where convenient as a means of clearing away human obstacles to his economic advancement at least as often as supposed savages used it as a last resort to defend their cultures and lands. Lack of conscience knows no societal bounds.

Victorio, no doubt with his people upon their sad peregrination, had avoided death from poisoned whiskey and perhaps had been completely untouched. Throughout his life there is no report of his ever being drunk, a state which among the Apaches carried no stigma of any kind. It is possible that he avoided whiskey entirely; some Indians did. His colleagues upon occasion became drunk, but if Victorio did no hint of it has survived. His probable abstemiousness is another indication of the self-control and wisdom that made him a great war leader and chief.

Steck urged that a treaty, one that the Senate could approve, "should be held . . . as soon as possible" with Mimbres and Mogollons alike, but he feared the inevitable time lapse occasioned by the complicated mechanism for getting such a pact ratified. "You might as well talk Greek to them as try to explain the delays," he grumbled.[39]

VI

Under Pressure

In the spring of 1858 a wanton attack on peaceful Indians gathered hard by Fort Thorn pointed up anew the pressures and mounting hostility between the races. It was of that lamentable series of clashes marking relationships from the earliest white contacts with Indians on many frontiers. In this case, the second such attack upon the Mimbres within three short years, thirty-six Spanish-Americans from Mesilla, led by one Juan Ortega, savagely assailed the camp by the agency and "butchered indiscriminately men, women, and children." First Lieutenant William Henry Wood, in command at Thorn, reported on April 7:

This morning about day break a party of armed Mexicans from Mesilla, charged into the Indian Camp.

Immediately on ascertaining what was going on, I ordered the Garrison under arms, and while the Rifles were saddling up, went out with the Infantry and succeeded in capturing the whole party, about half a mile from the post, as they were retreating with a number of little children whom they had made captives. . . . After disposing of the prisoners [who were disarmed and held under guard] a party was sent out to collect the dead bodies. They soon returned bringing in seven, three men, three women and one boy, all of whom we interred in rear of our burying ground. Three of the wounded . . . have been placed in Hospital. . . . This affair is but a repetition of the horrible massacre recently perpetrated by the same party at Doña Ana. . . . These Indians . . . I sincerely believe have given no cause for this cowardly outrage.[1]

Steck was absent from the agency at the time. Upon returning next day he filed his own report, saying in part:

The people living at the agency were aroused by the screams of Indians and . . . saw the [raiders] indiscriminately butchering Indians regardless of age, sex or condition. After the first attack the most of the Indians probably 30 in number ran for the woods near by and were followed by the assassins who seemed to take a fiendish delight in murdering innocent defenseless and unoffending women . . . The conduct of Lieut. Wood merits the highest praise. But for his promptness and energy the bloody work might have continued much longer. In fifteen minutes from the time he received information of what was doing he rushed into the midst of the outlaws drew his pistol and demanded of their leader immediate surrender. The prompt action of this officer has had a most excellent effect upon the Indians, many of whom saw him make the capture. It shows that . . . they will be protected. . . . So far as I can learn there had been no cause for this cowardly and murderous attack. . . . This is the same party of men who committed the outrageous murders in Doña Ana on the 7th of February 1855.[2]

Nothing had happened to them following that occasion, Dr. Steck noted, and he feared nothing would happen to them after these slayings. So far as existing records show, nothing did.

Assuredly there was exasperation on both sides, as well as criminal activities. Special Agent George Bailey of the Interior Department reported to Commissioner of Indian Affairs Charles E. Mix in November, 1858, that "the testimony of all who have any knowledge of the Apaches concurs in pronouncing him the most rascally Indian on the continent. Treacherous, bloodthirsty, brutal with an irresistible propensity to steal, he has been for years the scourge of Mexico . . . and grave doubts are expressed whether any process short of extermination will suffice to *quiet* him." In fairness it should be noted, however, that for sheer rascality the Apache would have been hard put to match that of numerous whites of both Mexico and the United States, his examples. Bailey continued:

"A part of the Mimbres Apaches passed Stein's Peak shortly before I reached it, with several hundred head of cattle which they had stolen in Mexico. A portion of this band moved with the cattle to the mountains, the remainder proceeded to Ft. Thorne. . . . The amount of property stolen annually by these Indians is incalculable. According to the returns of the United States Marshals there were stolen in New Mexico alone, between the 1st August and 1st October 1850, 12,887 mules, 7,050 horses, 31,581 horned cattle and 453,293 head of sheep."[3] He failed to point out that these alleged thefts were committed, not by Mimbres alone nor even in great part, but by other Indian tribes and bands, and by white rustlers of every variety, who generously sought when possible to shift blame for their deeds to their red brethren. Bailey was not overly perspicacious; cures he suggested were impractical and most of his ideas unimaginative, but he reflected the common view of that day in New Mexico. His mission probably had been prompted by a windy, sixty-six page pamphlet, *Indian*

Depredations in New Mexico, which Attorney John S. Watts published in 1858 to further the hopes for profits by numerous claimants (perhaps clients) alleging damages suffered.[4] Under certain circumstances the federal government would reimburse citizens for losses to Indian raiders.

It was to the advantage of those who lost stock to white rustlers, as well as to the thieves themselves, to lay such losses upon the Indian. If the thefts were by whites, the rancher received no redress from any source unless he could recapture his animals. But if he could show that Indians had stolen them he might recover something and, with a little judicious padding of his reported losses, could even turn a profit. The Indian would be unlikely to object too strongly at being blamed for stock thefts he had not committed, since he may well have been guilty of others and he could be executed but once.

In his *Annual Report* of August 6, 1858, Steck noted the "most friendly" relations with the Mimbres and Gila Apaches, saying that during the year "not a single depredation has been committed" on the main road to California east of the "Chilihauhua [Chiricahua] Mts and parties of from 2 to five men are now constantly traveling the road from the Rio Grande to Ft. Buchanan [in present-day southern Arizona] in safety." Despite abuses by citizens toward them, the Mimbres and Mogollons appeared willing to cooperate to maintain the peace, he reported.

Steck noted that he had "urged the propriety of uniting the Mogollon & Mimbres bands. . . . I encouraged such a removal and now many of the Mogollon Band are living with those of the Mimbres and have corn planted together and among them their old Chief Mangas Colorado." Almost as an aside he thus revealed a significant development among the Eastern Chiricahuas: their amalgamation into a single band, a development strengthened and continued from this time forward.

"The Mimbres, Mogollon & Mescalero Bands of Apaches are exceedingly poor and decreasing in number very Rapidly—as is the case with all wild tribes; they cannot bear contact with civilization, the exercise & excitement of the chase or marauding being gone they become indolent & contact vices which weaken & vitiate the system rendering it more liable to attacks of disease and less able to resist its influences hence many of them die from affections [*sic*] that ordinarily seldom prove fatal. . . .

"The Mimbres Band have been constantly exposed to the evil in-

61

fluences of intercourse with the Spanish population of the country who cannot be prevented from selling them whiskey." He said their mortality had been "terrible." "Of the men who numbered one year ago about 85 not less than one fifth have died during the year. The Mogollon Band having been exposed to the same influences . . . have suffered as severely. . . . The two Bands together cannot now muster 250 warriors, while in 1853 the Mimbres band alone with a day's notice could bring into the field over 300."

He recalled the "fixed policy of the Ind. Dep. to locate wandering tribes," adding that "this certainly is the only hope for the Apaches." He pointed out that agriculture alone could forestall their raiding and stealing and at "some distant day" provide a living for them. "The Bands best prepared for the change are the Mimbres & Mogollon," and again urged their relocation somewhere along the remote Gila River, although with the military on hand to "prevent improper intercourse with citizens." He thought the Mimbres and Mogollons could "at once be induced to remove," if that were decided upon.[5]

As though to stress the urgency of removal, white pressure on the Mimbres increased sharply that summer with a fresh attempt by one, Leonard Secaurus, of Mexico, to work the Santa Rita mines. Victorio's people deeply resented this.

"These mines were included in the Indian reserve provided for in the [1855] Treaty," noted Steck, "and when Mr. Secaurus took possession of the mines he done so without consulting the Indians or their agent. This course though impolitic he had a right to take as he holds a lease from the owners. The Indians were however, dissatisfied at the time and as the country had been given to them by treaty they thought they should have been consulted." At length the Mimbres were placated, "but the Mogollon Band are now threatening to interfere. I have frequently been told by Mimbres Indians that those on the Gila threatened to drive the people away from the mines, and today I was informed . . . that there is no doubt of their intention to do so if something is not done soon. . . . They seem to be friendly to americans, their hostility to the people at the mine arises from the fact that they know they are from the Republic of Mexico." Steck urged the superintendent to visit the area as soon as possible; perhaps he could head off trouble.[6]

On Christmas Day, 1858, Dr. Steck left the agency at Fort Thorn for an extended trip through Indian country. He stopped at the copper mines, where he found the Mimbres quiet and apparently satisfied.

He journeyed on, probably through Doubtful Pass, across the wide San Simon Valley, southwesterly to Apache Pass in the "Chilicagua [Chiricahua] Mts., one hundred & seventy miles from the agency on the road travelled by the Overland Mail to California."[7]

Steck continued, "At this place I found a band of Apaches called Janeros or Chilcagua Mt. Apaches [the central Chiricahuas]. They number about 50 men, 130 women and 400 children making a total of 600. This Band of Apaches, although living upon the main emigrant road to California, have committed no depredations upon the route for about two years. In order, therefore, to encourage them in that good behaviour, I collected the whole Band, and distributed among them a portion of the presents designed for the Coyotero and other Apaches.[8] After distributing the presents I visited Ft. Buchanan . . . on Sonoita Creek to the West." Dr. Steck returned to Apache Pass with Captain Ewell and some dragoons, and again remarked that the Chiricahuas numbered only fifty warriors, a figure probably too low. He added that they lived upon mescal and what they could steal in Mexico, but he warned them against raiding, noting that the chiefs "are aware of the power of the Govt. to crush them at any moment." Before too many years the Chiricahuas would abundantly disapprove that boast!

He then made the first important contacts with bands of the Coyoteros and Pinals. In the course of amicable and successful councils, he warned them against hostilities against the whites and urged them to live at peace with all their neighbors, red or white. He described his meetings as "most satisfactory" and said they "fully confirmed me in the belief that . . . the White Mt. Band of Coyoteros is the Best, and most reliable division of the whole Apache tribe."[9] In late March, 1859, he counciled with some other Pinal Apaches, twenty-five miles north of Tucson, also with satisfactory results.[10]

In his *Annual Report* for 1859, written in August, Steck for the first time officially lumped the Mimbres and Mogollons together as the "Gila Apaches," with headquarters in the "Buras," meaning Burro, Mountains.

He said that these Indians had selected, as a preferred site for a reservation if they must move, bottomlands along the Santa Lucia, now called Mangas Creek, a tributary of the Gila debouching about fifteen miles south of the Mogollon Mountains. "This valley is large enough to locate the Mimbres & Mogollon Bands upon together with the Mescaleros, if at a future day it should be thought advisable to remove them west of the Rio Grande. It is completely isolated being surrounded by mountains." He thought a permanent reservation should be patented for the Indians there, remote from civilization, yet easily supplied. "As long as they are permitted to rove about in small parties, petty thefts will be occasionally commited by them," he cautioned. "Situated as they now are they are compelled to roam about in small parties to obtain a subsistence and cannot be watched either by the agent or their chiefs. But secure to them a reservation, let this then be subdivided so as to give each head of a family a farm to cultivate, they would regard that as their permanent home & having something to lose would dred [sic] the consequences of a violation of their obligations."

The Chiricahuas he now estimated at one hundred warriors—double his earlier calculation—and said they had had very little contact with white Americans until the Overland Mail drove through the heart of their country. Since his visit, he pointed out, "no traveller has been molested upon the road through their country."

"This Band of Apaches roam about in small parties and have always been termed by the people the (Apaches Broncus) or wild Apaches. . . . This Band is intimately connected with those of the Mogollon Mts. by intermarriage & habits and if a reservation should be established they should at once be compelled to locate with them upon the Gila."

Colonel Bonneville had suggested, Steck recalled, locating a military post at "Lucero Spring," a suggestion "of the utmost importance." This post, at the spring probably named for Victorio, "would be within twenty-five miles of the planting grounds of the Indians, between them and the settlements, and within 8 miles of the present Overland Mail route to California. This post cooperating with two companies upon the San Pedro [in Arizona] and two near Tucson would induce the settlement of the country and in the event of war would be sufficient to chastise the Inds."[11] The site of Lucero Spring, or Ojo de Lucero, is not definitely known but appears to have been within a few miles southeast of the southeastern extremity of the Big Burro Mountains.[12] This would have been well within the range of the Mimbres.

This same year, incidentally, there was established a picket post, or outpost, of Fort Craig, called Ojo Caliente, on a low bench on the southern bank of the upper Alamosa River, just above a cleft where the river plunges into the Alamosa Mountains. This post, centered upon a square of adobe buildings, would later on become the agency headquarters for the Mimbres during their critical years, although now it was more a precautionary installation than anything. It always was lightly garrisoned.[13]

With no escort whatever, Steck in October went westward with presents once more, meeting about eight hundred of the Gila bands probably at Lucero Spring, and found his charges content. At the San Simon River, southwest of Stein's Peak, he distributed presents to about four hundred Chiricahuas and received from "Chees," or Cochise, three animals that had been stolen, exacting the promise of the chieftain that he would "watch over the interest of the mail coaches and travelers upon the great thoroughfare to California." He recommended again that the Chiricahuas be settled with Mangas and his people.[14]

Steck journeyed to Washington early in 1860, leaving his aide, Pinckney R. Tully, as acting agent.[15] When he returned he at once visited his Mimbres, finding them "behaving as well as usually, but in an unusually destitute condition," with problems once more beginning to mount. "Settlements have been made upon the Mimbres [River] & at the Coppermines and stations have been built every fifteen miles on the Overland Mail route, all of which seems to have driven the game out of their former hunting grounds & the cedar berry which other seasons formed a part of their subsistence this year has been an entire failure. Complaints have been made that they killed a few head of cattle about the Coppermines but considering their condition & that these people are operating in the heart of their country it was a matter of surprise that complaints of this kind have not been more frequent and upon a larger scale."

Steck reported that "these Indians complain very much about our permitting the people to settle in their country. They say they are occupying the best portions of it and fast running them out—and every word of their complaints are true. There are now at least forty settlers on the Mimbres, most of them with their families, and not less than one thousand souls living at or near the Coppermines. If some steps are not taken to set apart a portion of their country as a reserve they will have none worth having left. . . . Cannot something be done at the present session of Congress?" He urged a reservation, fifteen miles on each of four sides, upon the Gila, to include Santa Lucia Creek and springs. It would have included the present communities of Gila, Cliff, and Buckhorn, northwest of Silver City, the boundary line going north almost to Shelly Peak, west to near Jackson on U.S. Highway 180, and its southern boundary would have touched Bald Knoll. It is rolling grassy country, now grazed by cattle and farmed in the bottoms, but no amount of troops could have kept the Indians on it if they had decided to stray, as they very soon would have.[16]

In response to a query, Steck informed the commissioner that Indians proposed for this reservation would include: Mescaleros, 120 men, 600 women and children; Gila bands, including Mimbres, Mogollon, and Chiricahua, 300 men, 1,800 women and children.[17]

Steck warned anew that "a large proportion of the settlers and operatives in the copper & gold mines near Santa Rita del Cobre are americans, mostly irresponsible, little knowledge of Indians, & not patience sufficient to live amicably with hungry Indians—an eruption with the Apaches would be more to their taste & having little to lose in the event I fear difficulty every day, particularly as the Inds. situated as they now are cannot be prevented from getting drunk."[18] His gloomy forebodings were to prove accurate.

With the discovery of gold on Bear Creek and the mushroom development of the Pinos Altos diggings, a scant seven miles north of present-day Silver City, the relationships of Mimbres and whites entered a new, more savage phase, never to be reversed. It would bring dispute, disorder, bloodshed, and ultimate disaster.

VII

The Pinos Altos Rush

White settlement on the lower Mimbres River began in earnest in 1859 when about thirty Mexicans and Americans created a small community, planted one hundred acres in corn and beans, established two whiskey dispensaries, and called it Mowry City, after Lieutenant Sylvester Mowry, southwestern pioneer and visionary whose advertisements of the place for eastern publications included cuts of steamboats on the frequently dry Mimbres where no craft of any sort ever in fact existed.[1] This tiny village, invading lands of the Mimbres Apaches, was but the harbinger of the flood which poured in with reports of a gold strike on Bear Creek. The find was made by "Colonel" Jacob Snively, an adventurer of considerable experience, an inverate prospector who periodically struck it rich but never profited much from his luck and succumbed to a Yavapai arrow at last over in Arizona.[2] He made the strike in company with a prospector, Hicks, and an alleged killer named Birch, or Burch, after whom the community first was called Birchville. The name was changed to Pinos Altos for the tall ponderosas standing silent guard over the waiting wealth. Until today its mines have yielded about eight million dollars in gold, besides silver and, nearby, zinc and lead.[3]

Among those who swarmed in was Anson Mills, fresh out of West Point, later to become a brigadier general, who as a surveyor laid out the town, and James H. Tevis, hastening there from his new ranch on the lower Río Grande. Tevis built the first permanent structure at about the point where the creature which gave Bear Creek its name was shot from a tree. Tevis was luckier than Mills, or his imagination more active, for he later recalled making twenty-five to six hundred dollars a day from his claim, while Mills recalled taking out only three dollars a day. At any rate Tevis found his work profitable when he was not off fighting Indians somewhere.[4] There is no doubt that he was prominent in the strife that developed, conflicts that dug a deep chasm between Indians and whites, as profound as the canyons that bound the creeks about Pinos Altos, squarely athwart the Continental

67

Divide at 7,007 feet. It is on a point overlooking the head of Bear Creek to the north, Río de Arenas to the east, and Pinos Altos Creek to the west. The latter flows between the community and the Pinos Altos Mountains.

Because the prospectors sought color in the heart of country the Mimbres believed theirs, shot off the game, brought in whiskey mills and other accouterments of civilization, and, most of all, because of their thronging numbers, conflicts were inevitable. This was foreseen, and the army had swiftly established a post in the area, sending Major Isaac Lynde, Seventh Infantry, to the Mimbres. He arrived September 16, 1860, selecting a site near present-day Hurley, fifteen miles south of Santa Rita, twenty miles south of Pinos Altos, and a dozen miles west of the Overland Mail crossing of the river.[5] He recommended that it be called Fort Webster, but the secretary of war announced in December it would be named Fort McLane after Captain George McLane of the Mounted Rifles, killed by Navahos on October 13. Between Lynde's suggestion and the name assigned by Washington it had been briefly called Fort Floyd, after whom is unclear, though probably for War Secretary John Buchanan Floyd, later an incompetent Confederate brigadier general.

Even the military could not prevent clashes between the Apaches and the unruly, intemperate, and callous white miners.

On December 4, 1860, a band of Pinos Altos gold miners, probably under the guidance of Tevis, "attacked & killed some of the peaceful Indians at old Ft. Webster," Steck wrote Indian Superintendent James L. Collins. "This I have been anticipating for some time, as there are now and have been for some months, three or four hundred people at the Pino Alto Mines, a majority of whom were not taking out gold enough to support them. . . . What effect this will have it is impossible to say with certainty [although] the Mimbres band is to [sic] weak to make any formidable resistance. The only result I dread is that they will remove to the Republic of Mexico . . . and from there maraud upon the property of our people." Steck conceded that the Mimbres may have stolen a few animals from the miners, "but where one has been stolen by Indians, four have been stolen by white thieves." Steck said four Indians were killed and others wounded and fifteen women and children made prisoners. These were handed over to Fort McLane troops "and will be turned over to the Indians."[6]

Major Lynde added that twenty-eight miners had made the attack, headed by Henry Tibbets, who may be James Henry Tevis. "The excuse for the attack is that they have lost animals and they charge the Indians with stealing them, though they have no proof that this party has anything to do with it. I fear that this may lead to serious difficulty with these Indians."[7]

Tevis tells how the raid had come about and, with himself as guide, how it was conducted.

He wrote that the band of Apaches had killed and eaten a mule which they thought belonged to him, implying that he would have assented to it. But it was another's. The miners organized a company of "rangers," offered the leadership to Tevis, but he declined, saying that "prospectors were out all over the country, and the Indians were not molesting them, and that it would be far better to raise the money and pay for the mule than to risk war with them." However "the majority of the men were Texans . . . they wanted to fight. Seeing that they were determined to fight it out, I consented to go."

The posse picked up some barely broken horses and made their way under cover of darkness to the Mimbres Valley. The river was dry and Tevis scouted a *ranchería* next to a ranch owned by a German "in some way connected" with the tribe. The mounted party charged the camp and "out came the warriors like bees, and before they could form their line of battle we were upon them." The half-wild horses became unmanageable, however, and some were shot by Indian arrows. "I was only holding my ground with the men, but our six-shooters were having a telling effect on the Indian line." Tevis dismounted his men, and the Indians were joined by warriors from a nearby *ranchería*. Elías, the chief and an old acquaintance of Tevis, "sat on his horse, near the German's cabin, not over two hundred yards away, and cussed us in English—and in good English, too. I asked if any of the rangers could lift him out of his saddle, and one by the name of Davis . . . raised his gun, and before the smoke cleared away, Elias lay stretched on the ground. . . ." The rangers pursued the Indians up the river but ran into too much opposition and withdrew.

Major Lynde, at Fort McLane, had been advised of the affair by courier and sent Second Lieutenant John Sappington Marmaduke[8] with a detachment of Seventh Infantry with orders "to take charge of all captured stock and prisoners," Tevis recalled. "I was eager to get rid of the prisoners, but the stock I wanted in order to replace those stolen from the whites." He refused to release it until Marmaduke agreed to hold the animals while Tevis went to Pinos Altos, secured a list of stock allegedly stolen, and made it up from the Indian animals.

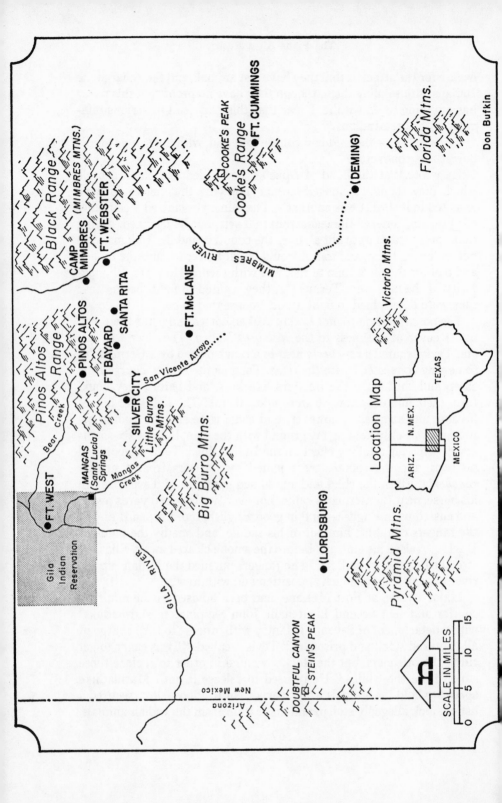

However, Victorio's people stole the stock back before Tevis fulfilled his mission, killing a few herders.[9]

Acting Agent Tully, trying to take rations to the Mimbres, found them furious and impossible to deal with, although they told him their version of events, differing considerably from the white accounts.

He called it a "very unprovoked attack" made "without the least possible cause or justification." The Mimbres, he believed, "are and always have been true to the Americans." At the outset of the fight "the Indians, believing that there must be some mistake, tried to get the Americans to hold fire a moment until some reason could be had for this very unexpected attack, but it appears that these men went to kill Indians and did not care much who nor where, so they killed them. Elias, one of the apache captains, and I believe the best indian in the tribe, done all he could to get to the Americans, to tell them who he was and ask them what they were killing his people for, but he could do nothing. He still kept going to the miners and they firing at him, until he was finally shot dead with three others." Most of the Apaches had promptly fled, it was reported, to Chihuahua, but "before they left they sent word to all the families on the Río Mimbres that they did not want any peace with the Americans, and that if the settlers on the Mimbres did not go away from there that they would kill them, and they took by force several animals . . . and killed one man . . . and I fear that we will have no peace for them. . . . The settlers on the Mimbres appear to think that those Indians had done nothing to deserve such treatment, in fact most . . . appear to think that these Indians were not the guilty ones." He added that he did not think "one half of the stealing is done by Indians."[10]

"This affair," Collins wrote to A. B. Greenwood, commissioner of Indian affairs, "may give some idea of the many difficulties with which we have to contend."[11]

There is no doubt that Victorio led his people on the warpath from that moment, since virtually all the Mimbres were out save the aged Mangas and a few of his followers. Most of the hostiles swept down into Mexico, raiding ranches, slaughtering whites whom they came across, depredating in every way, irreconcilable after the brainless and murderous Texan assault upon a peaceful encampment, where victims fell simply because the whites wanted to kill someone, guilty or not, and attacked upon the most flimsy of pretexts.

Thus begun, the troubles were compounded by an unfortunate incident that occurred in late February, 1861, in Apache Pass, and

71

which added to the hostile Mimbres the Chiricahua warriors under Cochise. The event, termed by Tully a "very badly managed affair," was indeed productive of much evil. "We have nothing else every day but Indian depredations to such an extent that we are hardly safe in our houses," and talking the Apaches into again accepting peace "is our only chance to live at all in this part of the Territory," Tully wrote.[12]

The story of Cochise's break with the whites is well known, but not so familiar is a contemporary version, with some fresh details, from the Mesilla *Times*, which condensed it from an account in the *Weekly Arizonian* of Tucson. Tully sent the clipping to Collins, since it contained "all I could write to you":

On Wednesday evening [February 7] the Overland Stage from the West was fired into some two miles the other side of Apache Pass by a large body of Indians. Some 15 or 16 shots were fired, but, owing to the darkness of the night, the driver—King Lyon———was the only person injured. He was shot in the leg. One mule was killed, another so badly wounded that it died on arriving at the station. After removing the dead animal, the coach proceeded on its way, and was again fired at once soon after starting, but without effect.

The stage from the East had arrived at the station ahead of time; and the occupants reported that in a narrow cañon they found the road obstructed with a large quantity of hay, probably placed there to be fired on the approach of the coach to stop it and afford light to enable them to shoot the occupants. . . .

A company of Infantry from Fort Buchanan, under Lieut. [George N.] Bascom, arrived at Apache Pass on the preceding Monday. He held a consultation with Cachees and his braves, demanding the surrender of a captive boy,[13] and some stock which had been stolen from [John] Ward's rancho [near Fort Buchanan]. Cachees was willing to deliver over the stock, but persisted in retaining the prisoner; whereupon Bascom took the chief and six other Indian prisoners; with the intention of holding them as hostages. Cachees, however, cut a hole through the tent in which he was confined, rushed by the guard, and made his escape, but not until he had been shot in the leg and had a rifle bent over his head by one of the soldiers. The next day, in spite of his severe injuries, he was on horseback again at the head of a party of Indians. They showed a white flag, and Mr. Jas. F. Wallace, driver on the Overland line, Mr. Chas. W. Culver, the Station keeper, and his assistant, Mr. Welch, finally resolved to go and confer with them. When within reach, the Indians attempted to seize them, and did succeed in capturing Wallace. Culver escaped, wounded, after knocking down two Indians. Welch also escaped, but when near the corral, was shot dead. The next day the Indians again appeared, leading Wallace with a rope around his neck and his arms pinioned.

Mr. A. B. Culver, brother of the wounded man, started immediately for Tucson. A short distance the other side of the station, he came upon the remains of a Mexican train, and the bodies of eight men probably murdered by the Indians. Two of the bodies were chained to the wheels of a wagon, where to all appearances they had been burned alive. All their animals had been stolen. The road was barricaded with rocks, etc., for a distance of over two miles, and one bridge almost entirely demolished.[14]

Soon some of the Mescaleros and a few Navahos joined in raiding and "thus the entire southern part of the tribe has been led on until they are now in open hostility," wrote Collins to Greenwood.[15]

As if the attack upon the more or less innocent Elías camp were not enough, truculent and irresponsible miners now alienated the great Mangas Coloradas, quite as needlessly. He had been the acknowledged head chief of all the Eastern Chiricahuas, and was closely associated with Cochise, leader of the Central Chiricahuas—some said they were brothers-in-law.[16] One would suppose that any man with normal acuity would have been concerned to keep an individual of his influence friendly, or at least pacified, but if such there were at Pinos Altos they were not heeded. Some of the more timorous began to entertain suspicions about him, rumors from their lively imaginations spread like fire, and soon the entire camp was jittery with the absurd conviction that Mangas sought to lure them, one by one (there were well over two hundred whites at Pinos Altos at the time) into the brush to be murdered, although no one at all had yet been killed in that manner. "The next time . . . that Mangas visited the camp, he was tied to a tree and administered a dose of 'strap oil,' well applied by lusty arms. His vengeance was . . . keenly aroused," and guerrilla fighting against the miners began, Mangas, it was said, even sending to Cochise for help in extirpating them.[17] But Cochise was otherwise engaged.

The Overland Mail was suspended because of Civil War uncertainties, and this emboldened the Mimbres and their allies, "for they believe that they caused its withdrawal," wrote Tully. Since soldiers had not been sent against them for the same reasons, he continued, "they finally concluded that the troops were afraid of them." By now the Indians had swept off "nearly every hoof of stock from the country near the copper mines, and Fort McLane . . . [and] the settlers are leaving the Mimbres Valley, their crops and houses are left at the mercy of the Indians.

"The Pino Alto gold mines have been entirely abandoned, but I am not sorry for this for the miners were the principal cause of the first difficulty with those Indians." Major Lynde growled that he would treat all Mimbres as enemies wherever he met them, but, Tully pointed out, since "his animals are all taken he can do nothing."[18]

VIII
War and Murder

In late March, 1861, it was determined to abandon the Overland stage line. Superintendent William Buckley informed William Sanders Oury, Tucson agent for the company,[1] and by April 1 the exodus had begun. One party engaged in this undertaking was ambushed near Doubtful Pass and every man slain, including Anthony Elder, a veteran frontiersman and Tevis' partner in a ranch eighteen miles north of El Paso.[2] It is probable that numerous incidents involved loss of life as the Butterfield Company shifted its route to the north, as the Pinos Altos mines were abandoned,[3] as Santa Rita became depopulated again, and as most of the isolated settlers and ranchers scurried for places of refuge. The Apaches once more held virtually undisputed domination over the region, even if briefly.

This condition had been greatly furthered by withdrawal of soldiers from New Mexico and Arizona frontier posts in order to concentrate them along the lower Río Grande, up which the Texas Confederates were now moving in some force. Fort McLane was abandoned July 3, 1861, after less than a year of service, the troops withdrawn to Fort Fillmore, on the river six miles below Mesilla.[4] Fort Breckenridge, at the junction of the San Pedro River and Aravaipa Creek, was destroyed by order July 10 and the troops moved west to Fort Buchanan on Sonoita Creek between the present-day towns of Patagonia and Sonoita. This post in turn was burned July 21 and the troops withdrawn east into New Mexico.[5]

On July 13, Steck wrote Collins from Las Cruces, as the Confederates threatened Fillmore, that "it may be many months before the presence of an agent will be needed here. I have therefore concluded to come to Santa Fe."[6] It was years before the Mimbres would have an agent of their own once more. Bloody times were ahead.

It is probable that the Indians knew little of the white man's fratricidal war. Many of them were convinced that the withdrawals signified a cowardly retreat in the face of red strength, but, whether or not they held this view, the damage was done in many areas, and they

75

were thoroughly aware of that. Their game had been killed off, their lives and culture disrupted, their old reliance upon a generally understandable nature was now impossible, the rations upon which they had come to depend and which alone kept them from raiding and depredation—to the extent that they *were* kept from it— were no more. But they still had life, and the inherited need to keep its flame aglow. No virile people ever starved when food was within reach, and it was available: in the possession of white men in small settlements, on isolated ranches, in Old Mexico, and north of the border, too. It was steal or starve, depredate or die of want. With free rations being no more, it was unthinkable to an Apache that he decline to seize what his people required. It would have been equally fanciful for a white American under the circumstances to have remained passive.

Yet the strife that ensued should not be overstressed. Cremony, who from design or imperfect knowledge frequently exaggerated, wrote in 1868 of Mangas Coloradas that

"the northern portions of Chihuahua and Sonora, large tracts of Durango, the whole of Arizona, and a very considerable part of New Mexico, were laid waste, ravished, destroyed by this man and his followers. A strip of country twice as large as all California was rendered almost houseless, unproductive, uninhabitable by his active and uncompromising hostility. Large and flourishing towns were depopulated and ruined. Vast ranchos . . . once teeming with wealth and immense herds of cattle, horses and mules, were turned into waste places, and restored to their pristine solitudes. The name of Mangas Colorado was the tocsin of terror and dismay throughout a vast region of country, whose inhabitants existed by his sufferance under penalty of supplying him with the requisite arms and ammunition for his many and terrible raids."[7]

And so on.

This has come down to us as the last word on an Apache chieftain with whom Cremony was acquainted personally, but it is magnified, distorted, and untrue in the whole and in many parts. Mangas was, indeed, the foremost leader of his band and recognized as over-all chief by the Mimbres and probably the Mogollons as well. He was friendly with Cochise, but he had no recorded control over the Central Chiricahuas, let alone the Southern Chiricahuas. Much of the destructive raiding in northern Mexico was conducted by the Pinals, with some help from various White Mountain, San Carlos, and possibly Southern Tonto bands, as well as by the Central and Southern Chiricahuas. The Eastern Chiricahuas, under Mangas and others, may have joined at times in raids on Sonora, but their principal field of activity in Old Mexico was in Chihuahua, and here they shared in the general deviltry with the Mescaleros and Comanches. Mangas was an effective leader of but a small part of all these peoples. He cannot fairly be blamed for all that happened in Mexico, in any but a very small portion of Arizona, or in southern New Mexico east of the Río Grande.

Mangas, it is true, was the most prominent leader of the Eastern Chiricahuas and, because of his size and manner—which many who observed him suggested was that of a grave, thoughtful, and unflappable leader of strength and vision—he was widely known, in fact and by rumor. But he was no more a superman than Cochise or Victorio, and little more influential. He no doubt encouraged much raiding and war, for that was the Apache way, and he must have been an extraordinarily persuasive and effective leader; through training and example his influence extended to the work of Victorio and others, but he was limited by the nature of his culture and the mores of his society. He was no emperor. There were none among the Apaches.[8]

On July 26, 1861, Lieutenant Colonel John R. Baylor, Mounted Rifles, of the Confederate forces, occupied Fort Fillmore and went on to capture Major Lynde's entire force of seven companies, near San Augustin Pass in the Organ Mountains, with virtually no resistance. Baylor proclaimed establishment of the Territory of Arizona, declared himself governor, and chose Mesilla as seat of his government. He was succeeded as commander by Brigadier General Henry H. Sibley on December 14, 1861,[9] but retained his self-proclaimed governorship of "Arizona," which by Baylor's proclamation of August 1, 1861, included southern New Mexico as far northward as the 34th Parallel, crossing the Río Grande midway between present-day Truth or Consequences and Socorro. Baylor's proclamation was confirmed by the Confederate Congress and signed into law by President Jefferson Davis, effective February 14, 1862.[10]

Victorio's people for months occupied territory which the Texans considered theirs by right of conquest, but the new invaders proved no more intelligent or adept in control of the Apaches than had other whites. Even less so.

Thoroughly infected with the Texas frontiersman's contempt for Indians, particularly hostile ones, Baylor had no sympathy whatever for the Apaches, and this attitude led to his downfall. To counter their rising hostility he organized two groups of volunteers, the Arizona Rangers, of thirty-five men, commanded by Captain George M. Frazer, and the Arizona Guards, thirty men, under Captain Thomas Helm. He sent them to reopen the road from Mesilla to Tucson and on March 20 wrote his famous letter of instructions to Helm, then at Tucson, saying in part:

I learn from Lieut. J. J. Jackson that the Indians have been in to your post for the purpose of making a treaty. The Congress of the Confederate States has passed a law declaring extermination of all hostile Indians. You will therefore use all means to persuade the Apaches or any tribe to come in for the purpose of making peace, and when you get them together kill all the grown Indians and take the children prisoners and sell them [into slavery] to defray the expense of killing the Indians. Buy whiskey and such other goods as may be necessary for the Indians. . . . Leave nothing undone to insure success, and have a sufficient number of men around to allow no Indian to escape. . . . I . . . look to you for success against these cursed pests who have already murdered over 100 men in this territory.[11]

Despite this heroic intent to execute his opponents by treachery, the situation worsened, and by mid-spring the Indians controlled almost all of Confederate "Arizona."[12] Indian Agent W. F. M. Arny, who had succeeded Steck, messaged the commissioner in late March that "Col. Baylor with 600 Texians are south of Fort Craig[13] and has his hands full with the Southern Apaches. . . . Gen. Sibley in command of the Texians has made communications to the Indians of New Mexico by Agents proposing to take them under his care and protection if they will cooperate with him. We hope he will not succeed, as *the Southern Apaches* are now at war with them (the Texians)."[14]

Because of his cruel order calling for the murder of the Apaches, it is said, Baylor was removed from office by President Davis. Union officials had used the directive to convince the Indians of the Confederate intent to exterminate them, hoping thereby to win their allegiance.[15] In a letter of December 29, 1862, Baylor defended his policy:

Outrages were committed frequently; the mails were robbed; in one or two instances the messengers were found hanging up by the heels, their heads within a few inches of a slow fire, and they thus horribly roasted to death. Others were found tied to the wheels of the coach, which had been burned. Upon the arrival of General Sibley's brigade these Indians stole from his troops 100 head of horses and mules. Accompanied by many native-born citizens of Arizona and New Mexico I followed the robbers' trail, which led me to the town of Carretas, Chihuahua [midway between Janos and Bavispe]. I thought myself justifiable in killing the Indians and recovering the animals.

He said he had just read a newspaper story to the effect that the Confederate Congress had declared a war of extermination against inveterately hostile Indians, and, "feeling convinced (as I do still) that such a policy was the only one suitable to the hostile and treacherous tribes, I acted on it."[16]

With this letter, Baylor sent along a shield he said he had taken from an Indian chief he personally had slain. Attached to the shield was a scalp "of a Miss Jackson, who had been murdered." or, by another account, of a "Texas lady named Woods."[17]

The Texan invasion of New Mexico was of brief duration, partly because of a lack of organization and too lengthy supply lines, but mostly because of the aggressive heroism of the Colorado Volunteers. What was possibly a contributing factor to its demise was the movement eastward of the so-called California Column of eighteen hundred men under Colonel James Henry Carleton, who became a brigadier general April 28. He took command of the Department of New Mexico September 18, 1862, and Colonel Joseph R. West that of the District of Arizona, which included the Mesilla Valley and, of course, the Mimbres country. West became a brigadier general of volunteers on October 25.

All these events were of little except peripheral concern or, for that matter, knowledge to the Mimbres and other Apaches, except as they provided opportunity for plunder and occasional combat. Baylor's statement that more than one hundred men had lost their lives to the hostiles within a few months of the Texas invasion, and similar reports from the Union side,[18] suggest there must have been numerous skirmishes during this period, although few of them became matters of record. An exception was the so-called Battle of Apache Pass, described, with his customary expansivenes, by Cremony,[19] but recounted in official and more conservative reports, as well.

As the California Column approached Apache Pass in late June, 1862, Lieutenant Colonel Edward E. Eyre was detailed with 140 men of the First California Cavalry to reconnoiter the route. On June 25 he encountered Indians, bearing a white flag, at the spring near the pass and expressed the desire of the whites for friendship with them. These no doubt were Cochise's Chiricahuas. Only later did he discover that three of his men who had wandered from the main body had been killed by Indians, and in a rare night attack, presumably by Apaches —who almost never fought after dark—his surgeon was wounded.[20]

A second advance party of 122 men under Captain Thomas L. Roberts of the First California Infantry left Tucson July 10 under orders from Carleton "not to attack the Indians unless the latter were the aggressors." Indians as allies were more important than Indians as enemies. Roberts, on July 14, entered Apache Pass with his infantry and two mountain howitzers and ran into an ambush which Cremony alleges was devised by Cochise and Mangas Coloradas. Among the warriors present, according to legend, were Victorio and one later to become noted as Geronimo. The volunteers had marched forty miles that day without water and were desperately thirsty when, for the first time, they came under hostile fire. They were half a mile short of the spring. An artilleryman was killed and a teamster wounded in the initial clash, when the Indians struck at the rear of the column. Other Apaches were positioned among the rocks high above the route. The howitzers were run up, though the gunners had difficulty elevating the muzzles sufficiently. At length, however, they brought enemy positions under fire.[21] The Indians continued their attack for several hours, killing a cavalryman and wounding another, and then withdrew.

Cremony credits "a prominent Apache who was present in the engagement," with the statement that three Indians were killed by musketry and sixty-three by artillery fire, a figure often quoted even though it is unbelievable. Carleton's official summary said: "Captain Roberts reports that the Indians lost ten killed," an estimate that might still be high.[22] Mangas himself was said by Cremony to have been wounded when he, with about fifteen warriors, attacked a six-man (he says seven) cavalry detachment sent by Roberts from the pass to contact Cremony and his supply train. It was camped at Ewell's Station, a stage stop and spring named for Baldy Ewell (by now a Confederate officer), about thirteen miles west of Apache Pass.[23] Several of the whites' horses were killed, one man was wounded, and another, John Teal, cut off. Teal wrote in his diary:

The indians then turned toward me. I had mounted & fired my carbine at them, they closed in around me, both mounted & on foot. The chief or commander of the indians was armed with a citizen rifle but was unwilling to fire at me without a rest so, after ralying his warriors, he ran for a rest & I after him but, on looking over my shoulder, I saw the mounted indians to[o] close to my rear for safety, so I turned on them & they scattered like birds. I turned again to tend to the old chief but I was to[o] late, he had got to a bunch of Gaita grass & was lying on his belly on the opposite side of the bunch with his rifle resting on the bunch pointed strait at me, which caused me to drop from the horse on the ground & the indian shot the horse instead of me. The horse left & I laid low sending a bullet at them whenever I had a chance. We kept firing till it was dark when a lucky shot from me sent the chief off in the arms of his indians.[24]

This chief, reportedly Mangas, was taken to Janos, where his wound was successfully treated by a Mexican physician.[25]

Carleton, finding it "indispensably necessary to establish a post" in Apache Pass, caused to be founded Fort Bowie, commanding the spring. The installation was named for Colonel George W. Bowie, California Infantry, and raised at the spring July 28, although later it was removed a short distance to the south. It became one of the most prominent posts during the Apache wars, and its ruins have been labeled a National Historical Site. It was abandoned as a military installation October 17, 1894.[26]

With arrival of the California Column at the Río Grande, and the departure of the Confederates down the river, a several-years' task of pacifying, or at least controlling, the roving Apache bands could commence. And it was sorely needed. On September 7, Collins reported to the commissioner that "the Navajos, and the Apaches in the southern part of the Territory, are still in a hostile condition. They have murdered many persons and robbed a large amount of property. No campaign has yet been put on foot against them nor will there be until our new commanding officer takes charge of the Department."[27] Carleton assumed control from Brigadier General E. R. S. Canby on September 18. He was to become the Union Baylor in his Indian attitude, feeling no empathy toward them, little understanding of them, no regard for or patience with hostile Indians of any description. He was described by Cremony, perhaps accurately, as one "whose unscrupulous ambition and exclusive selfishness had passed into a proverb, despite his acknowledged ability and apparent zeal."[28] On October 12 Carleton ordered that all Indian men were to be killed whenever and wherever they could be found.[29] Brigadier General West, in command of his district, read the directive carefully and absorbed its implications fully.

In issuing his General Orders I, directing the establishment of Fort West at the present Mangus [sic] Springs, which was to have been included in the Santa Lucia Reservation, Carleton stated: "Brigadier General West . . . will immediately organize a suitable expedition to chastise what is known as Mangus Colorado's Band of Gila Apaches. The campaign to be made must be a vigorous one, and the punishment of that band of murderers and others must be thorough and sharp."[30] Details were left to West. But the unfortunate directive compounded the evil done at Apache Pass two years earlier, which had loosed Cochise upon the whites, although it differed little from other incidents of record in the Southwest of those years, except in the prominence of the primary victim. The order soon became common knowledge, to the general approbation of southwesterners. It stirred within them great hopes. One newspaper approvingly commented that "General Carleton is taking vigorous steps to punish all the Indian thieves and murderers in this Territory; and already a heavy force, under General West, is ordered to take the field, and punish the Gila Apaches, under that notorious robber, Mangus Colorado."[31]

Several versions of the killing of Mangas on the night of January 18, 1863, are extant, but the most reliable appears to be that of Daniel Conner, an honest eye-witness, who had nothing to gain by distorting the facts.[32]

By this account, Joseph Walker, a veteran mountain man now prospecting through the Southwest, had decided to seize a prominent Apache as hostage to make more secure his journey westward with his party. The Walker band, accompanied by some soldiers, reached deserted Pinos Altos where, under a white flag, they captured Mangas, who had come in in good faith. They convoyed him to Fort McLane, where they encountered West and "his command," or part of it. Also present was a civilian, Corydon E. Cooley, who was to become one of the great scouts and characters of the Apache frontier in Arizona.[33] West pre-empted the prisoner under the pretext of obtaining satisfaction for some thefts of which Mangas may or may not have had any previous knowledge. But West also saw in this unexpected capture of the great Apache a godsend in view of the otherwise chimerical instructions of his chief.

According to a soldier, West clearly implied that he wanted Mangas shot,[34] and that night his guards tormented the chief until he protested, then killed him before Conner's eyes. The guards of course were not punished or reprimanded in any way, since their deed fulfilled West's wish. The general's official report of the affair, if Conner's account be trustworthy, was a fabric of lies from beginning to end.[35]

Mangas' huge head later was severed from his body, the tremend-ous skull boiled out and eventually secured by a phrenologist-lecturer, Orson Squire Fowler.[36] Its present whereabouts are not known.

The greatest tragedy of the affair was less the death of the aging chieftain than the lasting distrust generated on the part of Apaches toward white Americans and soldiers. In the view of one informed person, it had an even more deleterious effect than the notorious Sand Creek massacre of peaceful Cheyennes in Colorado, and obviously it was no less an act of treachery.[37] The distrust endured as long as the Apaches were influenced by their memories—as they are to this day—and had its repercussions so long as they were able to mount important hostilities against the American aggressors. Thus, the im-prudent and brutal decision of an unwise officer wrought untold misery and hardship upon uncounted innocent victims for long years to come. It first became apparent in the increased hatred, if that be possible, manifested by Cochise, one who knew well how to vent his malice,[38] and by Victorio, now swiftly coming to the fore, entering the vacuum created by the demise of the old warrior.

Following closely upon the execution of Mangas, Captain William McCleave killed eleven or twelve Mimbres near Pinos Altos, said by one who should have known to have been members of the family of Mangas waiting there for word of his release. It was said that "their scalps were afterwards worn as ornaments upon the bridles of the soldiers."[39] Captain Edmond D. Shirland slew nine others nearby. These latter killings were said to result when the Mimbres again sued for peace, returned to Pinos Altos, and, while eating a dinner "espe-cially prepared for them, they were fired on by the soldiers, some were killed, others escaped to the mountains. Since then I have heard of no overtures for peace, but I have heard of very many murders and robberies by them, even to the taking of Cavalry horses and [setting] at least two if not three companies afoot."[40]

Fort West was established February 24, 1863, at Mangus Springs,[41] and when the post herd was swept off, McCleave followed the raiders into Arizona and, striking a *rancheria*, said he had killed twenty-eight. Early in May, West announced that "the savages are pretty well cleared out from the headwaters of the Gila River," although, if so, they would return.[42]

Carleton pursued single-mindedly his extermination policy against the exasperating Apaches and Navahos, but the results were not decisive. He sought aid toward this end from the governors of Sonora,

Chihuahua, and Arizona, and official reports, not too reliable, listed 216 Apaches killed, compared with 16 whites, in a number of skirmishes.[43] But the war went on. Soldiers could not end it, because it was not a conflict for military glory, but for survival of a people. As long as the people lived, and were not fed by the usurpers of their land and resources, they must depredate—and be fought. The figures, official or otherwise, of Apache casualties are always suspect, unless they are calculated estimates of seasoned chiefs of scouts or other veterans whose experience and good sense warrant confidence. The value of military estimates depended upon the knowledge and trustworthiness of the officers concerned, and these qualities varied widely. One illustration is that, at the death of Mangas, the Mimbres and other Eastern Chiricahuas were believed to number about one hundred warriors; when Victorio finally went out in earnest, fifteen years later, his fighting men numbered about the same, or a few more. Even allowing for the maturing of youths in the interim, this would not leave too many warriors to have been slain in combat, but this calculation is contrary to official reports and estimates of casualties inflicted on this enemy. If all the Indians claimed in official reports to have been killed actually had been slain, and were laid end to end, they would extend to the nearer planets.

Perhaps it was due to the deteriorating Indian situation in New Mexico that the able Dr. Steck was reassigned to that Territory, this time as superintendent of Indian affairs, on May 23, 1863. He reached Santa Fe July 7.[44] With the admission of Arizona as a Territory February 24, 1863, New Mexico was cut in half and its Indian problems, although as plaguey as ever, were not quite so geographically impossible as they had appeared earlier. Steck reported in August that "except for the Navajoes & a part of the Southern Apaches, who are at war, the Indians of this Territory are in a satisfactory condition."[45] In his first annual report that year, Steck said that "the condition of the country was not fully recovered from the effects of the Texan invasion. During the occupation . . . all intercourse with many of the Indian tribes was entirely broken up. The military force was necessarily withdrawn from the frontiers to defend the Territory against the invaders, and the Inds. were then left without the controlling influence of its presence. This, of course, led to evil consequences that still exist to a greater or less extent."

He lumped the southwestern Apaches under the term Gila Apaches, as most persons did thereafter, and said that since the invasion they were at war "and still are." It was no longer correct to look upon any of the New Mexico tribes as nations, except the Pueblos, Steck observed, or to treat them as such.

There is not one of them . . . that is bound together by any general laws or social relationship. All are divided into fragments and these fragments of from 10 to 50 men are headed by some successful warrior [who] acts without any consulting with the mass, &, in time of war, recognizes no law but that of violence. There appears to be no distinguished chieftain among them who can concentrate and lead an undirected tribe in time of war or inspire their confidence and give them council in time of peace.

It has sometimes been said that Victorio immediately succeeded Mangas Coloradas as chief of the Eastern Chiricahuas,[46] but this was not the case. He was still evolving as a war leader, had a small band of devoted followers, but was not yet a major chief, although he was on the way. One who still "ranked" him, it might be said, was Delgadito, a "warlike man of great influence," second only to Mangas,[47] and one who might have been a powerful influence for peace if the whites had had the wit to use him thus, but during this period, he too, was slain. As in the case of other noted Apaches, his death has been variously described. Cremony, who knew him well, said that he was stabbed from behind by a Mexican with whom he was fording the Mimbres River.[48] The supposed autobiographical account of a later agent, John Philip Clum, says he was slain in a bloody fight near Pinos Altos in which, according to the book, forty whites and a dozen Apaches were killed.[49] This version is suspect, however, on several points. A history of Fort Craig asserts that Militia General Estanislao Montoya led a scout against supposed raiders and killed twenty Indians, including Delgadito, in 1864.[50] Be that as it may, Delgadito disappears from this time and it is probable that he was too prominent to have died peacefully without report of it reaching the whites.

Steck warned that "the policy of regarding the tribes . . . in the light of nations & holding treaties with them as such where there is no acknowledged head or power to compel the tribe to comply can be productive of no good." Therefore he urged the assigning of reservations, establishment of nearby military posts "not only to command their respect, but at the same time prevent the encroachments of settlers and the consequent evils that always result from a free intercourse with the white population." Generous rations would lure them to the reservations, he felt. "They will sign any paper presented whether they understand its contents or not, if they are offered plenty of beef in return." Feeding Indians, he argued, was cheaper than fighting them.

Besides, he continued, New Mexico's gold and other riches inevitably would draw in more adventurers. "If every Indian was a Spartan they could not long bear up against the resistless tide of emigration. Humanity then demands of us if we wish to save even a portion of this interesting people that they be located and to secure a home for them in the future, that their reservations be secured to them by patent as early a day as possible."

Military conquest of them was impossible, he believed, but even if it could be done, "fight them if you please untill you kill half the warriors in the field and capture every horse they own and you leave the women & children & those that are left less able to provide for themselves than when you commenced." Extermination would cost three million dollars annually, he calculated. To feed them would cost only one-twentieth of that.

Steck warned against perpetuating such "absurd" customs and beliefs as "killing the cattle & destroying all the property of any one who dies," or "moving their huts (if but a few hundred yards) upon the death of anyone in camp," and the "making of feasts of which they have a great number and the most extravagant of which is one made when a female child arrives at a marriageable age. The parents at this feast will sacrifice all the property they possess to feast the tribe, who dance & make night hideous with their songs for from five to ten days. With these and other barbarous customs in force among them it is hardly necessary to say they can make no progress." Instead, he urged that a "laudable desire to accumulate & retain property . . . must be cultivated."

He estimated that during the past three years citizens had lost 500,000 sheep; 5,000 horses, mules, and cattle; and over 200 lives to the raiding tribes. He urged that the Mescaleros, Jicarillas, and "the small band of Mimbres Apaches that still belong to this Territory" be gathered together at the Bosque Redondo on the Pecos River.[51]

IX

The Bosque Fiasco

Bosque Redondo was a "round wood" in name only. It was on the Pecos River, near present-day Fort Sumner, and Cremony, who was with the party which selected the precise site for a forty-square-mile reservation, described it as sixteen miles long by half a mile wide "and for several miles affording only a few scattered trees, which were by no means thick, even in the densest portion."[1]

The timber was cottonwood, and would soon become exhausted when the winters proved cold and thousands of destitute Indians were crowded among the barren trunks, seizing upon anything combustible for their little fires. Despite objections from the experienced Dr. Steck, Carleton envisaged massing all the Navahos, all the Mescaleros, and all the Mimbres he could catch onto the Bosque Redondo reserve. But, in point of fact, Kit Carson and troops under his direction could corral fewer than half the Mescaleros, no more than half the Navahos (and those the least troublesome),[2] and only a handful of Mimbres, and the reserve, which might have succeeded had Dr. Steck's recommendations been followed, was a dismal failure. It was to be abandoned within a few years, to the relief of practically everyone and the general agreement that it had become a "pandemonium of breech clouts and red skins."[3]

In May, 1868, crusty old General William Tecumseh Sherman visited Fort Sumner and talked with the unhappy Navahos at Bosque Redondo, hearing their complaints about their hopeless condition and agreeing with what he heard. He signed a treaty June 1, unraveling Carleton's misbegotten reservation and allowing the Indians to return to their own country.[4] The sprinkling of Mimbres who had been herded to the Bosque had long ago fled, and creation of the reserve did nothing to solve the state of constant warfare in southern New Mexico. The Gilas may even have gained a few recruits from Carson's Mescalero expedition, for on February 1, 1863, Carleton informed Washington that all the Mescaleros had been brought under control "except a few who have either run off into Mexico or joined the Gila Apaches." He gave no estimate of their number.[5]

The old Southern Apache agency was formally abolished June 30, 1864,[6] largely because the hostiles it was intended to serve were beyond reach. With the war back east all but over, Dr. Steck now received an intimation that the Indian war in southern New Mexico could also be terminated. He quickly proceeded to act upon his information until General Carleton rudely brought him up and made impossible, for the time being, a quiet solution to that grim problem.

Nowhere else in New Mexico history is there so clear-cut an illustration of how differently humanitarian interests and an autocratic military saw a single situation. Steck was a wise, if sometimes mistaken, essentially just man who truly had Apache interests at heart, even though he was afflicted to some degree with the opaque materialism of his times. Carleton, on the other hand, was unencumbered by the slightest impulse toward justice for the Indians, or any notion that they had basic rights as human beings. He stubbornly persisted in his ill-advised scheme to shunt them all over into eastern New Mexico, to the Bosque Redondo, out of sight and, hopefully, out of mind, where they could wither and disappear in so remote an area that not even the odor of their dead bodies would reach Santa Fe. He was peering west toward the developing gold fields and in any event would scarcely be troubled by any dying aroma from a doomed and inferior race.

Steck sent Indian Commissioner William P. Dole a letter from Justice Joseph G. Knapp of Mesilla in mid-February, protesting Carleton's ill-advised policy, and to it the superintendent added some comments of his own:

The account given here will apply to every part of the Territory where the Military Department have controll. General Carleton . . . commenced a war of extermination against the Apaches in this Territory and Arizona. The cry was *no Quarter* for the Apache, and the people are now suffering the consequences. I am told, Apaches have been fired upon and killed, when approaching camps of soldiers with a white flag, to ask for peace, and others who were invited in, and came promptly, were thrust into the guardhouse at Fort Cummings,[7] and afterwards murdered while in the Guardhouse in the most wanton manner. . . . It has recently been reported that these Indians are willing to make peace with the whites, and I am now making arrangements, by which I will get an interview with their chiefs. . . . It is high time the management of these Indians ... [is] taken from the military and placed in the proper department."[8]

Judge Knapp wrote that he had feared Carleton's policy would lead to a "general outbreak," and time had proven him right.

The "plan" as Gen. Carleton calles it, has now been in force (for two years), and though he is himself reporting that we have peace and safety throughout the land, the Indians in scattered bands are roving everywhere, and the property and lives of the people have to suffer for it. ... I say that the "plan" has proved the worst thing which could have taken place.

Towards the Apache the "plan" is executed by killing every one which can be seen—a war of extermination, reaching to the women and children. The Apache on his part returns life for life, when the soldier cannot be taken the citizen is taken. These in turn must go armed at all times. ... The consequence is that the Indians have much the best of the contest, and the citizens are the sufferers.[9]

A letter from Albert Bloomfield, another citizen of Mesilla, confirmed Knapp's report, and simultaneously brought Victorio again into full view, after a dozen years when his presence must usually be inferred with little tangible evidence, aside from a fleeting and casual hint now and then.

I lived at Pinos Altos ... on the 12th of January of this year, where on or about that time, several Indians appeared and commenced hallowing and making friendly signs. I then with other citizens, went out to meet them, and induced them to approach us, after which Captain [George H.] Cook, N.M. Vols., came up, and took the Indians three miles west of town where he was mining, with some of his soldiers. Shortly afterwards I followed the Indians to Capt. Cook's Camp and brought them to the town of Pinos Altos, and on Capt. Cook's request, I acted as interpreter. The Indians, among whom was Salvidor, son of Mangus Colorado ... told us they wanted to make peace with us, and that they would go back to their tribe, at their camp, a distance of three and a half days travel. They accordingly left and returned five days thereafter, bringing with them fifty-three warriors (59 in all), among whom were recognized the notorious Chief Riñon, Victorio, and two brothers of Salvidor ... as also [Mangas Coloradas'] widow. They enquired for Major [Dr.] Steck, and said they wanted to see him and make a chain between them and the whites that would never be broken. They expressed every confidence in Supt. Steck, that he alone of all the officials was a true man, and that they were willing to be guided by his advice in every thing and that they regarded him as a Father, who loved his red children. Whereupon Capt. Cook told them to make a Camp in the Town, and he would furnish them rations, until Supt. Steck could be sent for.

The Indians, however, fearing treachery, fled, although they hovered near the town, interested in further contacts with the whites, but afraid to make them.[10]

With these two letters, Steck also enclosed a petition signed by twenty-nine citizens of Mesilla, noting that there appeared to be a desire for peace on the part of the Mimbres and Gila Indians, and urging Steck to confer with the natives to that end.[11]

A month later the superintendent notified the commissioner that he would visit the Gilas, confident he could bring peace, but on March 20 he penned still another letter, explaining that Carleton had aborted the endeavor. The general was determined that he would round up the Southern Apaches and ship them off to the Bosque Redondo or there would be no peace, and this despite the obvious fact that the Pecos River experiment already was proving a colossal failure. Steck enclosed a copy of the general's letter in which he had "dictated the only terms on which peace can be had and in the next sentence adds that the 'Military department . . . should and *must* manage all affairs with them until the war is ended,' " adding that the Indians were "still in the hands of the Military *and will be until the Military commander makes peace with them upon his own terms.*" Steck believed that Bloomfield was correct in thinking that the Apaches at Pinos Altos feared "treachery on the part of the soldiers" because they before had been "treacherously dealt with, and at least two of their chiefs and about twenty of their people wantonly murdered by our troops and people." Yet Carleton, said Steck, declared he alone had the right to make war and dictate peace, delivered an ultimatum that they remove to Bosque Redondo and starve with their enemies, and said that they must accept his terms or be exterminated. "By this course the war must be protracted indefinitely," wrote Steck, "and the lives and property of our people be sacrificed."

He added, "There are no Indians in this Department *more faithful* than the Mimbres band of Apaches, when at peace." They had been at peace (with the Americans, at any rate) from 1854 to 1859, when "they were driven by the *treachery of our own people* into their present hostile condition." He charged that since the right to make treaties with the Indians lay with the Department of the Interior, Carleton had taken upon himself "rights that do not belong to him," and Steck further stated that "in my humble opinion, the Government has already had to[o] much of Military management of Indians . . . and that some decisive steps should be taken to correct these evils and the immense draft upon the Treasury consequent upon them."[12]

In sending his letter, with copies of his exchange with Carleton, Steck included a copy of a directive from Carleton to Captain Cook, urging him to convey to the Indians the general's ultimatum as the only plan "that can save the tribe from ultimate destruction." But Cook could not contact the Apaches again, for they sensed what to expect and "dare not trust the military."[13] Steck might easily have reached them, however. It was reported that the Mimbres waited two months for him to appear and negotiate an agreement in which they could have faith but, because of Carleton's intransigence, Steck could not come.[14] Carleton, upon hearing that the Mimbres sought peace, had sent Brevet Brigadier General Nelson Henry Davis to Pinos Altos to negotiate, but, although Davis did talk with Victorio, the venerable warrior Nana, and others, they were too wary for him, and would not go to the Bosque. Victorio was quoted by Davis as having said, "I and my people want peace—we are tired of war—we are poor and we have little for ourselves and our families to eat or wear—it is very cold—we want to make peace, a lasting peace . . . ," Davis adding that "this was the first time he had ever asked for peace." Victorio offered to go with Salvador, Nana, and an Apache named Acosta to the Bosque to look the place over, but then made excuses and refused to undertake the trip. In exasperation Davis blurted, in his report, "Death to the Apaches, and peace and prosperity to this land is my motto!"[15] The Mesilla editor, Judge A. E. Hackney, reported their allegations that "they had been treacherously dealt with by Carleton's command and dare not trust the military" again.[16]

Early in 1866 the Territory's legislative assembly memorialized Congress about depredations in New Mexico, asserting that from 1846 until 1866, with the exception of six years when records were not gathered, the Indians had caused almost 200 civilian casualties, including 123 killed and 21 made captive, along with stock losses estimated at $1,377,329.60, in addition to animals swept off and "not reported." These were apart from military losses in personnel and animals. There were frequent reports of attacks against soldier herds.[17]

Colonel Francisco P. Abreu reported from Fort Craig on May 4,

1866, that about fifty bow-armed Indians had run off thirty-one horses from a cavalry herd grazing a mile and one-half from the post. The colonel mounted some men on available mules and chased the hostiles toward the San Mateo Mountains, Victorio's favorite retreat, but couldn't catch them. "At present," sighed Abreu, "all the cavalry of this post is eight mounted men."[18] On June 6 a band of forty hostiles swept off thirty-six horses and five mules from Camp Mimbres.[19] The guard was mounted on the only four horses remaining in the "stables," and galloped in pursuit of the well-armed hostiles, but couldn't catch up. Sergeant Antonio Ruperts, Company C, First California Cavalry, in charge of the herding detail, said he had ridden to the river, a thousand yards from the animals, to bathe an aching head when the hostiles scooped up the stock. Carleton, "greatly mortified and pained"—and furious—upon receiving this fresh evidence that his extermination policy was developing imperfectly, wrote bitterly that "nothing can be said to extenuate such unpardonable carelessness and want of vigilance which led to so disastrous a result."[20] His frustration was evident in every word of his message.

A short time later fifteen Indians attacked herders near Fort McRae,[21] killed one, and ran off eleven horses and eight mules, although they failed to get the beef herd, Captain E. P. Horne reported. Again the hostiles escaped with their booty. Since this raid occurred east of the Río Grande, these may well have been Mescaleros.[22]

Civilians also suffered. The commissioner received a letter from the probate judge of Valencia County charging the Gilas had stolen fifteen horses and eight mules, although most of the stock was recovered. Dr. Steck estimated that two hundred Mimbres were all the Gilas remaining in New Mexico; they must have lived well during those days of ceaseless hostility.

Julius H. Graves, special Indian agent for New Mexico, early in 1866 investigated the situation, steadily worsening under Carleton's bumbling program, and from informed members of the legislature learned of their conviction that any attempt to force the Southern Apaches onto the Bosque ought to be given up. Instead, they argued, a reservation should be created for them somewhere on the Gila. The Apache bands could not get along with the Navahos, this testimony averred, since they had always been inimical "and are still so at this time."[23] But it was one thing to comprehend this, and quite another to convince the stubborn officer.

The situation grew more intolerable. George W. Nesmith, a nephew of Oregon Senator James W. Nesmith, wrote at the instigation of Hackney from Mesilla to Lewis Vital Bogy, nominated but not confirmed as commissioner of Indian affairs, about Carleton and his policies. "The Apaches west of the Rio Grande have upon several occasions made formal overtures for peace" without avail, he said, "the Bosque being the ultimatum. They are now at war, and meet with but feeble opposition from Gen. Carleton, and consequently the citizen whites suffer. . . . In more than one instance they have mounted themselves by stealing the horses of Cavalry companies, and thus well mounted they go where they list, without fear of molestation from foot soldiers." He realized Washington may have been misled into believing Carleton's policy was succeeding. "Were you here and [could] see how men travel from town to town, and hear from the lips of reliable citizens what little security there is in New Mexico for life and property, in consequence of a mistaken Indian policy, you would, I am sure, try to devise some way to give us peace with the Indians who, as well as ourselves, desire it if it can be had upon a practicable basis."[24]

Carleton had his many supporters, of course,[25] but the clamor for a reasonable settlement of the vexing Mimbres question continued to rise in southwestern New Mexico. Pinos Altos, resettled with the return of Union forces to the region, was in the heart of their country. Citizens of that battered community sent petitions in the late summer of 1866 to the *New Mexican*, a Santa Fe weekly, "to publicly express our entire concurrence" with the suggestion that the Mimbres be given a reservation in their own country, to "give peace to this section of the Territory." An accompanying petition, signed by others of Pinos Altos, said such a policy "will be most successful. They [the Indians] have long since desired peace on such a basis, and we have no reason to doubt but what they would gladly embrace the offer. The colonization of these Apaches . . . would give access to the richest metallic country east of the Rocky Mountains, if not indeed in the known world," and bring in swarms of settlers to assure by their numbers that the peace would be permanent.[26]

These and numerous similar statements must finally have had an impact at Washington, for on October 6, 1866, Carleton was ordered to join his regiment at San Antonio[27] and, said the *New Mexican*, an anti-Carleton journal, "it thus appears that our territory will be relieved from the presence of this man . . . who has so long lorded it amongst us. For five years or more he has been in supreme command in New Mexico, and during that whole time, has accomplished nothing for which he is entitled to the thanks or graditude of our people. . . . He has, however, succeeded in gaining for himself the detestation and contempt of almost the entire population of our territory."[28]

It was a day of journalistic vitriol and it is to be doubted that James Henry Carleton lost any sleep over such words, even if in part they were true. Steck also had departed the Indian service for private business, although the memories he left were far gentler and more appreciative, on the part of both red men and whites with whom he had been in contact. He was succeeded as superintendent of Indian affairs by A. Baldwin Norton.[29] Although there still was neither reservation nor agency in the southwestern part of the Territory, Luis M. Baca was appointed agent for the Apaches, if he could contact them, in the Pinos Altos vicinity, "about the only place at which an Indian agent could be stationed and be in the immediate vicinity of the Indians whose conduct he is to supervise."[30] Fort Bayard, whose establishment had been ordered by Carleton in 1866,[31] was hard by to lend him moral and, if needed, military support.

During this period the Indians pursued their roving habits, occasionally depredating across the border into Old Mexico,[32] as well as north of the line. In February, 1867, they were even reported to have swept down on the "Rio Mimbres settlement [the ancient, short-lived Mowry City] and effectively wiped it out so far as stock was concerned and burned some houses."[33] Norton requested a $27,000 appropriation in order to settle his Indians; lacking this, he pointed out, there would be no point in attempting to negotiate, since he would have nothing to offer.[34] Baca, apparently ineffective in contacting Victorio's band, was succeeded by John Ayres on July 25, 1868,[35] only a slight improvement, although he was agent during two critical periods. Apache depredations, accompanied by "distinguished atrocities," continued as the unsettled Indians were forced to pillage for their livelihood.[36]

X

The Good Agent Drew

Black-bearded Governor Robert B. Mitchell, tough veteran of the Civil War, stirred up the pot with his personal declaration against the Gila Apaches and, for good measure, the Navahos, by way of an executive proclamation of war on August 2, 1869. Never notably forbearing, he had threatened to shoot three hundred fifty men of his Union cavalry regiment in 1863 for alleged mutiny, thus winning the reputation of an "unyielding leader whose command bordered on the despotic."[1] That minor crisis over and done with, he became governor of New Mexico in 1866, bequeathing the Territory a turbulent three years in which, it is safe to assert, no one was bored, neither friend nor enemy. No man was neutral about Mitchell. There is little wonder that his declaration of war against intractable Indians was his last official act as chief executive; it generated clamor and protests from Congress, the State Department, the army, and even his "own official family."

Since the military had warned the Indians to settle down and many had not complied, said his proclamation, those still out were "outlaws." He therefore deemed it "his imperative duty to take immediate steps" in defense of the citizenry:

> In consequence of the constant depredations and the murder of our most esteemed and valuable citizens—cruelly murdered by the Navajo and Gila Apache Indian tribes—said tribes are hereby declared outlaws, and will be punished wherever found outside of the limits of their respective reservations (except under the immediate escort of the soldiery) as common enemies of the country.
>
> I do further authorize the citizens of the Territory to use sufficient force, in all localities, for the protection of its citizens, even should it result in the killing of every such depredators.

Secretary of the Territory William Frederick Milton Arny, who did not get on amicably with Mitchell anyway, sent a copy of the document to Washington, commenting that the general's authority

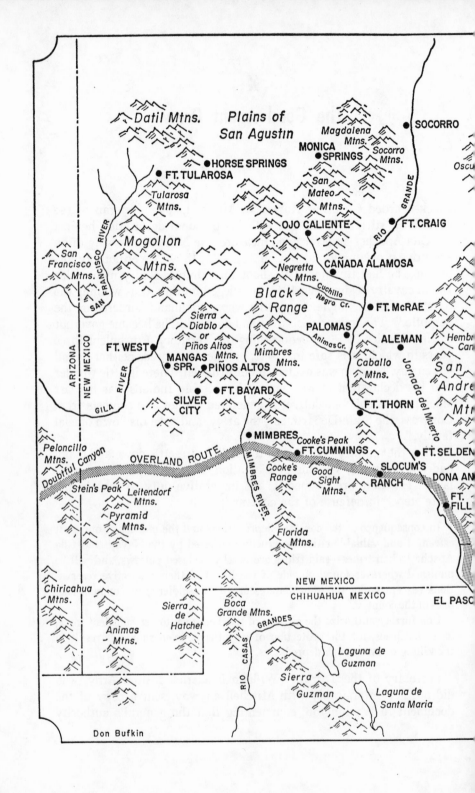

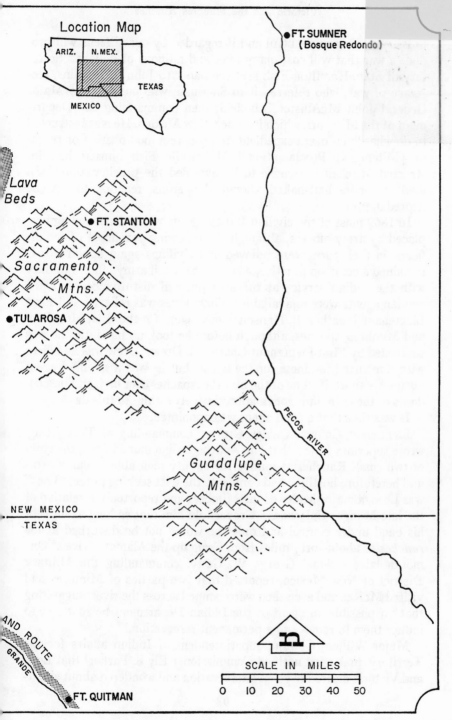

Location Map

ARIZ. | N. MEX.

TEXAS

MEXICO

FT. SUMNER
(Bosque Redondo)

Lava
Beds

FT. STANTON

Sacramento
Mtns.

TULAROSA

Guadalupe
Mtns.

PECOS RIVER

NEW MEXICO

TEXAS

AND ROUTE

GRANDE

FT. QUITMAN

SCALE IN MILES

0   10   20   30   40   50

Sites Important to Events Related

to issue it "is very doubtful and if regarded by our citizens will produce a war that will cost many lives and millions of dollars." Secretary of State Hamilton Fish sent the paper to John A. Rawlins, secretary of war, who referred it to Sherman, who passed it to Major General John McAllister Schofield, then commanding the Department of the Missouri, which included New Mexico. He was instructed to do what "you deem expedient, to procure a modification or repeal of [Mitchell's] Proclamation." Meanwhile Fish himself had instructed Mitchell "to cause to be annulled the proclamation."[2] So died one more half-baked, though dangerous, reaction to Apache depredations.

In 1869 most of the civilian Indian agents were suspended and replaced by army officers, although the following year most of the officers, in their turn, were relieved and civilians again appointed. It remained a common practice, however, to detail army officers to duty with the Indian service at times of unusual disturbances or when civilian agents were unavailable.[3] Thus Ayres was relieved and First Lieutenant Jonathan B. Hanson named agent for the Gila, Mogollon, and Mimbres Apaches, although before he took up his duties he was succeeded by First Lieutenant Charles E. Drew.[4] Drew was an officer with a reported fondness for the bottle, but he was a splendid agent during his short life, one of the best the Apaches ever had, and descendants of those Indians speak appreciatively of him to this day.

It was time that a good agent was appointed.

Lieutenant Colonel Cuvier Grover, commanding at Fort Craig, wrote superiors June 2 that "an Apache Indian named Locs, the chief of two small Rancherias numbering twenty men able to carry arms and heretofore hostile," had come into the post seeking peace. "Locs" was Loco, a major leader of the Mimbres and reportedly a relative of the late Mangas Coloradas.[5] Grover told him that so long as he kept his band under control and quiet he would not be disturbed at his *rancherías* about forty miles from Craig up the Alamosa River.[6] One month later Colonel George W. Getty, commanding the Military District of New Mexico, reported that two parties of Mimbres had visited McRae and even then were camped across the river, suggesting that "if possible an agent of the Indian Department be sent . . . to induce them to remove to a permanent reservation."[7]

Major William Clinton, superintendent of Indian affairs for the Territory, in August notified Commissioner Ely S. Parker[8] that Loco and Victorio desired to go on a reservation and wondered about shunt-ing them to the new Navaho reserve to the northwest. Agent Lorenzo Labadi, who had had experience at Bosque Redondo, was appalled at that idea and urged that the Mimbres be moved instead to the Mescalero country around Fort Stanton.[9] So it was to go. Down the years suggestions would be made from time to time that the Mimbres be moved to the east, to the west, to the north, and from Arizona to the Navaho reservation, to the Mescalero reservation, and even, so help us, to Oklahoma. Few ever seriously considered acceding to their simple request to remain where they were, in their traditional homeland where they had been raised, and whose mountains, valleys, deserts, and canyons they knew and loved. They must be moved. Why? Search the records from end to end, the thousands upon thousands of documents, and you discover no valid reason. There was no reason. It was simply that, since they desired to remain, they must be moved.

In his first annual report on September 3, 1869, to Commissioner Parker, himself an Indian, Drew related how he had begun his work, re-establishing relations with these wild natives who had been driven into hostility and had remained out now for eight years.

His initial contacts were with Loco and some of his warriors, Victorio lurking in the mountain recesses, suspicious no doubt, wary, perhaps afraid to come in. It requires little imagination to picture the smoky councils, the arguments between these two Mimbres leaders, at this time of approximately equal influence. Always, or nearly always, Loco, the elder, was for peace if it could be arranged; ever according to the surviving records, Victorio was less optimistic that it could be reached. He remembered clearly the many abortive attempts when the people were fired on by soldiers, even when bearing white flags, the whites' own symbol of peaceful intent. He no longer trusted this enemy. Victorio, the record shows, was never loquacious with the whites; he rarely talked much, and when he spoke it was with decision. He would compromise when he must, but no more than was forced upon him. If the whites proved treacherous, let them have war. Now they would offer food, peace, and a reservation? Let them prove it!

Drew had proceeded toward Fort Bayard, he wrote, "to endeavor to communicate with the Southern Apache Tribes of Indians." It had been left to his discretion "to stop at any place on the road to Fort Bayard, providing I could enter into communication with the Indians." At Craig he learned that some two hundred fifty Mimbres were camped along the Cuchillo Negro River, about twelve miles southwest of Fort McRae. At this post "I found some Mexicans who were willing to go to the Chief and endeavor to bring him in. After three days, Loco, Chief of the Mimbres tribe, came, accompanied by three warriors and four squaws. I then through the means of interpreters had a talk with them," learning that "Loco is willing to abandon the war path and says he can speak for all of his tribe. He says that they want peace and good peace and no lie (as he expresses himself). Loco also says that Lopez, one of the chiefs of the Gila Apaches who range in the Burro Mountains, is at his camp, and that Lopez's tribe are willing to come in after they see what becomes of Loco." Lopez meanwhile said that Loco could speak for him. The Mimbres added that they desired the right to plant along the Cuchillo Negro, as they used to do, before being driven away, and the right to hunt on the east side of the Mimbres Mountains, or Black Range. "They appear very willing to make peace, and I think that with proper care and by treating them honestly and justly the whole of the Apache Tribes may be brought in from the warpath," said Drew. He observed that some of Loco's men bore wounds, leading to the suspicion that they were guilty of recent depredations, as no doubt they were, since they had to survive.

"In my opinion no better place could be had to negotiate with them from than this [Fort McRae]; for should you go out to them with troops, they will hide and if you go alone you are not apt to return," continued Drew, accurately.

"Loco has promised to remain camped where he now is until I hear from this letter. Not having any funds or goods and no authority to promise anything it is impossible to carry out my instructions. . . . Loco . . . says he is contented to wait a month to hear from the Great Father. If this opportunity is lost it will be almost impossible to again allay their suspicions and I would beg that if anything is to be done with them, it be done as soon as possible."[10]

Depredators though they were, and despite their persistent raiding into Mexico, the Mimbres were not guilty of all charged against them. Milton B. Duffield, former United States marshal and now special agent for the Post Office Department,[11] wrote from Mesilla in mid-July that Apache Indians had captured two more mails between that place and Tucson, the third within eight days, killing two drivers. "The fact is they kill all they can, and have taken several mails. From La Messilla to Tucson, a distance of three hundred miles, there is not *one* mile in that distance, that is safe to travel on account of the murderous Apache."[12] However, Clinton wrote Parker that the "outrages" committed on mail carriers appeared upon investigation chargeable to Sonora Apaches rather than to either Mimbres or Central Chiricahuas, even though "the present condition of the Apaches of New Mexico is that of war."[13]

Drew followed up his original communication a month later with one reporting on a council he had held October 10 with Victorio, Loco, Lopez, Chastine, "and one whose name I cannot write or pronounce. The first three I had met twice before. The last are of the tribe known as the Mogollon-Apaches." They were all very suspicious, wary.

"There was some 40 warriors and I saw lookouts on almost every hill, besides a guard over their animals about half mile distant. The Council was held on the outskirts of a small Mexican town called Cañada Alamosa, which is the northern boundary of what they want for a reservation." Cañada Alamosa, from this time forward to figure regularly in Mimbres history, is today called Monticello. It was to become a focal point for Mimbres-white relations, and now it already was a full-blown community of Mexicans who apparently lived almost entirely by trading contraband with the Apaches for contraband in return—whiskey, largely, and arms, ammunition, and food, for stolen horses, mules, and cattle. Today the community, drowsing in a mile-wide valley on the Alamosa River, hard against the Sierra Negretta Mountains, is a sleepy, half-populated cluster of houses beneath giant cottonwoods which were sizable even in Apache days. The pattern of the old settlement and its typically Mexican plaza with the houses built around it is plain; once it was a meeting place for hundreds of Indians, scores of Mexican traders and *contrabandistas*, U.S. agents, and the military. To the north are the San Mateo Mountains. Westward, beyond the low Sierra Negrettas, glowers the Mimbres, or Black Range. To the east and south were unpopulated flats and breaks, extending to the Río Grande in the one direction, to Mexico in the other. The reason for the community's existence there was its never-failing spring, and the Alamosa River.[14]

Loco appeared to Drew to be the head chief who "does all the talking." A son of Mangas Coloradas, not a chief, perhaps the individual named Salvidor, also attended, but said little.

Drew reported that Loco promised all "will come in from the warpath if their Great Father will give them food & clothing." The officer found difficulty making them understand that he still had neither to give them right away, that the "Great Father" lived far away and it would take time for him to send the goods. The Indians insisted that

101

"I must hear pretty soon," because the cold was coming in and they were hungry. A Mexican informed the agent that the Mogollons, who dwelt up the canyon beyond Ojo Caliente, or Warm Springs, numbered about 84 warriors and the Mimbres 132, plus women and children. "He thought there must be 400 in all," wrote Drew, but he is not clear on what that figure would include. It is apparent, however, that until this time most estimates of the strength of the Mimbres were unreliable. Under pressure from troops, or for other reasons, many must frequently have filtered in among the Central Chiricahuas, the Sonora Chiricahuas, and perhaps other bands. Thus the numbers of the Mimbres available for any estimate would fluctuate markedly.

"They were very suspicious and all came well armed, a great many with guns, the rest with lances and bows," Drew reported. "I could not get them into town . . . on account of a citizen scout [or Indian-hunting party] of 25 men under Capt. J. M. Bullard."[15]

Bullard's party purportedly were trailing up some Apaches who had killed a woman and child near Pinos Altos. Drew reported that Bullard "behaved well and moved out of town at my request." Later that worthy conceded to Drew that he had not actually trailed the murderers, but, assuming they were from the Indian camp, had come directly there, then agreed it would be unwise to assail the Apaches in council with the officer. Thus still another savage "retaliatory" attack upon possibly innocent Indians was averted narrowly.[16]

"The Indians," Drew continued, "took every precaution to prevent a surprise and were very restless. . . . It is impossible to get near them with soldiers, they are so suspicious. . . . All the warriors I have seen are young and hardy and a great many of them have been wounded." The Apaches were gathering in such numbers they could give the troops much trouble if not granted food and clothing, and he now had been among them three times with nothing but promises, "and do not feel disposed to go again without something to give them."

At this conference the basic inclination of Loco toward peace and of Victorio to remain warily aloof was clearly evident. Victorio remembered well the fate of Mangas and of many another who had trusted the Americans. Even today the descendants of Loco and other Warm Springs Apaches remember this as the most remarkable difference between the two: Loco ever for peace, Victorio ready for war if forced. That is why Victorio was killed while Loco was shipped off under guard to languish away, cruelly neglected, in a distant and unpleasant country. Who is to say which was the wiser?

Drew concluded:

"Loco says he will keep what there now is [the Indians gathered] together where they now are . . . and will also try and get as many more of them as he can. I am certain Loco means peace, but he will have hard work to keep some of them, as I believe Victorio is not disposed to do if he can keep enough warriors with him. At present he has a very small band, and can do nothing unless some of the others get discontented. There will probably be depredations committed in different places by members of this same tribe, although they have to shoulder a great deal done by Mexicans. . . . But where they now are there are no roads or towns except Cañada Alamosa, and they [the Mexicans] are friendly to them. A beginning must be made if anything is to be done, and . . . now is the time to do it."[17]

Drew found communications with the superintendent at Santa Fe slow and unsatisfactory, and was frustrated by the lack of response to his reports. He wrote that "my instructions were to go get my indians together if possible. I have done so . . . and now I do not know what to do with them." He pointed out that where other officer-agents had gone to established agencies, dealing with reservation Indians, Drew must collect Indians that were on no reservation and had not been in contact with an agent for many years, and that he had only precarious and intermittent means to feed and care for them and must develop methods as he went along. Added to all this was the exasperating lack of specific responses to his suggestions, questions, and needs. It was enough to discourage a saint.[18] Captain George Shorkley, commanding at McRae, came strongly to his support in a Christmas Day letter to his district headquarters, urging Colonel Getty to back Drew and try to get some action out of the Indian Department. He pointed out that the lieutenant had arranged an understanding with Loco, Victorio, and others on October 10 and had promptly reported this action to superiors, filing a copy with the military. Repeatedly then he had asked for instructions, which had never arrived. In fact, "he informs me that he has not received even an acknowledgment of the receipt of his communications, much less the instructions asked for." The Indians, for their part, "have faithfully kept every condition of the agreement . . . and evince an earnest purpose of remaining permanently at peace . . . but they expect the issues of clothing, blankets &s., as agreed upon."

Shorkley wrote that Drew, "with a most commendable zeal has repeatedly visited them, and remained over night in their camp or village, and has so far kept them in patient waiting, although they have greatly needed these issues." If they did not receive the promised goods shortly, they must go back to depredating in order to live. Not only the Mimbres, Loco assured Drew, but he had been informed that even Cochise and the Chiricahuas would come in, if the Indians were only treated justly—and soon. In an endorsement Getty noted that a picayune sum, $2,800, finally had been granted Drew. It wasn't much cash, but at least it constituted an acknowledgment that the Indian Office approved what he was doing at the very real risk of his life.[19]

In developing a relationship with his wild charges, Drew, as had so many agents in the past, ran into difficulties not caused by Indians but the work of the shadowy elements most disruptive of frontier tranquility: those whites who desired no peace, those Mexicans who believed that the answer to unsettled conditions was the murder of any Indians they could catch, and those unscrupulous traders with their endless machinations. The fact that the traders in this case were noted figures in the region did not lessen the peril they posed to Drew's success, although it seems simple justice that in the near future one of them would himself become an agent and suffer from the identical difficulties he was to cause Drew. All three of these vexatious factions now descended upon this low-ranking officer who, better acquainted with his Indians each day, became more and more their partisan. He could see ever more clearly the many instances in which they were in the right and the whites in the wrong. White men not so familiar with the Indians and their difficulties and the injustices that befell them could never seem to appreciate this point of view. They did not wish to.

William L. Rynerson,[20] who had risen from sergeant to brevet lieutenant colonel with the California Column and apparently had absorbed Carleton's notions on how to handle Indians, wrote to the new governor, William A. Pile, whom he believed sympathetic,[21] calling attention to the "deplorable condition" of folks in Grant County "on account of Indian depredations." Rynerson, post trader at Baynard, told of engagements with Indians (with no apparent loss of life on either side) and said the hostiles were everywhere and the people "are in terror." He pleaded for deliverance from the ravages of "a merciless foe." Drew, commenting on the letter, conceded the depredations but denied they were committed by his Indians. He added:

From information received from reliable sources, I am compelled to believe that [parties] in the lower country is [sic] strongly opposed to any attempt to make peace with the Apaches, and especially to the placing of them on a reservation. No doubt they have their own reasons for their conduct. Letters received from disinterested parties living in the most exposed portion of the lower country, state that comparatively few depredations from the Indians have occurred this year, and certainly no reign of terror exists in that portion of the country.[22]

In the second place, writing to Major William Clinton, the superintendent, Drew complained:

Scouting parties from Chihuahua and who are paid a premium for Indian scalps are also allowed to hunt for Indians in the Territory [of New Mexico]. A party from Hanos [Janos] Chihuahua a few days since threatened to attack these Indians. They were warned by [brevet brigadier] Genl. [John Sanford] Mason, [commanding at Fort Bayard] not to do so, but they left the Mimbres [River] with the avowed intention of attacking the camp. . . . I remained in this camp two days to prevent such an outrage. It seems to me that some measures should be taken at once to prevent citizens of another Government with whom we are at peace, from committing outrages upon people that are looked upon by this Government as its wards. If allowed to [hunt] Indians at all in this country, they should be made to know that Indians on a reservation are not to be molested. It will be impossible to establish a permanent peace with those Indians if straggling bands of citizens from Old Mexico are suffered to roam at will and attack those Indians whenever and wherever found and under any and all circumstances. People, too, who hunt Indians only for a few paltry dollars they receive for the scalp. . . . A friendly Indian is worth as much as . . . any other.[23]

Drew reported that on January 1, 1870, he had visited the Indian camp, conferred with Loco. Victorio, Salvidor (the son of Mangas), and others, all expressing a willingness to do whatever was required. He estimated there were now about three hundred Indians in camp. Before his visit he had been informed that stock had been stolen from San José, Grant County, the citizens accusing Loco's band.

I informed Loco of the fact. He denied any knowledge . . . [and] sent Salvadore . . . and ten or twelve others to look for the trail. On the following day Salvadore reported to me the fact that he had followed the trail of the stolen cattle and that he was convinced that Navajoes or Mexicans stole the stock and if I would go with him or send some one he would track them to their camp in order to show that the Apaches did not have anything to do with it.

Drew added that

Mexican thieves are continually stealing from the citizens along the Rio Grande and then start in pursuit of the Indian. This is a notorious fact and time and again they have been opposed in their villainous effort to saddle their rascality on the Indians. These thieves hang around the camp of the Indians and see what mark and brands are on their animals, and then claim them as their property. This trick has been exposed on two occasions, and gives me a great deal of trouble . . . to keep down misunderstanding.[24]

This letter, at least, got some action. District headquarters warned commanders at all the southwestern posts, Forts McRae, Cummings, Bayard, and Selden,[25] that "armed parties of Mexicans, entering the United States for any purpose whatever . . . will be arrested and disarmed."[26]

By this time Drew had experienced the first two of the unholy trio of obstacles to peaceful management of southwestern Indians. He was now to encounter the third.

No sooner had Victorio, Loco, and the others agreed upon peace and settled their people openly at Cañada Alamosa or nearby than the traders lumbered in with their laden wagons to turn up an honest dollar, if they could manage it, but in any event to turn up a dollar. Licensed early in 1870 for this trade was a firm known as Jeffords & Brevoort,[27] headed by two notables of that frontier, Thomas J. Jeffords[28] and Elias Brevoort.[29] Apparently they became impatient with a watchdog Drew closely eying their operations and decided to get rid of him. On March 8 they sent a letter to the officer, then at Fort McRae. The communication seemed innocent enough.

They reported that Loco, on March 3, had returned from McRae very tired and

wanted us to get him some whiskey, when we told him, as we had repeatedly before, that we were not allowed to keep it, did not use it, and would not under no consideration give him any or procure it for him. He begd & begd & we continued to refuse, when he became very excited and very angry and stated that he did not understand how it was we refused to get him whiskey & said to him that if the agent, or great father at Washington, knew we gave, or sold him or his tribe whiskey we would be removed from here, stating that when he was at Fort McRae (night of 2d) that you procured *four* bottles of whiskey, which he & your self & perhaps some others drank, intimated that we were deceiving him &c. . . . We hope his statement may prove untrue though at the same time, the fact of his becoming so angry & being so much excited is almost proof that his statement is correct. We admit that it is a very strange affair, & requires an explicit explanation from you whether such is really the case, & if it will occur again in which case we are duty bound for our own protection to take notice of it through a different channel. . . . You will at once see the folly of your act if his statement be true & the critical position in which you have placed us. . . . You are probably not aware that any person who *gives* or *sells* whiskey to an indian subjects himself to indictment—a fine of five hundred dollars & ten years imprisonment.[30]

Drew immediately fired the letter on to Clinton, with one of his own, noting that he had received the communication "by special messenger" March 16.

I do not imagine that these gentlemen believe what they say and hence am at a loss to account for their action. I will state to you that there is not the slightest foundation for the story. So far from giving "Loco" whiskey, I took the trouble to go with him until he passed through Alamsita for the express purpose of preventing him from getting any. . . . After writing my letter to you in reference to the stories in circulation about these gentlemen, I told them what I had heard, and also that I had written you on the subject.

They denied it so emphatically that I left them under the impression that they had been misrepresented. On a second visit to Cañada [Alamosa] they seemed very friendly and I was beginning to form a better opinion of them, although from the first they have exhibited a disposition to dictate to me in a manner strangely at variance with their position. This spirit has at length culminated in the insolent and bullying letter enclosed. Such language I cannot and will not tolerate, and am compelled therefore to request that their appointment be revoked.[31]

Clinton hustled the letters on to Parker at Washington, with the explanation that Jeffords & Brevoort must have written "under excitement," though he did not doubt that Loco "told them what they report he did." Even so, that did not excuse their letter to Drew. Meanwhile, he asked Getty to have the Fort McRae commander investigated; Shorkley wrote March 29 that he had done so. "It seems positive that 'Loco' did not get the whiskey as stated," he reported as his "firm belief."

"I saw 'Loco' in the evening of the 3rd instant soon after he came to the Post and he was there I thought under the influence of liquor. Agent Drew took him to his quarters and kept him and his party over night. I again saw him the next morning and 'Loco' was entire sober and was so when he left the Post." He charitably added that " 'Loco' may have been misunderstood by Jeffords and Brevoort as he denies their statement." He concluded, "From my personal knowledge of the condition of Lieut. Drew's Agency I have no hesitancy in stating that I give his statement full credence."[32]

With Shorkley's report were two statements, one by Post Trader Frank Frenger at McRae who said he was the only one possessing whiskey in the area—legally—and he had seen Drew refuse Loco's request for liquor there, and had heard him warn others against granting it. Interpreter Robert C. Patterson, the other letter writer, was generally believed an able and intelligent man. He said he had accompanied Drew to Cañada Alamosa, called Jeffords' and Brevoort's attention to their statements, and asked Loco about the matter. "He said the statement was false, that he had not said so and did not get any whiskey. There was no mistaking his meaning in this. Loco," he added, however, "talks very bad Spanish and it is often difficult to understand him."[33]

In view of the report, Clinton, by Special Order Number 1, dated April 15, 1870, revoked the license of Jeffords and Brevoort to trade with the Cañada Alamosa Indians. As might be supposed, this nettled the pair considerably; *that* was not what they had had in mind at all.

Analyzing the correspondence and the incident from this perspective, it appears that Brevoort was the instigator and Jeffords merely went along with it. The writing resembles Brevoort's, for one thing, and Jeffords was never known to have engaged in any other such dispute during his adventurous and generally responsible career.

In a notarized statement Brevoort now added charges against Lieutenant Drew. Anything to get the license reinstated!

"We had *personally* seen the said Lieut. Drew give whiskey to Indians on a previous occasion," it said, and that they had communicated to him privately, intending to "rouse the said Lieut. Drew from the (we are pained to say) apparently drunken stupor, caused from almost constant dissipation or drunkeness since his arrival in the country & to bring him if possible to a true sense of his duties even at the risk of offending him." The letter formally alleged:

"1st. That he did give whiskey to two Apache Indians out of a bottle. This was on or about the 12th day of January last.

"2nd. That he has been under the influence of whiskey and drunk during the issuing of rations."

That he struck an Apache squaw for not interpreting for him, that he had been drunk with Loco, that he was always drunk, and so on, concluding with the revealing note that "Lieut. Drew has publicly stated that he did not personally like Mr. Brevoort."[34]

Hacienda del Carmen, one of Chihuahua's greatest, richest, and most durable ranches during Indian war days, from which, Mexican rumor insists, Victorio was seized as an infant by raiding Apaches.

The only known photograph of Victorio. It is believed that he lost his head band in a struggle to avoid having his picture taken and that he had to be held for the camera.

Courtesy National Archives

An artist's reproduction of the photograph, modifying Victorio's typically Indian appearance. The artist may have been influenced by the belief common in Mexico that Victorio was of Mexican ancestry.

Courtesy Museum of New Mexico

Black Range, or Mimbres Mountains, Victorio's favorite retreat.

Fort Webster, one of the earliest posts on the Mimbres River, was on the flat land of the valley. A canyon, right rear, leads to Santa Rita.

Stein's Peak was an important landmark on the Butterfield Overland Mail Route. The walls of the stage station, foreground, date from 1858. This area was the scene of much heavy action between Apaches, especially Mimbres, and whites.

Ruins (now gone) at Janos, Chihuahua, said to be those of the presidio.
The Mimbres were often in conflict with the residents of Janos, who may
have resorted to arsenic poisoning to try to rid themselves of the Indians.

Site of the first Mimbres reservation, on Santa Lucia Creek, now Mangas
Creek, in western New Mexico. The Indians were there only briefly
before discovery of gold nearby brought an influx of settlers and new
hostilities.

Doubtful Canyon Pass, through the Stein's Peak Range, where parties of whites were massacred by the Mimbres and other Apache bands from time to time.

Joseph Rodman West, who as brigadier general in the California Column gave the orders that resulted in the murder of Mangas Coloradas.

Colonel and Brevet Major General Thomas Casimer Devin, commander of the Eighth Cavalry, active in controlling the Apaches in the 1870's.

From Third Cavalry

Apache Pass, between the Dos Cabezas and Chiricahua Mountains, at its western approaches. The pass was the scene of many bloody encounters between Apaches and whites.

Fort Bowie, overlooking the Apache Pass trail, was one of the most important posts in Apache country. Its ruins are now a National Historic Site.

At the site of Fort Craig, above the Río Grande, trim stone ruins stand like tombstones. For many years Fort Craig was a key post in Apache country.

Cañada Alamosa, now Monticello, New Mexico, in the distance, along the Alamosa River. It was at the edge of the Mimbres' Ojo Caliente reservation.

Plaza at Monticello, formerly Cañada Alamosa. The church does not date back to Apache-Mexican times.

Clinton sent everything along to Parker, noting that since Jeffords and Brevoort had been fired as traders the statement might be taken with a few grains of salt. Clinton added that he had heard from other sources that Drew "had been denounced for drunkenness," although others contradicted these reports. He had cautioned the officer, he said. But, he added warmly, despite their truth or falsity, "Lt. Drew has managed the Indians under his control quite as well as could be done by a man of more temperate habits, and he certainly is the first Agent who has had them under control, at least for many years."[35]

Years afterward Victorio still remembered Lieutenant Drew as one of the Mimbres' best agents. In 1873 he asked General O. O. Howard, then trying to find them a suitable reservation, "for an Agent like the first one they had at the Cañada [Alamosa]." But he was dead.

In Drew's officer file in the National Archives is a copy of the report of his death, along with an endorsement by Clinton, both furnished eight years later to Drew's father, William A. Drew:

Parahe, N.M.[36]
June 5th, 1870

Maj. Wm. Clinton
Supt. Indian Affairs
Santa Fe, N.M.
Sir,
Lt. Drew died this morning under the following circumstances.
The Indians (Mescaleros) run off the herd belonging to J. H. Whittington's train. Lt. Drew with Lt. [Pendleton] Hunter and fifteen men started after them and when in the mountains could not find water. Lt. Drew with five men started back for this place. One of the men was left in the mountains and is supposed to have perished. All the others came in safe but Drew. He must have been within eight or ten miles from this place when he got lost and he has been wandering there for nearly forty hours. This morning the party sent out to find him, found him—he was alive but very weak. They gave him water and stimulants but could not revive him. After carrying him about four miles he died in the men's arms. From the time he left the mountains until this morning (nearly four days) he was without water. His body was brought in a few minutes ago and will be sent to Fort Craig for interment. His effects and papers are here and will be turned over to the Commanding Officer of Fort Craig.

The letter was signed "H. D. Hall," who cannot be identified.
Clinton's statement said, "It is a satisfaction to me, and should be to the friends of Lt. Drew, that notwithstanding the abuse heaped

upon him by his enemies, he died whilst in the strict discharge of his duty, and while he was endeavoring to recover property belonging to citizens of the country." It was a generous, apparently well-deserved tribute.

In the same statement Clinton reported that he had ordered First Lieutenant Argalus Garey Hennisee,[37] already agent for the Mescaleros, "where he has comparitively nothing to do," to take over the Southern Apaches at Cañada Alamosa as well.[38] He, too, proved an intelligent and worthy agent, and a harassed one. He reached Craig in June.[39]

Hennisee, in a letter on June 22, reported that the Southern Apaches numbered about 360, that they "could not hunt much for fear of being killed by whites," and that while it had been the practice to ration them for thirty days at a time, "I do not like that plan much for all the food is consumed or made into liquor within 10 days after the issue, giving the Indians an excellent chance to get hungry and insubordinate before the next issue. I think it would be much better to issue the food every ten days and to issue meal instead of corn to prevent them from making liquor which I understand cannot be so easily made from Meal."[40]

But Hennisee found more than corn to worry about. Mexican bootleggers at Cañada Alamosa, he soon learned, were peddling whiskey to the Indians. His able interpreter, Patterson, sought to break up their traffic, so they persuaded some Indians to steal about a hundred bushels of wheat from Patterson's farm.[41] In sending along Hennisee's report, Clinton urged that the agent be authorized "to prosecute these rascals to the full extent of the law. . . . So long as these people trade with the Indians . . . just so long will the Indians be thieves and uncontrollable by the Agent."[42]

In mid-September Hennissee reported his attempt to break up the "illegal traffic in whiskey, powder, lead, percussion caps, manta &c., which a large portion of the Mexican population of the country at and within the distance of sixty miles from Cañada Alamosa, N.M., have been engaged in with the Indians under my charge." He had quietly searched for evidence to support his suspicions. "I was informed and had good reason to believe that José Trujillo, the Justice of the Peace, and Juan N. Montoya, the constable . . . were the principal traders. . . . I concluded to prosecute these officials only" because there were too many others to gather evidence against.

"I issued rations to the Indians on Aug. 22d. . . . On the morning of

August 23d, before many of the Indians returned to the town, I searched the house of Juan J. Montoya and found about 28 gallons of whiskey in a barrel, which I poured upon the ground. I arrested Juan N. Montoya and Juan Montoya, who lives in the same house. . . . Juan N. Montoya purchased the whiskey from Juan N. Baca at Socorro, N.M., on or about Aug. 18th, and paid for it an U.S. Mule which he (Montoya) had received from the Indians." Montoya had revealed to an acquaintance that he intended to trade the whiskey to the Indians for ten mules. An informant told Hennisee that he had seen Trujillo "at his house, give whiskey to the Indian Chief 'Loco' and to five or six other Indians on the night of August 10th, the Indians all being drunk at the time, and that Trujillo told the drunken Indians that the Indian Agent and the Interpreter told them lies, that he (Trujillo) was their best friend. . . .

"I arrested Trujillo and intended to complete the search of his premises when he and Montoya, by virtue of their official positions, summoned a Posse Comitatus of about forty Mexicans, who were at hand for the purpose, and disarmed my party of men, which consisted of my interpreter, three soldiers . . . and Lieut. Thomas Blair. . . . Two carbines and three pistols were wrenched from the party by the Mexicans before it was possible to use them."

Hennisee said that his "intention was to kill, if necessary, any person who resisted," but that it was just as well it turned out as it did, because had a fight started "not one of my party would have escaped alive."

The lieutenant said he was chased out of town and went to Socorro to get a writ against Trujillo and Montoya and a writ of habeas corpus for Patterson, who had been arrested and still was at Cañada Alamosa. "The whole affair appears ridiculous, but as I succeeded in destroying a large portion of the whiskey which they had on hand I would again do as I did under like circumstances." He added that the Mexicans had been ordered to appear before a U.S. district court at Albuquerque, but doubted they would be convicted "as I think the Mexican witnesses for the prosecution will allow themselves to be bribed by the defense." It was extremely difficult to obtain a conviction "by an ordinary Mexican jury."

But that was not all of the officer's troubles.

Trujillo brought an action against him for assault before the Alamocito justice of the peace, and "I was tried, convicted and sentenced to imprisonment in the County Jail for three months." He appealed, of course. All of the Mexicans engaged in the illicit traffic said they believed he had acted from personal bias, he explained, "and I shall have to be very careful to escape personal injury." He went on that "I think that I can safely say that nearly every Mexican on the Rio Grande between Socorro and Mesilla who has much property has made it by trading with Indians. . . . The trading has been carried on for such a period and so many persons have made money by it that they look upon it as a natural right." He cited instances in which Indians had stolen stock, Mexicans refused to loan animals for the pursuit, and the stolen beasts ended by being traded for whiskey, lead, or other contraband. "The difficulty in recovering a stolen horse or mule from a Mexican is that the owner cannot go and take it without a writ, without the risk of being arrested, tried and *convicted* of being a horse thief, and before he can get the writ the thief is informed of the action, and the animal cannot be found." Hennisee said that the rations for the Indians still were insufficient to satisfy their hunger and prevent depredations. He urged that a reservation be created so that unsavory characters could be kept from them.[43]

Hennisee returned to Cañada Alamosa and met Victorio on September 20. The Apache assured him that "all the Indians would be in early the next day to receive rations," but for two days they did not appear because the Mexicans warned them the officer meant to demand that they return stolen horses and mules. "It seems that the Indians traded the mules to the Mexicans and after I searched for the whiskey . . . the Mexicans turned over the animals to the Indians for safekeeping and that the Indians still have them." Loco then came in, and the officer told him that no rations would be issued until the animals were given up. By this time there were some six hundred Indians at Cañada Alamosa; good treatment and rations continued to attract them.[44]

William Arny now was U.S. special agent,[45] in which office he toured the Indian country. He reached Paraje on October 16 and the next day accompanied Hennisee to Cañada Alamosa. With them went Patterson, "the efficient and energetic Interpreter who has known these Indians for a number of years," and Brevet Major Frederick William Coleman, who later would be forced to resign from the army for ordering soldiers to fire on peaceable Apaches while he, Coleman, was drunk.[46]

They met a few Indians at Cañada Alamosa, but the others were afraid to come in. On the nineteenth the four, with no escort, proceeded about four miles up the lovely canyon toward Ojo Caliente, the Indians watching them from the bluffs and hills all around. At last they were met by Victorio, Loco, Nana, and Tomascito, who asked four days to bring in the others. "I told them to hurry as it was important before cold weather to let the Great Father know what they proposed to do, and what they would require." They agreed to hasten.

"The next day a large cavalcade of Indians came in, headed by *'Cochise,'* the principal chief of the *White Mountain Apaches, Coyoteros* and *Chillicorias.*[47]

"We had present at this council all the principal chiefs of the various bands of Apaches except 'Cadette,' the head chief of the Mescaleros, who is on the warpath with the Comanches in Texas. . . . We had present 22 Chiefs and Captains and 790 Indians, of which number there were 96 of Cochise's band proper and his family, and 114 Mescaleros under 'Nane,' a head man who has left Cadette and desires peace." Arny reported that on the night of October 18 he had become "sick from poison eating canned peaches,"[48] but continued his report anyway.

" *'Cochise'* and the other chiefs confessed that they had been guilty of murders and thefts and gave me a history of his actions since 1860," or about the time of the Bascom incident.[49] "He said his people had been at war for ten years, and although they had killed many whites, they had lost many braves so that now he had more women and children to provide for than with a war he could protect, that he desired peace, would talk straight and wanted the government to talk and act straight with him. . . . He told me that if the government would feed his people and give them clothing that in a few months he would have all the Indians of his tribe in and at peace." He did not like the White Mountains nor the area around Camp Thomas,[50] and wanted to see how he would like Cañada Alamosa, Cochise told Arny. The special agent said that Hennisee had been "indefatigable" since becoming agent, with an increase in the number of Indians at his post each month. Victorio and others predicted that "in a month there will be 1,000 or 1,200 present to be fed and they will also require Blankets."

He believed "it is folly to urge these indians to make restitution of the stolen horses and mules. They have nothing with which to do it except a few horses which they ride and which they would not give up except with their lives, and these horses are without brands and

129

have not been stolen. . . . The Indians told me that the stolen animals were either killed and eaten by them or sold to the Mexicans." They had, indeed, become wise in ways to avoid accountability.[51]

In his "Report No. 8" to Parker on November 21, Arny said that the Southern Apaches had "during the last ten years, shown themselves to be the most savage, barbarous, and uncivilized Indians on this continent. Their exploits in the way of murder, robberies and torture are unparalleled in the history of any other tribe of Indians: they have robbed mails, burned Stage Coaches, have torn out, cooked and eaten the hearts of some persons, and have burned at the stake stage passengers and other prisoners who have fallen in their power; they have killed miners, and retarded the mining operations of one of the richest portions of the United States."[52] He estimated their numbers. Coyoteros and Central Chiricahuas: warriors, 340; women, 672; children, 466, for 1,478 Indians plus about 600 horses. Mimbres: warriors, 280; women, 370; children, 210; total, 860 plus about 400 horses. Mogollon and Gila bands: warriors, 130; women, 180; children, 230; total, 560 with about 260 horses. The grand totals for these bands, plus the Mescaleros, Arny put at 910 warriors with 1,502 women and 1,226 children, for an over-all total of 3,638 individuals with some 1,760 horses. His figures made no allowance for the White Mountain and other Arizona bands, except as the Central Chiricahuas and Coyoteros were included.

"The Southern Apaches have certainly been guilty of many atrocious acts," Arny conceded, "but they have not gone scot free as their census fully shows, and they feel it. . . . All these Indians now desire peace. . . ."

He urged strongly that a reservation be quickly set aside where they could be collected, protected, and led from barbarity into the paradise of civilization, for these Apaches still had never been on a reservation of their own, except for the brief attempt at Mangus Springs. Arny listed six possibilities: one might be near Camp Thomas [Fort Apache] in Arizona, out of the way of the settlements, with an abundance of wood, water, grass, and arable land. Or they could be collected at the old Santa Lucia reserve along the Gila. A third possibility was adjacent to the Mimbres River, the site that the Treaty of 1855 had sought to establish. However, because of the heavy influx of miners and settlers toward Pinos Altos and the "Silver Flats," or Chloride Flats (the future Silver City), Arny did not favor this.

A fourth possibility was where they now were, along the Alamosa

River between the San Mateo and Mimbres Mountains, "commencing two miles north of the Hot Springs [Ojo Caliente] and running thirty miles down the valley, and twenty miles in width." About three hundred acres of this valley were under cultivation by whites, Arny reported, about two thousand acres could be irrigated, and eight hundred acres otherwise cultivated, with additional resources to supply "every demand of the whole Southern Apache tribe. There are living on this land 52 families—46 residences, 2 Mexican mills, 193 persons," whose improvements might be purchased for about $11,000 and, since they had no clear title, they could readily be moved away.

In the fifth place, the Apaches might be moved to a reservation near Fort Stanton, east of the Río Grande, near which the Mescaleros had been collected, or, a final possibility, they might be moved to the Tularosa River, about eighty miles west of Socorro, "a suitable place being outside of all present settlements . . . the indians themselves I believe would prefer it to any other location." There they would be remote from "the vile whiskey sellers and more wicked traders in ammunition." Arny recommended a reservation along the Tularosa for the Mimbres, Chiricahuas, Coyoteros, Gila and Mogollon Apaches, "and for any other Apache bands who by mutual consent may agree to occupy it." He recommended that the government make no treaty with the Indians,[53] but that it go ahead and construct agency buildings along the Tularosa, meanwhile leaving the Apaches on the Alamosa while indoctrinating them mentally to accept the ultimate necessity of removing from evil influences. When the reservation was fully prepared to receive them, Arny further suggested, the Indians would be informed, with no negotiation, that they had a new home, a new reservation, and if found off it "they will be considered as at war, and be dealt with accordingly." This method would save much trouble and argument.[54]

Right now the Apaches at Cañada Alamosa were living hand-to-mouth. Patterson persuaded Hennisee to visit his fields with him. They found "a large quantity of corn had been taken and from the corncobs and shucks around the many little fires . . . I was convinced that it had been taken by the Indians." He again visited the fields later, and "saw the Chief Victorio and his family, about fifty yards from one of the fields, cooking and eating corn which evidently had been taken from the field that morning."[55] It was apparent that no healthy Indian family intended to go hungry with white men's corn fields all around.

With the autumn of 1870, management of the Indians was turned over by the army to civilian officials once more. Orlanda F. Piper took his oath of office October 28 to succeed Hennisee, and Nathaniel Pope on November 30 succeeded Clinton as superintendent of Indian affairs for New Mexico.[56]

XI

The Vincent Colyer Mission

After reading Arny's report, Indian Commissioner Parker directed Pope on November 12 to select a tract near Fort Stanton for a Southern Apache reservation, one far enough from their homeland to guarantee they would be dissatisfied with it. Noting that the Mescaleros "especially" had indicated readiness to learn to farm, Pope believed the Mimbres "can be made to support themselves in a very few years, and become an industrious and hard-working people."[1] In this he echoed misguided optimism of many another. The Fort Stanton idea was shelved before being put into operation.

The Indian Bureau, meanwhile, experienced difficulty in rationing the Indians collected. Vincent Colyer, secretary of the Board of Indian Commissioners, wondered formally just before Christmas if the War Department "cannot promptly issue an order for the officers commanding the Department of New Mexico to subsist the Apache Indians. . . . The President says the War Department has the power to issue such an order and . . . he, the President, will promptly sign it."[2] The necessary directive was formulated,[3] and from this time forward such a maneuver was often employed; it solved a recurring problem and did much to make the rationing of unsettled Indians reasonably adequate and continuous.

Under the improved system more and more Indians turned up at Cañada Alamosa, more than one thousand by mid-March,[4] although this had still to be formally designated a reservation. In fact, the Southern Apaches had still long months to wait for their first full-fledged reserve. White citizens, meanwhile, pointed to them as scapegoats for crimes committed anywhere within conceivable range, or even beyond it. In fact, Governor William A. Pile wrote the secretary of state in mid-April, "about twenty men and women have been murdered and horribly mutilated, within the last three weeks" by Apaches, according to his "official" information. He said that "outraged citizens" planned an attack upon Cañada Alamosa, which he would endeavor to stop.[5] A month earlier Pope had written Parker

133

reporting Pile to have urged that Cochise be lured upon a reservation, warning that "if there is no effort made in a peaceable way to stop the continued depredations of these Indians, I shall feel it my duty to adopt the best means in my power to protect the citizens of this Territory and punish the savages." Pope added that "I fully realize" the state of affairs in the south, that he had scrounged all the money he could, even personally going $9,000 in debt, to feed the Mimbres and keep them quiet. Rations, he pointed out, were about the best inducement to bring Cochise and his people in. However, he went on, the reported "depredations" were largely retaliation "for the killing of quite a number of Apache thieves and murders by scouting parties of soldiers and citizens." As elsewhere, murder begot murder, and Apaches proved not so different from other peoples. Besides, Pope confided, "a great many of the depredations charged to the Apaches of New Mexico are committed by White Mountain, Coyotero and Tonto Apaches of Arizona, the Sonora Apaches of Old Mexico, and by Mexicans."[6]

The citizens remained uneasy and dissatisfied. The deputy probate clerk at Ralston,[7] writing of the murder of Charles Southerland on his return from Chihuahua, grumbled that "milk and water, kid glove policies may do for some tribes but it is no go with the Apaches," and urged that the government "inaugurate more vigorous means of dealing with these wretches than feeding them good beef & bacon on the reservations."[8] He spoke for many.

Although the record is unclear, it is apparent that bands of armed men occasionally scoured the back country for Indians, seeking to prevent, or avenge, "depredations," which perhaps were committed as frequently by rustlers and border thieves as by Indians, although blame inevitably fell upon the Apaches. One by-product of this hyperactivity of the whites was the frightening away of the Indians from the tentative reservations and making it impossible for some time to persuade Cochise, perhaps the principal depredator among the Indians, to come in. He no doubt believed that to do so would invite his own murder and disaster for his people. Parker had directed Pope on March 8 to invite Cochise, Victorio, and other prominent men to Washington, but the invitation had to be delivered, and Cochise was elusive.

Piper was instructed to send three agents April 1 to attempt to locate him; they "returned without finding any trace of him or his people. It is thought he has gone to Chihuahua or Sonora . . . with most of the hostile Apaches, to avoid the numerous scouting parties of troops from the different posts. . . . If this is so, it will take some time to communicate with him." Pope added that he was sending a fresh seven-man party of Mexicans and Indians to find Cochise and "not to return without him," though the killing of more Apaches by armed civilians and troops would make the mission difficult.[9]

Pope visited Cañada Alamosa, conferred with Victorio, Loco, and Nana, extracting from them the promise that they would continue at peace, and received a new request from them for a reservation and regular rations. "I told them I was prepared to feed . . . *all* Apaches who might come in . . . also that they would be cared for and protected, so long as they listened to their agent and obeyed him." For two years now, the Apaches had heard such promises, Pope admitted, yet still they were destitute and near starvation. "During this time no doubt they have committed many depredations upon citizens, but I am satisfied" from personal investigation and reliable informants that much of the stealing credited to them "is done by Mexican and American horse thieves who infest southern New Mexico, and there is reason to believe a great deal of rascality is suggested to the Indians by persons who trade whiskey, manta,[10] &c., to them for stolen stock and who are active in running such stock to different parts of the Territory for sale."[11] About May 1, Piper moved his agency headquarters from Paraje to Cañada Alamosa and increased the frequency of rationing from two weeks to one, in order to more closely watch his charges.[12]

Pope's seven-man mission returned within a month reporting that they had found Cochise's family and camp "about 160 or 175 miles almost due west from Cañada Alamosa, and north of the Gila river in Arizona. It is impossible to fix the locality of this camp with any certainty as these messengers know little or nothing of the geography of this country and give very unsatisfactory accounts of their trip." Actually it is probable that the camp was in the Dragoon Mountains, west of Apache Pass and south of the Gila, not north. Anyway, Cochise was not there. He was raiding in Sonora and none knew when he would return.[13] The Indians he had left were "nearly naked, half starved and in constant fear of scouting parties of troops. They had been attacked three times lately and had made their camp in a narrow gorge of the mountains for safety." The agents had brought in about one hundred Indians, all they found at the camp except Cochise's immediate family, and Pope tried to find other messengers who would

135

return and await the arrival of the chief, to bring him in as well. But he admitted to "great difficulty" in finding anyone to go, "as the trip is a dangerous one."[14] Only Tom Jeffords would chance it.

He left Cañada Alamosa June 7 and returned about the 28, having found Cochise but having been unable to persuade him to come in. The Indian argued that "the country was filled with soldiers and he was now afraid to venture with his women & children at present, and as he could not take them with safety, he would not leave them." He "could not come till the troops were withdrawn from that country," but promised to "send word to all bands over which he had control and . . . would advise them to cease their depredations and make peace." Jeffords said he felt that Cochise knew of the Camp Grant massacre and "was influenced by it to some extent."[15] Pope said he would make one more effort to bring the great chief in.[16]

The reason for the repeated and urgent attempts to contact Cochise was that Vincent Colyer was preparing to visit the Territory on his extended peace mission, and Cochise was one of the Indians he most desired to meet.[17] He was believed a key to the pacification of the Southwest. That Colyer might anticipate difficulties, not only from the Indians, but from impassioned, often misinformed whites was obvious. The danger of a fresh Camp Grant incident in New Mexico was very real. Governor Pile warned in mid-June that "in all the Southwest part of the Territory, and especially along the line between this Territory and Arizona, there were serious troubles and constant hostilities between the Indians and citizens. A large party of armed citizens were on the point of leaving Silver City for the purpose of attacking the Indians at Cañada Alamosa and had I not gone there personally we would have had in this Territory a repetition of the Camp Grant affair in Arizona. Of course I stopped that proceeding by peremptory orders."[18] There was little wonder that Colyer, convinced that the Indians were the victims of unfair treatment, declined to even confer with whites. This distorted the perspectives he drew and rendered a good part of his mission less valid than it should have been.

Adjutant General Edward Davis Townsend on July 18, 1871, messaged commanding generals of the departments of the Missouri and Arizona, the military divisions of the Missouri and the Pacific, and the commissary general of subsistence, that President Grant had directed "so far as your resources will permit, assistance be given in provisions, and transportation and military protection to Mr. Vincent Colyer of the Indian Commission in endeavoring to collect the wild Indians of

New Mexico and Arizona, upon a reservation at Cañada Alamosa, and also to such Indians as may be induced to come in, both on the way and after arrival at the Reservation."[19]

As though to stress the dichotomy thus created, on the same day Probate Judge Richard Hudson of Grant County wrote from Pinos Altos to Piper at the Cañada. He reported new depredations, by Indians, of course, and leveled a clear threat of civilian action against the "reservation" Indians. He charged that Piper had obstructed citizens' efforts to recover stolen animals.

What we want to know is, whether our stock can be recovered or not, from Indians on your Reservation, when fully proved and identified, or if we are to be governed at the mercy of these thieving, murderous Apaches, who have a "House of Refuge" at Alamosa; if so, the sooner we know it the better, because the citizens of this country are determined to put a stop to it, and if they carry out their programme the Camp Grant massacre will be thrown entirely in the shade and Alamosa will rank next to "Sand Creek."[20]

Piper replied soothingly, reporting that Judge Hudson had been misinformed, that all the stock but one horse trailed to the reservation had been surrendered and any future thefts would be corrected when possible. He sent Hudson's letter, with a copy of his reply, to Pope, who commented August 3 that he had requested enough troops to stand by to prevent a repetition of the Arizona disaster. He wrote Hudson simultaneously, asserting it "my duty to endeavor to prevent by any and all means in my power, all attacks upon the Indians located at Cañada Alamos." He added that he considered this "an act of humanity for those who will necessarily suffer and retaliate for such unlawful act." He hoped Grant County citizens "will consider this matter in every light without prejudice before deciding to commit an act which would stand to their discredit hereafter."[21]

Piper sent still another mission July 31 to bring Cochise in if he could be found again. His delegation this time included Loco, an Indian the Chiricahuas knew and would trust, and José Trujillo, alcade, or justice of the peace, at the Cañada.[22] The delegation, of three Mexicans and three Apaches, returned August 21 without Cochise but with a tale of having run into Brevet Major General George Crook at Camp Apache and being rudely shooed home. Crook, on his first field tour after assuming command of the Department of Arizona, wrote that "as two of this party were recognized by several as being Cochise's worst men, and whom they knew to be ringleaders in some of his past

137

outrages . . . I felt very suspicious they were there in the capacity of spies; but as they could find out nothing of value and I did not want even a semblance of interference with the Peace Department, I did not arrest them."[23]

Piper was not so reserved in describing the incident to Pope. Trujillo reported, he wrote, that Crook abruptly ordered him back

and refused to recognize his authority to go to Cochise's Camp and threw his letter down in disdain saying that the Superintendent of Indian Affairs of New Mexico nor any of the Indian agents had any authority to send parties to Arizona. . . . He also says that they attempted to arrest his Indians, but Lieut. [William J.] Ross [Crook's aide] knew Loco and interceded for him. Gen. Crook would not let him get his rations which were at some distance from where he met the party. The Gen. told them that they were lucky to get back with their lives without rations. . . . Gen. Crook selected the route for him to return and told him not to go by any other."[24]

Pope sent Piper's letter to the commissioner, together with one of his own, asserting that Crook's action "caused me great inconvenience and delay in the discharge of my duties and will tend to weaken, if not destroy, any influence Agent Piper or myself may have over the Indians."[25] Apparently nothing was done about Crook's imperiousness.

Vincent Colyer originally planned two Apache reservations, one at Camp Grant, Arizona Territory, and the other near the eastern edge of Apache country, in New Mexico, but soon discovered that such a simplistic solution would not do.[26] He reached Fort Craig August 16,[27] and journeyed to Cañada Alamosa, finding the place deserted of Indians, the Apaches "frightened away by the threats from the residents at Rio Mimbres." The few he found were "the most scary Indians I have seen," stampeding at every rumor. "The day after our arrival I rode up the valley, and could see hundreds of their wicker wigwams standing, but not an Indian was to be seen." Gradually a few filtered in, mostly to draw rations, but the bulk remained aloof. Colyer felt it would be "preposterous" to buy out the three hundred or so Mexicans settled in the valley claimed by the Indians "when there are millions of acres of unoccupied land in the immediate neighborhood." Rather, he said, he would endeavor to find them "another place as near to Cañada Alamosa as practicable." With his reluctance to either buy out or run out the Mexican squatters, the Indians must be moved from their homeland, and difficulties and further bloodshed became more probable.

Colyer returned to Craig then on August 23,[28] and came back to the Cañada again with a party including guide Philip Gonzalez, Pope, interpreter John Ward, and a small soldier escort. They went 18.3 miles up the beautiful and picturesque canyon to Hot Springs, or Ojo Caliente, which the Indians considered the heart of their traditional country and which had the advantage of separation by the low mountains from the *contrabandistas* at the Cañada. At the springs they met Piper, Loco, and Trujillo, "examined the neighborhood . . . carefully, and finding the area of land capable of being cultivated far too small for the necessities of a tribe so large as this band . . . we were very reluctantly compelled to seek further." They arrived at Tularosa on August 29, "carefully inspected the valley and neighborhood of the Tularosa River, and finding the same to possess most of the requisites necessary for a home for the Indians, it being remote from white settlements, surrounded by mountains not easily crossed, sufficient arable land, good water, and plenty of wood and game, I officially notified Colonel Pope that I would designate it as an Indian reservation, agreeable to the authority given me. . . . I telegraphed to the Secretary of the Interior . . . to that effect, on the 29th of August."[29]

This and other actions of Colyer were approved by President Grant. On November 11, Adjutant General Townsend messaged Lieutenant General Phillip H. Sheridan, commanding the Military Division of the Missouri, informing him that the secretary of war directed that orders fix the boundaries of the Tularosa Reservation among others. "At all costs these Indians must have a chance to escape war," he cautioned. "Whilst they remain on the Reservation there is an implied condition that they should not be permitted to starve, and our experience is that the Indian Bureau is rarely supplied with the necessary money to provide food, in which event you may authorize the subsistence Dept. to provide for them."[30] That same day Townsend sought from Major General John M. Schofield, commanding the Military Division of the Pacific at San Francisco, his views on establishment of the suggested reservations. He desired the officer to consider them in the light of probable future railroad construction and, in a fatal and portentous sentence, added that he should take into account "the possible policy of a future concentration of all the Indians on one Reservation, abandoning the others."[31] This evil notion, so casually launched, was to generate more strife and bloodshed throughout the West than any other single disaster inflicted upon the Indians.

Sheridan issued his General Orders No. 8 on November 20, declaring the valley of the Tularosa, from the headwaters of the stream down its course thirty miles, and extending ten miles on either side, a reservation. The Southern Apaches were directed there immediately, where they would be protected while at peace but if found off of it without permission would be considered hostile.[32] Colonel Gordon Granger, commanding the District of New Mexico, was ordered to Cañada Alamosa to contact the Indians, giving them thirty days "in which to commence their movement" to their new home. With Superintendent Pope "if he will cooperate with you," Granger was directed to inform the Apaches "kindly, but firmly, of the necessities of the case," and what would happen if they refused. "It is above all things desirable that this movement of the Indians be accomplished peacefully and kindly, and without collision with the Indians or their agents which can be properly avoided." Granger was told to establish a post "at some suitable point" on the new Tularosa Reservation, "to be garrisoned this winter by one company of infantry, but to be so placed and planned that the post may be enlarged."[33]

Cochise meanwhile had come in of his own accord on September 28, settling his thirty warriors and their families at Cuchillo Negro, about a dozen miles south of Cañada Alamosa on the river of that name. Pope and Piper conferred with him,[34] found him anxious for peace, but unwilling to go to Tularosa for it. Piper said that "he does not make the selection of a reservation as a condition of peace," that his objection to Tularosa was not "on his own account, but on account of the desire of the chiefs that have been here for some time." Piper added that "I do not anticipate much trouble in getting the Indians to Tularosa,"[35] but opposition was mounting. Pope and Piper brought up the subject of a visit to Washington by Cochise, along with Victorio, Loco, Nana, Cadette of the Mescaleros, Miguel of the White Mountain Apaches, and others, but the Chiricahua "made so many excuses and objections to it that I was satisfied he did not consider it safe to go at that time." Pope added, "I therefore told him to think about it. . . . The success of the peace policy in this section is a question of *time* only."[36] He was overly sanguine.

Steadily Apache opposition to Tularosa mounted. Pope conceded October 17 that

during my last visit . . . the Indians . . . made many objections to removing to the Tularosa Reservation. The principal objections were that their present location suited them better, and that it was too cold at Tularosa, &c. I told them I did not come to argue the question, but to say to them that it was an order from the Department and must be obeyed; that the Agent would remove the Agency and provisions at once, and that no more rations would be issued at Cañada Alamosa. They did not refuse to go, but I think it may be difficult to overcome their objections for awhile. *Cachise* said he would leave the matter to *Victoria* and *Loco* as they had the largest number of people. . . . I think they will follow the Agency, when they get hungry, but it may be necessary to humor them till spring.[37]

Three days later the weary Piper messaged Pope that "I have used every argument in my power and made all the promises I dare to to induce the Indians to go to the new reservation. They positively refuse to go, saying that I may take the rations and give them to the Bears and Wolves, that they will do without." He urged that reconsideration be given to the location for the agency, warning that an Indian war, which might follow an attempt to use force, would be disastrous.[38] Obviously, in their continuous councils, Victorio and his people had mustered courage to reject the peremptory demands.

Pope, in passing Piper's communication along to Washington, added, "I have reason to think they are influenced by interested parties," that is, the Cañada Alamosa contraband merchants, but "I do not think it would be wise or practicable to move them by force." He said the Cañada Alamosa residents probably anticipated selling out to the government at a handsome profit if a reservation were located there; even if not paid for their miserable dwellings, they could then continue to prosper by illegal trading. "These Indians have been humored so much of late that they have become very exacting and dictatorial in their intercourse with the Agent. . . . I am loth to take any action that would furnish the least excuse for them to scatter, but I am as loth to humor them in their frivolous and unreasonable objections to the new Reservation." He thought it possible to move the agency and ration center to Tularosa, believing that most of the Indians eventually would go there, yet it might be "cheapest to locate the Reservation at Cañada Alamosa, purchase the town and improvements and remove all white settlers."[39] Again he asked for instructions.

Obviously difficulties were increasing; the situation needed clear assessment. Once again Colonel Nelson Henry Davis, assistant inspector general of the army, was sent from Leavenworth to New Mexico to "report as accurately as possible" on the situation. He stated there were about twelve hundred Indians at Cañada "under the noted Chiefs or headmen named *Victoria, Loco* and *Nanne*, whom he had met previously, and who were "nominally at peace, though guilty of having committed several murders and many thieving depredations."

The "great war chief," however, he believed to be Cochise, "the terror and curse of the people of Arizona and New Mexico [who has] caused the murder of more men, women and children and the loss of more property by theft, than probably any score of chiefs." He found Cochise "disposed to talk little of his past acts or course, and is represented as a dignified, commanding, able and shrewd leader." Some of the wild Chiricahuas continued to filter into the Cañada Alamosa vicinity, Davis said. Cochise would not consent to go to Washington, "but permitted his picture to be sent" in his stead.[40] Davis reported also that the Apaches declined to go to Tularosa and "it is not improbable that the employment of compulsory means or withholding their rations to effect this object will create serious trouble and scatter the most warlike portions of them far, again resuming their depredations."

Another factor, he pointed out, was the report that the vicinity of the proposed reservation was "a rich mineral region, which will doubtless soon be prospected and occupied by people seeking the precious metals, in spite of Indians and Indian reservations, and if the Apaches are located there in all probability serious trouble will ensue from this cause."

"Under existing circumstances," he concluded, "I deem it the wisest and best policy to allow these Indians to remain for the present at Cañada Alamosa as a matter of economy, and as calculated the more certainly to keep them quiet and to prevent their depredations." He added that Colonel Granger concurred in this view.[41]

After digesting this report and other communications, Interior Secretary Columbus Delano deemed it "expedient" to "permit the Indians to remain for the present at 'Cañada Alamosa,'" even though the Apaches were to be made to understand the concession was "limited, and that they must be prepared to remove as soon as possible." The agent was instructed to press this point home "with firmness."[42] It was a reprieve, not a pardon.

Agent Piper had ever more Indians to press it home upon. He reported in late October that his charges numbered now about nineteen hundred, though all were not Southern Apaches, of course. "One 'Coyotero' Chief of the name of 'Chiva' arrived here and brought with him 190 Indians. Cochise also says that a great many more will be in shortly."[43]

Tularosa

Southwesterners didn't think much of Vincent Colyer or his mission. One newspaper, after he had resigned his secretaryship of the Board of Indian Commissioners, hoped "the sanctimonious old humbug will take a situation as mail driver on the Tucson road for a few weeks," where he could hear the whir of an arrow or catch a bullet, as other men had.[1] Yet Colyer, visionary though he was, had accomplished much good, establishing a series of reservations which was to form the framework of the system for settling the Indians that is in existence to this day. He made a grave mistake, however, in selecting a reservation for the Mimbres Apaches on the Tularosa.

Already civil and military officials disagreed sharply over the viability of his work.[2]

Nevertheless, in late winter the decision finally was reached at Washington for the move to Tularosa—for the Apaches' own good, of course. On March 17, Pope reported that he and Colonel Granger, Colonel J. Irwin Gregg,[3] and Colonel Thomas C. Devin[4] reached the agency with the double view of informing the Indians of the decision and persuading Victorio, Loco, and Chiva to visit Washington. Neither was an easy mission. Two days later Pope confessed that "the Apache chiefs are afraid" to make the trip. He reported more fully on March 23:

On the 19th we held council with the chiefs separately and made known our business. I presented a letter from the Honorable Secretary of the Interior to "Cachise" inviting him, with "Loco," and "Victorio," to visit Washington, which was read and explained. . . . I used all the arguments and offered all the inducements at my disposal to persuade "Cachise" to go, but was unable to overcome his fear and distrust. He made so many excuses and objections, that we were satisfied it would be useless to urge him. . . . "Loco" was afraid to [go], but "Victorio" signified his willingness to go. As I did not care to send "Victorio" alone I gave them 6 days to decide, telling them I would send "Loco" and "Victorio" without "Cachise."

Col. Granger then . . . told the chiefs and their people to prepare to go to Tularosa on or before the first of May. Objections were made to the removal, but . . . most of [the reasons] were frivolous. The substance . . . is that they prefer Cañada Alamosa to Tularosa. . . .

I was more than ever convinced that the majority of these Indians are wholly under the control of the Mexicans, and a few Americans, living at Cañada Alamosa, and several other small towns in the vicinity, and that all the objections . . . have been suggested and fostered by [these persons], most of whom are supported indirectly by the Agency business.

He again recited the pernicious influence of the illegal traders and others, asserting it was "impossible to keep them away from the Indians," and supported in general the removal of the Apaches to Tularosa as best suited to solve the grave difficulties of managing them. Not all his arguments were specious. The only difficulty was that his solution would not work.

"I think it is advisable by all means to push the movement," he said. "I am inclined to think most of them will go peaceably when the agency and provisions are moved. Some, no doubt, will go to war, but energetic and prompt action by the troops will compel them to submit soon, and the lesson will benefit all the Apaches."[5]

Piper wrote Pope on March 28 that, after "a long and satisfactory talk" with Victorio and Loco, they had told him they would go to Tularosa, but not to Washington, [though] they would like to see their Great Father and that they are satisfied he is their friend." Their movement to Tularosa, they said, following lengthy councils with their people, was conditional upon Piper's sending to the Mescalero Reservation for Nana and a chief called Hiasha. Piper agreed to send his interpreter, Zebina Nathaniel Streeter,[6] to Fort Stanton, to "try and induce Nana and his party to return." Piper added that the removal would begin April 15 and "I am anxious to get to Tularosa as soon as possible, so that we may be able to do a little farming and gardening. I have sent a man out to Tularosa to see the condition of the buildings."[7]

Three days later the agent reported still another conversation with Victorio, who appeared anxious to do as the stubborn whites desired, no matter what his private thoughts may have been as to the wisdom of it. "He still says that he and his people will go with me to Tularosa," said Piper. Victorio "says that he will get all of his and Loco's bands together and then we will decide how they will go, over the mountains, or with the teams," by road. This would be a longer, but easier, way.

145

"I have every reason to believe they are sincere," Piper added, optimistically. "Victorio wishes me to say to you that he is talking straight and that they have no intention of going on the war path. He also says that they are few in number and could not fight long before they would all be killed by the soldiers. I promised them to send Mr. Streeter to Stanton to assist them in inducing Nana, Hiaska and their bands to return. He will start on the 2d of April."[8] Pope still, however, anticipated "more or less trouble" in moving the Indians. He said Piper had left Cañada Alamosa for Tularosa April 19 "but has failed to notify me how many (if any) Indians accompanied him." He added that Cadette, the Mescalero, had suggested that Loco, sent to Stanton with Streeter to pick up Nana, "means mischief." "I fear that Agent Piper may have been deceived by 'Loco' and 'Victoria,' and that there may be more trouble than was at first apprehended."[9]

But Piper arrived at Tularosa April 29 all right and on May 9 Pope reported that the agency had been removed there, even if the Indians had not.

Two companies of troops had been located near the agency for the protection of the Indians, if they showed up.[10] Their deadline to appear had passed, but, since they seemed inclined eventually to make the move, Pope delayed asking troops to beat them in, fearing this might precipitate unwelcome hostilities. Pope, in preparation, requested Devin to consider moving the new post some miles east of the agency because "the Indians can be more easily collected and controlled at the Agency in the absence of troops, . . . the location of the post upon a separate . . . military reservation will tend to prevent possible conflicts of authority in the future . . . and, [since] the intercourse between the troops and Indians is demoralizing to both, [it] should be avoided as far as possible."[11]

One week later Devin reported that about 350 Indians at last would gather at Ojo Caliente for the move, requesting transportation for their old and infirm. Victorio, who claimed never to have seen Tularosa before, returned from a cursory survey there and expressed himself as having "much pleasure and satisfaction with the new location," Devin reported.

Wagons already had left Fort Craig northwesterly for Monica Springs, at the base of the northernmost tip of the San Mateos where Devin and Pope expected to overtake them. From the springs they would send the vehicles southward to Ojo Caliente to pick up the aged Indians and the supplies, then move northwest again across the broad and flat San Augustin Plains with the horde of nomads toward the present Horse Springs. From there they would cross the Continental Divide at 7,312 feet and, reaching the Tularosa River, follow its canyon southwest to the site of the agency at present-day Aragon. No matter how reluctant the Indians had been to assemble for the move, they had never been "more peaceable than for the past three weeks," Devin reported. The move remained however "a matter which [must] be delicately managed in the present uncertain temper of the Indians, who have been very badly stampeded by the reports of the lying and unscrupulous Mexicans . . . whose interest it appears to be to render the new reservation a failure. The Indians have been led to believe that Tularosa is a trap. . . . I shall therefore make haste very slowly."[12] Yet on May 27 he could report that "I have just returned from Tularosa Valley and have the honor to report . . . that the new Apache Reservation is so far a complete success."[13] On the last day of the month Pope notified his superior that Victorio and Loco had ridden in on May 24.

It was seventy miles from Cañada Alamosa airline to Tularosa and perhaps one-third again as far by the way they must travel. Pope notified Indian Commissioner Francis A. Walker[14] in June that with an escort of sixteen Eighth Cavalry troopers and twenty wagons the move had commenced May 17. About fifty or sixty aged, women, and children rode, but most of the remainder, an estimated three hundred Apaches of Victorio's, Loco's, and Gordo's bands (Gordo was a Mogollon leader) accompanied by Jeffords and Streeter, preferred to traverse the mountains on horseback or afoot. They crossed a spur of the San Mateos and of the northern Mimbres or Black Range, passed south of the Luera Mountains, south also of the 9,000-foot crest of the Elk Mountains, and north of Loco Peak, plunging then down into the forested valley of the Tularosa where the agency was nearing completion. On arrival they "found Cheever [Chiva] there with 60 or 70 of his people." Chiva reported that "*Cachise* told him to take his [Chiva's] people to Tularosa, saying he would follow if they were well treated at the Agency. Cachise is said to be in the Mogollon Mountains [to the south], with less than 50 of his band . . . I considered it the wisest course to let him alone at present." Anyway, Pope added, "he is getting too old to successfully carry on a war."

About 400 Indians had reached Tularosa by the first of June and were "well pleased" with their new home; others were coming in daily, although some 250 were with the Mescaleros, and the troops scouted southern mountains to chase in any stragglers.[15]

Vincent Colyer's work, upon being implemented, soon developed obvious imperfections, and Washington decided upon a fresh mission to define and correct them. The question was, who would go? On February 29, 1872, Interior Secretary Delano reported that he had secured the consent of the undisputed first choice, Brigadier General Oliver Otis Howard, providing he could take along his aide, First Lieutenant Melville Cary Wilkinson.[16] Orders were issued at once. Howard, who had lost his right arm at the Battle of Fair Oaks, was commissioner of the Bureau of Refugees, Freedmen, and Abandoned Lands. He was named now by President Grant a special Indian commissioner charged with settling Indians permanently upon reservations, inducing the whites to treat them "with humanity, justice and forbearance," preserving the peace between whites and reds and "to consider the propriety of inducing the nomadic tribes . . . to unite and accept a reservation further East," the removal theoreticians being as mischievously at work as ever.[17]

Howard's peace theories being "strongly tinged with common sense,"[18] he was much better received by southwesterners than Colyer had been. He left Washington March 7, returned there briefly in June,[19] and was sent back to New Mexico in July to complete his work.[20]

Late that month he reached Tularosa and spent eight days talking with Victorio and the other major leaders. Already, he reported,

the Indians seemed to be generally discontented with their reservation, hundreds had left to get their living in the old romantic way; they complained of sickness and death amongst the children; the impurity of the water; coldness of the climate; the crops failing from early frost, and the complaints were aggravated by their superstitions, claiming that past races had been consumed by floods and other causes. Every death became a cause of alarm, and the cause of a quick abandonment of camping grounds. They all longed for Cañada Alamosa, near which the most of them had been born, and where they alleged Lieut. Drew promised them they should have their reservation when they first gathered from the mountains.[21]

Statistics tend to confirm his impressions. For example, Piper stated officially that the four hundred Apaches at Tularosa on August 8 had dwindled to three hundred by October 3.[22]

Howard had a long, private talk with Victorio about these and related matters. The Indian's views were contained in a letter Captain Coleman wrote six or eight months later, formally witnessed by Interpreter Robert H. Stapleton and a farming foreman named Stackpole.

The general, Victorio recalled, had said that at planting time, the spring of 1873, he would move the Indians back to Ojo Caliente, and that he would send them an agent they liked. They definitely did not like Piper. Victorio is said to have complained to Howard that "we mean no disrespect, but that Piper, the Agent, is getting old, and he had better go home and see his children and take care of them."[23] Howard further promised, Victorio said, that he would establish a large fort at Ojo Caliente, and would gather together all the Apaches at that place. In the meantime he urged Victorio to "keep quiet around here" and not to go away, that the soldiers were stationed there to protect them.

Howard particularly had asked Victorio to tell him all about Piper, and why the Indians did not like him, as well as other matters which perturbed the chief. Unfortunately, however, nothing of this was written down or, if so, preserved. Victorio did ask for an agent like the "first one" they had had at Cañada Alamosa, Lieutenant Drew, whom they all remembered fondly, and the general said that he would have a grand council, when he got home, and pick out "a good agent for them for good."[24]

Victorio was an honest man, and no doubt he told the truth. Howard confirms all that he said, but a difference arose over a slight misunderstanding. Howard had promised, as Victorio witnessed, to remove the reservation to Ojo Caliente providing *all* the Chiricahuas could be gathered there, but in the meantime he had seen Cochise in southeastern Arizona, been persuaded to give him a separate reservation in that area, and therefore was unable to collect the entire people at Ojo Caliente. In a letter to Ponce, Victorio, and Loco, sent by way of Captain Coleman early in 1873, Howard explained:

I am not the President or Great Father. I only obey orders. I told the Indians (my good friends) I would try to get all the apaches to say they would go to Cañada, and then I would come home to Washington and get Cañada set apart for a reserve. *Cachise* and his Indians were not willing to go there. The President will not set apart Cañada for a few Indians. Congress will not give the money to buy the land. . . .

"*Victoria* knows that I believed Cachise would go to Cañada but he did not go."[25]

However, the general, as he had promised, did talk to Cochise about moving to Cañada Alamosa, which the Chiricahua conceded he personally preferred. Howard had tried to contact him by messenger while at Tularosa, but to no avail.

In his 1908 book for young people, Howard lauds the influence for peace that Victorio represented at Tularosa. He wrote that Victorio, "the very first Indian I saw" at Tularosa, was "a good man who was troubled for his people," realized that "they were discontented and wanted to go on the warpath, and that it was better for them to keep peace." Victorio, he recalled, had eventually proven the key to his spectacularly successful mission to Cochise by arranging his meeting with Chie, son of Mangas Coloradas, and with Jeffords, the two making practicable the adventurous journey to the great Chiricahua leader.[26]

Before leaving Tularosa, the general took up a few housekeeping duties. He messaged Pope that "considering the discontent of the Indians . . . and the great importance of keeping them here without compulsion, I hereby authorize you to purchase and add to the ordinary ration Sugar and Coffee in amounts usually issued to soldiers, also (½) one half pound of Flour per day to each Indian."[27] Since the Apaches seemed adamant in their dislike of Piper, Howard granted him, for reasons of "health," a short leave, with an opportunity to extend it, and broadly hinted that he would urge the commissioner to find some less arduous work "for one so faithful and worthy as yourself."[28] This was not all polite twaddle. A student wrote, much later:

Piper's tenure as Indian Agent for the Southern Apache coincided with an exciting part of the agency's growth. The number of Indians under his charge grew from three hundred fifty to a high estimate of one thousand nine hundred. He faced the difficult task of gathering and keeping a nomadic group of warlike people quiet under trying conditions of a hostile citizenry, confusing and conflicting orders from his superiors, insufficient funds and insufficient supplies, and unscrupulous men who attempted to turn the Indians against him by blaming the agent for all their troubles. Added to this was the establishment of the Tularosa reservation against the Apache's wishes and breaking earlier promises made to the Indians that they would be able to remain on their old grounds at Cañada Alamosa. Piper fulfilled his duty, even though he had disagreed with the logic of disrupting the Indians by settling them in a different area.[29]

On November 8, John Ayres was renamed temporary agent and he the Apaches well liked,[30] in part perhaps because they could intimidate him and by unruly behavior have their own way, in at least some respects.

Howard, accompanied by Victorio, Jeffords, and some others, had journeyed to Cañada Alamosa and inspected it carefully, frankly viewing it as a better place for a reservation than Tularosa.

Had I been able to prevail upon Cochise and his Indians to go to Cañada, I should have recommended strongly a reservation there, the government buying up all the Mexican improvements. It is a fine country, just suited to the Indians, and the difference of cost of transportation of supplies between Cañada and Tularosa, would in four years exceed the purchase of the improvements. The Indians at Tularosa numbered less than three hundred when I was there. We would not be justified with so small a number, to ask for the proposed reservation.[31]

From Cañada Alamosa Victorio returned to Tularosa, and Howard, accompanied by Jeffords, Chie, and others, dropped a dozen miles south to the Cuchillo Negro, where they found a band of forty or more Apaches under Sancho, whom southwesterners considered an inveterate raider. In this camp was Ponce, an Indian whom Jeffords, Chie, and Howard wanted to accompany them to Cochise, since he was said to be a good friend of that Indian and would make more probable success of the delicate mission. In order to gain his services, Howard wrote out a pass for Sancho, granting him permission to remain where he was, in the vicinity of Cañada Alamosa, until the Cochise mission was concluded. He messaged the commanding officer at Fort Craig:

Having to take *Ponce* and another man (Indians) with me to visit the wild Indians [meaning Cochise], I have provided for his family and his people, here with them, about forty in all, more or less, until his return. Please notify Forts Tularosa, Cummings and Selden by mail, that they may not be disturbed by the Troops.

Sancho acts as head and has one paper of protection, and Jer-ma-chi-co [Ramon Chico, another head man] another for his (Ponce's) Camp. He will probably be away about 20 or 30 days, they must visit Cañada and all the region about here for food and hunting.[32]

This action by Howard led to a flurry of charges and recriminations and much exasperation on the part of other officers who had believed Tularosa was made the only reserve where the Southern Apaches might gather. On October 17, Piper reported to Pope that "the Indians under *Sancho* . . . are continually stealing stock and trading them to the Mexicans at Alamosa and other towns on the river. . . . I would recommend that his pass be annulled."[33] Pope, sending a copy to Colonel Granger, supposed that Howard "would approve of any action that might be necessary to stop this stealing . . . when he learns that the Indians have broken faith, but as he has two or three of this party of Indians with him in Arizona and is virtually at their mercy, it might not be advisable to take any action until his safety is assured."[34] Granger sent the messages to his superior, General John Pope at Leavenworth, who in transmitting them to his commander, Sheridan at Chicago, leaped to the conclusion that Howard "seems to have determined the complete abandonment of the Tularosa Reservation, and either their location elsewhere, or the privilege of wandering over the country at will with papers from him. . . . It is to be regretted that a consistent and stable course had not been pursued in the matter. . . . This unexpected action has, I think, greatly prejudiced any future undertaking of the kind by impairing the confidence, both of whites and Indians, in the adherence of the authorities to any plan whatever."[35]

Sheridan referred the matter to Sherman in the hopes that his superior might "ascertain in some way the intentions of the Indian Department." Sheridan growled that "the admirable system of civilizing and providing for the wild tribes is constantly being thrown into chaos by the impracticable, unbusinesslike actions of some of the men engaged in carrying it out. The settlement of these Indians on the Tularosa Reservation was in process of successful accomplishment . . . when interrupted by General Howard."[36]

Eventually the adjutant general summarized the situation, noting the creation of the Tularosa Reserve and stating that "a party of Indians under 'Sancho' and others were permitted to visit Cañada Alamosa, and the region about for food and hunting, by General O. O. Howard." The army was at a loss how to handle the situation in view of conflicting directives. This whole assemblage of papers finally reached Howard after his return to Washington, and he replied that "a total misapprehension seems to exist as to what I did in New Mexico." He said he had not really violated the order establishing Tularosa. "I found a small party of Indians under Ponce some one hundred miles from any reservation. Ponce had never been to Tularosa, but was willing to take his people there as soon as I was done with him. I could not have communicated with the wild Indians without him." He said he had expected to find Cochise in New Mexico, instead of Arizona, "& that Ponce would very soon return & move his people to Tularosa or Fort Stanton." He added that he had had no trustworthy officer at hand to escort the Indians to Tularosa.[37] Although Howard thus explained his actions, the incident did serve to confuse the gathering of Apaches at their reserve, although other factors contributed to muddy the waters. Tularosa was becoming an experiment of dubious viability.

General Pope, on December 11, made one last appeal for "instructions," pointing out that the army had gathered many Indians at Tularosa "after a great labor and considerable expense," while Howard had granted permission to "an indefinite number" of them to roam about and frustrated efforts of the troops to drive them in. "The result has been to put a stop to the removal of the Indians to the Tularosa Reservation as ordered, and the practical abandonment of the whole plan. It also has necessitated the re-occupation of Fort McRae . . . where many of the Indians still remain . . . by General Howard's permission." Even worse it "destroyed confidence both in whites and Indians of any stability in the action of the Government." However overstated, this communication points up some of the confusion which Howard's "explanation" did not allay.[38]

Howard had completed his mission to Cochise. He had left Cañada Alamosa September 20 with his aide-de-camp, Captain Joseph Alton Sladen, Jeffords, the two Indians, Chie and Ponce, and other persons, including two packers, an interpreter, and an ambulance driver, although the vehicle was forced to travel by the round-about road and thus was not very useful. It is possible that Streeter went along, perhaps as a packer. He claimed later in life that he had accompanied Howard, but there is no proof that he did so.

Captain Samuel S. Sumner, commanding at Bowie, messaged Crook and General Pope October 2 that Howard had struck Cochise's trail forty miles from Silver City and "followed it with two Indians and five white men (not soldiers)," until contacting the Chiricahuas. Howard, Jeffords, and Sladen then journeyed ninety miles farther, meeting Cochise in the Dragoons, "some four or five miles south of Tucson Road." Cochise, continued Sumner, "is anxious to make peace [and] himself has done no mischief since his return from New Mexico [Cañada Alamosa], but . . . some of his people separated from himself, have done so. He would like to go to Cañada Alamosa if he could prevail on all his people to go with him. . . ."[39]

Howard reported:

> We remained with him altogether eleven days[40] to enable him to bring in his Captains for a Council. Cochise himself favored the Cañada reservation, but notwithstanding the ascendancy he has gained over the Indians, he was not able to take them all there, and confessed that it would break up his band, a part being left to do mischief in Arizona, but he declared that he could gather in all his people, protect the roads and preserve the peace, if the Govt. would allow him the Chiricahua Country where his people have always lived. He plead that it was not right to restrain him and his band from going and coming like the Mexicans, but he yielded to my reasons for the necessity of limiting his reservation. . . .
>
> From what Cochise told me, I do not believe that all the wild Indians in that vicinity will come under control. There are some fifty men without families who are complete outlaws, who have been away from friendly and reservation Indians. It is evident that these Indians are the most desperate and difficult to control.[41]

These no doubt included some of the Southern Chiricahuas who normally lived south of the border, among them Juh, Geronimo, and others who would create unending trouble for the whites in years to come, all of them well known to Victorio and the Chiricahuas north of the line, and who occasionally would pillage and raid with him and other war leaders.

Howard set aside the Chiricahua Reservation to include the mountains named for the tribe, and the Dragoons and intervening valleys,[42] recommending that Jeffords, whom the Indians trusted implicitly, be named agent. Crook tried many times to secure a "written copy" of Howard's agreement with Cochise, but always failed.[43] There is no mention of such a document in any of Howard's writings or reports, and he explained later that "no formal treaty with Cochise and his band was made," although the agreement covered five major provisions to be fulfilled by the Americans, and two by Cochise, plus "other items of minor importance." The fact that it was verbal made it no less binding upon men of the character of Howard and Cochise, but created difficulties for others with responsibility for Indian-white relations in understanding what was expected of them and of the Chiricahuas.[44]

XIII

Tularosa Given Up

Captain Coleman reported from Tularosa that Chie and Ponce had returned there October 17 or 18, bringing news of the creation of a reservation for Cochise in Arizona, and thereby portending unrest and perhaps dissolution of the Tularosa arrangement.

> It would not surprise me at all, if (as soon as Cachise and his band are settled on their new reservation) Chie and Gordo, two captains now here, were to join him at that place, also the Mangas family headed by Lopez, another captain. Chie . . . is one of this family and is highly delighted with the new place. Chiva and Gordo are Coyotero Apaches, and really belong to Cachise's band, being only observors here.
>
> The balance of the Indians on this reservation formerly from the Cañada, are merely a mob. The Captains have very little, if any authority. Besides this, they are very jealous of Chiva and Gordo, and mortally afraid of Cachise for the reason that when he is around they are exceedingly small fry. . . . [Yet], if allowed to go back to the Cañada, they will be as they always were, drunk whenever they get a chance. If they remain here, they will be the same, except that here they have to brew their own beer, and at the other place they get whiskey.[1]

Depredations, allegedly by the Apaches, were causing growing recriminations against the Tularosa Indians by southwestern whites. For one thing, Sancho, who they believed should be on the reservation but wasn't, stole all the stock in sight, or so they claimed.[2] Although some of the depredations no doubt were caused by whites, and others incited by them in order to trade for stolen stock, still others probably were the result of Indian initiative. Since many of the Indians were not at Tularosa, and others traveled—and depredated—back and forth between that agency and the Chiricahua reserve, the settlers felt surrounded by thieves or worse.

It was often difficult to discover who was to blame for depredations. On November 11 a Fifteenth Infantry detachment, hauling logs four miles from Fort Bayard, found on the road a wounded Mexican who reported Apaches had attacked Brown's ranch. A soldier hurried to

155

the fort, reported the incident, and Second Lieutenant James Burke Hickey, sent to investigate, found Brown's body the next day, the victim perforated with six arrows, then shot in the head and badly mutilated, including "his privates." Colonel Devin reported that Brown "was known as one of the bravest men in this vicinity, and was probably entirely unarmed" at the time of the outrage. Two other men had been fired upon. The tracking party lost the trace in rocky ground and retired.[3]

But Devin, believing the trail could be picked up where the hostiles had crossed the Gila, sent another party of ten men of A Troop, Eighth Cavalry, under Sergeant James C. Cooney and a Mexican guide. They reached Tularosa November 19, reporting they had trailed the slayers from Brown's house to within five miles of the reservation. Captain Coleman and Ayres held a brief council and at ten o'clock the next morning a more formal one, with Victorio and other head men present. The Indians reported that some Coyoteros had passed nearby, but had not come in. "Whether this is a lie or no is the whole question," conceded Coleman. The only Indian known to have been absent from the reservation during the time in question was Colares, who, with a valid pass, had "proved to the satisfaction of all that he was not guilty."

"The chiefs said that they wished peace . . . and they thought it was hard, that they should be held accountable for what other bad Indians did. That this was not their country, and they were not able to stop other Indians being bad and it was not right to blame them for others." And about there it ended.[4]

A factor making management of Indians difficult was that control was divided between the military departments of New Mexico and Arizona, and these were in the separate divisions of the Missouri and the Pacific. After a discussion between the President and the secretaries of war and interior, Delano in December, 1872, formally suggested that the Chiricahua and White Mountain reservations be transferred to the District of New Mexico, along with Camps Bowie and Apache.[5] This plan looked fine theoretically, but seemed not so feasible to officers charged with policing the area. Sherman believed the move would "rather complicate than improve the actual relations of the Indians with their white neighbors." He urged that the action be delayed until Crook and General Pope could comment. Crook strongly opposed it[6] and so did Pope,[7] as did Sheridan by endorsement,[8] and Sherman repeated his objections. Thus the proposal, which seemed a viable solution to some officials, was canceled out by the men most concerned. But it suggested the exasperations generated by the uneasy and imperfect peace with the Apaches, who, for their part, were increasingly unhappy and discontented. Another disturbing element was that the Chiricahua Reservation, hard against the Mexican border, made it simple for young Indians to cross into and raid Sonora and Chihuahua. Schofield noted that "it appears to be, to say the least, a breech of good neighborhood towards Mexico to give to our common enemy peace and protection on our side of the border when he can with the greatest facility continue his war on the other side."[9]

This wrangle continued as long as the Chiricahua Reservation existed and, in fact, was largely the cause of its abandonment in 1876, although Howard insisted repeatedly that he had never given Cochise the "right" or permission to raid into Mexico. He ever believed that the chief refrained from doing so but was unable to control young warriors who pursued that exhilarating pastime indefatigably. The point with reference to Victorio is that many of the Mimbres doubtless joined in these raids, passing through the Chiricahua reserve to and from Mexico, and he could not control this, either, although presumably he seldom accompanied them. He felt himself getting old and beyond raiding age. Still, the avenue from Tularosa through the Chiricahua reserve to Sonora was well worn by the hoofs of war ponies and stolen stock and, from time to time, the softer, fearful tread of captives.[10] Thus, by encouraging an intolerable situation, these young Mimbres had a part in the final breakup of the Cochise reserve, the attempted concentration of his Indians upon San Carlos, and the beginnings of a removal policy by which their own people would be rudely taken to Arizona and their long bitter war with the whites finally made inevitable.

In late 1872, Benjamin Morris Thomas was named Southern Apache agent,[11] at the same time Levi Edwin Dudley succeeded Nathaniel Pope as superintendent of Indian affairs for New Mexico,[12] with an inspection trip to troubled Tularosa high on his agenda.[13]

Dudley left Santa Fe February 18, 1873, as new reports reached him of unruly behavior of the Indians "asserting their right to the control of the Agency, in some instances leaving the reservation in large numbers," making tiswin out of issue corn and getting drunk on it, "making threats of violence and using their best efforts to intimidate the agent," Ben Thomas, who had inherited the explosive situation built up under Ayres's incompetent leadership. By the time Dudley arrived, February 26, Thomas had succeeded in restoring a semblance of order, "but the Indians were still demonstrative, demanding that they should be removed to the Cañada Alamosa and refusing to accept their present reservation. I met the principal men," planned a council, and toured the reservation, talking to Indians. "I found that . . . Ayres had done much to bring about the present state of affairs," by encouraging the Apaches to believe they could return to the Cañada "and allowed them to run the Agency as they thought proper. Frequently they have taken cattle and other supplies provided for them from him by force and made the distribution to suit themselves." In the face of "the worst possible opposition," Thomas had restored order. "Many other much needed reforms had been introduced by Agent Thomas, and of course he had become exceedingly unpopular" with the Indians.[14]

The big council was held with Victorio, Nana, Chiva, Loco, Ponce, and others present, all sulky and morose.

Dudley explained why they could not return to Cañada unless they could persuade Cochise to come there. They concluded that this would be impossible. He asked, then, if they wished to go to the Chiricahua Reservation, and they replied no, that they could not live there. Fort Stanton? No. "I then told them that their only chance was to remain at Tularosa. They complained that they could not raise corn there, and I met this objection by asking if they had tried to raise anything, and they replied that they had not." Dudley explained that new types of seeds would be introduced and perhaps, after all, they could raise some crops. He distributed presents then, "and much to the surprise of all present, during the last hour of the council the greatest possible good feeling prevailed, and the Indians expressed themselves as willing to remain."

Just before his arrival one hundred young men of Victorio's band had left, probably for a raid in Sonora. This figure is interesting, for, while only a few years earlier Victorio had but a small following, his people since had increased markedly. This could not have occurred unless he had matured into a war leader of great good fortune and ability and a counselor whose wisdom was generally respected. "I asked him if he could secure their return," recalled Dudley. "He replied that he could if allowed to go after them with five men." The superintendent instructed Thomas to issue the necessary passes and hoped for the best.[15]

With the change of seasons a new threat arose: whiskey was being sold by the post trader at Fort Tularosa to the soldiers and already some drunken trooper had shot one Apache woman, which resulted "very nearly in an outbreak." On January 18, 1873, a Saturday night, two or three Indians, "probably drunk," were hanging about the laundress' quarters, annoying her, when she called the corporal of the guard. He ordered the Indians away, but they leveled rifles at him and he "ran for his life." The adjutant told him to take six men and, if threatened again, to fire upon them. Thomas arrived just as the shooting "at all the Indians in sight" commenced. The woman was shot in the arm, near the shoulder, and, although Dr. Henry Duane amputated the limb, she died. The incident, Thomas reported, "probably would not have occurred if the Commanding Officer of the Post had not at the time been disqualified for the discharge of duty by drunkenness," and probably because of the trouble generated Captain Coleman resigned from the army two months later.[16]

Noting that "the worst band of Indians in this Territory" was involved, Dudley "earnestly" recommended a ban on whiskey sales to anyone, because he felt that "the peaceful conduct of affairs at that Agency depends upon the exclusion of spirituous liquors."

Other than accidents, usually from gunshot wounds, the Apaches appear to have been remarkably healthy during this period. Doctor Duane[17] reported in late June that in six months he had had four cases of intermittent fever (perhaps malaria), seven of acute diarrhea, twenty of whooping cough, four of chronic rheumatism, four of conjunctivities, eleven cases of "inflammation of the lungs," six of "inflammation of the pleura," four simple fractures, four gunshot wounds, five incised wounds, and two lacerated wounds. Deaths were one from whooping cough, complicated by pneumonia, and two from gunshot wounds. "The Apaches are a hardy race," concluded the physician, "with good constitutions, consequently much of the diseases are light, readily amenable to remedies. They are virtuous," he added, "and there is no taint of syphillis among them." Most of the wounds, he pointed out, were caused while the Indians were drunk. He noted that the beef ration was probably insufficient, "particularly during the winter" and that coffee issues were unnecessary, since they rarely used it except to trade.[18] One would suppose that the spartan rations issued the Apaches would cause a serious dietary imbalance, affecting their general health and inducing physical lassitude as well as a tendency toward mental apathy. That these disorders did not markedly appear might be attributed to the fact that they tended to eat beef rare, consumed no pork at all, and supplemented their issued rations with such native and nutritious foods as mescal, piñon nuts, and so on.

Incidents marking increased estrangement between the whites and Indians began to appear at Tularosa. An Apache fired an arrow at Dr. Duane when he entered their camp in answer to a call. Another warrior directed an arrow at the interpreter and, for good measure, one at a beef herder. Still another leveled arms at Thomas himself. All of these incidents, he reported, were "without provocation and simply for their own amusement," but they made agency life interesting.[19] Depredations continued. Most of them appeared to call attention to Sancho, the raider no one could reform. And now, at long last, they were to generate a series of incidents culminating in Victorio's first outright defiance of the Americans since the Civil War, bringing him to open, if brief, hostility. Perhaps it exhausted his considerable store of patience, his belief that some sort of *modus vivendi* could be reached with the odd white race.

Early in July Apaches swept down on Shedd's ranch,[20] on the east slope of the Organ Mountains near San Augustin Pass, about twenty miles northeast of Las Cruces. Several head of horses were run off, toward the west.

Captain George W. Chilson of the Eighth Cavalry, commanding Fort Selden, mounted up ten men and pursued the raiders. "After following them four days and a half," he reported, "I struck them in a cañon, tributary from the southwest of the Cañada Alamosa, where an engagement ensued resulting in the loss of one man, Corporal Frank Battling of my Troop, killed; the killing of three Indians out of four who were seen, and the recovery of all the stock."[21] It was a hard fight and three troopers, First Sergeant James L. Morris, Sergeant Leonidas S. Lytle, and Private Henry Wills, won Medals of Honor. Among the Indians wounded was Victorio's nephew.[22] The surviving raiders fled for Tularosa.

A few days later Ben Thomas, riding past the Indian encampment, "heard loud lamentation and saw the Indians running to and fro as if they were terribly excited. I soon discovered Sancho, a notorious thief, whom I know to be off the reservation for two or three weeks, sitting under a tree with a wounded companion evidently recounting some adventure to a crowd of Indians." Thomas recalled that on previous occasions the principal men of the tribe had "often expressed a desire to have the bad thieves punished," and once, when Sancho had thundered in with a herd of stolen mules, "Victorio wanted to go with the Agent and soldiers and kill him." Thus he believed Victorio would help arrest the thieves now.

So Thomas brought Victorio and Loco into his office, telling them what he intended to do. To his astonishment "they replied that they were to be protected here, and that they would not allow one of their number to be taken." But on this occasion, perhaps unknown to Thomas, one of Victorio's relatives had been involved; family ties among the Apaches always were strong.

When Thomas pressed the chiefs, the Indians stormed from his office, "gave a signal at which the women and children all left the Agency and the men got their arms and mounted. Victorio then told me that if I wanted to fight he was ready, or if the soldiers wanted to come there and to fight, he was ready." The agent, at this show of strength, was helpless, but fortunately, within about an hour, Major William Redwood Price clattered into Fort Tularosa with three companies of the Eighth Cavalry and twenty-five Navaho scouts. He came promptly to the agency and had a meeting with the Indians, who had not expected this much force to appear so quickly—nor had Thomas. The Apaches had lost none of their bravado, however.

"All the warriors that were on the reservation (about fifty) were present, with their arms, and the talk was short and unsatisfactory and inclined to insolence on the part of the Indians," reported Thomas. They brazenly said their tiswin was about ready; they would go and drink it, and talk tomorrow. The next morning, however, they reported that some of their people were coming in from the Chiricahua Reservation and they must meet them. Then Victorio said he would talk to Price, but in a canyon, two miles from the agency, where it would prove difficult to surprise or surround him, and the advantage would be his. "The Col. [Price held a brevet rank of colonel for an Arizona Indian fight five years earlier] then took eighteen men, and we rode slowly down to the Indian camp . . . and went to Victoria's camp and found it deserted with everything that would be troublesome to carry remaining in the tents," i.e., wickiups. At a nearby *rancheria* about thirty women and children were found. Thomas sent one to call in Victorio, and when that chief did not appear requested Price to herd the noncombatants to the agency and hold them as hostages.[23]

Thomas composed a summary of events and formally requested Price to "council with the Indians and make arrests by force, if necessary."[24] Later in the day he added, in a second note, "As a result of the arrest of Indians . . . today, the rest of the tribe have fled to the mountains. I respectfully request that you [Price] follow them, and make every effort to open communication with the chiefs and enduce them to return to the reservation peaceably. . . . But if they insolently reject every reasonable proposition, I have to request that you take steps to protect the settlers adjacent to the old range of these Indians."[25] If they truly desired war, they could have it. But war they did not want, at least not yet.

Victorio's wounded relative and the Indian who had fired an arrow at Stapleton, "both bad men," were arrested by Price and held as hostages for a few days until the chiefs, including Victorio, finally decided to come in. The danger passed.[26] But there would be more confrontations, now.

The old question of removal continued to crop up. The government desired to close out the manifestly unsatisfactory Tularosa Reservation, perhaps as much for financial reasons as to benefit the Indians. Its population had varied from an average of 663 during the winter months to 330 in summertime,[27] when visiting, raiding, and roaming through the still largely uninhabited Mogollon and Black uplifts lured the Indians strongly. Yet the numbers of Indians located there were not inconsequential; they compared favorably with populations at many other reservations; it was poor economy that denied them the home range of their choice.

In May Dudley was informed by Washington that "inducements to reasonable extent may be held out to Apaches to go to Fort Stanton"; he tried to persuade them and was forced to report December 2 that while removal might be "very beneficial to the Government," still "it would be impossible to secure their removal by any means short of force."[28] Washington, it appeared, was not listening. By early 1874 removal talk again had grown loud, but suddenly there was a difference; perhaps, after all, they might be taken to Ojo Caliente, to which the Apaches would readily consent to go.

All during 1873, Price had been scouting the country with a double purpose: to prevent or punish depredations and to locate and chart possible wagon routes for the future, when population would seep into western New Mexico, as he believed inevitable. His scouts traversed more than five thousand miles, carefully noting waters, mountain ranges, and resources. He said he had found two good wagon routes, from Fort Wingate[29] to Horse Springs, east of Tularosa. He worked out three trails from Horse Springs and Tularosa south to Fort Bayard, although he admitted the two westernmost were impracticable without an expenditure of $100,000 because the country "is very rough and broken, abounding in high hills and deep and impassable cañons," impractical for wheeled traffic. A road from Horse Springs by way of Luera Springs to Fort McRae could easily be developed.

Price said that the Apaches rarely passed north of a line through Horse and Luera springs to Fort Stanton, because "they consider all country north of that line Navajo ground, of which tribe they stand much in dread." The Tularosa Indians, he added, "visit and spend much of their time with Cochise." Price told of a couple of minor depredations, including the running off of stock, by two boys trying to become raiders and warriors like their elders. The officer concluded his lengthy account by recommending that Fort Tularosa, moved to Horse Springs, be made a permanent post for two infantry companies, but not too permanent, as "the small number of Indians there may shortly consent, or ultimately be forced, to merge themselves" with others.[30]

General Pope supported the move of the post, adding that he thought the Mescaleros ought to be removed from east of the Río Grande to Tularosa.[31] It was high time to move some Indians somewhere!

Field commanders reported in February, 1874, that the Apaches were unusually quiet, although raids on Old Mexico continued, apparently, and the barter towns south of the border, where the Indians exchanged stolen stock for arms, ammunition, and liquor, were as busy as ever.[32]

First Lieutenant Henry Joseph Farnsworth reported from McRae that frequent scouts had thoroughly scoured the country on both sides of the Río Grande, demonstrating "that there are no Indians in this vicinity or, if there are any, that they travel in such small numbers as to leave no trace," and the most recent depredations were not committed by Indians anyway.[33] Captain Charles Steelhammer of the Fifteenth Infantry, commanding at Bayard, reported that continuous scouts during the winter revealed that "not a single Indian depredation has been committed in this section of New Mexico. A perfect quiet, such as has never before been known in Grant Co., has existed throughout."

Only once had Indians been reported, he said, and that from a not

163

very reliable source: a Mexican on January 30 said he had seen fifteen Indians going southward. "If this report was true," said Steelhammer, "it must have been Victoria . . . who is reported to have left about that time making for Sonora. He disturbed nothing, however, while passing down."[34] Yet Price was not fooled. He reported that he had "no confidence in the permanency of the present apparent gratifying condition of affairs." He explained his "theory" of handling Indians, based upon eight years of hard experience: "I believe and *know* that the most humane policy . . . is to never overlook or compromise a depredation committed by the Indians against the defenceless and scattered white settlers, nor to allow citizens to vent their vengeance against innocent or inoffensive Indians on a reservation."[35]

He knew that with spring, depredations would occur again. He wanted his men ready.

To keep the warriors on the reservations, General Pope ordered that "a small force of Cavalry (three or four companies) be kept in the field, constantly circulating during the summer, moving a few miles each day from waterhole to waterhole" so as to keep a close watch upon the Tularosa and Mescalero Apaches and be ready to act at any time in defense of the peace.[36] Dudley cautioned against these troops setting foot on the reservations themselves, since "Indians upon a reservation should see no troops except the permanent force" unless "open hostilities are actually begun by the Indians."[37] Whether the policy reduced depredations was a moot point.[38]

Price messaged commands that "*all* company cavalry officers [are] to become familiar with the country within a radius of a hundred miles" of their post, contribute toward a detailed map, chart their scouts accurately, and, if raiders came from Arizona as he anticipated, the country would be so crisscrossed with military trails as to frighten them off. Commanders were to take care of their stock, not break it down needlessly, and train men in use of the prismatic compass and odometer and the taking of topographical notes. "Different men in the companies will be instructed in packing, and officers will see that care is taken of the mules and that they are properly and carefully packed," with special attention to the fitting of their equipment.[39]

The dissatisfaction of the Mimbres with Tularosa continued, coinciding by this time with Washington concern, which, however, arose not from attention to Indian wishes but from economic considerations. Since Tularosa was an expensive proposition, all its cargo having to be freighted at high cost from the Río Grande towns, the interests of Indians and officials for once pointed in the same direction, and the Apaches got their hearing. On March 6, Dudley wrote Indian Commissioner Edward P. Smith,[40] sending along a newspaper clipping from the *Borderer* of Las Cruces dated February 21, 1874. It printed a letter from Fred Hughes, an employee of the Chiricahua Reservation, formerly at Cañada Alamosa, suggesting that the Indians at Tularosa and the Chiricahua Reservation might be gathered together at Ojo Caliente; if this could be done, Dudley observed, "much expense and trouble would be saved."[41]

Smith replied on the nineteenth, directing Dudley to journey to the Chiricahua Reservation, talk to Cochise and Agent Jeffords, and get their views on removal, pushing the idea, if possible. Dudley suggested he might as well inspect Ojo Caliente en route. "Of course that country will be filled with squatters as soon as it becomes known that there is a possibility of its being set apart as an Indian Reservation," he lamented, in recognition of the American's penchant for turning a dollar at government expense whenever possible. To forestall such an eventuality he issued an order, subject to approval, reserving that country "until it can be decided whether or not the Indians will remove there."[42] General Pope briefly intervened with the opinion that citizens of New Mexico might object if the dreaded bands were combined within that territory,[43] but his fears were allayed by both Dudley and Governor Marsh Giddings.[44]

The superintendent inspected Ojo Caliente, then went south to Fort Thorn, westward to Bayard, discovering there that Bullard, who had threatened Howard's Apache guide in 1872, had completely changed his mind "and now said that the peace effected with Cochise had, contrary to his expectations, been productive of the most beneficial results. I may as well remark . . . that the same feeling existed at all points visited," wrote Dudley. He added that the Chiricahuas also were of use in keeping the northern Apaches from depredating along the Tucson road and, if that were the only consideration, they might be left on their present reservation.

He grumbled that he did not recommend the journey from Bayard to Fort Bowie "as a pleasure trip," but he survived it. "I learned that Cochise was lying very ill in the Dragoon Mountains, about forty miles distant, and that it was feared he might die." He commented that "to hear fear expressed that the greatest and most warlike Apache might die sounded strange enough, but when I ascertained that the great chief retained in peace the wonderful power and influence he had exercised in war, and that he regarded his promises made to General Howard sacred and not to be violated upon any pretext whatever, I knew that it would be a calamity to the frontier to lose him from the ranks of living men."

Dudley digressed to express a view that the reservation should be closed out because, in addition to being an avenue for raiders bound for Mexico, there was too little arable land to enable the Apaches ever to become self-sufficient.

Tom Jeffords, still agent for the Chiricahuas, about this time messaged Smith, outlining one of the major problems at his charge.

A party of Indians [has recently] come . . . from the Tularosa Reservation . . . and from what I can learn from them, I believe in a short time we will be overrun with Indians from . . . the north. . . . The Indians will leave their reservation with their families and go on into Sonora or Chihuahua on a raid. Their families will then seek shelter on this reservation, they will intermingle with the Indians belonging here, and it makes no difference whether I feed them or not, they will not leave. The men who have gone into Sonora or Chihuahua raiding will soon return, camp in some of the mountains in the vicinity of the reserve, and after a while come in here and want rations. If I do not feed them, they will go again, and keep going as they did a year ago. I believe by feeding them and trying to keep them here, they would not be liable to do so much raiding. For that reason I am compelled to ask for instructions.[45]

In company with Jeffords, Dudley journeyed twenty-five miles west of Bowie to Sulphur Springs, there meeting Taza, the eldest son of Cochise and, within a few days, to become chief. The party went southerly to the leader's *rancheria.*

The camp was located on top of a high butte or foothill and commanded a view of the surrounding valley as far as the Chiricahua Mountains on the east and as far as the eye could reach to the North and South, while immediately in the rear was the great Dragoon Mountains. The place was well chosen for defence, and was probably selected with that view.

I found Cochise lying down, with his face toward the East and commanding from where he lay an extended view of the approaches to his camp. The instinct of the warrior to guard against surprise evidently still lingered with this dying man. The old chief was suffering intensely and I at first thought he would not outlive the night. I found a ready welcome as soon as his son explained who I was, for I had been expected; and when I gave him a photograph of General Howard and myself taken together my introduction to his favor was complete. The picture was frequently examined by the old chief during my stay and always followed by the warmest expression of feelings of affection for the General.

Soon after the arrival of Agent Jeffords and the interpreters I commenced a conversation. . . . I told Cochise that I regretted seeing him so ill and that I would not worry him then but would go away and come again when he was better; but he insisted upon hearing me then and said that he would soon die and that I had better also talk with the sub Chiefs. They were accordingly summoned. After talking for an hour I found Cochise so much exhausted that I decided to leave him for the time. During that night he was unconscious for several hours.

Dudley returned to Bowie and three days later again came to the camp. He found Cochise still alive, but failing rapidly, although he had a "much longer talk" with him.

While he expressed a preference for their location I became convinced that should he live Agent Jeffords would have but little difficulty in securing the removal of the Indians.

During the second visit I found Cochise mounted on his horse in front of his wickiup, having been lifted there by his friends, showing his determination and strength of will. I asked why he did so, and he replied that he wished to be mounted once more before he died. The agent [Jeffords] and myself both feared he might die while on his horse, and probably he would have preferred such a death.

Dudley added:

I am convinced that should you decide to remove these Indians Agent Jeffords can do so. . . . I have seen no man who has so complete control over his Indians as Agent Jeffords and I am sure that if they are removed he would be the best man to make Agent at Hot Springs. He does not answer all the requirements of an Agent. None that I have seen do fill the bill in every particular. Jeffords can and does maintain discipline, and he has the influence to bring Indians to his reservation and keep them there, and if they go away he generally knows where they have gone. If the Apaches can be taught to work, Jeffords is the man who can teach them.[46]

Expecting Cochise daily to die, Dudley lingered at his camp until June 3, when he commenced his return, passing that night at Sulphur Springs. The next morning a twenty-seven-man war party under Taza approached. Dudley demanded their purpose, and

We were informed that it had been ascertained that Cochise's illness was due to the fact that an Indian of the Chiricahua band had bewitched him,

167

and they were going for the witch to compel him to cure their chief. . . . I asked what would be the fate of the supposed witch if he failed to cure Cochise, and was told they would hang him in a tree and burn him to death. There seemed no way of stopping them at the time and they went on to the other camp and secured their man, and returned with him firmly tied upon his horse. The agent believed he could save his life at the proper time, and I have no doubt did so. Four days after my departure, viz June 8th, Cochise died and his son Taza became chief. The feeling of Taza is as friendly towards the settlers as was his father, but I fear he has not so much influence over the tribe.[47]

Regardless of the sentiment of Indians or whites toward removal to Ojo Caliente, the Chiricahuas never formally transferred there, and this may have contributed to its ultimate weakness and to later disaster, furthered by the inability of officials far removed from the scene and its strong personalities to modify the solutions they conceived.

Dudley favored the Ojo Caliente site for a Mimbres reservation. "I find no opposition on the part of any settlers . . . to the consolidation of the Apaches at this point," he wrote. Military officers agreed that they could probably be better controlled along the Alamosa than anywhere else. "I believe the place selected is one to which the Indians will gladly remove . . . where so many advantages exist for an Indian reservation. . . . I believe that Tularosa has been a failure from the beginning and ought to be abandoned. . . . In view of all the facts I therefore recommend that you direct the removal of the Southern Apaches . . . to the Hot Springs, and the establishment of the Agency at that place, at as early a day as practicable."[48]

Agent Thomas reported July 21 that, having been ordered to the new reservation, he would arrange for the necessary buildings there, freight equipment and supplies in, and "as soon as that is accomplished, will take the Indians to Ojo Caliente."[49] Tularosa would be but an unpleasant three-year memory for the Mimbres Apaches.

XIV

Concentration Begins

Don't put the Mimbres to work! So pleaded Agent Thomas in the summer of 1874, requesting of Commissioner Smith an exemption for his charges from a new order requiring Indians to labor if they wished to eat. He explained, "The Southern Apaches are yet too wild for the enforcement of this law. An attempt to enforce it now, would, I am sure, drive them all off the reservation, and they would then gain a subsistence almost entirely by stealing."[1] Victorio's people might be ready to give up raids and war and squat upon a reservation, but they were as yet unprepared psychologically for that civilized situation where the male performs hard drudgery instead of the woman.

An Indian inspector pointed out about this time that "the Apaches, like all wild Indians, are averse to work and inclined to war and pillage," adding that, "feeding them tames their nature, but fighting them only stimulates their savage instincts."[2] Yet there were signs of a possible metamorphosis. Thomas had reported last spring from Tularosa that "a large number of the Indians are now planting and some of the very worst men are the most active in farming operations. When I say the men are at work I do not mean that they are working the women simply."[3] Perhaps the millenium would arrive.

The Apaches had been moved from Tularosa back to Ojo Caliente in mid-summer, and Thomas managed to secure a detachment of ten infantrymen under a sergeant from Fort McRae, but he asked for "a company of Cavalry . . . or, if that cannot be, of twenty or even ten men, in preference to a full company of Infantry. Cavalry stationed at the Agency is very efficient in trailing stolen stock from the Indians, and also in keeping the Indians at home. Infantry is worthless for this service among the Apaches."[4] Therefore, a cavalry detachment was stationed there, initially under First Lieutenant Jonathan D. Stevenson, a veteran Indian fighter with years of experience; he had been badly wounded in a fight against the Walapais in the Cerbat Mountains of Arizona six years earlier.[5] Thomas, unlike some

169

agents, appreciated the military, got on well with it, and was grateful for its muscle.

He informed Colonel Gregg, now commanding the District of New Mexico, in July that the Indians were quiet and their "present peaceable condition was due to Major Price's actions last summer." He added that if Price's command had remained longer, "the result would have been more satisfactory." In this he differed from Inspector William Vandever, who had charged that Price's only impact had been to "scare nearly all the Indians away to the mountains." Thomas, in a formal rebuttal, affirmed in a letter to Price: "You gave me control of my Indians . . . which I have been careful to maintain ever since. . . . I do not claim full control of my Indians, but I do claim that you made it possible for me to effect very great improvement. . . . If you had given this reservation your undivided attention for two months longer the success would have been *nearly* complete."[6] In view of Thomas' character and record, his views must be accorded weight.

At the new-old Ojo Caliente reservation there were, by the end of the summer, about 400 Indians, including 175 men of fighting age, about 150 horses and mules.[7] John M. Shaw of Socorro was named agent for the Southern Apaches on September 17, accepted October 6, and took over November 15.[8] Thomas went to the Pueblos, where his wife could enjoy some amenities of life after years of uncertainty among the turbulent Apaches. Although more Indians usually were rationed at Apache reserves in winter than in summer, the figures released by Shaw of a steady rise from the 400 reported in mid-summer by Ben Thomas to 1,317 Indians a year later seem peculiar.[9] Since an agent was dispenser of rations and other goods, huge profits could be made by inflating the number of his charges—a situation not unknown on the frontier. This is not to assert that Shaw was dishonest, but an explanation of his figures would be helpful. Unfortunately, none survives, unless it be a later formal charge that he calculated the number of Indians he fed by the amount of beef they accepted, rather than issuing meat for the number of Apaches actually counted. In time, and with practice, the perceptive Apaches would eagerly seize advantage of such a system.

Agent Shaw was to prove a trial to his superiors in diverse ways and in nothing more than the windy reports he regularly filed. It must have taxed the patience of Commissioner Smith and others to read them, as they try the indulgence of students today. A sample, from his report of November 30, 1874:

170

I would like to inaugurate a system for the improvement, mental, moral and physical of this people, but on a sure basis that will insure success and place them upon the great highway of progress and civilization. This will necessitate more mature consideration than I have been able to devote to this subject as yet. I believe however that the first step has been taken to ensure success, they are on a good Reservation of their own choice where they can be taught the great and essential principles of civilization which to them are habits of industry in place of idleness, honesty in place of theft and robbery. The great means to effect this change I believe to be agricultural labor and tame them from their roving disposition and from dwelling in booths or tents to permanent abodes or houses. [etc., etc.]

One wonders what Mr. Shaw imagined previous agents had sought to do.

He did however appreciate that "the close proximity of this Reservation to the frontier settlements presents a difficulty and a serious one." He learned, as others had before him, that "it is almost impossible to prevent traffic with the Citizens and Indians are fond of whiskey and will trade when they can get it, or corn of which they make a sort of beverage that intoxicates and many of them get beastly drunk . . . Only yesterday one of the Chiefs was mortally stabbed in a drunken row."[10]

The year 1875 passed relatively quietly despite tensions and other influences toward disorder. Many of these were only peripherally related to his charges, but Shaw discovered they could have important influences upon his Indians. For example, there was the continuing problem of the neighboring Chiricahuas and the endless raids upon Mexico. Dudley, now a special commissioner of Indian affairs out of Washington, was asked for his views and replied in June that he had twice visited Cochise's band and had heard complaints against them. He pointed out, however, that

there are a large number of Apaches living in Sonora to whom many of the alleged depredations are undoubtedly chargeable. There is also many [Arizona] citizens who have little regards for law and who in my opinion commit many of these outrages and save their own precious lives by charging them upon Indians. . . .

There is another reason for these frequent complaints [from Mexico]. Formerly the Mexican Government allowed the Government of Sonora a specific sum of money for the purpose of protecting his people against the raids of Indians. That sum has been withdrawn and the officers of Sonora would like to have it restored, hence this constant howl.[11]

171

Even more sinister was the flowering of a fresh version of the "removal policy," by which most of the Apaches were to be concentrated at San Carlos, in Arizona. This was to lead to an interminable series of conflicts and wars, one of the most serious of which was that involving Victorio himself.

The concentration was urged by certain factions as an economy move, but probably was mainly planned to sweep the Indians from vast areas coveted by whites. In addition, there was little comprehension on the part of certain officials of the innate differences, jealousies, and incompatibilities between the various Apache bands, who for generations had lived aloof from one another. "They're all Apaches, aren't they?" was the oft-heard demand. "Speak the same language? In about the identical cultural stage? It would be better for the Indians, as well as for us, to bring them together where they could more swiftly become civilized, self-supporting, and a homogeneous people." So ran the arguments. Logical, surely, but specious, too, for Indian desires and traditions, frequently in opposition, were unsuspected or ignored. The removals began with the bringing of about fifteen hundred Indians from Camp Verde to San Carlos in 1875,[12] continued with the transfer of part of the White Mountain Apaches from Camp Apache to San Carlos in the summer of that year.[13] Still to come were the removals of the Chiricahuas and the Mimbres.

Among Shaw's concerns at Ojo Caliente were the white intruders, or profiteers, invading the reservation for financial gain. Should he use the military to oust them?[14] Then there was the "problem" of rations for his charges. Shaw was buying supplies increasingly lavishly, always ready with an explanation of why he did so.[15] He outlined for the commissioner his somewhat original theories of handling beef purchases,[16] justifying them in the one way he imagined close to Washington's heart—greater economy. His superiors were interested in financial savings, it was true, but also wanted the Indians fed, and doubts arose whether the Apaches under Shaw's administration were being fairly treated. Although Shaw had issued more flour and beef than any previous agent, according to his vouchers, he complained with rising urgency that supplies were running low, that he was forced to issue but half-rations, that he might trade sugar for flour to stave off disaster, and so on.[17]

Unable to elicit satisfactory replies, he journeyed to Santa Fe to see the territorial delegate to Congress, Stephen Benton Elkins,[18] complaining that he could get authorization for no more rations "and what was I to do?" He added, "I can keep them at peace on the Reservation if any living man can; but no man can keep an Indian starving and keep him in subjection." He said he had held a council and "the chiefs said they were contented, never so contented and happy as now, never had a 'tato' that treated them so well," that they wanted to do right but could not if starving, and "some of the chiefs even cried" in contemplation of catastrophes to come if the ration were not improved, disasters upon which Shaw dwelt at unconscionable length with rambling word pictures of the horrors and destruction inevitably to come.[19] Elkins passed the communication on to Commissioner Smith, with a note that Shaw's views were entitled to a hearing, since "he understands the Indian character as well as anyone I know."[20]

In response to a request, Shaw on March 29 sent a windy plea to Smith similar to that to Elkins, reminding the commissioner that "were you as familiar with their bloody history for the past twenty-five years as I am you could more fully appreciate the importance that attaches to this subject." He even suggested taking funds from the Mescalero Agency and applying them to his account, since, he said, he had been feeding many Mescaleros "who refused to go there."[21] It is difficult not to appreciate Shaw's anguish at the well's abrupt drying up, nor to erase the suspicion that he had been giving his charges only a bare minimum of a ration, the remainder of what he had spent going to other purposes, so that now the curtailment of funds would mean a real hardship to the Apaches, perhaps precipitating an outbreak—with no further profit to himself. This was suggested by harsh questions Washington later in the summer fired at him.

The removal of the Chiricahuas from Jeffords' reservation to San Carlos had long been discussed, but was precipitated by events that began when, perhaps because available rations were reduced, Jeffords permitted a small band to move west from the agency into the Dragoons to supplement their issued food by hunting. Nearby was a stagecoach station run by one N. M. Rogers and his assistant, A. O. Spence. They eked out their existence by peddling bootleg whiskey to Indians in return for loot from raids into Mexico, or so went the general belief. The Dragoons Chiricahuas were led by Taza, Cochise's son and a friend of Jeffords. After a dispute among themselves, Taza withdrew into the Chiricahua Mountains to the east, leaving in the

Dragoons about a dozen hardy Apaches under Skinya, a belligerent war leader. With Skinya was his brother, Pionsenay, a noted raider. Pionsenay traded some of his booty with Rogers for whiskey, got drunk, and wanted more liquor. When the station keeper refused to sell it, Pionsenay killed Rogers and Spence and seized some arms and ammunition. The next day other hostiles, probably still drunk, killed yet another white man and stole some horses. With Jeffords as guide, the troops cornered the raiders in the Dragoons, but couldn't dislodge them and withdrew.

There was no further action against them for some weeks, but the turmoil engendered flushed a number of Chiricahuas from the reservation. Some may have gone south into Old Mexico, but others were reported to head northeast to commiserate—and draw rations—with their close friends on the Ojo Caliente reserve. On April 15, Shaw forwarded two dispatches he had received to Washington, along with his own urgent plea. The first said that "all the Indians from the South have gone to the Hot Springs Reservation. Look out for Indians in New Mexico."[22] The second, quite as alarming, was dated the following day, and warned similarly, "the Southern Chiricahuas have left for Tularosa," which, Shaw explained, meant his agency.[23]

These communications, he informed Smith, revealed "the critical stage of things here. By this dispatch you will see a large portion of the Chiricahua Indians are coming here. If I had rations to issue I could conciliate them and doubtless prevent an Indian war. My Indians are distressing me with their cries of want and suffering for food. What shall I do to prevent an outbreak among them?"[24] The Chiricahuas from Jeffords' reserve did not come directly to the agency, however, lurking instead in nearby mountains and raiding when necessary—those who did not plunge at once into Mexico.

Information of the Chiricahua disturbance had promptly reached Victorio's people, of course, and "many of them have left," Shaw reported a week later. Earlier he had demanded more troops as a precautionary measure, and these provoked "great fright and fires at once blazed on all the mountain tops and caused great alarm." He heard that the Mescaleros, too, had gone out. "I am doing my best to keep them quiet, but three parties were here yesterday and to-day, reporting my Indians on the Rio Grande and that they were stealing stock."[25] Strains and dissension rippling outwards from the Chiricahuas caused disputes and conflicts among Shaw's Indians. "They had a fight among themselves," he reported. "Killed three chiefs and wounded a large number yesterday. They had another fight, only one killed. This will cause a division among them and make my work still more difficult." Almost all the soldiers had been withdrawn now; he was without any real protection,[26] but fortunately Victorio, Loco, and the bulk of his Indians remained quiet, if morose, willing to live quietly if only they were fed.

Colonel Edward Hatch,[27] of the black Ninth Cavalry, commanding the District of New Mexico, reported he would leave Santa Fe by stagecoach April 17 for Fort McRae and the Ojo Caliente Reservation and explained his disposition of troops to meet the emergency should it spread to his territory. Major Albert P. Morrow,[28] a lithe, blue-eyed cavalryman just under six feet in height, commanding at Fort Bayard, was ordered up to Ojo Caliente. An additional cavalry company was ordered from Fort Selden to McRae, the company at McRae to join Morrow. Wagon trains with strong infantry guards, fortuitously at Craig to load ordnance for Fort Union, were diverted to old Fort Tularosa. Another company of cavalry was held in reserve at Santa Fe. "The rapid communication furnished by the new line of telegraphs from Fort Selden [to Santa Fe] and couriers [from Selden] to Bayard have enabled me to concentrate the troops so rapidly on the Southern Apache Agency. It will have the effect to control these Indians . . . and may possibly have the effect to frighten the Chiricahua Indians into coming in. . . . The Inspector of Indian Bureau Jno. Kimball . . . thinks it will be impossible to do anything with the Indians from Camp Bowie until they are punished."[29]

Hatch reached Ojo Caliente on the twentieth, finding the Apaches "extremely defiant. They were all well armed with Springfield, Winchester or Sharps rifles and carbines, Colts and Smith and Wesson Revolvers, the women and boys with muzzle loading arms and well supplied with ammunition. They declared openly that the Government had acted in bad faith, that no meat had been issued to them for four weeks, that many of their young men were away on raids for horses and mules and it was better for them all to go than to remain and starve." So much had Shaw's perplexing mismanagement accomplished.

"Some of the Chiricahua Indians engaged in the massacre . . . had reached the Southern Apache Indians at the same time the troops arrived. . . . Had it not been for the timely arrival of the troops [they] would have precipitated the Southern Apaches into a war and resulted most disastrously to the unarmed settlers." Hatch, noting that ponies already had been shod with rawhide for the warpath, added:

"The chiefs, Victoria, Loco, Sanchez, Rafael, Nana, declared their intention was to secure a peace with Sonora and then raid upon our Territory." Victorio grimly declared they could do better by war on the United States than they could do at peace with this country and war with Sonora. Our territory was now rich and Sonora poor, he explained, logically. Shaw added privately to Hatch that he believed this idea had been planted among the Indians by persons interested; it would not only bring profit to Sonora, being at peace with the Apaches, but more sinister profits as well.

"They said all the other Apaches would join them, that the Indians had fully calculated upon this should open hostilities occur," continued Hatch. By the sheerest good fortune the officer at that moment received information that the army would feed the Indians, no matter what the Indian Bureau did, and that would hold them upon the reservation for the time being. "It is not probable that they would have left quietly," he remarked, "and war must have resulted."

"The leading chiefs stated openly that however much they might be inclined to keep the peace, it was impossible for them to hold their young men who would raid for horses and mules, that the sale was a ready one among the Mexican towns, and through this means they were enabled to supply themselves with excellent arms and ammunition." The chiefs would be compelled to go to war to retain their influence, he added, although under duress they often saw to it that stolen horses were returned or made good. Not only the Southern Apaches but also the Mescaleros were raiding widely, Hatch added.

He had planned to break Morrow's command into small detachments, using the Navaho scouts, and scour the country for raiding parties whose members "would be killed or arrested when caught in the act, even if followed on the Reservation," but Pope warned that this might generate active hostilities, and Hatch canceled his order.

"The Indians are now in a better condition to resist than they ever were," he pointed out. "They require watching." He urged establishment of a summer camp on the Gila for three companies to watch the passes and the "natural track of the Southern Apaches" when they moved about.

The colonel grumbled that the Indians were no further advanced toward civilization than when they first came upon a reservation, and the reserve itself was a place of concealment for stolen property, besides drawing "a disreputable class of traders." The Indians were undisciplined, raiding upon settlers and into Mexico, and should be disarmed, although "the attempt to disarm them might result in driving them to Sonora," and they should be "compelled" to work. The agents had no control over their charges, Hatch decided, perhaps reflecting upon Shaw himself.[30]

General Pope, endorsing Hatch's report, agreed that "there is no doubt that these Indians should be disarmed and any ponies in excess of what are needed around their camps should be taken from them, but" he added, "it is equally necessary that they should be regularly and sufficiently fed."[31]

Amid all the uncertainty and weighty concern over a possible explosion at the Ojo Caliente Reservation, with its unfed, hungry warriors, ill-kept promises to them, the unsettling arrival of battle-tested fighters from Arizona, and other complications, comes a most incongruous note. Like a jest from some base comedian interrupting Macbeth in his mad scene, there is a droll suggestion that the Tonkawas and Lipans be removed from Fort Griffin, Texas, to the New Mexico reserve! The Apaches could not even get on with other Apaches, and there was not enough food for those now concentrated at Ojo Caliente, yet here came a serious suggestion that Indians still more disparate be crowded in among them. Fortunately, this undistinguished scheme was never implemented.[32]

Because rationing remained a problem, Shaw reported on May 8 that he had "ordered all Indians belonging to other tribes and reservations to return to their own homes, or at least to leave this Reservation. ... (one) small party have come in with stock which makes them very shy about visiting the Agency. ... I shall use every lawful means to prevent collision with the troops, for if once started the consequences will be disastrous. If they could be separated [from the peaceable Indians] it would do some of them good to feel the strong arm of military force against them, but they are very suspicious and the late movement of the military has created a state of great uneasiness amongst them." The whiskey that Rogers and Spence had bootlegged had flooded the Southwest with aching trouble from which it would not soon recover.

Developments at the Chiricahua Reservation had reached a climax. John P. Clum,[33] agent at San Carlos, was ordered May 3, 1876, to "proceed to Chiricahua; take charge of Indians. ... If practicable remove Chiricahua Indians to San Carlos,"[34] in accordance with a

Washington decision of May 1.[35] On second thought, nudged along by Governor Anson P. K. Safford of Arizona, Interior asked the secretary of war for military assistance in case Clum requested it. On May 13 the agent, noting that "the murderers in the recent outbreak . . . are all on the reservation drawing rations and no effort is made to arrest them," said he would attempt to pick them up, "and desire such support in arms or troops or both as will enable me in case of outbreak to subdue them without protracted war." Secretary of War Alphonso Taft caused General August V. Kautz, commanding troops in the Department of Arizona, "to furnish all military assistance necessary,"[36] and this was virtually the last instance on record of amicable cooperation between Clum and the military in Arizona.

Kautz swiftly and intelligently deployed "all the Cavalry of this Department and the Indian Scouts, deeming it economy to make such display of force, as would cause the Indians to submit . . . or if they resisted, to conquer them as speedily as possible." Seven companies of cavalry and two of Indian scouts from Apache and Verde were concentrated at Camp Grant, and three more companies of cavalry at Fort Lowell, Tucson, directed to accompany Clum to Bowie. One detachment of three cavalry companies was stationed at Sulphur Springs, west of Bowie, and another of four companies in the San Simon Valley, east of the Chiricahua Mountains. Kautz himself went to Bowie to sit in on the discussions between Clum and the Chiricahuas.

It is not the province of this work to describe in detail the removal of the Chiricahuas and dissolution of their reservation. On the morning of June 6 Clum counciled with Taza and his people. In keeping with his promise to his dying father to do as Jeffords advised, Taza agreed to remove to the San Carlos Reservation, selecting old Fort Goodwin as their home. Juh, Geronimo, and Nolgee, bitterly intractable Chiricahuas usually perhaps affiliated with the Southern, or Sonoran, division of the tribe, agreed initially to remove. But the next day they were found to have fled, killing their dogs to avoid alerting the whites, abandoning their old and decrepit people, and hastening southward.

The flight activated Kautz's two outlying detachments. He directed them to scout southward along the east and west faces of the Chiricahua Mountains, cutting for sign. The western party, under Captain George M. Brayton and with Al Sieber as chief of scouts, had a minor brush with a few returning raiders, but found no trace of the principal enemy, although it rounded the southern end of the mountains and worked part way north along the eastern slope. The other detachment, under Major Charles E. Compton, failed to carry out its orders well and allowed the hostiles to escape. Pionsenay, badly wounded in a fight with Taza when the latter refused to go to war instead of to San Carlos, surrendered with many women and children. These, with numerous aged, brought the total willing to transfer to 325. Pionsenay was turned over to a law officer for investigation of murder, but escaped, and Clum reached his reservation with the remainder, including only 60 warriors, on June 18.

Kautz cited evidence that only the one party of hostiles, the bands of Juh, Geronimo, and Nolgee, had left the reservation. He concluded that "the number of Indians pertaining to the Chiricahua Reservation has been greatly exaggerated," Jeffords claiming that he had been feeding from 750 to 900.

"When I inquired where they were in detail, his explanation was not satisfactory," said Kautz. He said Jeffords "spoke of the Southern Chiricahuas as having gone to Sonora and stated their number to be two hundred and nine. 'Gordo' with about thirty to sixty had come from the Warm Spring or Mimbres Apache Reservation three years before, and had remained until the killing of Rogers and Spence, when he moved away to Stein's Peak. . . . Agent Jeffords claimed also that quite a number of Indians had recently been killed in Sonora, but taking his figures in detail and summing them up, I could not make more than five hundred and fifty. . . . It is probable that the Chiricahuas proper have never . . . exceeded four hundred."[37]

It is possible that Kautz was correct in his surmise and that Jeffords had been overstating his rationing by 100 per cent or more. It is also conceivable that Jeffords was correct in his figures. Indian Inspector William Vandever had reported two years earlier that Jeffords issued rations "every fifteen days to Captains of bands, to heads of families, or to single individuals just as the Indians desire," believing that system best, and also rationing such visitors as the Mimbres and, presumably, raiding parties of the White Mountains, Pinals and others going to or from Mexico or perhaps merely at the reservation for a visit. Vandever said that at the time he was there, included among Jeffords' Indians were "three or four hundred who properly belong to Tularosa and other reservations. The last named Indians leave their reservations upon any pretext . . . and go to Chiricahua, where they are received and rationed."[38] It would be unfair to assume, on the basis of Kautz's figures alone, that Jeffords was dishonest or that he was not rationing as many Indians as he claimed to be. There is also the possibility that he issued more than the skimpy ration allowed, obtaining the additional food by overstating the number of Indians. This, in addition to making them more content, would be an act of humanity, rather than duplicity.

Scarcely had the Chiricahua Reservation been closed when some of its people turned up at the Ojo Caliente reserve where, in addition to complicating the rationing procedure, they caused friction and occasional bloodshed and added to the general instability that was to mount until it led into a series of explosions.

"Parties of Chiricahuas are arriving and I wish to know what action to take respecting them," Shaw reported on June 16. "The Indians report several killed [on the former reservation] and there is a good deal of excitement, and should I order them away I fear some of these [Mimbres] Indians would go with them and take to the mountains and cause great trouble. . . . It is quite a critical time."[39] A week later he reported that Gordo and more than fifty others had arrived. "Others are reported in the mountains near here and are expected in; I think there are more on the reservation than have reported."[40] On July 3 he messaged that twenty-five more had come in, "some young bucks are here on the reserve that have not reported,"[41] and July 17 about seventeen more showed up.[42] On July 21 an additional forty arrived, including Geronimo and his wife.[43] It was not an easy matter handling them. Shaw reported on July 14 that the visitors were "troublesome," adding that Loco, "my reliable chief, in trying to keep them in order was attacked by one and he was obliged to shoot him in self defense. This caused great excitement."[44] He enlarged on his difficulties: "Some of these Chiricahua Indians are young warriors or single and with good arms and well mounted. They are very haughty and difficult to manage. . . . They evidently have the idea they can do as they please. . . . The party last arrived informs me there is a number left for Sonora from Chiricahua."[45]

In all, then, about 135 of Jeffords' Indians had reported in at Ojo Caliente, more were suspected to be hiding out on the reservation and in nearby mountains, and still others had gone down into Sonora, perhaps to join their intractable cousins. The "removal" of the Indians from the Chiricahua Reservation had succeeded in emptying that reserve, but instead of collecting its population at San Carlos or anywhere else, it was dispersed over an enormous extent of country, and tumult and disorders became inevitable.

XV
The Mimbres Removed

Agent John Shaw sent in his resignation June 19, stating no reason,[1] although the disarray in his accounts may have been a factor. On August 15, James Davis of Allegheny County, Pennsylvania, was appointed agent, accepting August 31 and reaching Ojo Caliente October 15.[2] Meanwhile, the commissioner on September 4 took Shaw to task for several things. He charged him with issuing enough beef in 134 days to have lasted by regular issue 200, for calculating the number of his Indians "from the amount of beef issued, rather than the amount of issues from the number of Indians as fixed by actual count." This, said S. A. Galpin, acting commissioner, "shows a lack of judgment on your part, or an absence of business qualifications essential to the proper conduct of the affairs of an Indian Agency, and an extravagance in the issue of supplies, either wilfully or ignorantly, not warranted by the most liberal construction of the rules governing the management of your duties as Indian Agent." The communication demanded answers to a long list of questions, and asked Shaw to supply "a roll of the Indians both by bands and families."[3]

Shaw never answered the complaints specifically, according to surviving records, but one year later did send a census roll which had been taken in May, 1876. No previous census, he averred, had ever been made. "It was a very difficult task," was incomplete, and "no complete census could be made owing to the unsettled condition of the Indians at that time; owing to failure of supplies and presence of Troops many had left for the mountains and other Reservations and but few having recognized names, could not be enrolled without being present." This perhaps was Shaw's way of getting out of an embarrassing situation in which he may have been "rationing" many more Mimbres Apaches than at that time existed.

But his census is very revealing, the best record available of those Indians then considered as belonging to the Mimbres reservation. Victorio heads the list, with one wife, five children, and four other dependents. His son Washington had one wife and no children but

181

three other dependents. Other well-known names included Lopez, Mangus, Gordo, Bisine, Ramon Chico, Nana with one wife, seven children and a dependent, Loco with three wives, three children, twelve dependents including two orphans, Dolores, Sancho, Gavinda, and Benito. The total number of Indians listed was 916, including men, women, and children.[4] Incidentally, the presence of Gordo at Ojo Caliente in May, 1876, is difficult to square with the information Kautz reported that this Indian and his people had been on the Chiricahua Reservation for years prior to the uprising there.

Trouble again was building on the Ojo Caliente reserve. Complications seemed to pile one upon another.

Shaw, still agent, reported September 8 to the commissioner:

I am under the painful necessity of reporting that on the 4th inst. a company of soldiers and Navajo scouts under command of [Second] Lieut. [Henry Haviland] Wright [Ninth Cavalry] came upon the Reservation unbeknown to me, and attacked the village of Victoria, principal chief, consisting of twenty-seven *rancherias*[5]; and without cause or provocation of any kind sacked and burned the entire village and destroying all their property, provisions and cooking utensils and (corn fields in great measure), Indians barely escaping with their lives, and this without cause or provocation of any kind, the Indians being perfectly orderly and not even accused of having done anything wrong.

The precise circumstances surrounding this raid are unclear, but Shaw said he was hard put to "keep them from avenging the outrage."[6] Some of the Apaches fled to the mountains, where they felt safer, and it was well they did so. Exactly one month later a

party of citizens (supposed to be) made a raid upon the reservation . . . and drove off a herd of horses belonging to the Apaches. The Indians are very much enraged and no doubt will retaliate. . . . Some will no doubt join the Indians that are roaming and depredating on Sonora; strange Indians appear at the agency and as suddenly disappear. Until those that remained in the mountains from the Chiricahua Reservation are driven in or brought in, they will cooperate together, and cause trouble. I counted nine strange Indians to-day.[7]

When he turned over the agency October 16 to Davis,[8] no doubt it was with a sigh of relief.

During these months the army was far from idle. Its detachments scoured the dry mountains and rumpled basins in all directions for hostiles or Indians off the reservation who should be on it. Captain

Henry Carroll, Ninth Cavalry, left Fort Selden September 12 with twenty-five men of Company F, reaching Solcum's ranch, southwest of the Sierra de las Uvas,[9] that evening, marching on throughout the night, and arriving at the barren, parched Florida Mountains after sunup, a total distance of fifty miles. The grass was good, though there was little wood, most of it scrub oak, and no surface water. "The command was supplied with water by making holes with tin cups in the gravel and sand found in Ravines," reported Carroll. "This supply was exhausted in two hours, and it was necessary to secure more water or leave the Range." Yet the scout was continued, and the second day a trail of a few raiders was struck, followed up, and two wounded Indians discovered, who escaped after winging a trooper. Watering away from the range, Carroll resumed his scout and struck two Indians driving stolen horses, killed one, recapturing eight horses. "The Indians in question were armed with the improved Sharps Carbine Cal. 50 metallic ammunition. They had no bows, arrows or spears, their horses were packed with fresh beef, and many of them shod with rawhide shoes, some of which were worn out," Carroll found. He scouted thoroughly the course back to Fort Cummings and the Mimbres River, then east to Slocum's ranch, north to a spring possibly in Horse Canyon, on the north slope of the Sierra de las Uvas sometimes used by depredators, and east again to the Río Grande.

"The reports of Indian depredations, I believe, are much exaggerated, and in my opinion rancho-men are much to blame for these reports by harboring disreputable characters in their premises who are, in my opinion, much worse than the Indians," concluded the captain.[10]

More of a striking success was the hard scout led by Second Lieutenant John Anthony (Tony) Rucker,[11] among the most active of the army's Indian hunters and, in this instance, very lucky. On December 2 James Hughes had wired Kautz from Tucson that Apaches had swept off twenty-one horses from his ranch near old Camp Crittenden. Kautz sent the information to Bowie, and when Rucker returned from escort duty he was assigned to investigate. He left Bowie December 11 with ten enlisted men and thirty-four Indian scouts for Crittenden, about one hundred miles southwest of the post on Sonoita Creek. He reached there on the seventeenth, followed the trail of the stolen stock back easterly again for about 230 miles to the summit of the Stein's Peak Range. Out of rations and with worn-out stock, he returned to Bowie to refit, leaving the post January 4 once more, again with his thirty-four scouts and this time taking seventeen enlisted men and a surgeon. On January 7 he picked up the trail where he had left it. The next morning he sent his guide, Jack Dunn, with the scouts to follow the trail southeast across the wide Lower Animas Valley, which he called the "valley-de-las-playas," with its alkali flats, toward the Leitendorf Hills, the northern extension of the Pyramid Mountains, and himself moved out with his command at about 3:00 P.M.

At sundown a courier reached him from Dunn with the welcome news that fresh Indian sign had been struck. Rucker reached the Leitendorf Hills about 9:00 P.M., where another courier from Dunn awaited him "with the information that he had found the camp of a large body of hostile Indians. I then dismounted the Cavalrymen and had the animals tied up, leaving a guard of 6 men with them." With the rest of his men he silently marched six miles southeast, made contact with Dunn, and laid low until 3:00 A.M., then moved another four miles southeast and stopped, still four miles short of the enemy camp. It was about forty miles south of Ralston, later Shakespeare, or somewhere around the northern end of the Animas Mountains. Rucker directed Dunn with the Indian scouts "to take a portion to the westward of the Indian Camp on a hill commanding the camp, and about 150 yards from it, with instructions to open fire at daylight."

To avoid alarming the Indian Camp I did not go on with the soldiers until very near daylight, when I proceeded and took a position on a hill northward of the hostile camp distant about 300 yards.

Dunn had opened fire before I reached the latter point. As soon as Dunn commenced firing the hostile Indians rushed from their lodges and sought shelter behind rocks, and returned the fire briskly. I then opened with a reverse fire upon them from my position. The firing continued for about two hours and twice during the engagement Scout Dunn with several Indian Scouts charged the hostile positions but were driven back with the loss of Indian Scout Corporal Eshin-e-car, severely wounded. Then with a simultaneous charge from both points we carried the enemy's position.

The hostile Indians fled in every direction and I was unable to pursue them, owing to the exhausted condition of my command.

During the engagement 3 Indian Scouts were directed to drive off the captured herd of animals to a position of safety, which they did.

After the engagement the bodies of 10 hostile Indians were found dead, and from the indications observed there was a large number wounded.

One Indian boy, about 5½ years old, was captured alive near the camp. The boy has since been identified as a nephew of Ger-an-i-mo (the Chiricahua Chief).

Rucker reported that the party of thirty-five warriors had captured equipment that was identified as formerly belonging to the Chiricahua agency.[12] This was perhaps the first heavy punishment those Indians ever had suffered from troops, although it would not be the last. In relaying the report to his Whipple headquarters, Captain Curwen B. McLellan, commanding at Bowie, stressed that "too much credit can not be given [Rucker] for the indefatigable manner in which he has performed the duties assigned him."[13] Kautz, in his endorsement, added that the Indians "were the particular band that ran away from the removal of the Chiricahua Reservation," at the time estimated to number but twenty-five men, women, and children, but since calculated by the San Carlos agent as two hundred, including thirty warriors. "Lieut. Rucker's success is regarded as the first chastisement which the Chiricahuas have ever received, and he deserves great credit."[14]

But this affair in southwestern New Mexico was far more meaningful than a skillful pursuit and battle. Shortly after the first of the year 1877, rumors began to circulate that the fugitive Chiricahuas were either on the Ojo Caliente Reservation or were drawing recruits and sustenance from it. Agent Davis reported January 13 that the Indians "still refuse to be enrolled and counted. . . . The only way I can compel them . . . would be to have a company of soldiers stationed here and refuse them all rations."[15]

There were rumors that the wounded Pionsenay, a fugitive from Arizona authorities, had reached Ojo Caliente and was secretly harbored there. Davis reported January 27 that "there is no Indian here known by [that] name," but added there were two Indians called Ponce, "one of whom may possibly be the Indian referred to."[16] Pionsenay at this time, however, may have been fully recovered and raiding in Sonora.

Davis resigned in early April,[17] having had his fill of trying to manage the turbulent Apaches, and Dr. Walter Whitney, a physician, became acting agent pending appointment of a successor or dissolution of the reservation. He reported February 28 that he understood about 250 Chiricahuas had come to his agency, most not remaining long and only about 100 being there at the time he wrote. "The balance . . . joined a band that never has been on a reservation, and these, with small parties who leave the San Carlos, Mescalero and Warm Spring reservations, are the depredators" who kept the Southwest in turmoil.[18]

185

First Lieutenant Austin Henely,[19] a hard-fighting Sixth Cavalry Irishman with enlisted service in the Civil War and a commission by way of West Point, messaged Kautz March 17 that "I saw Geronimo at the Warm Springs Agency yesterday. He had just returned from a raid with one hundred horses, was very indignant because he could not draw rations for the time he was out." In relaying this message to the commissioner, Governor Safford said: "I have had good reasons to believe for some time past that the renegade Chiricahua Indians were making the Warm Springs Agency a rendezvous where they go for rest and rations, to go forth on raids at their pleasure. In the recent raids made in southeastern Arizona nine men were killed, and over one hundred horses and mules were taken. There must have been over one hundred Indians connected with the raid. . . . I am and have been for some time of the opinion that the Agent at the Warm Springs is entirely unqualified. . . . Those Indians should be removed and all concentrated at the San Carlos."[20]

In a later message Safford urged Commissioner Smith, "Please order Agent Clum by telegraph to remove renegade Chiricahuas to San Carlos."[21] The very next day Smith acceded, wiring Clum, "If practicable take Indian Police and arrest renegade Chiricahuas at Southern Apache Agency. Seize stolen horses in their possession; restore the property to rightful owners; remove renegades to San Carlos and hold them in confinement for murder and robbery. Call on military for aid if needed."[22]

John Clum was delighted. This operation, enlarged to include the Mimbres as well, would, if he could bring it off, concentrate the Apaches west of the Río Grande—or those who could be caught, at any rate—under his control at San Carlos, and this pleased his ambition and his vanity. In addition, it promised to be an exciting, perilous task, and, being very young, he exulted in its challenge. He readied his chief of Indian police, Clay Beauford,[23] his aide, Martin A. Sweeney,[24] and on March 31 wired the commissioner, "I start a company of Indian Police for New Mexico tomorrow. Another company will join me at Silver City. I have asked Gen. Kautz and Hatch to cooperate and will overtake Police at Silver City."[25] Two days earlier he had messaged Kautz at Prescott, "Your cooperation is earnestly desired in the capture of renegade Indians and the seizure of stolen stock which I am about to undertake. I start for Tucson tomorrow and will overtake Indian police at Silver City."[26] Kautz, who had no particular love for Clum anyway, tersely replied, "The

Southern Apache Agency is in the Department of Missouri, commanded by General Pope, whose troops are stationed within a few miles of the agency, at Fort McRae and at Fort Craig. Application should be made to General Pope at Leavenworth, or General Hatch at Santa Fe, N.M., for such troops as may be needed by you."[27]

John Clum, his explosion point always attached to a very short fuse, received this message as a rebuff and began to fume, although for the moment he put his anger aside. On April 2 he contacted Hatch at Santa Fe, outlining his orders.

"I desire your cooperation, and respectfully request that you guard the borders of said Indian Reservation to prevent escape of stock or Indians, and also that you will concentrate sufficient troops in the vicinity of the Reservation to enable me to dictate terms to the Indians and to meet any resistance they may offer."[28] Smith had asked the secretary of interior to outline the problem to the secretary of war and solicit cooperation. Pope therefore had wired Hatch to "use such available force, Cavalry and Infantry . . . as may be practicable . . . to assist the Indian Agent. . . ."[29] Hatch at once let Clum know that nine companies, eight of them cavalry, had been ordered to the Ojo Caliente vicinity. "This is the great military cooperation I have long desired," approved Clum. "The prospects are bright."

He had promised to leave Tucson April 5 by stage, expecting "hearty cooperation of New Mexico troops," adding as a needle, "Arizona military are useless."[30] The same day he charged in a message to the commissioner that Kautz "has made newspaper charge against me and the Indian Dept. which are entirely unfounded. . . . I demand an investigation. . . . I will prove Genl. Kautz guilty of criminal inactivity," and so on,[31] repeating next day that until an investigation was ordered "my usefulness is at an end."[32] But there was no time for idle amusements of that sort, and Clum hastened on to Silver City, learning as he left Tucson that renegades "from Hot Springs" had just stolen four horses from a stage station ahead of him, at San Simon, driving them south.[33]

The little agent reached Fort Bayard the second week of April, informing the commissioner that he would leave the fifteenth with 103 Indian police, reaching Ojo Caliente the nineteenth. He added that "Hieronemo and nearly two hundred stolen horses yet on reservation," and, as an afterthought, fired one more shaft: "Kautz has done nothing to protect Arizona Border; General Hatch is doing all in his power."[34]

187

Just before leaving Bayard on the fifteenth he added, "My scouts inform me only six hundred Indians at Hot Springs, including renegades. I advise movement of all to San Carlos."[35] He received telegraphic instructions from Washington April 17 to effect the removal of all the Indians, not merely the Chiricahua renegades, if he could do it,[36] and John Clum, of course, was convinced he could.

He took the precaution, however, of seeking an objective opinion on whether it was feasible, particularly since he desired to accomplish it before the troops were in position so that later he could boast of it as a feat of his Indian police, one in which soldiers had no part. Therefore he requested of Whitney "the exact number of men, women and children . . . together with information as to the approximate location of the various bands and parties. I would also like your views as to the expedience of disarming the Indians of this reservation and would also be glad to know your opinion regarding the proposed removal of these Indians to the San Carlos Reservation."[37] Whitney replied that he estimated there were 175 men, 200 women, and about 250 children, nearly all "located within a distance of five miles" or scattered about, "constantly changing camps."

"The Indians will naturally object strongly to being removed from their old home, but I do not think they will endeavor to resist by force, but no doubt many will try to escape," he wrote. "Whether they succeed will depend upon the disposition of the troops and the energy of the Indian scouts, of which you are the best judge. If the policy of the Hon. Commissioner in regard to the concentration of all Indians on a few reservations is to be carried into effect, no time more favorable than the present can be selected."[38] With this welcome assurance, Clum set in motion his plan.

Surprisingly he secured agreement of the uncertain Mimbres and their guests to remove,[39] although his later memoirs of this operation bear evidence of after-the-fact editing. For example, his article on Victorio gives very little information on this individual, since, at the time, Clum had not heard too much about the chief, perhaps barely noticed him, and thus assembled little information to later record. By contrast, his account of the taking of Geronimo, then just coming into prominence, is magnified in deference to his later fame.[40]

He wired the commissioner April 21, "Arrived here last evening. This morning arrested Hieronemo and two other prominent renegades [Gordo and an unnamed Chiricahua], this after counted all Indians here. Todal present four hundred and thirty-four. My opinion at least fifty remained in camps, as many as forty now raiding in Sonora and Arizona."[41]

Later he amplified this communication in a message to Major James Franklin Wade, Ninth Cavalry, commanding troops in the vicinity. He had arrived, he said, had a talk "with the principal chiefs," arrested Geronimo and others, and counted the Indians, though he did not confine the Mimbres. "I instructed all to come in to daily count during such time as I might remain here. This they promised to do and told me that a few, perhaps fifty, who were not at count yesterday would be in to-day. This morning I was informed that some had gone to the hills, but would be in to count. . . . I have just had the count which was ordered yesterday and only one hundred and seventy-five men, women and children were present. I am informed . . . that 'Loco,' 'Skinya,' and two other chiefs are camped about twenty miles east of the agency, and that they say they will be back to-morrow morning." He added that he didn't think they intended to come in and therefore informed Wade they were considered "insubordinate and hostile" and the officer was requested to "punish them as hostile Indians."[42] Before this could be done, however, the Indians filtered back for the daily counts and that minor emergency dissipated.

Clum asked Whitney two days later the "probable number of Indians who have been drawing rations at this Agency recently, and who are now raiding in Sonora and Arizona." Whitney replied that "from information given me by Indians, there is now in Sonora under the leadership of 'Pionsenay,' about ten fully grown males, and under 'Nolgee' about the same number. In addition to this number from fifteen to twenty men now absent at last issue."[43]

Clum reported April 25 that "I had a short talk with the principal men and they readily consented to move to San Carlos. I hope to start with them on the 30th inst."[44] Thursday, the twenty-eighth, he informed Washington that Wade would provide an escort,[45] and Hatch agreed to guard the agency buildings at Ojo Caliente after their departure,[46] which was fortunate. They would be needed again.

Hatch wired Kautz April 27 that "Indian Agent Clum, with all Hot Spring Indians, and renegade Chiricahuas with guard of cavalry from my district are now enroute to San Carlos Agency. Will be at Arizona line about May fourth. Can you relieve my Cavalry guard of two companies and furnish three wagons to haul Chiricahua prisoners, who are in irons, to replace my wagons?"[47] The New Mexico escort normally would be bound by the Arizona border.

Clum reported to the commissioner May 1 that 453 Indians left Ojo Caliente that day with Sweeney in charge. "I go by road with [seventeen] prisoners (in wagons) & join indians at Silver City. Military authorities concur with me that removal is completely made. Gen. Hatch & Col. Wade have acted splendidly & aided me greatly," although he was not yet through with Kautz. On May 7 he reported that the Indians had reached Silver City, "everything working excellent. Will complete success. Chiefs are here as I write. Will move on tomorrow." Later, he added, "Expect to be at San Carlos with Indians on eighteenth."[48]

Captain William M. Wallace, commanding at Bowie, had wired Clum on May 6, "Please inform me where and when you will cross the Arizona line. I desire the information because troops from this Dept. are to relieve the escort from N.M. at the line."[49]

This gave Clum his opening. Haughtily he replied, "For the information of the Department Commander [Kautz], I wish to say, no escort has been asked from Arizona, nor will any be accepted."[50]

New Mexico and Arizona commanders, embarrassed, smoothed the matter out between themselves,[51] but Kautz bundled up the exchange of communications and fired it up through channels, with his own explanation. Major General Irvin McDowell, commanding the Military Division of the Pacific, in the first endorsement, "inviting attention to the discourtesy of Agent Clum," referred it to General Sherman, who, in a second endorsement wrote for the information of the secretary of war that "Agent Clum had no business to decline the escort tendered by Genl. Kautz. Thereby he compelled the Escort from New Mexico to enter the Department of General Kautz. Military Commands like State lines are real necessities, which an Indian Agent has no right to disregard. . . . Agent Clum by personal & official discourtesy does not help to smooth over difficulties already great enough."[52]

Long weeks later, after he had left the Indian Service, Clum received a communication "directing" him to reply to the officer's charges of discourtesy and so on. Eagerly he did so, ripping into Sherman's charge that he had "no business" creating such military havoc and, for good measure, flailing away at the battered Kautz once more. He reiterated his dubious claim that with his Indian police he could pacify the Southwest without the military and keep it calm.[53] He might have been able to do it with those Apaches he could persuade to remain at San Carlos. But these did not include the wilder spirits. There were too many inbred animosities, jealousies, fears, and hatreds to make possible a permanent settlement of all together. Many Apaches would consent to it, but others would not. Victorio, for one, would not.

XVI
Bust-out!

John Clum resigned around the turn of the year, a new agent was named, then Clum withdrew his resignation, and the President his appointment of a replacement.[1] He resigned again on April 4, and in May a successor was selected; nothing came of that, either.[2] Now there arose a new twist in his tempestuous career as agent: Kautz preferred charges against him for corruption and mismanagement, perhaps in rebuttal to Clum's many charges against the officer.

The commissioner ordered Indian Inspector William Vandever to look into affairs at San Carlos. He dutifully did so, concluding that "it seems to me that it is about time for you to begin to lose confidence in the sincerity or justice of Army officers' frequent charges of corruption and dishonesty against the Indian office or its agents. As fast as one set of charges are found to be unfounded they make others in the most imperious manner and in total disregard of truth; I only wish that they could themselves be called to account for the numerous frauds and rascalities that they are known to commit with impunity. . . . To set such a set of fellows to watch Indian issues is unjust to every man in your service."[3]

When army officers nevertheless were ordered to inspect the agency, Clum, as was to be expected, went into orbit. He messaged the commissioner tersely June 5, "I will not submit to inspection by the Army. I am ready to transfer my property. How soon can I be relieved?"[4] The commissioner attempted to mollify him, but Clum retorted, "I will not submit for a moment to this surveillance. It is an insult to the honor, integrity and manhood of an agent and I should resent it as such. The Indian service has competent inspectors and we do not require watchmen from the army to inspire purity and justice."[5] As an afterthought he suggested June 9 that if the department "will increase my salary sufficiently & equip two companies of Indian police I will volunteer to take care of all the Apaches in Arizona. The troops can be removed."[6] This suggestion fell flat. On June 19 from Tucson Clum repeated, "I cannot be inspected by the Army. A mixture of civil and military rule will result detrimental to the best interest of all concerned and is ultimate failure. Either let the civil officers be the sole rulers or if they are incompetent transfer the exclusive control to the Army. . . . I want exclusive control and means to enforce the same or I want nothing."[7] He received no satisfactory reply and on the Twenty-third wired, "[First] Lieut. [Lemuel Abijah] Abbott has gone to San Carlos as inspector under new order of things. As you have not intimated to me any disposition to rescind this obnoxious edict I respectfully inform your office that precisely at twelve o'clock noon on July first I sever all official relations with your Department. . . . No military officer can inspect San Carlos until after July first unless I am sooner relieved."[8] And, promptly at noon, July 1, "I mounted my favorite horse and hit the trail for Tucson, leaving the Indians and the affairs of the agency in charge of my chief clerk [Sweeney] and Indian Inspector Vandever. Thirty-five years elapsed before I again returned to San Carlos."[9]

Although Victorio is pictured by Clum as going willingly to San Carlos with his people, he could not have intended to remain there indefinitely, perhaps just long enough to see what the perplexing agent had in store for him there. That he intended sooner or later to return to Ojo Caliente, in peace or in war, is evidenced in the fact that he and his people cached their good arms there before leaving.[10] This was in the best tradition of Apache wiliness or, it may be, foresight. General Crook often mentioned this custom in support of his conviction that disarming them was virtually impossible and, in any event, would be unwise. Other thoughtful men, army officers and civilians, tended to agree.[11]

Victorio either selected, or was assigned, old Camp Goodwin,[12] six miles west of the present Fort Thomas, as the place for his people to settle. It was an unfortunate choice, although perhaps not more so than some others in the San Carlos area. Malarial, barren, unattractive, with no good hunting grounds nearby but plenty of enemies among their cousins, it was a *ranchería* for unhappiness, not where a creative and satisfying future might develop.

Kautz, second guessing perhaps, said he had "foreseen that the Warm Spring Indians would not stay even if well treated without a force that could compel them to stay. So many antagonistic bands thrown together, will cause numbers to leave from fear of enemies among their own people."[13] Added was the faulty rationing policy which kept the Indians hungry and restless,[14] and Victorio's later

193

admission that the main reason for his bolt was "on account of continual fighting with the Coyotero Apaches" to the point that "they preferred living anywhere" to San Carlos.[15]

But another contributing factor was Pionsenay, the relentless raider who was responsible for the slaying of Rogers and Spence, had been wounded, escaped from a law officer, raided again, and now lurked around the southern boundary of the huge reservation. On May 4 two Chiricahuas who belonged to his band showed up at abandoned Ojo Caliente and were turned over to the military, but not for long. Two nights later their guard dozed, and they escaped. Another raider, captured later, said that Pionsenay himself with seven others had come to the southern edge of the Ojo Caliente reserve, learned of the removal of the Mimbres, and followed them toward Camp Goodwin.[16] On August 28 Pionsenay, Nolgee, and their followers, about eighteen in all, swept in to within four miles of the subagency where Ezra Hoag was issue clerk and the subagent in charge.[17]

They sent word that they wanted a talk and would surrender, but Hoag replied that he had no authority to negotiate; their surrender would have to be unconditional. So Pionsenay and his fellows stole five horses and faded into the wilderness, at times wandering the more secluded reaches of the San Carlos reserve itself. First Lieutenant Gilbert E. Overton, Sixth Cavalry, set out on their trail, but he might as well have sought the wind. At length Nolgee surrendered with three companions,[18] but he had no intention of remaining listlessly in camp. Pionsenay, who remained out, was reported to have spent August and September in close contact with Victorio's people.[19] He was not an influence for tranquility. No doubt it was this wild Indian who helped crystallize Victorio's strengthening intent to bolt. "Pionsenay wields a great influence over all of them, and they fear him worse than the devil," reported Hoag.

Loco is said to have explained later that they left because of the unjust removal of the Mimbres from their own country, for which, he said, Indians have as much affection as whites; secondly, the manner of their removal, which was unnecessarily harsh, a number being ill with smallpox and other ailments; and, thirdly, the neglect of them by Indian Department officials at the branch agency, by which he meant that reduced rations, causing hunger, added to their discontent.[20]

From July 1, when Clum left, until the arrival of the new agent,

Henry Lyman Hart of Washington County, Ohio,[21] affairs at San Carlos were conducted by Vandever, who came to detest the military with almost the former agent's fervor, and Sweeney, not an uncontroversial figure, either. None of this boded well for the unsettled Apaches, who required, now as never before, a firm and knowledgeable hand. Veteran Indian man Jeffords, whose contacts with the Chiricahuas were unrivaled, warned in August that the Warm Springs and some others were restless and might jump the reservation. Possibly it was this which induced Hart to bring them in closer to San Carlos.[22] Hart had scarcely settled in, however, when the explosion came.[23]

By chance there was a greater than usual concentration of troops in the vicinity. Second Lieutenant Robert Hanna, with Companies B and M, Sixth Cavalry, and Company D of Walapais scouts from the northwest under the veteran guide Dan O'Leary, had reached Fort Thomas at the end of a long scout from Camp Huachuca. Tony Rucker also had arrived at Thomas from Bowie with eighteen enlisted men of Companies H and L, Sixth Cavalry, and twenty-three Indians of Company C. Captain Tullius C. Tupper had come in from Camp Grant September 2 with Company G, Sixth Cavalry. He was told the previous night by Lieutenant Abbott that he "knew of no occasion for the immediate use of troops," a judgment shattered within hours by the bolt of the Mimbres.[24]

Under Victorio and Loco the Mimbres on September 2 stole horses from the White Mountain Apaches to mount their people and swept away from old Camp Goodwin, most of them heading north. Pionsenay and his people of the central Chiricahuas, accompanied initially by a few of the Mimbres, went east at the same time, following up the Gila, seeking no doubt to round the San Simon Valley, gain the Peloncillos, and race southward toward sanctuary in Sonora. Victorio's people may have had no clear idea where they were going at first, but sought to avoid troops to their east and their White Mountain cousin-enemies to the northeast; after all, they had stolen some of their horses. Victorio and Pionsenay did not rejoin.

General McDowell, commanding the Division of the Pacific, messaged the adjutant general that he learned from Hoag, via Abbott, that "Warm Springs left because Pionsenay ordered them to go," and suggested that Nolgee also had fled, although Hart's decision to move the Indians closer in may have been a factor.[25] Vandever, who had left San Carlos just before the *émeute*, reached Mesilla September 12 and contributed a discordant note: "Warm Spring Indians have left reservation. . . . Jeffords . . . stirred them up to insubordination. He can be convicted on Indian testimony of furnishing whiskey to Indians. . . ."[26] Kautz investigated the charge, receiving a report from Abbott that "I am inclined to believe the report false and malicious. Vandever is very bitter against Jeffords and it is quite likely his prejudice has affected his judgment. . . . Vandever is responsible for their not having been properly fed and kept well in hand and is probably more to blame . . . than any one else. . . . I do not suspect Jeffords in the least of having influenced the Warm Spring Indians to leave the reservation but on the contrary think his conduct . . . commendable. . . . I am only surprised that today there is an indian left on the reservation."[27]

Victorio and his people now were in full flight.

In his summary of the incident, Hart said that the Indians, numbered by various authorities up to about 310, burst out, "taking with them a number of horses and huge quantities of flour &c. they had saved from their rations; they were pursued the next morning by volunteers from the agency who overtook them at Ash Creek [north of the subagency, hard against Natanes Mountain] and fought them until all their [the volunteers'] ammunition was expended. The volunteers recovered twenty-eight animals, captured thirty women and children, and all the provisions in the camp."[28] Later Hart said he sent out a "party of Indian police under command of a chief, Es-kin-e-la,"[29] which joined military commands also in pursuit.

The Indian police returned last evening [September 17] and reported that on the 10th inst. they caught up with the renegades and fought them until dark, killing one man and eleven women and children and capturing thirteen women and children and six horses;[30] the chief Es-kin-e-la reports that the Indian police and scouts were always one day ahead of the soldiers and when they caught up with the Southern Apaches at the foot of the Mogollon Mountains there were only five of the scouts with the agency police; the larger portion being behind with the officers and the pack train, and that they did not arrive at the scene of action until the fight was over; the whole of the party of the Southern Apaches would have been taken had the police been supported, but as Es-kin-e-la had only twenty-three men with him altogether he could not surround the renegades and when the scouts did come up, there was not sufficient daylight to follow the trail of the fugitives.[31]

Later military reports fleshed out the preliminary sketch.

The New Mexico troops were not idle. Major Wade was reported "scouting actively with all his troops in the Mogollon Mountains," with E and C companies, Ninth Cavalry, scouting the Black Range to the east. "The effects of these scouts have been to force Hot Spring Indians north," toward Fort Wingate, where I Company of the Ninth was ordered to "receive Indian prisoners" in case they gave themselves up. Pope believed they would and urged that, when they did so, it would be best to move them quickly from Wingate to Ojo Caliente once more as "the cheapest place to feed them," even if they were to be returned eventually to San Carlos.[32]

Most of the military operations had been directed against those Indians fleeing easterly up the Gila.

During the night of September 2–3, when a courier reached Thomas from Goodwin with the hurried report that the Ojo Caliente Indians had bolted, Tupper had informed Hanna and Rucker, barely arrived after hard scouts, to be ready to leave at "daybreak" with their commands and ten days' rations. The command moved to Hoag's sub-agency, where Es-kin-e-la joined with his seventeen Indian police and a man called by Tupper, Bowe.[33] The Tupper command, now consisting of sixty Indian scouts with about seventy soldiers from B, G, H, L, and M companies, Sixth Cavalry, and forty-five pack mules, went northeast of the Gila from Fort Thomas and scouted the fearfully rough country eastward, apparently on the trail of Pionsenay's people, or part of them with a few Mimbres, to the south of the main band of fleeing people.

Hanna reported they went a dozen miles up the Gila to Apache Crossing, near the present town of Bryce, on September 3. The next day they continued a dozen miles northerly, where they rejoined their scouts and continued twenty-eight miles more in a northeasterly direction. On September 5 they scrambled up the "very rocky cliffs" of the Gila Mountains and paused at the head of Río Bonita to graze their stock, then continued until dark. The country, reported the lieutenant, was "very rough," the distance marched about twenty-five miles. The sixth they traveled eight miles due east to Eagle Creek, grazed their stock a couple of hours, then continued east fifteen miles over "very rough country having to walk most of the time up and down rocky and steep hills"—sore punishment for cavalrymen! Total distance, twenty-three miles. But the next day was even worse, thirty miles north and north-easterly to a small tributary of the San Francisco River, Blue Creek perhaps. "About sundown scouts jumped a

197

party of Indians travelling and brought in three (3) animals. Hostiles hid in the brush and got away in the dark." The next day, September 8, the scouts went ahead and about an hour before sundown struck the enemy again "and had a running fight for about ten miles until about ten o'clock at night. Killed five Indians and captured four squaws, two children, and one Indian boy."

Not all of the killing was of fugitives, however. Hard-pressed by pursuit and wild to get away, the hostiles picked up what stock they could find and occasionally killed white people to get it. Hatch reported that twelve men "certainly" had been killed, perhaps more.[34] It is not clear whether these were slain by Pionsenay, who needed much stock to see him safely into Mexico, or by elements of the Warm Springs who accompanied him on the first leg of the frenzied flight, before swinging off to the northeast, but the supposition is that they were killed mainly by the Chiricahuas.

One of the women Hanna reported captured proved a good informant. She revealed details of the Indians' flight thus far, reporting that two were killed in the Ash Creek fight with Diablo's party. The trail of the group she had been with (not the main body of fleeing Mimbres) had divided, she said, part under Pionsenay making for Mexico, the rest, perhaps under Chiva, swinging northwest through incredibly rough mountains and lava beds, toward Fort Wingate. The trail was almost impossible to follow, "split up in every direction." On the ninth the command reached the San Francisco, and on the tenth moved down it a short distance, awaiting the tireless scouts who came in and "reported having killed seven (7) Indians and brought in six (6) captives, one squaw and five children." By the thirteenth the outfit, by easy marches, had reached the Gila again and turned down it toward base. The Mimbres had gotten away. So had Pionsenay.

John Rope, a White Mountain scout who was one of those chasing Victorio into New Mexico, told Grenville Goodwin the story of their lengthy expedition. He said that the Warm Springs had bolted when Victorio and his warriors ambushed and killed a chief of the White Mountain Apaches and his family. The chief earlier had slain one of Victorio's band, so their action had been one of normal revenge. Rope maintains that the Mimbres killed some whites in addition to those slain by Pionsenay's band. His account vividly describes the work of the Apache scouts from the viewpoint of one of them, and the rugged nature of such soldiering.[35]

Hanna's formal report of the operation estimated there were "about 50" in the fleeing band Tupper trailed eastward, adding substance to the theory that most of the Warm Springs had fled north, seeking to round the populous White Mountain *rancherías* by way of the west and north, and that the party Tupper followed included Pionsenay's Chiricahuas and a small group of Mimbres. He added that captured informants revealed Pionsenay was making for "a stronghold they claim to have in the Sierra Madre Mtns., somewhere in the vicinity of Janos, in Chihuahua." This, he added, "coincides with information I had previously received from Mexicans in Sonora. The latter claimed to have followed the Indians into this place and stated that they had been defeated by the Indians there."[36]

Rucker's typically terse report merely outlined the scout. Tupper's was more detailed. He agreed with Hanna that the captured informant reported Pionsenay was heading south, but added that the others, the Mimbres, "were trying to make their way to their old reservation or vicinity where they expected to live"—so did Victorio's band love their homeland and so were they lured by it; anything would be an improvement over the abysmal miseries of San Carlos! Tupper concluded that even his iron-tough scouts were about exhausted, "footsore, moccasins worn out, patched and repatched, many with sprained ankles," so he had been forced to head back. From Pueblo Viejo, on the Gila near present-day Safford, Sam Bowman took the San Carlos police back to the reservation, and Tupper returned to Camp Grant.[37]

First Lieutenant William H. Hugo out of Fort Bayard meanwhile had taken up Pionsenay's trail and chased that flying Chiricahua southward, deep into Mexico, pushing the band "so closely as to force them to kill nearly all their extra stock," and not abandoning the trail until thirty miles south of Janos, where it plunged into the Sierra Madre. On the way back, Hugo scoured the Hachita, Animas, Pyramid, and Burro ranges and was sure "no Indians have gone south" since Pionsenay.[38]

While ranking officers assured each other that the Warm Springs Apaches would soon be brought to heel,[39] those closer to the scene worked feverishly to bring this happy conclusion about. Hatch reported September 22 that he had been occupied "in securing the main thorough-fares, mines and ranches, and pushing out scouting parties." All the cavalry from Fort Union had been ordered to Ojo Caliente, he said, a company of cavalry from Wingate ordered south, infantry drawn from Union, Fort Craig and Fort Marcy at Santa Fe, sent to

Ojo Caliente "to guard . . . Indians if they surrender." Major Wade was busy at Bayard and Hatch himself headed for Ojo Caliente to inspect the situation first hand.[40]

It is apparent that the Mimbres desired above all to return to Ojo Caliente. They loved that open, well-grassed country with flowing water, springs and rills, and the forested mountains all about, but they dared not chance it until they had learned the temper of the whites and whether the determination persisted to return them to hated San Carlos, among their enemies. Troops were everywhere, even poking into the lava and pine wildernesses where neither roads nor settlements, mines nor armed posts had ever been established. Victorio's choice was plain: stay in their retreats and face ultimate destruction in one manner or another, or sound the enemy whites cautiously, to see what could be worked out. If there was a division of thought about this among the fugitive Mimbres, Victorio no doubt favored going it alone, and Loco was for diplomacy, for such were their natures. If so, this time Loco won.

Hatch, reaching Ojo Caliente on September 29, reported to Whitney that Victorio, Loco, and Chiva had contacted officers at Wingate and said they would bring their people in within four or five days perhaps. Hatch added that he proposed, if they did so, to bring them back to Ojo Caliente and ration them. He hoped such kind treatment would prove a lure so that "the balance who left San Carlos will also be brought in without an extended campaign."[41]

Whitney, still at the former agency, wrote his brother at Washington, D.C., asking that he sound the Indian commissioner and learn if he could what was planned for the Mimbres now. "I do not think these Indians can be kept at San Carlos without much trouble; it only remains to let them stay here [at Ojo Caliente], or move them to the Ind. Territory," he sighed.[42]

XVII
Uncertain Interlude

Inspector Vandever wired the commissioner September 29 that "one hundred and fifty Warm Spring Indians, who recently stampeded from San Carlos, reported near Wingate, wanting to surrender. I recommend that they be received, disarmed, and dismounted, and sent to Ft. Stanton reservation by the military, and there kept under surveillance until further orders."[1] Send them anywhere but the place they wanted to go—home. C. W. Holcomb, the acting commissioner, thought Vandever was right and suggested to the interior secretary that "the necessary instructions" be issued, but fortunately this notion was not then implemented. The fact was that no one had any idea what to do with these Apaches except move them somewhere.[2] Agent Fred C. Godfroy of the Mescaleros reported there had been "secret emissaries from the Warm Spring Indians" among his people, although he had been "unable to discover the object of their visits. I can only presume that they desire to obtain aid and men from this Agency," but there is no evidence that they succeeded, if that, indeed, was their purpose.[3]

Hatch, at Ojo Caliente, learning of the presence of at least part of Victorio's band near Wingate, hurried two Navaho scouts there with directions that "all Apaches who may come in and give themselves up, forward to this point, or inform them that if they come in here they will be taken and rationed. . . . It is extremely important not to have the Apaches affiliate with the Navajoes and live on the Navajo Reservation."[4] Not only might they disaffect their cousins, but, once scattered about that reservation, might not be concentrated again for a long time.

Kautz estimated October 4 that approximately 50 warriors were out,[5] among the more than 300 Mimbres who had fled San Carlos with Victorio, plus the Chiricahuas. His was probably an underestimate. Shaw's census, returned September 3, listed 181 "heads of families," presumably men of fighting age, although there were a few women, probably widows, listed. There is no way to tell how many of these actually were included, since, in Apache usage, sex can not always be determined from the name. Nevertheless, with perhaps 5 per cent of the Warm Springs warriors off prowling somewhere, it would seem that an estimate of fifty warriors was too low, even if 150 might be too high.

The next day Kautz reported that Loco "and 144 of the Warm Spring Indian renegades" had offered to surrender at Wingate.[6] This "offer" was made late in September when two Ojo Caliente chiefs cautiously approached the post. On September 29 Thomas V. Keam, or Keams, an English immigrant and a good Indian man,[7] with the chiefs and five Navahos, left the fort heading south across the lava beds and continuing for about ninety miles, as nearly as Keam could calculate. This would have taken them to the vicinity of the Mangas Mountains, just north of their old reservation of evil memory at Tularosa.

On October 3 they "arrived in the vicinity of their camp due south of Ojo del Gallo,[8] finding them scattered over the mountains," Keam reported. He sent out for them and by noon they had gathered, 179 men, women, and children. "I then held a council with and informed them my purpose was to take them all to Fort Wingate. The Chiefs had told me some of them intended to [go] back into the mountains. These I requested to step aside and separate themselves from the others at once, as I would be responsible only for those who went with me and conducted themselves right, and would have troops sent after those that left." His bluff worked. "The dissatisfied then came to me individually and said they were tired of running over the mountains and being bad men, that they would also go with me and remain with their chiefs. I then issued them what rations were furnished me, and instructed them not to leave the trail without first obtaining permission, which I found they complied with."

En route back, Keam held frequent councils with them, the Mimbres expressing their detestation for San Carlos, seeking Keam's influence in obtaining them a reserve elsewhere, offering to work—anything. Just no more concentration.[9]

Captain Horace Jewett, Fifteenth Infantry, commanding at Wingate, reported on the eighth that "Loco, Victorio, with 187 Apache Indians, are now encamped at West Springs on this reservation. I still have them in charge of Mr. Keam," whose official position was that of post interpreter. Jewett said he had had a council with the Mimbres "and think it better to keep them in their present status, and through them to influence some more to come in who are now wandering in the mountains." He believed it better not to send the Indians with troop escort to Ojo Caliente "until every effort is exhausted to obtain those that may be in this vicinity." He added that he had imposed stringent conditions upon them to avoid their mingling with the Navahos or soldiers. The Mimbres might be persuaded to stay at Wingate, or they would readily return to Ojo Caliente, "but under no circumstances will they willingly go to the San Carlos reservation."[10]

Sure enough, once the big band was settled near Wingate, fed, and allowed to remain, other Mimbres still in the mountains indicated that they, too, desired to come in. Jewett reported October 11 that he had "sent out two parties to bring in indians that had not surrendered themselves, one in charge of Mariana, Navajo Chief, the other in charge of Juan Navajo. Each of these Navajos has two Apaches with them. . . . They will be absent about 12 days and I expect that they will bring in with them 56 additional indians, that will make the total of 247 Warm Spring Indians that I expect to have as prisoners here in 12 days." Vandever arrived, Jewett reported, and, while leaving management of the prisoners to the officer, "seems to think, that their being taken back to Ojo Caliente, in the face of their being removed from there by the Government, displays a weakness on the part of the Government in yielding to the demands of the indians, that will establish a bad precedent in the management of Indian affairs. San Carlos and the Indian Territory seem to be the two points to one of which he thinks they should be sent."[11] Pope urged that the Indians be sent to Ojo Caliente, not permanently, "but it is a favorable point at which to assemble them," and from which they could be sent elsewhere as desired. Sheridan, noting that 233 had come in by October 30, asserted that "they will be sent to Ojo Caliente."[12]

Hatch informed Pope October 11 that the principal Mimbres chiefs had surrendered and he ordered them "under guard to Ojo Caliente," assigning what infantry was available, 25 men, for guard duty over them. He said he had done this because he could "probably gather the scattered bands, some of whom are in the Mescalero Agency at Stanton, others scattered in small bands hiding from the troops in adjacent mountains," most readily at their old home. The best estimates showed about 200 Indians collected near Wingate, leaving almost 100 unaccounted for of those who had fled, and about 250 missing from those originally taken to San Carlos, minus the few captured women and children picked up during their flight.[13] Some of the missing may have gone to Mexico with Pionsenay, but where were the others? Where but among the soaring mountains and breaks of the wilderness, journeying to their friends on other reservations or engaged in wholesome raiding in Mexico or somewhere else. Truly the concentration policy, as regards Victorio's people at least, was a fiasco. Still, Victorio himself and Loco, generously giving the Great Father another try, had come in, and that was heartening.

"When these Indians are in our hands," said Hatch, confidently, "we can devote our attention to the Chiricahuas and renegade Indians now living in the mountains of Sonora and Chihuahua. These Indians occupy these mountains as an asylum for raiding New Mexico and Arizona. . . . Our troops have already followed one party into these mountains, obliging these Indians to abandon their stock.[14] I see no other way of compelling these Indians to come to terms than by punishing them in their strongholds."[15] Imaginative as this idea was, it would not be undertaken until 1883, when General George Crook would lead a surprisingly successful expedition into the Sierra Madre to break up the recalcitrant bands.[16]

Pope messaged Chicago on October 18 that he had ordered the surrendered Mimbres dismounted and disarmed, no doubt unaware that this meant nothing to them, since they had cached their best arms at Ojo Caliente before removal. He directed their return to Ojo Caliente for the time being.

"The Indians have an invincible objection to returning to San Carlos Agency, preferring to go anywhere else. . . . I am not entirely sure about the good policy of sending them to the Stanton reservation," because it would make the Mescaleros difficult to control with the small garrison there.[17] He reassured superiors on the twenty-sixth that "I have no intention of recommending the retention of these Indians at Ojo Caliente" indefinitely, however.[18] Hatch, sensitive to how the wind blew, assured Pope October 28 that "I do not consider a reservation set aside exclusively for the Warm Spring Apaches necessary." He pointed out that it was "useless to send them to San Carlos . . . if they are not to be strictly watched and held there by force. It is less trouble for us to guard them in New Mexico and less expensive than to hunt them out of the mountains whenever they choose to leave the reservation." He thought that if the army must guard the tribe, the Mescalero Reservation might be preferable. "These Indians cannot be trusted and wherever they are sent must be watched closely."

The Indian Territory was a possibility, "but the same surveillance would be required there over them."[19]

Pope reviewed the possibilities and on November 5 listed the advantages and disadvantages of the various sites. He believed that it was impossible to keep them at San Carlos without constant guard, that if sent to Fort Sill they might prove a catalyst for troublesome elements among much larger bands of Indians, and concluded it perhaps would be best to send them to the Mescaleros, although this was not a perfect solution, either.[20] Nana already was on that reservation. Godfroy reported that "whilst a few young bucks, about 8 or 10, desire to join the Warm Spring Indians among whom they have some relatives, the majority are against any such move."[21] It would not be until Victorio was roaming free as guerrilla leader that many of the Mescaleros would slip away to join him.

By early November the bulk of the Mimbres was being moved from Wingate to Ojo Caliente, reaching there November 9 or 10.[22] While they could not know all the reasoning, arguments, suggestions, and abortive plans concerning them, they no doubt realized that the outlook was dreary. For some reason wholly beyond comprehension of the native mind, the whites considered them contumacious, when all they desired was to go home and live quietly in the old ways and remain as aloof as possible from their inscrutable hosts.

Whitney received them kindly, sought funds to clothe them properly, recommended that their relatives still at San Carlos be permitted to come to Ojo Caliente, and said he believed it was "impracticable to remove to Indian Territory until Spring."[23] A few months of grace, at any rate. Hatch bustled in to assess the situation. He reported that the 250 Indians present, disarmed and dismounted, were counted at a daily roll call and appeared tranquil. Wade, who met him thirty miles from Fort Bayard, believed that raids were likely during the winter, however, from that nucleus of Apaches below the line, and Hatch ordered another cavalry troop to report to the major for duty, just in case.[24]

By the end of November Whitney revealed that the number of captives had risen to 260, among them 52 warriors, "probably all the So. Apaches now in this part of the Territory." They told him that "they left the San Carlos reservation because they were abused by other Indians, being nearly all unarmed, that they had no intention of going on the war path, and were seeking a place of safety and went to the Navajo country, not daring to come here on account of the troops

205

etc. stationed at this point." He added that this was probably true, since "no troops were nearer them than several days march . . . until they surrendered voluntarily at Wingate," and that the Indians skirmished with by Tupper's troops, losing some killed, had been "Chiricahuas who struck south." The Warm Springs' sufferings, Whitney concluded, began because of "the Chiricahua Indians being allowed to come here at the time [the Chiricahua Reservation] was broken up."[25]

Dr. Whitney, being as confused as everyone else about the intentions of the Indian Bureau regarding Ojo Caliente, asked December 13 how long he would be needed there, since he had been directed to report to the Navaho agency.[26] The army, too, was becoming restless in the lack of any decision as to what was to be done with the Mimbres. Immediately after New Year's Day, Hatch formally inquired "if it is the intention to retain the Hot Spring Indians at Ojo Caliente," because, if so, they ought to go to work, and, if thus directed, needed tools.[27] Sheridan, passing the communication along to Washington, commented that "as the motives which control the Indian Bureau in their objection to these Indians remaining at the Warm Spring reservation are unknown to me, I can only say that . . . it would be best to let them remain at the Warm Springs and I so recommend."[28] Sherman growled that "I doubt the wisdom of collecting at Fort Sill too many Indians of different and incongruous types. We are unable to maintain garrisons of sufficient strength [now] to prevent Indians from breaking away in search of game or food." In addition, he added an argument he knew would be compelling: "It will cost a round sum of money, because they will have to be escorted nearly 1,000 miles."[29] Secretary of War George W. McCrary, reading this, asked Sherman to refer the subject back to Pope, who replied that "I entirely concur in the opinion of the General of the Army that it will be highly injudicious to send these Indians to Fort Sill," and Sheridan, always sensitive to opinions of his superior, agreed: "To send the Warm Spring Indians to the Indian Territory would in my opinion be the worst policy of which the Indian Bureau could be guilty."[30] But the views of the military did not carry undue weight with Indian officials. Commissioner Ezra A. Hayt, after summarizing such opinions, pointed out that since it had already been decided to sell public property at the agency, and would be inconvenient to alter such arrangements, "the necessary orders be given for their removal to Fort Sill."[31] Carl Schurz, secretary of the interior, concurred.[32]

Fortunately, however, other views prevailed and this notion ultimately was dropped. If Victorio, Loco, and the others knew of it, they must have heaved sighs of vast relief. They may even have seen the ultimate sale of their horses with equanimity;[33] they could get others, when they needed them. They knew all about picking up what horses and mules they required.

If the whites were uncertain about the future of these Indians, the Mimbres themselves were gloomy about the outlook. On January 9, Whitney wrote the commissioner that the Apaches "desire that some of their chiefs and head men be allowed to go to Washington and have a 'talk' with the 'Great Father' relative to the future disposition to be made of them, &c." The agent pointed out that "when the hardships they have undergone for the past eight months are considered, it seems but natural that they should desire an opportunity to make known their grievances and receive some assurances." He asked that he be allowed to bring a five-man delegation to the capital.[34] This was never done with the Mimbres, although the Chiricahuas and other bands were accorded the dubious privilege. Why should the Mimbres be brought to Washington to seek justice when justice had nothing to do with them, and no one yet was certain how to deal with such stubborn people?

The Apaches, with their strong family ties, began to fret about their relatives left at San Carlos, now supposedly numbering 143, including 22 men, 63 women, 29 boys, and 29 girls.[35] Their supplications gave the army another chance to point out that these Indians after all were Indian Bureau responsibilities, not those of the War Department. Keam messaged Captain Ambrose Eugene Hooker, commanding troops at Ojo Caliente, that the chiefs "have again in council anxiously requested me, to ask the Commanding General that measures be taken to restore to them those of their families still retained at San Carlos." He sent along a list of the family members there, including thirteen of Loco's people, but none for Victorio or Nana.[36]

Still the whites would decide nothing. Living under this mortal uncertainty, the Indians remained touchy, trying to cooperate but not knowing quite how to do it or whether their tentatives were productive. Their bare necessities were taken care of slowly, by bureaucratic processes,[37] but that was all. In late June, Pope again wondered "why the Indian Bureau has not before this resumed charge of these Indians,"[38] and Sheridan added a typical cavalryman's endorsement: "These indians have been held as prisoners since last October and the Indian Department should have resumed control of them long since.

Unless they are taken charge of soon by that Department I shall recommend that they be turned loose."[39] If anything would jar the bureaucrats into action, it was a threat such as this. The Interior Department complained it was not its fault that the military still had charge of the prisoners. It had long ago suggested that they be sent to Fort Sill, and hadn't the army objected to that? Hadn't the army insisted on taking them to Ojo Caliente pending disposition? "It is not the fault of this office that the question was not settled at a much earlier period," countered Commissioner Hayt,[40] to which Sherman bluntly replied that it made no difference whose fault it was. The question now was who would pay for their rations, clothing, and all that. "I advise these prisoners be turned loose with their own tribe," he concluded, "as I suppose they are no worse than the remainder of the tribe."[41]

It might be simplest to return them to San Carlos after all.

Preparations were commenced to that end, especially military arrangements, since the Indians could not be expected to go willingly.[42] On July 22, Sherman ordered that the Ojo Caliente prisoners "be turned over to authorized representative of the Indian Bureau and a guard sufficient to ensure their safe transit to San Carlos be furnished."[43] Not until August 31 could the paper work be completed and instructions issued to Colonel Hatch, however.[44]

Captain Charles Steelhammer, Fifteenth Infantry, commanding at Ojo Caliente, had been reporting on the remarkably cooperative attitude of the Mimbres, and their deep fears that they were to be removed. His dispatch is touching when one considers the plight of the people enmeshed in heartless bureaucratic processes determined to return them to the one place above all others they dreaded to go:

I found everything in most excellent condition. The Indians appear reduced to absolute obedience, yet no harshness is used. When I look back upon the condition of these Indians a year and a half ago and contrast it with their present, it seems almost incredible that such a long step in their civilization could have been taken in so short a time. Everything connected with the Indians at Ojo Caliente is done well and with that regularity, precision and temperance which breed obedience and contentment.

The Indians wished me to say that they are happier than they ever have been were it not that they feared removal and that if the Government would permit them to remain where they now are they would gladly accept only one-half of their present ration, provided the Government would in the beginning furnish a few necessary tools and teach them how to till the ground.

Steelhammer added that the decision to drive them back to San Carlos had not yet been communicated to them.[45]

Yet it may be that they were not quite so docile as they appeared to the captain, at least not all of them. Secretary of State William M. Evarts told Schurz on September 11 that the minister to Mexico had been informed of a raid "by Indians from South West New Mexico, into Chihuahua, which, it is alleged, resulted in the murder of about seventy Mexicans and the capture of a large number of horses and other property." If the report was accurate, it is probable that the raid was by Mimbres, since the other Chiricahuas most frequently fell upon Sonora. And even if this raid were not by Mimbres, some of them soon would descend with all their fury upon that country.[46]

Agent Hart asked for thirty-five Indian scouts to assist in the removal, along with twenty-five assigned to his agency in case of trouble during it.[47] On September 18 Hatch issued the fateful orders: "At the request of the Interior Department . . . the Warm Spring Indians, numbering 266 souls . . . will be returned to their proper agency at San Carlos." Captain Frank T. Bennett,[48] Ninth Cavalry, was assigned to escort them, and a thankless task it was. He arrived at Ojo Caliente in mid-October and called the Mimbres in so that the movement might commence. But "about eighty Indians about forty men balance women and children with three chiefs got scared and took to the mountains and are still out." Bennett was ordered to use "every means" to bring them back, the adjutant for the district informing Leavenworth that "force will be required" to collect and move them, although they would "go anywhere else" except San Carlos.

Bennett scoured the mountains, finding no one, and on the eighteenth brought his tired troopers back to the springs, reporting he could not catch the fugitives and suggesting that he take the 186 still remaining to San Carlos anyway. On October 20 he was directed to do so.[49] He finally left with 169 Indians, picked up four more en route, and started off.[50] It was a miserable trip.

Bennett had reached Ojo Caliente October 10, he said in a summary of his actions. He had kept his soldiers in ignorance of their ultimate destination lest word be leaked to the Apaches, but found that "the Indians had known for ten (10) days or more" of the transfer, though "nobody knew how they got their information." They had been camped one and one-half miles from the agency. Bennett called a council, trying by "every argument I could to make them as satisfied as possible to move," but found them "very much opposed to going."

Victorio and Toggi (perhaps this was Tomacito) had gone to Wingate on a four-day pass, and the Indians would make no decision until they returned. Bennett agreed to wait. The two returned on the twelfth and came in for a talk.

They made very strong protests against going, and said that they could not live at San Carlos, that the Indians there were unfriendly to them, were constantly abusing them, and imposing on them, and had even killed some of them, that the water there didn't agree with them, that their arms, and horses were taken away from them and given to unfriendly San Carlos Indians, that they were willing, and wanted to do as the the Government wanted them to, but asked, and implored that they either be left at Ojo Caliente or given some other good place away from San Carlos.

Bennett had his orders and could not negotiate. On October 14, Victorio said all right, since the Great Father willed it, they would go. They began to move down to the agency. Loco as well agreed and came in. Toggi, however, with two or three companions fled. Bennett ordered Lieutenant Henry Wright, who had much experience chasing and fighting Apaches, in pursuit, meanwhile putting Loco and another chief who had come in under guard. This may have precipitated the explosion.

A Mescalero woman who had requested that she be permitted to return to her people at Stanton was granted her wish. But instead she mounted a pony and galloped up the canyon toward the Indian camp, "hallooing at the top of her voice that the soldiers were coming, and going to kill them all, and for all to leave . . . and save their lives. A stampede followed."

Lieutenant Wright pushed them hard but, beyond picking up a woman and three children and sighting from a distance one warrior, never glimpsed the enemy. The next day he was sent out again and, in another direction, Second Lieutenant Charles W. Merritt, Ninth Cavalry, searched the mountains and grassy hills, but neither had any luck. On the evening of October 22, however, Sanchez, one of the Indians who had fled, cautiously slipped in and said that Victorio would bring in the fugitives within two days, if Bennett would assure their safety. He did so, but they failed to arrive, their wariness overcoming their desire to submit. Not only that, but seventeen members of Sanchez' following also escaped, "crawling out between the sentries I suppose as none of the sentries saw them going." Victorio went raiding south into Mexico, according to report.[51]

Bennett left Ojo Caliente October 25 with his 169 captives, including Loco, and his train of six six-mule wagons, bound for Fort Apache by way of the San Augustin Plains, old Fort Tularosa, and the White River. "During the night of Oct. 28th there was considerable excitement in camp caused by outside Indians who had escaped from Ojo Caliente hallooing to the Indians I had," but it was impossible to send out troops, since he needed every man to hold the Indians he had and their beef cattle and horses. Three men did surrender to him during the trip, probably because their families were prisoners. On November 6 Bennett camped on the south fork of the White River, two and one-half miles from Fort Apache.

It started to rain and snow, the storm continuing four days. "The Indians suffered terribly, and the roads were so muddy and bad that it was impossible to travel." The road to San Carlos became a morass; the wagons could not move. Bennett needed pack mules, but they could not be issued without authorization from the department commander at Whipple, and the telegraph lines were down, as they frequently were. Finally he received permission by courier on November 15. That same day Dan Ming,[52] veteran frontiersman and chief of police at San Carlos, arrived with thirty-eight Indian police and instructions from Agent Hart to transfer the prisoners. Bennett wired his district headquarters at Santa Fe for permission, but those lines were down, too. Finally on November 19 he resumed his trek to San Carlos, but shortly received the sought-for permission to turn his Mimbres over to Ming. With considerable pleasure he handed over twenty men, seventy-eight women, and about seventy-five children and put about for Fort Wingate, reaching there December 1 after a trip of 719 miles and various adventures.[53] The Apaches reached San Carlos November 25. Of the fugitives, however, fifty were men— warriors, already depredating.[54] A well-informed correspondent told readers of the *Arizona Star* of Loco's observation that the Mimbres "had as much love as other nations" for their own country, and while Loco and many women and children had been returned to San Carlos, "Victorio has kept his word, and the result is he has laid waste and stricken terror into the whole valley of the Rio Grande. . . . If Victorio's band had been left at Ojo Caliente . . . all would have been at peace where now terror reigns and mourning, in many households." He charged that the attempted removal had been "unjust" to Victorio and his people—surely a novel sentiment for a white southwesterner of that day to proclaim.[55]

211

Some of the fugitives, rather than lurk like wolves in the mountains or raid into Mexico, had made for the Mescalero Agency. Godfroy wired November 1 that a family of Hot Springs Indians wanted to come in and said others prowled about who also would come in if permitted.[56] One complicating factor was the Lincoln County "war" then raging; there were "so many desperadoes traveling around and so much trouble and fighting that the Indians are thoroughly frightened" and avoided surrender. His clerk, Morris J. Bernstein, had been shot down in the course of that swirling guerrilla embroglio.[57] Yet Godfroy managed to hold a council with Ojo Caliente Indians in early November. They numbered three men, two women, and a child, "none of whom appear to be persons of note," but who told him.

There were forty-nine men with their women and children hiding in the mountains, who want to come here and live, that the Government has not kept faith with them insomuch that Mr. Vincent Colyer and General O. O. Howard (we judge them to be these gentlemen by the description the Indians give) promised them when they went to Ojo Caliente they should live there always and be well provided for. They state that when they had a good agent he was taken away from them and an old man [Piper?] who, if he knew would not understand their wants was made Agent, and to use their own expression was "like an old woman." When they could stand the whims of this agent no longer he went off. They then had a young man (a doctor) [Ben Thomas] as Agent who they could not get along with. They were then placed in charge of the military and now are required to remove to San Carlos . . . and cannot live at peace with the Indians there. These Indians . . . beg hard to be allowed to come in here and promise that they will be peaceful and obedient.

Godfroy told them to bring their people in and he would write for instructions. "I respectfully recommend that their request be granted as half the battle is gained when the Indians are contented," he said.[58]

So on December 3 fifty-two came in, including eighteen men. They were "very destitute and much emaciated and beg to be allowed to remain here. . . . The principal men appear to be very intelligent and request me to ask you to have them visit Washington and lay their case before you in person." Among them were Nana, Sanchez, Raton, and Little Captain—but not Victorio, still off raiding. The commissioner approved Godfroy's recommendation and on the tenth five more young men came in, promising others would follow once it was apparent they might live with the Mescaleros in peace. "Thus far all of them have behaved very well," the agent acknowledged.

The decision to accept these Indians, however, was not communicated to the military, for shortly Second Lieutenant Millard Fillmore Goodwin handed Godfroy his orders to arrest the "fugitive" Ojo Calientes and dispatch them to San Carlos.[59] This threat came to nothing, but the situation would never become serene while the whites were in control, the Apaches became convinced. Yet on January 23 nine more Ojo Calientes came in, including Tomacito. There were now sixty-eight of them living with the Mescaleros.[60]

To confuse the issue, others had surrendered to Lieutenant Merritt, now in command at Ojo Caliente, and on his own authority he gave a pass to two of them with permission to visit Fort Stanton and bring back "all Southern Apache Indians that desire to come in and surrender themselves up as prisoners of war."[61] This fresh complication disturbed anew his harassed superiors, and he was called to task for usurpation of authority[62] until some time later when he explained that among his newly surrendered prisoners was the dreaded Victorio himself and told why he had taken the initiative he had. Hatch gleefully wired Leavenworth that Victorio "and twenty-two of the Warm Spring Apaches" had surrendered, that Merritt expected fifty or more to follow their example, and wondered "what disposition shall be made of these Indians? They say they prefer death to being sent back to San Carlos." In an endorsement Sheridan ominously noted that "similar information was communicated in reference to the tone and temper of the Cheyennes while they were prisoners at Fort Robinson."[63]

Merritt summarized what had happened at Ojo Caliente:

On the evening of [February] 7th, Victorio and twenty-two other Warm Spring Apache Indians . . . alarmed the camp by their hallooing. I immediately ordered the company to hold itself in readiness and sent for an interpreter (by name Kelley[64]). I went out to where Victorio was, and he said he wanted to have a talk with me. I appointed the next day. . . . On the following day I went out I should judge, at least one-half mile and sent up my interpreter to tell him I was ready for a talk, to come down.

He said he would not come down, for me to come up where he was. At that time he was on the highest mountain on the right as you leave Ojo Caliente.

The Lieutenant mulled the proposition over, conferred with Kelley, since Victorio had insisted they come without arms and without escort. But it was talk or no surrender, so Merritt and Kelley climbed the mountain and met the feared Apache chief. Merritt

213

told him what I would do if he came in and gave himself up as a prisoner of war (I would here state that it would have taken a Regiment of Cavalry to have captured him and his band for there were only a few present, the remainder of the his band, and horses, were some eight or ten miles away at that time). . . . He asked me if he could send to Stanton Reservation and tell his other people to come in. I asked him how many he wanted to go and for how long. He said two for fifteen days. I said I would give him a pass, but did not want the Indians to be over the time specified in the pass and that they should not molest anyone while away. They left and . . . were very prompt to return at the very hour. . . .

The depradations which have been committed on the River and the surrounding country have been done by Nanna and his band . . . for I have information from a man . . . who lost fifteen horses and followed their trail into the camp of Nanna, who is on the Stanton Reservation, and recaptured them. Nanna says that Victorio was never there but went direct from here to Old Mexico with the twenty-two who came in with him, and I am convinced myself from the appearance of Victorio and his party and from the stock etc. they have in their possession they have been to Old Mexico. . . .

Victorio would not have stayed here one hour if I had not given him permission to send to Stanton for Nanna and his band, for it was understood by Nanna and his party that Victorio had gone to Old Mexico to get horses and ammunition for the whole party, for a summer's campaign. Nanna was only waiting for Victorio to get back and then he was to join Victorio from Stanton Reservation. . . . In my opinion if those Indians are allowed to come from Stanton Reservation there will be no trouble in the future and less in moving them. If they are not allowed to come in here openly and surrender as prisoners of war, there is nothing to prevent them visiting Victorio secretly, and in going and coming committing depredations and thereby making the Indians here restless and uneasy. It is the wish of the majority to come in here and not stop or stay at Stanton Reservation.[65]

Upon reading Merritt's well-reasoned explanation, Hatch messaged Pope that "I believe his action should be approved" after all, and Pope concurred. Hatch sourly added that "if it is the intention to remove this band" to San Carlos, "I respectfully ask that one of the companies of Arizona Indian Scouts be sent for them. . . . We may as well accept the fact that many of these Indians must be killed."[66]

With this blunt warning, Schurz gave in and on March 7 told the secretary of war that the Ojo Calientes might, after all, be turned over to Samuel A. Russell, newly appointed agent at the Mescalero Reservation, although Russell protested that the Mimbres were "a wild troublesome people" whom he would not accept without direct orders to do so. It is only fair to add that he later changed his mind about their natures. Initially he feared that they "would add largely to the troublesome element" among the Mescaleros if they came and said he would *very much* prefer not to receive them at this agency."[67] Commissioner Hayt sought to calm his fears, noting that they had proven generally peaceable when fairly treated "but they had a very strong aversion to being placed upon the San Carlos reservation. . . . This feeling was not without cause; they do not affiliate well with [those] Indians . . . and are friendly with yours. . . . It is believed you will have no trouble with them, and will therefore receive and take charge of all who may find their way to the agency or who may be delivered to you by the military."[68]

But now Victorio complicated matters afresh.

When told by Lieutenant Merritt that it had been decided to transfer his band from Ojo Caliente to Stanton, he may have misunderstood and thought that, instead of to the Mescaleros, he was to be returned to the hated San Carlos. He shouted that "he would die first!" With a whoop he gathered his people and plunged once more into the wilderness, heading north this time into the forested San Mateos.

"I shall at once send Cavalry company from Union and Indian Scouts to Ojo Caliente and with the Cavalry now there hunt up and endeavor to capture these Indians before they begin to commit depredations," sighed Hatch. "It is reported several renegades from San Carlos are in the mountains with Victoria."[69] He grimly added later that when, and if, he captured them he would turn the whole band over for delivery to San Carlos where they would "give us less trouble than to guard them at the Mescalero Agency." Besides, San Carlos was out of his district.

Hatch had spoken, however, without referring the matter to the Indian authorities, who acidly pointed out that when they had desired to return the Apaches to San Carlos, the military objected, and when they tried to accord their views with the army's and send them to Mescalero, the soldiers agreed but the Indians objected, whereafter the army now objected as well and had returned once more to the San Carlos idea. This time the Indian authorities were holding firm; when captured, Victorio must go to Stanton.[70] First, though, he must be taken.

Hatch visited the Mescalero Reservation on May 12, met Nana and Tomas, or Tomacito, whom he found "contented and willingly planting small crops of corn." He believed "they might induce Victoria

215

and his band . . . to come in" so he dispatched Tomacito with five runners into the San Mateo Mountains, looking for him, "probably too late." Already Victorio once more was depredating toward Mexico, with other dissatisfied warriors from San Carlos and elsewhere, although "fortunately" they were encumbered with women and children, some lately swept off from the Arizona reserve. This might encourage them to come in, a great saving to the government, if it could be brought about.[71]

Victorio apparently had fled west, ravaging as he went, before turning south. Four herders were killed and fifteen mules taken near Silver City, two other men slain in southern New Mexico, and troops ordered into the field from an arc of posts: Bayard, Bowie, Wingate, Grant, and others.[72] Some thought they had chased the wily chief into Old Mexico, but in truth no one knew where he was. Second Lieutenant Guy Howard, Twelfth Infantry, picked up scouts at San Carlos, and pursued what he thought were the Mimbres across the San Francisco River and sixty miles up over the Mogollon Mountains into New Mexico, forcing them to abandon animals and considerable property.[73] There Captain Charles D. Beyer, Ninth Cavalry, with Company C and part of Company I, dashed in upon the trail and chased the fleeing fugitives into the Black Range to the east, where he had a sharp fight on May 29, capturing their camp, supplies, and all their animals. He wounded five Indians, two fatally, and lost one man killed, two wounded, and three horses. He thought he had turned the Indians toward Old Mexico, perhaps to recoup their stock losses, but the Black Range must still be scoured. Six companies of the Ninth Cavalry moved toward the mountains from various posts to hunt them out if any were still there.[74]

Wherever they had gone, word reached them that the decision had been not to transfer them to San Carlos after all, but probably to the Mescaleros. On June 24, Victorio sent a runner from the Black Range to the agency across the Río Grande. Russell assured the courier of "my friendly feelings" and sent word to Victorio that if he would bring in his band "they should be protected and cared for." On June 30, Victorio at last did come in with twelve warriors, but they were "very suspicious and fearful of being deceived; begged me to be candid with them and that if I intended to send them to San Carlos to tell them so now." Russell reassured them, told them that if they would "be good Indians," stay on the reservation, they would "have no more trouble."

216

"They then urged me in the strongest manner possible to try and get their families here," whereupon Russell most earnestly asked the commissioner to arrange this, "believing that it will be the end of all the long and serious trouble with the Warm Spring Indians." With gifts Victorio and his party left "in good spirits," to bring in their people.[75]

Other Ojo Calientes already in also had urged the agent to send for their families "and (as white men often do) give as a reason for drinking" the fact that they were alone.[76]

Victorio's surrender created problems, although perhaps not major ones. It aroused a natural jealousy between the Ojo Calientes and Mescaleros and it caused uneasiness on the part of nearby white settlers who feared the noted war leader might stir up antiwhite sentiment. Russell asked for a slight increase in patrols about the reservation, but took no other precautions.[77] He said that Victorio had told him frankly that he wanted "peace and quiet, has pledged himself to obey my wishes in everything, and only asks that he should not be sent to San Carlos. I do not anticipate any necessity for troops here more than about thirty days—perhaps sixty days."[78] By late July Russell estimated he had 145 Ojo Calientes on his reserve.[79]

Then, on the thirtieth, he wired the commissioner a most ominous question, one that revealed a matter that was to climax Victorio's life, end peace in the Southwest, bring on war, destruction, endless campaigns—and disaster for the Mimbres Apaches and their disintegration as a people.

"Three indictments have been found against Victoria in Grant County, N.M., two for horse stealing and one for murder. There is little if any doubt but an effort will be made to arrest him," reported Russell. He explained that he had offered Victorio "protection" if he would come in. Hatch had given the same assurance. But now, in case civil authorities showed up with the warrants, what was he to do?[80]

In some way Russell's discovery about the warrants was communicated to Victorio, already suspicious, with much reason to be distrustful of white promises, and ready to bolt. Not being aware of Victorio's knowledge, Russell was flabbergasted when the Mimbres chief broke out for the last time. It was long before the agent learned the true reason.

XVIII
War!

(Telegram)

MESCALERO AGENCY, TO COMMISSIONER INDIAN AFFAIRS, WASHINGTON, D.C. AUG. 21ST 1879. WARM SPRING INDIANS HAVE ALL LEFT THIS RESERVATION GOING WEST. WILL PROBABLY TRY TO INTERCEPT THOSE SUPPOSED TO BE ON THE WAY FROM SAN CARLOS. HAVE INFORMED THE MILITARY.

RUSSELL, AGENT.[1]

Thus was signaled the final break of Victorio with the whites who sought to take over his homeland. So began his *émeute*, his last, wild fight against "progress," or what was considered that by the general population of that day, and too often of this. Victorio was an atavist, an anachronism. He would not submit to the disintegration of his people and therefore he must be destroyed. Already he had been driven to the ragged edge of endurance; now he must perish. But Victorio would contest that implacable verdict. While he drew breath he would continue his gallant, hopeless struggle. Dimly he had come to realize he could never, never, fully conciliate the relentless whites, so cruel and yet frequently so kind, but so unaware of the desirability of the variations of men and cultures, seeking in all things conformation to their own particular mores and even more to their skin color and garbled ancestry; so filled with primeval arrogance and those material lusts that propel human beings into conflict one with another—those things, surely, and their blindness, but mostly their simple lack of empathy. Lieutenant Charles B. Gatewood, who, as few others, "knew all the circumstances, always said that any man of discretion, empowered to adjust Victorio's well-founded claims, could have prevented the bloody and disastrous outbreak of 1879."[2] But there was no such man, at least in a position of authority.

Now Victorio led his people straight as an arrow for the Black Range.

Agent Russell on August 22 reaffirmed the break, adding, "I can-

218

not tell certainly what prompted this movement, but have no doubt
it was through the influence of Victoria. You will not be more surprised than I was, when I became satisfied that they had gone. They
had been repeatedly assured that their families would be here before
winter, and appeared delighted at the prospect." He speculated about
the probable cause of their flight.

"About four weeks ago, one of Victoria's party killed a Mescalero
Indian. An investigation of this satisfied me, *and the Mescaleros*,
that it was clearly a case of self-defense and no trouble grew out of it.
About two weeks since another of his men, when drunk, killed a
Mescalero woman, and bid defiance to Mescaleros and every body
else. . . . This created some feeling (very naturally) among the Mescaleros, but so far as I could hear no *threats*." Russell added that he
recently had talked with Victorio and his party, insisting that they
must be industrious and peaceful, and they had reassured him. "While
I am satisfied that there is not a more turbulent tribe of Indians in
the United States . . . I frankly admit my disappointment and regret
for this exodus."[3]

Not for two months did Russell learn the true reason for the outbreak, a cause which seems to us too trivial to have provoked so much
bloodshed and expense, conflict and tragedy, but nonetheless a tiny
hinge of history. He wrote the commissioner on October 18 that "in
a conversation with Mr. [Albert J.] Fountain, an attorney of Mesilla,
N.M., I learned . . . the true reason why Victoria left the reservation. . . .

"Victoria heard of the indictment against him in Grant County,
or as they say, that *a paper* was out against him. *Three days* afterward Judge [*Warren*] *Bristol*, Mr. Fountain, prosecuting atty. and
others passed through this reservation (passed the agency) to a point
some eighteen miles east of this Agency on a pleasure excursion (hunting & fishing). The Indians were acquainted with those persons, knew
their official positions, and convinced their visit [had a connection
with] 'this paper' referred to, and believed that Victoria (and perhaps his people) were to be arrested," fled from white control forever.[4]

Victorio, who is never known to have slain a white American from
the time his people first came upon a reservation at Cañada Alamosa
until this explosion, knew well that it would be impossible for an
Indian to receive a fair trial in southwestern white courts, and may
have believed that his arrest would mean his execution or prolonged

confinement—to an Apache an equivalent fate. Or perhaps he did not actually comprehend the legal process but understood that the paper signaled an intent by his enemies to seize him, and that was enough. Very likely he was not guilty of the specified charge; perhaps it had been Pionsenay who had done those things, but Victorio was well known to the whites; *ergo*, it must have been he or, at any rate, he probably had committed other crimes as bad. The Indians knew from long experience that so reasoned the whites. Thus, escape and war had been the only possible answers.

Among the ironies were the facts that the families of his people were at that moment being removed from San Carlos to the Mescalero Reserve, and that a plan finally had been proposed to move the Mimbres back to Ojo Caliente where all of them might have been collected permanently in their old homeland.[5] Had this been suggested one month earlier, or at any time before that, the catastrophe might have been averted. Colonel Hatch agreed that this move might be accomplished readily. The old agency was intact, the lands not yet overrun by squatters, and, despite assertions by previous agents to the contrary, the officer believed there was "agricultural land sufficient to sustain 1,000 Indians, and [enough] grazing [for] 200,000 head of sheep and 25,000 head of cattle" in the vicinity.[6]

Second Lieutenant George Washington Smith, Ninth Cavalry, holding the lowest rank of his life but a veteran Indian fighter who would die within two years at the hand of Nana, chased Victorio to the Río Grande but could not catch him. No one could come up with Victorio when he was on guard.[7]

Russell, of course, was exasperated. "On leaving the Reservation the Warm Spring Indians had stolen ten or twelve horses at Three Rivers," he informed the commissioner. "The Warm Spring Indians neither *respect* nor *fear* the Military and it would do them good to be severely *thrashed*, if such a thing is possible. It seems not to have been heretofore. It appears to me that the frequent *'trailing'* of these Indians by the Military, without (so far as I know) ever catching any only encourages them. They learn to feel that they can escape them."[8] However harsh his criticism of the army, it was but a sampling of what that service would endure for the next year from the civilian press and populace.

Victorio and Nana, who had fled the Mescalero reserve with him, began their work at once, sweeping in upon the herd of Captain Ambrose Hooker's Company E, Ninth Cavalry, at Ojo Caliente, killing

Standing like a sentinel, a rock-adobe wall marks the site of old Fort Cummings, long an important post in the Mimbres country.

Ojo Caliente, site of the agency and post that figured largely in Mimbres Apache affairs during the 1870's. Through the cleft in the center background runs the Alamosa River and the trail to former Cañada Alamosa, Fort Craig, and Fort McRae.

Fort Tularosa, to which the Mimbres were removed from Ojo Caliente for two miserable years, was on this flat tract. Rubbish of the fort and agency litters the ground.

Geronimo, who fled from an action in southern New Mexico to the Ojo Caliente reservation, precipitating the removal of the Mimbres to San Carlos and the long chain of events that led to Victorio's final guerrilla campaign. The photograph was taken in 1886 by Camillus S. Fly at Tombstone.

Mariana, Navaho leader, who was instrumental in getting Mimbres who had bolted from San Carlos to surrender at Wingate.

Courtesy Ben Wittich Collection, Museum of Santa Fe

Major Albert Payson Morrow, key commander against Victorio's Apaches, in a contemporary photograph.

Courtesy National Archives

Major General Augustus P. Blocksom, who as a second lieutenant led scouts against Victorio and saw arduous service in New Mexico, 1879, and Arizona, 1880.

From Third Cavalry

Lieutenant Charles B. Gatewood, who commanded Indian scouts against Victorio and fought that Indian repeatedly.

Courtesy National Archives

Company A, Apache Indian Scouts, Lieutenant Charles B. Gatewood in center, just returned from a long campaign against Victorio, 1880.

Courtesy Gatewood Collection, Arizona Pioneers Historical Society

James A. Maney, who as commanding officer of Company A, Apache Indian Scouts, actively chased Victorio for many months.

Courtesy National Archives

Colonel Edward Hatch, commanding Ninth Cavalry during the campaign against Victorio, 1879–80.

Courtesy National Archives

Joaquín Terrazas, who destroyed Victorio at Tres Castillos. This picture was made about 1900.

Courtesy Juan Manuel Terrazas

Poet-scout Jack Crawford headed a three-man mission that penetrated Mexico to within a mile of Victorio's hostile camp, but had to abort the effort to bring the Apaches in when his guides refused to go on.

Courtesy Mrs. Buford Richardson

Carrizal, Chihuahua, home community of the Mexicans massacred by Victorio in 1879.

Candelaría Range in northern Chihuahua was Victorio's major Mexican base during his years of raids and warfare. The site of a horrible double massacre of Mexicans by Victorio's warriors is on the far (north) side. The El Paso–Chihuahua road and railroad are visible to the lower right.

Aerial photograph by the author

Diorama, "Grierson at Quitman Canyon," in the Fort Davis National Historical Site Museum depicts the colonel's fight for life atop Devil Ridge in August, 1880, against Victorio's warriors, who considerably outnumbered the small army detachment.

Courtesy National Park Service

This is the view that Colonel Terrazas had from atop the north peak of Tres Castillos. The south hill, at right, is where the climactic battle took place.

Tres Castillos, from the east looking west. Victorio's people made their last stand on the hill to the left. The hill to the extreme right is the one Terrazas climbed to spot the approach of the hostiles.

Cave at the north end of the south hill of Tres Castillos. According to Colonel Terrazas, two Apaches hid here and fired upon Mexican attackers until the Apaches were slain. The cave is just large enough for two men to lie in and goes back about ten feet.

Cerro Mata Ortiz, a peak about fifteen miles north of Galeana, Chihua-hua, where Juan Mata Ortiz was trapped and slain by Apaches under Juh and Geronimo.

all the guard, numbering five soldiers and three civilians, and running off sixty-eight horses and mules, including the captain's personal mount. The raiders were estimated to number about forty.[9] A few days later Major Morrow, commanding at Fort Bayard, reported there had been another disastrous clash near McEver's ranch,[10] south of Hillsboro, a mining camp west of the Río Grande. "We had a five hour fight with all of one hundred Indians," the officer reported. "We have ten killed and several wounded. All our stock is gone. I sent every available soldier out."[11]

The number of hostiles was not certainly known. Hatch's head-quarters informed Pope that Victorio had forty-three men when he left the Mescalero Reservation, was reported to have forty when he wiped out Hooker's guard at Ojo Caliente, and Morrow estimated he had one hundred men at the McEver's ranch fight. Since "no information of other Indians being out," he might have been joined by Southern Chiricahuas and other warriors from Mexico, or the estimates could have been wrong.[12] Troops had been pulled in from everywhere to meet the threat. Gatewood, who during the coming six or seven years would see more arduous field duty against the Apaches than perhaps any other officer, was ordered in from Arizona with his Apache scouts.[13]

The racket of battle was all but drowned out by the howls of civilians across southwestern New Mexico, each certain he had been abandoned and was surrounded by murderous warriors. Major General Lewis Wallace, the governor,[14] wired Washington, "Indians committing horrible atrocities in Grant County. Not enough regular troops. Please give me federal authority to put three or four companies Volunteers in the field."[15] George McCrary, secretary of war, soothingly replied, "the Department is without any information as to nature of outbreak or number of hostiles. . . . I am compelled to decline giving orders to raise volunteers."[16] Wallace should have known better. Grim experience in the Southwest had shown abundantly that volunteers might verbally wreak the utmost devastation among the hostiles, but in practice they were lucky if they ever saw any—or unlucky, as the case might be. For example, one company of New Mexico militia accompanied Morrow's command on a later occasion into the San Andres Mountains, trailing hostiles. But they "left on the eve of going into action, stating their horses had broken down though they had marched on fresh horses one day, a less distance than the troops," commented Hatch. "It is reasonable to draw another

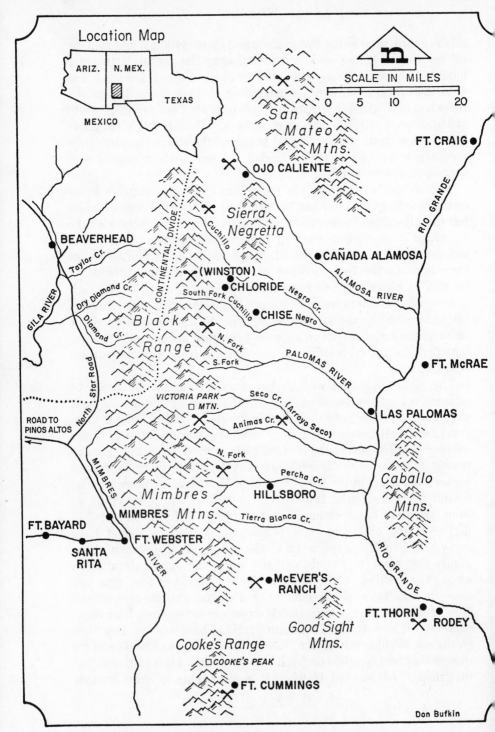

East Face of Black Range, or Mimbres Mountains

conclusion. That was the last ever seen of them. I have therefore concluded we can look for little or no assistance from them."[17] His judgment was shared by most army regulars.

Not all the depredations were committed north of the border, although it appeared as yet that the Mimbres were not swinging south in any great strength. Consul Louis H. Scott at Chihuahua City sent in a petition from former Governor Luis Terrazas, one of the major landholders and stock raisers in Chihuahua state, complaining of specific raids and the inability of his people to confront them so long as the raiders were supplied in the United States. It should also be mentioned that many southwesterners believed that the Apaches were armed and supplied by unscrupulous Mexican traders south of the line. No one knew which was the fact, though probably both charges contained elements of truth. Scott's communication cited raids from the northeast by Mescaleros, and from the west by Southern Apaches led by Juh, an Indian who "has a terribly bad reputation."[18]

But if Victorio had not dipped into Mexico, he continued to build the dread of his name north of the border. On September 23 Morrow informed Hatch:

[First Lieutenant Byron] Dawson, [Lieutenant] Wright and [Second Lieutenant Matthias W.] Day, struck Victoria's trail at head of Sierra Blanca Cañon two days old on sixteenth. Followed it to head of Las Animas River, where on the eighteenth they run upon the Indians who held a strong position. Troops were virtually caught in a trap. Capt. Hooker[19] with his company, and [First Lieutenant William H.] Hugo's came up and took part in the fight. After fighting all day the troops were compelled to withdraw under cover of darkness with a loss of five men killed and one wounded, and thirty-two horses killed and six wounded. I have sent [Second Lieutenant Augustus Perry] Blocksom and Gatewood with their Apache scouts, and [Second Lieutenant Robert T.] Emmet with his Navajoes to the scene of action, and follow immediately myself with all available men of the post. My cavalry will be principally dismounted.... Victoria is said to have about one hundred and forty men. Two Navajo Indians and one citizen were killed in the fight.[20]

So states the dry initial report, but the event was more lively than Morrow indicated.

The Animas River, or creek, flows from the Continental Divide in the Black Range eastward toward the Río Grande. Its headwaters feather out into a number of creeks and bottoms at an elevation of around seven thousand feet. It was in this maze of canyons that the fight occurred, forty or fifty miles southwest of Cañada Alamosa. In his later summary, Major Morrow said that, when advised that the Mimbres had broken out, he sent troops under Lieutenant Wright to the Socorro Mountains, west of the town of Socorro; Captain Beyer to the Caballo Mountains, east of the Río Grande from present-day Truth or Consequences, and troops under Lieutenant Hugo toward Ojo Caliente. When he heard that Hooker had lost his horses, he sent a courier after Beyer, pulling him back to the west side of the river, and ordered him to pick up the trail of the raiders. He sent Captain Dawson and Lieutenant Day to McEver's ranch to contact Beyer, and pulled Wright in from his fruitless search of the Socorros, directing him, too, to report to Dawson at McEver's.

Dawson already had found and was pursuing Victorio's trail, however, and Beyer, now reinforced, followed him up, but Dawson fell into the Indian ambush, and a strong trap it was. Dawson later escorted Morrow over the site.

"I will merely state that it took me one hour and twenty minutes to ascend to the Indian camp and under fire it would have been an *absolute impossibility* for *any* number of men to have taken the position by storm as it was as much as my command could do to take it without having any body on top to shoot at us," Morrow reported. He said that Dawson would have been annihilated but for the timely arrival of Beyer and that, in pulling the whole command out, Beyer "did the only thing that could have been done under the circumstances."[21]

Late in the fight, when the troops were ordered to withdraw as best they could, Lieutenant Day refused to leave his wounded, advanced alone against hot opposition six hundred feet and "carried a disabled soldier away under a heavy fire, for which offense the commanding officer, Byer [Beyer], wanted to have him tried by court martial, and for which the Congress of the United States gave him a gold medal."[22] A Dr. Kennon, who accompanied the troops as volunteer medical officer, scanned the scene with field glasses when they were shot out of his hands, although he was uninjured. The Apaches captured the hospital train and the personal baggage of most of the officers, wrote a correspondent. Truly this was a resounding triumph for Victorio, who had yet to taste defeat.

Pope reassured Sheridan on the twenty-sixth that there were "plenty of troops . . . now out," that he doubted there would be reports of any more depredations, and that Victorio "will be sure, I think, to be caught."[23] However Pope rated in military ability, he scored low for prognostication. Morrow could have enlightened him about the prospects, for the major was becoming instructed in the rugged impossibility of striking Victorio if the Apache did not wish to be caught. He told of his difficulties in his lengthy report, Gatewood elaborated upon it in his reminiscences, and while Victorio never was quoted on the matter in the public prints, he must have laughed with a flash of white teeth in his brown face when he thought about it.[24]

At Bayard, upon hearing on September 22 of the Dawson-Beyer fight, Morrow mustered his forces, numbering 191 enlisted men, 6 officers and 36 scouts, of whom the last and 73 soldiers were dismounted, and headed east. He camped the first night at Thompson's ranch on the Mimbres. From there he sent Gatewood and Blocksom with the scouts looping through the Black Range toward its eastern face, searching for the *rancherías* of the hostiles. Gatewood wrote that the scouts, equipped with pack mules, "proceeded straight across the Mimbres Mountains," while Morrow's soldiers, accompanied by vehicles, had to take "the wagon road around by old Fort Cummings" to McEver's ranch and back up Dawson as he moved once more to find and attack Victorio's camp. If everything were timed correctly, the Gatewood-Blocksom scouts would come in on the camp from the west while the soldiers attacked from below, and the Apaches would be caught in a vise. But Victorio was too sharp for such a clumsy trap. "The movement was executed satisfactorily, but the enemy was no longer there, having been gone about three days," Morrow glumly reported.

He now commenced the supremely difficult feat of trailing and occasionally skirmishing with the acrobatic enemy, campaigning along the all but untraversable eastern face of the Black Range, working northerly, plunging into the mountains here and there, trying to overrun some discovered camp. The slow-moving troops never were an equal match for the nimble Apaches, but it was a good lesson for the major. As Crook once pointed out, one might frequently engage in "battles" with the Apaches and never see one, only the puffs of smoke revealing their location. But for the scouts, the hunt would have been futile.

Blocksom's Apaches picked up a trail four miles north of McEver's ranch in the Arroyo Seco,[25] but as the courier arrived about dark, Morrow went into camp. Next morning he ordered the dismounted men, now eighty-three in number, to start out under First Lieutenant

Ballard Smith Humphrey, while he inspected the site of the late engagement with Dawson as guide. The following day, Sunday, he came upon Blocksom's horses and pack mules under guard a dozen miles northeast of Arroyo Seco. He learned that the lieutenant with the scouts had moved out at 1:00 A.M., working cautiously in toward the mountains, and, under cover of thick darkness, had surrounded another of Victorio's camps. Same result. "The Indians had decamped," reported Morrow. Gatewood graphically describes the hard scouting necessary to find and keep the hostiles' trail, living on tough mule meat and bacon, slopping through mud and rain much of the time and alternately suffering from thirst, lying over "in narrow gorges and cañons" in the daylight hours, daring to build only tiny fires lest smoke or glow warn the enemy, all the time scrambling over terrain of incredible ruggedness.

On Monday, the twenty-ninth, the scouts once more worked along the trail, Morrow with the command following

in the direction of the Cuchillo Negro [Creek]. After marching over very rough country, a distance of 8 miles, found our scouts awaiting us with the information that they had found the hostiles and unfortunately for us, had been seen by them. Although it was 5 P.M. I ordered an immediate attack, knowing that Victoria would not wait until morning. The Indian scouts under Blocksom and Gatewood rushed immediately to the assault and got possession of the hostile camp. The troops followed under fire from the surrounding hills. The firing was kept up until after ten o'clock when I ordered the command to go into camp. No one was hurt on our side, in this affair. Three hostiles were killed and left in their camp. Fifteen horses saddled and packed and a lot of loose stock captured.

Morrow reported that among the sixty horses and mules taken were a dozen of Captain Hooker's stolen animals,[26] but Victorio could readily seize more. In passing along Morrow's report Hatch opined that Victorio "is determined to fight it out on this line, and so is Morrow," and that he had "no fear for final result," though it might be a long time coming.[27]

Describing this fight, Gatewood reported that the scouts had

located Mr. Victorio and his "outfit" encamped in a deep cañon. They saw each other about the same time, and the fun began. The firing, of course, brought up those in rear "double quick." From the small number of scouts first seen, the hostiles thought themselves already the victors and became quite saucy and facetious, daring them to come closer, and even inviting them them to supper. My first sergeant, Dick, answered "We are coming," and when old Vic's braves saw forty odd scouts and many soldiers, white and colored, come tumbling down the side of the cañon into their camp, they stayed not on the order of their going out of it. . . . Result: two bucks and a squaw on their side; on our side, nothing. They managed to drive their stock away with them, and as they carry very little plunder on the warpath, their camp was not worth much after we got it.

At daybreak next morning, a vedette, or mounted guard, on a bluff overlooking the camp was killed and the hostiles began a hot fire, first on the scouts camped about a mile above the main body, then upon the Morrow camp itself. The canyon where the scouts were bivouacked, wrote Gatewood, "was perhaps 800 feet deep, with steep and rocky sides covered with pine, oak and heavy underbrush. The other camp [Morrow's] was in a sharp bend of the cañon lower down." After a single shot there came a volley, "suddenly increasing into more shots and more volleys, with shouts of command, all doubled and trebled in reverberations up the valley, until it was one roar of pandemonium that was enough to set a nervous person wild. . . ." Morrow describes the action, beginning with the dawn attack and continuing intermittently through the day, as a pursuit by the scouts and soldiers of "retreating hostiles" who, as "soon as driven from one position seeking another in rear" until, at 3:00 P.M., he ordered the command to saddle up and move over to the head of the Cuchillo Negro, where there was water. Gatewood's version is livelier and makes clear that the hostiles ran the troops out of the Black Range in a daylong fight:

Having gotten our men under arms, Blocksom sent me with twenty men on foot to report to Colonel Morrow [down the creek a mile] as soon as possible, and away we went. More noise and more excitement, until I didn't believe there was a sane man in the country, except the Corporal, who coolly informed me after awhile that I was sitting on the wrong side of a rock to be safe from cross-fire. Up to that time, it seemed to me, we would all be killed for every man had lost his head, and was yelling with all his might and shooting in the air. But once anchored on the right side of the rock, I was astonished to see how cool they were, and how steady was their aim, some even laughing and joking. . . . We were above Morrow's camp on the inner side of the bend of the cañon, while the enemy held the outer side. . . . Nothing but puffs of smoke could be seen over there, at least by me."

Some scouts, working country four or five miles distant, had heard the firing and, although the terrain was "exceedingly rough," swung in on the rear of the assailants within an hour. Morrow advanced a line of troopers up the canyon opposite Gatewood's party, Blocksom swung in on the left, and with the scouts they drove the enemy to higher ground where "it was useless to try to follow," Gatewood believed. The hostiles waved breech clouts and made other gestures of derision at their enemy. The command, when starting its withdrawal, was harassed all of the way out of the mountains.

"Getting the animals out of this cañon was no easy matter," Gatewood recalled. "The trail we came in on was too steep" to go out by, "and a new one had to be broken." Blocksom took the advance, Lieutenant Wright the rear, and Gatewood was in the center, the scouts serving as flankers. A terrified surgeon first accompanied Blocksom and, when the advance was fired upon, dashed back to Wright; when that element was struck, he sought safety with Gatewood and, when that lanky officer came under fire, decided to leave the army and go into private practice if he ever escaped. He did.

Gatewood makes clear that the column was under sporadic fire all the way to the Cuchillo Negro. The hostiles no doubt concluded they had routed the troops; an objective study finds their view accurate. One more win for Victorio.

The Apaches had suffered a number of wounded, however, among them Victorio's son, Washington,[28] and traveled slowly. The scouts captured a woman and child on October 1. She said she had become lost, and passed along the information that Victorio planned to head for the Mogollon range, to the west. Morrow settled down, probably on upper Silver Creek, and sent out the scouts to find the enemy camp, if possible. They returned at sundown that same day and reported that the elusive hostiles were only four miles "from the camp from which we had routed them," wrote Morrow, repeating his optimistic assessment.

At moonrise he ordered Blocksom and his scouts to get behind Victorio, while at 12:30 A.M. he himself began his approach from the east. Both commands were to strike at daylight. They did. They found fires burning, surrounding trees festooned with strips of freshly killed beef, the hills "strongly fortified at every possible point," and no hostiles. "The slippery enemy had again eluded us," sighed Morrow, adding that it was just as well. "Had Victorio held his position nothing but artillery could have dislodged him except at a fearful sacrifice of life. He certainly would have killed half the command before we could have taken his position." He sent out the weary scouts once more on the trail. They returned October 3 and reported that, as the

244

captured woman had suggested, it led toward the Mogollons by way of Malpais Creek.

Morrow believed that the trail would cross the North Star Road[29] in making for the Mogollons. Since he was but fifteen miles southwest of Ojo Caliente, he made for there to draw rations, and ammunition and shoe some horses and mules. He sent to Bayard for more men, reporting to headquarters that Victorio seemed headed for the Mogollons and might then swing south through the Burro Mountains for Mexico.[30] Morrow left Ojo Caliente October 5, a Sunday, and marched to Shaw's ranch on the North Star Road, probably about thirty-five miles distant, perhaps in the vicinity of Beaverhead or north of there. He left the ranch next day and followed the road southerly, cutting for sign, to Sherman's Canyon, where he met 113 men up from Bayard in response to his orders. They were officered by Captain George A. Purington, Ninth Cavalry, Second Lieutenant James A. Maney,[31] Fifteenth Infantry, who was to see a great deal of Indian fighting and now commanded San Carlos scouts, and Captain Beyer. From Purington Morrow learned that the Apaches had not crossed the road after all, at least to the south, and could still be to the east somewhere, or Morrow himself might have unwittingly missed their trail. He sent the scouts back to discover where they had gone and laid over, awaiting their report.

They returned on Thursday, reporting that the trail, sure enough, had crossed his and led northeast into the San Mateo Mountains which, next to the Black Range, was Victorio's favorite uplift. Morrow sent 110 worn-out men back to Bayard, along with Blocksom's used-up scouts, whose tour of duty was about over anyway. Morrow had become a little disillusioned with them, despite their hard work. He charged that "several days were lost in following blind trails" due to inefficiency of Blocksom's Apaches, who wanted to return to Arizona rather than stay beyond their enlistment period and fight Victorio some more. Morrow infers that the entire expedition west of the Black Range was actually unnecessary and could be laid to false information. If true, and if the mistaken reports were deliberate, it would be one of the very rare instances in which Apache scouts proved untrustworthy.[32]

The major returned to Ojo Caliente with his reduced command. Gatewood reported that his scouts had determined Victorio's party had now moved south, out of the San Mateos, hurrying down along

245

the eastern face of the Black Range, reversing Morrow's laborious path northward, and heading for Old Mexico, having completely encircled the army forces chasing them.

On October 12, Morrow reported, he "followed trail to Chase's Ranche[33] on the Cuchillo Negro." On the thirteenth, camp was broken in a driving rain, but the trail could still be followed. It led south to the Palomas, eight airline miles distant but half again as far over the rough terrain. A four-day-old *rancheria* was found there, and Morrow hastened south another four miles to camp at some waterholes, probably on Seco Creek, or the north fork of that generally dry watercourse. The rain continued all next day, though Morrow started his scouts at dawn and followed about 11:00 A.M. with his command, marching until 5:30 P.M. over a "fearfully rough" country, by reason of which he lost five horses and a mule. Nevertheless, he plunged along next day, south about eighteen miles by trail through the "placer diggings" which were the embryonic Hillsboro, where Mr. Chase, or Chise, caught up and reported a "squaw trail" paralleling his, though two miles to the east. "But I was on the main trail and would not leave it, knowing they would all come together eventually." Chase also informed him of the burning of McEver's ranch, perhaps in retaliation for its use as a base, and Morrow camped close to the charred ruins.

Sometime after midnight a civilian dashed into the bivouac and reported Indians killing people at Lloyd's ranch. A score of volunteers from Mesilla had set out to hunt down the Apaches and, on October 13, near the ranch, less than three miles southwest of abandoned Fort Cummings, they were ambushed. Six of them, including W. T. (Bill) Jones, were killed and the whites buried them at the foot of a mountain since named Massacre Peak in their memory. Over near Slocum's ranch, in Magdalen Canyon on the trace from Mesilla to Cummings, a wagon train and its eleven teamsters were destroyed.[34] Other attacks and looting were reported at Santa Barbara, now Hatch, or at Colorado, now Rodey, on the Río Grande, but details were contradictory. "At 6:30 [P.M.] runners came in from Gatewood," reported Morrow, "confirming somewhat" the reports of attacks on Lloyd's and Solocum's ranches and "reporting trail going toward Florida Mountains."

It was not certainly known that these murderous assaults were the work of Victorio's warriors; Morrow thought some of them might have been committed by a band of fifty Apaches up from Mexico under Juh. This may well have been, although one could not rule out collaboration between the two leaders, and Juh was not heard from again independently this year.[35] If Juh and Geronimo made a destructive raid into this area while Victorio and his people were coming south, they must have then joined forces, for there is some evidence that the doughty southern Chiricahuas were with Victorio in the hard fight to come, though there is no proof.[36]

All of the determined campaigning and actions generated an expectable uproar in the territorial press and among the politicians and those who hoped to profit in some way from it. On October 14, Governor Wallace and half a dozen other citizens wired Pope that "murdering by Indians still goes on in the South. Some nineteen (19) men are known to have been killed in the last twelve hours. Morrow & his brave soldiers are fighting & doing their best, but they are not enough. The people at Santa Fe at a meeting appointed a committee of public safety for the whole Territory. In behalf of Committee & people we respectfully ask issue of rations for five hundred (500) men who we will put in the field forthwith and no charge to Government except rations."

In forwarding this plea through channels, Pope resignedly said that "if the citizens will allay all excitement & at the small cost of rations which can be readily furnished, I suggest that [their plea] be granted for a limited time, it being impossible under present circumstances to send any more troops to that region now."[37] He had not, however, taken into account the reaction from the old curmudgeon.

The request was refused, Sherman snorted. He could not resist adding, "we have no lawful right to issue rations to allay the excitement of the people of Santa Fe. Who is threatening the safety of the people there? Has Col. Morrow called for help—if so he must be reinforced by every soldier subject to our joint command. . . . What Indian enemy is there to call for reinforcement of five hundred men at Santa Fe? I don't understand the case at all. It is too serious a matter to be made a farce of."[38] So much for Wallace's latest suggestion that armed civilians help out somewhere.

Morrow and his command joined Gatewood and the scouts at Cummings October 18 and sent a party to hurry along the supply train he had requested from Fort Bayard. The detail found the train on the Mule Springs Road[39] and brought it in at midnight. Couriers meanwhile had arrived from Captain Henry Carroll at Ojo Caliente, reporting in for duty with his Ninth Cavalry detachment. Morrow believed Victorio was still thinking in circles and ordered Carroll to join in trapping him, if that were the case.

247

As I was sure that Victorio would try to enter the Mogollon Mts. by his old trail by the Hatchet Mountains,[40] Mule Springs,[41] & San Francisco River, I sent orders to Captain Carroll to move at once down the North Star Road to Diamond Creek[42] where he would be joined by Lieut. Maney & his Indian scouts. He would then take Victorio's old trail through the Mogollon Mountains toward the San Francisco River, go to Mule Springs, thence still on the old trail to the Burro Mountains where, if Victorio had gone that way, his column would have struck him about the same time I would by following Victorio's trail.[43]

However, the main trail led south, and on the nineteenth Morrow sent Gatewood and his Apaches toward the Florida Mountains, following with his own command the next day and camping at Beyer's Spring,[44] a midpoint on the east slope of the Floridas and the only free water in that parched range. On October 21 he joined his scouts camped in the Tres Hermanas range to the south, directly upon the Mexican Line. They had hesitated to cross the border without orders to do so, although Victorio was under no such restriction. Morrow determined to risk an international incident and follow him. At daybreak Gatewood's scouts and Second Lieutenant Charles M. Schaeffer with a Ninth Cavalry detachment set out, Morrow following at 9:00 A.M. The main unit made camp at Palomas Lake, about four miles south of the line, and Morrow hurried couriers after Gatewood, telling him of a smoke he had seen in the Potrillo Mountains,[45] but they could find no enemy there.

However, Morrow was sure he had not been mistaken. He took his command to the range and discovered a four-day-old camp with "evidence of several wounded." The hostiles had used up the water, so it was a dry camp for the soldiers. Three miles farther the next day, October 26, they found another deserted camp. No water there, either.

Men and horses were beginning to suffer severely from thirst. A few small potholes with driblets of moisture did little to refresh them. Yet on October 27 the dogged Morrow set out again on the trail, leading southward into the desert, toward distant Janos and the Sierra Madre beyond. Before sundown the scouts reported that they had seen dust "just entering the mountains."[46]

"I halted the column & rode up and satisfied myself that it was made by mounted Indians. I sent the scouts ahead to reconnoitre the ground and as soon as it was dark enough to hide my dust, followed. I was anxious to get to the Corralitos River[47] which I knew to be somewhere in the direction in which I was marching and probably not more than five or six miles distant

(I had no guide who knew the country). My horses and mules were dropping down every mile, for want of water. Upon approaching the mountains where I had seen the dust my scouts came running back with the report that the Indians were fortified on the hills in front, on either side of the trail ready to open on me so soon as the command should have entered well into the Cañon.

I immediately turned the head of the column to the left, moved up under cover of the mountain, dismounted and prepared to fight on foot. . . . The mules and horses cried so loudly and persistently for water, that our presence was quickly discovered."

His scouts, whom he had sent to investigate the hills, were fired upon and Morrow immediately advanced his main force.

We had no trouble in dislodging the enemy from the two hills which they then occupied as we took them in rear and their breastworks were made to face the trail which led through the cañon; they leaped over the works, across the cañon trail, and into the works on the opposite hills; we kept up a lively fire and followed at a run until we commenced to ascend the hill upon which they were fortified and in a strong force, where we had to take it slowly, owing to the difficulty of climbing. When we had reached within about thirty yards of the top, and all exposed in the bright light of a full moon, they opened upon us with a rattling volley, with slight effect, however, as they fired too high. Three of the scouts were hit, one killed and two wounded. We tried persistently to advance, but could not do it. I then tried to flank [the] hill and sent Lieut. Gatewood around to the right to attack and the moment he opened fire I was to advance. He succeeded most gallantly in getting up within ten feet of the breastworks and held his ground there until he got out of ammunition. The enemy were in the meantime rolling rocks down upon him during his siege.

Gatewood, in describing this hard fight, revealed additional details from the viewpoint of one heavily engaged.

"The whole top of the mountain was a fringe of fire flashes," he recalled. The Indians were well armed with "improved Winchester rifles," and plenty of ammunition. "Nearer and nearer to the top of the ridge approached the flashes from Springfield carbines, and the reports from the Winchesters above were so frequent as to be almost a continuous roar." Suddenly the attackers came against a twenty-foot palisade which they could not scale, and the hostiles began to roll huge stones down upon them. The situation was hopeless for assault, and the men withdrew, while Captain Charles Campbell was ordered to flank the enemy and drive him into the others' guns. But

Campbell[48] failed, because of a confusion of orders, he later insisted, and Gatewood and six men, sent to scout Campbell's way for him, were ordered back; they bounded down the hill under heavy fire.

A lull developed; "the only noise" Gatewood later wrote, "was the tum-tum beaten by Victorio himself all during the fight, accompanied by his high keyed, quavering voice in a song of 'good medicine.' He was at this juncture holding forth to our scouts, trying to persuade them to desert and join his men, and together they would kill the last white and black soldier present. He didn't succeed."[49]

"I tried again and again to take the works in my front, but could not succeed," reported Morrow, "opposed as much by natural obstacles as by the enemy." About 1:00 A.M. he discovered his men were in such pitiful condition, after seventy hours with virtually no water, long marches through burning heat, and hard fighting almost all night, "that unless they had water very soon I would have to take my whole command back on foot," for the stock would have utterly given out. It was doubtful if many men would be able to return. He broke off the engagement.

Morrow's official loss was one killed and two wounded, but Gatewood remembered that "our loss was several soldiers killed and six or seven wounded," in addition to the scout killed and his favorite Apache sergeant, Jack Long, wounded. "He killed two Chiricahuas later to make up for it," wrote the lieutenant. The officer recalled that Nana later had told him the hostiles had "lost several killed and had quite a number wounded," and that "there were fully 150 bucks against us, being recruited from renegade Navajos, Mescaleros, Comanches and Lapans [Lipans], in addition to the Mimbres."[50]

If Gatewood was correct in his figure, it is probable that Juh and Geronimo were in the fight; representatives from other tribes mentioned would have been minimal, one or two renegades from each at most.

In his report Morrow said his command consisted of eighty-one enlisted men and eighteen scouts, but about half the soldiers had been left with the stock and to hold the hills "from which we had driven the enemy." Thus, he said, "only about forty men were or could have been engaged and we were outnumbered three to one." He added that the "entire credit" for expulsion of Victorio from New Mexico should be given the Apache scouts, "as I know that without the assistance of Indians the command would never have been able to follow Victorio's trail."

It was twelve miles to the river. Morrow made thirty-five miles the next day, October 30, to Lake Palomas, reached Beyer's Spring in the Floridas the following day, and from there returned to Bayard. Once more the troops had fought with Victorio and had little but bitter experience to show for it.

XIX
Double Massacre

Morrow notified superiors of his arrival back in southern New Mexico and his scattering of detachments at various posts in anticipation of Victorio's return, which he believed would not be long delayed. He also wanted two mountain howitzers, something like requesting baseball bats for a flea hunt. But Victorio did not fight like other Apaches. Morrow recalled the battle on the upper Animas, the action on the Cuchillo Negro, and more recently the engagement in the Chihuahua mountains, in each of which cannon would have been useful, at least until the first round was fired. He asked, too, for fifty more pack mules from California, so "I could make a pack train that will outlast Victoria."[1]

Pope reasoned that Victorio had shown too much strength to have drawn only from the Mimbres. The general thought not of Juh's Southern Chiricahuas initially, but of the Mescaleros. "As a considerable number of the Indian men from the Mescalero Agency are absent from their reservation and believed on excellent authority to have been with Victoria . . . I request that the Agent . . . ascertain precisely what Indians are away and when they return that he furnish a list of them to the Commanding officer at Fort Stanton in order that they may be arrested as soon as we can assemble there sufficient force to do it . . . and punished."[2]

Russell would deny that any substantial number of his charges were absent or with Victorio, but the army would nurse its suspicions and eventually, blunderingly, act upon them. In the end it would become evident that the army was at least partially correct, and some of the young men did indeed operate with the Mimbres chief, though perhaps not as an autonomous band.

The New York *Sun* reported in early November that "Victorio, the leader of the Warm Spring Apaches has, at length, turned and rent his pursuers. On Sunday last [November 9], he ambushed a company of fifty men from New Mexico, who were on his trail, and killed thirty-two of them, the other eighteen, wounded, escaping to tell the story."[3]

252

Although the facts were garbled, the statistics were almost correct.

After his stubborn fight against Morrow, which some might consider an Apache triumph since the Indians held their ground and the troops failed to dislodge them, Victorio removed his band ninety-five miles eastward to the Candelaría Mountains. This prominent east-west uplift, like a great-headed stone caterpillar, its eyes brooding over the El Paso–to–Chihuahua road passing below its very nose, was a favorite recruiting place for the Apaches. On its northern slope is a natural water tank, since called the Tinaja de Victorio, with excellent reason, for here was enacted one of the bloodiest massacres in the history of Apacheria.

Victorio and his band had gathered close by this water, the women building the *ranchería*, the men no doubt lazying about, gossiping, smoking, laughing about recent adventures, while the few wounded nursed themselves as they might, in what shade they could find. A lookout signaled that a party of Mexicans approached and instantly the Indians disappeared among the rocks, out of sight of passers-by. No sound escaped them. They waited.

The Mexicans had been sent to scout the mountains for hostiles. They had been armed and dispatched by the mayor of Carrizal,[4] thirty-three miles to the south of the Candelaría range. The story of what happened to these eighteen men and those who followed them is revealed in several dispatches. The first, from Rural Judge A. Jaquez of El Carmen, the hacienda-settlement where some say Victorio was born, asserted in part:

Just at this moment (10:30 P.M.) I had sent an armed force to the town of Carrizal, on petition of the mayor of said town for the uses described in the following communication [to me]:

"Town of Carrizal....:

"There have just now arrived here twenty men of the ones I sent to the succor of others which I had previously sent, and these have informed me that they have returned horseless, and the Indians have killed fifteen of their number while they were burying eighteen of the first force, killed also by the Indians. . . . The dead bodies remain on the field unburied, on account of the Indians having taken an advantageous position on the 'Tinaja de la Candelaría' overlooking the main road between El Paso and La Salada. . . . I believe that only by mustering a competent force of about 200 men, can the dislodgement of the Indians from their present position be attempted, or the burial of the dead which I repeat are more than thirty. . . . I enclose a list of the dead, as far as it is known."[5]

Lieutenant George Wythe Baylor, Sr., a younger brother of John R. Baylor, who had been Confederate "governor" of Arizona,[6] commanded a detachment of Company C, Frontier Battalion, Texas Rangers, and reported from Ysleta, Texas, his connection with the gruesome affair:

After Major Morrow's defeat the Indians, probably 200 in number, came down about 55 miles due west of here, and camped in the Candelaría Mountains, a group of peaks surrounded by open plains. They had splendid water, grass and plenty of game, and probably intended to winter, but a party of 15 Mexicans—the best citizens of Carisal—finding a trail, followed it and were led into an ambuscade and all killed.

The scene of the conflict was perfectly horrible. I saw in one little narrow parapet, which the beleaguered Mexicans had hastily thrown up, seven men piled up in a space 6 x 7 feet. The Indians had shown great cunning . . . The trail passed a low place between and commanded by, three rocky peaks. The Mexicans were fired upon from one side just as they reached the crest of the mountains; they had evidently dismounted and ran into the rocks on the opposite side, when the Indians began killing the horses that they had tied, and opened fire on them from nearly overhead and a peak out to one side. They were all killed. A letter written by them asking for help was found outside their breastwork, and near the body of two men who had evidently attempted to escape but were riddled by balls.

Thirty-five more men—nearly the entire fighting force of Carisal—went out to look for their kindred, and the Indians so managed as to drive them into the same slaughter pen, and eleven of them were killed, near the same spot, three ran some distance and their bodies were not found. We buried 26, and 3 were still missing.

Our command consisted of 42 men from El Paso under Jesus Vargas; 25 from Guadalupe under Francisco Escajera; 18 from San Ignacio, 13 from Saragossa; the rangers and 4 volunteers from this side. Near the Candelaría Mts. we were joined by 11 men from Carisal; 15 from Lucero and 41 Infantry from Carmel, making about 179 mostly armed with breech-loading arms. So if Victoria had been there we could have made a pretty good fight, but the sign showed they had only remained there about two days after the slaughter of the Mexicans.

We found 10 saddles of the dead men, hid in the rocks. The muzzle loading guns and swords were all broken, showing that Victoria is well supplied with arms. The trail led off North again, and the Indians are probably making back for New Mexico where we will soon learn of more murders."[7]

James B. Gillett, veteran Texas Ranger who accompanied Baylor, said Victorio's camp was on the north side and almost atop the Candelaría range, where he had a view of country any enemy would have to cross. From here half a dozen Indians raided the settlement of San José, stealing ponies. The citizens, spotting a trail of only a few Indians, organized under José Rodriguez and the party of fifteen followed to the north side of the range between two rocky peaks where, unbeknown to them, Victorio had laid his ambush. To the north were only a few boulders, but to the south the hills "were very broken, rising in rough tiers of stones. The Apaches hid in these rocks and awaited their victims. . . . As soon as they were between the two parties of Indians concealed on each side of the pass, the Apaches on the north side of the trail fired a volley at them. The Mexicans thereupon made for the rocks on the south side, when the redskins in the cliffs above opened fire on them. Caught in this death trap, the entire force was massacred."

Gillett saw "where one Mexican had got into a crevice from which he could shoot anyone coming at him from the east or west. He was hidden also from the Indians in the cliffs above him, but his legs were exposed to the warriors on the north side and they had literally shot them off up to his knees. I also found seven dead Mexicans in a small gully, and on a little peak above them I discovered the lair of one old Indian who had fired twenty-seven shots at the tiny group until he had killed them all, for I found that number of .45–70 cartridge shells in one pile." The second party then suffered the fate of the first. Gillett noted that the bodies were laid in a crevice where they would be secure, he added, since neither coyotes, buzzards, nor crows would consume them, although they would eat corpses of Yankees, Indians, or Negroes. Perhaps something in their diet made their bodies unpalatable.[8]

Dr. Mariano Samaniego,[9] well informed, wrote from El Paso, Mexico, on November 21 that one Tiburcio Madrid

has just arrived from La Tularosa[10] and says the Indians arrived there on the 13th inst. with the horses, arms and saddles which they took away from the poor people of Carrizal. Dr. [Joseph H.] Blazer has also been to see me and to whom I have a power of attorney to claim any stock belonging to [Luis Terrazas, Gabriel Aguirre] and me. He tells me there are over a hundred head of horses with [Terrazas'] brand, but that he did not dare to claim them for fear of his life. The traders at Tularosa were waiting to buy the booty from the Indians, the articles robbed from our poor countrymen and friends. It is unbearable that the U.S. should allow their Reservations to be nothing less than a safe area for murderers and thieves. . . . I wish a severe chastisement could be given to these Indians, right over there.

This is the only way left us to get rid of them. I believe it could be done since the U.S. forces recently crossed over and have been repulsed by the same Indians.[11]

Dr. Samaniego's urging of a retaliatory expedition by Mexicans to raid the Mescalero Reservation and kill Indians never was implemented, but his testimony that Apaches had brought Candelaría loot to Tularosa is interesting, since it suggests that some Mescaleros, at least, were with Victorio at that affair or possibly raiding for horses in Mexico at the same time. Russell conceded as much, while denying that many of his Apaches, if any, were with the Mimbres hostiles. He reported in late November that more than fifty of his Indians were absent, "a larger number than ought to be away, but a much less number than are represented by some of our local papers to be off the reservation."

The newspapers claimed that these absent Indians were with Victorio, Russell added, but "how any one can claim to know this certainly I am at a loss to know. It is easy to discriminate between a Warm Spring Indian and a Mescalero *when near them*, but impossible, I think, to do so at any considerable distance." The Mescaleros themselves vehemently denied any of their people were with the Mimbres. "Those that have recently returned, all claim to have been in Old Mexico, and admit that they were there to steal horses," the agent acknowledged. "They appear to think there is no wrong in going there for horses; say that it is a long distance and in another country and that they *have always done so*, &c."[12]

American consul Louis H. Scott at Chihuahua City, sending a copy of Dr. Samaniego's letter to Governor Wallace in order to prompt punishment for the Apaches, added observations of his own.

Juh, he said, had come to Casas Grandes[13] in early summer with a band of eighty warriors "who were but indifferently armed," though, because "there was no means to fight them," they remained unmolested. Since then, wrote Scott, they had depredated on both sides of the border "and even engaged at one time in a fight with U.S. Troops." This may have been the battle with Morrow. "About forty-five of Victoria's Indians, under that Chief . . . committed fearful ravages" and joined up with Juh and Geronimo, wrote Scott. He said that the Candelaría massacre "was supposed to have been done under Geronimo," although all other authorities say it was the work of Victorio and, if Geronimo was present, it was in a subordinate capacity. "A

256

few days after this, at Salada, they captured a train which they destroyed, killing all connected therewith.[14] On the 23d inst. they attacked Galeana,[15] killing two men and taking away sixty horses. The day following they came down in force on San Lorenzo killing three more and capturing three hundred horses which had been gathered at that place for the purpose of driving them nearer to Chihuahua for protection. From San Lorenzo they went to Santa Clara, dividing their forces on the way, one body, I suppose, to drive out the stolen stock, the other to continue their depredations." The group which moved the stock might have been those Dr. Samaniego reported to have reached Tularosa with stolen animals. Scott said he would urge General Geronimo Trevino, who had reached Chihuahua with five hundred federal troops, to drive the Apaches out of Mexico, his movement to be coordinated with one by Morrow in order to entrap the hostiles. "They should be kept on the jump until they surrender, or are exterminated," wrote Scott. Luis Terrazas, who lost two-thirds of the horses stolen, had just been renamed governor and "is dreadfully in earnest and will wage a bitter war against them."

Scott suggested a private arrangement between Wallace and Terrazas for a mutual crossing of the border in order to pursue and fight the Apaches, who, according to the general impression in northern Mexico, "have killed one hundred and fifty persons within the past six weeks," Scott concluded.[16]

He followed up this letter to Wallace on December 3 with one to Secretary of State William M. Evarts, who sent it over to Carl Schurz of Interior. Scott urged a "hearty cooperation in a war of extermination . . . with a mutual understanding that a party after hostile Indians shall pass the boundary line as often as it may be necessary." This arrangement could easily be made with Chihuahua and Sonora, he thought, and "with perfect safety." An informant had told him that many Apaches had arrived at Casas Grandes, some of them being identified as Victorio's Indians, although not that chief himself. "Chief Josh [Juh?] claims to have been in the fight when they captured—so he says—a whole wagon load of ammunition from the soldiers. He lost two of his principal chiefs in this or some of his other fights." These two may have been Tomacito and Toribio, whom Gatewood said were killed in late 1879.[17]

If you drive them out of New Mexico and Arizona they will take refuge in the mountains of Chihuahua and from these fastnesses they will from time to time raid forth and depredate across the line, and will probably be good Indians [in Mexico] so long as it is [politic] for them to do so. But if they are attacked from both sides of the line at once, and learn to their sorrow that there is no more line to shield them, they may be content to go back and surrender their arms and ponies and stay on their reservation.

One may study the Indian character, and moralize over his lamentable condition, but his ideas are not firmly fixed on the Indian question until he has been chased by them, and then his mind is settled on the question forever.[18]

In a still later communication Scott gives the best evidence available that Victorio and Juh had joined forces for the fight against Morrow, the Candelaría massacres, and perhaps in southern New Mexico even before.

Following the breakup of the Chiricahua Reservation, he reported, Juh settled in Mexico, raiding occasionally, making his headquarters in the "mountains near Casas Grandes." He had been reliably informed that Juh "sticks pretty close to the mountain and does not like to talk or be interviewed, but he has at times told of his exploits." He had accepted Victorio's forty-five warriors with his own band, more numerous but not so well armed, although Victorio had "plenty of ammunition and needle guns in abundance" to correct that deficiency. About the time of the Morrow fight or before, Juh had joined Victorio, reported Scott, although "these two worthy cutthroats have not been able to agree for years and personally are not friends. After their fight with Morrow, they crossed to the Candelaría Mountains, where they got in their terribly bloody work on the Carrizal party."

Scott reviewed subsequent depredations, reporting that after these Juh had asked for peace near Casas Grandes and, since the government had no means to fight him, was relatively unmolested there.

"Victoria never asked for peace, but went right to work, killing everyone he could find. The entire country north of the city [Chihuahua] is demoralized and they claim Victoria has a large band with him," although not more than 150 at the outside.[19] Colonel Orlando B. Willcox, now commanding the Department of Arizona, seemed to imply some awareness of the cooperation between the hostile leaders, as well.[20]

If southwesterners were implacable in their hatred for Victorio, others farther removed were more charitable and cognizant of the unjust treatment which had goaded him onto the warpath. The New York *Sun* remarked editorially that Victorio's band had been "shifted hither and thither from Agency to Agency without their consent and against their protest" and, in one case even among Indians inimical to them. "These various changes . . . involved transfers of hundreds of miles and in no case produced anything but discontent."[21] Now, Consul Scott warned, northern Mexico "will be crowded with renegade Indians who will sue for peace here [in Mexico], and will do their raiding into the U. States . . . unless they are exterminated or driven out."[22]

Settlers were increasingly irate as weeks passed and the hostiles roamed wild. One civilian, H. C. Campbell, wrote Secretary Schurz direct from Lincoln, reminding him that "the life of one good citizen laboring to develop the lands or mines of our Territory is worth more to humanity than a whole race of such miscreants," a view Victorio would not share. Campbell warned that even then "this band is moving north from Old Mexico," committing fresh depredations, and if Victorio ever got into the malpais country of broken lava flows west of Stanton "he can hold it against great odds," particularly since "the Army offers so little resistance." But Campbell had the solution: "I would say break up all tribal relations and scatter them so that it will be impossible to ever get together again. Let each State take so many, put them on farms or at trades and if they will not work and accept civilization let them starve and go down, the sooner the better."[23]

It was winter now, the grass was poor, the ponies thin, Mexico in an uproar, and many of the ranches had been swept clean of stock. It was time for the warriors, or some of them, to think of the easy reservation life again. So Juh, Geronimo, and about eighty of their people broke away from Victorio and went to the Guadalupe Mountains, forty miles east of the southern Chiricahua Range. There they permitted the veteran scout, Archie McIntosh,[24] Captain Harry L. Haskell, aide-de-camp to Willcox, and Tom Jeffords, assisted by friendlies, to contact them. They readily agreed to surrender.[25]

"The talk was very satisfactory," reported Haskell. "The Indians say they have heard General Willcox has always treated their people well and they have come in to live at peace, that they shall not go on war-path nor break out from the agency, that they have not been with Victoria and do not know where he is."[26] A scattering of white lies would do no harm, Juh and Geronimo figured, but Willcox had had no personal experience with these turbulent spirits and was delighted. He messaged the Mexican consul at Tucson that the Indians would be "treated fairly as long as they behave themselves," and believed

259

they might be "used as auxiliaries for the subjugation of hostile bands."[27] These Chiricahuas never joined forces with Victorio again, it should be mentioned, although Juh bloodily avenged his rival's death, as we shall see.

Toward the end of the year Scott once more urged concerted action against the hostiles in view of an offensive planned by General Trevino.[28] Pope instantly ordered his troops to be braced and sought cooperation from Arizona to that end. "The Governor of Chihuahua wishes the cooperation of our troops, and thinks the point where they will be probably needed is the Florida Mountains," he mused. "It's very essential not to permit the Indians to be driven north into our territory." Morrow moved into position, and Willcox ordered scouts and a strong force under Colonel Eugene Asa Carr, a veteran Indian fighter, although inclined to be contentious when there was not sufficient field duty to keep him from his writing desk.[29] Hatch informed Willcox that Terrazas reported from four hundred to five hundred men under Trevino moving "against hostile Indians who are now in the Laguna de Guzman and Santa Maria," and had requested cooperation. Already one prospecting party in the Floridas had been jumped, with a man killed and two wounded, by Apaches estimated to number thirty.[30] A group of Mexican merchants reaching Las Cruces reported that they too had been attacked in the Floridas, their animals stolen but later recovered.[31]

Unfortunately, at this point the threat of Indian trouble on the Pecos River of eastern New Mexico sapped some of the strength Morrow had counted upon.[32] Trevino informed Santa Fe on January 10 that about "100 Indians and their families" were heading for Mesilla, east of the Florida Mountains, "after committing great depredations," and that was the end of his operations against them.[33]

Pope about this time wondered officially what to do with captives, if his troops or the Mexicans picked up any, Sherman replying that if the Mexicans took prisoners north of the line they should be treated as if captured by American troops. The point, he did not bother to add, was to catch some.

General Pope, meanwhile, broached the most delicate subject of all: disarming and dismounting the Mescaleros, who, he firmly believed, were the wellspring for Victorio's strength, weapons, animals, and moral support.

The Mescaleros, he said, like all Apaches "are a miserable, brutal, race, cruel, deceitful and wholly irreclaimable. Although for years they have been fed by the Government and 'civilized' by their Agent, they are in no respect different from what they were when the process began." There was no game in their country and "they can do nothing with arms & horses except rob and murder and surely it is the merest common sense to take away from them what they can use for no purpose except a harmful one."[34] This idea, so implanted, was to flourish and eventually flower, to no particular detriment of the hostiles, but bringing generally undeserved misery upon the Mescaleros and probably strengthening Victorio's band just when its power had begun to wane.

Despite the careful placement by Pope and Willcox of their forces along the border, Victorio and his people slipped easily across, heading north. Morrow, from battered McEver's ranch, wired on January 9 that "I am on a large trail going towards the Black Range. Expect to strike the Indians in two days. My command is not all together. I expect Dawson to overtake me tomorrow night. Beyer with his command has gone astray . . . I fear he is on a wild goose chase."[35] Carr, however, with his command on the alert in southeastern Arizona, never saw a trace of a hostile at this time.[36]

Morrow caught up with Victorio on Percha Creek, west of Hillsboro, and a sharp fight lasted from 2:00 P.M. until sundown. "He made a strong stand and evidently thought he could check us, but he finally gave it up and went off on the jump," messaged the exuberant major, complaining anew about the "inexpressibly" rough country. "Expect to strike him again today or tomorrow on the Animas or Cuchillo Negro." He reported several hostiles killed or wounded, and his own Sergeant D. J. Gross killed, a scout wounded.[37] Hatch, aware of Victorio's demonstrated agility, messaged Major David Perry, who had brought a detachment to Bayard from Arizona, to contact Judge Hudson at Mimbres and see whether that well-informed individual had heard anything about the Apaches' movements in his direction,[38] but nothing came of this and Perry left for home.[39]

Morrow chased Victorio north along the eastern face of the Black Range, reversing the direction of his previous campaign, but not following so closely that the Mimbres could not swing by Ojo Caliente. On January 16 they came to within fifteen miles of the old agency and sent word to their friend, Andy Kelley, that they would like to surrender, but not to any military officer, "as [Victorio] said they had deceived him so often he could not trust any of them, and [he] wanted me to find out what terms of peace he could get . . . and when I heard from Washington to let him know." There were about sixty warriors, well armed and mounted, Kelley reported, adding that as he had known them for the past nine years "and the Indians know I never deceived them and they will believe me, I can give you information that the Indians have not been treated fair." Kelley added that the Mimbres were then in the San Mateos,[40] a fact Morrow was about to learn for himself.

He once more caught up with Victorio in that range on January 17. In a brisk engagement Second Lieutenant James Hansell French, Ninth Cavalry, was killed, two scouts wounded, and Victorio escaped without loss, so far as the major knew.[41] He returned to Ojo Caliente for fresh rations and a few hours of deserved rest. Arizona forces continued to scout the rugged country along the New Mexico line, but still they found no hostiles there.[42]

Morrow himself was plagued by an overabundance of Apaches. Victorio and his people, failing to surrender at Ojo Caliente and to secure permission to remain there, now turned south once more, retracing the beaten route down the east face of the Black Range. They had split into two bands, perhaps the better to ravage the countryside for stock and food, but came together on Animas Creek west of Las Palomas, a tiny community at the mouth of the Palomas River. Here Captain Carroll and Captain Louis H. Rucker, both of the Ninth Cavalry, struck them sharply, losing a man killed, three wounded, and some horses, but chasing the Indians across the Río Grande, down the right bank of which Morrow was hurrying with his own command. Captain Hooker also was due in from the west, over the Blacks, having found no hostiles on their western slopes.

The three commands plunged across the river to scour the mountains to the east and prevent, if possible, Victorio's making contact with the Mescaleros. Men from Fort Bliss, near El Paso, and Stanton, were called in; it seemed possible that the frustrating struggle might at last be ended. Half of the hostiles were said now to be afoot, their stock captured by Morrow's scouts, though if they could steal enough horses they might dash once more for Mexico. Mexican units were alerted to that possibility.[43]

Well, Morrow did come up with Victorio again, in the San Andres Mountains just west of the White Sands, on February 3. "After a sharp fight, our loss one killed and four wounded," he reported. "The Indians were routed, escaping during the night," possibly, he thought, gaining the west bank of the Río Grande again,[44] but they did not, in fact, try to do this. The word "routed" was the customary euphemism meaning the soldiers had lost contact. It happened frequently. In this instance Morrow had attacked with five companies of cavalry plus Indian scouts in a canyon northwest of Aleman.[45] "Victorio's men were stationed in squads of fifteen and twenty upon the sides of the cañon. Major Morrow succeeded in driving them from place to place, until night came on, when the firing stopped on Victorio's side. . . . A number of Indians were killed by the troops, but the number was not ascertained."[46] Six days later Captain Rucker overtook the Indians again, still in the San Andres, "strongly fortified in a narrow and rough canyon. The troops were received by a heavy fire, under which several horses and men fell. Perceiving their advantage, the Indians charged the troops, who gave way, and retreated in pell-mell order; the Indians in turn became the pursuers and drove the troops across the river. In the retreat rations and bedding were abandoned, which the Indians secured."[47] Clearly things were getting out of hand once more. Hatch himself came down to southern New Mexico to take charge, first ordering two companies of the Ninth Cavalry, 140 men under Captain Charles Parker, into the theater from Santa Fe.[48]

No one knew for sure, but the Mimbres might be breaking westward, and the Department of Arizona took fresh precautions lest the remaining dependents of the hostiles be forcibly extracted from San Carlos or break free. Hatch thought it might be a good idea now to bring these dependents to Ojo Caliente. They might lure Victorio in. They could even be turned loose when they surely would be collected by the hostiles and so encumber them as to make their entrapment and annihilation or capture more possible. Pope agreed with this reasoning. "It will greatly expedite matters to put the families where Hatch asks. I also urge that they be sent to Ojo Caliente," he said.[49]

Hatch, in his formal request, said the return of the Indian women and children to Ojo Caliente might well "terminate an Indian war" which otherwise would continue indefinitely.[50] Sherman informed Pope he had been unable to get a clear decision about it from the Interior Department and its reaction ultimately was negative, a fact Pope regretted "extremely." "To leave families at San Carlos is simply to prolong hostilities and be the occasion of the unnecessary death of both white men and Indians—if not of white women and children. To feed the families of Victoria's band at San Carlos, Arizona, whilst Victoria and the warriors of that band are raiding in New Mexico seems unaccountable."[51] Sherman once more sought to persuade Interior to alter its decision,[52] but to no avail. It would not admit that the concentration policy upon which it had embarked was a disaster. The Indians must meet Interior's terms or fight to the death. And this the Mimbres did.

Uncertainty as to the whereabouts of the hostiles caused Arizona officers again to nervously shuffle forces about on the border. Second Lieutenant Timothy A. Touey was sent with a Sixth Cavalry company to Bayard. Gatewood and his scouts were alerted for a possible movement east.[53] Then, when Hatch complained that "all the fight had been taken out of his [Hatch's] scouts," Willcox directed Carr to send in some Indians with Touey.

Pope's suggestion for disarming and dismounting the Mescaleros, meanwhile, gained support. Schurz on February 11 formally concurred, although he thought the Indians might keep the best of their horses for agricultural purposes, reschooling them from wild raiding to pulling plows and wagons. It would be no different for horses than for Indians, the changes perhaps no less distasteful.[54]

Reaching Ojo Caliente in late February, Hatch composed a defense of the gallant Morrow who had come under savage civilian attack for his inability to exterminate the hostiles. Hatch stressed the almost superhuman endurance, dedication, and fighting capacity of cavalrymen pursuing Victorio:

Major Morrow's command shows that the work performed by the troops is most arduous, horses worn to mere shadows, men nearly without boots, shoes and clothing. That the loss in horses may be understood, when following the Indians in the Black Range the horses were without anything to eat five days except what they nibbled from Piñon pines, going without food so long was nearly as disastrous as the fearful march into Mexico of 79 hours without water. All this, followed by forced marches over inexpressibly rough trails, explains the serious mortality among the horses, many of them from the states, and unacclimated.

Major Morrow has over-exerted himself to such an extent as to produce a dangerous hemorrhage. Long night marches have been made on foot by the troops in their efforts to surprise the Indian camps. Morrow deserves great credit for persistency with which he has kept up the pursuit and without the foot Indians and constant vigilance must have fallen into ambuscades, resulting in the destruction of his command. The Indians are certainly as strong as any command Major Morrow has had in action. We always fight in extended skirmish line. The Indian line is always found to be of same length and often longer, extending in some actions more than two miles. Hence the effort to extend his flanks with the object of surrounding him fails.

The Indians select mountains for their fighting ground and positions almost impregnable, usually throwing up some rifle pits where nature has not furnished them, and skillfully devising loop-holes. . . . The Indians are thoroughly armed and as an evidence they are abundantly supplied with ammunition, their fire in action is incessant, and nearly all the horses and mules they abandon on the march are shot. It is estimated they have killed from 600 to 1,000 since the outbreak. . . . It is impossible to describe the exceeding roughness of such mountains as the Black Range and the San Mateo. The well-known Modoc Lava beds are a lawn—compared to them.

He added that the "Mountain Hotchkiss is simply invaluable. It knocks the stone fortifications down readily," although there had been no report as yet that this artillery piece had come into action against hostiles.[55] The Arizona command planned to forward a gatling gun, a primordial machine gun, to forces operating in New Mexico, but there are no reports of its having been used in combat.[56]

Hatch's communication went all the way to Sherman, who gruffly responded that nobody expected the impossible. He said he was "well satisfied with the operations of the troops . . . [and] knows the difficult nature of the country. . . . There is no need for great haste, only to prepare for the coming of the Emigrant and to subdue those Apaches in the course of time."[57] Take it easy, Morrow—just keep up relentless pressure. But to maintain pressure upon Victorio would require further superhuman efforts. There was no other way.

In preparation for what he hoped would be a final, decisive stroke, Hatch streamlined his organization, creating three battalions under experienced, Apache-wise commanders. The first battalion, with five companies from the Ninth Cavalry and one attached from the Sixth, he placed under Morrow. The second, of four Ninth Cavalry companies, was to be under Captain Carroll. The third, with three Ninth Cavalry companies, a detachment from the Fifteenth Infantry, and a company of Navaho scouts, would be commanded by Hooker.[58] Forces in Texas under Brevet Major General Benjamin Henry Grierson, the noted Civil War cavalry raider, were organized to help out,[59] and Arizona units, too, were prepared, among them Gatewood's scouts.[60] The Mescalero, as well as the Mimbres, problem, was to be settled finally by this massive agglomeration of forces.

Even while these extensive preparations were under way, there was a fresh indication that the Mimbres might surrender. Russell wired the commissioner on February 26 that "two of Victoria's Indians reported . . . as being near here, suing for peace and word was sent them to come in and they were assured of protection and permission to return. They refused to come, wanted Capt. Steelhammer, myself & interpreter to go to them. We declined. The Indians refused for two days to come here and left sending word that they wanted to treat with me and not the military. I will not do this unless so instructed. They represent Victoria's camp to be within sixty miles of here."[61] Negotiations might still be possible but only on terms which assured the hostiles of good faith, and these conditions the whites would not meet, so nothing came of this endeavor, either.

Yet Agent Russell believed hostilities could be ended, just as he continued to have faith in the good intentions of the Mescaleros, despite army convictions to the contrary.

On March 3 Ca-bal-le-so (Caballero), principal chief of the Mescaleros, secured a five-day pass to contact Victorio and bring him in. On the tenth he sent the expired permit in with his wife, saying he would come later, but he did not. On March 8, San Juan, a subchief, asked for a pass to go hunt up Ca-bal-le-so, believing him killed, perhaps. "I represented to him that if Victoria's people had killed Ca-bal-le-so, they would kill him, and any others that might be with him. He claims that he could learn Ca-bal-le-so's fate without danger to himself," so Russell finally gave him a five-day pass. He did not return, either. It was rumored that Victorio had come within a day's ride of the agency, seeking to learn whether he could come in. If not, "he would attack the agency," it was threatened. Captain Steelhammer, learning of this warning, gathered 451 soldiers at the Mescalero center, "ample for any emergency."

Victorio's camp, it was understood, remained where it had been, "some fifty or sixty miles distant," that is, in the San Andres near a spring in upper Hembrillo Canyon, on the east side of the crest of the range.

"Today [16th] I learn by what I consider reliable authority, that about thirty-five Mescalero Indians have gone to join Victorio, part of them taking their families with them," Russell acknowledged. He noted that Hatch earlier had urged him to gather all the Indians with their stock to "the Indian Agency as early as the twelfth of April . . . as I shall be forced, owing to the alliance of many of the Mescaleros with Victorio's band, to consider all Indians not at the Agency hostile." Russell believed the Mescaleros would never consent to losing their animals "and if accomplished by force, the Indians will afterwards retaliate upon the people in this country."[62]

Russell asked instructions in case Hatch sought to disarm and dismount his Indians, warning that most of them would leave the reservation if they suspected what was to happen. He added that "I do not believe that any considerable number of Mescaleros has been with Victoria until recently [although] for a few weeks past he has been so near, that there has been constant communication between them. His success[es are] well calculated to encourage others who are at all evil disposed to join him. In addition to this, the Mescaleros are all afraid of him." Ca-bal-le-so, he added, at long last had returned, having been told by Nana that the Mimbres would settle at Ojo Caliente, if permitted.[63]

Depredations and raiding continued. About 120 horses were run off from San Antonio, south of Socorro.[64] On March 22 forty Indians killed eight persons, including the father of a territorial senator, near Santa Barbara, then swung down on a sheep camp on Tierra Blanca Creek above McEver's ranch and slew eight or ten more.[65] On the twenty-sixth two men were killed and a boy captured fifteen miles west of Polvedra, ten miles north of Socorro.[66] A newspaper reported that on March 29 about sixteen of Victorio's Indians stole twenty horses from Hillsboro while eighty-five soldiers under Beyer were on one side of town, Lieutenant Wright with Indian scouts on the other, the raiders passing between them. It was reported years later that Victorio had led his warriors right through Hillsboro while miners cowered fearfully and made no audible protest.[67]

The army, however, was not so idle as the civilians believed, Hatch continuing preparations for a huge operation east of the Río Grande. There is evidence that his main target was the Mescalero reserve and that only on the eve of his undertaking did he perceive that Victorio's camp lay directly in his path. While he had a major force mustered, he might give that hostile a climactic blow, as well. Yet this attack was to fail, through no fault of the soldiers, and the operation against the Mescaleros, although initially more successful, was to prove in the end a dismal failure as well by adding to Victorio's strength, rather than sapping it.

XX

The Mescaleros Disarmed

From Cuchillo Negro, tiny adobe settlement west of the Río Grande named for a great Mimbres leader of the past, Hatch issued his "Special Orders No. 18," assigning his three battalions for blows he fully expected to deliver against Victorio and the Mescaleros.

Captain Carroll with the second battalion was to cover the northeast and east side of the San Andres Range, a narrow, north-south system of rocky and generally arid peaks. Captain Hooker with the third battalion was to cover the west side and try to assure that Victorio, once flushed out, did not dash across the river and back into the Black Range. Hatch himself, with the first battalion, was to move into the mountains and bring Victorio to a fight, hopefully a climactic one.[1]

Colonel Grierson had been ordered from Fort Concho,[2] in mid-March, with what Tenth Cavalry companies he could gather, toward the Mescalero Reservation, to arrive there April 12. He collected five companies of cavalry, a detachment of the Twenty-fifth Infantry, in all 280 men and officers, and moved up from the southeast.[3] Although his destination was the agency, it was expected that he would block the escape of any Mimbres to the east or southeast from the San Andres, and perhaps even prevent them from fleeing onto the reserve, if he arrived in time. Grierson did not get in on the San Andres fight, but did participate in the operation against the reservation Mescaleros.

With troops all but encircling the mountains and reservation, how could Victorio escape? As he had ever done before: by a combination of the fortunes of war, luck, his sagacity, and his natural elusiveness, factors he shared with all of history's great guerrilla commanders.

According to Tommy Cruse, a second lieutenant with Captain Curwen McLellan, the glowering Scot of the Sixth Cavalry, Carroll's men had consumed some chemically charged water at the outset of their march, were made ill, then moved south to another spring the captain recalled, but found no water there, and at long last, suffering

268

badly from the effects of the gypsum and their long dry marches, staggered into Hembrillo Canyon[4] but found the springs held by Victorio and his men. The troopers were surrounded immediately and heavily pummeled.[5] Hatch was aware that Victorio was camped in or near Hembrillo Canyon, and Carroll may have been informed, but, if so, the desperate need for water outweighed any risk, and he moved in anyway.[6]

Carroll had split his command, no doubt hunting water, and went into the fight with Companies D and F, totaling seventy-one men, of whom each fourth man held the horses and packs, so that fewer than fifty were actually engaged. They fought all night and until about 9:00 A.M. April 8.

Hatch, too, had split his command meanwhile, sending McLellan and the Arizona troops and scouts directly from Aleman up to the crest of the San Andres above Hembrillo Canyon, while with the remainder Hatch marched southeast to enter the mountains well south of the canyon, search known trails for signs of the enemy, and move north through the range until he was struck. Reaching the crest, McLellan heard distant firing and sent couriers after Hatch, while preparing to plunge down from the rim and attack the besieging Indians. Carroll's Companies A and G, in the meantime, had come up and supported their commander, now heavily wounded by bullets in the right shoulder and in the leg; seven of his men also were wounded, two mortally.

When McLellan gained the crest of the mountains, just at dawn, he "found the Indians were there in force. Occasional shots were being fired but it was some time before I could discover to whom this fire was directed." He then detached his pack train and horses and ordered the scouts, commanded by Gatewood, Maney, and Second Lieutenant Stephen Crosby Mills, Twelfth Infantry, to the assault "and gallantly they went into action. In less than half an hour we discovered Captain Carroll with his company in a helpless condition . . . completely at the mercy of the savages. The enemy was strongly posted and had full control of what little water there was. . . . At 7:30 A.M. every available man of my command was engaged, and the fight was continued with varied success until about 3:30 P.M. when the enemy was routed from every point. . . . The loss to the enemy was three known to be killed, and no doubt a number of wounded."

Dour McLellan might be, but he was scrupulously fair, and he gave full credit for the relief of Carroll to his young officers: Gatewood,

269

Touey, Cruse, Mills, and Maney and, of course, to the Indian scouts they led.[7]

"It is universally admitted that but for the arrival of McLellan . . . Carroll would have been badly whipped and most of his men killed," reported an observer.[8]

When the Scot's couriers finally reached him, Hatch left the mountains and hastened north along their western front, thinking that the hostiles were trapped and the assault forces needed all the help he could bring. In so doing he missed an opportunity to cancel Victorio out for good. Flowing south through the mountains from the Hembrillo Canyon fight, Victorio and his people observed Hatch and his troopers, inexplicably to them, back out of the mountains and hurry north, but he had a bad fifteen minutes until the soldiers passed a short distance away. A subsequent reconnaissance revealed how narrowly the parties missed each other, one going south, the other north.[9] Well to the south and free of danger, Victorio's band split, some going east toward the Mescalero agency, the others west, to cross the Río Grande and once more gain the Black Range.[10]

"The Indians were as strong as the troops," Hatch summarized for Pope, "and had thrown up with much labor stone rifle pits, where there were not natural defenses. . . . Victoria with his band and nearly every fighting man of the Mescaleros, and some Comanches, were in the fight." Another observer, a civilian, reported that "a number of the ponies captured in the fight belong to the Comanche Indians and are branded with their brands, showing conclusively that the Comanches own them." He estimated the hostiles at "three or four hundred," an obvious exaggeration.[11]

Hatch believed that "Victoria was undoubtedly present & from the number of Indians there is not a question the Mescaleros were in the fight. . . . I recognized in one of the Indians killed a Mescalero." He thought the enemy numbered two hundred warriors.[12]

A non-army observer uncharitably concluded that "the Indians won the fight,"[13] and it would be difficult to refute this, but Sherman was elated, wiring Sheridan to

convey to Genl. Hatch my congratulations. . . . I want him to go on patiently and persistently, make if possible an end to these annual outbreaks. In pursuing hostiles he . . . must not allow his enemy to claim a safe refuge in an Indian Reservation. He may treat them as hostiles wherever found, and when made captive they should be deprived of arms and horses and held as prisoners of war. . . . Such as can be identified with murders and robberies will be surrendered to the civil authorities for trial and punishment, the rest after a fair investigation will probably be sent to work in the stone quarries at Fort Leavenworth."[14]

Even if he had known of such a cruel and implacable directive, however, Victorio could not have fought or campaigned more effectively.

Scouts having located the trail of part of Victorio's force heading toward the reservation confirmed Hatch's determination that those Indians must be dealt with, and he thought he now had sufficient force to do it. In addition to Grierson's 280 men and scouts, he had L Company of the Sixth Cavalry, and Companies A, B, D, E, F, G, H, J, K, L, and M of the Ninth and three companies of Indian scouts, or 430 men under his immediate command; the grand total was 710 armed men,[15] probably more than all the Indians, men, women, and children, on the Mescalero reserve.

Hatch arrived at Tularosa following the "largest trail," on the morning of April 13, a Tuesday. He rested his command on the fourteenth and then moved toward the reservation.[16] Grierson had "arrived on time." Everything was in readiness and the operation was successfully carried out, as Hatch reported on April 15,[17] but Agent Russell told the story in more detail.[18]

In response to Hatch's earlier demand, and at Russell's request, those Mescaleros who had "not identified themselves with Victorio" had moved in close to the agency, bringing their stock, by mid-April, pending arrival of the commander "with about one thousand soldiers...."

"A majority of these troops . . . passed unexpectedly . . . by and very near to these Indians. Although the Indians had been told of their coming, they did not expect so many, and became very alarmed. . . . In consequence . . . most of them moved their camp farther back in the mountains, more inaccessible, but not farther from the agency."

Hatch now informed Russell he intended to disarm and dismount the Mescaleros, Russell replying that, if they had known that, they would not have come in at all. They did so only because they trusted their agent.

"Col. Hatch replied, 'I will turn my Indians loose on them.' "

Russell then said he could probably get their arms and horses peacefully, if they would be returned after the "present troubles were over," and to this Hatch "clearly and unequivocally assented." The Indians then were asked to move still closer to the agency, which they

271

did. They were counted, 309 in all, suggesting that many were too frightened to come in at all. When Captain Steelhammer with a company moved to disarm them, "they were again very much alarmed and scattered in some measure." Complicating the delicate situation was the merciless, relentless vigor of the Apache scouts. Under Gatewood they intercepted a party of Mescaleros they thought were running off stock, although perhaps they were merely rounding it up, and killed two. This tended to affright further the bulk of the people. Some bolted and in an ensuing fight seven more were killed. From thirty to fifty warriors escaped.

Using his influence, Russell succeeded in gathering some arms, and Nautzillos, who had become principal chief when Ca-bal-le-so left to join Victorio, went out to call in the most scattered. Seeing how many had fled, however, he himself failed to return, although Russell stressed that "no one doubts his sincerity." Perhaps he had fled when Steelhammer's men opened fire upon some Mescaleros and frightened more of them. On May 20, Nautzillos finally justified Russell's confidence by returning, bringing in four warriors, four women, and a child. So far as was known, he had taken no part in depredations or hostilities.[19]

Despite the agent's assurance that those Indians who obeyed his call would be well treated, Hatch ordered a search of all their possessions for "contraband." Soldiers "found a few pistols, and a small amount of ammunition, and I have reason to believe plundered the Indians of much that was valuable to them," Russell complained. He wondered whether the action of some of the Mescaleros justified "the *total* and *complete* violation of each and every pledge" given the Indians on the part of Colonel Hatch.

Russell's full, factual report, interpreted by the military as charging unnecessary harshness, even cruelty, on the part of Hatch, was sent to Washington, where the secretary of the interior requested an explanation of the War Department, and that secretary of Sherman. The general replied May 8 that the Indian Bureau had assented to disarming and dismounting the Mescaleros "and I do not believe that Genl. Hatch would sanction acts of unnecessary cruelty." He urged that "the fullest confidence be given to Genl. Hatch. . . . Undue sympathy for these savages amounts to aiding & abetting a common enemy" and would make it more difficult to secure peace.

Russell defended his report as evolving from "my duty to write you a full and candid statement of all that occurred. . . . I re-affirm each and every statement made," adding that Hatch would probably deny nothing he said. The agent agreed with Sherman's concern over undue sympathy toward a "common enemy," but added that "I do feel and express sympathy for those that are at peace, and obedient to the requirements of the Government."[20]

Hatch reported that of sixty-five Mescalero warriors who attempted to escape, ten were killed, thirty got away, and others were being chased. They had fled with the understandable impression that "they were to be tried and hung," since Hatch believed they had "nearly all been with Victorio."[21] About two hundred horses and mules were taken by the troops, the latter turned over to the pack units and what Texas horses could be identified given to Grierson to take back to his post for their original owners, if they could be found.[22]

As might be supposed, the loosing of the most able and virile warriors created fresh turmoil in surrounding areas. "The Indians are at war," complained one harassed civilian. "Many did not come in and are murdering and stealing all around that vicinity. I went there and returned at the peril of my life, as it is most dangerous to travel. Two persons were shot down within a mile of the Agency while I was there. The buckboard mail has stopped running and mail is being carried on horseback, on account of the danger. . . . During fourteen years' residence in New Mexico I have never seen such dangerous times. There are now enough troops here to end the war but they themselves admit it will take a campaign of from 3 to 6 months. In the meantime life and property will be most unsafe."[23]

Some Mescaleros were struck in Dog Canyon, in the Sacramento Mountains, several being killed but most trailed toward the Guadalupe Mountains on New Mexico's southern boundary with Texas;[24] obviously they had not intended to join Victorio, since he had not gone that way. Grierson scouted for them, as they were on the route of his return. Hatch, still primarily concerned with Victorio, the arch-rebel, sent Morrow with the second and third battalions back across the Río Grande to scour the Blacks and San Mateos, intending to follow as quickly as he could.[25]

One thing he had learned: "The only way to put an end to Indian hostilities," was with scouts. His Arizona Apaches had been called back by Willcox, and Hatch, convinced he must have more, pleaded for permission to enlist two additional companies of fifty Indians each. It was "absolutely necessary," he argued, and if he had them he could end the troubles "forever," and do it this same season. General Pope agreed with him. "It is easy to break up large bodies of Apaches, but they scatter in small parties all through the mountains & have to be hunted out almost individually. The foot Indians are just the men for this," he noted approvingly.

But the request ran into red-tape trouble. It was impossible. Sheridan noted that the division was authorized but two hundred scouts. The Department of the Missouri, in which New Mexico was a unit, had fifty, and the others were needed elsewhere. Previously Hatch had suggested that Navahos be armed and rationed but not enlisted, to get around this limitation, but the attorney general had ruled that Indians "cannot be employed except regularly enlisted as soldiers," canceling out that idea. Sherman therefore decided that the "aggregate number of Indian scouts [requested by Hatch] cannot be granted, without subtracting an equal number of soldiers [from] the Army itself. This is simply impossible; therefore this request must be denied."[26]

Hatch would have to struggle along as best he could with what regular scouts regulations permitted. But Hatch had been correct, even though he could not have foreseen that within a month the scouts, unassisted by any soldier, would fight the pivotal battle with Victorio and send him reeling down the road to disaster.

XXI

"We Will Eat Victorio Up!"

When Victorio lunged back to the west side of the Río Grande, he stirred the settlers to half-hysteria, half-frenzy. A newspaper reported thirteen herders killed and 100,000 sheep scattered in the distant Mogollons. Cooney's mining camp in that range was attacked April 29.[1] Morrow hurried detachments to scout the range and the country along the San Francisco River, but they never saw an Indian, only their deadly work. One hundred armed civilians combed the Mogollon Range for the elusive chieftain, or so they said. "The cry is for arms," proclaimed Captain Henry H. Humphreys, Fifteenth Infantry, in command at Bayard. "More would go if they had arms. Reports place Indian force as high as four hundred, as low as one hundred and fifty, and again also at two hundred and fifty. . . . If the half telegraphed is true, the situation looks grave." Captain Daniel Madden, Sixth Cavalry, scouted the border between New Mexico and Arizona, but he made no contact, either.[2]

Grierson, meanwhile, after his fifteen-hundred-mile scout, returned to Fort Davis May 9, expecting to reach Concho the twentieth, well pleased with the performance of his men. He had scouted southeastern New Mexico "in a most thorough manner, crossing and recrossing, and passing through" the Sacramentos and Guadalupes, his men killing two chiefs, shooting three other Indians, capturing five women and two children, recovering about fifty head of stock and a Mexican captive from the Indians.[3] Scarcely had he returned to Concho when Pope urged that he be sent back to Stanton, since Hatch was far west of the Río Grande with broken-down horses and Victorio was suspected ready to swing back across the state toward the Mescalero Reservation again. Grierson was spared this redundant duty, however.[4]

Not only western New Mexico but eastern Arizona had its alarm. Captain Adam Kramer, Sixth Cavalry, was reported "fighting Victorio near Rocky Cañon [asking] for assistance. Victorio appears about ninety strong."[5] It was not Victorio, as it turned out. It was

275

Washington, his son, fully recovered from his wound, and he did not have ninety men with him, but fourteen. His purpose was unclear, though he may have tried to spring the Mimbres women and children from San Carlos and lead them into the mountains where the warriors lurked. If that was his intent, he failed. But he stirred up the hornets, just the same.

Washington assailed a camp of "peaceful" Indians, Juh's and Geronimo's bands, whose last contact with Victorio's people had been as allies in Old Mexico. Perhaps the fiery son of the Mimbres leader desired to drive them out on the warpath with his companions; attacks with such a purpose were not unknown. If so, his effort was fruitless. This time Juh and Geronimo were not ready for trouble.

Kramer, bringing along what cavalrymen he could gather in a hurry, outdistanced his scouts and lashed into the enemy, but "we received a volley from the hostiles compelling us to withdraw to a reasonable distance, where I skirmished with them until the arrival of my scouts, whereupon the enemy broke and ran, gained their animals, and made off at a run," he reported.[6] His losses included a sergeant, Dan Griffin, killed, one scout badly wounded, and some animals. Kramer pursued the fleeing raiders nine miles, clashed with them once more. They broke it off then and escaped, reaching Victorio's camp in the New Mexico mountains without losing a man, so far as was known.

Hatch meanwhile wired Pope from Tularosa[7] of his arrival, his command having been "pretty thoroughly over the Mogollon Mountains," finding numerous flocks of sheep deserted by terrified herders who had been "on good terms with the Indian until the present," but now were being slain indiscriminately because, Hatch believed, they were not competent in their own defense. "It is my opinion twenty resolute men, armed, can round up all the sheep west of Ojo Caliente. The herders have made no effort to defend themselves." He supposed the Apaches had killed about two hundred sheep, for food, no doubt. Hatch reported his stock was "so broken down can no longer pursue rapidly, hence Victoria may escape me," although the Indian's trail was littered with dead animals and he himself was "nearly dismounted." He did not know whether Victorio would go west or east, and neither did the chief, probably. Hatch intended to scout the San Mateos and other ranges with his men afoot. A captive who had escaped from Victorio reported that that leader "has Comanches with him," but they could have been only a few, if any.[8]

Hatch called for more troops, fresh troops, and Pope and Sheridan searched for some that might be moved in,[9] but the urgent necessity was erased by the one decisive victory over the Mimbres leader in the campaign to this point—and that not by troops, but by scouts, unaided and unsupported, and led by a relatively inexperienced white chief of scouts at that.

"Our scouts and a few men with them attacked camp of hostiles at daylight yesterday morning at head of Palomas River. Chief of Scouts reports officially killing thirty-one (31) men & scouts in the fight claim to have killed fifty-five," Hatch wired Pope from Cañada Alamosa on May 25.[10] He said the scouts' chief "is considered reliable," and reported attacking the enemy at dawn, May 23, having been sent out after Hatch had reached Ojo Caliente from the west, his regular troops exhausted.

News of the victory flashed like lightning through the gathering gloom surrounding Apache affairs in New Mexico and, indeed, marked the true turning point in the Victorio campaign, although no one as yet could determine that.

Official dispatches for the most part are terse, uncommunicative, and perhaps unreliable on this incident, while the report of the chief of scouts involved is valuable and revealing. He was Henry K. Parker,[11] a Texan who reported on May 26 to Hatch:

I am just in from Black Range or head of Palomas River. After taking up trail on the 21st I located Victorio's camp on the 23d, and jumped him on the 24th at daybreak. For fear things may reach you wrong I will give you a correct account of fight. On 23d, about 10 A.M., I located their camp. I then moved off of trail and stopped in rear of his camp. From there sent out scouts, two and three at a time, to learn the lay of the camp and the best way to jump it. At sunset they return and pronounced the camp favorable to jump. I sent 20 scouts entirely around their camp and 30 in rear. I then took 10 scouts on opposite side, that leaving only the way they came in for their escape, which I knew an Indian would not do—take back trail. We creeped [sic] all night and daylight found us in fifty yards of his camp. The 30 scouts in rear of camp opened on them at daybreak, killing several men, women, and children; the men ran and left their guns, a great many of them. They ran up in the direction I was in. When near enough to fire, we fired a volley into them. This turned them back towards 20 scouts up the cañon. They fired on them, and they turned back to where they were fired on at first. They then intrenched themselves while we fired on them. The firing was kept up by scouts all the while, though hostiles would make squaws stand the fire while they intrenched. They got in a very small place between two large rocks, and women and children were killed at point of rocks, while *men*, those that could get intrenched could not be got out and only put squaws out to be killed by scouts. We fought all [that day. After] getting in, there was, I presume, 30 men in there and about 8 or 10 squaws. The [next] day, our ammunition giving out, we left for want of water, after killing about 30 men and women and children, and capturing 74 head of stock.

Victorio was there and talked to scouts all day. Scouts say he was shot in the leg. This I only have their word for, but the former I saw and know to be correct, and can vouch for. There is other things concerning fight which I fail to mention, as I leave this evening to overtake Major Morrow's command, as I understand he has gone to follow me; however, we gained a complete victory, killing several and losing no scouts.

H. K. PARKER
Chief of Scouts

None of our scouts were hurt.

H.K.P.[12]

Morrow, reporting on his activities at this time, told how he had scouted the Mogollons, then worked north into the Datil Mountains above old Fort Tularosa and picked up a hostile trail, on which he had sent Parker and his Indians. They traced it to near Ojo Caliente, going in there, presumably for rations or to await orders. "General Hatch told me that Parker, with the Indian scouts was [at Ojo Caliente] when he arrived, but that he had ordered him out immediately to stick to the trail, and keep along with the hostiles and harass them until the troops could come up, and if an opportunity offered to jump them."[13] Morrow appeared astonished that Parker, after his fight, "*had come in on my trail and was following me up*," though what else the chief of scouts could do under the circumstances was not clear. Hatch afterward reported that when he had reached Ojo Caliente he found that "Parker came off the trail he had been ordered to take, saying he was worn out, and it was with great difficulty that I forced him to the point," that is, to follow up the trail.[14] It is obvious that Parker was not a veteran chief of scouts, and that there was much confusion, but there would be more. From the official reports we thus get one side of the picture, but it is fleshed out in a subsequent newspaper account which casts a different light. It came "from one who took part in the pursuit of and fight with the Indians on the headwaters of the Palomas[15] . . . and on whose statements we can rely."

Parker was reported to have had about seventy-five scouts,[16] the figure no doubt inflated, and he had been in the Southwest for some years. His brother, Thomas Parker, lived in Chihuahua and knew the warlike Apaches well.[17]

According to this newspaper account, which may have originated with Parker himself, he approached Morrow on the San Francisco River on May 17 and, since the soldiers' stock was broken down, asked permission to take his scouts and see what they could turn up. Morrow said, "You see the condition we are in. Go. I have no orders to give you. Do the best you can." He was given eight pack mules and four days' rations and scouted southeasterly toward the Black Range. On the first day the tired mules gave out, so he ordered the rations cooked up and parceled out among the Indians, each to pack his own. On the fourth day, May 21, he reached Ojo Caliente and found Hatch there. The officer listened to his report, then told him to "go out and kill one or two Indians. He wanted something done to keep things going until he could get the troops in shape to pursue," said the newspaper.

Parker drew three days' rations, again divided them up, and started south, along the east face of the Black Range.

On the 2nd day out he spotted a camp of hostile Indians, and immediately moved up into the mountains to escape observation. He then sent out scouts to find out the best way to get at the camp without attracting attention; just at sunset his scouts returned and reported that they had found just the place....

Capt. Parker, with more true military skill than has yet been shown by officers . . . began to carry out his plan for an attack. He ordered Sergeant Jack Long (an Indian)[18] to take 20 of the scouts and cautiously go around to the other side of the camp, to stop the hostiles in case they made a break in that direction to get away. Sergeant Jim was instructed to take 30 men and move up immediately above the camp, while the Captain took 11 picked men and crept up to the side opposite the position taken by Jim. Capt. Parker instructed Jack Long not to fire a shot until the Indians came down the canyon; he also ordered the scouts with him not to fire until the hostiles ran up on them. Sergeant Jim had orders to get as near to the hostiles as he could and open fire on them at daylight.

The Indians had a sentry out on the side next to Jim's position, and Jim selected a man to kill him, while the balance fired down into the camp. According to orders, Sergeant Jim opened fire at daylight, and the hostiles broke up [to] the position held by Capt. Parker. A galling fire sent them back into the canyon, and they ran down it, gathering together as they ran,

279

when they came plumb upon Sergeant Jack Long's command and received a fire that drove them pellmell back to their camp.

The hostiles then commenced fortifying, supposing that they were surrounded, being fired upon from all sides; those who got into the fortifications fought desperately until night. Many were killed before they could reach the fortifications. Firing was kept up.

Victorio was wounded, but when the scouts called to the women of the camp to "come out and they should not be hurt," the women derisively shouted back that "if Victorio died, they would eat him, so that no white man should see his body!" Surely he held great devotion from his followers.

The assailants held their position all night and in the morning Parker sent a Mexican packer to Hatch asking more ammunition. Late in the afternoon, his men's rounds being about expended, he pulled them back five miles to water. He remained there two nights and one day, awaiting ammunition and rations, although he began to suspect that his courier had been killed. Then he took his command to Ojo Caliente.

There he was assured that his courier indeed had come in, reported, and been assigned to Lieutenant Maney's pack train, which had moved to Camp French.[19] Parker followed it there, located his packer-courier, who said he had reported to Hatch, who had immediately left for Fort Craig to wire "the celebrated message that his column . . . had struck the Indians" with some slight assistance from the scouts.[20] Parker inquired of officers at Camp French the reason for the delay in following up the victory, but "no satisfactory answer could be had, they merely replying, we do not know, we are not in command."[21]

Estimates of the damage Parker did to Victorio vary widely, ranging from the fifty-five hostiles reported slain by the *Chronological List* down to the "ten or twelve" estimated by Cruse (who may have counted warriors only). He added that, "whatever the number actually killed it was a deadly blow to Victorio, as he lost some of his best men."[22] The army generally was casual about the fight; how could it have been otherwise when, after all the hard campaigning, the decisive action was fought with not a regular involved? The officers, including Hatch himself, attempted to share the credit for the success, however little they had had to do with it.

From his breakout in 1879 until now Victorio had never been trapped, never clearly defeated. But from this time forward his star was in decline. Although he would win his other engagements, until the final one, they would more and more resemble rear-guard actions of a force growing gradually weaker. Victorio was discovering what Cochise had learned before him: you could whip the soldiers time and again, but they were too many and so well supplied and reinforced that they would wear you out. The ancient lesson, from the time of Hannibal and before, was that brave and superbly led forces could win the battles, but the blundering, fumbling onrush of endless numbers with unlimited supplies, aided by dogged persistence, would win the wars. Victorio had no source for more men. His supplies were hard to come by. All he possessed in abundance were spirit and courage, relentless determination—and the right. And these were not enough.

Hatch reported that Morrow "came up the day following the attack of the scouts, taking up the pursuit, when the Indians broke in some three parties, the largest crossing at Fort Cummings, all going toward Mexico."[23]

Sherman told Sheridan to "encourage Genl. Hatch all you can to persevere in the destruction of those Apaches. . . . Assure Genl Hatch of our entire confidence, and that he must do the best he can regardless of newspaper clamor, which has no effect whatever on us here in Washington, where we are so used to it." He informed McDowell at San Francisco that "destruction of the hostile Apaches is necessary to enable the proprietors to build the Southern Pacific Railroad." Sherman had no stock in the road, but believed it "so important to the whole country" that brushing aside a few abused Indians should not delay it.[24]

As soon as Parker had pulled back, Victorio and his people melded west into the Black Range, then broke south. About one hundred, perhaps more, burst across the old road near Fort Cummings, making for Mexico. A group of twenty-five plunged south by way of Goodsight Peak, midway between Cummings and Slocum's ranch, also bound for Chihuahua. The parties still in the Blacks, reported Hatch, were so small as to be inconsequential, although Morrow "struck one about Cook's Cañon [southwest of Cummings], killed two, wounded three, capturing their stock" and continued searching for small bands expecting to drive them to Mexico. If Grierson would bring his Tenth Cavalry and hold the country east of the Río Grande, Hatch thought he could "settle Victoria's band" or what remained of it to the west.[25]

But Grierson was not ordered there and soon would have his own hands full with Victorio.

Hatch now conceded that "the surprise made by the scouts on the twenty-fourth is more serious to the hostiles than at first supposed." He thought those Indians racing south were "Mexican Indians, and not . . . Victoria's main force," but the "Mexican Indians," led by Juh and Geronimo, remained at San Carlos and would raid and fight no more with Victorio. Those Apaches plunging south were Victorio's people, all right, or at least those still able to travel swiftly. Many of the severely wounded must have been left in the secluded reaches of the Mimbres Mountains, to their own devices. Lieutenant Maney, still commanding Parker's scouts, reported that those Indians making for Mexico did so "for the benefit of the wounded," or those who could travel.

The third main band of Apaches swept down the familiar route early in June, slaying five men they chanced to stumble across at the west end of Cook's Canyon on their way, but otherwise too hurried to commit depredations. "There has been no depredations in the Mimbres Valley, or the river & the mines about Hillsboro which are the important points to protect where there is much stock & many unarmed people," Hatch reported.[26]

Morrow followed one band of Apaches almost to the line, reporting that their trail led toward Palomas Lake,[27] and the next day, in a sharp clash with stragglers hurrying south with stolen stock, killed ten, wounded three, and recaptured some animals. This was a more significant victory than the figures suggested, for among the slain was Washington, the vigorous son of Victorio who had raided widely and savagely in close imitation of his famous father.[28] And on this successful note ended the conflicts between Victorio's people and Hatch's troopers in southern New Mexico, for now the Apaches were across the border. They would make no further raids in their homeland while Victorio lived, although they would fight farther east.

Morrow persisted in his scouts for stragglers in the Black Range, picking up a few Mescaleros, who explained that Victorio had never permitted them to surrender before. Many of the Mescaleros, Hatch believed, had accompanied Victorio into Mexico. They might try to cross the lower Río Grande above old Fort Quitman,[29] he reasoned, returning thence through the Guadalupe Mountains to the Mescalero agency, although "this depends on whether the Mexicans attack them."[30] Hatch's speculation was sound, but it appears that most of the Mescaleros remained with Victorio, although they sought once more to get him to surrender at the agency, their only hope. He seems to have tried this, but his attempt was aborted, as shall be seen.

Hatch's belief that some of the Mescaleros with Victorio were being held as virtual prisoners was relayed to Agent Russell, who called some of the leading men into council. He asked if they would send messengers to "those of their people who were with Victorio, to say to them that if they wanted to surrender they could do so now, but that this would be their *last chance*." They replied, "We are not going to Victorio's Camp; we think the Indians that joined Victorio deserve to be killed. Victorio used to send messengers to us every two or three days to ask us to join him, but we wouldn't do it; we are not going to have anything to do with it." Yet, Russell pointed out, "these people [his own Indians] are prisoners." Something should be done for them.[31]

Rumors continued in these confused days, some wildly improbable, such as that reaching the War Department that the Utes, Apaches, and Navahos planned to combine forces in a general uprising.[32] The military commanders in the field were occupied with more rational problems. Hatch pleaded for Washington to rapidly negotiate an agreement permitting him to chase the Indians deep into Mexico. "Time is an element of the greatest importance," he urged. "The great bulk of the Indians have gone into Mexico and are now in the mountains near [Janos]. They are merely there with their sick and wounded, and as soon as recuperated will return. It is important that they should be followed and allowed no rest." The Department of State communicated with the U.S. minister at Mexico City, but on June 22 he replied that the "Govt. of Mexico declines consent to our troops following Apaches across the border," and he could do no more,[33] although late in the summer limited agreement was reached.

Hatch meanwhile came up with a fresh estimate of the forces now with the Mimbres.

Agent states that he had present at one time at the Agency, five hundred and fifty-three, but may not have included all the Indians. There are now prisoners, mostly women and children, two hundred & eighty-five. With Victoria two hundred and sixty-eight. Victoria had fifty-three when he first left the reservation. Indians from Mexico one hundred renegades. From Arizona, Comanches & others, seventy-five. Total force four hundred and ninety-six, of which women and children, one hundred and sixty. Killed in various engagements, one hundred, leaving present strength of hostiles two hundred & thirty-six warriors. Parties who claim to know more than myself make the hostiles much stronger.

Pope believed Hatch had overestimated. He informed Sheridan:

As there were no Indians out from San Carlos Agency and only eight Comanches (two men and six women) reported absent, his estimate must be . . . reduced by seventy-five, leaving two hundred and sixty-one as his estimate of the hostile Indians, which varies but little from my own. If one hundred of these have been killed during his campaign, there remain only one hundred and sixty-one hostiles, all of whom were supposed to be now in Old Mexico.[34]

The task of scouting for the wild Mimbres now befell Grierson. He must scour repeatedly the West Texas country between Fort Davis and El Paso, from the Río Grande to the Guadalupe Mountains,[35] an immense area, not dissimilar in many respects to southern New Mexico, almost as waterless and with even less population. His forces never returned to the Mescalero agency, where the Indians, still "nominal prisoners," were unhappy with even that status. Yet Pope and others defended such control over the Mescaleros as necessary to avoid "any possibility of [their] getting in with Victoria's band. . . . To release these is simply to re-enforce the hostiles now out and utterly destroy any hope of getting them in. . . . These Indians are nothing but savages and . . . they are irreclaimable. . . . There seems to be no sufficient object in conducting military campaigns against these savages if they are to be released as soon as caught and especially if one half of them is to be released whilst the other half is still . . . committing murders and depredations."[36]

Victorio, of course, had to raid to live. He or some of his bands operated deep into Chihuahua, at one point striking within thirty miles of the city itself. They traded at Gallego, about seventy-five miles north of Chihuahua City. Hatch again suspected that if they tried to recross the line they would do so below Quitman.[37]

With military operations against him dormant for the time being, attention once more was drawn to the possibility of Victorio's surrender. Agent Joseph C. Tiffany, controversial figure in charge of San Carlos, suggested it to Colonel Carr, commanding field forces in southeastern Arizona, and described his conversation to this end in a communication to the commissioner in midsummer. Tiffany had pointed out that the military campaign had been unfruitful "and the failure [was] calculated to encourage disaffected Indians to go upon the warpath." Carr wondered if, in the event of negotiations with Victorio, Tiffany would receive him at his agency.

"I told him, yes, provided he came in in good faith, but that I did not believe he would consent to come in, as he knew he would be in danger of his life from the San Carlos Indians . . . [who] had vowed to shoot him upon the first opportunity anywhere." Some of the San Carlos Indians had even applied for permission to go kill the hostile, but Tiffany had not encouraged this.

Carr told Tiffany that he personally was not in favor of dealing with Victorio, but that Colonel Willcox, department commander, seemed to incline toward it.

Tiffany suggested sending a group of San Carlos Indians out to capture or kill Victorio, and this idea intrigued both Willcox and Hatch. They asked for details.

On July 16 Tiffany replied: "I believe a party can be organized on this reservation who would capture or kill Victorio in less than four months from date. But I should object to their being placed under command of 1st or 2nd Lieuts. . . . It would be well for an officer of experience to accompany them, who would move and live as they do in order to keep them from marauding, or give military advice if needed or requested." Tiffany added that if the commissioner approved he would look around "cautiously" for 100 to 150 Indians for the mission, adding that "I believe good will come of it, either in bringing Victoria to terms of getting rid of him altogether." The hostiles were expected back across the border shortly, the agent added, "the recent rains having started the grass" to support their ponies.[38]

Hatch, who had had more experience with Victorio, or at least with chasing him, than any officer except Morrow, did not feel that the Indian yet was beyond surrender. He assured Carr, after he had learned of Tiffany's initiative, that his capitulation was feasible. "The Mescaleros who are with him are anxious to return to the Reservation," he pointed out, adding, however, that "I don't believe Victoria will ever live at San Carlos; if he surrenders it should be unconditionally. Jeffords can undoubtedly manage Victoria," anywhere it might be decided to settle him.[39]

Hatch reported July 16 that Victorio was in the mountains in Old Mexico about one hundred miles west of Eagle Springs, Texas. Eagle Springs is at the base of the Eagle Mountains, about fifteen miles southwest of Van Horn, and Hatch's calculation would place the hostiles either in their old Candelaría camping ground or more to the southwest in the Sierra de la Magdalena. He believed that the "Mexicans intend to attack them about the fifteen inst.," under command of Colonel Adolfo J. Valle, who had messaged that he had 320 cavalry and 150 infantry "and has authority to cross the line" from United States officials.[40]

Sheridan was informed, slightly prematurely, that Victorio had crossed the Río Grande by July 22, making for Eagle Springs and closely pursued by Valle's command. The truth was that Valle and Victorio had collided; Grierson moved from two points on Eagle Springs, hoping to cooperate with the Mexicans and entrap the hostiles.[41]

The reasons for Victorio's moving north at this time, into the inhospitable country of West Texas, are obscure, but perhaps the Mescaleros with him had persuaded the chief once more to attempt to reach their old reservation, or at least to gain the Guadalupes, where in the rugged fastnesses they might stand off their persistent enemies. Victorio was in relatively unfamiliar country now, although it was well known to the Mescaleros. He was far better acquainted with the northern Mexico terrain westward of the line from El Paso to Chihuahua; if he had ever raided into this eastern country the fact has not been recorded. Entering this unfamiliar area was a mistake. Victorio must soon have realized this.

Grierson wired General Edward O. C. Ord at San Antonio on July 24 that he had received reports "to the effect that an engagement occurred about three days ago between Mexican troops and Victoria's band at Ojo del Pino, Mexico,[42] in which six soldiers were killed." The Indians, he said, were reported "to have a large number of horses and cattle. The river is high and difficult to cross," but he believed the Apaches might attempt it somewhere near Quitman. Grierson's Pueblo scouts and his Tenth Cavalry detachments warily waited.[43]

Valle reported that a few days later his forces killed four Indians while losing a man killed, three wounded, and ten horses slain, still in the Pinos Mountains. They then moved a bit northwest, into the low Sierra de Fierro, adjacent to the Sierra San Martín del Borracho, where Valle intended to make a major effort to destroy them.[44] But Victorio did not wait. Despite the peril of the swollen river, he with part of his band, about sixty in all, braved the Río Grande, crossed successfully, and attempted to move north along Quitman Arroyo, dry at this season, between the Eagle and Quitman mountains, ranges seared by the blazing sun and rising to about sixty-five hundred feet, except for Eagle Peak, one thousand feet higher. In this movement they almost bagged their biggest game, for they trapped a small detachment commanded by Colonel Grierson himself July 30, giving him a very bad time until rescue arrived.

"I was encamped with a small party at the point which they intended to pass," the colonel reported later: "Having learned at one A.M. this morning of their probable approach, I fortified the position with such means as were available." He had selected a position on present-day "Devil Ridge," on the right bank of the arroyo, to make his stand. Grierson

sent orders to Capt. [Charles D.] Viele at Eagle Springs, and Captain [Nicholas] Nolan at Quitman to proceed immediately to that place. At four A.M. a detachment of thirteen men under [Second] Lt. [Leighton] Finley reported to me, previously to which I had but seven men, including three teamsters. At about nine A.M. the Indians were observed approaching rapidly in force. They were vigorously repulsed and our position held until the arrival of Capt. Viele at about eleven A.M. with his company and a part of Company G, Tenth Cavalry, and upon his approach a sharp action took place between the troops and the Indians, in which the latter were severely punished and [First] Lieut. [Samuel R.] Colladay wounded and one man of Company E killed and eight animals. In the entire engagement, which lasted about three hours, seven Indians were killed and many wounded. Upon the approach of Capt. Nolan's Company, the Indians fled rapidly to the Rio Grande, none having gone north. The Mexican troops returned to the Rio Grande opposite Quitman on the twenty-eighth, being entirely out of supplies. They are now moving down the River and are opposite here.

Grierson did not think the Indians would make another attempt to move north by that route.[45]

It is probable that only the lightness of the force he could muster prevented a major blow against Victorio, but now he was back in Old Mexico again. Grierson reported on August 3 that Victorio probably was camped in mountains along the river. He sent the information to Valle, who was reported moving downstream; "I presume he is now opposite Ojo Caliente,[46] and I have sent couriers to again communicate with him. The last report received from scouts, states that the river has risen since the Indians crossed back into Mexico, and it is now only passable with great difficulty, being higher than it has been heretofore this season."[47]

Valle, at this point, required rations and supplies more than he

287

needed trouble with Victorio, and pulled out for the south. Perhaps a briefly flaring revolution in the interior of Chihuahua called him back. At any rate, Victorio, accompanied now, Grierson estimated, by 125 to 150 warriors, crossed the river by August 3 "and is passing north, towards Vieja Pass, Van Horn or Bass Cañon,"[48] and Grierson was left alone to handle him. "My troops are now moving rapidly to get in his front," he reported. "Indians evidently striking for Guadalupe or Sacramento" mountains.[49] The officer notified Colonel George P. Buell, now commanding at reactivated Fort Cummings, who hurried his troops to the Río Grande and sent scouts into the San Andres Mountains to await Victorio's possible arrival. Morrow continued scouting for stragglers in the high broken mountains to the west.[50]

Some Mexican forces, perhaps irregulars, followed the hostiles across the Río Grande for a brief clash on the afternoon of August 10,[51] but this apparently was with a foraging party from Victorio's main band, still pushing north. Grierson moved parallel with them, although careful to keep a range of mountains between him and the hostiles, to shield his presence. Logically they would have moved north along Quitman Arroyo, rounded Devil Ridge where Grierson had had his narrow escape, continued north toward Dome Peak and the northwestern extremity of Sierra Diablo. This is speculation, since the military dispatches attach place names unidentifiable with certainty today to features of the area.

Grierson arrived at Rattlesnake Springs, probably on the southwestern slopes of the Sierra Diablo, for he reported climbing "the rough and precipitous cliff" of the range, two thousand feet high, after their long, hard march, in order to set a trap. He had covered sixty-five miles in less than twenty-four hours and was far enough in advance of the Indians to lay his ambush carefully. Two companies of the Tenth Cavalry under Captain Viele were placed on either side of a ravine and lay quietly, awaiting the enemy.

About 2:00 P.M. the straggling column of Indians approached, the eager soldiers holding their fire until they saw that the wary enemy would come no nearer when they loosed the first of eight volleys. The Apaches melded instantly back among the rocks and clambered upward to assess the situation. Learning the small number of troops, they launched a desperate attack, seeking to gain control of the precious waterhole. Grierson, in anticipation of this, had concentrated troops nearby and, before the Indian attack developed, two companies under First Lieutenant Thaddeus Winfield Jones attacked from a new direction, flushing the Indians from cover. They gained the rough slopes at a distance, where they stationed themselves, beyond reach of soldier fire. Neither party had the vigor to renew the fight. For two hours all was still.

At four o'clock a supply train escorted by Captain J. C. Gilmore and a detachment from the Twenty-fourth Infantry, a black outfit, rounded a point of mountains eight miles southeast, heading for the waterhole, the men apparently ignorant of the fight in progress, most of them riding in the wagons and hence invisible to the Indians. Unable to resist such a rare opportunity for loot, the Apaches, or a party of them, swooped down upon the lumbering wagons, but were discomfited when uniformed soldiers leaped from every wagon and met them with a fire that killed one and wounded others. A second party of attackers also was repulsed.[52]

Fought off, denied the sorely needed water, Victorio's party was collected and eased off for the Carrizo Mountains, between the Sierra Diablo and the Sierra Blanca, northeast of Quitman. It had not been a good expedition for Victorio; the omens were darkening. "The haste with which he fled," reported Grierson, exultantly, "fully attests the energy, pluck and earnest activity of the troops." That and the Indians' need for water, he might have added. Grierson continued: "Victorio goes back into Mexico with badly demoralized and considerably lessened force, and with a loss of from fifty to one hundred animals, and of his supply camp, which was captured . . . and consisted of about twenty-seven head of cattle," plus laden pack animals. Grierson noted that his troops had now twice forced the Indian back across the river, and in this he was correct, even if Victorio was not pushed there. The two engagements represented repulses for the hostiles, not defeats.

Captain Nolan trailed the Indians almost to their crossing of the Río Grande, ten miles below Quitman,[53] "going south towards Pass in the mountains across the River," or along the east side of the Sierra Guilman. "The whole outfit has crossed, including cattle, horses & families," Nolan reported,[54] suggesting the troops had not stripped them as completely as reported.

Dr. Manuel Samaniego, who had revealed the grisly Candelaria massacres earlier, reported in mid-August that Victorio was back in that range, nursing his wounds, no doubt sullenly wondering what now to do. His warriors had made a pass at Santa María, a small town, killing two Mexicans incidentally to their sweeping up loose horses for transportation and food, but otherwise they molested no one, remaining aloof. Colonel Valle was still engaged in suppressing revolutionists in southern Chihuahua and Durango. Grierson's patrols watched the known springs and waterholes in West Texas and scouted for sign. There were rumors—that the Indians never heard, of course—that Governor Luis Terrazas might personally lead troops against them, though he was not the Terrazas they must watch, but Joaquin, Luis' cousin.[55]

No more would Victorio range north of the border, although some of the Mescaleros en route back to the reservation would attack a stage near Quitman within a few days, mortally wounding Brevet Major General James J. Byrne, a Civil War veteran now employed by the Texas Pacific Railroad,[56] and bronco Apaches from the Sierra Madre, raiding in New Mexico, would ambush another stage, slaughtering three men and, in a brush with pursuing troops, kill a soldier, two scouts and wound two more.[57] Victorio had no part in these or related incidents.

Pueblo scouts dispatched by Grierson trailed the Mimbres to the Candelaría range, reporting the band "in a very crippled & demoralized condition, having their wounded with them & their stock played out as an evidence of which they were nearly all marching on foot driving their animals, avoiding their usual trails . . . & skirting the rough broken country. . . . The Indians crossed the road leading from El Paso to Chihuahua only a few hours after Col. Valle with a small detachment had passed south towards that place." Grierson estimated the Indian loss in the two Texas fights and other skirmishes at "certainly not less than thirty killed & wounded, very probably forty & . . . they are not now in condition to act in a body against any organized force."[58]

The rest in the Candelaría range was good for Victorio's wounded but bad for morale. Wars and raids were amusing and the rightful occupation of a man, providing loot and high adventure, but this war had settled into dreary campaigns with less and less plunder, more and more soldiers against them north and south of the border, and no end in sight except a bullet, perhaps soon. It is not to be wondered that the Mescaleros, who at this time may have represented 30 to 50 per cent of his strength, desired to leave and make their way by stealth and long dry marches back to the reservation, where they would filter in among those who had remained. Unless their agent was wiser than most agents they had known, no white man would be aware they had arrived, or where they had been.

So Ca-bal-le-so one day saddled his horse and ordered his people to come along. Victorio, fingering his worn rifle, disputed the Mescalero's right to leave. An argument ensued, became heated, and Victorio killed the other. The Mescaleros stayed. Victorio's band, while slowly dwindling, would not be destroyed in that way.[59]

On August 28 about thirty hostiles swept away two hundred horses belonging to Dr. Samaniego, driving them at a mad gallop toward Lake Guzman, while another party of sixteen Indians was reported burning down a house within a dozen miles of the Mexican El Paso; it was hard to tell from the report what raiders—if any—were involved in this incident.

The military north of the line was not idle during these weeks. Jack Crawford, who had won the title of "poet scout" with his verse, and now was stationed at Fort Craig, was told by Hatch in August to scout the Sacramentos, then go to Cummings and report to Buell, who at this time was organizing a considerable expedition into Mexico after Victorio. He thought, however, that a contact with the hostile might be productive and told Crawford he had conceived a "very dangerous mission," to send a scout with an Indian and a Mexican to find the Apache and try to induce him to surrender once more.

Since no other scout would undertake the assignment, Crawford volunteered. With him went Navaho Charlie, an Apache who knew Victorio well, and Casimero, "a fearless little Mexican,"[60] the party being escorted to the line by Lieutenant Maney and some scouts.

Parting with Maney, Crawford rode south, loosing smoke signals from hilltops, "hoping to catch the eye of the band we were hunting," hoping that the signs would be returned. They were not.

"On the evening of the third day we camped on Lake Santa Marie [María], a lovely body of water at the base of the San Blas Mountains," or just south of them. The night was so beautiful, Jack recalled, that he had composed a sentimental poem of three verses and as many choruses by the light of moon and campfire. Next day the party trailed the Victorio band, which had left the lake country, toward the Candelaría Mountains.

At every camping place . . . I noted the absence of the remains of game, and as large game was abundant in the country . . . I was satisfied that the band was out of ammunition. . . .

On the second day . . . we reached the Candelaría range, and much to my gratification while sweeping the country with my field glass I discovered Victorio's camp [which was on the north side of the range, near the Tinaja de Victorio]. I at once pushed forward to within a mile of his camping place, and gave Navaho Charlie explicit instructions to enter the camp, explain to the old Chief our mission and bring himself and not more than two of his warriors out to meet me and have a talk. To my astonishment and dismay he absolutely refused to go. He would give no explanation of his conduct. Coaxing and threats alike failed to move him. . . . In my anger I would have taken desperate chances and have gone myself into the hostile camp, but I knew not enough of the Apache tongue to intelligently converse with Victorio, and he nor none of his warriors could speak English.

Thus he reluctantly turned toward El Paso, reported by telegraph to Buell, then met him at Palomas, just south of the line and north of the lakes, and with the force returned to the Candelaría Range, where they found that Victorio had moved eastward, toward his rendezvous with destiny. Crawford crossed the Río Grande, went southeast of Quitman to Indian Hot Springs, recrossed into Mexico, and was nearing the Sierra San Martín del Borracho when he was ordered back by Buell, who was withdrawn from Mexico. "The government of the United States was rid of a troublesome foe, and General Terrases several thousand dollars richer through turning back our troops and capturing the hostile band," concluded the scout.[61]

Buell had received permission from Washington to cross the line in pursuit of the elusive hostiles. On September 1 he had reported that, since Victorio was rumored "not to exceed four or five days from us," he would mount a massive campaign against him, taking "all available Cavalry from Thomas, Grant, Lowell, Huachuca and here [Cummings]. Probably make up 200 men . . . [plus] two Indian [scout] companies, Mills and Stanton's, with their Pack Trains, also Lowell Pack Train now at Thomas," along with wagon transportation as far as the line, including a 400-gallon water wagon he had invented. Maybe Juh or Natchi would come along as volunteers, Buell speculated.[62]

This expedition, of huge dimensions for Apache warfare, did penetrate Mexico, but another body of armed whites, about the same size, was being organized far down in Chihuahua,[63] and this was the force that fate would bring into conflict with Victorio and send him implacably down into cold death.

XXII
Tres Castillos

Joaquín Terrazas was six feet tall, slender, energetic, a chain smoker of cigarettes, and somewhat vain. He had been fighting Apaches for a long time. One authority even believes him to have been a scalp hunter, a class including such characters as James Kirker and John Glanton,[1] but, while it is not clear that Joaquín Terrazas would stoop to such disreputable associations, he was, in any event, an Indian hunter with many years of experience, sagacious, persistent, and with an acquired mercilessness toward those whom he considered the enemies of all civilized mankind.[2]

Colonel Valle had returned from his operations in the south, stationing his cavalry at Carrizal and the infantry at the El Carmen Rancho, when Governor Luis Terrazas, alarmed and no doubt irritated at the continued reports from the north of depredations, ordered the two officers to take the field and operate together until the Indians were destroyed. On August 22 or 23 he called Valle to his home, where that officer found Joaquín already in conference with the governor and was introduced to him. Luis reviewed the growing reports of depredations by Victorio's warriors "who have now returned to the Lagunas," west of Candelaria. Despite the fact that the state's funds were low, as they generally were, Luis Terrazas had determined to stop hostilities "by any means." The governor said he could add three or four hundred armed civilians to Valle's regulars, and had ordered Joaquín to go along because he was familiar with the country, had a good fighting record, and had agreed to serve under Valle.

Valle was dubious. He protested that his troops were worn out, his horses broken down, and his equipment in such bad repair that, even if they found Indians, the results could not be favorable. Joaquín, on the other hand, was eager for the mission, anxious to be off. It suited his restless, driving temperament.

"Of the 100 horses which have returned from this [Valle's] campaign, at least 50 are in good enough condition to continue," he

293

argued. "The dismounted cavalry can go out on foot; they are used to operating as infantry. And the infantry itself is always ready for battle, especially after a few days' rest," which they now had enjoyed. Joaquín added that enough other horses could be raised from different garrisons and ranches to mount sufficient men, in any case. He believed a force of five hundred, "more than whatever number the Indians may have," could readily be assembled. If the Indians were at the Lagunas as reported, it would be only forty or fifty leagues—about one hundred miles—from Carmen and less than that from Carrizal, Galeana, or Corralitos. The campaign, he urged, "ought to proceed right away."

Valle objected still. He didn't know the people Joaquín spoke of and could not command them effectively; perhaps he recalled how bitterly Victorio had fought in the Sierra de los Pinos, and one taste was enough. "I'll have no part of it," he said, flatly. If Valle would not go, there was no point in Joaquín's urging it further, Terrazas conceded, and asked to be excused.

But the next morning he was directed to be at the governor's house again that evening, without fail.

"You see that Colonel Valle does not wish to take part in the campaign," Luis told him. The governor had decided nonetheless that the operation "should be done, and it will be done." He had secured a pledge of two hundred men from the political chief of Ciudad Guerrero, 111 miles by road west of Chihuahua City, and would immediately send rifles and ammunition for that number, money to hire mules, and supplies to pack them with. Orders had been issued to the political heads of Bravos[3] and Galeana, 30 miles southwest of Casas Grandes, to raise what troops they could. Luis' directive stated that "the government will pay four reales to the infantry and six to those who brought a horse and will pay rewards for Indian scalps, and the capture alive of women and children, according to the law, and 2,000 pesos for Victorio, dead or alive." It added that "all civilians enlisting for this campaign" would be under Joaquín's command. The expedition, Luis Terrazas directed, would form up at Galeana. He told his cousin to march the next day for San Andrés, 27 miles southwest of Chihuahua, collecting civilians to join with those of Guerrero and Galeana.

Early on August 25, Terrazas left Rancho la Huerta, where the interviews had taken place, with two soldiers, a servant, and a friend, and arrived at San Andrés before sunset. It is said that Joaquín Terrazas always took four white horses with him. One he rode, the other three being led or driven for fresh mounts as needed.[4]

The people of San Andrés, disorganized because of a recent abortive rebellion, were unenthusiastic about the proposed campaign, but at length the officer recruited twenty-seven. He reached Guerrero on August 31; the expected civilians had not yet arrived. He waited for them until September 6, when he left for Galeana, instructing the community leader to send them along when they showed up, that he would await them either at Galeana or to the north, or leave directions there how they might join him. The restless Terrazas rode on then to Namiquipa, fifty miles due north of Guerrero, where he found the civilians not ready to campaign, either. The town president assured him that those who would go would join with the main force from Guerrero, when they came through.

Terrazas continued to Santa Clara, twenty-three miles straight east of Namiquipa, and to Ortega, eight miles north of Santa Clara, where he gathered some men, then to San Lorenzo, thirty miles north of Ortega, and to El Carmen rancho, eleven miles farther northeast. At walled El Carmen, an island of defense and civilization for north-central Chihuahua, Terrazas heard of Buell's expedition forming up to drive down upon the lakes. He found at El Carmen men ready to join his force but awaiting arms from Chihuahua City. He sent messages to the men of Bravos on the Río Grande to come south to the Laguna de Patos, just north of present-day Villa Ahumada, to scout for Indians and to await instructions.

The tireless Terrazas went west then, fifty-five miles by road through San Buenaventura to Galeana, and from there forty miles northwest to Corralitos, where he expected to meet with the political chief who was trying to gather men.

He met him there, Juan Mata Ortiz,[5] a hard-bitten old Indian fighter who, within two years, was to be most cruelly done to death by Juh and Geronimo in retaliation—unplanned no doubt—for Terrazas' destruction of Victorio. No thought of that grim possibility crossed the minds of the two avengers as they mapped their campaign. Joaquin named Mata Ortiz his second in command.

With his slowly growing force Terrazas moved eastward to the Santa María River, which flowed from the south into Santa María Lake. He now had, in addition to those men he had brought with him, fewer than 50, about 119 whom Mata Ortiz had gathered, plus about

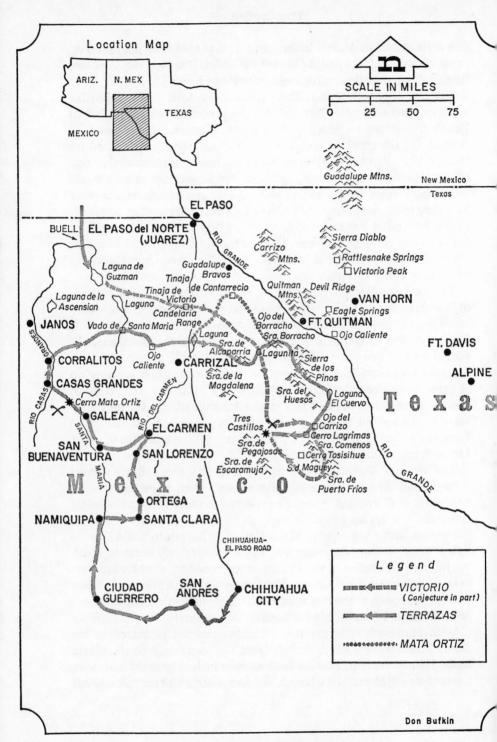

The Battle of Tres Castillos

50 additional cavalrymen. Mata Ortiz reported that he had scouts at the lakes hunting for the hostiles, and noted that United States forces were moving in that direction, too. Orders were left at Corralitos for the lakes scouts to follow up the command's trail when they returned. They did so, joining at Vado de Santa María, fourteen miles south of the lakes, reporting that they had found no Indians, only the tracks of ten horses heading east.

Terrazas now commenced searching for his enemy in earnest. He had his scouts working hard, and moved twenty miles southeast to the Ojos Calientes, then twenty-six miles farther east, to the Laguna de Patos, where he had instructed the men from Bravos to meet him. He arrived there September 28.

By now Joaquín had completed what would have been a full campaign for a lesser soldier, about 350 miles by his circuitous route from Chihuahua City, having to hustle up his own fighting force as he went and that from frequently reluctant civilian officials and an unenthusiastic citizenry who could not see why they should be marched to a distant area to fight Indians posing no immediate threat to themselves or their property. Yet he *had* collected men, seen that they were armed, arranged for supplies, scanty as they were. Now, after all this herculean effort, he was prepared finally to set out upon the real purpose of the operation: the hunting down of an elusive, dreaded, and apparently tireless enemy every bit as resourceful as Terrazas himself. Victorio would learn, however, that he was not the only fighter with courage, wiliness, and tenacity in Chihuahua that autumn. The two were antagonists well matched.

Terrazas sent out his scouts that same night, telling them to thoroughly work the Candelaría Range; if they found Victorio there, to steal silently away and let the officer plan the attack. The scouts left about dusk. They returned with the dawn. They had discovered no Indians. But they had found a trail leading east.

No one can know what was in the mind of Victorio, why he led his people out into the desert, toward no fixed goal. He was aware that the country beyond the Río Grande was seething with soldiers. He knew of the great force Buell was even then moving down from the northwest; perhaps he had learned this from spies among the San Carlos Indians, who regularly visited him, for it is to be remembered that some of the Mimbres had been returned there and dwelt still upon that great reservation. Victorio may have known, too, of the Terrazas command driving in from the west and southwest. The only truly safe

297

retreat for wild Indians now was the Sierra Madre, and Victorio knew that well—so why did he elect to go in the opposite direction? Why, indeed? There is no simple answer.

He led an exodus from the land and places he knew into the blazing wilderness. Toward a promised land? He could not have believed that. Perhaps the Mescaleros with him, who knew that country, persuaded Victorio that he and his followers could survive at peace out there. It may have been his own idea. He was getting old. Perhaps he was tired. He had whipped his pursuers, his tormentors, time without number, but their hordes were inexhaustible, and his warriors were few and becoming weary. His was an exodus to nowhere, from the land of broken hopes to the land of no hope whatever. So toward the east Victorio led his people, his men almost out of ammunition, driving before them the beasts to be their food, a crawling multitude under a pillar of dust there were no eyes to see save those of the vultures ever wheeling in the cloudless, burning sky, awaiting their turn, which was coming.

At the Laguna de Patos, meanwhile, there arrived at last 100 civilians from Guerrero, several more from Carrizal and the stalwarts from Bravos. By September 29, Terrazas commanded 350 men.

That day and the next they reshod their horses, brought in what little food Carrizal could offer. Terrazas ordered more supplies to follow him from El Paso del Norte, the present Juárez. He moved out on October 1, commanding one column, Juan Mata Ortiz the other. Mata Ortiz went northeast, making for the tanks of Cantarrecio, thirty-eight miles distant, expecting to meet there the additional supplies from El Paso. Then he would cross the plains southeast, paralleling the Río Grande although inland from it ten or twenty miles, following a trail which today is a truck road leading to the Wells of Borracho, thirty-five miles beyond Cantarrecio. Terrazas directed him to scout all the ranges along his route.

With his own column the colonel left the Sierra de Alcaparría, twenty-five miles southeast of Laguna de Patos, from there to scout the Sierra de Fierro and cross the chaparral plains to Borracho, to reach there when Mata Ortiz planned to arrive.

However, midway between the ranges of Alcaparría and Borracho is a small lake called the Lagunita, and here Joaquín Terrazas made his first important strike. The muddy banks and environs of the pond were a morass of tracks of men and animals. Victorio had camped here. In the gathering darkness Terrazas could not be sure which way the hostiles had gone. Eight butchered animals were strewn about, and his men helped themselves to some of the meat.

Believing that the Indians might have gone to the Sierra San Martín del Borracho, Joaquín pushed on that night, approaching the range cautiously. He contacted Mata Ortiz at dawn on the fifth, neither having struck the enemy. From Borracho they sent scouts south-easterly to the long line of hills known as the Sierra de los Pinos, where Valle a few weeks earlier had learned that fighting Victorio was not for him. They scoured other ranges, as well.

Terrazas had made a mistake leaving the Lagunita without working out Victorio's trail—perhaps he had no Indians who could do this—and now he had no idea where the enemy had gone. He remained at Borracho until the seventh of October, receiving the supplies from Paso del Norte, as well as reports from his scouts that the mountains within their reach were clean of hostiles. He moved out then, working southeasterly to the southernmost of the Pinos Mountains, where it was reported Victorio had camped earlier in the summer. He believed he was now north and perhaps east of the Indians, but couldn't be sure.

The slender colonel was not alone hunting Victorio, even here.

Buell's couriers had contacted him at Laguna de Patos, and Lieutenant Maney and his San Carlos scouts, with a Ninth Cavalry company under Lieutenant Charles Schaeffer, joined Terrazas briefly in the Pinos Mountains, but the Mexican officer was suspicious of the Apaches and on the night of October 9 advised Buell that "the further advance of American troops into the Territory of Mexico would be objectionable," so the American officer withdrew.[6] Meanwhile, Colonel Carr had scouted the country west of Corralitos to Janos, finding that "no hostiles were, or had been, this side [to the west] of that line."[7]

Even irregulars from the north had joined in the climactic search.

"On September 17, 1880, Lieutenant Baylor with thirteen rangers, myself included, entered Mexico," wrote James Gillett. They were joined by volunteers from various Mexican and Texan towns until they totaled more than one hundred, scouting the scattered ranges until Terrazas came up with them. They had joined Schaeffer, Maney, and Henry Parker, his chief of scouts, who had scored the signal victory over Victorio in May, now close to fulfilling his promise to prove the nemesis of the noted warrior.

Terrazas informed them that since the trail was headed south, deeper into Chihuahua, "he thought it best for the Americans to return to the United States. I was present at this conference and I at once saw my chance for a scrap with old Victorio to go glimmering."[8]

From the Sierra de los Pinos there is a chain of mountains leading due south: the Huesos, Carrizos, Comenos, Magueys, and Puerto Frios, all more or less in the same system like a north-south wrinkle on the seamed face of the desert. Terrazas moved toward the northern point of this range, intending to work south along it, for perhaps the enemy was there. Just above the northernmost portion of the chain is a lake, and he sent his scouts to examine it for signs that hostiles had visited it.

On the night of October 8 a courier informed him that the scouts had learned that the Indians indeed had passed by the shore of the laguna, apparently bound either for Cerro Lagrimas (Hill of Tears) or perhaps for the Tres Castillos (Three Castles). Both lay to the southwest, Lagrimas about twenty-seven miles, and Tres Castillos forty-five. Terrazas sent a runner to warn Carrizal that the hellhounds once more were heading that way, and to warn as well Gallegos, the Hacienda de Aguanueva, and other places.

The colonel now cut his force by ninety civilians, "who seemed to him worthless" in view of the swift marches that probably lay ahead. With his column reduced to 260 men, whose names are preserved, he marched to El Cuervo, the point at the south end of a tiny system of lakes of which Laguna is the largest, arriving at midnight of the ninth. Tracks of some hostiles were pressed into the mud by the lake, but with the dawn they were revealed to be those of only a few Indians, leading in the direction of Cerro Lagrimas. His blood warming, however, with this fresh trace of the enemy, Terrazas pushed south to the Ojo de Carrizo, between Cerro Lagrimas and Sierra del Carrizo to the east. Here he divided the few supplies and again split his forces. Mata Ortiz, with one column, worked south to Cerro Tosisihua, fifteen miles, hunting sign of the main body of hostiles, while Colonel Terrazas, with the other, struck due west for the Llanos de los Castillos (Castle Plains). Before separating they agreed upon signals in case either party should find fresh sign or sight Indians, and a point of reunion, if neither did.

Terrazas scouted all night, seeking sign amongst the chaparral. At dawn on October 13, leaving the brush, he cut tracks of three animals, at the edge of the Llanos de los Castillos. They came down from the north, appearing very fresh. While his main force camped concealed

300

in the chaparral, scouts worked onto the plains until, little more than a league out, they came across the trail of the main body of hostiles. The sign showed that they had passed within a few days, seeming to make for Tres Castillos.

The colonel hastened a messenger to Mata Ortiz, ordering him up under cover of darkness from Tosisihua, sent other couriers to Carrizal to hurry up supplies, and detached about fifty men to scout the Castillos that night, to see whether Indians were there. They returned at dawn, reporting no hostiles, but plenty of tracks. Mata Ortiz came in. He had found nothing. A false alarm led Terrazas and a small detachment to the south, where tracks had been reported leading east from Tres Castillos toward the Ojo de Carrizo, but, finding nothing, the party turned west toward the Castillos, scouting as they moved, intending to join Mata Ortiz, who was making directly for that place across the plains.

Terrazas arrived at the Castillos with his eleven-man detachment, at 2:00 P.M., October 14, his horses about worn out.

The Tres Castillos, of three major and some minor bare rock protrusions, the most elevated less than one hundred feet above the surface of the plain and the entire northeast-southwest range being scarcely half a mile in length, are the home today, as a century ago, of nesting eagles, rattlesnakes, and a gila monster or so. At their base are mudflats filled in October by hard summer tempests to form three ponds, one to the south, another to the east, and a smaller pool to the west. When full they attract ducks and countless crested quail, rabbits, and other small game. Antelope even today browse the surrounding plains, which are broad and unpeopled. Ten or fifteen miles southwest lies the Sierra de la Pagajosa, and beyond it the Sierra de las Escaramuzas, the closest major range. Neighboring uplifts in other directions are twice as far and the Tres Castillos stand alone, on the flat sink of the plains named for them, an unmistakable landmark as far as they can be seen. Aside from the rain collects, there is no water there in quantity, although a tiny spring or seep on the southernmost hill, the largest, has stained the brown stone. In October, when the ponds are full and there is plenty of water for people, stock, and wildlife, the site is an oasis, isolated, remote, and secure—except on October 15, 1880.

Terrazas climbed one of the three major hills, searching the horizon with his binoculars.

Dust! A blur to the south above the chaparral, about four leagues, or ten or twelve miles distant. Then another dust cloud, now that his eyes were alert to the barely distinguishable mist, and still later another. He studied the signs for half an hour, convincing himself that people were approaching the Castillos. He directed his escort to remain at the site, searching it well and, as the Indians approached, to make for a rocky hummock a mile or two north, not so high as the Castles, but still a landmark, concealing themselves there until his force arrived. The colonel warily rode off then, meeting Mata Ortiz and the two commands about midway from their last camp to the Tres Castillos.

The force was formed for the march in closed columns, with a front of 20 men, the only way they could hide the number which made up the command," wrote Terrazas, thinking that if the Indians observed but a score of men approaching they might stand and fight.

As the sun set the command, in said order, neared the Cerros de los Castillos, where already had arrived two of the groups of Indians who had raised the dusts. [When about one thousand yards distant, the Indians sighted the oncoming column, and about thirty warriors burst toward them.]

As the Indians came to within 400 meters, running as swiftly as they could, two of the Arisiachic [Tarahumares] dashed ahead of the column, shooting into them, the foremost one fell, and the rest turned back to the mountains, where most of the Indians remained.

As the assault force ran toward the hills, it split into separate commands, Mata Ortiz taking the right wing around to the north, and Terrazas the left, and so they encircled and collided with the main body of Apaches who had taken to the rocks. "Shooting back and forth with the Indians, they pushed the enemy onto the Cerro del Sur [the southern, most massive of the three main peaks], while almost all of the Indian horses were captured, many saddled and packed." The Mexicans swept around the southern peak, separated by some yards from the small central protrubrance, which a few of the Mexican soldiers used for cover.

Meanwhile, the remaining Indians, a small number whose dust Terrazas had observed when he scouted the range earlier, fled at the start of the fight. The other two bands, or what was left of them, were entrapped on the south peak. "Most of the night the Indians attempted to shoot their way from the peak, but were thrown back," wrote Terrazas. At about 10:00 P.M., some leagues to the south, a sudden blaze flared up while the entrapped Indians gathered brush, the only combustible material on the mountain, and kindled a response.

302

Terrazas dispatched about thirty riders toward the distant blaze. They ran into the Indians, but after a sharp skirmish returned, reporting they had dispersed them in the chaparral. There were no known casualties in this brief fight.[9]

"About midnight the death song of the Indians on the peak began to be heard, continuing with agonizing cries for more than two hours," Terrazas wrote. Nevertheless, throughout the night the Indians were busy, building the familiar rock defenses, ever a mark of Victorio's fights. When dawn burst over the plains the battle resumed, more ferociously than before.

"Immediately they were attacked by fire and hand-to-hand assault, with the result that among the fighters were found warriors and boys pleading for their lives, some of them being saved by this circumstance," wrote the colonel. In his initial report he said the Apaches were "fortified and made a desperate resistance. The Indians fought fiercely to the last, sustained by very advantageous positions which they had prepared during the night and which were taken by us by assault, our force throwing itself upon theirs, fighting man against man, the combatants wrestling with each other and getting hold of each other's heads." In his memoirs he added, "The warriors were killed, among the rocks, remaining only two of them in a cave, well armed and with plenty of ammunition, who, with no thought of surrender, held out for more than two hours before they were killed, this despite the fact that their lives were offered them by means of Indians already prisoners."

This cave, at the north end of the south hill, just large enough for a couple of warriors and protected by boulders from most direct fire, is a secure, though hopeless, retreat. By 10:00 A.M. they, too, had been slain. The cave has been thoroughly dug out by treasure hunters, but in it we found one .44-40 cartridge case, a probable relic of that bloody fight. This, with other cartridge cases of that era found elsewhere around the south peak, are all but geography that remains of the great battle today.

Terrazas had lost three men killed: Nicanor Aguilar and Serapio Muñoz from San Andrés, and Luis Rubio from Guerrero, and ten men wounded, four seriously. He had slain and scalped (for the bounty) seventy-eight Indians, of whom sixty-two were warriors and the remainder women and children, taken sixty-eight prisoners,[10] and recovered two captives, Felix Carrillo, twelve, of Belen, New Mexico, wounded in the leg, and Felipe Padilla, ten, of Padillas, near Belen.

He also had recovered 120 horses, 38 mules, and a dozen burros. In his report Terrazas cited for gallantry Juan Mata Ortiz, Rodrigo García, and Mauricio Corredor, captain of the Arisiachic force of Tarahumares Indians. It is noteworthy that he made no mention of Mauricio as having killed Victorio, a feat for which posterity has generally credited him (he was honored by the government for having done so), nor did Terrazas know which Indian was Victorio, nor, for that matter, positively that Victorio had been among the slain until he was so informed by the two Mexican boys recaptured and the fact was confirmed by Indian prisoners.

It is obvious that no one knew who had slain the great guerrilla, nor precisely how he was killed. The various stories of his death—that he was mounted upon a white horse,[11] that he dropped after repeated wounds while directing the defenses,[12] that he was the last man killed defying his enemies from the peak of the mountain[13]—all reflect the imagination of the writer rather than the facts of that grisly day. Terrazas said that after he was told Victorio was leader of the party, and which Indian he was, that fact was confirmed by prisoners. "The indian Victorio is of the dead, according to the signs by which he is known," he reported in a communique that same day to Luis Terrazas, "according to those who tell me, those who knew him and the testimony of the captives, besides the wearing apparel and personal accoutrements which I have recovered, and which . . . would only be carried by an Indian chief of some importance." Terrazas himself had never seen Victorio before.

As might be supposed, Indian versions of the death of Victorio vary widely from the official Mexican version. One old Apache tale has it that Victorio was captured, then slain by boiling in oil, which, although preposterous, suggests the still-lingering hatred between the races.[14]

First Lieutenant William Henry Beck, Tenth Cavalry, interviewed by a newspaper, told the most savage account of the death of Victorio, a story he said he had picked up south of the border.

After the surrender, Terrazas ranged ten of the bucks in line and asked where Victorio was. They stolidly refused to answer and were immediately shot. Another ten shared the same fate, and so the match proceeded until thirty-seven braves had been disposed of. The thirty-eighth man, a half-breed Mexican Apache, threw up his hands and promised to reveal the spot if his life were spared. Accordingly he conducted Terrazas to the ravine

304

where Victorio lay wounded mortally, surrounded by his squaws. To make a sure thing of it, however, Terrazas commanded his orderly to kill him, and that functionary speedily sent him to the happy hunting grounds.[15]

Beck might have believed this yarn, but it is impossible, since there is no ravine near Tres Castillos where a wounded Indian could hide, nor did Victorio have more than one wife.

Mescaleros filtering back to their agency gave their version of what had happened: "The first attack made on him by a portion of the Mexican forces, was repulsed," they said. "After being entirely surrounded by Mexican troops he fought from his defenses until [his] ammunition was exhausted when, by command,[16] they all eased to their feet, throwing up their hands as token of surrender. All not captured were then killed. All the captured women and children were distributed as peons."[17]

The most extended Apache version was told by James Kaywaykla to Eve Ball, long-time confidante of descendants of these and other hostiles, who has interviewed many and recorded their recollections. Kaywaykla was a grandson or grand-nephew[18] of Nana and, at the age of four, was in the battle of Tres Castillos. Being then a child, he could not clearly recall every circumstance in later life, but added to his memories were the recollections of his people, some of them adults who escaped the massacre, and his version therefore deserves great weight. A graduate of Carlisle Indian School, he was an educated, intelligent informant.

He said that the Apaches, whom he believed to number four hundred,[19] were camped one day southeast of Tres Castillos, where they butchered thirty head of beef, dried the meat, and then set out for Tres Castillos, from which they hoped to cross northern Chihuahua to Sonora and the Sierra Madre. Nana suggested leading a band on a search for ammunition, but Victorio demurred, saying he needed Nana to manage the rear guard in the event of an attack by soldiers known to be operating in that country. The straggling line of Indians, with Nana in the rear with some warriors, marched northwest all day. They came to "the long sand dune around which we must pass to reach the lake" at the eastern foot of Tres Castillos. Between the dune and the foothills was a "very narrow passage," and through it the Indians moved to make their camp, hard by the *cerros* (hills), some of the women taking the horses to water. Shots abruptly sputtered beyond the lake. Instantly all was commotion. James, seized by his mother, was rushed to "a little bench," where she looked back. "There was less firing, just a few scattered shots. I knew that the chief and his guard were out of ammunition."

As the Apaches climbed into the rocks, shod horses, carrying Mexicans, dashed to and fro, cutting down any who had not gained the safety of the rocky peaks. Kaywaykla's mother crawled with the child among the rocks, huddling in a crevice between two huge boulders while a Mexican soldier, so near they might have touched him, smoked a cigaret, ground out the stub with his heel, and stalked away.

"When he was out of hearing we left our refuge and crawled up the mountain. There were still occasional shots in the valley. Horses moved back and forth and I knew our people were being hunted down and killed. But I heard no cries, for they were Apaches."

The fugitives came across another woman and a girl. James's mother knew of a tiny arroyo crossing the bench. The other woman would not try escaping that way, sure they would be caught, but Kaywaykla's mother, urging the child ahead of her, began the attempt and they made it; the other two did not escape.

"All night we toiled up the mountain, stumbling, falling, struggling toward the summit. . . . At dawn we crossed the ridge and started down the west slope." They met other stragglers, a wounded warrior, some women and children, and eventually Nana and his men. Seventeen had escaped the battle. The little band of survivors made their way to the Sierra Madre.

In one account Kaywaykla said Victorio committed suicide by knife rather than be captured,[20] and this seems generally accepted among Apaches today. In addition to Nana's party of seventeen, another small group, about fifteen, was away on a raid, and still another minor group of Mescaleros was off hunting and missed the battle. Victorio's remarkable sister, Lozen, who "had the power" and could determine the direction and distance of the enemy, was not with the band, and thus Victorio had no warning of the proximity of the Mexicans until the fight began, so believe the older Apaches.[21] Thus he was surprised, and so he perished.

The principal difficulty with Kaywaykla's account is geographical, but perhaps it can be made to conform to the terrain; it is a revealing and valuable insight into this great engagement. Having visited Tres Castillos twice and thoroughly explored the peaks and environs, I do not believe any sand dune such as he describes now exists or did exist, although to a child a long, low hill might seem a dune. Perhaps the "narrow passage" he described was that between the two lakes, the eastern and the southern, rather than between the lake and a dune. Most of the features mentioned in Kaywaykla's recollections of the early part of the fight can be discerned, with slight adjustments. The hills are skirted by benches, particularly to the east and between the two principal uplifts. There is a small arroyo nearly crossing the bench, or saddle, between the north mountain and that to the south, where the major fight took place. There are huge connecting boulders all about, offering such shelter as James and his mother sought while the soldier smoked his cigaret close by.

The greatest difficulty comes with his description of climbing the mountain all night until they reached safety with the dawn beyond the ridge. The Tres Castillos are such small protruberances that this would not be possible. One can clamber to the top in a matter of half an hour, and with soldiers everywhere there would have been no safety on the far side. What must have occurred, it seems to me, is that once beyond the hills the mother and son, together with a few other survivors, struggled through the darkness across the southwestern plains to the Pegajosas or, more likely, beyond them to the mountain range called Escaramuzas, whose crest they could have reached during the single night and beyond which they would have found safety.

Unfortunately, James Kaywaykla is no longer living, and this theory cannot be checked with him. With this slight modification, however, his recollections fit the geography remarkably well.

XXIII
Afterward

Nana directed Ka-ya-ten-nae, the influential warrior who became a subchief, back to Tres Castillos as soon as the Mexicans had left, to search the site and bury as many victims as he could, James Kaywaykla later reported. Ka-ya-ten-nae subsequently married James's mother, becoming the boy's stepfather.

Ka-ya-ten-nae found that many [bodies] had been burned. The advance guard had fought as long as one bullet remained. The three men remaining with Victorio[1] had followed the example of their chief and died by their own knives. Their bodies had not been mutilated so identification was sure. They piled rocks upon those four bodies, but were unable to render a like service to the others. When the hunters returned, Grandfather [Nana] led his remnant of people westward to the Sierra Madre, the Blue Mountains of the Apaches.[2]

Washington was informed officially of Victorio's destruction by Juan N. Navarro, Mexican consul at New York City, on directions of his government. The event was termed a "noteworthy feat of arms which will exert so great an influence over the tranquility of both frontiers."[3]

Several sources report that the "vengeance" of the Apaches upon the Mexicans was ferocious and costly, but without advancing much solid evidence of this. Gillett wrote that Nana and his band killed more than two hundred Mexicans before joining other Chiricahuas in the Sierra Madre, but with a lack of detail.[4]

"The young warriors of Victorio's band are striking terror into the Mexicans, having killed twenty-five since the massacre. I understand Terrazas struck only the squaw camp with a few old men in it," was the message from a scout named Riley[5] from Mesilla on December 9.

It was not long before the Mescaleros who had been with Victorio cautiously sought to return to their Fort Stanton reservation. Russell reported on November 22 that "thirteen Indians: six men, five women and two children, came in. . . . Some of the men have been immediately around the Agency for several days, the others, 15 to 20 miles away. A few days since three of them stood near their horses within fifty yards of the Commanding officer who, at the time, was at the camp of the friendly Indians." A few nights later they reported to George W. Maxwell, post trader, that they wanted to come in and would do so if the military would not kill them. Receiving assurances, they surrendered and were housed in two tents lent by Russell and were rationed by him. "Although these Indians did not admit to the officer that they had been with Victorio (evading the question) they do admit it to Mr. Maxwell, and say that there are only seven or eight Mescalero Indians out now, that most of the rest were killed, died, or were taken prisoners, and add that the few now out will soon be in."[6]

Captain Casper H. Conrad, Fifteenth Infantry, commanding at Stanton, listed the Mescaleros killed or captured during the Tres Castillos fight as including Blanco, his wife and child; Anton Chiquito, his wife; and others, together to the number of sixty men, women, and children. One of the subchiefs, San Juan, came in.[7] Muchacho Negro[8] and his band of six men, five women, and two children were away with Nana's group or another party and missed the massacre.[9] Hatch noted in an endorsement that "the number of Mescaleros [with Victorio] was always supposed to be greater than the number" reported by Conrad,[10] but it appears that Conrad's figures were approximately correct.

Others surrendered from time to time, even as late as 1882;[11] some continued to provoke turmoil and unrest, leading Pope to suggest anew that the whole tribe be removed to Indian Territory, where, it was hoped, their militant presence "would have a powerful effect in restraining the ardor of the invaders" or white squatters upon that territory presumably reserved for Indians.[12] On August 11, 1882, Sergeant Na-tu-go-liu-je and Private Patricio of the Indian police captured an Indian in "an important arrest." "The captive is known to the Indians here and also to the Interpreter as one of Victoria's principal warriors and that he left here with Victoria in 1879." His name, not clearly decipherable, appears to be "Josecique."[13] This Apache might have been old Josecito, first heard of in 1853 when he signed the treaty.

Nine soldiers were ambushed south of Carrizal after their part in the big fight, and one of them, having in his possession a saddle and personal effects of Victorio, was hacked to pieces, according to a newspaper.[14] Yet the publication was not sure whether the seemingly indestructible Victorio actually had been killed after all, asserting the matter "is still an open question."[15]

Returning Mescaleros assured the military and their agent that Victorio indeed was dead,[16] but suspicions to the contrary persisted. Jack Crawford expressed skepticism.[17] One report said that Victorio not only was still alive, but was trying to induce Navahos to join him in new raids.[18] Agent Tiffany, of San Carlos, heard the rumors and took them up with the one Indian best able to discover the truth and whom he knew to be completely trustworthy: Loco, a cochief with Victorio for many years and closer to the great guerrilla than any other ranking Apache who had come in.

On April 13, 1881, Tiffany reported to the commissioner:

> For some time old Loco . . . has been interviewed by me privately, that I might find out whether Victorio was really dead, and being suspicious that some of the hostiles were in communication with some of his band I asked him to inform me. Yesterday evening he came for a private talk, and said Victoria was dead, and the band would come in to this reservation under him [Loco] as chief if I would promise them safe protection from being turned over to the military to be killed, and if the Govt. would not allow me to give them protection, to let them know so they could get away and go somewhere else, that they would behave themselves and never go out again, and Loco would be responsible for them.[19]

So it was true, on the best possible authority. Victorio was dead.

Colonel Terrazas already had been acknowledged throughout northern Mexico the conqueror of this scourge of the frontier, although the suspicion persisted north of the border that Victorio was taken so easily only because he had too little ammunition to put up a good fight.[20]

Terrazas' triumphal entry with his forces into the City of Chihuahua was reported by a *Chicago Times* correspondent, reprinted in the *Daily New Mexican*:

> The whole city turned out—all classes and conditions. The housetops were covered, the balconies were alive, and banners were flying from all the masts. The bands played, and from the church and cathedral towers the bells rang out in tuneful clamor. . . . [Beyond the city] we could discover some black objects against the sky like waving plumes of the knights of old. The signal is given and the column moves forward, and behold! these waving plumes are the ghastly scalps of the fallen enemy, held aloft to the gazing crowd, who yell and cry, and follow along perfectly wild with

excitement. They are on poles about ten feet long, carried by the victors four abreast. We count them, seventy-eight in number, sixteen of which are women and children. I had of course expected to see some scalps, but here I saw a long black line of terrible looking objects worse by far than I had supposed. The whole head of hair had been in most cases taken.

First came an immense throng of people, men, women, and children, pushing each other to and fro, mad with excitement. Then came a band, whose music was drowned from time to time by the plaudits of the populace. Then came Colonel Terrassas [sic] and his staff of officers, looking worn and travel-stained. Immediately after came the prisoners mounted upon ponies and mules. They were all women and children, from old age to infancy, except one Comanche whose life was spared by Cruz, the scout. After the prisoners came the scalp bearers and pack trains. The men were bloody and dirty in the extreme, as a natural consequence; but they could not equal the Apaches, who for filth, dirt, and mean looks surpassed anything I ever saw or could imagine. . . . This campaign will cost the state not less than $50,000 cash outlay [for scalps]. The scalp of Victorio, tinged visibly with gray, was carried by the man who was given the credit of shooting him. . . .

About 1 o'clock the procession halted before one of the large prisons or camp yards, and the prisoners dismounted and passed in. The next day all the smaller children, up to girls of 13 years of age, were given away, and, strange as it may seem, they have been taken into the best and wealthiest families in the city. Governor [Luis] Terrassas took two, a boy and a girl. One gentleman took three. They have been cleaned up, and are much improved in appearance. . . . The women are all confined in the city prison. . . .[21]

The slayer of Victoria has been presented with a suit that is neat and not gaudy, either. The short jacket is of crimson broadcloth; the vest and pants of black doeskin, trimmed with silver face; the hat a magnificent white fur broadbrim, and covered with spangles. He is a peaceful Tarahumare Indian, and bears his honors quietly.[22]

Terrazas was promoted to full colonel in the Mexican Army for his feat.[23]

An elaborate monument in recognition of his conquest of Victorio was erected in the city of Chihuahua, a monument almost unique in all of Mexico, for Indian fighters, even successful ones, were not customarily so honored in that country. There is no monument, plaque, or anything of that nature in the dusty, unprepossessing community of Galeana to the memory of Juan Mata Ortiz, for example, who fully shared in the battle against the Apache,[24] although its forlorn little plaza is named for him.

311

For all his experience in fighting the Apaches, Juan Mata Ortiz fell into a typical one of their traps, and cruelly perished.

A band of Apaches on November 13, 1882, drove off some horses from near Galeana, operating too brazenly, too slowly, to have been anything but a lure to draw out the whites, but Mata Ortiz, veteran Indian fighter that he was, pounded out from the community with twenty-one men, chasing the Indians fourteen and two-tenths miles toward the ridge dividing the Galeana country from that of Casas Grandes. The Apaches kept just far enough ahead with their loot to draw the Mexicans on. Suddenly the pursuers were attacked by the main body of Apaches under Juh and Geronimo and, too late, Mata Ortiz saw that he was trapped. He led his force to the top of a pointed hill, since known as Cerrito Mata Ortiz, and there the doomed men tried to dig in. But the stony soil—the hill is littered with small, broken limestone boulders and has very little free earth—defied their efforts. One by one they were picked off, until a single man escaped (let go by Geronimo, it was reported, in order to bring more Mexicans into the trap), and only Mata Ortiz remained alive.

The nature of his death is uncertain, but that he died that day there is no doubt, as did also two of the Apaches.[25]

The death of Victorio marked the mid-point, rather than the end, of the Apache wars of the Southwest, but never again were fighters in such numbers to roam and ravage that country, nor were they again to be so ably led and managed except, perhaps, in a minor way by Juh.

Victorio had been lucky very often, it was true, but he also was astute, and there is little doubt that as a guerrilla leader he possessed a rare genius.

No one taught Victorio tactics, unless it was the enemies with whom his world was fairly bursting. But that he grasped them well is evident. Gillett said he often discussed Victorio with army officers, who agreed that he "displayed great military genius." One of them, Major Andrew Jackson McGonnigle, who had fought through the Civil War and against Sioux and Apaches afterward, "considered Victorio the greatest Indian general who had ever appeared on the American continent."

The ranger himself had inspected twenty-five or more of his camps. "He was very particular about locating them strategically, and his breastworks were most skillfully arranged and built," wrote Gillett. "If he remained only an hour in camp he had these defenses thrown up.''[26] Many others who fought him commented on the skill and enduring quality of his rock shelters.

Victorio learned early to seize and hold superior positions, greater in elevation than those of his adversary. He neglected this matter twice only, in the Parker fight and at Tres Castillos, and each time he suffered for it.

The Indian chose always to resist where wild, rough country was at his rear, into which he would disappear when he was through fighting or if his defenses seemed about to be turned. Again, it was lack of such a situation on the broad and barren plains surrounding the rocky hummocks of Tres Castillos that led to his destruction. Although he had no quartermaster department, Victorio was careful always to supply his people with all the ammunition they could carry and to keep their larder mobile and ready to bolt. This food supply, of course, consisted largely of cattle and horses. When he butchered an animal, he festooned pack stock with fresh meat, so that if the camp must be quickly abandoned, the rations would move with the people.

Victorio was concerned that his intelligence be accurate. At the Candelaría Range he regularly posted a lookout on the highest point overlooking the El Paso–Chihuahua road. In air so luminous the observor could see anyone approaching thirty or forty miles in either direction. Even in the disputes and differences around Ojo Caliente, Victorio made it a practice to remain beyond reach until the way was safe. He might remain aloof on a mountaintop until he was very sure. Never was Victorio a lounger around the agency or military posts. He remained apart, ever vigilant, wary, even when nominally at peace. He could not be surprised. Nor is there any indication that he consumed much alcohol. Loco went through a period when he drank what whiskey he could get, and so did other chiefs, but not Victorio. In his fifty-five or sixty years of life there is no record that he ever lost control of himself through whiskey or any other dissipation. He had but one wife, but the loyalty shown him by others of his people, women as well as men, was astounding.

No white man knew him well, although many made contact with him frequently.

Victorio kept his people in line and peaceful when he pledged to do so, but that was in return for rations and a reservation, not because he loved, cared for, or was concerned about the white man. He was an Apache, a man apart—the greatest of Apaches of his time

313

perhaps—and he would have been a bulwark of peace had he been dealt with fairly. He killed rather than see his strength dissipated, as when he shot Ca-bal-le-so rather than permit him to take his people off, but other Mescaleros then remained with him to the end.

He died because his luck had run out. That was the main thing. He was trapped by an enemy he feared little, out of ammunition or almost so, on a rocky upthrust where his wiliness was meaningless, a position easy to surround, impossible to defend without arms.

And he and his people "died fighting like brave men."[27] But the war they carried on had taken the lives of several hundred men, women, and children and had cost the United States easily several millions of dollars.

General Sherman, in his Annual Report for 1881, said, "I do not know the reasons for the Interior Department insisting on the removal of these Indians to Arizona. They must have been very cogent to justify its cost to the settlers and to the government. Victorio's capture is not very probable, but his killing, however cruel it may be, will be done in time."

It was done. The record is not one in which other Americans should take pride.

BIBLIOGRAPHY

Manuscript Materials, Unpublished Documents, Collections

Ayres, John. "Ancient Santa Fe, 1883," Bancroft Library, HHB [P-E 5].
Ball, Eve. Interviews, correspondence with author, 1965 to present.
Brevoort, Elias. Reminiscences, Brancroft Library, HHB [P-E 5].
Crook, George. Documents from Tours of Duty in Arizona, 1871–75 and 1882–86, Rutherford B. Hayes Memorial Library, Fremont, Ohio.
Erbe, Marie. "Orlanda F. Piper, Agent for the Southern Apache Agency, New Mexico, 1870–1872," Presbyterian Historical Society, Philadelphia.
Farmer, Malcolm F. "New Mexico Camps, Posts, Stations and Forts," n.d., compiled and mimeographed under direction of the Library, Museum of New Mexico, Santa Fe.
Griswold, Gillett M. "The Fort Sill Apaches: Their Vital Statistics, Tribal Origins, Antecedents." Unpublished manuscript courtesy Field Artillery Museum, Fort Sill, Oklahoma, 1970.
Howard, Oliver Otis. "Indian Troubles in Arizona and New Mexico (1872)," Bancroft Library, HHB [P-D 6].
Loring, L. Y. "Report on Coyotero Apaches, Camp Apache, Arizona Territory, 1875," Bancroft Library, HHB [P-D, 5].
Montes, Bertha. "The Great Chieftains," in possession of C. L. Sonnichsen, University of Texas at El Paso.
Shapard, John A. Interviews, correspondence with author, 1969 to present.
Steck, Michael. Papers, Zimmerman Library, University of New Mexico, Albuquerque.
Terrazas, Joaquin. Career Military File, Secretario de Guerra y Marina, Archivos de la Nación de Mexico, Mexico City.
United States Government, National Archives and Records Service. Old Military Records Division: Selected Documents Relating to the Activities of the Ninth and Tenth Cavalry in:
    The Campaign Against Victorio, 1879–1880, AGO, Letters Received, 6058–1879, Record Group 94;
    AGO, Microcopy 666, Letters Received, 2465–1871, Roll 24, Correspondence relating to Vincent Colyer's mission to the Apaches;
    AGO, Microcopy 666, Letters Received, Roll 123; Correspondence

relating to the agreement with Cochise . . . negotiated by Gen. Oliver O. Howard;

AGO, Microcopy 666, Letters Received, 2576–1876, Roll 265, Correspondence relating to the removal of the Chiricahua Apaches to the San Carlos Indian Agency, Arizona, 1876–77;

AGO, Microcopy 666, Letters Received, 1827–1877, Roll 326, Correspondence relating to the arrest and removal of Geronimo's band of renegade Chiricahua Apache Indians from Hot Spring, N. Mex., to the San Carlos Indian Agency, Ariz., 1877;

AGO, Microcopy 666, Letters Received, 5705–1877, Correspondence relating to military operations against the Warm Springs Indians who fled from the San Carlos Indian Agency, Ariz., 1877–79;

AGO, Record Group 393, Records of U.S. Continental Commands, 1821–1920, Department of Arizona, *Miscellaneous Papers re. Victoria Campaign*, Roll 36;

AGO, Record Group 393, Letters Sent, District of New Mexico, 1881–83;

Clum, Henry R., personal military file; Drew, Charles E., personal military file; Hennisee, Argalus Garey, personal military file; Morrow, Albert P., personal military file; Steen, Enoch, personal military file;

Office of Indian Affairs, Microcopy 234, Letters Received, 1824–80, Arizona Superintendency, 1863–80;

Office of Indian Affairs, Microcopy 234, Letters Received, 1824–80, New Mexico Superintendency, 1849–80;

Returns from U.S. Military Posts, 1800–1916, Microcopy 617, Forts Apache, 1870–87, Roll 33; Bascom, 1863–70, Roll 81; Bayard, 1866–94, Rolls 87–88; Bowie, 1862–82, Roll 129; Buchanan, 1856–62, Roll 156; Conrad, 1851–54, Roll 246; Craig, 1854–55, Rolls 261–62; Cummings, 1863–66, Roll 275; Doña Ana, 1849–51, Roll 320; Fillmore, 1851–62, Roll 366; Hatch's Ranch, 1856–62, Roll 464; John A. Rucker, 1878–80, Roll 556; McRae, 1863–76, Roll 710; Ojo Caliente, 1879–82, Roll 877; Rio Mimbres, 1863–66, Roll 1025; Selden, 1865–82, Rolls 1145–1146; Socorro, 1849–51; Roll 1202; Stanton, 1855–87, Rolls 1216–1218; Thorn, 1854–59, Roll 1271; Tularosa, 1872–74, Roll 1300; Webster, 1852–60, Roll 1407; West, 1863–64, Roll 1410; Wingate, 1862–82, Rolls 1448–1449; McLane, 1861, Roll 1522.

————. Social and Economics Records Division: *Treaty Between the U.S. and part of the Apache Nation of Indians, 1855.* 10 Stat. 979–81.

————. Cartographic and Audiovisual Records Division: Map of District of New Mexico, 1875, drawn by Lieutenant C. C. Morrison, 6th Cavalry, Acting Engineer Officer, Record Group 77, W 197-1; Map of Southern New Mexico, May, 1881, prepared in the Chief Engineer Office of the

Department of Missouri, Record Group 393, Dept. No. 12; Map of Southwestern New Mexico, 1882, prepared under supervision of First Lieutenant Thomas N. Bailey, Record Group 393, Dept. No. 15.

Government Publications

Biographical Directory of the American Congress 1774–1927. Washington, Government Printing Office, 1928.

The Centennial of the United States Military Academy at West Point, New York, 1802–1902. 2 vols. Washington, Government Printing Office, 1904.

Chronological List of Actions, &c., with Indians, from January 1, 1866, to January, 1891. Washington, Adjutant General's Office, 1891.

Federal Census—Territory of New Mexico and Territory of Arizona: Excerpts from the Decennial Federal Census, 1860, for Arizona County in the Territory of New Mexico, the Special Territorial Census of 1864 Taken in Arizona, and Decennial Federal Census, 1870, for the Territory of Arizona. Washington, Government Printing Office, 1965.

Heitman, Francis Bernard. *Historical Register and Dictionary of the United States Army, from its Organization, September 29, 1789, to March 2, 1903.* 2 vols. Washington, Government Printing Office, 1903.

Hodge, Frederick Webb. *Handbook of American Indians North of Mexico.* 2 vols. Washington, Government Printing Office, 1907.

Matloff, Maurice, ed. *Army Historical Series: American Military History.* Washington, Office of the Chief of Military History, United States Army, 1969.

Medal of Honor Recipients: 1863–1963, Prepared for the Subcommittee on Veterans' Affairs of the Committee on Labor and Public Welfare, United States Senate. Washington, Government Printing Office, 1964.

Orton, Brig. Gen. Richard H. *Records of California Men in the War of the Rebellion, 1861 to 1867.* Sacramento, State Office, 1890.

Pamphlet Accompanying Microcopy No. 234, Letters Received by the Office of Indian Affairs, 1824–80. Washington, National Archives Microfilm Publications, 1966.

Record of Engagements with Hostile Indians Within the Military Division of the Missouri, from 1868 to 1882, compiled from official records. Washington, Government Printing Office, 1882.

Royce, Charles C., comp. "Indian Land Cessions in the United States," *Bureau of American Ethnology, Eighteenth Annual Report, 1896–97.* 2 parts. Washington, Government Printing Office, 1899.

Swanton, John R. *The Indian Tribes of North America.* Washington, Government Printing Office, 1953.

35 Cong., 1 sess., Sen. Exec. Doc. 11, II Serial 920.

39 Cong., 2 sess., *Senate Report* No. 156, Serial 1279 (1865).

U.S. Board of Indian Commissioners. Peace with the Apaches of New

317

Mexico and Arizona. Report of Vincent Colyer, Member of Board—1871. Washington, Government Printing Office, 1872.

War Department, *Annual Reports of the Secretary of War,* 1878–79. 46 Cong., 2 sess., House Exec. Docs., *1879–1880;* Volume II, Number 1, Part II, Volume I. Washington, Government Printing Office, 1880.

War Department, *Annual Reports of the Secretary of War,* 1879–80. 46 Cong., 3 sess., House Exec. Docs., *1880–81;* Volume II—War, Number 1, Part II, Volume I. Washington, Government Printing Office, 1881.

Newspapers

Albuquerque, New Mexico, *Daily Journal.*

Globe, *Arizona Silver Belt.*

Las Cruces, New Mexico, *Thirty-Four.*

New York *Sun.*

New York Times.

Prescott, *Arizona Miner.*

Prescott, *Arizonian.*

Santa Fe, *Daily New Mexican.*

Silver City, New Mexico, *Enterprise.*

Silver City, New Mexico, *Grant County Herald.*

Silver City, New Mexico, *Southwest.*

Tucson, *Arizona Star.*

Tucson, *Weekly Arizonian.*

Yuma, *Arizona Sentinel.*

Zanesville, Ohio, *Times Recorder.*

Primary Sources

Arny, W. F. M. *Indian Agent in New Mexico: The Journal of Special Agent W. F. M. Arny, 1870.* Ed. by Lawrence R. Murphy. Santa Fe, Stagecoach Press, 1967.

Ball, Eve. *In the Days of Victorio: Recollections of a Warm Springs Apache.* Tucson, University of Arizona Press, 1970.

Bartlett, John Russell. *Personal Narrative of Explorations and Incidents in Texas, New Mexico, California, Sonora, and Chihuahua, connected with the United States and Mexican Boundary Commission During the Years 1850, '51, '52, and '53.* 2 vols. New York, D. Appleton & Company, 1854.

Betzinez, Jason. *I Fought With Geronimo.* Harrisburg, Pennsylvania, The Stackpole Company, 1959.

Clarke, Dwight L., ed. *The Original Journals of Henry Smith Turner with Stephen Watts Kearny to New Mexico and California, 1846.* Norman, University of Oklahoma Press, 1966.

Clum, Woodworth. *Apache Agent: The Story of John P. Clum.* Boston, Houghton, Mifflin Co., 1936.

Conner, Daniel Ellis. *Joseph Reddeford Walker and the Arizona Adventure.* Norman, University of Oklahoma Press, 1956.

Corbusier, William T. *Verde to San Carlos: Recollections of a Famous Army Surgeon and His Observant Family on the Western Frontier 1869–1886.* Tucson, Dale Stuart King, 1968.

Cremony, John C. *Life Among the Apaches.* San Francisco, A. Roman & Company, 1868; reprinted, Tucson, Arizona Silhouettes, 1954.

Crook, George. *General George Crook: His Autobiography.* Ed. by Martin F. Schmitt. Norman, University of Oklahoma Press, 1960.

Cruse, Thomas. *Apache Days and After.* Caldwell, The Caxton Press, 1941.

Davis, Britton. *The Truth About Geronimo.* New Haven, Yale University Press, 1929.

Emory, William Helmsley. *Lieutenant Emory Reports: A Reprint of Lieutenant W. H. Emory's Notes of a Military Reconnaissance.* Introduction and notes by Ross Calvin. Albuquerque, University of New Mexico Press, 1951.

Frazer, Robert W., ed. *Mansfield on the Condition of the Western Forts 1853–54.* Norman, University of Oklahoma Press, 1963.

Gillett, James B. *Six Years with the Texas Rangers: 1875 to 1881.* New Haven, Yale University Press, 1963.

Hamlin, Captain Percy Gatling, ed. *The Making of a Soldier: Letters of General R. S. Ewell.* Richmond, Virginia, Whittet & Shepperson, 1935.

Howard, Oliver Otis. *Famous Indian Chiefs I have Known.* New York, the Century Company, 1908.

———. *My Life and Experiences Among Our Hostile Indians.* Hartford, Connecticut, A. D. Worthington & Company, 1907.

McNitt, Frank, ed. *Navaho Expedition: Journal of a Military Reconnaissance from Santa Fe, New Mexico, to the Navaho Country, Made in 1849 by Lieutenant James H. Simpson.* Norman, University of Oklahoma Press, 1964.

Marion, John H. *Notes of Travel Through the Territory of Arizona, Being an account of the trip made by General George Stoneman and others in the Autumn of 1870.* Ed. by Donald M. Powell. Tucson, University of Arizona Press, 1965.

Meriwether, David. *My Life in the Mountains and on the Plains.* Ed. by Robert A. Griffen. Norman, University of Oklahoma Press, 1965.

Mills, Anson. *My Story.* Washington, privately printed by Byron S. Adams, 1918.

Pattie, James O. *Personal Narrative of James O. Pattie.* Ed. by Timothy Flint. Chicago, Donnelley and Sons, 1930.

Terrazas, Joaquin. *Memorias del Sr. Coronel D. Joaquin Terrazas*. Juárez, Escobar Hermanos, 1905.

Tevis, James H. *Arizona in the '50's*. Albuquerque, University of New Mexico Press, 1954.

This Is Silver City, New Mexico: The Silver City Enterprise in the Year 1891. Silver City, The Enterprise Company, 1967.

Watts, John S. *Indian Depredations in New Mexico*. Washington, D.C., Gideon Press, 1958; reprinted, Tucson, Territorial Press, 1964.

Secondary Sources

Almada, Francisco R. *Diccionario de Historia, Geografía y Biografía Chihuahuenses*. Chihuahua, Talleres Gráficos del Gobierno del Estado, 1927.

Altshuler, Constance Wynn, ed. *Latest from Arizona! The Hesperian Letters, 1859–1861*. Tucson, Arizona Pioneers' Historical Society, 1969.

Athearn, Robert G. *William Tecumseh Sherman and the Settlement of the West*. Norman, University of Oklahoma Press, 1956.

Bancroft, Hubert Howe. *History of Arizona and New Mexico*. San Francisco, The History Company, 1889.

———. *History of the North Mexican States and Texas*. 2 vols. San Francisco, The History Company, 1889.

Barnes, Will C. *Arizona Place Names*. Tucson, University of Arizona, 1935; 2nd ed., 1960.

Barry, Louise. *The Beginnings of the West: Annals of the Kansas Gateway to the American West 1540–1854*. Topeka, Kansas State Historical Society, 1972.

Baylor, George Wythe. *John Robert Baylor: Confederate Governor of Arizona*. Tucson, Arizona Pioneers' Historical Society, 1966.

Brandes, Ray. *Frontier Military Posts of Arizona*. Globe, Dale Stuart King, 1960.

———, ed. *Troopers West: Military & Indian Affairs on the American Frontier*. San Diego, Frontier Heritage Press, 1970.

Clendenen, Clarence C. *Blood on the Border: The United States Army and the Mexican Irregulars*. New York, The Macmillan Company, 1969.

Cullum, George W. *Biographical Register of the Officers and Graduates of the U.S. Military Academy at West Point, N.Y.* 8 vols. Boston, Houghton, Mifflin and Company, 1891–1910.

Deibert, Ralph Conrad. *A History of the Third United States Cavalry*. Harrisburg, Pennsylvania, Telegraph Press, 1933.

Diccionario Porrua: Historia, Biografía y Geografía de Mexico. 2nd ed. Mexico City, Librería Porrua, 1965.

Dictionary of American Biography. 22 vols. New York, Charles Scribner's Sons, 1958.

Ellis, Richard N. *General Pope and the U.S. Indian Policy.* Albuquerque, University of New Mexico Press, 1970.

Farish, Thomas Edwin. *History of Arizona.* 8 vols. San Francisco, The Filmer Brothers Electrotype Company, 1915–18.

Faulk, Odie B. *Too Far North ... Too Far South: The Controversial Boundary Survey and the Epic Story of the Gadsden Purchase.* Los Angeles, Westernlore Press, 1967.

Frazer, Robert W. *Forts of the West: Military Forts and Presidios and Posts Commonly Called Forts West of the Mississippi River to 1898.* Norman, University of Oklahoma Press, 1965.

Glass, Major E. L. N., comp. and ed. *The History of the Tenth Cavalry: 1866–1921.* Tucson, Acme Printing Company, 1921.

Goodwin, Grenville. *The Social Organization of the Western Apache.* Tucson, University of Arizona Press, 1969 (copyright, 1943).

Gregory, J. N. *Fort Concho: Its Why and Wherefore.* San Angelo, Texas, Newsfoto Yearbooks, 1957.

Grinnell, George Bird. *The Fighting Cheyennes.* Norman, University of Oklahoma Press, 1956.

The Handbook of Texas. Ed. by Walter Prescott Webb, H. Bailey Carroll, and others. 2 vols. Austin, Texas State Historical Association, 1952.

Herringshaw, Thomas William, ed. *Herringshaw's National Library of American Biography.* 5 vols. Chicago, American Publishers' Association, 1909.

Heyman, Max L., Jr. *Prudent Soldier: A Biography of Major General E. R. S. Canby 1817–1873.* Glendale, California, The Arthur H. Clark Company, 1959.

Horn, Calvin. *New Mexico's Troubled Years: The Story of the Early Territorial Governors.* Albuquerque, Horn & Wallace, 1963.

Hunt, Aurora. *The Army of the Pacific: 1860–1866.* Glendale, California, The Arthur H. Clark Company, 1951.

———. *James H. Carleton, Frontier Dragoon.* Glendale, The Arthur H. Clark Company, 1958.

Keleher, William A. *The Fabulous Frontier: Twelve New Mexico Items.* Rev. and enlarged ed. Albuquerque, University of New Mexico Press, 1962.

King, James T. *War Eagle: A Life of General Eugene A. Carr.* Lincoln, University of Nebraska Press, 1963.

Lister, Florence C. and Robert H. *Chihuahua: Storehouse of Storms.* Albuquerque, University of New Mexico Press, 1966.

Lockwood, Frank C. *The Apache Indians.* New York, The Macmillan Company, 1938.

Lutrell, Estelle. *Newspapers and Periodicals of Arizona 1859–1911.* Tucson, University of Arizona, 1950.

McGaw, William Cochran. *Savage Scene: The Life and Times of James Kirker, Frontier King*. New York, Hastings House, Publishers, 1972.

Macleod, William Christie. *The American Indian Frontier*. New York, Alfred A. Knopf, 1928.

McClintock, James H. *Arizona: Prehistoric, Aboriginal, Pioneer, Modern*. 3 vols. Chicago, The S. J. Clarke Publishing Company, 1916.

Moorhead, Max L. *The Apache Frontier: Jacobo Ugarte and the Spanish-Indian Relations in Northern New Spain, 1769–1791*. Norman, University of Oklahoma Press, 1968.

Mullin, Robert N., ed. *Maurice G. Fulton's History of the Lincoln County War*. Tucson, University of Arizona Press, 1968.

National Cyclopedia of American Biography. 20 vols. New York, James T. White & Company, 1898–1926.

Ogle, Ralph Hedrick. *Federal Control of the Western Apaches, 1848–1886*. Albuquerque, University of New Mexico Press, 1940.

Oliva, Leo E. *Soldiers on the Santa Fe Trail*. Norman, University of Oklahoma Press, 1967.

Opler, Morris E. *An Apache Life-Way*. Chicago, University of Chicago Press, 1941; New York, Cooper Square Publishers, Inc., 1965.

Pearce, T. M., ed. *New Mexico Place Names: A Geographical Dictionary*, assisted by Ina Sizer Cassidy, Helen S. Pearce. Albuquerque, University of New Mexico Press, 1965.

Powell, William H. *List of Officers of the Army of the United States from 1779 to 1900, Compiled from Official Records*. New York, L. R. Hammersly & Co., 1900; reprinted, Detroit, Gale Research Company, 1967.

Raht, Carlysle Graham. *The Romance of Davis Mountains and Big Bend Country: A History*. El Paso, The Rahtbooks Company, 1919.

Reeve, Frank, and Alice Ann Cleaveland. *New Mexico: Land of Many Cultures*. Boulder, Colorado, Pruett Publishing Company, 1969.

Sachs, Benjamin. *Be It Enacted: The Creation of the Territory of Arizona*. Phoenix, Arizona Historical Foundation, 1964.

Sanita, Frances, ed. *The Apache*. Arizona State Teachers College Bulletin, Vol. XX, No. 1. Flagstaff, 1939.

Schilling, John H. *Silver City-Santa Rita-Hurley, New Mexico*. Socorro, New Mexico, State Bureau of Mines and Mineral Resources, 1967.

Shinkle, James D. *Fort Sumner and the Bosque Redondo Indian Reservation*. Roswell, New Mexico, Hall-Poorbaugh Press, Inc., 1965.

Smith, Cornelius C., Jr. *William Sanders Oury: History-Maker of the Southwest*. Tucson, University of Arizona Press, 1967.

Sonnichsen, C. L. *The Mescalero Apaches*. Norman, University of Oklahoma Press, 1958.

Stanley, F. *Fort Craig*. Pampa, Texas, The Pampa Print Shop, 1963.

Stern, Madeleine B. *Heads & Headlines: The Phrenological Fowlers*. Norman, University of Oklahoma Press, 1971.

Stratton, Porter A. *The Territorial Press of New Mexico 1834–1912*. Albuquerque, University of New Mexico Press, 1969.

Thomas, Alfred Barnaby. *Teodoro de Croix and the Northern Frontier of New Spain, 1776–1783*. Norman, University of Oklahoma Press, 1941, 1968.

Thrapp, Dan L. *Al Sieber, Chief of Scouts*. Norman, University of Oklahoma Press, 1964.

———. *The Conquest of Apacheria*. Norman, University of Oklahoma Press, 1967.

———. *General Crook and the Sierra Madre Adventure*. Norman, University of Oklahoma Press, 1972.

———. "The Military Pack Outfits," *Brand Book Number One*, Ray Brandes, ed. San Diego, The San Diego Corral of the Westerners, 1968.

Twitchell, Ralph Emerson. *The History of the Military Occupation of the Territory of New Mexico from 1846 to 1851 by the Government of the United States*. Chicago, The Rio Grande Press, 1963.

———. *The Leading Facts of New Mexico History*. 2 vols. Albuquerque, Horn & Wallace, 1963.

Underhill, Ruth. *The Navajos*. Norman, University of Oklahoma Press, 1956.

Ungnade, Herbert E. *Guide to the New Mexico Mountains*. Denver, Sage Books, 1965.

Utley, Robert M. *Frontiersmen in Blue: The United States Army and the Indian, 1848–1865*. New York, The Macmillan Company, 1967.

Wagoner, Jay J. *Arizona Territory 1863–1912: A Political History*. Tucson, University of Arizona Press, 1970.

Walker, Francis Amasa. *The Indian Question*. Boston, J. R. Osgood and Company, 1874.

Watson, Dorothy. *The Pinos Altos Story*. Silver City, New Mexico, The Silver City Enterprise, 1960.

Webb, Walter Prescott. *The Texas Rangers: A Century of Frontier Defense*. Boston, Houghton, Mifflin Company, 1935.

Wellman, Paul I. *The Indian Wars of the West*. New York, Doubleday and Company, 1947.

Who Was Who. Chicago, The A. N. Marquis Company, 1943.

Articles and Essays

Amsden, Charles. "The Navaho Exile at Bosque Redondo," *New Mexico Historical Review*, Vol. VIII, No. 1 (January, 1933), 31–50.

Ayres, John. "A Soldier's Experience in New Mexico," *New Mexico Historical Review*, Vol. XXIV, No. 4 (October, 1949), 259–66.

Ball, Eve. "The Fight for Ojo Caliente," *Frontier Times*, Vol. XXXVI, No. 2 (Spring, 1962), 22–23, 40.

Bender, A. B., "Government Explorations in the Territory of New Mexico 1846–1859," *New Mexico Historical Review*, Vol. IX, No. 1 (January, 1934), 1–32.

Bloom, Lansing B. "Bourke on the Southwest, II," *New Mexico Historical Review*, Vol. IX, No. 1 (January, 1934), 33–77.

Bloom, Lansing B., ed. "Historical Society Minutes, 1859–1863," *New Mexico Historical Review*, Vol. XVIII, No. 3 (July, 1943), 247–311.

Brophy, A. Blake. "Fort Fillmore, N.M., 1861: Public Disgrace and Private Disaster," *Journal of Arizona History*, Vol. IX, No. 4 (Winter, 1968) 195–218.

Chávez, José Carlos. "Extinción de los Apaches: Victorio," *Boletín de la Sociedad Chihuahuense de Estudios Historicos*, Vol. I, No. 10 (March 15, 1939), 336–46.

Clum, John P. "Apache Misrule," *New Mexico Historical Review*, Vol. V, No. 3 (July, 1930), 221–39.

———. "Geronimo," *New Mexico Historical Review*, Vol. III, Nos. 1,2,3 (January, April, July, 1928), 1–40, 121–44, 217–64.

———. "Victorio," *Arizona Historical Review*, Vol. II, No. 4 (January, 1930), 74–90.

"Cochise," Tucson *Weekly Arizonian*, September 17, 1870; reprinted, *Arizoniana*, Vol. I, No. 3 (Fall, 1960), 24.

Crawford, Jack. "The Pursuit of Victorio," *Socorro County Historical Society: Publications in History*. Vol. I (no number), February, 1965, 1–8.

Crimmins, Colonel Martin L. "Colonel Buell's Expedition into Mexico in 1880," *New Mexico Historical Review*, Vol. X, No. 2 (April, 1935), 133–42.

Espinosa, J. Manuel, "Memoir of a Kentuckian in New Mexico 1848–1884," *New Mexico Historical Review*, Volume XIII, No. 1 (January, 1937), 1–13.

Gatewood, Charles B. "Campaigning Against Victorio in 1879," *The Great Divide*, April, 1894, 102–104.

Jones, Calico. "Victorio's Vengeance Raid," *Real West*, Vol. XIII, No. 81 (April, 1970), 31–35, 55, 77.

Kaywaykla, James, as told to Eve Ball. "I Survived the Massacre of Tres Castillos," *True West*, Vol. VIII, No. 6 (July–August, 1961), 22–23, 38.

———. "Nana's People," *True West*, Vol. X, No. 6 (July–August, 1963), 20–21, 66–67.

Lyon, Juana Fraser. "Archie McIntosh, the Scottish Indian Scout," *Journal of Arizona History*, Vol. VII, No. 3 (Autumn, 1966), 103–22.

Mehren, Lawrence L., ed. "Scouting for Mescaleros: The Price Campaign of 1873," *Arizona and the West*, Vol. X, No. 2 (Summer, 1968), 171–90.

Myers, Lee. "The Enigma of Mangas Coloradas' Death," *New Mexico Historical Review*, Vol. XLI, No. 4 (October, 1966) 287–304.

———. "Fort Webster on the Mimbres River," *New Mexico Historical Review*, Vol. XLI, No. 1 (January, 1966), 47–57.

———. "Military Establishments in Southwestern New Mexico: Stepping Stones to Settlement," *New Mexico Historical Review*, Vol. XLIII, No. 1 (January, 1968), 5–48.

Oates, Stephen B. "The Hard Luck Story of the Snively Expedition," *The American West*, Vol. IV, No. 3 (August, 1967), 52–58, 77–79.

Opler, Morris E. "A Chiricahua Apache's Account of the Geronimo Campaign of 1886," *New Mexico Historical Review*, Vol. XIII, No. 4 (October, 1938), 360–86.

Phelps, Frederick E. "A Soldier's Memoirs," ed. by Frank D. Reeves, *New Mexico Historical Review*, Vol. XXV, Nos. 1–4 (January, April, July, October, 1950), 37–56, 109–35, 187–221, 305–27.

Rasch, Philip J. "The Death of Victorio," *The English Westerners' Brand Book*, Vol. II, No. 3 (April, 1960), 9–10.

Reeve, Frank D. "The Federal Indian Policy in New Mexico, 1858–1880," *New Mexico Historical Review*, Part II, Vol. XIII, No. 1, (January, 1938), 14–62; Part IV, Vol. XIII, No. 3 (July, 1938), 261–313.

Rope, John. "Experiences of an Indian Scout," ed. by Grenville Goodwin, *Arizona Historical Review*, Vol. VII, No. 1 (January, 1936), 31–68.

Ruhlen, George. "Kearny's Route from the Rio Grande to the Gila River," *New Mexico Historical Review*, Vol. XXXII, No. 3 (July, 1957), 213–30.

Sachs, Benjamin. "Arizona's Angry Man: United States Marshal Milton B. Duffield," *Journal of Arizona History*, Vol. VIII, Nos. 1, 2 (Spring, Summer, 1967), 1–29, 91–119.

Smith, Ralph A. "Apache Plunder Trails Southward, 1831–1840," *New Mexico Historical Review*, Vol. XXXVII, No. 1 (January, 1962), 20–42.

———. "Apache 'Ranching' Below the Gila, 1841–1845," *Arizoniana*, Vol. III, No. 4 (Winter, 1962), 1–17.

———. Book Review, *Pacific Historical Review*, Vol. XXXVIII, No. 1 (February, 1969), 94–95.

———. "The Scalp Hunt in Chihuahua—1849," *New Mexico Historical Review*, Vol. XL, No. 2 (April, 1965), 116–40.

Tarin, Don Jesus, as told to José Aceves. "Who Was Victorio?" *Frontier Times*, Vol. XXXVII, No. 5 (August–September, 1963), 24–25, 71.

Walker, Henry P., ed. "Soldier in the California Column: The Diary of John W. Teal," *Arizona and the West*, Vol. XIII, No. 1 (Spring, 1971), 33–82.

Worcester, Donald E. "The Beginnings of the Apache Menace of the Southwest," *New Mexico Historical Review*, Vol. XVI, No. 1 (January, 1941), 1–14.

NOTES

FOREWORD

1. Frederick E. Phelps, "A Soldier's Memoirs" (ed. by Frank D. Reeves), *New Mexico Historical Review*, Vol. XXV, No. 2 (April, 1950), 120–21.

2. Grenville Goodwin, *The Social Organization of the Western Apache* (hereafter cited as *The Western Apache*), 554.

CHAPTER I

1. Frederick Webb Hodge, *Handbook of American Indians North of Mexico*, I, 63. John R. Swanton, *The Indian Tribes of North America*, 329, follows Hodge in this opinion.

2. Morris E. Opler, *An Apache Life-Way*, 1–2; Goodwin, *The Western Apache*, 1.

3. This view has a surprisingly wide acceptance in northern Mexico. It first was expressed to me by Oscar Flores, a Chihuahua rancher, businessman, and attorney, who directed me to Tres Castillos, scene of Victorio's fatal battle.

4. Ralph A. Smith, "Apache Plunder Trails Southward, 1831–1840," *New Mexico Historical Review*, Vol. XXXVII, No. 1 (January, 1962), 25.

5. Bertha Montes, "The Great Chieftains," a manuscript in possession of C. L. Sonnichsen, who kindly supplied me with a copy. Miss Montes is a niece of Eugenio Baeza, in 1948 the owner of Tres Castillos. Her paper, written for an English course at Texas College of Mines, El Paso, in 1948, has notable inconsistencies; they may be due to the differing traditions which she traced, yet they reflect the rampant incongruities in the stories told by Chihuahuans and which tend to becloud whatever factual basis they may have. For instance, she says that Padilla was captured just months after seizure of the boy who became the chief, was held only four years, yet reported extensively upon the war leader Victorio (who must still have been a child) and upon his mature resemblance to an adult Padilla earlier had known at El Carmen. She also places the kidnapings in the late 1790's. This would make Victorio upwards of eighty at his death, which is impossible.

6. National Archives and Records Service, Old Military Records Division, Office of Indian Affairs, 1824–80, Microcopy 234, Letters Received, New Mexico Superintendency, 1849–80 (hereafter cited as LR NMS, with roll number), Roll 579-1880, N50, Ritch to Schurz, second enclosure.

7. For a brief description of the great haciendas of Chihuahua in those years, see Florence C. Lister and Robert H. Lister, *Chihuahua: Storehouse of Storms*, 74. Hacienda del Carmen was renamed Colonia Ricardo Flores Magón for a Mexican revolutionary who died while serving a twenty-year sentence at Leavenworth Penitentiary. *Diccionario Porrua: Historia, Biografía y Geografía de Mexico*, 2nd ed., 597. It is on the paved highway from Buenaventura to El Sueco, where the road crosses the Carmen River.

8. LR NMS, Roll 548, N235, Meriwether to Office of Indian Affairs, January 27, 1857; Steen to Claiborn, January 1, 1857; Steck to Meriwether, January 3, 1857. *Ibid.*, N255, Meriwether to Manypenny, March 31, 1857. The possibility of Costales' having been slain by a relative is suggested by the similarity of the names of murderer and victim. Steen to Claiborn, cited above.

9. Ralph A. Smith, "Apache 'Ranching' Below the Gila, 1841–1845," *Arizoniana*, Vol. III, No. 4 (Winter, 1962), 4. José Carlos Chávez, "Extinción de los Apaches: Victorio," *Boletín de la Sociedad Chihuahuense de Estudios Historicos*, Vol. I, No. 10 (March 15, 1939), 340 n.

10. Michael Steck to Meriwether, September 12, 1855, Steck Papers, Zimmerman Library, University of New Mexico, Albuquerque; Steck reports Mimbres bringing back forty-two prisoners. Frances Sanita, ed., *The Apache*, Arizona State Teachers College Bulletin, 6. Swanton says that any Apache population increase was due to "captives taken by these people from all the surrounding tribes and from the Mexicans," *Indian Tribes*, 330. "The forays and conquests of the Apache resulted in the absorption of a large foreign element [including] Spanish . . . ." Hodge, *Handbook of American Indians*, I, 66. Bartlett to Stuart, February 19, 1852, speaks of "many" captives, not only held then by the Apaches, but some sold elsewhere into slavery by them; Bartlett asked of the governor of Sonora a list of children stolen in Chihuahua and Sonora, the assembling of which was a formidable task. LR NMS, Roll 546, B81. "There can be no doubt that a large strain of Mexican blood became incorporated in several of the Apache tribes, for even hundreds of Mexican women were brought northward . . . as were countless children." James H. McClintock, *Arizona: Prehistoric, Aboriginal, Pioneer, Modern*, I, 179.

11. Don Jesus Tarin, as told to José Aceves, "Who Was Victorio?" *Frontier Times*, Vol. XXXVII, No. 5 (August–September, 1963), 24–25, 71.

12. LR NMS, Roll 572–1877, NMS992, Shaw to Smith, September 3, 1877.

13. Goodwin, *The Western Apache*, 523.

14. Jason Betzinez with W. S. Nye, *I Fought With Geronimo*, 24.

15. Goodwin, *op. cit.*, 523.

16. Gillett M. Griswold, "The Fort Sill Apaches: Their Vital Statistics, Tribal Origins, Antecedents," manuscript at the Field Artillery Museum, Fort Sill, Oklahoma, 144.

17. Reprinted in the *Arizona Sentinel* of Yuma, November 1, 1879.

18. John H. Marion, born in Louisiana about 1836, arrived in Arizona via California in 1864. He owned and edited a succession of newspapers, becoming Prescott's best-known newspaperman. In the words of one historian, "his newspapers formed an inseparable part of the pioneer days of Arizona." He died July 27, 1891. John H. Marion, *Notes of Travel Through the Territory of Arizona*, ed. by Donald M. Powell, 3–11; Estelle Lutrell, *Newspapers and Periodicals of Arizona 1859–1911*, 90–91. See also Dan L. Thrapp, *Al Sieber, Chief of Scouts*, 50–53f.

19. Betzinez, op. cit. 50.

20. To my knowledge he is first so identified in 39 Cong., 2 sess., *Senate Report No. 156*, 305.

21. Opler, *An Apache Life-Way*, 468.

22. Interview with author, August 23, 1965.

23. John A. Shapard to author, October 11, 1969.

24. See note 8 above.

25. C. L. Sonnichsen, *The Mescalero Apaches*, 159.

26. For this brief discussion of Apache life, see Opler, *op. cit.*, 5–139; Goodwin, *The Western Apache*, 428–521.

27. Goodwin, *op. cit.*, 463.

28. Opler, *op. cit.*, 350–51.

29. McClintock, *Arizona*, 179.

30. Dan L. Thrapp, *The Conquest of Apacheria*, 311; Britton Davis, *The Truth About Geronimo*, 140.

31. Daniel Ellis Conner, *Joseph Reddeford Walker and the Arizona Adventure*, 220–21.

32. Goodwin, *op. cit.*, 554–55.

33. The foregoing is from Opler, *op. cit.*, 134–39.

34. These facts have been well established by ethnologists. See Opler, *op. cit.*, 140–51; Goodwin, *op. cit.*, 284–93.

35. LR NMS, Roll 561, NM D356, Duane to Thomas, June 29, 1873.

36. LR NMS, Roll 572, NM S992, Shaw to Smith, September 3, 1877.

CHAPTER II

1. Donald E. Worcester, "The Beginnings of the Apache Menace of the Southwest," *New Mexico Historical Review*, Vol. XVI, No. 1 (January, 1941), 5.

2. Morris E. Opler, "A Chiricahua Apache's Account of the Geronimo Campaign of 1886," *New Mexico Historical Review*, Vol. XIII, No. 4 (October, 1938), 360n.

3. See the Costansó-Mascaró map of 1780, redrawn in Alfred Barnaby Thomas, *Teodoro de Croix and the Northern Frontier of New Spain, 1776–1783*, facing p. 82. Max L. Moorhead, in *The Apache Frontier: Jacobo Ugarte and the Spanish-Indian Relations in Northern New Spain, 1769–1791*, also discusses this problem, 170.

4. Thomas, *op. cit.*, 64–67.

5. *Ibid.*, 134.

6. *Ibid.*, 146, 164.

7. Moorhead, *op. cit.*, 140.

8. *Ibid.* On p. 70 Moorhead argues that the Mimbres were named by the Spanish after the "Mimbres Mountains," but more likely the mountains and the people both were named for the Mimbres River, "mimbres" meaning willows in Spanish. The river heads in the Black Range, and sinks into the earth near present-day Deming, or below the old Overland stage crossing, according to James H. Tevis, *Arizona in the '50's*, 106–107. The Mimbres Mountains are today's Black Range, a notable 100-mile-long narrow upfolding, rising to more than 10,000 feet in a peak named for Victorio, north of present-day Kingston. The lower, or southern, end of the range, still called Mimbres Mountains on some maps, now is considered an extension of the Black Range. Herbert E. Ungnade, *Guide to the New Mexico Mountains*, 132–34. Moorhead reports that the Apaches on the eastern slopes were frequently allied with the Faraones, probably a Mescalero band (see Hodge, *Handbook of American Indians*, I, 453), while the other Mimbreños were often found with the other Chiricahuas, or Gileños, by which he apparently means the Mogollons, White Mountains, or Pinals, for purposes of hostilities against Nueva Vizcaya and Sonora. By the nineteenth century this distinction had been lost. Moorhead lists those 18th-century Mimbres chieftains whose names were known. *The Apache Frontier*, 172–73.

9. Moorhead, *op. cit.*, 184–91.

10. *Ibid.*, 285.

11. John Russell Bartlett, *Personal Narrative of Explorations and Incidents in Texas,*

New Mexico, California, Sonora, and Chihuahua, connected with the United States and Mexican Boundary Commission During the Years 1850, '51, '52 and '53 (hereafter cited as *Narrative*), 234–36.

12. See John H. Schilling, *Silver City-Santa Rita-Hurley, New Mexico*, 24–26; Ralph Emerson Twitchell, *The Leading Facts of New Mexican History* (hereafter cited as *New Mexico History*), I, 475; Hubert Howe Bancroft, *History of Arizona and New Mexico* (hereafter cited as *Arizona and New Mexico*), 303; Ungnade, *Guide to the New Mexico Mountains*, 29–30; and numerous others. Now an open pit operation of the Kennecott Copper Corporation, fifteen miles east of Silver City, the main pit is 1,000 feet deep and more than a mile across, one of the largest mines in the world. All of the original diggings have been excavated as part of the larger work.

13. See James O. Pattie, *Personal Narrative of James O. Pattie*, 65–74; Frank Reeve and Alice Ann Cleaveland, *New Mexico: Land of Many Cultures*, 201 f.

14. Smith, "Apache Plunder Trails Southward, 1831–1840," *New Mexico Historical Review*, Vol. XXXVII, No. 1 (January, 1962), 30–31.

15. Ralph A. Smith, "The Scalp Hunt in Chihuahua—1849," *New Mexico Historical Review*, Vol. XL, No. 2 (April, 1965), 116–40.

16. Smith, "Apache Plunder Trails Southward, 1831–1840," *loc. cit.*, 33–34. See also his "The Scalp Hunt in Chihuahua—1849," *loc. cit.*

17. William Cochran McGaw in his *Savage Scene: The Life and Times of James Kirker, Frontier King*, probably the best over-all account of the scalp-hunting business and one of its principals yet published, quotes Johnson's report of April 24, 1837, to the governor of Chihuahua to the effect that his party killed twenty Apaches, including three chiefs: Juan José, Marcello, and Juan Diego, wounded fifteen or twenty others, including women and children, and lists the seventeen scalp hunters, in addition to Johnson, who were involved. See also Smith, "Apache Plunder Trails Southward, 1831–1840," *loc. cit.*, 33–34; Ralph A. Smith, untitled book review, *Pacific Historical Review*, Vol. XXXVIII, No. 1 (February, 1969), 95.

18. Paul I. Wellman, in *The Indian Wars of the West*, 254, says that he was named a subchief by Mangas Coloradas at that time, but he was far too young. Subchiefs were not named by chiefs in any event.

19. John C. Cremony tells this story, which he said he received from an "intelligent Mexican" of Sonora, in *Life Among the Apaches*, 30–32. From lack of any official support, and on the basis of the traditional Apache fighting methods, the story would seem greatly exaggerated, if there is any truth to it at all. Yet following the assassination the mines did abruptly close and remained shut down for a score of years, no doubt because of Apache hostility. William Helmsley Emory, *Lieutenant Emory Reports: A Reprint of Lieutenant W. H. Emory's Notes of a Military Reconnaissance*, 97–98.

20. I am aware that Mexicans and other Latin Americans also consider themselves "Americans," and are truly such. Yet in the lack of any other satisfactory word to signify Anglos and Negroes of United States origin, in this work the term "Americans" means whites and blacks from north of the Mexican border.

21. Ralph Emerson Twitchell, *The History of the Military Occupation of the Territory of New Mexico from 1846 to 1851 by the Government of the United States*, 86–89. See Dwight L. Clarke (ed.), *The Original Journals of Henry Smith Turner*, 83–87, entries for October 15 to October 20, 1846, for the day-by-day account of the progress of Kearny's expedition, the meeting with Mangas, and relationships with the Apaches.

22. A mountain that Emory named for Captain Benjamin D. Moore of the First Dragoons, shortly to be killed at the battle of San Pasqual, in California.

23. Kearny's route to the Gila has been skillfully worked out and is presented, with excellent maps, by George Ruhlen, "Kearny's Route from the Rio Grande to the Gila River," *New Mexico Historical Review*, Vol. XXXII, No. 3 (July, 1957), 213–30. This shows his crossing of the Black Range to be fifteen miles south of so-called Emory Pass, at Parks Pass.

24. William Helmsley Emory, *Lieutenant Emory Reports*, 96–101.

25. Jack Hays was one of the more noteworthy Texas Rangers. Born in Tennessee in 1817, he arrived in Texas shortly after the Battle of San Jacinto, served four years on the frontier against Mexicans and Indians, and in 1840 was made captain of a Ranger company. He was colonel of a regiment of Texas volunteer cavalry during the Mexican War, winning distinction in the battle of Monterrey. In 1849 he emigrated to California, serving as Indian agent to the Gileños en route. He acquired considerable properties and interests in the San Francisco Bay area, and died in Alameda County in 1883. Walter Prescott Webb, *The Texas Rangers: A Century of Frontier Defense*, 67–80; *Dictionary of American Biography* (hereafter cited as DAB).

26. *Pamphlet Accompanying Microcopy No. 234, Letters Received by the Office of Indian Affairs, 1824–80*, 2–4.

27. LR NMS, Roll 546, NM 1106, Hayes to Ewing, January 3, 1850.

28. John A. Shapard, Jr., reports this incident on the basis of conversations with Moses and Raymond Loco, in a manuscript under preparation on Chief Loco.

29. J. M. Washington to Adjutant General, Washington, D.C., September 24, 1849, *Report of the Secretary of War, 1849–50*, 111.

30. LR NMS, Roll 546, B81, Despatch No. 35, Bartlett to Stuart, February 19, 1852; Bartlett, *Narrative*, 226–39, 300–354.

31. See Odie B. Faulk, *Too Far North ... Too Far South: The Controversial Boundary Survey and the Epic Story of the Gadsden Purchase*, for a study of the Bartlett Commission's work.

CHAPTER III

1. Not July 1, 1852, as the treaty itself states.

2. John Greiner, born at Philadelphia September 14, 1810, was state librarian of Ohio when appointed Indian agent in New Mexico in 1849. In 1865 he became editor of the Zanesville, Ohio, *Times*, wrote many songs, and died May 13, 1871. He was credited with writing "Tippecanoe and Tyler, Too," a noted political song-slogan of the Zachary Taylor epoch, but this was in error, although he did write "Old Zip Coon" and other popular jingles of the day. Greiner and Sumner became embroiled in a dispute over who was the actual superintendent of Indian affairs for the Territory, a dispute not unique in the long and occasionally troubled association between the Interior and War departments over Indian matters. Norris F. Schneider, feature writer for the *Times Recorder*, Zanesville, Ohio. LR NMS, Roll 546, G43, Greiner to Lea, July 31, 1852, with enclosures.

3. Calhoun, New Mexico's first territorial governor, had spent twenty months there as Indian agent before becoming governor March 3, 1851. A Mexican War veteran, he was a farsighted, able leader who, deathly ill, left the Territory with a coffin he had caused to be constructed and died on the Kansas plains en route east, probably on June 30, 1852. Louise Barry, *The Beginning of the West: Annals of the Kansas Gateway to*

the American West 1540–1854, 1107. Calvin Horn, *New Mexico's Troubled Years: The Story of the Early Territorial Governors*, 21–33.

4. From the earliest American occupation, military scouts were directed against the Gila Apaches, by which were meant the Mimbres as well. See, for example, in the Old Military Records Division of the National Archives Records Service, Returns from U.S. Military Posts, 1800–1916, Microcopy 617 (hereafter cited as *Posts*, with roll number), Roll 320, Doña Ana, monthly return for August, 1851.

5. Fort Webster was established at Santa Rita January 23, 1852, named for Secretary of State Daniel Webster. On September 9 it was moved to the Mimbres River bottoms, eight or nine miles east. It was abandoned militarily December 20, 1853, perhaps upon the recommendation of Colonel Joseph K. F. Mansfield, who in the spring of 1853 had formally inspected the Department of New Mexico, suggesting Webster's removal westerly to the Gila. Upon abandonment, however, its garrison was sent east to Fort Thorn, established December 24, 1853, at Santa Barbara (now Hatch), a hundred miles up the Río Grande from El Paso. Other posts later were briefly named Fort Webster. Lee Myers, Fort Webster section, "Military Establishments in Southwestern New Mexico: Stepping Stones to Settlement," *New Mexico Historical Review*, Vol. XLIII, No. 1 (January, 1968), 6–8. Report W. Frazer (ed.), *Mansfield on the Condition of the Western Forts 1853–54*, 25–26; Robert W. Frazer, *Forts of the West: Military Forts and Presidios and Posts Commonly Called Forts West of the Mississippi River to 1898*, 104–105, 106–107; *Posts*, Roll 1407, Fort Webster, monthly returns, January, September, 1852.

6. LR NMS, Roll 546, N25, Calhoun to Lea, January 31, 1852.

7. LR NMS, Roll 546, N44, Calhoun to Lea, April 6, 1852.

8. Treaty text dated July 1, 1852, between the United States and "part of the Apache Nation of Indians," in 10 Stat. 979–81, Record Group 75, Social and Economics Records Division, National Archives and Records Service.

9. LR NMS, Roll 546, G41, Greiner to Lea, July 31, 1852.

10. Luke Lea, born in Tennessee, where he served as secretary of state, moved to Mississippi and served a term in the state legislature, ran for governor and was badly defeated, and was appointed commissioner of Indian affairs, serving from July 1, 1850, until March 24, 1853. He was a nephew of Luke Lea of Tennessee, an Indian agent at Fort Leavenworth, who died in 1851. Information from Richard S. Maxwell, assistant director, Social and Economics Records Division, National Archives and Records Service.

11. The historian Hubert Howe Bancroft, a firm believer in Manifest Destiny, in a most interesting passage admits that there were Indian rights in matters of this kind. "I do not deny . . . that the Apaches had often been grossly wronged," he wrote. "Much may be urged, moreover, against the right of a foreign race to take from the Indians their country, and very little in defence of Spanish or English treatment of the aborigines from the beginning. . . . I do not blame the Apaches for defending their homes and liberties in their own way. . . ." *Arizona and New Mexico*, 563n.

12. LR NMS, Roll 546, N70, Greiner to Lane (no date, but written September 30, 1852).

13. *Ibid.*

14. LR NMS, Roll 546, N82, Lane to Lea, December 31, 1852.

15. Enoch Steen, born in Kentucky, joined the mounted rangers in Missouri in 1832 and transferred to the First Dragoons the following year. He was cited for gallantry in the battle of Buena Vista, Mexican War, and in 1849 was "severely wounded" in an

Apache fight near Doña Ana. He retired as a lieutenant colonel in 1863 and died January 22, 1880. It is probable that Stein's Peak and Stein's Pass in southwestern New Mexico, both famous sites in Indian war days, were named for him, although *New Mexico Place Names: A Geographical Dictionary*, ed. by T. M. Pearce, 160, says they were named for "Captain Steins," otherwise unidentifiable. Steen's military record, National Archives and Records Division. Francis Bernard Heitman, *Historical Register and Dictionary of the United States Army, from its Organization, September 29, 1789, to March 2, 1903*, I, 919.

16. Mescal, not to be confused with a modern Mexican drink of that name, was the fleshy leaf base and trunk of various species of agave, roasted in pit ovens until it became a sweet, nutritious, and highly desirable food. It was used by several Indian tribes and was a staple among some Apache bands. Because it grows only in certain areas and was gathered at certain times of the year, its collection was a social event on the Apache calendar. Mescal pits, generally circular, were six to twenty feet in circumference, a foot to three feet in depth. The pit was lined with stones, a fire built, and the mescal laid in and covered with grass and earth. After steaming for a couple of days, the pit was reopened; the mescal was ready for immediate use, or it might be stored almost indefinitely. It was an article of trade with tribes that lived outside the mescal area. Hodge, *Handbook of American Indians*, I, 845–46.

17. Opler, *An Apache Life-Way*, 464–71; Goodwin, *The Western Apache*, 164–85.

18. LR NMS, Roll 546, N128, Sherman to Lane, May 30, 1853.

19. *Ibid.* Agent Steck appeared to believe, however, that Mangas was chief of the "Mogollon Band," allied to, but not identical with, the Mimbres. Since the two bands constituted the Eastern Chiricahuas, Mangas must have been over-all chieftain, and Delgadito at this time the chief of the Mimbres, but the two were closely associated. For example, Mangas agreed to endorse anything Delgadito assented to in the Treaty of 1855. Victorio's subband at this time may have been under Delgadito or a mixture of the two which ultimately combined. A later investigator in an official report in 1858, however, said the Apache bands in southwestern New Mexico included the "Mogollones, Mangus Colorado's band, the Apaches of the Mimbres and the Mescaleros," suggesting that Mangas' band then was intermediate between the Mogollons and the Mimbres. LR NMS, Roll 548, no number, Steck to Collins, November 25, 1857. LR NMS, Roll 549, no number, Bailey to Mix, November 4, 1858.

20. Born at Hughesville, Pennsylvania, October 6, 1818, Steck was graduated from the Jefferson Medical College, Philadelphia, about 1843, then practiced medicine at Miffenville, Columbia County, Pennsylvania, for six years before going to New Mexico in 1849 as a contract surgeon with the army for two years. He returned to Washington in 1852. With the recommendations of ethnologist Henry Rowe Schoolcraft, Professor Joseph Henry, director of the Smithsonian Institution, and Commissioner of Indian Affairs Luke Lea, he was appointed Indian agent to New Mexico by President Millard Fillmore and returned at once to the Territory. When Fillmore was succeeded by Pierce in early 1853, however, Steck went back to Washington to settle his accounts. Again, influential men came to his support and, upon urging of Governor Lane and George W. Manypenny, new commissioner of Indian affairs, he was reappointed, later being again appointed by President James Buchanan. He returned to Pennsylvania following the Texan invasion of New Mexico early in the Civil War. In 1863 he was appointed by President Abraham Lincoln superintendent of Indian affairs in New Mexico, serving until May 1, 1865, when he resigned. Later he became interested in mining operations

in New Mexico, ran unsuccessfully on the Greenback ticket for lieutenant governor of Pennsylvania, and died at Winchester, Virginia, on his birthday in 1883. Steck Papers, 209–11; Aurora Hunt, *James H. Carleton, Frontier Dragoon,* 286n. David Meriwether, *My Life in the Mountains and on the Plains,* ed. by Robert A. Griffen, 159n.—inaccurate in part, but correctly identifying Steck as "genuinely interested in the Indians' welfare."

21. Steck from Lane, July 11, 1853, Steck Papers.

22. LR NMS, Roll 546, N148, Lane to Manypenny, July 29, 1853.

23. Steck to Lane, August 13, 1853, Steck Papers.

24. LR NMS, Roll 546, N176, Smith to Meriwether, September 5, 1853.

25. *Ibid.*

26. *Ibid.,* A421, Smith to Meriwether, September 10, 1853.

27. LR NMS, Roll 547, N200, Meriwether to Manypenny, November 30, 1853.

28. *Ibid.,* N205, Meriwether to Manypenny, December 14, 1853.

29. This apparently innocuous move, for reasons of white convenience, of the agency from the Mimbres River to Fort Thorn on the Río Grande was to have profound effects upon the Eastern Chiricahuas. The reason for this was that it tended to draw the Mimbres toward the eastern slope of the Black Range, to be closer to the agency and its largess, such as it was, while the Mogollons, more remotely situated, inevitably gravitated toward the White Mountain bands and others of their relatives, in eastern Arizona. Thus, with the death a decade later of Mangas, the strongest bond between the bands, the Mimbres were more isolated than they ever had been and, being more proximate to the white influx, increasingly fell prey to contentions they had never sought. This led remorselessly to their final destruction.

CHAPTER IV

1. Abstract of Issues to Apache Indians during quarter ending December 31, 1854. Steck Papers.

2. Steck to Manypenny, January 31, 1855. *Ibid.*

3. LR NMS, Roll 548, N264, Meriwether to Manypenny, April 13, 1857.

4. Many of the places bearing the name Lucero in New Mexico no doubt reflected Spanish families of that name, particularly in the northern part of the state or along the Río Grande. A possible exception is Lucero Mesa, in Valencia County. T. M. Pearce (ed.), *New Mexico Place Names: A Geographical Dictionary,* 93.

5. For examples of the military activity against Gila and Mogollon Apaches from Fort Thorn, see monthly returns for March and April, 1856, and March, 1857, when four men were killed or died of wounds following a fight. *Posts,* Roll 1271.

6. LR NMS, Roll 547, N298, Steck to Meriwether, August 22, 1854. The same letter is in the Steck Papers.

7. Notes, labeled by Steck as basis for a talk to the Gilas, August, 1854, Steck Papers.

8. *Ibid.,* Steck to Meriwether, October, 1854 (day of the month not given).

9. *Ibid.,* Steck to Meriwether, January 22, 1855.

10. *Ibid.,* Steck to Meriwether, April 13, 1855.

11. *Ibid.,* Meriwether to Steck, April 28, 1855.

12. *Ibid.,* Steck to Meriwether, May 15, 1855. In his autobiography, Meriwether says this treaty was negotiated by him in 1856. *My Life,* 256–59. However, his contemporary correspondence shows the date to have been 1855. LR NMS, Roll 547, N467, Meriwether to Manypenny, June 26, 1855. *Ibid.,* Meriwether Annual Report to the commissioner, September, 1855. Bancroft, *Arizona and New Mexico,* 660n. Twitchell, *New Mexican History,* II, 302f.

13. LR NMS, Roll 547, N467, *op. cit.*

14. Steck to Manypenny, July, 1855, Steck Papers.

15. *Ibid.*, Steck to Meriwether, September 12, 1855.

16. *Ibid.*, Abstract of provisions issued to Apache Indians at Apache Agency by M. Steck, Ind. agent, during the quarter ending September 30, 1855.

17. LR NMS, Roll 547, L631, Steck to General Land Office, October 4, 1855.

18. *Ibid.*, N557, Meriwether to Manypenny, December 12, 1855.

19. *Ibid.*, N467, Meriwether Annual Report.

CHAPTER V

1. Davis, born in 1820 in Pennsylvania, became a lawyer, served in the Mexican and Civil wars, and rose to the rank of brevet brigadier general. He came to New Mexico in December, 1853, as United States attorney for the Territory, served on a volunteer basis as private secretary to the governor and his companion on several trips through the area, and held a variety of posts. Eventually he returned to Doylestown, Pennsylvania, where he unsuccessfully ran for Congress, published a newspaper, and held public positions. He died in 1910. Meriwether, *My Life*, 156n–60n.; Heitman, *Historical Register of the U.S. Army*, II, 361. *Who Was Who.*

2. LR NMS, Roll 548, W2, Davis to Manypenny, November 15, 1855.

3. Steck to superintendent of Indian affairs, December 22, 1855, Steck Papers.

4. *Ibid.*, Steck to Davis, January 9, 1856. *Ibid.*

5. *Ibid.*

6. *Ibid.*, Davis to Steck, January 21, 1856.

7. LR NMS, Roll 548, N53, Steck to superintendent of Indian affairs, February 15, 1856.

8. See monthly report for March, 1856, in *Posts*, Roll 261, Fort Craig, for the start of this expedition.

9. LR NMS, Roll 548, N100, Steck to Davis, April 6, 1856.

10. LR NMS, Roll 548, N182, McClelland to Jefferson Davis, with enclosures, September 25, 1856.

11. *Ibid.*, Garland letter.

12. *Ibid.*

13. Steck to Manypenny, October 28, 1856, Steck Papers.

14. *Ibid.*, Matthew L. Davis to Steck, July 9, 1856.

15. For further on Dodge, see Meriwether, *My Life*, 198n.; Ruth M. Underhill, *The Navajos*, 103–105; Robert M. Utley, *Frontiersmen in Blue: The United States Army and the Indian, 1848–1865*, 165–66, and references cited.

16. Meriwether to Steck, November 28, 1856, Steck Papers.

17. LR NMS, Roll 548, N235, Claiborne to Nichols, January 2, 1857.

18. *Ibid.*

19. *Ibid.*, enclosure: Steen to Claiborne, January 1, 1857.

20. Meriwether to Steck, March 24, 1857, Steck Papers.

21. LR NMS, Roll 548, N235, Meriwether to commissioner, January 27, 1857.

22. *Ibid.*, N256, Meriwether to Manypenny, March 31, 1857.

23. Steck to Meriwether, March 14, 1857, Steck Papers.

24. *Ibid.*

25. *Ibid.*, Steck to Bonneville, March 14, 1857.

26. Utley, *Frontiersmen in Blue*, 155.

27. Lee Myers, "Military Establishments in Southwestern New Mexico: Stepping

Stones to Settlement," *New Mexico Historical Review*, Vol. XLIII, No. 1 (January, 1968), 13.

28. Percy Gatling Hamlin (ed.), *The Making of a Soldier: Letters of General R. S. Ewell*, 82.

29. Steck to Bonneville, March 14, 1857, Steck Papers.

30. Myers, "Military Establishments," *loc. cit.*, 9–13.

31. *Ibid.*, 14. 35 Cong., 1 sess., Sen. Exec. Doc. 11, II, 135–41. This document reprints official dispatches of the campaign, including reports of actions by Miles and Ewell. In the latter report, two officers and seven enlisted men are revealed wounded, none mortally: Lieutenant Steen struck by "an arrow (in the corner of the eye)" and Second Lieutenant Benjamin Franklin Davis, First Dragoons, "shot in the knee in a personal encounter with an Apache." Corporal Anderson, Company G, First Dragoons, was "twice seriously wounded (arrow and bullet)"—clearly the Coyoteros were worthy foes. See also Utley, *Frontiersmen in Blue*, 155–57; Thomas Edwin Farish, *History of Arizona*, II, 30; Ralph Hedrick Ogle, *Federal Control of the Western Apaches: 1848–1886* (hereafter cited as *Western Apaches*), 38–39f.; Hamlin, *The Making of a Soldier*, 82–83.

32. LR NMS, Roll 548, C1196, Collins to Denason, September 30, 1857.

33. *Ibid.*, enclosure, Bonneville to Collins, September 23, 1857.

34. Frank D. Reeve, in "The Federal Indian Policy in New Mexico, 1858–1880," *New Mexico Historical Review*, Vol. XIII, No. 3 (July, 1938), 281, argues that Bonneville's lyrical impression of the region hastened the Apache-white confrontation by bringing in whites and consequently increasing pressure.

35. Reeve, *op. cit.*, 281, tells of illicit trade by Apaches with stock stolen in Mexico for whiskey and ammunition in New Mexico. Steck to Collins, May 6, 1857, Steck Papers, discusses the probable intent of the Mimbres in going to Janos at this time.

36. *Ibid.*, Steck to Collins, May 16, 1857.

37. *Dictionario Porrua*, 1761.

38. LR NMS, Roll 548, N264, Padilla to Meriwether, November 9, 1856, received by Meriwether from Janos in April, 1857.

39. LR NMS, Roll 548 (no number), Steck to Collins, November 25, 1857.

CHAPTER VI

1. LR NMS, Roll 549, C1485, Wood to Nicholls, April 17, 1858.

2. *Ibid.*, Steck to Collins, April 18, 1858.

3. *Ibid.*, no number, Bailey to Mix, November 4, 1858.

4. The sixty-six-page report, published in 1858 at Washington, lists losses in the hundreds of thousands of dollars allegedly caused by Indian raids.

5. Annual Report, August, 1858, Steck to Collins, Steck Papers.

6. *Ibid.*, Steck to Collins, September 27, 1858.

7. On March 3, 1857, Congress passed an act providing for the transcontinental mail service. The postmaster general approved a contract September 16, 1857, with John Butterfield and associates to carry a letter mail twice weekly between St. Louis and San Francisco. The service began on September 16, 1858, under the corporate name, The Overland Mail Company, but it soon became commonly known as the Butterfield Overland Mail. Its stations usually were about fifteen miles apart. One of them was at the eastern end of Doubtful Pass; ruins of it still remain. Another station was at the spring in Apache Pass, a point Steck now had reached.

8. Tevis was agent at the Apache Pass stage station at this time and writes of Dr.

Steck's visit, but his account is oddly garbled and its trustworthiness uncertain. James H. Tevis, *Arizona in the '50's*, 110–14; 168–69. He says, for example, that there were four thousand Indians present, which is not credible. He writes that Dr. Steck was virtually driven away by Cochise because he had brought few presents, when Dr. Steck does not even mention Cochise, nor any such incident, and said the presents given were taken from those intended for other Indians. Tevis writes as though the visit Steck made afterward with Baldy Ewell and the dragoons was an entirely separate occasion, but Steck shows it to have been part of the same journey. Steck adds that this was his first visit to them, made at the direction of Collins to assure safety to the newly developed "great thoroughfare to the Pacific" opened by the Overland Mail Company. Annual Report, August, 1859, Steck Papers. Yet the Tevis narrative is of interest and he presents many novel and perhaps true incidents of life among the Chiricahuas.

9. LR NMS, Roll 549, C1931, Steck to Collins, February 1, 1859.

10. *Ibid.*, C2126, Steck to Collins, April 8, 1859.

11. Annual Report, August, 1859, Steck Papers.

12. Myers, "Military Establishments," *loc. cit.*, 14–16, 42n. 37.

13. Frazer, *Forts of the West*, 101. *Posts*, Roll 877, has entries from this post, but only for the years 1879 to 1882.

14. LR NMS, Roll 549, C288, Steck to Collins, November 25, 1859.

15. Tully to Steck, April 10, 1860, Steck Papers.

16. LR NMS, Roll 550, S201, Steck to Greenwood, Washington, May 11, 1860. On May 14, 1860, the commissioner approved Steck's suggested Santa Lucia Reservation, but only a few Indians ever moved there. In 1861, when Texan troops invaded New Mexico, the agent was forced to flee and the reserve was not again occupied. On August 28, 1867, it was ordered restored to the public domain. Charles C. Royce (comp.), "Indian Land Cessions in the United States," *Bureau of American Ethnology, Eighteenth Annual Report*, II, 822–23. Santa Lucia Spring, today on a highway marker called "Mangus Springs," lies in the same lovely valley as it did a century ago, with the idling stream flowing between wooded banks and the springs (there are several) bordered by ancient cottonwoods. There is a pinpoint settlement there, owned by a single rancher.

17. LR NMS, Roll 550, S203, Steck to Greenwood, Washington, May 14, 1860.

18. Steck to Collins, March 10, 1860, Steck Papers.

CHAPTER VII

1. Silver City *Enterprise*, May 22, 1885; Pearce, *New Mexico Place Names*, 105–106. For details of Mowry's establishment of the community named for him, see *This Is Silver City, New Mexico: The Silver City Enterprise in the Year 1891*, 60–61.

2. Jacob Snively, born in Pennsylvania about 1815, was of German origin. He was educated, later became a surveyor, and reached Texas early enough to fight in the revolution; become paymaster general, secretary of war, adjutant and inspector general for the Texas armed forces; and be made a colonel by President Sam Houston on February 16, 1843. He led an abortive raid against a well-escorted Mexican caravan on the Santa Fe Trail, was taken with his party by the then Dragoon Captain Philip St. George Cooke, and hustled back to Texas sans almost all the weapons of his party. He struck gold in paying quantities at Pinos Altos in 1860. In 1858 he had made the strike that resulted in the founding of Gila City, Arizona, as a boom camp. He was killed March 18, 1871, about twenty miles east of Wickenburg, still prospecting. *Federal Census—Territory of New Mexico and Territory of Arizona*, 1870. Will C. Barnes, *Arizona Place Names*, 1st

ed., 412–13. McClintock, *Arizona*, I, 189–90. Tevis, *Arizona in the '50's*, 190. Hubert Howe Bancroft, *History of the North Mexican States and Texas*, II, 371–72. *The Handbook of Texas*, II, 631–33. Leo E. Oliva, *Soldiers on the Santa Fe Trail*, 43–48. For a good résumé of the expedition against the Santa Fe Trail, see Stephen B. Oates, "The Hard Luck Story of the Snively Expedition," *The American West*, Vol. IV, No. 3 (August, 1967), 52–58, 77–79.

3. Ungnade, *Guide to New Mexico Mountains*, 131. Pearce, *New Mexico Place Names*, 122. Tevis, *Arizona in the '50's*, 190–205. Anson Mills, *My Story*, 58–59. Constance Wynn Altshuler (ed.), *Latest From Arizona! The Hesperian Letters, 1859–1861*, 93, 96, 99. Schilling, *Silver City*, 12–13.

4. Tevis, *op. cit.* Mills, *op. cit.*

5. Myers, "Military Establishments," *New Mexico Historical Review*, Vol. XLIII, No. 1, 16–20. *Posts*, Roll 1522, lists some scouts against Indians. An added hardship of frontier soldiering appears on the return for May, 1861, when scurvy was reported to have afflicted half the command of most companies, due, of course, to a lack of fresh vegetables and fresh meat in the diet.

6. LR NMS, Roll 550, B842, Steck to Collins, December 14, 1860.

7. LR NMS, Roll 550, Lynde to Steck, December 14, 1860.

8. John Marmaduke, born March 14, 1833, in Missouri, was a six-foot West Pointer who had served in the Mormon Campaign of 1857. Despite the fact that his father favored the Union, John joined the Confederate Army as a colonel in the Civil War, becoming a major general after hard fighting at Shiloh and west of the Mississippi River. He was elected governor of Missouri in 1884 and successfully fought for railroad regulation and other progressive measures. He died December 28, 1887. DAB.

9. Tevis, *Arizona in the '50's*, 206–18.

10. LR NMS, Roll 550, C910, Tully to Collins, January 3, 1860 (*sic*).

11. *Ibid.*, Collins to Greenwood, January 13, 1861.

12. *Ibid.*, C984, Tully to Collins, February 17, 1861.

13. This was the youngster, Felix Ward, later known on the southwestern frontier as Mickey Free. See Thrapp, *The Conquest of Apacheria*, 16f. and 16n.

14. This information, included in the clipping Tully sent Collins on February 17, 1861, came from Howard L. Bickley, superintendent of the Overland Mail Line, who knew of the incidents firsthand.

15. LR NMS, Roll 550, C991, Collins to Greenwood, March 3, 1861.

16. LR NMS, Roll 557, Arny to Parker, October 24, 1870.

17. So says Cremony in *Life Among the Apaches*, 172–73. Numerous writers have followed him in this. See, for example, Farish, *History of Arizona*, II, 125–26; Wellman, *The Indian Wars of the West*, 286–88, etc. Cremony is not overly reliable, particularly when estimating enemy losses, but there is no reason to doubt that this incident, or something like it, occurred.

18. LR NMS, Roll 550, C1231, Tully to Collins, June 2, 1861.

CHAPTER VIII

1. Tucson, *Arizona Star*, July 20, 1879. Cornelius C. Smith, Jr., *William Sanders Oury: History-Maker of the Southwest*, 122.

2. Tevis says that Elder was killed when a party of 122 men was massacred southeast of Stein's Peak Stage Station, which was just east of the peak at the eastern entry to Doubtful Canyon. *Arizona in the '50's*, 218. No such large party ever was wiped out

there, and it appears possible that Tevis meant to write 12, instead of 122. If so, it may be that these victims are identical with the thirteen victims Cremony reported having found between Doubtful Canyon and Apache Pass the following spring, but which did not include Elder. *Life Among the Apaches*, 171–75. However, Cremony apparently confuses the incident which *he* reports with the fate of the Free Thompson party, in an encounter which also occurred in the vicinity of Doubtful Canyon, but involved six men, not thirteen. See Thrapp, *The Conquest of Apacheria*, 19–20; Ray Brandes (ed.), *Troopers West: Military & Indian Affairs on the American Frontier*, 30–33. Carleton, incidentally, reduces Cremony's thirteen to nine, in Richard H. Orton, *Records of California Men in the War of the Rebellion, 1861 to 1867* (hereafter cited as *California Men in the War*), 64.

3. There is a report of an attack by five hundred Apaches under Cochise and Mangas Coloradas on Pinos Altos in September, 1861, in which the miners killed a dozen Indians. There is no supporting evidence, however, and in view of Tully's assertion that the mines had been abandoned several months earlier, plus the incredibility of the figure cited, the report must be discounted as a fable, although there was an attack on a later settlement there, as we shall see. Schilling, *Silver City*, 13.

4. Fillmore, established September 23, 1851, was occupied briefly by Texas Confederates and reoccupied by Union forces in 1862. It was abandoned as a permanent post October 10 of that year. Returns for the early years reflected much Indian activity. Gila Apaches were active in 1857, according to the monthly returns, and in a sharp skirmish in March of that year Brevet Captain Alfred Gibbs, later to become a brevet major general, received a severe lance wound in the abdomen from Mimbres Indians, but recovered. Frazer, *Forts of the West*, 99. *Posts*, Roll 366. See also A. Blake Brophy, "Fort Fillmore, N.M., 1861: Public Disgrace and Private Disaster," *Journal of Arizona History*, Vol. IX, No. 4 (Winter, 1968), 195–218.

5. Ray Brandes, *Frontier Military Posts of Arizona*, 21–24.

6. LR NMS, Roll 550, C1286, Steck to Collins, July 15, 1861.

7. Cremony, *Life Among the Apaches*, 177–78. John W. Teal, a soldier in the California Column who knew Cremony well, wrote in his diary for June 25, 1863, of the officer that "I do not believe any thing he says except when he says he wants whiskey." Henry P. Walker (ed.), "Soldier in the California Column: The Diary of John W. Teal," *Arizona and the West*, Vol. XIII, No. 1 (Spring, 1971), 49.

8. It should be noted that Ray Brandes, in his essay "Mangas Coloradas: King Philip of the Apache Nation" in *Troopers West*, comes to the opposite conclusion, and he has done more thorough and more extended research on Mangas than anyone else. Documentation will be awaited with interest, however, for his statements that Mangas operated around Tucson, frequently visited Santa Fe, and once broke through a twenty-foot wall in an attack upon a Mexican village. These tenets are difficult to accept on the basis of my own research.

9. Aurora Hunt, *The Army of the Pacific: 1860–1866*, 52–56.

10. Benjamin Sachs, *Be It Enacted: The Creation of the Territory of Arizona*, 62–63.

11. George Wythe Baylor, *John Robert Baylor: Confederate Governor of Arizona*, 13.

12. *Ibid.*, 12.

13. Fort Craig, about twenty miles south of the present San Antonio, New Mexico, on the west side of the Río Grande, was established April 1, 1854, and designed originally for two companies, although it sometimes housed more. It, too, was frequently the base

Notes

for Indian operations. *Posts*, Roll 261, the monthly return for July, 1860, tells of a brisk fight at "the Cañada Alamosa," where Victorio's people later would settle. See also Frazer, *Forts of the West*, 98; F. Stanley, *Fort Craig*.

14. LR NMS, Roll 551, A512, Arny to Dole, March 28, 1862.

15. Baylor, *John Robert Baylor*, 14.

16. *Ibid.*, 14–15.

17. *Ibid.*, 15, 32.

18. A report from the Executive Office at Santa Fe said that losses during the calendar year 1862 "principally to the Navajoes and Apaches" totaled, for eight counties, 40 killed, 23 wounded, 6 captives, 419 horses, 1,863 cattle, 30,729 sheep, 874 goats, 71 burros, 32 "other animals," 140 mules, for a total value of stock lost of $247,026.17. LR NMS, Roll 551, A43, newspaper clippings undated but with letter dated January 17, 1863.

19. Cremony, *Life Among the Apaches*, 153–67, 175–76.

20. Hunt, *The Army of the Pacific*, 226–27. Orton, *California Men in the War*, 64.

21. Walker, *Diary of John W. Teal*, 41n.

22. Cremony, *op. cit.*, 164. Orton, *op. cit.*, 64.

23. Barnes, *Arizona Place Names*, 149.

24. Walker, *op. cit.*, 41.

25. Cremony, *op. cit.*, 176. Farish, *History of Arizona*, II, 142. Hunt, *Army of the Pacific*, 151.

26. Frazer, *Forts of the West*, 4.

27. LR NMS, Roll 551, C1832, Collins to Dole, September 7, 1862.

28. Cremony, *op. cit.*, 198.

29. Jay J. Wagoner, *Arizona Territory 1863–1912: A Political History*, 20.

30. Myers, "Military Establishments," *New Mexico Historical Review*, Vol. XLIII, No. 1, 21.

31. LR NMS, Roll 551, A43, unidentified newspaper clipping.

32. For this writer's conclusion that Conner's is the most trustworthy version, see Thrapp, *Conquest of Apacheria*, 20–23. Lee Myers in "The Enigma of Mangas Coloradas' Death," *New Mexico Historical Review*, Vol. XLI, No. 4 (October, 1966), 287–304, examines the several versions and appears to come to the same conclusion, although he questions certain of Conner's details; these, however, apparently are errors of memory, not of untruthful intent. His crediting the Walker party with the initiative in the capture of Mangas, although doubted by Myers, appears to me more probable than the reverse. Conner's edited version is told in his *Joseph Reddeford Walker and the Arizona Adventure*, 34–42. Another version of Conner's account is in McClintock, *Arizona*, I, 176–77, followed by a version from another source, p. 178.

33. Thrapp, *op. cit.*, 103n.

34. Myers, *op. cit.*, 299–300; McClintock, *op. cit.*, 178.

35. Myers, *op. cit.*, 295–97. Joseph Rodman West, born at New Orleans September 19, 1822, was graduated from the University of Pennsylvania and served in the Mexican War. He moved to California in 1849 and engaged in newspaper work in San Francisco. He entered the Union Army as a lieutenant colonel, was promoted to brigadier general of volunteers October 25, 1862, and brevetted major general January 4, 1866, for "faithful and meritorious service," being mustered out at San Antonio. He went to New Orleans, held several positions, was elected U.S. senator for one term, died at Washington October 31, 1898, and was buried in Arlington National Cemetery. *Herringshaw's Library*

of American Biography, V, 646. *Biographical Directory of the American Congress 1774–1927*, 1683–84.

36. McClintock, *Arizona*, I, 177. Fowler, born October 11, 1809, at Cohocton, New York, was a member of a New York publishing house and the author of numerous works on physiology, mental health, sex, and phrenology. He died August 18, 1887, at Sharon Station, Connecticut. *Herringshaw's Library of American Biography*, II, 499. Madeleine B. Stern, *Heads & Headlines: The Phrenological Fowlers.*

37. LR NMS, Roll 554, Hackney to Boggs, November 24, 1866.

38. LR NMS, Roll 558, Pile to Fish, June 19, 1871.

39. Hackney to Boggs, *op. cit.*

40. *Ibid.*

41. In its brief lifetime of just under one year, Fort West was the center for continuous Indian activity. On one scout a detachment "discovered a rich gold region." McCleave's scout after Indians who ran off sixty-five horses resulted in a fight "near the Río Bonita," when the stock was recovered and, for good measure, a number of Indian ponies seized. The soldiers lost First Lieutenant Albert H. French, D Company, First California Cavalry, wounded, and a soldier killed. Before they returned, provisions gave out and "for a number of days they endured great hunger and fatigue, eating their own horses & marching over a rocky country barefooted." Soldiers were ever being picked off, wounded or killed, and fights were virtually monthly affairs. The post was abandoned January 8, 1864. *Posts*, Roll 1410. Myers "Military Establishments," *New Mexico Historical Review*, Vol. XLIII, No. 1, 21–25.

42. Utley notes that Victorio's turn to lead his people now was approaching. *Frontiersmen in Blue*, 252.

43. Thrapp, *The Conquest of Apacheria*, 31.

44. LR NMS, Roll 551, S123, Steck to Dole, July 23, 1863.

45. *Ibid.*, S144, Steck to Dole, August 28, 1863.

46. Frank C. Lockwood, *The Apache Indians*, 222, for example.

47. LR NMS, Roll 546, A421, Smith to Meriwether, September 10, 1853. Delgadito, whose Apache name was Tudeevia, sometimes spelled Dudeevia, was also reported to have been killed in 1855, obviously an error. Griswold, *The Fort Sill Apaches*, 144.

48. Cremony, *Life Among the Apaches*, 84.

49. Woodworth Clum, *Apache Agent: The Story of John P. Clum*, 31.

50. Stanley, *Fort Craig*, 84.

51. Annual Report, 1863, September 15, 1863, Steck Papers.

CHAPTER IX

1. Cremony, *Life Among the Apaches*, 200. *See* James D. Shinkle, *Fort Sumner and the Bosque Redondo Indian Reservation*, for a general history of the reserve and vicinity.

2. Bancroft, *Arizona and New Mexico*, 730.

3. LR NMS, Roll 554, G81, Hackney to Boggs, January 31, 1867. Bosque Redondo was established by executive order January 15, 1864. The Navahos and some Apaches were moved to it, but the bulk of the Apaches, mostly Mescaleros, fled in 1865. A treaty with the Navahos, June 1, 1868, provided for a reservation in their old country, and Bosque Redondo was abandoned, its area being termed surplus July 21, 1871. Royce, *Indian Land Cessions*, 830–31. For an examination and analysis of the Navaho period there and related events, see Frank D. Reeve, "The Federal Indian Policy in New Mexico, 1858–1880," *New Mexico Historical Review*, Vol. XIII, No. 1 (January, 1938), 14–49.

4. Robert G. Athearn, *William Tecumseh Sherman and the Settlement of the West*, 202–206. Bancroft, *op. cit.*, 732–33; Charles Amsden, "The Navaho Exile at Bosque Redondo," *New Mexico Historical Review*, Vol. VIII, No. 1 (January, 1933), 47–48.

5. *Ibid.*, 40.

6. LR NMS, Roll 552, S487, Steck to Maxwell, September 15, 1864.

7. Cummings, established October 2, 1863, fifty-three miles west of the Río Grande and fifteen miles northeast of present-day Deming, was on the Mesilla-Tucson road at Cook's Springs, in dangerous Indian country. *Posts*, Roll 275, recounts an endless series of Apache raids on the post's livestock, scouts, affrays, and Indian attacks on travelers in its vicinity. Samples: "Frequent scouts . . . during month, without any casualties worth of note." "Privates Charles Williams and Jim Kelly . . . attacked by Indians 8 miles west. . . . Williams was killed instantly with a lance. Kelly escaped, badly wounded." "Indians broke into Stage Co. Corral; Sentinel reported Indians fired several shots in corral, killed one mule, shot a horse with an arrow, left without making alarm," etc. etc. Cummings was one of very few walled forts in the West; it was evacuated in 1873, reoccupied in 1880 and occupied variously thereafter, transferred to the Interior Department in 1891, and the site now is in private hands. Frazer, *Forts of the West*, 98.

8. LR NMS, Roll 552, S606, Steck to Dole, February 15, 1865.

9. *Ibid.*, Knapp to Dole, February 4, 1865.

10. *Ibid.*, S624, statement by Bloomfield, February 10, 1865. Manuscript copy, Mesilla, February 10, 1865, Steck Papers.

11. *Ibid.*

12. LR NMS, Roll 552, S625, Steck to Dole, March 20, 1865.

13. *Ibid.*, Roll 554, G81, Hackney to Boggs, January 31, 1867.

14. *Ibid.*

15. Bancroft, *Arizona and New Mexico*, 744n.–45n. LR NMS, no roll number, D98-1865, N. H. Davis, Santa Rita Copper Mines, to Ben C. Cutler, AAAG, District of New Mexico, Santa Fe, May 3, 1865.

16. Hackney to Boggs, *op. cit.*

17. LR NMS, Roll 553, A68, memorial to Congress.

18. *Ibid.*, A106, Abreu to DeForest, May 4, 1866.

19. *Ibid.*, C340, Nichols to DeForest, June 6, 1866.

20. *Ibid.*, C218, Carleton to Burkett, June 22, 1866.

21. Established April 3, 1863, McRae was three miles east of the Río Grande and was intended to stop Indian depredations along the Jornada del Muerto and elsewhere. It was virtually abandoned October 30, 1876, except for a small detachment. It was about thirty-seven airline miles south of Craig, opposite Alamosa near the mouth of the Alamosa River. Many Indian-fighting episodes occurred in its vicinity. For example, on September 10, 1865, a small detachment chased Indians who had driven off post animals westward, overtook them in the Mimbres Mountains, recovered the animals plus Indian ponies after a sharp clash in which an officer and two soldiers were severely wounded. These were almost certainly Mimbres Apaches. Frazer, *Forts of the West*, 100. Malcolm F. Farmer, *New Mexico Camps, Posts, Stations and Forts*, 4. *Posts*, Roll 710.

22. LR NMS, Roll 553, D438, Horne to DeForest, September 28, 1866.

23. *Ibid.*, no number, Ellison to Graves, January 30, 1866.

24. *Ibid.*, H453, Nesmith to Boggs, November 17, 1866.

25. Hunt in *James H. Carleton, Frontier Dragoon*, for example, gives him sympathetic though generally fair treatment on this matter, 274–91.

26. LR NMS, Roll 553, N105, Robert Walsh et al. to Manderfield and Tucker, August 11, 1866.

27. Hunt, *op. cit.*, 344.

28. LR NMS, Roll 553, clipping dated October 27, 1866.

29. *Ibid.*, no number; Norton was commissioned February 17, 1866.

30. LR NMS, Roll 554, C134, Chaves to Browning, March 27, 1867.

31. LR NMS, Roll 553, N10, General Orders 23, September 15, 1866. Bayard, adjacent to present-day Silver City, had actually been established August 21 when a company of California infantry arrived at the site, and was not abandoned as a military post until 1900. Around it swirled Indian operations for almost a third of a century. The post was one of the most famous during the Indian wars, ranking with Whipple, Bowie, Craig, and Cummings in that respect. Frazer, *Forts of the West*, 95–96. Myers, "Military Establishments," *New Mexico Historical Review*, Vol. XLIII, No. 1, 35–40. *Posts*, Rolls 87–88.

32. LR NMS, Roll 554, H20, Foutts to DeForest, November 24, 1866.

33. *Ibid.*, G81, Hackney to Boggs, February 4, 1867.

34. *Ibid.*, N34, Norton to Boggs, March 4, 1867.

35. *Ibid.*, A535, Ayres appointment dated July 25, 1868. John Ayres, born at New York City in 1827, went to sea at thirteen, rounded Cape Horn, and remained in sail until 1849, when he landed in California. Arriving in May, he worked in the mines until 1861, when he enlisted in Company D, First Cavalry, California Volunteers. He was in the fight at Picacho Pass, continued on to New Mexico, was commissioned by Carleton, and, after serving as agent to the Southern Apaches, became an agent to the Utes. He was still alive in 1884. John Ayres, "Ancient Santa Fe, 1883," manuscript in The Bancroft Library, HHB [P-E 5]. This was reprinted as "A Soldier's Experience in New Mexico," *New Mexico Historical Review*, Vol. XXIV, No. 4 (October, 1949), 259–66.

36. LR NMS, Roll 555, H707, Heath to Browning, July 23, 1868.

CHAPTER X

1. Horn, *New Mexico's Troubled Years*, 117.

2. This matter is contained in LR NMS, Roll 556: A321, Townsend to Schofield; A323, signed by Arny, including the proclamation text; A350, Fish to Rawlins.

3. *Pamphlet Accompanying Microcopy No. 234, Letters Received by the Office of Indian Affairs, 1824–80*, 4.

4. Charles Edward Drew was born in 1840 in New Hampshire and enlisted at Lawrence, Massachusetts, in 1861, becoming a first lieutenant in the Twenty-Sixth Massachusetts Infantry on September 23. He transferred to the Thirty-Fourth Infantry of the Regular Army in 1866 and was made a first lieutenant on July 31, 1867. He was court-martialed at Holly Springs, Mississippi, in November of that year on a series of charges alleging corruption, found guilty, and sentenced to be cashiered. But the President overruled the court because of the suspicious nature of the evidence against him and "his manifest innocence of any intentional misconduct," and he was restored to duty. He received his commission as agent for the Southern Apaches at New York's Astor House on July 20, 1869, proceeding immediately for New Mexico. He went about his duties in a most intelligent and dedicated manner, and his early death was tragic. LR NMS, Roll 556, D369, Drew to Parker, July 20, 1869. Drew's military file in the Old Military Records Division, National Archives and Records Service.

5. John A. Shapard to author, December 4, 1969.

6. LR NMS, Roll 556, G149, Grover to Getty, June 2, 1869.

7. *Ibid.*, G167, Getty to the superintendent of Indian affairs, July 3, 1869.

8. Parker, a full-blooded Seneca and an Iroquois chief, was a civil engineer who became acquainted with Grant before the Civil War and served under him in several capacities during that conflict, rising to brevet brigadier general. He served as commissioner of Indian affairs for two years, "a stormy tenure," and then retired to his prepublic life profession of engineering. Born in 1828, he died August 31, 1895. *Who Was Who. National Cyclopedia of American Biography*, V, 330. *New York Times*, July 5, 1969.

9. LR NMS, Roll 556, C3920, Clinton to Parker, August 5, 1869. Fort Stanton was established May 4, 1855, and, after brief Confederate occupation, rebuilt at its present site about five miles southeast of Capitan after 1868. It was constructed to control the Mescaleros and became a major Indian post, fully as important as Craig and Bayard. It today is a tuberculosis sanitarium. Frazer, *Forts of the West*, 103–104.

10. LR NMS, Roll 556, C481, Drew to Parker, September 3, 1869.

11. Duffield was a noted southwestern figure and a competent, if hard-bitten, frontiersman. Benjamin Sachs, "Arizona's Angry Man: United States Marshal Milton B. Duffield," *Journal of Arizona History*, Vol. VIII, Nos. 1, 2 (Spring, Summer, 1967), 1–29; 91–119.

12. LR NMS, Roll 556, N388, Smith to Rawlins, July 19, 1869.

13. *Ibid.*, C395, Clinton to Parker, August 9, 1869.

14. Mrs. John (Mary Ann) Sullivan, then fifty-six, one of the major landholders of the community, which is twenty-five miles northwest of Truth or Consequences, said in an interview October 7, 1969, that "my great-grandfather, Victoriano Chavez, lived here 130 years ago and said the spring was flowing then, had never been known to dry up, and never has been known to since. My husband's grandfather, also named John Sullivan, was a soldier discharged at Fort Craig and came here in the nineteenth century, when it was known as Cañada Alamosa. He renamed it for his birthplace, Monticello, New York."

15. This was probably James Bullard, who, with his brother John, discovered in 1868 the silver deposit later known as Chloride Flat that led to the founding of Silver City, New Mexico, a community incorporated in 1876. The Bullards had come to New Mexico from Missouri in 1866. John was killed by an Apache February 11, 1871. Both brothers occasionally led scouts against Indians, but James was the more prominent in this pursuit. Frederick E. Phelps, then a second lieutenant in the Eighth Cavalry, described him as "our civilian, but not civil guide (he was about as morose, insolent and foul-mouthed a brute as I ever saw)." Bullard nearly aborted General O. O. Howard's mission to Cochise to bring peace to that part of the Southwest by threatening to shoot the officer's Apache guide, without whom he could not have contacted the veteran Chiricahua leader. Later, Bullard was said to have changed his mind and conceded that the mission had been beneficial to the region, despite his earlier antagonism toward it. Frederick E. Phelps, "A Soldier's Memoirs" (ed. by Frank D. Reeve), *New Mexico Historical Review*, Vol. XXV, No. 1 (January, 1950), 54–55 and 54n.–55n. Schilling, *Silver City*, 4–5. *This Is Silver City, New Mexico, 1888–1889–1890*, 4. Twitchell, *New Mexican History*, II, 436–37. Oliver Otis Howard, *My Life and Experiences Among Our Hostile Indians*, 191–92 (hereafter cited as *Among Our Hostile Indians. Ibid., Famous Indian Chiefs I Have Known*, 121–22. Office of Indian Affairs, Microcopy 234, Letters Received, 1824–80, Arizona Superintendency, 1863–80, in the Old Military Records Divi-

sion, National Archives and Record Service (hereafter cited as LR AS, with roll number), Roll 10, D1002, Dudley to Smith, June 30, 1874.

16. LR NMS, Roll 556, C612, Drew to Clinton, October 11, 1869. *Ibid.* Roll 557, Rynerson to Pile, November 22, 1869.

17. Drew to Clinton, October 11, 1869, *op. cit.*

18. LR NMS, Roll 556, C648, Drew to Clinton, October 23, 1869.

19. *Ibid.*, Roll 557, A664, Getty to commanding officer, Department of the Missouri, January 4, 1870. *Ibid.*, A688, Drew to Clinton, October 5, 1869.

20. Rynerson, born in 1836 in Hardin County, Kentucky, was no man to trifle with. He shot and killed the territorial chief justice, John P. Slough, in the lobby of a Santa Fe hotel on December 17, 1867, and was acquitted. Later he became involved in the Lincoln County War. Twitchell, *New Mexican History*, 412 and n., Robert N. Mullin (ed.), *Maurice G. Fulton's History of the Lincoln County War*, 72–73, and additional references.

21. For Pile's attitude toward the Indian problem and reaction to it, see Calvin Horn, *New Mexico's Troubled Years*, 143–44.

22. LR NMS, Roll 557, C801, Drew to Clinton, December 12, 1869.

23. *Ibid.*, C840, Drew to Clinton, January 5, 1870.

24. *Ibid.*

25. Fort Selden was located a mile and one-half east of the Río Grande, about twelve miles above Doña Ana; it was established May 8, 1865, and permanently abandoned in 1889. Frazer, *Forts of the West*, 102–103.

26. LR NMS, Roll 557, C847, Headquarters, District of New Mexico, January 14, 1870.

27. *Ibid.*, C907, Clinton to Parker, February 5, 1870.

28. Thomas Jonathan Jeffords, by reason of his friendship with Cochise, is one of the best-known southwestern frontier figures. Born in Chautauqua County, New York, in 1832, he arrived at Taos in 1859 and in 1862 guided the California Column from Tucson to Fort Thorn. He is said to have taken part in the battle of Valverde, near Fort Craig. After the war, as a stage driver, he was ambushed by the Apaches, but escaped, though wounded. He became superintendent of mails between Fort Bowie and Tucson and is said to have lost fourteen men in sixteen months to Indian hostility. He then negotiated his one-man pact with Cochise, and began a friendship never broken while Cochise lived. Jeffords will appear later in this narrative. He died in Pinal County, Arizona, February 19, 1914. Thrapp, *Al Sieber, Chief of Scouts*, 218n.

29. Brevoort, born in Michigan in 1822, reached New Mexico in 1850 and had long been a trader to the Indians, also traveling extensively through the Southwest and in Old Mexico. He was proud of once having ridden a single horse three hundred miles in three days. See a manuscript by Brevoort about his New Mexico experiences, The Bancroft Library, HHB [P-E 5]. See also the note in *New Mexico Historical Review*, Vol. XVIII, No. 3 (July, 1943), 288, n.112.

30. LR NMS, Roll 557, C1150, Jeffords and Brevoort to Drew, March 8, 1870.

31. *Ibid.*, Drew to Clinton, March 17, 1880.

32. *Ibid.*, Shorkley to AAG, District of New Mexico, March 29, 1870.

33. *Ibid.*, Patterson statement, no date.

34. *Ibid.*, C328, Jeffords and Brevoort to Clinton, May 12, 1870, with endorsement by Clinton.

35. *Ibid.*, Clinton endorsement.

36. Paraje, nine miles north of Fort Craig, was near the present-day San Marcial. The townsite has been submerged by the waters of Elephant Butte Lake. Pearce, *New Mexico Place Names*, 117.

37. Hennisee was born January 16, 1839, at Trappe, Talbot County, Maryland, and was appointed a first lieutenant, First Eastern Shore Maryland Infantry, in 1861. He fought at Gettysburg, joined the Regular Army in 1867, and retired on his birthday, 1903, as colonel of the Fifth Cavalry. He was described by Major General Elwell S. Otis as "a careful and painstaking officer" and by Colonel E. V. Sumner as possessing "good talents, character and soldierly requirements." He needed such qualities, as much in dealing with disreputable characters who sought to profit from the Indians as with the Apaches themselves. Hennisee's military file in the Old Military Records Division, National Archives and Records Service.

38. Drew's military file, *loc. cit.* LR NMS, Roll 557, C1472, Hall to Clinton, June 5, 1870.

39. *Ibid.*, C1437, Clinton to Parker, June 29, 1870.

40. *Ibid.*, Hennisee to Clinton, June 22, 1870. This liquor, called tiswin, or tizwin, was a mild, fermented beer, manufactured and drunk by the Apaches on social and other occasions and sometimes even used as a food. Briefly, the corn is soaked, sprouted, dried, and ground, and this is mixed in water and kept in a warm place to ferment. Its production was probably an early Apache art, but with refinements imported from the Spanish or Mexicans. A good description of its making is in Opler, *An Apache Life-Way*, 369–70. See also Hodge, *Handbook of American Indians*, I, 456, under "Fermentation." Apache "tiswin drunks" caused much tumult on the reservations, thus the manufacture of the drink frequently was proscribed by agents, and attempts to eradicate the beverage and its use led to endless strife.

41. LR NMS, Roll 557, C1732, Hennisee to Clinton, September 15, 1870.

42. *Ibid.*, C1755, Clinton to the commissioner of Indian affairs, September 30, 1870.

43. *Ibid.*, C1730, Hennisee to Clinton, September 16, 1870.

44. *Ibid.*, C1755, Hennisee to Clinton, September 30, 1870.

45. For a biographical treatment on Arny, see *Indian Agent in New Mexico: The Journal of Special Agent W. F. M. Arny, 1870* (ed. by Lawrence R. Murphy), 7–12; for his diary of the visit to the Mimbres Apaches, *ibid.*, 54–58.

46. LR NMS, Roll 562, D616, Thomas, "Report from Southern Apache Indian Agency," April 1, 1874; LR AS, Roll 10, 1629, Morrill to Whipple, March 29, 1874. Yet John Gregory Bourke, often a discerning judge of character, called Coleman "an able and companionable gentleman," and, again, "a very fine officer." Lansing B. Bloom (ed.), "Bourke on the Southwest, II," *New Mexico Historical Review*, Vol. IX, No. 1 (January, 1934), 40 and 40n. Born in New York and a Civil War veteran with two brevets for gallantry, Coleman resigned from the army in 1874 and died July 16, 1902. Heitman, *Historical Register of the U.S. Army*, I, 316.

47. Arny here means the Central Chiricahuas, the only band over which Cochise actually was chief. Cochise, the next day, explained that Victorio and Loco were head chiefs of the Mimbres. Arny, *op. cit.*, 57n. The appearance of Cochise at Cañada Alamosa was the first of several during which he held conferences with white officials. Contacts between the whites and Cochise culminated in the famous meeting with General Howard in 1872. These contacts correct the commonly held view that Cochise was intractably hostile from 1861 to 1872. He certainly was aloof, but frequently could be contacted during this period; it is probable that Jeffords could have brought Cochise to Howard

as readily as he conducted Howard to Cochise for their noted meeting in the Dragoons.

48. LR NMS, Roll 557, A1579, Report No. 8 of W. F. Arny, November 21, 1870.

49. In early 1861.

50. Cochise had visited Camp Mogollon, the later Fort Apache, in the White Mountains of Arizona on about August 30, 1870, conferring with Brevet Lieutenant Colonel John Green. Tucson *Weekly Arizonian*, September 17, 1870, reprinted in *Arizoniana*, Vol. I, No. 3 (Fall, 1960), 24. Camp Mogollon had been named Camp Ord until August 1 of that year, and was renamed Camp Thomas on September 12. It was named Camp Apache in 1871 and Fort Apache in 1879. Frazer, *Forts of the West*, 3.

51. LR NMS, Roll 557, A1502, Arny Report No. 7, October 24, 1870.

52. Their gravest sin, he no doubt felt.

53. No treaties were made with Indian tribes after 1871, following which date the Indians were treated as wards of the government, not independent nations. William Christie Macleod, *The American Indian Frontier*, 536.

54. Arny, Report No. 8, *loc. cit.*

55. LR NMS, Roll 557, C1952, Hennisee to Clinton, November 25, 1870.

56. Piper, from Macomb, Illinois, was a Presbyterian layman, prominent in civic affairs, a onetime police magistrate, alderman, and insurance agent, but with no particular experience or aptitude in handling the wild Apaches. His appointment was part political and part due to his religious affiliation. He was sponsored by the Presbyterian Board of Foreign Missions. Marie Erbe, "Orlanda F. Piper, Agent for the Southern Apache Agency, New Mexico, 1870–1872," manuscript in possession of The Presbyterian Historical Society, Philadelphia. Correspondence with the McDonough County Historical Society, Macomb, Illinois. Frank D. Reeve, "The Federal Indian Policy in New Mexico, 1858–1880, IV," *New Mexico Historical Review*, Vol. XIII, No. 3 (July, 1938), 293. Nathaniel Pope, born in Missouri, was a nephew of Brevet Major General John Pope, who commanded the Department of the Missouri, which included the District of New Mexico, from 1870–83.

CHAPTER XI

1. LR NMS, Roll 557, P592, Pope to Parker, December 7, 1870.

2. *Ibid.*, A1598, Colyer to secretary of interior, December 23, 1870.

3. Reeve, *op. cit.*, 293–94.

4. The "count" of Indians for rationing at this time rarely was a sure indication of how many were in the vicinity, since most agents did not require that the Indian collect rations in person, but merely that someone collect for him. This was partly because they were afraid of their charges, and also because of the truculent refusal of many Indians to comply with any order that they be counted in person. Thus, it was possible and, in times of short rations highly probable, that double or triple rations were collected by individuals claiming they were drawing also for others. Accurate counting of Indians, begun by such soldiers as Crook, often revealed discrepancies between the number of Indians "rationed" and the number actually present. This is no proof that the agents profited from the difference; excess rations may as frequently have gone into the bellies of Indians actually on hand, or have been traded by them to unscrupulous whites for arms, ammunition, and the like. Rations distributed at the Southern Apache agencies fluctuated from a few more than three hundred to almost two thousand. It appears unlikely that the food and other goods issued there were so lavishly distributed as to have attracted many Indians from other reserves.

5. LR NMS, Roll 558, A298, Pile to Fish, April 28, 1871.

6. *Ibid.*, P1540, Pope to Parker, March 18, 1871.

7. Ralston, later renamed Shakespeare, was a mining camp three miles outside present Lordsburg, New Mexico. It is now a ghost town.

8. LR NMS, Roll 558, P167, Peck to Butler, March 27, 1871.

9. *Ibid.*, P213, Pope to Parker, April 21, 1871.

10. Manta, in this sense, means cloth used for clothing and other purposes. It was a standard trade item with the southwestern Indians.

11. LR NMS, Roll 558, P224, Pope to Parker, April 21, 1871.

12. *Ibid.*

13. This report is good evidence that Cochise was not the Indian whose party killed First Lieutenant Howard B. Cushing in the Whetstone Mountains on May 5, 1871, as so often is alleged. The Apache who figured in this incident most likely was Juh. See Thrapp, *The Conquest of Apacheria*, 77.

14. LR NMS, Roll 558, P275, Pope to Parker, May 24, 1871.

15. Jeffords' bill for this mission was $500, a generous, but not lavish, reward for successfully completing a perilous undertaking on which he furnished his own mules and supplies. It reflected, also, Jeffords' singular monopoly of such enterprises. He was virtually the only American who could penetrate Cochise's strongholds at will and return safely. LR NMS, Roll 558, P536, Pope to the commissioner, October 8, 1871. *Ibid.*, Piper to Pope, October 8, 1871.

16. *Ibid.*, P319, Pope to Parker, June 28, 1871.

17. For the background to the Peace Commission, its organization, mission, and work, see Ogle, *Western Apaches*, 86–91. Colyer was born in New York City, September 30, 1824, and became an accomplished artist. He became colonel of a Negro regiment he had raised in the Civil War. Afterward he held a number of benevolent positions. Under Grant he served as Indian commissioner, visiting Alaska as well as the Southwest. "His character was as noble as his disposition was amiable." He died at Rowayton, Connecticut, July 12, 1888. *National Cyclopedia of American Biography*, VII, 541. President Grant, on July 14, said he would direct the War Department to assist Colyer settle the Indians. Office of the Adjutant General Microcopy 666, Letters Received (hereafter cited as LR AG, with roll number), Roll 24, 2465–1871, Grant to Belknap, July 14, 1871. B. R. Cowen, acting secretary of the interior, on July 21 ordered Colyer "to proceed to New Mexico and Arizona Territories, and there take such action as in your judgment may be deemed wisest and most proper for locating the nomad tribes . . . upon suitable reservations. . . . The Department invests you with full powers. . . ." *U.S. Board of Indian Commissioners. Peace with the Apaches of New Mexico and Arizona Report of Vincent Colyer* (hereafter cited as *Colyer Report*), 6–7.

18. LR NMS, Roll 558, A464, Pile to Fish, June 19, 1871.

19. *Ibid.*, A453, Townsend to the commanding general, Department of the Missouri, July 18, 1871. *Colyer Report*, 7.

20. LR NMS, Roll 558, C542, Hudson to Piper, July 18, 1871.

21. *Ibid.*, Pope to Hudson, August 3, 1871.

22. This probably is the same Trujillo who sought to cause trouble for Agent Hennisee over the whiskey matter. Whatever his moonlighting activities, Trujillo's close acquaintanceship with the Apaches made him a logical man to send after Cochise.

23. Crook to adjutant general, September 4, 1871, Letterbook 1, No. 1, Crook Collection, at the Rutherford B. Hayes Memorial Library, Fremont, Ohio.

24. LR NMS, Roll 558, C570, Piper to Pope, August 21, 1871.

25. *Ibid.*, P431, Pope to commissioner, August 16, 1871.

26. LR AG, Roll 24, 2695–1871, Colyer to Delano, July 31, 1871.

27. Unless otherwise stated, this summary of Colyer's visits with and actions toward the Cañada Alamosa Indians is based upon the *Colyer Report*.

28. Before leaving for the northwest, he conferred with two "sorry-looking, half-starved" Chiricahuas who had left Cochise twenty-five days before. "Cochise had a fight while he was sick, his band were whipped and had got scattered; he had retired up to the inaccessible part of the mountains, having first killed his horses and taken them up with him for food. Some five or six of the Apaches had been killed. They were Papagos or Mexican scouts who had attacked them." Later a brother of Cochise came in for "a good peace," indicating he would stay. *Colyer Report*, 10. LR AG, Roll 24, 3920–1871, Colyer to Schofield, October 20, 1871.

29. Tularosa River, which joins the San Francisco at present-day Reserve, New Mexico, comes down from the northeast through a high, mountainous country that is fairly remote, even today. The agency was to focus upon a site just east of present-day Aragon, elevation 7,312 feet, with timbered hills on all sides and a flat of varying width bordering the river, where corn cultivation and other light farming is done to this day. Truly it was an isolated valley, unattractive even to whiskey sellers for that reason, but it was cold and distant from their homeland, and the Mimbres never liked it.

30. LR AG, Roll 24, 3896–1871, Townsend to Sheridan, November 11, 1871.

31. *Ibid.*, Townsend to Schofield, November 11, 1871.

32. *Colyer Report*, 55–56; LR AG, Roll 24, General Orders 8, no number.

33. *Colyer Report*, 57–58.

34. LR NMS, Roll 558, P477, Pope to commissioner, October 7, 1871.

35. *Ibid.*, A529, Piper to Davis, September 30, 1871.

36. *Ibid.*, P491, Pope to commissioner, October 9, 1871.

37. *Ibid.*, P501, Pope to commissioner, October 17, 1871.

38. *Ibid.*, P521, Piper to Pope, October 20, 1871.

39. *Ibid.*, Pope to acting commissioner, October 26, 1871.

40. This is an interesting statement, if factual. No photograph or painting from life is known to exist of Cochise, but Davis' report suggests that one was sent to Washington in 1871. It may some day be located.

41. LR NMS, Roll 558, A629, Davis to AAG, headquarters, Department of the Missouri, October 25, 1871.

42. LR NMS, Roll 558, C969, Delano to Clum, November 7, 1871.

43. *Ibid.*, P537, Piper to Pope, October 24, 1871.

CHAPTER XII

1. LR NMS, Roll 559, unnumbered, undated, unidentified clipping.

2. LR AG, Roll 24, 3920–1871, Schofield to Sherman, October 23, 1871.

3. Brevet Major General Gregg, born at Bellefonte, Pennsylvania, July 19, 1826, served in the Mexican and Civil wars and at this time commanded the Eighth Cavalry. He died at Washington on January 6, 1892. *National Cyclopedia of American Biography*, X, 497.

4. Tommy Devin, major general of volunteers in the Civil War, was born December 10, 1822, at New York. He now was lieutenant colonel of the Eighth Cavalry. For an

amusing glimpse of him, see Phelps, "A Soldier's Memoirs, I," *New Mexico Historical Review*, Vol. XXV, No. 1, 52–54. Devin died at New York April 4, 1878.

5. LR NMS, Roll 559, P766, Pope to Walker, March 23, 1872.

6. Streeter is one of the intriguing, and enigmatic, southwestern frontier figures. Born in New York State, he arrived in Apacheria after a most adventurous life. Later, it is said, he fought with the Apaches against the whites in several engagements, was outlawed, and finally shot in a Sonora village. In this reference Streeter no doubt was a Spanish-English interpreter rather than Apache-English, for it is doubtful whether he had yet mastered the Indian language to any extent. Thrapp, *The Conquest of Apacheria*, 279–80.

7. LR NMS, Roll 559, P786, Piper to Pope, March 28, 1872.

8. *Ibid.*, P788, Piper to Pope, March 31, 1872.

9. *Ibid.*, P819, Pope to Walker, April 29, 1872.

10. Company K, Fifteenth Infantry, left Craig April 26 and reached Tularosa April 30, opening the post; Troop H, Eighth Cavalry, left Craig April 29 and arrived May 5, while Coleman assumed command July 1. *Posts*, Roll 1300. The many artifacts lying around the site of the post and, perhaps, of the later agency, suggest it once was a populous place. To the east, where the river emerges from a canyon, the valley is protected by timbered ridges. A mile to the west, beyond the linear community of Aragon, the valley opens into a basin, half a mile or so broad and still wider where an intersecting creek joins from the north. Bounding the basin northward are sandstone bluffs. The valley flats, of varying width up to half a mile, extend southwestward for five or six miles before the mountains close in again near Apache Junction. Westward rises a jumbled mass of forested mountains reaching into the White Range of Arizona. Before the fort was completed, it was removed to Horse Springs, nineteen miles east. It was abandoned November 26, 1874. Frazer, *Forts of the West*, 105.

11. LR NMS, Roll 559, no number but follows P840, Pope to Walker, May 9, 1872.

12. *Ibid.*, P840, Devin to Sartle, May 9, 1872.

13. *Ibid.*, W1647, Devin to AAAG, District of New Mexico, May 27, 1872.

14. Walker, born at Boston in 1840, was a brilliant economics theoretician and educator who served "with great ability" as Indian commissioner from November, 1871, to December, 1872. "He injected common sense and honesty into the administration of Indian affairs." He was professor of political economy at Yale and president of the Massachusetts Institute of Technology from 1881 to 1897. One of his books was *The Indian Question*, published in 1874. He died in 1897. DAB.

15. LR NMS, Roll 559, P890, Pope to Walker, June 5, 1872.

16. Wilkinson, born in New York, served in the Civil War. He won a brevet as major against the Nez Percé Indians in the Chief Joseph campaign. Killed by Chippewa Indians in the "battle" of Leech Lake, Minnesota, October 5, 1898, he was the last U.S. serviceman to be slain by hostile Indians during the conquest of a continent. Heitman, *Historical Register of the U.S. Army*, I, 1037.

17. LR AG, Roll 24, 807–1872, Delano to Howard, March 4, 1872.

18. Bancroft, *Arizona and New Mexico*, 564.

19. Howard, *Among Our Hostile Indians*, 124–76. George W. Cullum, *Biographical Register of the Officers and Graduates of the U.S. Military Academy at West Point*, *N.Y.*, II, 576, 577. DAB, IV, 94.

20. LR AG, Roll 24, 2663–1872, Grant to adjutant general, July 3, 1872.

21. *Ibid.*, 4728–1872, Howard to Walker, November 7, 1872.

22. LR NMS, Roll 560, W496, Piper to Coleman, October 9, 1872.

23. Erbe, "Orlanda F. Piper, Agent for the Southern Apache Agency, New Mexico, 1870–1872," Manuscript in possession of The Presbyterian Historical Society, Philadelphia.

24. LR NMS, Roll 573, A678½, Coleman et al., statement, January 12, 1873.

25. LR NMS, Roll 560, D378, Howard to Coleman, included in Dudley to commissioner, March 15, 1873.

26. Howard, *Famous Indian Chiefs I Have Known*, 112–36. There is no hint here, nor in Howard's other writings and communications, that he ever considered Victorio to be anything but an Apache—no suggestion whatever of any Mexican parentage. Surely Howard would have heard, had the story that Victorio was a Mexican been current in 1872. Obviously, it was not.

27. LR NMS, Roll 559, P153, Howard to Pope, September 5, 1872.

28. *Ibid.*, P172, Howard to Piper, September 16, 1872.

29. Erbe, *op. cit.*

30. This was Ayres' second experience as agent for the Southern Apaches. His first, as we have seen, was in 1868.

31. LR AG, Roll 24, 4728–1872, Howard to Walker, November 7, 1872.

32. *Ibid.*, 4130–1872, Howard to commanding officer, Fort Craig, September 19, 1872.

33. *Ibid.*, 4507–1872, Piper to Pope, October 17, 1872.

34. *Ibid.*, Pope to Granger, October 24, 1872.

35. *Ibid.*, Pope to Sheridan, October 28, 1872.

36. *Ibid.*, Sheridan to Sherman, November 7, 1872.

37. *Ibid.*, Howard to secretary of war, November 27, 1872.

38. LR AG, Roll 24, 5070–1872, Pope to Sheridan, December 11, 1872.

39. LR NMS, Roll 559, P167, Pope to Walker, October 11, 1872, including letter, Sumner to Pope, October 2, 1872.

40. In a statement dictated for the historian Hubert Howe Bancroft, Howard said he had spent thirteen days with these Indians. Oliver Otis Howard, "Indian Troubles in Arizona and New Mexico (1872)," manuscript in the Bancroft Library, HHB [P-D 6].

41. LR AG, Roll 24, 4728–1872, Howard to Walker, November 7, 1872.

42. The reservation was set aside by Executive Order on December 14, 1872, and canceled by Executive Order on October 30, 1876. It was bounded generally by the New Mexico border, the Old Mexico border for fifty-six miles west, the western slope of the Dragoons, and from Dragoon Springs northeastward to the New Mexico line at the Stein's Peak Range. Royce, "Indian Land Cessions," 860, 888, and Arizona Map II.

43. *General George Crook: His Autobiography* (ed. by Martin F. Schmitt), 177.

44. Howard's summary of his "treaty" with Cochise was penned for the commissioner. LR AG, Roll 24, 3988–1873, Howard to commissioner, September 23, 1873.

CHAPTER XIII

1. LR NMS, Roll 559, P187, Coleman to AAAG, District of New Mexico, October 18, 1872.

2. *Ibid.*, P181, Pope to Walker, October 25, 1872; Piper to Pope, October 17, 1872.

3. LR NMS, Roll 560, W611, Devin to AAAG, District of New Mexico, November 12, 1872.

4. *Ibid.*, P290, Ayres to Pope, November 21, 1872. *Ibid.*, Roll 561, W668, Coleman to AAAG, District of New Mexico, November 20, 1873 [*sic*].

5. LR AG, Roll 24, 5055–1872, Delano to Belknap, December 11, 1872.

6. *Ibid.*, 838–1873, Crook comments on proposed transfer, February 2, 1873.

7. *Ibid.*, 120–1873, Pope to Townsend, January 14, 1873.

8. *Ibid.*, first endorsement. Sherman's concurrence is the second endorsement; his original remarks are in LR AG, Roll 24, 5173–1872, Sherman to Belknap, December 17, 1872.

9. *Ibid.*, 5312–1872, Schofield to adjutant general, Washington, December 26, 1872.

10. This dispute is reflected, for example, in LR AG, Roll 24, 783–1873, Howard to Schofield, January 6, 1873, and accompanying documents; 831–1873, Crook to AAG, San Francisco, February 11, 1873, etc.

11. Born July 25, 1843, in Warren County, Indiana, Thomas was one of the better agents to serve the Mimbres Apaches, but, because he was inflexible and could not be intimidated, the Indians never liked him nor his administration as they did Ayres and other weaker agents. Recollections of today's descendants of those Indians reflect such views. A Presbyterian, Thomas was trained as a dentist and went to New Mexico for his health in 1870. The following year he entered the Indian service; he followed his Southern Apache service with duty at agencies for the Pueblos, Utes, and Jicarilla Apaches, besides supplying special services at other agencies. For all of them he served intelligently and usefully. In 1883 he went to Tucson for a few years as register of the land office, but in 1889 was named secretary of the Territory of New Mexico and came back to Santa Fe. He died October 2, 1892. It was said of him that he was "a man of forceful character and high ideals . . . some administrative ability, with a conscience that never permitted him to swerve from what he deemed right." Twitchell, *New Mexican History*, II, 503–504.

12. Dudley, born in Vermont and from New York appointed superintendent of Indian affairs for New Mexico on December 14, 1872, continued in that post until abolition of the superintendency in 1874. He later served as special commissioner of Indian affairs, ably performing the dangerous and difficult removal of the Camp Verde Indians to San Carlos in the early spring of 1875. Thrapp, *Al Sieber, Chief of Scouts*, 159–69. Dudley was a brave man, willing to assume responsibility and undertake great hardships to carry it out, all the while complaining about his hard lot. Information from Richard S. Maxwell, assistant director, Social and Economics Division, National Archives and Records Service.

13. LR NMS, Roll 559, D192, Dudley to Walker, December 19, 1872.

14. Dudley cited as one instance of the source of Apache dislike for Thomas the reformation in beef rationing which Dudley had ordered Thomas to make. Under this ruling Indians were issued butchered beef, instead of animals on the hoof, "thereby preventing the inevitable fight among the Indians about the distribution and securing to each person their proper share. Mr. Thomas carried out this instruction in the face of the worst possible opposition of the Indians and the predictions of others that it could not be done. Many other much needed reforms had been introduced by Agent Thomas, and of course he had become exceedingly unpopular with those under his charge." LR NMS, Roll 560, D378, Dudley to commissioner, March 15, 1873.

15. *Ibid.*

16. *Ibid.*, Roll 562, D616, Thomas to commissioner, report, April 1, 1874.

17. Duane died at Tularosa January 21, 1874. *Ibid.*, D129, Thomas to Dudley, January 23, 1874.

18. *Ibid.*, Roll 561, D356, Duane to Thomas, June 29, 1873.

19. *Ibid.*, D417, Thomas to Dudley, July 25, 1873.

20. Apparently this secluded ranch, which was in Mescalero, not Mimbres, country, here got a dose of its own medicine, since it was "notorious as a clearing house for stolen stock," according to common knowledge. Mullin, *Fulton's History of the Lincoln County War*, 84.

21. LR NMS, Roll 561, W1013, Chilson to Price, July 17, 1873.

22. *Ibid.*, Roll 562, D616, Thomas to Price, July 30, 1873.

23. *Ibid.*, Roll 561, D417, Thomas to Dudley, July 25, 1873. *Ibid.*, W1013, Price to AAAG, District of New Mexico, July 25, 1873. *Posts*, Roll 1300, return for July, 1873.

24. LR NMS, Roll 561, D417, appendix A, Thomas to Price, July 24, 1873.

25. *Ibid.*, appendix B, Thomas to Price, July 24, 1873. *Ibid.*, D376, Dudley to commissioner, August 1, 1873.

26. *Ibid.*, Roll 562, D616, Thomas to Price, July 30, 1873.

27. *Ibid.*, Roll 561, D499, Thomas report on status of reservation, no address.

28. *Ibid.*, D889, Dudley to Smith, December 2, 1873.

29. Wingate, in northwestern New Mexico, was established near the headwaters of the Río Puerco in 1860, closed out by reason of the Confederate advance early in the Civil War, re-established at the present San Rafael in 1862, and moved to the former site in 1868, then being titled Wingate. It still is in use by the Army Ordnance Department. Frazer, *Forts of the West*, 108–109.

30. LR NMS, Roll 563, W641, Price to AAAG, District of New Mexico, December 13, 1873.

31. *Ibid.*, Pope to Drum, January 9, 1874.

32. LR AG, Roll 123, 480–1874, Vandever to commissioner, January 23, 1874.

33. LR NMS, Roll 563, 1498, Farnsworth to commanding officer, Troops Operating in Southern New Mexico, February 15, 1874.

34. *Ibid.*, Steelhammer to Price, February 21, 1874.

35. *Ibid.*, Price to AAAG, District of New Mexico, February 28, 1874.

36. *Ibid.*, Roll 562, D687, Pope's Special Orders 54, Department of the Missouri, April 14, 1874.

37. *Ibid.*, Dudley to commissioner, June 20, 1874.

38. A contrary view is expressed by Agent Thomas. See LR AG, Roll 123, 2913–1874, Gregg endorsement to Vandever report, July 6, 1874.

39. LR NMS, Roll 563, 1498, Price to Steelhammer, February 21, 1874. For details on how army pack units were organized and operated, see Dan L. Thrapp, "The Military Pack Outfits," *Brand Book Number One* (San Diego Corral of the Westerners), 181–90.

40. The Reverend Edward P. Smith, born in Connecticut and graduated from Yale, was described as of "strong mind, excellent judgment . . . with a wide knowledge of men and the world and good business ability." He was agent for the Chippewas and related peoples in 1871, appointed commissioner of Indian affairs in March, 1873, and served until December 11, 1875. He was one of the more able Indian commissioners of the nineteenth century. Information from Richard S. Maxwell, assistant director, Social and Economics Records Division, National Archives and Records Service.

41. LR NMS, Roll 562, D254, Dudley to Smith, March 6, 1874.

42. LR AS, Roll 10, D339, Dudley to Smith, March 28, 1874. The Ojo Caliente Reservation, a rectangle twenty-five by thirty miles, was created by Executive Order on April 9, 1874, soon after Dudley's letter reached Washington. The reserve's boundaries were modified by Executive Order on December 21, 1875, and the area restored to public

domain, also by Executive Order, August 25, 1877. Royce "Indian Land Cessions," 874, 882, 890.

43. LR AS, Roll 10, D425, Pope to Giddings, April 12, 1874. *Ibid.*, E-50, Dudley to Elkins, April 14, 1874.

44. Giddings, a Connecticut-born Michigan Republican, was appointed governor in 1871 and died in office, June 3, 1875. He was born in 1816. Horn, *New Mexico's Troubled Years*, 150–71.

45. LR AS, Roll 10, 1698, Jeffords to Smith, June 7, 1874.

46. *Ibid.*, D1002, Dudley to Smith, June 30, 1874. In this lengthy report he describes fully his journey to Cochise and related matters.

47. *Ibid.* For Jeffords' announcement of Cochise' death and accession of Taza, see LR AS, Roll 10, I-705, Jeffords to Smith, June 10, 1874. Taza, born about 1843, never married and had no children. He was one of a delegation of Apaches taken to Washington, D.C., in 1876, and died there of pneumonia on September 26 at the approximate age of thirty-three. All others of his relatives are recorded and their biographies traced in the Fort Sill genealogy. Griswold, *The Fort Sill Apaches*, 132–33.

48. This was one of Dudley's final duties as superintendent of Indian affairs for New Mexico. He was "retired" from that position in mid-June. The New Mexico superintendency was abolished June 16, 1874, after Congress failed to provide funds for it. Lawrence L. Mehren (ed.), "Scouting for Mescaleros: The Price Campaign of 1873," *Arizona and the West*, Vol. X, No. 2 (Summer, 1968), 173 n.9. Supervision of a number of agencies by a single superintendent was discontinued everywhere during the 1870's; it was completed by 1878. Thereafter all agents reported directly to the Bureau of Indian Affairs at Washington. *Pamphlet Accompanying Microcopy No. 234, Letters Received by the Office of Indian Affairs, 1824–80*, 4.

49. LR NMS, Roll 563, T411, Thomas to Smith, July 21, 1874.

CHAPTER XIV

1. LR NMS, Roll 563, T483, Thomas to Smith, August 7, 1874.

2. LR AG, Roll 123, 480–1874, Vandever to commissioner, January 23, 1874.

3. *Ibid.*, 2913–1874, Thomas to Price, May 29, 1874.

4. LR NMS, Roll 563, T592, Thomas to Smith, September 21, 1874.

5. *Ibid.*, Roll 565, W28½, Special Orders 125, Headquarters, District of New Mexico, December 12, 1874. Thrapp, *The Conquest of Apacheria*, 48–51.

6. LR AG, Roll 123, 2913–1874, Price to AAAG, District of New Mexico, June 13, 1874. *Ibid.*, Thomas to Price, May 29, 1874.

7. LR NMS, Roll 563, T616, Thomas' reply to questionnaire, no date, but 1874. This census states there were no "Indians of mixed blood" on the reservation, suggesting once again that if Victorio was white, or half-white, that fact was unknown to Thomas and others who were best qualified to judge.

8. *Ibid.*, Roll 562, I-1038, acting secretary of interior to commissioner, September 17, 1874; Roll 563, S1411, Shaw to Smith, October 6, 1874; Roll 563, S1652, Shaw to Smith, November 15, 1874.

9. See series of Shaw's monthly statements, LR NMS, Roll 565: S114, December 24, 1874, rations to 460 Indians; S116, December 31, to 500; S813, May 6, 1875, to 693; S866, May 13, to 729; S960, May 27, to 903; S1063, June 10, 1875, to 1,317 Indians.

10. LR NMS, Roll 565, S1134, Shaw to Smith, November 30, 1874.

11. LR AS, Roll 13, D257, Dudley to Smith, June 4, 1875.

12. Thrapp, *Al Sieber, Chief of Scouts*, 156–69. William T. Corbusier, *Verde to San Carlos: Recollections of a Famous Army Surgeon and His Observant Family on the Western Frontier 1869–1886*, 261–80.

13. Lockwood, *The Apache Indians*, 211–12.

14. LR NMS, Roll 565, S815, Shaw to Smith, May 6, 1875.

15. *Ibid.*, S1199, Shaw to Smith, June 24, 1875.

16. *Ibid.*, S1284, Shaw to Smith, July 26, 1875.

17. *Ibid.*, Roll 568, S250, Shaw to Smith, March 24, 1876.

18. Born in Perry County, Ohio, September 26, 1841, Elkins arrived in New Mexico as a young attorney after the Civil War, settling first at Mesilla and then at Santa Fe. He held public positions of increasing importance, was elected territorial delegate in 1873 and re-elected in 1875. Always politically inclined, he served as secretary of war in Benjamin Harrison's administration and for three terms as U.S. senator from West Virginia, to which state he had removed. He died January 4, 1911. Although he became one of the most prominent and active political figures in New Mexico, he remained a controversial figure, then and now. Twitchell, *New Mexican History*, II, 401n.–402n. Porter A. Stratton, *The Territorial Press of New Mexico 1834–1912*, 84–85. William A. Keleher, *The Fabulous Frontier: Twelve New Mexico Items*, 122n.–23n.

19. LR NMS, Roll 566, E45, Shaw to Elkins, March 29, 1876.

20. *Ibid.*, Elkins to Smith, April 7, 1876.

21. *Ibid.*, Roll 568, S270, Shaw to Smith, March 29, 1876; S335, Shaw to Smith, April 6, 1876.

22. *Ibid.*, S330, Shaw to Smith, April 15, 1876, with enclosures from Marrill and Hughes detailing the outbreak.

23. *Ibid.*

24. *Ibid.*, Shaw to Smith, April 15, 1876.

25. *Ibid.*, S337, Shaw to Smith, April 17, 1876.

26. *Ibid.*, S341, Shaw to Smith, April 22, 1876.

27. Born at Bangor, Maine, December 23, 1832, Hatch served in the Civil War, took part in Grierson's great Mississippi raid, and rose to brevet major general. In his lifetime he took part in forty battles. "He was an able soldier, a man of decision, firm of character and with a well-balanced judgment." He died April 11, 1889, from effects of an accident. DAB.

28. Morrow was born March 10, 1842, at Payson, Illinois, enlisted as sergeant of the Seventeenth Pennsylvania Infantry on February 18, 1861, and rose to become colonel of the Third Cavalry at his retirement in 1892. He died in Gainesville, Florida, January 20, 1911. He was captured during the Civil War, paroled, and was wounded severely at the Battle of Dinwiddie Court House in 1865 and suffered throughout his army career from rheumatism, arthritis, and related ailments, although he was a persistent, active, effective soldier. Morrow's military file, National Archives and Records Service. During his last year of active duty he participated in a series of battles against Mexican bandits, marauders, and "would-be revolutionists" from Fort McIntosh, Texas. He was an important officer in the Victorio campaigns. Ralph Conrad Deibert, *A History of the Third United States Cavalry*, 76.

29. LR NMS, Roll 569, W569, Hatch to Pope, April 16, 1876.

30. LR NMS, Roll 569, W703, Hatch to AAG, Fort Leavenworth, May 20, 1876.

31. *Ibid.*, first endorsement, by Pope, June 8, 1876.

32. *Ibid.*, W516, secretary of war to secretary of interior, April 27, 1876.

33. Born September 1, 1851, near Claverack, New York, Clum was a member of the Dutch Reformed Church, at that time charged with supervision over the Apaches. There may have been other influences helping him obtain the position, at twenty-two, of San Carlos agent. Henry R. Clum, a Civil War veteran who was distantly related to him, worked for the Indian service during this period and was acting commissioner of Indian affairs at times in the 1870's. Henry was born March 30, 1830, at Brunswick, N.Y., and died at Washington on April 13, 1904. He enlisted in the Fifth Wisconsin Infantry, rising to captain. He transferred to the fledgling Signal Corps when it was formed in 1863, reaching the brevet rank of lieutenant colonel. He was in command of Signal Corps works in the Department of Virginia and North Carolina and then was transferred to Signal Corps headquarters at Washington for the remainder of the war. John Clum also began his government career in the Signal Corps. He was named an observer to its newly organized meteorological service in 1871 at Santa Fe. Nepotism was not unknown in government service. George A. Clum, hired briefly as a schoolteacher at San Carlos in 1875 (at the payment of $1,200 a year), was John Clum's brother. Clum was appointed San Carlos agent February 27, 1874, arriving at his post August 8. It is said that he was aghast to find, upon his arrival at that desolate Gila River outpost, the heads that army units had secured from slain renegades but, if so, he quickly became inured to it. He soon proudly reported that his Indians themselves had secured the heads of five renegades and shortly thereafter brought in a sixth. Clum was brash, impudent, contentious, and nearly impossible to get on with, and he hated, or at least despised, the army. But he also was brave, intelligent, reliable in action, probably honest, and, in sum, a fine agent. He died at Los Angeles May 2, 1932. The facts of his life are well known from *Apache Agent*, a biography-autobiography compiled by his son, Woodworth Clum. See also Thrapp, *The Conquest of Apacheria*, 162–65; Henry R. Clum's military service record, National Archives and Records Service; death certificate of Henry R. Clum, District of Columbia, April 14, 1904, No. 154,445; information from Mrs. A. J. Thomas, Jr., Columbia County Historical Society, Kinderhook, New York; LR AS, Roll 13, C710, May 1, 1875, announcement of George Clum's new position; *ibid.*, Roll 16, C25, his resignation, December 13, 1875; *ibid.*, Roll 10, C680, C753, Clum's report of heads brought in.

34. John P. Clum, "Geronimo," *New Mexico Historical Review*, Vol. III, No. 1 (January, 1928), 9.

35. LR AG, Roll 265, 2653–1876, Galpin to secretary of interior, May 8, 1876.

36. *Ibid.*, 2641–1876, Sherman to Schofield, May 15, 1876.

37. This lengthy report is in LR AG, Roll 265, 4396–1876, Kautz to AAG, San Francisco, June 30, 1876.

38. *Ibid.*, Roll 123, 480–1874, Vandever to commissioner, January 23, 1874.

39. LR NMS, Roll 568, S476, Shaw to Smith, June 16, 1876.

40. *Ibid.*, S486, Shaw to Smith, June 23, 1876.

41. *Ibid.*, Roll 568, S530, Shaw to Smith, July 3, 1876.

42. *Ibid.*, S574, Shaw to Smith, July 17, 1876.

43. *Ibid.*, S594, Shaw to Smith, July 21, 1876.

44. *Ibid.*

45. *Ibid.*

CHAPTER XV

1. LR NMS, Roll 568, S524, Shaw to Smith, June 19, 1876.

2. *Ibid.*, Roll 566, D448, Davis to Smith, August 31, 1876. *Ibid.*, D580, Davis to Smith, October 16, 1876.

3. *Ibid.*, Roll 568, Galpin to Shaw, September 4, 1870 [*sic*: 1876].

4. *Ibid.*, Roll 571, S992, Shaw to Smith, September 3, 1877. Victorio, according to Griswold, had four sons, three of them killed during his war; the youngest, Istee, aged about ten in 1880, was not with Victorio but with Loco's Apaches at San Carlos and thus missed the conflict and probable death at that time. Victorio also had one daughter. Some of his descendants are buried at Fort Sill, and at least one is still living, at this writing, and resides in New York City. Griswold, *The Fort Sill Apaches*, 144–45.

5. He means dwellings, instead of *rancherías*.

6. LR NMS, Roll 569, S717, Shaw to Smith, September 8, 1876.

7. *Ibid.*, S838, Shaw to Smith, October 8, 1876.

8. *Ibid.*, S857, Shaw to Smith, October 16, 1876.

9. Ungnade, *Guide to the New Mexico Mountains*, 145. The ranch, often used by scouting parties of troops, was about twenty-five miles westerly from Las Cruces on the road to Fort Cummings. Map of Southern New Mexico, prepared in the Chief Engineer Office of the Department of the Missouri in May, 1881, Record Group 393, Dept. No. 12, at National Archives and Records Service, Cartographic and Audiovisual Records Division.

10. LR NMS, Roll 569, W1180, Carroll to post adjutant, Fort Selden, September 22, 1876.

11. Tony Rucker, a son of Brigadier General Daniel Henry Rucker, army quartermaster general, was a brother-in-law of General Sheridan. Born in Albuquerque, he was a cadet for two years at West Point, but did not graduate. He was commissioned a second lieutenant of the Sixth Cavalry July 27, 1872, and in the Southwest became perhaps the most aggressive and successful leader of expeditions, sometimes long and grueling, against the Apaches. He drowned with First Lieutenant Austin Henely on July 11, 1878, in White River Canyon, in the Chiricahua Mountains, during a flash flood. The circumstances are somewhat controversial. A military camp, canyon, and settlement were named for him. *Arizona Miner*, July 19, 1878. Barnes, *Arizona Place Names*, 2nd ed., 48–49. John Rope, "Experiences of an Indian Scout" (ed. by Grenville Goodwin), *Arizona Historical Review*, Vol. VII, No. 1 (January, 1936), 44–46. Heitman, *Historical Record of the U.S. Army*, I, 849.

12. LR AG, Roll 265, 1005–1877, Rucker to AAG, Bowie, January 14, 1877, with accompanying documents.

13. *Ibid.*, McLellan to AAG, Prescott, January 15, 1877.

14. *Ibid.*, Kautz comments attached thereto, January 29, 1877.

15. LR NMS, Roll 570, D64, Davis to Smith, January 13, 1877.

16. *Ibid.*, D86, Davis to Smith, January 27, 1877.

17. *Ibid.*, D1323, Schurz to commissioner of Indian affairs, April 10, 1877.

18. LR AS, Roll 18, A203-1877, Stevens to Smith, April 2, 1877, with enclosures.

19. Born in Ireland in 1848, Henely enlisted in the Civil War, then went to West Point. Like Rucker, he was an active, aggressive officer, and with Rucker he drowned July 11, 1878. Heitman, *op. cit.*, I, 523. *The Centennial of the United States Military Academy at West Point, New York 1802–1902*, II, 267.

20. LR AS, Roll 18, A131–1877, Safford to commissioner, March 18, 1877.

21. *Ibid.*, A175–1877, Safford to Smith, March 19, 1877.

22. LR AG, Roll 326, 1927–1877, Smith to Clum, March 20, 1877.

23. Beauford, or Buford, whose real name was Welford Chapman Bridwell, was born in Maryland in 1848 and at fifteen fought with Pickett at Gettysburg. After the Civil

War he enlisted in the Fifth Cavalry, winning a Medal of Honor for heroism. He was with the San Carlos police for several years, later became a ranchman, and was prominent at other pursuits. He died at Los Angeles February 1, 1905. Thrapp, *The Conquest of Apacheria*, 167n.

24. Sweeney, a redheaded Irishman and onetime prize fighter, had been fifteen years a cavalry sergeant, was termed by Clum "honest, industrious, good-natured, fearless," and was of great help to him. He was reported later to have been killed at Tombstone. *Ibid.*, 164–65 and 164n.–65n.

25. LR AG, Roll 326, 2265–1877, Clum to Hatch, April 2, 1877.

26. *Ibid.*, 3063–1877, Kautz to AAG, San Francisco, May 11, 1877, including telegram, Clum to Kautz, March 29, 1877.

27. *Ibid.*, Kautz to Clum, March 31, 1877.

28. Clum to Hatch, April 2, 1877, *loc. cit.*

29. LR AG, Roll 326, 2265–1877, Pope to commanding officer, District of New Mexico, April 3, 1877.

30. LR AS, Roll 18, S204, Clum to commissioner, April 4, 1877.

31. *Ibid.*, S224, Clum to commissioner, April 6, 1877.

32. *Ibid.*, S225, Clum to commissioner, April 7, 1877.

33. *Ibid.*, S223, Clum to commissioner, April 6, 1877.

34. *Ibid.*, S263, Clum to commissioner, April 14, 1877.

35. *Ibid.*, S279, Clum to commissioner, April 15, 1877.

36. *Ibid.*, S398, Clum to Wade, April 21, 1877, mentioning telegraphic instructions to remove all Indians, dated April 17, from commissioner of Indian affairs.

37. *Ibid.*, S553, Clum to Whitney, April 20, 1877.

38. *Ibid.*, Whitney to Clum, April 20, 1877.

39. For a résumé of Clum's recollections, penned many years after the event, but loosely based upon his copies of correspondence of the time, see Thrapp, *The Conquest of Apacheria*, 172–75.

40. John P. Clum, "Victorio," *Arizona Historical Review*, Vol. II, No. 4 (January, 1930), 74–90. *Ibid.*, "Geronimo," *New Mexico Historical Review*, Vol. III, Nos. 1, 2, 3 (January, April, July, 1928), 1–40, 121–44, 217–64.

41. LR AS, Roll 18, S315, Clum to commissioner, April 21, 1877. The rather dramatic story of his capturing Geronimo and persuading the Mimbres to remove is well known. See Thrapp, *The Conquest of Apacheria*, 172–75; Lockwood, *The Apache Indians*, 218–24; Clum, *Apache Agent*, 215–49; Ogle, *Western Apaches*, 172–75.

42. LR AS, Roll 18, S398, Clum to Wade, April 21, 1877.

43. *Ibid.*, S553, Whitney to Clum, April 23, 1877.

44. *Ibid.*, S398, Clum to commissioner, April 25, 1877.

45. *Ibid.*, S331, Clum to commissioner, April 28, 1877.

46. *Ibid.*, S327, Clum to commissioner, April 27, 1877.

47. LR AG, Roll 326, 3063–1877, Hatch to Kautz, April 27, 1877.

48. LR AS, Roll 18, S369, Clum to commissioner, May 1, 1877. *Ibid.*, S394, Clum to commissioner, May 7, 1877. *Ibid.*, S395, Clum to commissioner, May 7, 1877.

49. LR AG, Roll 326, 3063–1877, Wallace to Clum, May 7, 1877.

50. *Ibid.*, Clum to Wallace, May 7, 1877.

51. *Ibid.*, Hatch to Kautz, May 8, 1877.

52. *Ibid.*, Sherman endorsement, June 1, 1877.

53. LR AS, Roll 18, C1109, Clum to commissioner, July 28, 1877, a lengthy exposition of Clum's position—and attitude.

CHAPTER XVI

1. LR AS, Roll 18, I-8, Interior Department memo, January 3, 1877.

2. *Ibid.*, S557, Clum to commissioner, June 19, 1877, in which Clum refers to his telegram of April 4 requesting he be relieved.

3. LR NMS, Roll 572, V78, Vandever to commissioner, June 4, 1877.

4. LR AS, Roll 18, C640, Clum to commissioner, June 5, 1877.

5. *Ibid.*, S505, Clum to commissioner, June 6, 1877.

6. *Ibid.*, S525, Clum to commissioner, June 9, 1877. See also *ibid.*, S553, Clum to commissioner, May 28, 1877, for enlargement upon Clum's notions of the superiority of his control over the Apaches to that of the army.

7. *Ibid.*, S557, Clum to commissioner, June 19, 1877.

8. *Ibid.*, S576, Clum to commissioner, June 23, 1877.

9. Clum, "Geronimo," *New Mexico Historical Review*, Vol. III, No. 2 (April, 1928), 124.

10. LR AG, Roll 366, 6111-1879, Hatch to AAG, Fort Leavenworth, September 8, 1879. *Ibid.*, 6341-1877, Abbott to AAG, Prescott, September 22, 1877.

11. In 1883 Crook wrote, "The disarming of Indians is very generally believed to be the first step in solving the Indian problem, and it is often insisted on as the one condition precedent to placing them on reservations. In my judgment this is an error. In the first place it is impossible to disarm Indians. Individuals may be taken in certain instances at such disadvantage as to make it possible to get their arms, but with whole bands or tribes this is hardly possible. I knew that the Chiricahuas had an abundance of the best arms, and yet when they came into our camp, thinking very likely that I would demand the surrender of their arms, many of them were armed only with lances, and others with very indifferent guns, which would have been given up had I demanded them. The result would have been, they would have considered that we were afraid of them, their arms would have still been in their possession, and we would have lost their confidence. . . . Neither is it possible to prevent Indians from obtaining arms and ammunition; in this country money will buy anything. . . . There is another reason; the Indian knows better than any one else, how necessary arms are for his protection. He has discovered that the Government does not prevent the disreputable class of white men with which he is surrounded from committing depredations upon his reservation, or punish them for their acts. He concludes that he must protect himself. Deprive the Apache Indians of their arms, and in a short time there would not be a hoof of stock on the reservation. . . ." Annual Report, 1883, Crook Collection.

12. Camp Goodwin, established June 24, 1864, was six miles west of Camp Thomas, which dated from August 12, 1876, and was named a fort May 18, 1877. A town of that name still exists there. Both were on the south side of the Gila River. Goodwin, twenty-eight miles airline distance east of San Carlos, was abandoned by the military on March 14, 1871. It subsequently became a subagency, or branch agency, of San Carlos. Barnes, *Arizona Place Names*, 182; 2nd ed., 127, 129, 132-33. Brandes, *Frontier Military Posts of Arizona*, 32-34, 67-69.

13. LR AG, Roll 366, 6341-1877, Kautz to adjutant general, U.S. Army, September 28, 1877.

14. *Ibid.*, Abbott to AAG, Prescott, September 22, 1877.

15. *Ibid.*, 6629–1877, Keam to Jewett, October 8, 1877.

16. LR NMS, Roll 572, S475, Whitney to Smith, May 8, 1877.

17. Hoag, nicknamed "Sunken Nose" by the Apaches, was born in Pennsylvania about 1838 and at this time was single. He was described by Clum as "very efficient," "judicious," and a man "of sterling character" who, wrote Clum, probably "never owned a gun. All of the Indians liked Ezra Hoag. He was just and sympathetic, and the Indians— including the 'wild Chiricahuas' were his friends, and he was their friend." On the other hand, he was also described as a drunkard. He was working at Fort Defiance on the Navaho Reservation in 1870. Clum said he appointed Hoag to the newly created subagency in 1875, but the list of employees, dated July 7, 1877, says he commenced service July 1, 1877, at $1,000 a year. John P. Clum, "Apache Misrule," *New Mexico Historical Review*, Vol. V, No. 3 (July, 1930), 228, 234, 236. Ogle, *Western Apaches*, 190.

18. LR AG, Roll 366, 5749–1877, Martin to AAG, San Francisco, September 3, 1877.

19. *Ibid.*, 3633–1877, appendix E, diary entry for September 8, 1877. This informant said that for ten days prior to the outbreak Indians had been filtering away from San Carlos unbeknown to officials.

20. *Arizona Star* (Tucson), March 29, 1880.

21. Hart, appointed June 29, accepted July 9 and reached San Carlos August 21. He has been called a "tactful" man and, by the military, "evidently a gentleman and man of sense," whose interest however, quickly wandered from his charges to mining properties in the vicinity. It is not clear whether, in sum, he was a good or a bad agent. He remained two years. Ogle, *op. cit.*, 183n., 184. LR AS, Roll 18, H313, Hart to Smith, July 9, 1877. *Arizona Star* (Tucson), July 6, 1879. LR AG, Roll 366, 5749–1877, Martin to AAG, San Francisco, September 3, 1877. *Ibid.*, 3424–1879, McDowell to adjutant general, army, May 29, 1879.

22. *Ibid.*, 6341–1877, Abbott to AAG, Thomas, September 22, 1877.

23. *Ibid.*, 6526–1877, Kautz, first endorsement, to War Department, September 22, 1877.

24. The account of the subsequent developments, unless otherwise noted, is based upon Tupper's report, LR AG, Roll 366, 3633–1877, Tupper to post adjutant, Camp Grant, September 18, 1877; Rucker's brief report, *ibid.*, September 20, 1877; Hanna's report, *ibid.*, September 28, 1877; Hanna's diary, *ibid.*, September 3 to 14.

25. *Ibid.*, 5705–1877, McDowell to adjutant general, Washington, September 11, 1877.

26. *Ibid.*, 5807–1877, Vandever to commissioner, September 12, 1877.

27. *Ibid.*, 6341–1877, Abbott to AAG, Prescott, September 22, 1877.

28. *Ibid.*, Kautz to adjutant general, Washington, September 28, 1877.

29. This Indian was Diablo, said by Goodwin to be "credited unanimously by the Apache of his group as being the greatest White Mountain chief of his time." A noted warrior, he had frequently led his people in raids against the Navahos and other enemies. In 1864 when Camp Goodwin was established "this chief was the principal representative for the White Mountain Apache in a council held with army officers which established a peace between them and the Americans. Again, in 1867, he gave the Americans permission to construct a road from Fort Goodwin [*sic*] to White River and erect another military post, Fort Apache." He was the equivalent among his people of Cochise among the Chiricahuas, and obviously was a fit challenger to Victorio and Loco. Goodwin, *The Western Apache*, 10–11. He was said by Assistant Surgeon Leonard Young Loring to have been in 1875 thirty-five years of age, "noted for his desperate encounters," his "daredevil character," and his frequent killing of his enemies, his many wounds, but he

"has always been friendly towards the whites and gives promise by his behavior to remain so." L. Y. Loring, "Report on Coyotero Apaches, Camp Apache, Arizona Territory, 1875, manuscript in the Bancroft Library, HHB [P-D, 5].

30. It is not clear whether this fight is the same as that previously mentioned on Ash Creek. If so, the Indian police joined Tupper's command afterward, and went on with the troops.

31. LR AG, Roll 366, 6606–1877, Hart to commissioner, September 18, 1877.

32. *Ibid.*, 6271–1877, Platt to AAG, Fort Leavenworth, September 6, 1877.

33. This was probably Sam Bowman, a noted figure during the latter Apache conflicts. He was part Negro, part Choctaw, illiterate but brave and reliable. He is said to have been murdered several years later. Thrapp, *Al Sieber, Chief of Scouts*, 400.

34. LR AG, Roll 366, 6186–1877, Hatch to AAG, Fort Leavenworth, September 22, 1877.

35. Rope, "Experiences of an Indian Scout," *Arizona Historical Review*, Vol. VII, No. 1, 58–68.

36. See Dan L. Thrapp, *General Crook and the Sierra Madre Adventure*, for the story of how this stronghold eventually was penetrated and emptied of hostiles.

37. Tupper Report, September 18, 1877, *loc. cit.*

38. LR AG, Roll 366, 6186–1877, Wade to AAAG, Santa Fe, September 22, 1877.

39. *Ibid.*, 5836–1877, Sheridan to Townsend, September 18, 1877.

40. Hatch to AAG, Fort Leavenworth, September 22, 1877, *loc. cit.*

41. LR NMS, Roll 572, S1116, Whitney to Smith, September 29, 1877.

42. *Ibid.*, S1214, Whitney to brother, October 1, 1877.

CHAPTER XVII

1. LR AG, Roll 366, 6150–1877, Vandever to commissioner, September 29, 1877.

2. *Ibid.*, Holcomb to secretary of interior, October 1, 1877.

3. LR NMS, Roll 570, M792, Godfroy to Smith, October 1, 1877.

4. LR AG, Roll 366, 6629–1877, Hatch to commanding officer, Wingate, September 30, 1877.

5. *Ibid.*, 3633–1877, Kautz to AAG, San Francisco, October 4, 1877.

6. *Ibid.*, 3885–1877, Kautz to AAG, San Francisco, October 5, 1877.

7. Born at Truro, Cornwall, England, in 1843, Keam was a sailor for some years before reaching San Francisco, where in 1862 he enlisted in the First California Volunteer Infantry; he was mustered out at Santa Fe in 1865. Later he served briefly as a second lieutenant under Colonel Christopher Carson, operating against the Navahos. Keam became Wingate interpreter in 1877 and moved to Ojo Caliente with the Mimbres, resigning March 15, 1878. He then lived with the Hopis for some years. He died at Truro, November 30, 1904. His name also is spelled Keams. Barnes, *Arizona Place Names*, 230–31.

8. This spring probably was in the Gallo Mountains, west of the Mangas Mountains, and not the Ojo del Gallo near Grants.

9. LR AG, Roll 366, 6629–1877, Keam to Jewett, October 8, 1877.

10. *Ibid.*, Jewett to AAAG, Santa Fe, October 8, 1877.

11. *Ibid.*, 6802–1877, Jewett to AAAG, Santa Fe, October 11, 1877.

12. *Ibid.*, 6734–1877, Sheridan to Townsend, October 30, 1877.

13. Hatch gave the breakdown this way: originally turned over to San Carlos Agency, 464; supposed to be out raiding at the time of removal, 25; total: 489. Surrendered at

Wingate, 233; will come in to Wingate in addition, about 17; at Ojo Caliente, 2 children; came in to Ojo Caliente, 3 men; driven back to San Carlos by the troops according to San Carlos agent, 143; killed by troops, 20; at Stanton Reservation with Nana, 19; total: 437. Number out raiding, 52. Hatch added that "it is claimed at the time of their removal there were 120 living off the reservation. This is possible, but I have never been able to make them more than 60." LR AG, Roll 366, 6969–1877, Hatch to AAG, Fort Leavenworth, October 28, 1877. LR NMS, Roll 572, S477, Whitney to Smith, May 26, 1877. The only doubtful note is Hatch's figure of 143 driven back to San Carlos by troops; I have found no confirmation of this figure nor any suggestion that more than a sprinkling were "driven" in. There were no troops after them from Arizona save Tupper's command, and it encountered no such number of fugitives.

14. Probably referring to Lieutenant Hugo's chase.

15. LR AG, Roll 366, 6629–1877, Hatch to AAG, Fort Leavenworth, October 11, 1877.

16. For the story of this remarkable expedition, its origins, and how it was conducted, see Thrapp, *General Crook and the Sierra Madre Adventure*.

17. LR AG, Roll 366, 6629–1877, Pope to Drum, October 18, 1877.

18. LR NMS, Roll 572, 6802–1877, Pope, October 26, 1877, second endorsement.

19. LR AG, Roll 366, 6969–1877, Hatch to AAG, Fort Leavenworth, October 28, 1877.

20. *Ibid.*, Pope to Drum, November 5, 1877.

21. LR NMS, Roll 570, M854, Godfroy to Hayt, November 7, 1877.

22. *Ibid.*, Roll 572, S1325, Whitney to commissioner, November 10, 1877.

23. *Ibid.*, S1443, Whitney to commissioner, November 15, 1877.

24. *Ibid.*, 7499–1877, Hatch to AAG, Fort Leavenworth, November 21, 1877.

25. *Ibid.*, S1465, Whitney to Hayt, November 30, 1877.

26. LR AG, Roll 366, 1245–1877, Whitney to Hayt, December 13, 1877.

27. *Ibid.*, 321–1878, Loud to AAG, Fort Leavenworth, January 2, 1878.

28. *Ibid.*, Sheridan second endorsement, January 14, 1878.

29. *Ibid.*, 888–1878, Sherman, second endorsement, no date.

30. *Ibid.*, 1245–1878, Sheridan, fourth endorsement, no date.

31. *Ibid.*, Hayt to secretary of interior, letter of transmittal, February 2, 1878.

32. *Ibid.*, 888–1878, Schurz to secretary of war, February 5, 1878.

33. *Ibid.*, 126–1878, Steelhammer to AAG, Santa Fe, December 17, 1877.

34. LR NMS, Roll 575, W320, Whitney to Hayt, January 9, 1878.

35. LR AG, Roll 366, 1160–1878, Pope endorsement, no date.

36. *Ibid.*

37. *Ibid.*, Schurz to secretary of war, no number, May 11, 1878.

38. *Ibid.*, 4563–1878, Pope endorsement, June 20, 1878.

39. *Ibid.*, Sheridan endorsement, June 24, 1878.

40. *Ibid.*, 5398–1878, Hayt to secretary of state, July 30, 1878.

41. *Ibid.*, Sherman endorsement, August 2, 1878.

42. *Ibid.*, 5144–1878, Watkins to Hayt, July 16, 1878; Leeds to secretary of interior, July 17, 1878; Schurz to secretary of war, July 18, 1878. LR NMS, Roll 573, I-1234, Schurz to commissioner, July 18, 1878.

43. *Ibid.*, Roll 575, W1305, Townsend to commanding general, Chicago, July 22, 1878.

44. *Ibid.*, W1786, Sheridan to Townsend, no date.

45. LR AG, Roll 366, 6037–1878, Loud to AAG, Fort Leavenworth, August 16, 1878.

46. *Ibid.*, 1495–1879, Merritt to AAAG, Santa Fe, February 20, 1879.

47. LR NMS, Roll 575, W2017, Hart to commissioner, September 9, 1878.

48. Bennett was a tough soldier, well qualified for this task. Born in Ohio, he enlisted in the Civil War and rose to rank of major before his retirement in 1889. He was brevetted for gallantry at Chicamauga, and died June 21, 1894. Heitman, *Historical Register of the U.S. Army*, I, 211.

49. LR AG, Roll 366, 7500–1878, Loud to AAG, Fort Leavenworth, October 18, 1878.

50. *Ibid.*, 8779–1878, Hart to Abbott, November 24, 1878.

51. *Ibid.*, 1495–1879, Merritt to AAAG, Santa Fe, February 20, 1879.

52. Daniel Houston Ming, born near Louisville, Kentucky, February 23, 1845, reached Arizona in 1872 and became a noted stockman. He served as chief of Indian police at San Carlos for a time and was packer in the Philippines in 1899. He died at San Francisco, November 12, 1925. Thrapp, *The Conquest of Apacheria*, 180n.

53. The story of Bennett's adventures is told in his lengthy report, LR AG, Roll 366, 8935–1878, Bennett to AAAG, Santa Fe, December 4, 1878.

54. LR AG, Roll 366, 8914–1878, Hart to Abbott, November 26, 1878.

55. *Arizona Star* (Tucson), two-part article signed "Palomas," March 29 and April 6, 1880.

56. LR NMS, Roll 573, G483, Godfroy to commissioner, November 1, 1878.

57. *Ibid.*, G507, Godfroy to Hayt, November 7, 1878.

58. *Ibid.*, G519, Godfroy to Hayt, November 13, 1878.

59. *Ibid.*, G567, Godfroy to Hayt, December 13, 1878.

60. *Ibid.*, Roll 576, G44, Catanach to Hayt, January 24, 1879.

61. LR AG, Roll 366, 1495–1879, Merritt pass for two Indians, January 21, 1879.

62. *Ibid.*, 1495–1879, Loud to Merritt, February 15, 1879.

63. *Ibid.*, 925–1879, Sheridan to Townsend, February 13, 1879. Sheridan referred to the outbreak of the Cheyennes from Fort Robinson, January 9 to 22, 1879. See *Chronological List of Actions, &c., with Indians, from January 1, 1866, to January, 1891*, 46; George Bird Grinnell, *The Fighting Cheyennes*, 414–27.

64. This was Andrew Kelley, also known as Andy Kelly, prominent pioneer in southwestern New Mexico. He had worked for the Ojo Caliente Agency for years, was well known to the Indians, and they trusted him. LR NMS, Roll 579, K135, Kelley to secretary of the interior, January 20, 1880.

65. LR AG, Roll 366, 1495–1879, Merritt to AAAG, Santa Fe, February 20, 1879.

66. *Ibid.*, Hatch, first endorsement, February 26, 1879.

67. LR NMS, Roll 576, R229, Russell to commissioner, March 27, 1879. *Ibid.*, R257, Russell to commissioner, April 5, 1879.

68. LR AG, Roll 366, 2774–1879, Hayt to Russell, April 16, 1879.

69. *Ibid.*, 2398–1879, Hatch to AAG, Fort Leavenworth, April 18, 1879. *Ibid.*, 2544–1879, Hatch to Fort Leavenworth, April 23, 1879.

70. *Ibid.*, 3337–1879, Schurz to secretary of war, May 20, 1879.

71. *Ibid.*, 3672–1879, Hatch to AAG, Fort Leavenworth, May 26, 1879.

72. *Ibid.*, 3416–1879, McDowell to adjutant general, Washington, May 29, 1879.

73. *Ibid.*, 3443–1879, McDowell to adjutant general, Washington, May 31, 1879.

74. *Ibid.*, 3615–1879, Whipple to adjutant general, Washington, June 6, 1879. *Posts*, Roll 877 (Ojo Caliente), May, 1879.

75. LR NMS, Roll 577, R467, Russell to commissioner, June 30, 1879.

76. *Ibid.*, R440, Russell to commissioner, June 21, 1879.

77. *Ibid.*, R484, Russell to Purington, July 3, 1879.

78. *Ibid.*, Russell to commissioner, July 3, 1879.

79. *Ibid.*, R527, Russell to commissioner, July 24, 1879.
80. *Ibid.*, R548, Russell to commissioner, July 30, 1879.

CHAPTER XVIII

1. LR NMS, Roll 577, R506, Russell to commissioner, August 21, 1879.
2. Thomas Cruse, *Apache Days and After*, 157–58.
3. LR NMS, Roll 577, R625, Russell to commissioner, August 22, 1879.
4. *Ibid.*, R771, Russell to commissioner, October 18, 1879. Sonnichsen, in *The Mescalero Apaches*, 162–63, has an interesting account obtained from informants who learned the facts firsthand, but Russell's dispatches suggest that he was ignorant of their intention to leave until after they had done so.
5. LR AG, Roll 366, 6111–1879, Hatch to AAG, Fort Leavenworth, September 6, 1879, with enclosure. *Ibid.*, Hatch to Hayt, September 6, 1879.
6. *Ibid.*
7. LR NMS, Roll 578, W2011, Purington to AAAG, Santa Fe, August 23, 1879. Smith entered the Union Army as captain in 1861 and rose to brevet rank of lieutenant colonel. He resigned in 1866, and rejoined in 1873 as a second lieutenant. He was a bold fighter, and his rashness led him to his death against Nana's raiders on August 19, 1881. Heitman, *Historical Register of the U.S. Army*, I, 898; Thrapp, *The Conquest of Apacheria*, 215.
8. LR NMS, Roll 577, R663, Russell to commissioner, September 5, 1879.
9. *Posts*, Roll 877 (Ojo Caliente), September, 1879. This entry also contains details of an interesting series of skirmishes between mail detachments and Victorio's men during September.
10. McEver's ranch, a focal point for Indian fighting during these months, was at the site of the present Lake Valley, seventeen miles south of Hillsboro. Twitchell, *New Mexican History*, 11, 439n. Both communities, together with Winston and Chloride, also frequently mentioned, were east of the Black Range.
11. LR NMS, Roll 578, W2047, Pope to Townsend, September 18, 1879. In the *Chronological List*, p. 47, the figure is shown as nine civilians killed in actions at McEver's ranch and Arroyo Seco, to the north. According to *Record of Engagements with Hostile Indians Within the Military Division of the Missouri, from 1868 to 1882*, 92, ten "citizens," that is, civilians, were killed.
12. LR NMS, Roll 578, W2078, Loud to Pope, September 21, 1879.
13. *Ibid.*
14. Lew Wallace, even then working on his great novel, *Ben-Hur: a Tale of Christ*, was a soldier of considerable experience. He had been second lieutenant in the Mexican War and had risen to major general of volunteers in the Civil War; he had performed a number of important services for the government and various agencies. He was governor of New Mexico from 1878 to 1881, during a turbulent period. DAB.
15. LR NMS, Roll 578, Wallace to McCrary, September 17, 1879.
16. *Ibid.*, McCrary to Wallace, September 18, 1879.
17. Record Group 94, Selected Documents relating to the activities of the Ninth and Tenth Cavalry in the campaign against Victorio, 1879–1880 (hereafter cited as VP, with serial number), AGO, Letters Received, 6058–1879, 1567–1880, Hatch to AAG, Fort Leavenworth, February 25, 1880.
18. LR NMS, Roll 577, State-1855, Scott to Seward, September 19, 1879.
19. This was Beyer, not Hooker.
20. VP, 6323–1879, Loud to AAG, Fort Leavenworth, September 23, 1879.

21. VP, 379–1880, Morrow to AAAG, Santa Fe, November 5, 1879. This very long report covers Morrow's activities from August 31 to November 1, 1879, including his fruitless campaigning after Victorio in New Mexico, and his fight with that Indian in Old Mexico late in October. Unless otherwise cited, it is drawn upon for the reconstruction of those events.

22. Charles B. Gatewood, "Campaigning Against Victorio in 1879," *The Great Divide*, April, 1894, 102. *Medal of Honor Recipients: 1863–1963*, 632. Silver City (New Mexico) *Herald*, reprinted in *Arizona Star*, October 1, 1879.

23. VP, 6324–1879, Pope to Sheridan, September 26, 1879.

24. Gatewood, who never saw Victorio in person, unless in a distant fire fight when characteristics could rarely be detected, wrote in 1894 that Victorio at this time was a "palsied, aged and decrepit chief, who was barely able to accompany the squaws and children in their forays." This description should not be taken too seriously in the light of unqualified assertions by agents, army officers, and others who dealt directly with him that he was vigorous, able, and the true chief of the Mimbres. Gatewood wrote from memory fifteen years after the campaign, made mistakes in dates and other details, and in his recollections may have confused Victorio with Nana, already an old man, though still vigorous. Gatewood wrote that the "real plotters . . . were Nanye [Nana], Tomas [Tomacito?] and Torivio," or Torribio, perhaps from the Spanish verb, "turrar," meaning to toast or broil, reminiscent of what Apaches sometimes did to their captives. Turrivio and his son, Turrivio Filho, or junior, were listed in Shaw's census of 1876. Turrivio was said, on uncertain authority, to have been Victorio's son-in-law and to have been killed in 1880. Calico Jones, "Victorio's Vengeance Raid," *Real West*, Vol. XIII, No. 81 (April, 1970), 32–33. Gatewood, however, says both he and Tomás were killed in 1879.

25. Today's Seco Creek, a Río Grande tributary between Animas Creek and the Palomas River.

26. VP, 6528–1879, Sheridan to Sherman, October 4, 1879.

27. VP, 6718–1879, Hatch to AAG, San Francisco, October 7, 1879.

28. VP, 379–1880, Morrow report, as cited. One is intrigued by Washington's name, and speculation as to its origin naturally turns to some possible connection between this son of Victorio and Major John Macrae Washington, brevet lieutenant colonel, a Mexican War veteran who was military and civil governor of New Mexico from October 11, 1848, until October 23, 1849. See A. B. Bender, "Government Explorations in the Territory of New Mexico 1846–1859," *New Mexico Historical Review*, Vol. IX, No. 1 (January, 1934) 9 n.32. He was drowned Christmas Eve, 1853, when the steamer *San Francisco* upon which he had embarked at New York for San Francisco was flushed by a giant wave. He was described by one who knew him as a "very positive, brave & efficient officer." J. Manuel Espinosa, "Memoir of a Kentuckian in New Mexico 1848–1884," *New Mexico Historical Review*, Vol. XIII, No. 1 (January, 1937), 7. Heitman, *Historical Register of the U.S. Army*, I, 1007. Frank McNitt (ed.), *Navaho Expedition: Journal of a Military Reconnaissance from Santa Fe, New Mexico, to the Navaho Country, Made in 1849 by Lieutenant James H. Simpson*, in which the story of Washington's New Mexico service is summarized. In correspondence, McNitt said that surviving military records of the period "are so few and incomplete" that it is impossible to say with certainty whether there ever was any contact, either at Santa Fe or in Southern New Mexico, between the officer and the Apache, adding, "in either case I have nothing at all that supports such a conjecture. . . . I cannot think of anything

Washington did during his one year of command that could have endeared him or made him otherwise deserving of great respect, in the eyes of Apaches. . . ." McNitt to author, December 30, 1971. If there was a connection, this would suggest that the Apache Washington was born about 1848 or 1849, and would have been in his early thirties at his death in 1880. This would tend to confirm Victorio's birth date of about 1825, which would have made him about twenty-three at the time of Washington's birth.

29. This road, named for the North Star Mine, led northerly from near Mimbres on the Mimbres River, following present-day State Route 61, to above Beaverhead. Morrow believed the Indians would have to cross it either at Diamond Creek, twenty-two miles south of Beaverhead, or at Malpais Creek, probably present-day Taylor Creek, about ten miles north of Diamond Creek. The Mogollon Mountains are then about thirty miles directly west.

30. VP, 6536–1879, Sheridan to adjutant general, Washington, October 8, 1879.

31. Maney, born in Tennessee, was a West Point graduate who in 1893 killed Swedish-born Captain Alfred Hedberg, also of the Fifteenth Infantry, and was indicted for it. Apparently he was exonerated, for he became captain four years later and in 1902 was major of the Seventeenth Infantry. Hedberg had been cashiered in 1873 but was reinstated in 1888. Heitman, *Historical Register of the U.S. Army*, I, 519, 687. Captain Jack Crawford, "The Pursuit of Victorio," *Socorro County Historical Society: Publications in History*, Vol. I (no number) February, 1965, 4.

32. VP, 6782–1879, Sheridan to Townsend, October 18, 1879.

33. This was probably the place today called Chise, on the middle Cuchillo Negro.

34. Ungnade, *Guide to the New Mexico Mountains*, 137.

35. The reports are very contradictory and incomplete. The *Chronological List* cites six men killed at Lloyd's ranch, the location of which is uncertain, and eleven killed at Slocum's ranch, about midway between Mesilla and Cummings, both incidents on October 13. Gatewood, in "Campaigning Against Victorio," *loc. cit.*, says that Bill Jones and his posse of fourteen men from Mesilla were all killed. See LR NMS, Roll 578, W2239, Loud to AAG, Fort Leavenworth, October 14, 1879; VP, 6782–1879, Sheridan to Townsend, October 18, 1879.

36. LR NMS, Roll 580, N13, Scott to Wallace, November 29, 1879. Adjutant General Office, Microcopy 666, Roll 36, Miscellaneous Papers re. Victoria Campaign (hereafter cited as AG, MP 36), Scott to Hunter, November 28, 1879.

37. LR NMS, Roll 578, W2237, Pope to Sheridan, October 16, 1879.

38. *Ibid.*, Sherman to Sheridan, October 16, 1879.

39. This route followed the river south about twenty miles below the village of Mimbres, then turned east, crossing the divide between the Black Range and Cook's Peak Range, and followed Mule Springs Creek southeast to the old Butterfield Road east of Fort Cummings.

40. In southwestern New Mexico, west of the Florida Mountains.

41. Northwest of the Burro Mountains.

42. Where Morrow himself had been twelve days earlier.

43. VP, 379–1880, Morrow Report, as cited.

44. Called Byer's Spring on modern topographical maps.

45. These mountains, which Morrow places about twenty-five miles distant from his camp, might be the Sierra Boca Grande, nineteen miles air distance southwest from Lake Palomas, or Sierra de los Marcos, farther west. Gatewood, in "Campaigning Against Victorio," *loc. cit.*, says that they marched southeast, then southerly, but in

stating that they ended up twenty miles from Janos and eighteen miles from water at a peak across a plain to the west suggests that instead they marched southwest, then southerly.

46. From the above calculation, this range, which Gatewood calls the "Guzman Mountains," might be the Cerros de la Cal (Limestone Peaks), about twenty-one miles north of Janos. See Map of District of New Mexico, 1875, in the Cartographic and Audiovisual Records Division, National Archives and Record Service, which places them immediately southwest of Lakes Guzman and Santa Maria.

47. He no doubt means the Casas Grandes River which, if my deductions are correct, ran parallel to his course a short distance to the east.

48. "Since resigned," said Gatewood, *op. cit.*, 103.

49. *Ibid.*, 104.

50. *Ibid.*, 104.

CHAPTER XIX

1. LR NMS, Roll 578, W2409 Hatch to AAG, Fort Leavenworth, November 4, 1879.

2. *Ibid.*, W4204, Pope to Sheridan, November 4, 1879.

3. Clipping included with LR NMS, Roll 582, W1354, Evarts to Schurz, June 28, 1880.

4. Carrizal, a sun-blasted sprinkling of one-story light gray adobe structures scattered around a gravelly plaza of indeterminate shape, is on a tributary of the Río Carmel and was best known to an earlier generation of Americans as the site of the only major engagement between soldiers of Brigadier General John J. Pershing's Villa Punitive Expedition and Carranzista forces, June 21, 1916. American losses were twenty-three men, including ten soldiers and two officers killed, all of the Tenth Cavalry; the Mexican losses were never publicly stated. Clarence C. Clendenen, *Blood on the Border: The United States Army and the Mexican Irregulars*, 306–12.

5. LR NMS, Roll 577, S2424, with Schurz to Evarts, December 3, 1879.

6. Baylor, *John Robert Baylor: Confederate Governor of Arizona*, 17. *The Handbook of Texas*, I, 123–24.

7. VP, 277–1880, Baylor to Jones, December 3, 1879.

8. James B. Gillett, *Six Years with the Texas Rangers: 1875 to 1881*, 161–69.

9. Born in 1831, Samaniego was a political and at times military leader in northern Mexico, at times acting governor of Chihuahua. He died in 1905. *Diccionario Porrua*, 1374.

10. The Tularosa meant here was not the site of the abortive Mimbres reservation in western New Mexico but the settlement a dozen miles north of present-day Alamagordo, just west of the Mescalero Reservation.

11. Filed with LR NMS, Roll 580, N13, Wallace to Schurz, December 29, 1879.

12. LR NMS, Roll 577, R871 and R881, Russell to commissioner, November 25 and 27, 1879.

13. Casas Grandes, a lovely, heavily shaded community on the river of that name, is on the site of an ancient Indian community so highly developed as to give its name to a culture which archaeologists have traced widely through the Southwest. Only nine miles southwest of raucous, noisy New Casas Grandes, the old town retains much of the leisurely, comfortable air of early Mexico. It is centered around two plazas, the older of which is the smaller. The river, bounded by bluffs rising ten or fifteen feet above the

water, touches the town to west and north. Casas Grandes was a favorite trading point for the Southern Chiricahuas, and it was here Juh died in a fall in 1883.

14. Scott heard that about a dozen men were slain in this incident. AG, MP 36, 232-1880, Scott to Hunter, November 28, 1879.

15. Galeana, thirty miles southeast of Casas Grandes, is a dusty village typical of northern Mexico, with a neglected plaza and a few stores shaded by giant trees along the highway. It is on the Río Santa Maria. In the late nineteenth century it was among the more populous centers of upper Chihuahua.

16. LR NMS, Roll 580, N13, Scott to Wallace, November 29, 1879.

17. Gatewood, "Campaigning Against Victorio," *The Great Divide*, April, 1894, 102.

18. LR NMS, Roll 577, S2424, Scott to Hunter, November 14, 1879.

19. AG, MP 36, 232-1880, Scott to Hunter, November 28, 1879.

20. LR NMS, Roll 582, W1354, Willcox to Prieto, November 8, 1879.

21. *Ibid.*, New York *Sun*, November 8, 1879.

22. AG, MP 36, 3973-1879, Scott to Evarts, November 7, 1879.

23. LR NMS, Roll 576, C1244, Campbell to Schurz, December 6, 1879.

24. Juana Frazer Lyon, "Archie McIntosh, the Scottish Indian Scout," *Journal of Arizona History*, Vol. VII, No. 3 (Autumn, 1966), 103-22.

25. *Arizona Star*, December 30, 1879; January 7 and 8, 1880. These state that an eventual total of 108 Indians surrendered.

26. LR NMS, Roll 581, W67, Haskell to AAG, San Francisco, January 9, 1880.

27. *Ibid.*, W1354, Willcox to Prieto, January 31, 1880.

28. *Ibid.*, Roll 580, N13, Scott to Wallace, November 29, 1879.

29. See James T. King, *War Eagle: A Life of General Eugene A. Carr*, 183-226, for a study of this interesting man in Arizona at this time.

30. AG, MP 36, no serial number, Loud to commanding officer, troops in the field, Camp Grant, Arizona Territory, January 4, 1880.

31. *Ibid.*, Humphreys to Carr, January 13, 1880.

32. *Ibid.*, Loud to commanding officer, as cited.

33. *Ibid.*, Humphreys to Carr, January 10, 1880.

34. VP, 280-1880, Pope to AAG, Chicago, January 9, 1880.

35. VP, 238-1880, Loud to AAG, Fort Leavenworth, January 10, 1880.

36. AG, MP 36, no serial number, Martin to Carr, January 11, 1880.

37. *Ibid.*, Hatch to Carr, January 14, 1880.

38. *Ibid.*, Perry to Carr, January 16, 1880.

39. *Ibid.*, Perry to Carr, January 17, 1880.

40. LR NMS, Roll 579, W135, Kelley to secretary of interior, January 20, 1880.

41. VP, 414-1880, Morrow to AAAG, Whipple, January 18, 1880.

42. AG, MP 36, no serial number, Martin to Carr, February 8, 1880.

43. VP, 828-1880, Hatch to AAG, Fort Leavenworth, February 2, 1880. *Posts*, Roll 88 (Fort Bayard), January, 1880.

44. VP, 928-1880, Hatch to AAG, Fort Leavenworth, February 5, 1880.

45. The place is called "Kane" in AG, MP 36, no serial number, Martin to Carr, February 8, 1880. It may have been near Caine's ranch, fifteen miles north of Aleman and ten miles west of the San Andres Mountains, or in a canyon east of Caine's.

46. *Arizona Star*, February 12, 1880. *Chronological List*, 49. In a letter to his friend, Steelhammer, at the Mescalero Reservation, Morrow wrote, "I am heartily sick of this

business and am convinced that the most expeditious & least-expensive way to settle the Indian troubles in this section is to employ about one hundred & fifty Apache Indian Scouts and turn them loose on Victorio without interference of Troops except general instructions from the officer conducting the campaign. I have had eight engagements with the Victorio Indians in the Mts. since thier [sic] return from Mexico and in each have driven and beaten them but there is no appreciable advantage gained they run but make a stand on another point where possibly ten men can stand off a hundred, kill a number and loose [sic] none. I hear that some Comanches (about 170) have come up from Sill with the intention of joining Victorio. . . . This rumor confirms what Victorio said to Mr. Kelley at Cañada Alamosa the other day 'Nana has just been to the Mescalero and Comanche countries and says that the Troops will have more than they can handle in a few weeks.' . . . I leave here [Tularosa] tomorrow and will stick to Victorio's trail so long as a serviceable animal or available soldier is left but I still think that the pursuit is an unsuccessful one. . . ." Morrow to Steelhammer, from Tularosa, N.M., February 8, 1880; copy supplied to author by Lieutenant Colonel David Perry Perrine, Third Infantry.

47. *Arizona Star*, February 17, 1880. This fight is not reported in the *Chronological List*.

48. *Arizona Star*, February 17, 1880.

49. VP, 2407–1880, Hatch to AAG, Fort Leavenworth, February 20, 1880; VP, 1214–1880, Pope to Sherman, February 24, 1880.

50. LR NMS, Roll 582, W471, Hatch to AAG, Fort Leavenworth, February 25, 1880.

51. *Ibid.*, W625, Pope to Sherman, March 25, 1880.

52. *Ibid.*, W430, Crosby to Schurz, March 30, 1880.

53. AG, MP 36, no serial numbers, Martin to Carr, February 9, 1880; Martin to Carr, March 5, 1880; Willcox to Hatch, March 5, 1880.

54. VP, 1065–1880, Schurz to secretary of war, February 11, 1880.

55. VP, no serial number, Hatch to AAG, Fort Leavenworth, February 25, 1880.

56. AG, MP 36, no serial number, Haskell to Carr, March 2, 1880. A gatling gun was a manually operated weapon with several revolving barrels. It was developed during the Civil War but not adopted by the army until 1866. There was much uncertainty over how and when its use might prove of value. Matloff, Maurice (ed.), *Army Historical Series: American Military History*, 293.

57. VP, 1567–1880, Sherman, third endorsement to Hatch report on Morrow, March 12, 1880.

58. VP, no serial number, Hatch, General Field Orders No. 1, February 23, 1880.

59. VP, 5012–1880, Grierson to AAG, San Antonio, May 21, 1880.

60. AG, MP 36, no serial number, Willcox to Hatch, March 5, 1880.

61. LR NMS, Roll 580, Russell to commissioner, March 16, 1880.

62. *Ibid.*, R342, Russell to commissioner, March 27, 1880.

63. *Ibid.*, Russell to commissioner, March 16, 1880.

64. *Ibid.*, N185, Montoya to Wallace, March 23, 1880.

65. *Ibid.*, N178, clipping dated March 26, 1880.

66. *Ibid.*, Chavez to Wallace, March 27, 1880.

67. *This Is Silver City*, 44.

CHAPTER XX

1. VP, no serial numbers, Sherman inquiry, April 19, 1880; Hatch's Special Field Orders, No. 18, April 5, 1880.

2. At the present San Angelo, Texas. Built of fieldstone, it is remarkably well preserved and is said to be the best existing example of a frontier fort in Texas. It was established in 1867 and abandoned June 20, 1889. Frazer, *Forts of the West*, 147. J. N. Gregory, *Fort Concho: Its Why and Wherefore*.

3. VP, 5012–1880, Grierson to AAG, San Antonio, May 21, 1880. This very long and detailed report covers Grierson's entire operation from March 18 to May 8 and is drawn upon here for his part in the Mescalero incident.

4. It is not clear from the record whether Carroll came down the east or the west side of the San Andres from Malpais Spring, but it is perhaps more likely that he came down the east side.

5. Cruse, *Apache Days and After*, 70–77.

6. VP, 3993–1880, McLellan to post adjutant, Bowie, May 16, 1880. This detailed report describes McLellan's role in the Hembrillo fight and Mescalero operation, and is drawn upon here.

7. *Ibid.*

8. S. H. Newman filed a series of dispatches to *Thirty-Four*, a Las Cruces newspaper for which he was publisher. They concern the Hembrillo Canyon fight and subsequent events at the Mescalero Reservation. They are gathered in LR NMS, Roll 580, N227. This dispatch was dated April 11, 1880.

9. Cruse, *Apache Days and After*.

10. Thrapp, *The Conquest of Apacheria*, 194–97.

11. LR NMS, Roll 580, N227, Newman, dispatch of April 9, 1880, in *Thirty-Four*.

12. VP, 2207–1880, Hatch to Pope, April 8, 1880.

13. LR NMS, Roll 580, N227, Newman, dispatch of April 10, 1880, in *Thirty-Four*.

14. LR NMS, Roll 582, W755, Sherman to Sheridan, April 12, 1880.

15. *Ibid.*, Roll 580, N227, Newman, dispatch of April 11, 1880, in *Thirty-Four*.

16. VP, 2341–1880, Hatch to Pope, April 10, 1880. VP, 2320–1880, Sheridan to Townsend, April 16, 1880.

17. VP, 2472–1880, Hatch to Platt, April 15, 1880. VP, 2475–1880, Hatch to Platt, April 17, 1880.

18. Russell's detailed report is in LR NMS, Roll 580, Russell to commissioner, April 17, 1880.

19. VP, 3416–1880, Hatch to Pope, May 27, 1880.

20. LR NMS, Roll 580, R573, Russell to commissioner, June 4, 1880.

21. VP, 2422–1880, Sheridan to Townsend, April 20, 1880.

22. VP, 2475–1880, Hatch to Platt, April 17, 1880.

23. LR NMS, Roll 580, N227, Newman, dispatch of April 22, 1880, in *Thirty-Four*.

24. VP, 2496–1880, Sheridan to Townsend, April 23, 1880.

25. VP, 2669–1880, Hatch to Pope, April 24, 1880.

26. VP, 2697–1880, endorsements by Pope, April 28, 1880; Sheridan, April 29, 1880; Sherman, May 4, 1880.

CHAPTER XXI

1. Sonnichsen, *The Mescalero Apaches*, 185–86.

2. VP, 5553–1880, Humphreys to AAG, Fort Leavenworth, May 7, 1880.

3. VP, 3138–1880, Grierson to AAG, San Antonio, May 9, 1880.

4. VP, 3229–1880, Hatch to AAG, Fort Leavenworth, May 19, 1880, and Pope's first endorsement thereon, May 20, 1880. *Ibid.*, 3218–1880, Sheridan to Townsend, May 22,

1880. *Ibid.*, no serial number, Sheridan to Pope, same date. *Ibid.*, 3721–1880, Ord to Sheridan, May 26, 1880.

5. VP, 3239–1880, Loud to AAG, Fort Leavenworth, May 8, 1880.

6. *Arizona Star* (Tucson), May 9, 1880. The *Star* reprinted his official report textually.

7. This was old Fort Tularosa, rather than the Tularosa near the Mescalero Reservation.

8. VP, 3229–1880, Hatch to AAG, Fort Leavenworth, May 17, 1880.

9. VP, 3296–1880, Sheridan to Townsend, May 26, 1880. *Ibid.*, 3661–1880, Pope to Sheridan, May 26, 1880. *Ibid.*, 3325–1880, Sheridan to Townsend, May 27, 1880.

10. VP, 3334–1880, Sheridan to Townsend, May 27, 1880.

11. Parker appears in history for a brief period, then disappears. He is first mentioned in the Globe *Arizona Silver Belt* as leading Indian scouts out of Bayard, an item reprinted in the Tucson *Arizona Star* of October 8, 1879. The Tenth Census, 1880, for New Mexico, Vol. I for Grant County, p. 82, says that Parker was white, aged twenty-six, a Texan with a Pennsylvania-born father and Illinois-born mother, and that is all the biographical information on Parker I have been able to turn up, except that he had a brother, Thomas, of Chihuahua and later of Silver City, and probably a nephew, George, of the latter place. Official records show that he was hired July 1, 1879, at San Carlos, initially probably as a packer but soon to become a chief of scouts. He was such under Second Lieutenant James A. Maney in November and December, 1879; with Morrow in January, 1880; with Maney in February, 1880; with Morrow in March, 1880; with Maney April through July, 1880; again was chief of scouts with Maney from August 1 to October 21, 1880; and was on the payroll for the first half of 1881, either as packer or as chief of scouts. *Reports of Persons and Articles Employed and Hired at Fort Bayard and Fort Cummings*, for periods cited, no serial number, no citation number, District of New Mexico, 1880, 1881. There is an outside possibility that this Parker may have been Knight Parker, born at Bowling Green, Kentucky, December 8, 1858, who died at Globe October 25, 1935, but if so his descendants are unaware of any such activity on his part. Knight Parker is not known to have had the first initial H. The Ninth Census, for 1870, lists him at eleven years of age, as living at Dallas, Texas, with the first name of Knight, and no preceding initial.

12. War Department *Annual Reports of the Secretary of War*, 1879–80, 46 Cong., 3 sess., House Exec. Doc., 99–100.

13. *Ibid.*, Morrow Report, June 27, 1880, 101–103.

14. *Ibid.*, Report of Colonel Hatch, August 5, 1880, 93–98.

15. The Palomas River heads in the Black Range and flows into the Río Grande between Cuchillo Negro Creek and the Animas and North Seco Creek. One report said that the fight was just below the "box canyon" on the Palomas.

16. Cruse, *Apache Days and After*, 84.

17. AG, MP 36, 232–1880, Scott to Hunter, November 28, 1879.

18. Sergeant Jack Long figured in Gatewood's fight with the hostiles on the upper Cuchillo Negro—almost this same area—and his appearance in this fight suggests that Parker may have been chief of scouts during the earlier engagement.

19. The exact location of this temporary post is unknown, but it was between Hot Springs (present-day Truth or Consequences) and Palomas. War Department *Annual Reports, loc. cit.*, Morrow Report, 102. No doubt it was named for Lieutenant French, who had been killed a few months earlier in the San Mateos.

20. Hatch later explained that troops being sent to him drew him to Craig at this

time, though he had ordered Morrow, with four companies, to follow up the scouts' success quickly; in view of the deplorable condition of the command, however, haste was impossible. VP, 4071–1880, Loud to AAG, Fort Leavenworth, June 7, 1880.

21. *Arizona Star*, June 5, 1880, reprinted from the Silver City (New Mexico) *Southwest*.

22. *Chronological List*, 50. Cruse, *Apache Days and After*, 84. Cruse may have meant warriors only, not counting others killed.

23. War Department *Annual Reports, loc. cit.*, Report of Colonel Edward Hatch, 98.

24. VP, no number, Sherman to Sheridan, May 28, 1880. *Ibid.*, Sherman to McDowell, May 22, 1880.

25. VP, 3625–1880, Loud to AAG, Fort Leavenworth, June 7, 1880. VP, 3889, Military Division of the Missouri, 1880, Pope to Whipple, June 2, 1880. VP, 3935, Military Division of the Missouri, Ord to AAG, Chicago, June 3, 1880.

26. VP, 3453–1880, Sheridan to Townsend, June 3, 1880.

27. VP, 3528–1880, Sheridan to Townsend, June 8, 1880.

28. *Chronological List*, 50. *Record of Engagements*, 95. VP, 3528–1880, *op. cit.* Henry Parker, chief of scouts in the field in New Mexico, wired J. J. Longwell, chief of scouts at San Carlos, on June 5, 1880, from Fort Cummings, ". . . Had fight today; killed three hostiles, no scouts hurt. . . . Victorio's youngest son killed today," suggesting that Parker was in the fight or heard about it first hand. *Grant County Herald*, June 8, 1930.

29. Quitman, on the left bank of the Río Grande about seventy miles below El Paso, was established September 28, 1858, to protect the stage and emigrant routes. Traces of these well-worn roads still are visible. The post, of adobe, "was usually in a poor state of repair." It was variously occupied by Union and Confederate troops, was abandoned for a time, re-established January 1, 1868, and permanently abandoned January 5, 1877. Frazer, *Forts of the West*, 157–58. Gillett, in *Six Years with the Texas Rangers*, 181, said that the overland stage company had a station there in 1880. A reduced-size "replica" of it at Interstate 10 and local road 34 is interesting and includes many relics from the site of the old fort, a few miles southeast.

30. VP, 4449–1880, Military Division of Missouri, Hatch to AAG, Fort Leavenworth, June 8, 1880.

31. LR NMS, Roll 580, R601, Russell to commissioner, June 10, 1880.

32. VP, 3663–1880, Loud to AAG, Fort Leavenworth, June 8, 1880. VP, 3672–1880, Pope to Whipple, June 11, 1880.

33. VP, 5691–1880, Morgan to Evarts, July 24, 1880. *Ibid.*, Ruelas to Morgan, July 23, 1880. *Ibid.*, Morgan to Ruelas, July 24, 1880. See also VP, 4233, Military Division of the Missouri, various communications; VP, 3787–1880, Sherman's second endorsement, no date; VP, 6369, Military Division of Missouri, 1880, Valle to Brinkerhoff, August 9, 1880, and Hatch's second endorsement thereon.

34. VP, 3939–1880, Hatch to Pope, June 16, 1880; Pope to Whipple, June 21, 1880.

35. VP, 4731, Military Division of Missouri, Pope to Sheridan, July 1, 1880.

36. LR NMS, Roll 582, W1611, Pope to Whipple, July 19, 1880.

37. *Ibid.*, W1565, Hatch to AAG, Fort Leavenworth, July 13, 1880.

38. VP, 6595, Military Division of Missouri, Tiffany to commissioner, July 20, 1880, with enclosures, including transmittal note from Sherman via Drum, August 31, 1880.

39. VP, 5906–1880, Hatch to AAG, Fort Leavenworth, September 11, 1880. In this favorable reaction, Hatch volunteers to go himself on this perilous mission, which he regarded as offering possibilities of success.

40. LR NMS, Roll 582, W1613, McDowell to commissioner, July 26, 1880.

41. VP, 4509–1880, Sheridan to adjutant general, Washington, July 22, 1880.

42. Ojo del Pino was a spring in the Sierra de los Pinos, forty miles southwest of Eagle Springs and across the Río Grande.

43. VP, 4633–1880, Ord to AAG, Chicago, July 24, 1880.

44. VP, 5747, Military Division of Missouri, Grierson to AAG, Chicago, August 1, 1880.

45. VP, 4805–1880, Grierson to AAG, Chicago, August 2, 1880.

46. Now called Indian Hot Springs, on the river southwest of Van Horn, Texas.

47. VP, 4932–1880, Brinkerhoff to AAG, San Antonio, August 3, 1880.

48. Grierson gives Victorio a spread of one hundred miles. Vieja Pass is thirty-five miles due south of Van Horn and thirteen miles northeast of the Río Grande. Bass Canyon is unidentified.

49. VP, no serial number, Grierson to AAG, San Antonio, August 3, 1880.

50. *Ibid.*, Hatch to AAG, Fort Leavenworth, August 8, 1880.

51. VP, 5074–1880, Hatch to AAG, Fort Leavenworth, August 12, 1880.

52. VP, 6209, Military Division of the Missouri, 1880, Grierson to AAG, San Antonio, August 14, 1880. This fight, described by Carlysle Graham Raht in *The Romance of Davis Mountains and Big Bend Country*, 262, in accordance with the fiction that soon surrounded it, was not an ambush within an ambush, but a double action, one following the other. Thrapp, *The Conquest of Apacheria*, 204–206 and 205n.

53. VP, 5138–1880, Hatch to AAG, Fort Leavenworth, August 14, 1880.

54. VP, Military Division of the Missouri, Hatch to AAG, Fort Leavenworth, August 15, 1880.

55. Juan Manuel Terrazas Sanchez to author, October 19, 1970.

56. *The Handbook of Texas*, I, 260, reports him killed August 22, but this cannot be, as Grierson reported the incident in a dispatch dated August 19 from Eagle Springs. He implies the attack was made by Victorio's warriors before they crossed the river into Mexico, but Mescaleros were more probably the authors of the deed. Gillett in *Six Years with the Texas Rangers*, 181–82, says Byrne was killed August 9, but he must mean August 19.

57. Thrapp, *The Conquest of Apacheria*, 207.

58. VP, 5373–1880, Ord to AAG, Chicago, August 27, 1880.

59. VP, 7442–1880, Hatch to AAG, Fort Leavenworth, December 4, 1880.

60. This "Casimero," not otherwise identified, might have been Streeter, the former interpreter from Craig who, now with a price on his head from Arizona for his relationship with the Apaches, had fled to Mexico. He would not have returned under his own name, but was known to use the name Cassimiro, or some spelling variant, in Mexico and, if he had slipped back into New Mexico, might have gone under that alias. He was small and perfectly fluent in Spanish. Also, he knew Victorio personally.

61. Crawford, "The Pursuit of Victorio," *Socorro County Historical Society: Publications in History*, Vol. I, February, 1965, 1–8.

62. Buell's lengthy, interesting report, including many details of the hunt for Victorio, was edited by Colonel Martin L. Crimmins and published: "Colonel Buell's Expedition into Mexico in 1880," *New Mexico Historical Review*, Vol. X, No. 2 (April, 1935), 133–42. See also AG, MP36, 2715–1880, Buell to AAG, Fort Whipple, September 1, 1880.

63. VP, 6763, Military Division of the Missouri, 1880, Grierson to AAG, San Antonio, September 2, 1880. VP, 7079, Military Division of the Missouri, 1880, Pope to Sheridan, September 20, 1880.

Notes

CHAPTER XXII

1. Smith, "Apache Plunder Trails Southward, 1831–1840," *New Mexico Historical Review*, Vol. XXXVII, No. 1 (January, 1962), 23–24.

2. Unless otherwise specified, the narrative follows Joaquin Terrazas, *Memorias del Sr. Coronel D. Joaquin Terrazas*, 72–82. Terrazas, born April 16, 1829, at a ranch called Labor de Dolores in Chihuahua, began fighting Apaches early in life, becoming "one of the men to whom civilization owes most for the extinction of the barbarians." He was wounded in a battle at the northern lakes where the Apaches were wont to repair with their four-footed loot. Terrazas fought with the Liberals in the War of Reform which followed the announcement of Benito Juárez' Constitution of 1857 and was prominent in the struggle against the French interventionists a decade later. As a loyal supporter of the government, he subsequently helped put down various revolutions. By 1880 he was a veteran, thoroughly seasoned, having been a soldier all of his life and taken part in innumerable hard fights and campaigns, winning encomiums from officers under whom he served. Joaquin Terrazas died October 8, 1901; his *Memorias* were published four years later. *Diccionario Porrua*, 1566. Francisco R. Almada, *Diccionario de Historia, Geografía y Biografía Chihuahuenses*, 698–99. See also Terrazas' military career file, Archivos de la Nación de Mexico, Secretario de Guerra y Marina. This contains certain facts and figures about the Victorio battle.

3. This was Guadalupe Bravos, on the Río Grande (Río Bravo del Norte), on the right bank, thirty-three miles downstream from present-day Juárez.

4. Gillett, *Six Years with the Texas Rangers*, 184.

5. Juan Mata Ortiz was born about 1820, perhaps at Galeana or in northwest Chihuahua, and for forty years took part in expeditions against the Apaches, being described by Smith as a scalp hunter like Joaquin Terrazas. The two had met before this campaign, no doubt, for Mata Ortiz, as *commandante*, had fought with Luis Terrazas at Avalos in 1876 and was a well-known soldier. He several times was elected political chief of the canton of Galeana. Juan Mata Ortiz was to be killed by Apaches November 13, 1882. Almada, *Diccionario de Historia, Geografía y Biografía Chihuahuenses*, 438–39. Smith, "Apache Plunder Trails Southward, 1831–1840," *loc. cit.*, 23f.

6. VP, 6513–1880, Buell to AAG, Fort Leavenworth, October 19, 1880.

7. AG, MP 36, 3264–1880, Carr to AAAG, Whipple, October 10, 1880.

8. Gillett, *Six Years with the Texas Rangers*, 183–86.

9. Nana led this party out on the plains; some say he had been sent by Victorio to forage for ammunition and livestock. That may be true, or it may have been that he and his party simply had not joined when the battle erupted, or perhaps, as one witness reported, he had commanded the rear guard of Victorio's band and fled at the outset of the fight.

10. Terrazas is said to have earned $17,250 from the scalps and $10,200 from the captives he had taken. Smith, "Apache Plunder Trails Southward, 1831–1840," *loc. cit.*, 34. For an English translation of Terrazas' official communique of the fight, see the *Daily New Mexican* (Santa Fe), October 23, 1880, and for his added details, *Daily New Mexican*, October 30, 1880. For a summary of this campaign and battle, see Philip J. Rasch, "The Death of Victorio," *The English Westerners' Brand Book*, Vol. II, No. 3 (April, 1960), 9–10.

11. Gillett, *Six Years with the Texas Rangers*, 188. Gillett reported that Victorio was slain in the initial attack and this loss, plus the absence of Nana, so demoralized the

others that they proved easy prey. When they heard of it, the Rangers "felt thoroughly disgusted and disappointed at missing the great fight."

12. Wellman, *The Indian Wars of the West*, 391–92.

13. Numerous writers.

14. John A. Shapard to author, December 4, 1969, reporting interview with Loco's descendants.

15. Albuquerque *Daily Journal*, December 27, 1880.

16. Whose command, Victorio's or the Mexican commander's?

17. LR NMS, Roll 582, W1739, Buell to AAAG, Santa Fe, November 30, 1880.

18. The relationship is variously given. See "I Survived the Massacre of Tres Castillos," by James Kaywaykla, as told to Eve Ball, *True West*, Vol. VIII, No. 6 (July–August, 1961), 22, and "Nana's People," by James Kaywaykla, as told to Eve Ball, *True West*, Vol. X, No. 6 (July-August, 1963), 20, for examples. Kaywaykla's account is expanded and graphically presented in Eve Ball's *In the Days of Victorio: Recollections of a Warm Springs Apache*, 93–103.

19. If this figure is accurate, many more Apaches escaped the massacre than was supposed, since those slain and the prisoners, plus Nana's band, which got away, totaled only about one hundred and fifty.

20. Eve Ball, "The Fight for Ojo Caliente," *Frontier Times*, Vol. XXXVI, No. 2 (Spring, 1962), 40.

21. Lozen, Mrs. Ball was told, was known to the Apaches as the "woman warrior"; she was a medicine woman, or shaman, and considered fully the equal of male fighters in every way. While one authority was told that "women never go on raids" (Opler, *An Apache Life-Way*, 333), another, equally diligent, reported that women were known to go with war parties sometimes (Goodwin, *The Western Apache*, 224, and 537: "In very rare instances women even went to war and helped fight and kill the enemy"), supplying Lozen with perfectly good credentials. But most important was her "power." Kaywaykla said that several times he had seen her search out the direction and distance of the enemy. "Standing with uplifted face and outstretched arms, palms up, she sang:

Upon this Earth
On which we live
Ussen has Power.
This Power he grants me
For Locating the enemy.
I search for that enemy
Which only Ussen, Creator of Life
Can reveal to me.

"As she sang, she circled clockwise moving slowly until a tingling in the palms of her hands caused her to pause. Her outstretched arms pointed toward the enemy, and the intensity of the sensation indicated their proximity or remoteness." Kaywaykla reported that her palms became almost purple when they designated the direction of pursuers. Ball, "The Fight for Ojo Caliente," *loc. cit.* See Ball, *In the Days of Victorio*, for a greatly expanded account of this remarkable woman. She is pictured in a group photograph in the book, p. 196.

CHAPTER XXIII

1. Kaywaykla always denied that Victorio had many warriors with him at the final battle. Most, he believed, were on other missions.

2. Kaywaykla, "Nana's People," *True West*, Vol. X, No. 6 (July–August, 1963), 20–21, 66–67.

3. VP, 6835–1880, Hay to Ramsey, November 9, 1880.

4. Gillett, *Six Years with the Texas Rangers*, 189.

5. This could be John H. Riley of Lincoln County War note, then living near Las Cruces and at loose ends. Mullin, *Fulton's History of the Lincoln County War*, 4.

6. LR NMS, Roll 580, R1135, Russell to commissioner, November 23, 1880.

7. Reportedly becoming a Christian, he died in about 1885. Sonnichsen, *The Mescalero Apaches*, 215–16.

8. This Indian, still living in 1908, was a member of a posse which tracked down and killed an Indian slayer of a white man that winter. *Ibid.*, 234.

9. LR NMS, 442–1881, Office of Indian Affairs, Conrad to post adjutant, Fort Stanton, December 1, 1880.

10. *Ibid.*, Hatch, second endorsement, Santa Fe, December 13, 1880.

11. LR OIA, 15391–1882, H. H. Llewellyn to commissioner, August 15, 1882.

12. VP, 7447–1880, Pope, first endorsement, Hatch to AAG, Fort Leavenworth, December 6, 1880.

13. Llewellyn to commissioner, August 15, 1882.

14. *Daily New Mexican* (Santa Fe), November 21, 1880.

15. *Ibid.*, November 24, 1880.

16. LR NMS, Roll 582, W1739, Buell to AAAG, Santa Fe, November 30, 1880.

17. *Daily New Mexican*, November 12, 1880.

18. *Ibid.*

19. LR OIA, 6607–1881, Tiffany to commissioner, April 13, 1881.

20. *Arizona Star* (Tucson), October 21, 1880, reprinting item from Galveston, Texas, *News*.

21. Most of these prisoners, women and children, never returned to the United States, and their descendants live in Mexico today as almost indistinguishable elements of that country's population. One of the descendants of the prisoners taken at Tres Castillos, Albert Azua, fifty-six in 1968, told me of their lives in Chihuahua before he emigrated to this country in about 1920. Interview, October 25, 1968, at Plainview, Texas. M. Romero, of the Mexican Legation at Washington, officially informed the State Department April 23, 1895, that the prisoners "following the custom adopted in such cases, were distributed among various families of the State. Some of these Apaches adopted civilized life and others took flight, but at the present time none of the Indians captured in that battle are in prison." AGO, 13672–1895. On August 15, 1903, Superintendent James A. Carroll of the Mescalero Reservation said in his annual report that an investigation of a rumor of remnants of Victorio's band living in Mexico uncovered thirty-seven of them "occupying a narrow canyon in the Guadalupe Mountains about twenty miles east of Zaragoza, a station on the Mexican Central Railroad. They were in wretched circumstances, having to depend almost entirely on game and herbs and the sale of curios. They were anxious to remove to this reservation," but attempts to effect this were fruitless. *Annual Reports of the Department of the Interior, 1903: Indian Affairs, Part I, Report of Commissioner and Appendices*, 214, in the Social and Economics Records Division, National Archives and Records Service.

22. December 2, 1880. The date of the original story is not given; the pseudonym of the writer was merely "Consular." Mauricio Corredor, the Tarrahumare credited with slaying Victorio, also was given a nickel-plated rifle which, according to legend, he later

used to kill American Captain Emmet Crawford in the Sierra Madre. Thrapp, *The Conquest of Apacheria*, 341–42. Smith says that Mauricio, too, was a scalp hunter of much experience. "Apache Plunder Trails Southward, 1831–1840," *New Mexico Historical Review*, Vol. XXXVII, No. 1 (January, 1962), 23.

23. Adjutant General's Office, Record Group 393, Letters Sent, District of New Mexico, 1881–83, 153–1881, Hatch to AAG, Fort Leavenworth, April 19, 1881, in Old Military Records Division, National Archives and Records Service.

24. Florence C. Lister and Robert H. Lister in *Chihuahua: Storehouse of Storms*, 166n., say that a railroad settlement south of Casas Grandes was named for him, but it is not shown on the most detailed map of Chihuahua known to me.

25. One legend is that he was burned alive. See Lister and Lister, *op. cit.*, 166. But this is improbable, since there is not enough wood in that country to build a fire capable of consuming a body, and there is no indication that a century ago it was more plentiful. Since Mata Ortiz was well known to the Apaches, however, there is no reason to doubt that some ingenious method of execution was employed, particularly since Juh participated. He was fat, it has been reported, and would have been about sixty at his death. The best account of the fight is in Betzinez, *I Fought With Geronimo*, 93–96. I am indebted to Arnaldo Balencia Gallegos, proprietor of the Rancho Santa Maria near Galeana, for guiding me over the site.

26. Gillett, *Six Years with the Texas Rangers*, 186–87.

27. Barnes, *Arizona Place Names*, 23.

INDEX

377

299; Hembrillo Canyon fight, 268–71;
career of, 365n.
Mangas Coloradas: 3, 11, 23, 35ff., 42, 48,
52ff., 65, 84, 89, 98, 101, 102, 150, 155;
meets Kearny command, 21; bold raider,
24–25; signs treaty, 26ff.; Wingfield's description, 32; fights Mexicans, 32–33;
aloof from council, 42ff.; settles with
Mimbres, 61; truce with miners, 61;
whipped by miners, 73; Cremony's char-
acterization, 76–77; wounded at Apache
Pass, 80–81; murder of, 82–83; succes-
sors, 85; his chieftainship, 332n.; Pinos
Altos "attack" discounted, 338n.; Bran-
des' evaluation of, 338n.
Mangas Creek: see Santa Lucia Creek
Mangas, José: seeks Dodge, 52
Mangas Mountains, N.M.: 202
Mangus, son of Mangas Coloradas: 11, 182
Mangus Springs, N.M.: 81, 83, 130
Mansfield, Joseph K. F.: 331n.
Manypenny, George W.: 38, 47, 51
Mariana (Navaho chief): 203
Maricopa Indians: 34
Marion, John: 7; biography, 327n.
Marmaduke, John Sappington: 69ff.; bi-
ography, 337n.
Mason, John Sanford: 105
Massacre Peak, N.M.: 246
Mata Ortiz, Juan: second in command to
Terrazas, 295–97; hunt for Victorio,
298–300; joins Terrazas at Tres Castillos,
301–302; in Tres Castillos battle, 302–
304; few honors for, 310–11; cruel death
of, 312; biography, 373n.; various accounts of fate, 376.
Maxwell, George W.: 309
Meriwether, David: 37, 39, 40, 47, 51, 53,
56; becomes governor, 33; policy on
captives, 37; summons council, 42ff.;
dispute over mining grants, 45–46
Merritt, Charles W.: 210, 215; dispute
over pass, 213; obtains Victorio's surrender, 213–14
Mescal: 332n.
Mescalero Apaches, Reservation: 3, 7, 19,
33, 45, 46, 54, 61, 63, 73, 77, 92, 99, 125,
126, 129, 131, 133, 140, 145, 163, 164,
173, 174, 181, 201, 203, 210, 237,
250, 262, 265, 268, 275, 284, 285, 286,
298, 306, 310, 314; population, 34; summoned for council, 42ff.; Meriwether's
population estimate, 46; removal sug-

gested, 66; Bosque Redondo suggested,
86; Bosque experiment, 87–93; population (Arny), 130; some Mimbres prefer, 148; raiding, 176; and Mimbres,
204–207; Mimbres filter in, 212ff.; Russell opposed, 214–15; Victorio comes in,
216–20; Mescaleros aiding Victorio, 252;
justify horse theft, 256; disarming of
proposed, 260–64; with Victorio, 266–
67; Hatch plans against, 267; disarming
attempted, 271–74; few captured in
Black Range, 282–83; Russell attempts
to recall hostiles, 283; depredations,
290; Victorio kills Ca-bal-le-so, 290–91;
Mescalero version of Victorio's death,
305; filter back to reservation, 308–309
Mesilla, N.M.: 49, 52–53, 59, 75ff., 88ff.,
100, 128, 195, 219, 246, 260, 308; citizens
petition for peace, 90
Mexicans: 134; thefts by, blamed on
Apaches, 42; raid U.S. Apache lands,
44; nine killed by Dodge slayers, 52;
steal Delgadito's horses, murder Costales, 52–53; threaten Cañada Alamosa,
105; ruses against Indians, 105–106;
counter Tularosa move, 147
Mexican-Apache relations: 16, 21; in war,
11; Croix-Ugarte success, 16–17; after
Mexican revolution, 17–18; scalp hunting, 19–20; disperse friendly Gilas, 22;
Mangas explains, 24–25; Mangas protests, 27ff.; peace and treachery, 28;
fighting with Mangas, 32–33; Mexicans
threaten Cañada Alamosa, 105
Mexico: see Chihuahua, Sonora
Mickey Free: 337n.
Miguel (White Mountain chief): 140
Miles, Dixon Stansburgy: 54; Bonneville
expedition, 54ff.
Mills, Anson: in Pinos Altos rush, 67
Mills, Stephen Crosby: 292; in Hembrillo
Canyon fight, 268–71
Mimbres Apaches: 8, 16, 20, 38, 40ff., 53,
55, 61ff., 76, 93, 98ff., 131, 133, 144, 157,
164, 172, 179ff., 252, 265; band names,
3–4; Spanish names of, 6; census of, 15;
early hostility, 16–17; at peace in 1787,
17; contact Kearny command, 20–21;
Jack Hays, agent, 21–22; boldest Sonora
raiders, 24–25; depredations, 26ff.; first
treaties, 26ff.; population of, 30; Wingfield tributes, 32; Steck visits, 33ff.;
numbers of, 34; depredations, 34–35;